BLITZKRIEG TO DESERT STORM

BLITZKRIEG TO DESERT STORM

The Evolution of Operational Warfare

Robert M. Citino

UNIVERSITY PRESS OF KANSAS

© 2004 by the University Press of Kansas
All rights reserved

Published by the University Press of Kansas (Lawrence, Kansas 66045), which was
organized by the Kansas Board of Regents and is operated and funded by Emporia
State University, Fort Hays State University, Kansas State University, Pittsburg State
University, the University of Kansas, and Wichita State University

Library of Congress Cataloging-in-Publication Data

Citino, Robert Michael, 1958–
    Blitzkrieg to Desert Storm : the evolution of operational warfare /
Robert M. Citino.
        p. cm. — (Modern war studies)
Includes bibliographical references and index.
    ISBN 978-0-7006-1300-7 (cloth : alk. paper)
    1. Operational art (Military science)—History—20th century.   2.
Military history, Modern—20th century.   I. Title.   II. Series.
    U163.C54   2004
    355.4′09′045—dc22   2003020208

British Library Cataloguing-in-Publication Data is available.

Printed in the United States of America

10 9 8 7 6 5 4 3

To my daughter Laura

Contents

Illustrations

BLITZKRIEG TO DESERT STORM

Introduction

The Day the World Changed

It was 7:00 P.M. on the evening of May 20, 1940, as the first column of German vehicles clattered into the French town of Abbeville at the mouth of the Somme River. They were the spearhead of 2nd Panzer Division, part of General Heinz Guderian's XIX Panzer Corps. Considering that Europe was in the midst of a great war, the town was quiet. An occasional Allied plane would appear overhead, but there was no organized French resistance here. A little later that evening, the "Spitta Battalion" of 2nd Panzer, named for its commander, pressed on from Abbeville and drove the twenty kilometers to Noyelles on the Atlantic coast, occupying it without incident. The men of the unit were tired, but exhilarated. They had reason to be. They had just finished one of the most audacious maneuvers in the history of modern warfare. Having negotiated the difficult, winding trails of the Ardennes forest, they had been part of a massive German armored force that had broken through a weakly defended portion of the French lines at Sedan on May 13. Since then, they had driven at top speed, nearly unmolested, clear across the rear of an immense Anglo-French army in Belgium. In ten short days of action, Spitta's men had covered more than two hundred miles, and in fact they had done the last sixty since morning. The battalion's arrival at Abbeville and Noyelles spelled doom for the Allied forces to the north. They were now trapped, cut off from their supply base in France, hemmed in on all sides by a combination of the Germans and the sea, and, consequently, not long for this world.[1]

Lieutenant Colonel Spitta undoubtedly knew that he had just taken part in a victorious battle. What he might not have realized was that his drive from the Ardennes to Noyelles heralded a new age in military history. Upper echelons in the German army knew. Consider the testimony of the German Panzer Group commander, General Ewald von Kleist:

> I was halfway to the sea when one of my staff brought me an extract from the French radio which said that the commander of their 6th

1

Army on the Meuse had been sacked, and General Giraud appointed to take charge of the situation. Just as I was reading it, the door opened and a handsome French general was ushered in. He introduced himself with the words, "I am General Giraud." He told me how he had set out in an armored car to look for his Army, and had found himself in the midst of my forces far ahead of where he had expected them to be.

Kleist concluded, with some understatement, "This was a sidelight on the apparent unexpectedness of our arrival."[2]

Indeed, the German army (Wehrmacht) had just done something that no army in the world had been able to do for decades. The campaign in France, designated by the Germans as Case Yellow (*Fall Gelb*), was the sort of operation that planners on both sides in World War I had aimed at repeatedly but had failed to carry off. The feint to the north, the disguised main thrust to the south, the encirclement of an entire enemy army in what German staff officers called a *Kesselschlacht* (cauldron battle), the destruction of the enemy's entire field force in a single seamless campaign, at negligible cost — such things seemed to belong to a bygone era, to the age of the great Field Marshal Helmuth von Moltke, or the Emperor Napoleon, or perhaps even the "warrior king," Frederick the Great. It was, to put it simply, a decisive victory — something that had become all too rare of late. One German military analyst called it nothing less than a "modern Austerlitz," a battle that marked "a new epoch in military history."[3]

The shock was understandable. The world had not seen anything like it for some seventy years. Starting in the late nineteenth century, stalemate had become the predictable outcome when great armies clashed. The Boer War, the Russo-Japanese War, the Balkan Wars, World War I: all featured campaigns that fell far short of the goals that their commanders had set. When victory came, it was typically a victory of attrition, a peace of exhaustion. So expensive were these stalemated wars that defeat often plunged the losing side into political and social revolution — Russia in 1905 and again in 1917, Austria-Hungary and Germany in 1918.

Case Yellow was different, a clever plan executed by a highly mobile, agile military instrument, led by officers who understood the potential of new technology, especially the tank and the airplane. It changed forever the way the world's armies fought. It changed the way they planned for wars and what they expected to achieve from them. It should be noted, moreover, that the Germans had achieved this revolution, amounting to nothing less than a restoration of the art of war, with a mere ten panzer divisions and ten motorized divisions, a small fraction of the more than one hundred divisions they mobilized for the campaign in the west.

The Work

Blitzkrieg to Desert Storm offers a detailed, operational-level look at battlefield developments from 1940, the year of the stunning German victory in France, to 1991 and the successful Coalition assault in Operation Desert Storm. It starts at the point that my previous book, *Quest for Decisive Victory: From Stalemate to Blitzkrieg in Europe, 1899–1940*, ended. That earlier work demonstrated how difficult it had become to achieve decisive battlefield victory in the age of the mass army, the rifle and machine gun, and rapid-fire artillery. Although the infantry-based armies of the early twentieth century could generate enormous firepower, they were relatively immobile. With their voracious supply needs tying them tightly to the railroad, they were incapable of carrying out the sort of elegant maneuvers that were the stock-in-trade of the great nineteenth-century captains like Napoleon or Helmuth von Moltke. Because cavalry was increasingly unable to carry out a decent reconnaissance or conduct a pursuit, armies of the day tended to blunder into one another. At this point, a mutual bludgeoning began. Both sides took and inflicted huge, often crippling casualties. Even if they managed to achieve a local success, the underdeveloped state of communications technology (based around the telegraph) rendered the command and control of these masses highly problematic. Although opportunities might arise in the course of the campaign, they often went unexploited. This was the particular problem that bedeviled so many military operations in World War I.

During the interwar period, the German army arrived at solutions to most of these problems. Motor technology (tank, truck, and airplane — both tactical and transport) solved the mobility problem. Radio enabled the commanders to exercise much more effective command and control. It was not, however, a simple case of new inventions and new technology leading to an obvious military revolution. The victory in 1940 was the result of a long period of trial and error, doctrinal experimentation carried out not just in theoretical work but in a detailed and exhaustive series of maneuvers, exercises, and war games.

As the next fifty years would show, Case Yellow proved a difficult thing to copy. Operational-level warfare after 1940 was immensely more complex than that which had preceded it. The new dominance of ground vehicle and aircraft meant an enormous strain on the logistics network. Previously limited to supplying ammunition and food, a task that had proved difficult enough over the years, it was now responsible for slaking the nearly unlimited thirst of thousands of fuel tanks, as well as for delivering the spare parts that a hard-driving mechanized army required in abundance. Gasoline and lubricants — not the speed of an army's tanks — became crucial factors limiting a modern army's mobility.

Many other problems made victories in the style of Case Yellow the exception rather than the rule. Because mechanized operations could, potentially, cover much vaster distances than old-style campaigns, command and communications still remained an area of concern and continue to elude neat solutions to the present day. Success on the operational level also required mastery of the third dimension: air power. Whether acting as the eyes and ears of the commander on reconnaissance missions, plastering enemy ground formations with bombs, or ranging deep into the rear to interdict supplies and reinforcements moving up to the front, aircraft had become indispensable to combat on the operational level.

This meant, however, that effective use of combined arms, difficult enough to achieve when it was merely a matter of coordinating infantry and artillery, had now become exponentially more difficult. Operations had become a very intricate minuet, with fast-moving mechanized columns, infantry, artillery (now mechanized as well), and aircraft all playing an essential role. Because the music was so much more complex, the conductors of the orchestra, the officers, required more and better training than ever before; so too did the musicians, the men and units that were performing the most complex military operations in the entire history of war.

Any analysis of post-1940 operations must touch on all these areas. What is the role of mobility? Is it more or less important than firepower? What sorts of advantages does better, more realistic training bestow? How important is doctrine? What types of command and control mechanisms work best on the modern battlefield? Do victorious campaigns, and the armies that achieve them, share certain characteristics? Finally, is it possible to discern long-term trends in operational warfare?

Opening with Germany's decisive victories in the first years of World War II, the book begins with the reassessment forced on every army in the world by the new German doctrine of mechanized warfare. During the war's opening campaigns (1939–1940), the German armed forces (Wehrmacht) solved the problem that had bedeviled military planners since 1914: how to keep moving on the modern battlefield; how to maintain the momentum of the advance even in the face of the withering firepower generated by modern armies; and, finally, how to limit the mobility of one's enemy.

In the new German scheme of military operations, highly mobile, massed formations of tanks (panzers), working in close cooperation with the air force (Luftwaffe), proved capable not only of blasting through static enemy positions on the tactical level, but of sustaining their operational advance into open country, moving forward vast distances every day, linking up far behind enemy lines, and then trapping and destroying hostile formations in great battles of encirclement. At the same time, the German armed forces also made a dramatic breakthrough into airmobility. In Scandinavia, the Netherlands, and Crete, German units entered battle by transport aircraft, glider, and paradrop, perhaps the true operational innovation of the war's early years. The world would call the entire package *blitzkrieg* ("lightning war"), although the Germans themselves did not use the term in any kind of precise way. It was the basis for the dramatic German victories in Poland and France, and for the first year of the invasion of the Soviet Union — victories that still stand at the pinnacle of the modern military art.

Much of the rest of the war (1941–1945), in fact, can be seen as an attempt by the Allies (Great Britain, the Soviet Union, and the United States) to assimilate the new German methods, integrating them into their own traditions, and finally creating a new synthesis. The U.S. Army, for example, had literally to create an armored force out of nothing, once the Germans had shown how essential massed tank formations had become to modern military operations. Both the British and the Soviet armies had done a great deal of work with tanks and mechanized units in the interwar era but now found that the gap between their experiments on the maneuver ground and the reality of war had grown wide indeed.

Nevertheless, all the Allied powers confronted the Wehrmacht with a great deal of confidence. The Soviet counterattack at Moscow in December 1941 was just one part of a huge, theaterwide counterstroke that Josef Stalin was sure would crush the German army once and for all. So was the Soviet counterstroke at Stalingrad in November 1942. Likewise, from the start of its involvement, the U.S. Army seemed to think that winning the war was a fairly direct matter of assembling a massive force for a cross-Channel invasion. It seemed to give much less thought to what the force would actually do once it was in Europe, except for the vague thought of destroying the German army. As early as 1943, field officers and men were already mocking "the annual 'collapse of Germany' predictions" that emanated from the staff.[4] In Field Marshal Bernard Law Montgomery, the British army had perhaps the ultimate optimist, one who promised to take the city of Caen on the first day of the Normandy landings and "knock about a bit there."

In fact, it proved to be a little tougher than that. It is not simply a question of whether there was ever an "Allied blitzkrieg." Blitzkrieg was a German phenomenon based on the traditions and heritage of German military history. But all too often, the U.S. and Soviet armies, especially, seemed to rely on their enormous quantitative superiority in manpower and matériel, simply bludgeoning their way forward in bloody campaigns of attrition. Even quite late in the war, when it was clear that the overall verdict was not in doubt, the Allies had a hard time erasing the German army's qualitative edge, an advantage derived from several factors: a more talented officer corps, more effective methods of command and control, and a better grasp of maneuver on the operational level. Cases in point are the incomplete victories at El Alamein (by the British) and Stalingrad (the Red Army), and the Cobra-Falaise campaign (the U.S. Army). None of these great Allied victories was as complete as it might have been, and all seem replete today with the aura of missed opportunities.

The same might be said for the entire spectrum of conventional military conflict the world over since 1945. The search for rapid, decisive battlefield victory in the German style survived, but it proved, by and large, to be an elusive and often frustrating search. In this analysis of operations, we examine the Korean War, especially its highly mobile first year. It featured the drive of the North Korean People's Army down the Korean Peninsula, the United Nations' dramatic riposte at Inchon, and the entry of the Red Chinese into the conflict. The war featured a schizophrenic performance on the part of the U.S. Army, from the high of Inchon and the drive to the Yalu to an ignominious rout at the hands of a Chinese force consisting almost exclusively of light infantry. The Chinese, for their part, squandered numerous opportunities to turn successful battles into decisive victory.

During the Arab-Israeli Wars of 1947, 1956, 1967, and again in 1973, the Israel Defense Force (IDF) showed the world that it had become the mobile force par excellence, and irony of ironies, the heir to the German Wehrmacht. Although those wars also showed the limits of what can be achieved through operational triumph, the IDF's victories are still worth analyzing — models of slashing maneuver, quick decision making, and expert coordination of land and air power. The 1973 war, however, showed that the Arab states had finally grasped some of the realities of operational-level warfare. The fright that the combined Egyptian and Syrian assault threw into the mighty Israeli army still reverberates in the Middle East.

The U.S. Army's longest war of the post-1945 era presents a very different kind of picture. The Vietnam Conflict continues to exert its fascination on Americans of all political stripes and is still, in every way, highly controversial. Not subject to dispute is this: despite overwhelming superiority in technology, firepower, and communications, and despite victory in every major encounter, the world's most technologically sophisticated field force was, in the end, unable to defeat a communist insurgency in South Vietnam. Nevertheless, the Vietnam experience, including extremely impressive operations like the relief of Khe Sanh (Operation Pegasus), would continue to inform U.S. doctrine in ways some might find surprising.

Wars in the Third World showed the same varied pattern. There was a series of conflicts, for example, between the two hostile offspring of the British raj: India and Pakistan. Although most were indecisive, they did include one of the twentieth century's most successful campaigns, the Indian army's lightning drive into East Pakistan in 1971. It was a truly impressive victory that led to comparisons in the world press with the great German triumph in 1940. To their credit, the Indians seemed to be less impressed than many observers, with their army's Chief of Staff demurring on the Rommel comparisons. Nevertheless, the campaign resulted in the dismemberment of India's chief geo-strategic rival and the creation of an independent Bangladesh. The 1980s, by contrast, brought the senseless and extended bloodletting of the Iran-Iraq War, proof positive that modern weaponry alone does not a blitzkrieg make. Given Western strategic interest in the Near East, this was a closely watched war. The eventual Iraqi triumph led Western analysts into some of the most embarrassing judgments ever committed to paper extolling the fighting qualities of the Iraqi army — qualities that would suddenly appear quite ephemeral in 1991.

That same decade also witnessed one of military history's great intellectual revivals, this time in the U.S. Army. It was a time in which innovative staff officers took a hard look at the army's weapons, doctrine, and procedures, post-Vietnam, and found them wanting. The result was the writing of new field manuals, the development of new war-fighting doctrines (first "active defense" and then "AirLand Battle"), the introduction of new weaponry, and new, intense methods of training. The army soon had a chance to demonstrate its sharply honed war-fighting abilities in 1991. During Operation Desert Storm, the U.S.-led Coalition forces planned and executed an operation that dismantled a large, entrenched defending force with virtually no friendly casualties.

Like *Quest for Decisive Victory*, *From Blitzkrieg to Desert Storm* concentrates on that level of war between *tactics* (the movement of battalions, companies, and squads on the battlefield) and *strategy* (the realm of the politico-military leadership of the respective warring nations).[5] The German army has traditionally placed emphasis on this intermediate level of war, usually called the "operational" level. Involving the movement of corps and divisions, it might be described as the analysis of the campaign (rather than the battle or the war). Nowhere else is the creativity (or lack thereof) of the higher commander so important to the outcome. Both tactics and strategy are essentially sciences; warfare on the operational level is an art. A commander may feint in the center with one corps while massing overwhelming forces on one or both flanks; he might employ surprise, or take advantage of the terrain to march a force into position in the enemy's rear. The tradition in the German army was for the commander to "shape" the campaign so that it resulted in a great battle of annihilation. His primary task was to concentrate overwhelming strength at the decisive point of the battle, the "point of main effort" or *Schwerpunkt*, rather than frittering away his forces on diversionary thrusts or nondecisive sectors of the theater. A well-conducted campaign would have a *Schwerpunkt* that defined it, gave it shape and meaning.

Operational commanders, then, must do more than simply assemble divisions, corps, and armies, and march them off in the general direction of the enemy. Rather, they must have an end result in mind at the start of the operation, one that involves the destruction of a considerable portion of the enemy's fighting power. It is difficult to conceive of any other goal worthy of assembling a modern army, with its 200,000 or so troops, its mountains of expensive equipment, and the vast amount of supplies it consumes on a daily basis (starting with an average of two hundred tons of grain per day). Yet, as we shall see, warring nations have all too often done exactly that — sent huge forces off in a general direction without any clear conception of what they would do when they arrived. Armies that are particularly successful on the operational level — the German army in the early years of World War II, the Soviet army in the later years, the Israel Defense Force, perhaps even the Indian army in its 1971 blitz into East Pakistan, and the U.S. Army in Desert Storm — have always thought of ways to shape the campaign so that they confront the adversary on advantageous terms, rather than simply crashing into the enemy's main body.

One assumption of this work is that operational success is far more a result of "soft factors" than of technology per se. The Germans, for example, owed much of their operational advantage to a highly flexible, decentralized doctrine of command known today as *Auftragstaktik* (mission tactics), although it too is a term that the Germans seldom used.

The higher commander decided on a general mission *(Auftrag)*, passed it on to subordinate commanders in a short, concise order, and then left it up to them to decide the means and methods of achieving it. He was not to draw up a detailed plan for all possibilities and contingencies — an impossible thing to do, in any event, given the rapid pace of the modern machine-driven battlefield, where the overall situation could change by the minute.

In a broader sense, no law or set of laws can ever explain any phenomenon as messy, chaotic, or bound up with chance as operational-level warfare. Starting in the 1980s, the U.S. Army became enamored of general theories of military operations. Concepts like "operational art," "maneuver warfare," "asymmetric warfare," "dislocating" the enemy's "centers of gravity," and "getting inside the opponent's decision cycle" soon became buzzwords, and so did the simple English adjective "deep."[6] Such theoretical approaches to war are completely divorced from the actual history of military campaigns of the modern era. If the last century teaches us anything, it is that military operations have proven remarkably resistant to attempts at codification. It is impossible to apply methods of systems analysis to their workings. Each campaign has unique features, and only a great deal of close historical analysis can help us to understand it. There is still wisdom in the words of the Chief of the German General Staff, Count Alfred von Schlieffen, who once advised his officer corps that "a book lies before each man who wishes to become a commander, and it is entitled Military History."[7]

As with all my books, this one has been the beneficiary of some very helpful people. As always, Randy Talbot, my former graduate student at Eastern Michigan University and now a Staff Historian at the U.S. Army Tank-Automotive and Armaments Command (TACOM) in Warren, Michigan, has been a tremendous aid to me. Collin Boyd and Jacob Hamric, current graduate students, continue to stimulate my thinking with good questions. A collective "thank you" is in order to the entire staff at the U.S. Army Military History Institute (MHI) at Carlisle Barracks, Pennsylvania. Not only are they fiercely dedicated professionals, they also work overtime to make sure that the MHI is a welcoming and friendly home for scholars. The reading room at the MHI is one of the historical profession's very special places. Specifically, I would like to thank Dr. Richard Sommers, the chief of the Patron Services Division at the MHI, who invariably takes time out of his day to inquire into the state of my research. Louise Arnold-Friend, librarian in the Historical Services Division, never misses a single occasion to be helpful, and she can talk hockey with the best of them! Archivists Kathy Olson and David

Keough answered every request for help with knowledge and patience. Mr. Keough gave me a guided tour of the "Vietnam Room" in the MHI basement, introducing me to a truly vast documentary collection. James Corum and Jonathan House read the manuscript and offered a great deal of encouragement and advice, and I am exceedingly grateful to both. They spent so much time and energy helping me on this project that one must ask where they find the time to do so much excellent work of their own. As always, I would like to thank Barbara and Charles Jelavich. As the years pass, I look back on my days with them at Indiana University more and more fondly. Finally, thank you to my beautiful wife, Roberta, and my daughters, Allison, Laura, and Emily. Their love and support are what keeps me going. Of course, any failings in the work are mine alone.

1

Toward World War II:
The Quest for Decisive Victory

World War II in Historical Memory

It seems ironic. By virtually every measurement, World War II was far worse than its immediate predecessor. World War I, with its death toll of twenty million, probably killed more human beings than all previous wars combined. Unfortunately, the same can be said of World War II: its fifty million victims outnumbered all the dead in the entire previous history of war, and that includes World War I. Although the scope of both wars was vast, involving as it did all the continents except Antarctica, Europe was very much the epicenter of World War I. The second was legitimately a "world war," with immense battles fought not only in Europe but also in regions as far-flung as the North African desert, the Arctic Ocean, the islands of the Pacific basin, and the Asian mainland. Both wars featured the targeting of civilian populations for military action, but the zeppelin raids on London during World War I were nothing but a grisly foretaste of what was to come in the next war, when entire cities, along with their populations, were literally incinerated by attack from the air. Moreover, while both wars featured the use of ever more effective weapons, the finest that modern industrial technology could design and produce, it was World War II that bequeathed to humanity the nuclear weapons that could destroy civilization in a few short seconds. World War II was, in short, a disaster: for Europe, for the world, and for the human race.[1]

Still, World War II today enjoys an entirely different, and better, historical reputation than World War I. Few analysts ever refer to it as meaningless, as they routinely do to World War I. Few use it as an object lesson in the futility of war, and it certainly did not lead to the sort of mental and emotional hand-wringing that was a feature of Western life during the 1920s and 1930s. The literature of World War II is, by and large, of an entirely different character than that of the first. There is no World

War II equivalent to *All Quiet on the Western Front*. World War II, despite
the horror, despite the death and destruction, still occupies a place in the
Western imagination as the "crusade in Europe," the "mighty endeavor,"
and, of course, the "good war."[2]

On one level, of course, we have Adolf Hitler to thank for that. Although
historians are generally willing to spread responsibility for great conflicts
in as many directions as possible, that has by and large not happened with
this war.[3] Ridding the world of National Socialism, along with the racial
and militarist values that it championed, is a tough thing to criticize, whatever mixed motives the Allies might have had for actually fighting the war.
A second, related reason, at least from the perspective of American historians, is that the war resulted in the rise of the United States to superpower
status. It capped the seemingly triumphal process that had begun with the
war against Spain and that had continued through American intervention
in World War I in 1917–1918. The spectacle of a reluctant, isolationist-
minded giant finding itself dragged inexorably to the pinnacle of world
power does have its attractions, and American historians and politicians
alike have not been immune to its lure.

But there is another reason for the "good press" that historians have
given this war. It has little to do with the cause for which it was fought
or the political results it brought. It is instead a function of the nature
of the fighting. Rather than a static war of trenches, barbed wire, and
machine guns, this was a war of tanks and aircraft, of extremely high
mobility and the inherent drama that mobility offers. World War I featured huge armies doing little more for the middle two years of the fighting than hunkering down in their trenches and hurling shells at one
another, but World War II was a conflict of rapid maneuver, bold thrusts,
and encirclements. It was a war whose progress could be charted through
a path of catastrophic defeats and decisive victories. Both of these views
are stereotypes, of course. World War I saw repeated campaigns of movement on the eastern front, and World War II certainly had its moments
of stalemate, even trench warfare. Nevertheless, the overall images linger
in the Western consciousness.

The opening years of World War II brought a dramatic end to two debates that had been raging within European armies for years. First, the
dramatic German victories in Poland and France, and the first year of the
war with the Soviet Union established beyond a reasonable doubt that
mechanization was a prerequisite to success on the modern battlefield.
The tank, its strengths and weaknesses, had been at the center of a great
debate among military planners during the two interwar decades. But the
debate suddenly became moot after the great German victory in France.

Tanks and aircraft had played a starring role in Germany's early dramatic victories, and all Germany's neighbors — enemies and neutrals alike — suddenly saw the light regarding their necessity.

Second, and much more broadly, the success of Germany's panzer and air forces had demonstrated that decisive battlefield victory of the sort that had eluded the world's armies since the days of the elder Helmuth von Moltke was still a possibility. Modern armies, apparently, were not doomed to fight bloody, grinding battles of attrition, as they had from 1915 to 1917. They could, once again, maneuver, strike, penetrate, and pursue. They could destroy their adversaries, rather than simply maul and be mauled in turn. They could fight what the Germans traditionally called *Bewegungskrieg* (the war of movement).[4] The days of stalemate, trenches, and the iron grip of the machine gun had suddenly ended. A new era of mobile and decisive warfare had arrived. For six years, the action on all fronts was fast and furious. Armies on both sides experienced the thrill of decisive victory, carrying out dramatic advances hundreds of miles into enemy territory and achieving the encirclement and destruction of vast enemy forces. This was war as understood in the days of Napoleon, and it is interesting to see how instinctively the world responded to its drama.

The scenes crowd upon one another. German panzers reaching the English Channel on May 20, 1940, after breaking through the French lines at Sedan and carrying out an audacious dash across the rear of the Allied armies fighting in Belgium. The German drive into Soviet Russia in 1941, featuring the greatest annihilation battles in the history of warfare, yet falling tantalizingly short of total victory. The Red Army, pounded nearly to extinction in 1941, reviving in 1942 and coolly turning the tables on the Germans at a place called Stalingrad. The Western Allies breaking out of their Normandy bridgehead in August 1944 in Operation Cobra, lunging clear across western Europe in a single campaign and reaching the very borders of Germany itself. The real reason that World War II has continued to touch the historical imagination of both scholars and nonscholars alike is that it was so much more exciting.

The Supremacy of Fire? Problems of Command, Control, and Information, 1860–1914

To explain the impact of World War II on its contemporaries, it is necessary first to discuss the fifty years that preceded it. Starting in the late nineteenth century, it was clear to military analysts that a fundamental problem had arisen in the conduct of military operations. Although campaigns were becoming larger, bloodier, and costlier than ever before, they were also becoming curiously indecisive. Virtually every great campaign from 1899 onward followed the same general pattern: offensive operations started out in promising fashion and then bogged down short of victory. This development reached its zenith, or perhaps nadir, in World War I, a conflict that began as a series of mobile campaigns in which all the combatants sought an operational decision through maneuver warfare and then soon degenerated into a series of static, grinding battles of attrition. It seemed to many that the disastrous course of the war, and the immense casualties it generated, had sounded the death knell for military operations as they had been traditionally conceived since the days of Napoleon: a series of maneuvers in the open field designed to culminate in a decisive battle against the enemy's main force.

The inability to achieve decisive victory was due to a number of factors. Contemporary discussion of the problem usually pinned the blame on the increase in defensive firepower brought about by new weapons: the rifle (especially in its breech-loading form), the machine gun, and new forms of rapid-fire artillery. The new weaponry, so the argument goes, could inflict such severe losses on the attacker that old-style Napoleonic assaults were doomed to fail. Even if, somehow, the attack had succeeded in reaching the enemy's position, defensive fire left the assault troops well and thoroughly mauled, with their units intermingled and their chain of command disrupted by key officer casualties.

Although there is some truth to the traditional argument, the breakdown of operations actually involved far more complex problems of command and control. These included the rise of mass armies, so large that they had lost the ability to maneuver in any real sense; the absolute dependency of these hordes on the railroad; and the static nature of the telegraph net, making it nearly impossible for the commander to conduct a mobile offensive or to control the dispersed masses, especially when they were in contact with the enemy or under fire.[5] Equally important to the breakdown of operations was the increasingly problematic issue of information, in its broadest possible sense: the gathering and dissemination of intelligence; the formulation and distribution of orders; and the maintenance of liaison between the units fighting at the front and the command structure. Imprecise, insufficient, or late information had always played a role in battle, of course, but the problem had intensified as the armies had grown.[6]

Information problems could show up in many forms. The difficulty of insufficient information, or none at all, occurs repeatedly in campaigns of the era. For the best example, one need look no further than the masterpiece of the great Prussian commander Helmuth von Moltke, his victory over the Austrians at Königgrätz in 1866.[7] It comes as a bit of a shock to historians of the campaign to realize that, on the very eve of the battle, Moltke wasn't even sure *on which bank* of the mighty Elbe River the Austrians were deployed.[8] The Boer War of 1899–1902 was fought in a theater of war bigger than France and Spain combined, served by three single-track railroads, much of it without telegraph, and large sectors still unmapped.[9] At the battle of Colenso, the link between British commander Sir Redvers Buller and his assault units was a system of pennants and the unreliable heliograph. During the Russo-Japanese War, in the midst of their leisurely pursuit of the Russians after the battle of Liaoyang, the Japanese were actually surprised by a range of mountains they encountered.[10] Nor did either side in that conflict ever solve the problem of the *kaoliang*, a variety of millet that grows ten to twelve feet tall, high enough to hide sizable forces from prying eyes.[11]

As for wrong information, the connoisseur has a true smorgasbord of examples from which to choose. In the Boer War, on two separate occasions, at the Modder River and at Colenso on the Tugela River, the British launched assaults into the teeth of entrenched Boer forces.[12] Both times, they were misinformed as to the true course of the river they were facing, as well as the location of its crossing points. In the First Balkan War, the Turks believed that the Bulgarian army would launch an opening strike directly against the fortress of Adrianople. They therefore planned to reinforce the fortress in the opening days of the war. In fact, the Bulgarians deployed an entire army well to the east of the fortress. The war opened with the Bulgarians driving deep into the Turkish right flank and rear, catching the Turkish main body moving up to Adrianople completely unaware and routing it.[13]

Finally, there was a problem that we today find familiar: too much information. Although the telegraph was immobile and inflexible, it did manage to generate thick reams of dispatches that had to be decoded, typed, and placed on the commander's desk. During the opening weeks of World War I, this mountain of confusing reports proved to be completely beyond the comprehension of all the commanders involved; more than a few of them (Sir John French of the British Expeditionary Force; German 8th Army commander Max von Prittwitz; Russian 2nd Army commander A. V. Samsonov, and the supreme German commander, Helmuth von Moltke the Younger) cracked completely under the strain.

It is difficult to defend Moltke's prosecution of the 1914 campaign, but it is easy to sympathize with him. Especially toward the end, during the battle of the Marne, Moltke lost control of the operation. Alone in his office, far from the front, carrying the fate of Germany on his slumped shoulders, his desk piled high with a mountain of paper that he did not even have time to read, let alone digest, he was the first victim of a new twentieth-century problem: information overload. Anyone who has ever sat down at the computer and found three hundred unread e-mail messages understands his problem. Moltke reacted by "pressing the delete button," in a sense, abdicating his command and sending Colonel Richard Hentsch on his fateful journey to the front, with orders to "coordinate a general withdrawal," if necessary.[14] The Hentsch mission ended with the retreat of the German right wing back to the Aisne River and the end of German hopes for a rapid victory in 1914.

The Death of Operations, 1915–1917

All the preceding problems reached their culmination during the trench years of World War I, from 1915 to 1917. Those who argue that the problem was mainly one of firepower certainly have a case. New and ever heavier artillery came into action, forcing the infantry on both sides to dig trenches to survive. The machine gun, the "concentrated essence of infantry," could literally sweep the field clean of attackers, turning the assault zone into a "no-man's land" that no enemy could cross. Again, unfortunately, there are several examples from which to choose. An English historian might look to the first day of the battle of the Somme, when German machine guns annihilated hapless waves of British infantry as they tried to "assault" across no-man's land. A French or German scholar might call forth the battle of Verdun, with the men on both sides sitting under an unceasing rain of high-explosive shells, literally ground up in the "mill on the Meuse." British military analyst Basil Liddell Hart, who built an entire career on exploiting these horrors, once described the foot soldiers of the war as being "yoked like dumb, driven oxen to the chariot of Mars," and it is an apt image.[15]

Even here, however, problems of intelligence, information, and command and control of the mass army played a crucial role. A close look at the war's worst "slaughter battles" — Gallipoli, Verdun, and the Somme — show how close each of the offensives came to succeeding. At Gallipoli, the British 29th Infantry Division landed around the southern tip of the peninsula, Cape Helles, hitting five separate beaches simultaneously (designated, left to right, Y, X, W, V, and S). At four of the five landing sites, the landings met a hail of fire from well-prepared Turkish forces, enduring an orgy of slaughter and barely getting ashore. At Y Beach, however, less than an hour's march northwest of the cape, two thousand men managed to land without a shot fired. They then sat there for eleven hours while confusion, administrative muddle, and lack of orders prevented them from exploiting a success that would have cut off all the Turkish defenders farther down the peninsula. The disaster at the other beaches left them in a precarious perch, and eventually they reembarked. Likewise, the landing of the Australian-New Zealand Army Corps (ANZAC) at Gaba Tepe met little opposition. Patrols penetrated three and a half miles inland, where they could actually look clear across the peninsula to the Narrows — the operational objective of the campaign. Unfortunately, command paralysis, lack of intelligence, and unfamiliarity with the terrain now conspired to halt the advance. The pattern was repeated in the subsequent landing on August 6, at Suvla Bay to the north of Gaba Tepe. The force landed without incident, as well it should have, there being a complete absence of Turks in front of it. Then it failed to push inland. In all these landings, numerous objectives could have been had simply by advancing toward them on the first day. A week later, they could not be had for tens of thousands of casualties.[16]

It brings us no closer to understanding the phenomenon if we simply blame the man on the spot. Sir Ian Hamilton, the force commander, had no idea what was happening on shore, nor, with the technology of the day, could he. Often criticized for being aboard ship as the landings were taking place, he wouldn't have been any better served by being ashore. This is not to argue that the failure at Gallipoli was foreordained. It is simply an appeal for higher, systematic analysis of these well-known battlefield failures. Historians have tended to personalize the entire process: this commander failed at a crucial moment, zigged when he should have zagged; that commander was too old or infirm or simply having a bad day. What one can't help but notice is that these same explanations keep popping up again and again for every battlefield failure in history.

Similar things happened the first day on the Somme. Analysis of the entire campaign tends to focus on the opening fiasco, as the 4th Army under General Henry Rawlinson went "over the top" to its doom. But as bad as the casualties were on that terrible day, it must be pointed out that at several places in the attack sector, the British came within a hair of breaking through the German positions altogether. Overwhelming German firepower crushed the center of the assault, but that was far from true on the flanks. On the far right wing of Rawlinson's offensive, the 30th Division, consisting of new battalions of "Pals" from Manchester and Liverpool plus four battalions of regular troops, stormed and

occupied the German line with few casualties. Along with a French success on their right and a successful advance by the 18th Division on their
left, it seemed as if the 30th Division just might have found the key to
the entire German position on the Somme. The village of Montauban,
one of the first-day objectives, lay in their path. They stormed it. The
Germans fled from their last trench behind the town ("Montauban
Alley") into a wide valley, and a few of the Pals pursued them there, capturing two field guns whose crews had been too slow to get away. Most
of the division could now see something that few soldiers in the war
would ever see: clear, open terrain without an enemy, green fields, woods.
Then, of course, in an all too familiar scenario, they waited for orders
to advance, orders that never came. By the time word had gotten back
to Rawlinson about this success, the disaster in the center of his line
occupied all his attention. The command mechanism of the 4th Army
was working on other problems. The Germans managed to rush reinforcements to the Montauban sector and to reform their line.[17]

In a sense, the positional warfare of the trench years simplified the
command and control problems of the mass army. The enemy was there,
directly to the front; friendly forces were here, facing them. A fairly
simple regimen of trench raids could gather all the information one could
possibly need. "Command and control" of a trench force was child's play
compared to warfare under more mobile conditions. Units hunkered
down in a trench were always under control. But to what purpose? Even
assaults that broke into the enemy's defenses got stuck once there,
because of the same complex set of problems that had bedeviled military
operations since Napoleon's day. The real issue was how to restore operational mobility.

Rebirth: The Interwar Military Revolution

During the interwar period (1919–1939), the German army found a
solution.[18] It managed to develop a war-fighting doctrine that shattered
the trench deadlock once and for all. At its heart were highly mobile
armored (panzer) formations working in close cooperation with aircraft.
By now, it is a well-known fact that the Germans themselves did not
coin the term *blitzkrieg* (lightning war).[19] In fact, they were much more
likely to use the term *Bewegungskrieg*. Still, *blitzkrieg* does have some utility in describing a wildly successful operational doctrine employed by
the German army in the opening days of World War II. It had a profound influence on the war-making doctrine of the nations it fought, at

least in the sense of convincing them to form large tank and aircraft fleets. It still informs the operational doctrine of every modern army in the world and was especially important to the U.S. Army's development of the AirLand Battle doctrine. We may define blitzkrieg, then, as a doctrine of employing mechanized units (including air units) on a grand scale to defeat, pursue, and destroy entire enemy armies within a two-to-four-week span of time. With the old command problems solved, or at least eased, by the invention of the radio, the Germans were able to restore the *campaign* — an interconnected series of maneuvers and battles aimed at the defeat of the enemy's main field force — to its rightful place in military affairs. In so doing, they set a standard to which, consciously or unconsciously, every later army has aspired.

Why did the Germans succeed where others failed? The tank was, after all, first developed in Great Britain, and the British were far ahead in the field-testing of mechanized units. Their Experimental Mechanized Force was undergoing trials as early as 1927, at a time when the Germans did not possess a single tank or military aircraft because of the disarmament clauses of the Treaty of Versailles.[20] The same might be said for the French, Russians, and Italians; even a lesser power like Poland had some tanks in its arsenal.

To understand the German achievement, we must look first to the past. Although there is a tendency to view blitzkrieg — with its dependency on machines and its rapid pace — as a modern manifestation, in fact the Germans based their mechanized doctrine on a very old and very traditional view of war. They traced it back to Frederick the Great, Carl von Clausewitz, and the elder Helmuth von Moltke, and it had survived even the recent experience of World War I. The Germans saw themselves as engaged not so much in innovation as in restoration of their classical doctrinal traditions.

What were they? First, there was the flexible doctrine of command that had been developed in the nineteenth century. The Germans saw no certainty in war. "Strategy," Moltke once wrote, "is a system of expedients," and on another occasion, "No plan survives contact with the enemy's main body." While it was on the march, an army had to be ready for anything, not hamstrung by rigid orders. "Only the layman perceives the campaign in terms of a fixed original conception, carried out in all details and rigidly followed until the end," he wrote.[21] His solution was a system that is often called *Auftragstaktik* (mission tactics) today, although that, too, is a term the Germans themselves used seldom, if at all.[22] The commander devised the mission (*Auftrag*), but left the methods and means of achieving it to the officer on the spot.[23] There was no need for long, detailed orders. Instead they should be crisp, clear, and short. In fact, they did not even have to be written down; the German army made more extensive use of verbal orders than any other force in the world. In the wars of German unification, for example, Moltke's touch was light indeed. Often, his army commanders did what they thought was correct and reported it to him afterward. On several occasions in the 1866 campaign, armies of more than 100,000 men went a day or two without any orders at all — an incredible notion by our modern standards.

Second, the Germans already viewed the operational level as the normative level for conducting warfare. A commander was expected to do more than simply oversee a strategic buildup of forces in a theater in order to overwhelm his opponent. Crammed into an unfortunately tight spot in central Europe, ringed by enemies and potential enemies, the Germans had neither the time nor the manpower for such an approach. Likewise, an emphasis on tactics might lead to local success but not the rapid victory Germany needed in any likely wartime scenario. German staff officers had been conceiving war in operational terms — that is, at the level of the campaign — for nigh on two centuries. There were two types of operations: the static "war of position" (*Stellungskrieg*) and the "war of movement" in the open field (*Bewegungskrieg*). The former was sterile, bloody, and likely to lead to a war of attrition, something the Germans dreaded. It was unsuited for achieving rapid and decisive results. It was, indeed, a degenerate form of warfare, mechanical and dull, that allowed the commander little scope for creative decision making.[24] It was a German axiom that an army commander in a *Stellungskrieg* had less authority or opportunity to shine than a regimental commander under more mobile conditions.[25] Mobile warfare, as embodied in the campaigns of Frederick the Great, Napoleon, and the elder Moltke, was the only means to win the quick and decisive victory Germany required. Battles like Rossbach (1757), Friedland (1807), or Königgrätz (1866) were intellectual touchstones for German officers in the interwar period. The German task in the 1920s and 1930s, then, was not to "invent" something new. It was merely to return war to the fruitful path of *Bewegungskrieg*. Tanks, aircraft, and all the new technologies being investigated in the period were nothing more than means to that end. This is a crucial distinction between the Germans and the British or French, for example.

A third tradition was the unique nature of German military culture. Although in many ways the interwar period was the age of the enthusiast, always preaching the wonders of some new weapon or doctrine, one sees very little of it in German military writings. German officers prided themselves on avoiding *Einseitigkeit* (one-sidedness) in their discourse. Claims that this or that new weapon had revolutionized the art of war were simply foreign to their way of thinking. They had a perfectly sound conceptual framework for understanding war, they believed: *Bewegungskrieg*, the war of movement on the operational level. There had been no fundamental change in the nature of war. The nature of war was unchanging, as per Clausewitz: it was, and is, an act of violence to compel an enemy to do one's will. The only point at issue was how to resurrect the war of movement and once again fight campaigns of decisive victory. While the rest of the armies in the world were essentially trying to reform their tactics, the Germans were looking at war's operational level.[26]

Another example of the German disdain for one-sidedness was the conspicuous lack of an "all-tank school" in Germany. Mobility could only be restored through the combination of all weapons working in harmony. Warfare could still aim at decisive results, but only on a combined arms battlefield. There was no mechanization debate in Germany; machines had become indispensable. The light mortar, light and heavy machine guns, motorized and mechanized vehicles of all sorts (tanks, trucks, armored cars, motorcycles, gun carriages, and especially aircraft) had an important role to play, and contemporary warfare had become unthinkable without them. But just as there was no real debate on mechanization, there was never a significant body of opinion making overly extravagant claims on behalf of the tank. No German officer ever argued that tanks working alone on a battlefield would be capable of much of anything, save rolling off to their own destruction. Tanks had to work in harmony with the other weapons, whose standards of mobility had been raised up to their own.

The Radio: *Funkübung,* 1932

One area generally ignored in a historical discussion of combined arms is the radio. Although the strengths and weaknesses of the tank were the obsession of most contemporary military discourse, radio was the real breakthrough of the period. The days of the runner, the unreliable telegraph, and Morse code were gone, replaced by direct voice messages from the commander to subordinate and vice versa. It was not the result of a single invention but was instead a gradual process. The large and unwieldy "unquenched" sets of the wartime period gave way to smaller high-frequency sets, and manual tuning yielded to the crystal. Although

Panzerkampfwagen

Motorisierte
Nachrichten

Mot. Schützen

Funk

Kradschützen

Artillerie mot.

Fernsprecher

Pioniere mot.

Panzerabwehr

Flieger

Aufklärungs Abt. mot.
Pz. Spähwagen

Reiter

Kav. Geschütz

Radfahrer

Rückwärtige Dienste mot.

Aufbau und Einheiten der Schnellen Truppen

More than just tanks: A portrait of Germany's mobile troops, including cavalry, motorcycles, and bicycles. From *Die Wehrmacht* 3, no. 17, August 16, 1939, p. 2.

the British were the first to make tactical use of them in their tanks, the Germans worked to grasp their operational possibilities. For the first time, a commander could monitor his own and the enemy's dispositions in real time and be able to use that information to direct far-flung battlefield action, enabling divisions, corps, even entire armies "to wheel like companies" on the battlefield of the future.[27] The military revolution of the interwar era was as much one of information and intelligence as of new equipment and weaponry.

The summer of 1932, for example, saw the Reichswehr undertaking an exercise designed to test the skills of the radio troops in the event of a war. This *Funkübung* (radio exercise) differed from earlier, purely technical, exercises among the signal troops by reason of its size, scope, and operational character.[28] Radio exercises had taken place in the Reichswehr before, but they typically taught the trainee how to solve problems arising from technical difficulties, such as insufficient range or malfunctions. This exercise, by contrast, focused on problems arising from the operational situation. It placed modern operational concepts, especially leadership in the mobile battle, in the foreground to investigate the technical problems they posed for the signal troops, and it laid special stress on the key role of the radio in a war of movement. This required a large number of men and a large amount of equipment — some 300 officers, 2,000 men, 450 vehicles, 88 complete radio sets, and 300 horses, as well as a large neutral radio and telephone net for the directors and umpires.

The situation postulated a mobile invasion by Red (Czechoslovakian) forces of Blue (German) territory, breaking out on May 20 of some future year. Red assembled Army Group A on both sides of the Elbe near Leitmeritz, with orders for a swift advance up the Elbe to Dresden and eventually to Berlin. To the left of the army group was an independent 1st Army deployed in the Karlsbad region, consisting of eight infantry divisions, two cavalry divisions, an "armored unit" (*Panzerverband*), and a mountain brigade. Its orders called for a rapid blow in the direction of Erfurt to prevent unified action by forces in northern and southern Germany and to seize armaments factories in the central part of the country. In response, Blue deployed a border defense force (*Grenzschutz*) between the Danube and Elbe at the beginning of June, with sector headquarters in Nürnberg and Chemnitz. The border defenses were to fight a delaying defense and retire sector by sector.

Red forces crossed the border on June 1, and by June 5 Army Group A was nearing Dresden. The 1st Army easily broke through Blue's border defense cordon; a Red Cavalry Corps (1st and 2nd Cavalry Divisions) was already northwest of Zwickau, and infantry units had reached the line

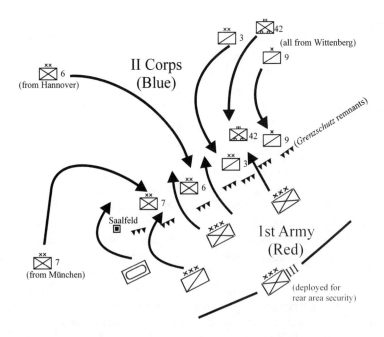

The Reichswehr's Radio Exercise *(Funkübung)*, summer 1932: Meeting engagement between Red 1st Army and Blue II Corps.

Hof-Plauen. Red's armored unit entered Bayreuth, and its patrols were as far west as Kulmbach. But Red also had to deploy an entire army corps (the III) in its rear to deal with an uprising by the German civilian population that had already developed into a series of guerrilla operations. Thus, as Red advanced, its rearward communications became increasingly threatened.

To oppose the Red advance, Blue's Army Command assembled II Corps, composed of the 6th and 7th Infantry Divisions, arriving by rail from Hannover and München, respectively; the 3rd Cavalry Division, coming up from Wittenberg; and new units like the 9th Cavalry Brigade and the 42nd Infantry Regiment, a motorized unit. The corps had orders to screen the Leipzig-Halle-Jena industrial region and maintain communication between northern and southern Germany. Unfortunately, by the time most of the corps had assembled, Red armor had already reached Bamberg and was wheeling north, threatening to envelop the newly arrived 7th Infantry Division at Saalfeld. The rest of the Blue command also found itself threatened by forward Red units as the latter drove quickly to the north. The first task of the exercise was for each Blue unit to radio its position and readiness for combat, as quickly as possible, to II Corps headquarters in Münster.

The Red and Blue signal services each had unique problems. Red's situation was that of a systematic and well-planned advance and attack, directed from the beginning by a definite and strict operational conception. Its radio net, therefore, bore the same stamp; it was "prepared calmly and systematically from the beginning." Blue had to improvise, both technically and tactically. Its rapidly and haphazardly inserted regular units found themselves intermingled with border defense units, forced to cooperate in a common strategy of delaying defense. The difference in organization and equipment between their signal units led to a great deal of friction. Moreover, Blue had to maintain communications in the face of overwhelming Red superiority in the air and far-ranging Red armored units. Red, too, faced problems, notably the civilian uprising in its rear areas that threatened to choke off its telegraph communications altogether.

As in all German maneuvers, the exercise ended with a final discussion (*Schlussbesprechung*), led by the inspector of the signal troops, General von Bonin. He began by remarking that the problems posed by the exercise, especially those on the Blue side, were seldom seen in peacetime training. But "a future war will require us to master them," he said. Signal troop training had until then concentrated on operations up to divisional size. The exercise had confirmed that communications within the division were generally good. But signal troops had much less practice in operational-level communications. This, too, had been evident. It had taken almost one full day of the exercises to make the operational net (that is, between the component divisions and the corps headquarters) fully functional. In a real war, however, the smooth flow of radio traffic within the first twenty-four hours might be crucial.

Bonin saw another danger, as well, what he called the "bureaucratization" of the radio service. A radioman was not simply a factotum who encrypted, handled, and decoded other people's messages. He had to be completely immersed in the operational situation and its requirements, and free of the "spirit of the filing cabinet." In many cases, he would be the one to decide what to send and what not to send. Not all messages were equally important. For example, the arrival of an eagerly awaited message from a reconnaissance battalion required breaking in on a less important transmission. The entire "soul" of the radio unit, he said, from commander down to operator, must be permeated with the idea of rapid transmission. In keeping with the army's tradition, Bonin wanted radio messages kept short. There was no time in a rapidly changing situation for long-winded reports or detailed orders.

The *Funkübung* of 1932 is important not for any specific lesson it taught or technical glitch it uncovered. Rather than being viewed as a test bed, the exercise should be seen as a training tool, in which German officers gained experience in the process of radio communication among divisional, corps, and army headquarters. The goal was not something new, but something that the Germans had long realized was a problem for modern mass armies: smooth command and control on the operational level. Germany led all interwar armies in the frequency and detail of such operational exercises, as well as the painstaking analysis afforded to them.

The pages of the interwar German literature were likewise filled with discussions of the role of information and the importance of the radio. The new mechanized *Bewegungskrieg* would be fast paced and hard driving. It would require quick decisions on the part of all ranks, as well as close contact between command and forward elements. The lead essay in a 1935 issue of the semiofficial *Militär-Wochenblatt* spoke of an ongoing "reorganization of warfare."[29] Information was the departure point. "Today," wrote the anonymous author, "there are more eyes on the enemy." Even more important, what they saw could be immediately and effortlessly reported over great distance. New technologies were lifting the fog of war, replacing it with secure knowledge. It was no longer possible, to give just one example, to hide that old tactical staple, the 4–5 km per hour infantry flank march. At the present time, troops could be photographed, wrote the author; very soon, television technology would be available. In union with long-range reconnaissance aircraft, television would give the commander even more certitude about enemy dispositions and intentions.

In 1936, General Heinz Guderian published an article in the General Staff journal, *Militärwissenschaftliche Rundschau*, that explored the cooperation of tanks with the other arms. He argued that "intelligence forces intended for cooperation with the Panzers must primarily be radio troops." Radio would be essential for maintaining communications in all directions: from the divisional commander down to his regiments and independent detachments; between the various division commanders; above to the fliers (both reconnaissance and tactical); and back to the corps and army headquarters. In the new, complex, three-dimensional battlefield, maintaining an adequate flow of quick and reliable information was not a luxury. Indeed, the "rapidly changing conditions of battle" as well as "the necessity for the commander to be far forward" meant that he had to have "highly mobile, fully armored, all-terrain intelligence vehicles" at his disposal.[30] The tank-aircraft-radio marriage was yet another form of combined arms.

The problems of radio communication received even closer attention in a 1938 article in the same journal. Colonel Fuppe claimed that signal troops were not simply technical personnel, with a narrow training in the operation of certain types of equipment. Rather, they had to be seen as field officers, thoroughly schooled in the operational and tactical situation, ready to employ their radio assets at the point of main effort. This *Funkschwerpunkt* would almost always be found with the mechanized forces. The need for radio would always be more urgent here than it would be with the traditional arms. The war of movement would place a heavy strain on communications, especially when it came to the far-flung insertion of panzer or motorized troops and to the cooperation of land and air assets.[31] Fuppe viewed radio primarily as a facilitator for the new arms. There were, however, just as many officers arguing for radio's usefulness in making the traditional arms more effective, enabling closer cooperation between infantry and artillery, for example.[32]

The German army was the first to realize that radio communications for transmitting both orders and intelligence were not simply desirable as far as the new mobile formations were concerned. Instead, the radio was absolutely indispensable. "It is part of the unique character of motorized and mechanized units that they can only be commanded with the assistance of technical means of communication," wrote Major Friedrich Bertkau. "The masses of motor vehicles in their extraordinarily long columns or widely dispersed battle formations, the noise of the machines, the difficulty of observation from inside the tank, the speed of movement, the rapid change of the battle situation, the special difficulty in moving at night — all these demand a technical solution to command problems."[33] Only the radio could provide an instantaneous way to report the situation back to the commander and to send relevant orders to the troops. From the start, the German principle for the new panzer division was a radio in each command station and each vehicle of the unit, from the smallest motorcycle to the heaviest tank, with specialized command vehicles designed to carry radio equipment, both senders and receivers. Tank warfare on the operational level, in other words, was unthinkable without the radio.

During the interwar era, the German army solved the problem of operational indecisiveness. The solution blended the old and the new. On one hand, German success was due to traditions like a flexible doctrine of command, a positive orientation toward the operational level of war, and a strong prejudice in German military culture against intellectual one-sidedness (*Einseitigkeit*) in thought and discourse. On the other, the Germans had a high appreciation for the importance of communications and the role that the new technology such as radio could play in controlling a sprawling mass army. The German doctrinal achievement in the inter-war era grew out of specific German traditions. These included a flexible system of command and an emphasis on the operational level of warfare, as opposed to the strategic or the tactical. In the end, the Germans fused traditional operational doctrine and modern mechanized equipment into decisive victory in the opening year of World War II and in the process revived the art of warfare on the operational level.

Bewegungskrieg in Poland: Case White

The campaign in Poland offered proof of the military revolution. The operational plan for Case White featured concentric drives by two widely separated army groups — five full armies — operating from Pomerania and East Prussia in the north and from Silesia and occupied Slovakia in the south. The Wehrmacht deployed in two main forces: Army Group North (General Fedor von Bock) and Army Group South (General Gerd von Rundstedt). Their operations resulted in the formation of two great pincers: 4th Army advancing from Pomerania and 8th and 10th Armies advancing from Silesia forming one; 3rd Army from East Prussia and 14th Army from Slovakia forming another. The maneuver caught most of the Polish army in a fantastic *Kessel* ("cauldron," or encirclement). The Poles lost 65,000 men killed in action, 144,000 wounded, and 587,000 prisoners of war. The advance was incredibly rapid, with the German panzer forces reaching the outskirts of Warsaw on September 8. By September 19, only the capital held out — the Germans, in fact, spoke of the "Eighteen Days' Campaign."[34] Surrounded and under constant aerial bombardment, Warsaw fell September 27. Although there were, as in any large-scale operation, a few missteps here and there, the new radio-commanded, machine-driven *Bewegungskrieg* worked practically to perfection.

The new stability of command afforded by the radio allowed the Germans to break in, through, and out of the principal Polish defensive positions at the border. The Polish decision, undertaken for political rather than operational reasons, to defend every inch of the country's overlong border assisted the Germans, but nevertheless the Wehrmacht's achievement was impressive. In contrast to virtually every campaign fought since the days of Napoleon, German momentum did not flag but actu-

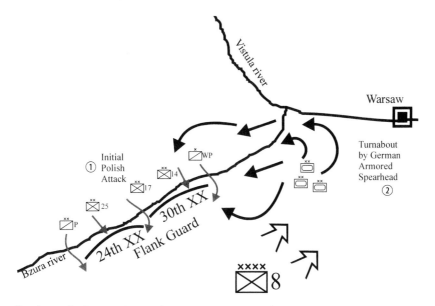

Battle on the Bzura, September 9–12, 1939: Polish attack and German counterattack.

ally increased as the first week of the campaign passed. Elements that had stalled previous campaigns — fortifications like the ones at Modlin outside Warsaw, for example — were now simply crushed by air attacks. Dive-bombers, or *Stukas*, proved especially effective. Massed into a "Close Battle Division" of 160 aircraft, they destroyed the Modlin position, cracking what would have been a tough nut indeed for ground forces alone.[35] No longer, as in previous campaigns, did armies have to pause while the heavy siege guns rolled up.

The campaign was quick, the pace relentless, and the manner of giving orders had to keep pace. The past two decades of work on short, crisp orders bore fruit. Captain Hans von Luck ordered his company into action against the first Polish defensive position he encountered on the evening of September 1, 1939, with a simple verbal order: "No. 1 and No. 2 platoons attack. No. 3 platoon in reserve, the heavy platoon to give fire-cover." He soon found that he had to add, "Everyone follow me."[36]

Although the huge body of literature on this campaign virtually ignores them, the Poles fought bravely and well. They even launched a major counterattack along the Bzura River west of Warsaw, on September 9–12. Units of the Polish Poznan Army under General Tadeusz

Kutrzeba (the 14th, 17th, and 25th Infantry Divisions and the Podol-
ska and Wielkopolska Cavalry Brigades) hit the overextended German
24th and 30th Infantry Divisions strung out along the Bzura, where
they were serving as the northern flank guard for the advance of the
German 8th Army (General Johannes Blaskowitz).[37] The attack achieved
total surprise and made good progress at first, capturing some 1,500
German prisoners from 30th Division alone. It certainly caused anxious
moments at German headquarters, both on the army and army group
levels. Nevertheless, superior operational mobility on the part of the
Germans turned the tables dramatically. German reinforcements were
soon on the way, including the mass of 8th Army's armored units.
Diverted instantaneously from the drive on Warsaw, they shifted their
axis 180 degrees almost effortlessly — an object lesson in the command
advantages of the radio. The insufficiency of the Polish radio net, meanwhile, forced the Polish attackers to act in isolation, without support
from forces in the rest of the country — who were having troubles of
their own, to be sure. Faced with concentric attacks from all four points
of the compass, the mass of the Polish attackers was soon hemmed into
a small pocket on the Bzura, along with remnants of Army Pomorze who
had retreated from the northwest under the hammer blows of Army
Group North. Subjected to unremitting attack by the Luftwaffe and
punished heavily by mobile German artillery, in a hopeless strategic situation, more than 100,000 men surrendered by September 21. At this
point, 8th Army did it again: shifting its axis of advance 180 degrees for
the second time in a week and hurrying back toward Warsaw.[38]

Case Yellow

The offensive in France and the Low Countries was even more impressive.[39] Featuring a grand diversion in the north (Bock's Army Groups
North) and a main panzer thrust through the supposedly impassable tank
country of the Ardennes forest in the south (Rundstedt's Army Group
South), it blasted a hole through the French lines at Sedan. From here, the
panzers drove to the sea across the rear of the Allied forces in Belgium,
reaching the English Channel and achieving a complete encirclement of
the enemy. Besides tanks, the campaign featured well-integrated air power,
used both tactically and operationally; assault by airborne infantry (*Fallschirmjäger*) to secure airfields, ground installations, and bridges; even a
direct assault by glider-borne infantry on Fort Eben Emael, the modern
Belgian fortress guarding the left bank of the Albert Canal.

The Ardennes thrust was extremely risky. It involved a massive force, including seven of Germany's ten panzer divisions. Getting a column of mechanized and motorized vehicles some fifty miles long through the winding trails and old growth of the forest was the trick. The problem of traffic control alone was a prodigious one, and there was a great deal of concern on the part of the Germans as to what might happen if the Allied air forces decided to show up. The Allies did not consider the Ardennes good tank country, however, and thus had left it nearly undefended. Brushing aside small units of Belgian motorized cavalry, the panzers got through, unmolested, in just two days.

And then came the assault, as the mass of the German armored force smashed into one of the most weakly defended points in the French lines. Three panzer corps had arrived on the Meuse: XV Corps under General Hermann Hoth in the north, concentrated between Namur and Dinant; XLI Corps under General Reinhardt in the center, at Monthermé; and XIX Corps under General Guderian in the south, massed in front of Sedan. Each encountered some tough fighting, but, with the French under constant attack by dive-bombing aircraft (the *Stuka*) and German artillery, each managed to get across the river and break through the French defenses. It was all quite methodical. In Guderian's sector, the XIX Corps chief of staff, Colonel Walther Nehring, dusted off the orders used in a recent war game, crossed out the dates, changed an item here and there, and used them almost verbatim.[40]

The German pursuit across northern France will always stand as a high water mark for armored forces. Never pausing, never letting the foe regroup, the panzer forces raced across the open country of northern France to the sea. The Allies, their original plan of battle thoroughly mangled and suddenly finding large enemy forces well to their rear, never did manage any sort of coordinated response. There were two local counterattacks by the French 4th Armored Division under the command of General Charles de Gaulle, the first toward Montcornet (May 17) and the second toward Crécy (May 20), as well as an attack by two British armored columns near Arras on May 21.[41] None of them did anything to break German momentum, however. A potentially more serious problem came from within the German high command. So rapidly were the panzer divisions advancing that, at one point, the Chief of Staff, General Franz Halder, actually ordered them to halt, to let the supporting infantry divisions catch up. The German command had reason to be nervous. The panzer forces were like a huge arrow, strung out over a hundred miles of terrain and pointing toward the coast, but only three to five miles wide. Under the guise of a "reconnaissance in force," however, Guderian continued the advance. The victorious drive ended, as we have seen, with the Spitta Battalion pulling into Noyelles on the Atlantic Coast.

This was a victory of tanks, to be sure, but tanks that operated with supporting arms of equal mobility, in units that were commanded by men who understood the operational potential of their new mobile units and who communicated with them, with each other, and with higher headquarters through the instantaneous medium of radio. Airpower had proved itself to be a full partner in military operations. No longer a luxury or piece of exotica, it had become indispensable to any possible scheme of operational-level warfare. Holding together this complex modern field force, coordinating air assets, mechanized spearheads, follow-on infantry, and the huge supply chain necessary to feed them all, was the radio. Along with the tank and the airplane, it was one of the three makers of this revolution in military affairs. Hardware was important, certainly, but only in that it allowed the Germans to bring concepts of leadership and command that had been simmering for decades to near-perfect fruition. The Germans had redesigned the "chariot of Mars," so that it could be controlled, guided, and driven. It ran on gas, oil, and, just as important, radio-transmitted information.

The German Achievement

In the last twenty years, there has been a great deal of interest in the German army. Both scholars and soldiers — academics and "operators" — have spent a great deal of energy and ink attempting to analyze the true nature of the German achievement during the interwar period, parsing it in every conceivable way, trying to unlock the secret to its success. General Hans von Seeckt, the chief of the Army Command during the 1920s, is probably better known to the world today than he was at the time, and the same might be said for a host of other German military thinkers. The use (and as some have suggested, abuse) of German military terms is quite common in today's U.S. Army, a sign of the importance placed on the Polish and French campaigns in the formulation of U.S. military doctrine, and especially AirLand Battle. It is difficult to pick up the professional literature of the past decades without running into terms like *Auftragstaktik*, *Kesselschlacht*, and, of course, *blitzkrieg*.

On the surface, this is perfectly understandable. The German army of the interwar period offers a classic model of how an army can innovate during peacetime. The Reichswehr faced a set of constraints that were unprecedented in military history. The disarmament clauses of the Treaty of Versailles left Germany with an army of only 100,000 men (of whom no more than 4,000 could be officers). It dictated the organization and armament of the force: seven infantry and three cavalry divisions, without any "offensive weapons" such as tanks, aircraft, or heavy artillery. It prohibited conscription, so that the force consisted of long-term volunteers (twelve years for the men, twenty-five years for the officers), stipulations that theoretically made it impossible for the Germans to accumulate a trained reserve. It abolished the Great General Staff, as well as the *Kriegsakademie* that had trained it. Finally, in a move that had to impact military readiness, it saddled Germany with an enormous reparations bill, at the same time as its territorial clauses removed a full 30 percent of the German national tax base.[42]

Despite all the constraints that politics and economy may place on an army, the Germans never forgot the words of the old student song, "die Gedanken sind frei." Thoughts are free. They are free in the sense of costing nothing, not an inconsiderable factor in times of tight spending, but also free in the sense of being unconstrained by nature. Versailles could disarm Germany physically, a process that extended from breaking up German tanks to closing down the German staff college, but it failed miserably at disarming Germany mentally. A foreign observer at the Reichswehr's 1924 fall maneuvers made this very point. Having just witnessed five days of intense mobile warfare, Blue and Red forces aggressively seeking each other's flanks and rear in a highly realistic wartime scenario, U.S. Colonel Allen Kimberly ended his dispatch to the War Department by noting that, although Germany was to all intents and purposes disarmed by the Versailles treaty, "her brains were far from disarmed."[43]

There are great dangers, however, in viewing the German advances of the interwar period as a simple list of propositions to copy. They were dependent on a whole host of factors that are unlikely ever to obtain in precisely the same way again. The Germans used radio, for example, to transmit short, concise orders, creating a highly sensitive and responsive structure of command and control. This was a major competitive advantage in the opening campaigns of World War II. Higher German units (divisions, corps, and armies) moved faster, reacted more quickly, and changed directions more easily than their Polish, British, French, and Soviet adversaries. In fact, it might be argued that the Germans never relinquished the advantage in this area, however badly they were eventually beaten in others.

This tradition of short, crisp orders arises not in the 1920s, however. It goes back at least as far as Moltke the Elder, as an aspect of his flexible tradition of command. Flexible command, in turn, arose out of the sudden rise of the mass army earlier in the nineteenth century and the inability of period commanders to control the huge forces under their command. In fact, the entire doctrinal package of *Bewegungskrieg* aimed at achieving the most rapid victory possible, an imperative for Germany, with its uncomfortable geographic situation. It was certainly not as pressing for an island nation like Great Britain or continent-spanning powers like the United States or the Soviet Union. All these armies have their own traditions, culture, and benchmarks of success.

To use the Germans as a historical model, the first imperative is to get the history right. A careful survey of German military literature in the interwar period, the weekly *Militär-Wochenblatt*, for example, reveals some interesting facts. What is most noteworthy is what is absent. *Auftragstaktik*, the term used by so many armies today to describe flexibility of command, seems missing in action, although the Germans do recommend *Biegsamkeit* (the common noun for "flexibility") as a desirable aspect of command. *Blitzkrieg*, a term the Germans adopted only after it was introduced by their enemies in World War II, appears nowhere at all. Nothing could be further from the German military mentality than making a fetish out of a word or phrase. No rule of war could be universally valid for all times and places. *Kein Schema!* ("Not a formula," or "Not a hard and fast rule") was one of the most common admonitions of the German staff, along with a contempt for *Patentlösungen* ("patent solutions" or "pat answers"). Seeckt himself warned in an article about the use of *Schlagworte* — "catchphrases" or "buzzwords." They could easily become a substitute for creative thought, he argued. A person wedded to a buzzword might, after all, become *einseitig*, perhaps the worst term of opprobrium in the German military vocabulary.

If German operational thought of the interwar years was a result of a uniquely German intellectual milieu, perhaps it is not easy for modern armies to copy it. It might be as difficult as ordering someone to "think German" or "be German." Any educated person would laugh at the notion. This is not to say that modern armies cannot innovate as well as the Germans, train in ways even more effective than the Germans, or learn from the German experience. It is to say that attempting to bottle a German secret for operational success, or to follow a German script for successful innovation, is probably doomed to failure and that German usages and concepts must be handled with care.[44] What is required instead is to analyze German concepts carefully in their historical context; translate them, not only into English words, but into American practice; and then decide whether they are helpful in terms of doctrine.

The German military intellect prided itself on synthesizing existing ideas in ways that incorporated them into the fundamentally traditional concept of operational-level maneuver warfare. In other words, it built its innovation on top of a structure in which it already had a great deal of confidence. No army can innovate unless it first undertakes a careful study of what is worth preserving.

What, then, is to be done for a modern army interested in innovation? A good place to start is with military history. Commanders who want to fight maneuver warfare on the operational scale should be thoroughly familiar with its history. The distinctive problems facing the modern army have their roots in the late nineteenth and early twentieth centuries, an age that saw a dramatic growth in the size of armies; increased, and apparently insurmountable, difficulties in commanding and controlling them; and a vast increase in the lethality and range of weapons. Yet how many officers serving today are conversant in the campaigns of the Russo-Japanese War of 1904–1905, the Balkan Wars of 1912–1913, or the Spanish Civil War of 1936–1939, let alone the dozens of campaigns of the two world wars? All of them are highly instructive in the problems (and opportunities) of operational-level warfare. All offer concrete examples of the never-ending search for decisive victory. They are the forerunners of contemporary and future campaigns, and their commanders faced many of the same problems that characterize the modern battlefield. If, as Petrarch held, history is philosophy taught by example, then military history is doctrine taught by example. And for those who require a German imprimatur for any military idea, there is an article in the *Militär-Wochenblatt* from 1931 stressing this very point.[45]

2

In Search of the Impossible:
The German Operational Breakdown in
World War II, 1940–1942

The Germans clearly held an operational advantage in the first two years of World War II. Little that they tried failed. The victory in Poland started the cascade. Scandinavia would be the next site of a decisive German operation, although the drama of Case Yellow would steal its thunder. The panzer drive across northern France was the most spectacular military maneuver since the days of Napoleon. The legend of the Afrika Korps in the Western Desert, a bold airdrop onto the British-held island of Crete, the epic of Operation Barbarossa, the vast double envelopment that led off Operation Typhoon — it is an impressive and, some might say, incomparable list.

The improbably easy victory in France and the Low Countries, however, "the greatest annihilation battle of all time,"[1] set a standard that the Wehrmacht was unable to match. Even well-conceived and successful operations — General Erwin Rommel's lightning drives across North Africa toward Suez in 1940 and 1941, the devastating thrust into the Soviet Union at the start of Operation Barbarossa, for example, or the drive on Moscow in the fall of 1941 — contained just enough friction to stop them short of the kind of victory that the Germans expected and needed. When rapid victory eluded them, we see German planners, for all their vaunted operational capability, more and more at sea about how to proceed.

It was more than insane national leadership, more than simply losing a war of attrition — being outnumbered, outproduced, and eventually flattened by their enemies. As important as those strategic factors were in the final result of the war, German operations must also bear their share of the blame for the final outcome. By 1942, the Wehrmacht was already launching a vast operation into the southern Soviet Union (Case Blue)

36

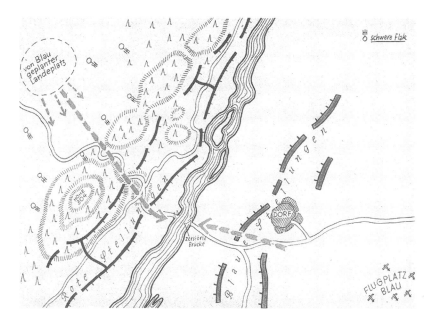

German scheme for an airborne landing: Blue (Blau) vs. Red (Rot). From *Die Wehrmacht* 3, no. 9, April 26, 1939, p. 4.

that was so seriously flawed as a concept that it should never have begun. The next summer, the best that the German General Staff could come up with was a lumbering strike at the most obvious spot on the map, Operation Citadel against Kursk. The German response to the Allied breakout from Normandy in August 1944 was the disastrous thrust toward Mortain, putting the last remaining armored reserves in the western theater into a noose from which few escaped. The story of German operations in the war was one of slow, steady decline. Put another way, the Germans did achieve a "revolution in military affairs" in 1940, but it proved to be both contingent — dependent on a host of unique factors — and extremely fragile.[2]

Germany Ascendant: Norway and Crete

Although we tend to think of tank warfare when we discuss the virtues of the Wehrmacht in World War II, there is far more to the story. The invasion of Poland in 1939 and the campaign in the West in 1940 relied heavily on the tank, but the Germans fought other, equally impressive campaigns in the war's opening years. Yet neither the Norwegian campaign in April 1940 (Exercise Weser) nor the airdrop on Crete (Operation Mercury) in May 1941 has received the attention from military historians that it deserves. Timing is everything, after all, and both these campaigns stand in the shadow of events that immediately followed them: Weser by Case Yellow, and Mercury by Operation Barbarossa. Still, both were crucial milestones of twentieth-century history, representing a breakthrough into an entirely new area of warmaking: airborne operations.

In April 1940 the period of inaction since the fall of Poland, the "Phony War" as it was known in the United States, came suddenly to an end. The Wehrmacht launched an invasion of Denmark and Norway.[3] The purpose of the campaign was threefold. First, in a general sense, occupation of the Scandinavian coast secured Germany's northern flank and protected the Reich from threats emerging in that direction. Second, Germany needed to protect its iron ore supply, mined in neutral Sweden, in the Kiruna ore fields, shipped by rail to the Norwegian port of Narvik, then by steamer down the Norwegian coast to Germany. Finally, German naval chief Admiral Erich Raeder saw the Norwegian coast, with its numerous protected inlets, or fjords, as a useful base for submarine operations against Great Britain. British thoughts, interestingly enough, were running in the same direction. First Lord of the Admiralty Winston Churchill had already ordered plans drawn up to mine Norwegian waters, perhaps even to send an occupation force to Norway.[4]

As in so many other cases this early in the war, the Wehrmacht beat its enemies to the punch. Exercise Weser was a blitzkrieg of a sort, although there were hardly any tanks involved at all. Rather, this was blitzkrieg by sea and air, one of the most complex undertakings in military history up to that point. Denmark, for example, was the target of several well-coordinated landings on the morning of April 9, 1940, including the first paratroop landing in military history. It was a small group, just ninety men, siphoned off from the main landings to the north in Norway at the last minute. Their mission was to secure the long bridge linking the Gedser ferry terminal to the Danish capital, Copenhagen. It was a picture-perfect landing and a bloodless capture of the bridge's small garrison. Other air landings took place at Aalborg, in the far north of the Jutland Peninsula, with its important airfield. There were virtually simultaneous naval landings at (from west to east) Esbjerg, Thyboron, Middelfart, Nyborg, and Gedser, which secured these objectives against minor resistance. Finally, a land drive, two motorized brigades,[5] and an infantry division swept up the Jutland Peninsula and, by the end of the day, had covered the entire length of Denmark, well over three hundred miles, linking up with the paratroop forces and securing the whole country.[6] Five naval landings, two airborne drops, and a vigorous drive by land were all accomplished in practically perfect coordination and split-second timing — even the lack of serious opposition by the Danes does not make this operation any less impressive. A German analysis from 1941 seems justified:

> The success of the Danish undertaking was new proof of the value of the German General Staff. Under the leadership of their commanders, a few dedicated officers immersed themselves in quick, precise, and tireless preparation. Because the preparatory work was correct and secrecy maintained, the plan worked out in action like a precision watch.[7]

The Danes capitulated in four hours, and who can blame them?

The Germans had nearly the same level of success in much larger Norway. That same morning saw six simultaneous sea-borne landings, moving north to south: Narvik, Trondheim, Bergen, Kristiansand-Arendal, Oslo, and Egersund; a paratroop landing at Stavanger, to seize the nearby air base at Sola; and a combined air and sea landing at Oslo. German troops in the first wave numbered somewhat less than nine thousand all told, but they made up for their small numbers by appearing seemingly everywhere along the coast, all at once.[8] They did not come by transport craft. Since the dispersed nature of the various landings placed a premium on rapidity and precision, warships, not transport vessels, carried the first wave. Because some of the ships did not have sufficient fuel to reach their destinations, the navy pre-positioned tankers, disguised as merchant ships, at strategic points along the route. Likewise, an "export group," consisting again of disguised merchant vessels, was to be put into the various Norwegian ports before the invasion, carrying vital equipment and supplies for the landing troops.[9]

The landings were not without incident. A Norwegian floatplane spotted the German naval group coming into Kristiansand. Headed by the cruiser *Karlsruhe*, it had originally intended to dispatch a battalion in patrol boats to the shore to capture the two island forts guarding entrance into Kristiansand fjord. That was now clearly impossible. The commander of the *Karlsruhe*, in a pattern that would come to characterize this campaign, had to call in the Luftwaffe. A force of seven Heinkel medium bombers arrived, and when they were unable to get the job done, a larger force of sixteen managed to silence the guns on both forts and as a bonus blew one of the Norwegian ammunition dumps sky high.[10] Heavy air attacks also featured in the Stavanger/Sola and Bergen landings.

There was also one genuine disaster for the Germans: the loss of the heavy cruiser *Blücher*.[11] Sailing into Oslo fjord at a reckless twenty-five knots, with Nazi party and Gestapo personnel actually on the fantail as a band played, the ship came under shell- and torpedo-fire from the Norwegian fortresses guarding the Dröbak narrows. There were multiple torpedo hits on its hull, and then a gigantic explosion. *Blücher* rolled over and sank, with the loss of a thousand men, some intended for the Oslo landing itself. German paratroopers heading toward Fornebu airfield near Oslo had to turn back, and it seemed that the crucial assault on the capital was in serious trouble. Rescuing the situation was a second wave of German transports, which had intended to land at Fornebu airfield once the paratroopers had secured it. Apparently resisting recall orders, the commander of the transport wing landed at the airfield anyway. There was minimal resistance — the Norwegian defenders had obeyed their orders to retreat. The happiest men at Fornebu were the pilots of a flight of ME-110s who were nearly out of fuel and who were supposed to land at the airfield once airborne forces had secured it. They had watched the entire strange affair with amazement, one eye, no doubt, on their increasingly frightening fuel gauges.[12] Enough troops landed at Fornebu that by the evening of April 9, the German invaders had secured Oslo, along with all their other objectives. Luftwaffe units now staged forward and were operating from Norwegian bases by the end of the day. Again, the timing and precision of the landings, the cooperation between land, sea, and air, would have been impressive achievements even for a peacetime exercise.

Norway was not yet secure, however. From Oslo, the Germans had to launch a land drive to relieve the occupied posts on Norway's west coast.[13] Norwegian units in the interior blocked them from overland supply, and once the German navy had lost strategic surprise, the seas were firmly in the hands of the Royal Navy. It was a fascinating campaign, in which tiny German forces made the long slog up Norway's mountains and valleys against a game but outclassed Norwegian force. Whenever the Germans found themselves held up, however, they called on air support that was well nigh irresistible. With the Germans in total control of the air, the bewildered defenders never did form a cohesive resistance.

Unlike their behavior during the invasion of Poland, the Allies tried to help Norway. Within a week of the invasion, taking advantage of

British staff work done in preparation for an invasion, they began landing forces north and south of Trondheim. On April 16, the British 146th Infantry Brigade and the French 5th Demi-Brigade of Chasseurs-Alpins landed at Namsos, 127 miles north of Trondheim.[14] Two days later, the British 148th Infantry Brigade landed at Aandalsnes, about the same distance to the south of the city. Together, they were to advance on the key German position in central Norway and eliminate it.

In fact, the "Trondheim pincer" was a debacle. Command and control for the Allied landings was a nightmare, and each of the on-site commanders actually had to report back to London or Paris. The deficiency of their equipment and their general lack of military deportment shocked even the Norwegian forces, who, after all, had a week of fighting the Wehrmacht under their belt by this time.[15] The immediate threat was the Luftwaffe, which placed both forces under constant and heavy air attack. Hitler gave the Luftwaffe orders to destroy the port and rail facilities of the two towns "without consideration for the civilian population," and this is essentially what it did.[16] The Namsos force, under General Carton de Wiart, did begin a desultory advance down toward Trondheim, reaching Steinkjer, about halfway there. Here, under constant pounding from the air, threatened by small parties of Germans to his west, and under harassing fire from German destroyers active in Trondheim fjord, Carton was stopped cold and eventually fell back on Namsos. It was a harrowing march and countermarch for the Allies, who had brought no antiaircraft guns with them to Norway.[17] Failing to exert any real pressure on Trondheim, both forces soon reembarked and departed Norway altogether: the Aandalsnes force on April 30–May 2, the Namsos group on May 1–3.

Another landing did much better. On April 15, the British 24th Guards Brigade landed on the island of Hinnory, near Narvik. This landing, combined with a devastating naval attack that sunk all ten German destroyers anchored there, meant that the German defenders (3rd Mountain Division under General Eduard Dietl) were hard pressed to hold the town.[18] With Dietl's force operating well outside the Luftwaffe's air umbrella, the German art of war seemed much less artful. The two German divisions pushing up from Trondheim (2nd Mountain Division and 181st Infantry Division) were nearly three hundred miles away as the crow flies, and the Allies were able to disrupt and delay the advance with small parties landed from the sea. The Allies, by now a robust force of British, French, Norwegian, and Polish troops, attacked and actually took Narvik on June 3. Dietl retreated to the mountains in a seemingly hopeless position, contemplating death or imprisonment for the duration of the war.[19] Once the great German offensive had opened against France and the Low Countries, however, Narvik was suddenly very much a backwater to the Allies. They had taken Narvik simply to use it as a port of embarkation for home.[20]

Histories have tended to portray Exercise Weser as a naval campaign. In fact, it was what we today would call "triphibious": involving air, land, and sea assets working in harmony. Not one had failed. The amphibious side — both planning and execution — was quite impressive. This, of course, was not an area in which the Germans had any real experience or historical tradition. The loss of much of Germany's surface fleet, particularly its destroyers in action around Narvik, was regrettable but also unavoidable. Of course, units of the army had fought with their usual skill. Their mission had called for aggressive attacks without the usual panoply of modern equipment. Tanks played a small role in this campaign, but the German infantry had proved its mettle, if anyone doubted it.

The real difference in Norway, however, was airpower. The Luftwaffe made this victorious campaign possible. The X Fliegerkorps was an omnipresent force in this campaign. It broke up Norwegian resistance and fortified positions in the crucial first hours; it spearheaded the German land forces in their two-pronged drive from Oslo through Gudbrandsdal and Ostersdal to effect the linkup with Trondheim, a tough little campaign all its own; it kept the highly superior Allied naval forces at bay for much of the campaign; and, above all, once the Allies had made seaborne landings, it convinced them that Norway was an inhospitable place in which to carry out military operations. At the start of the campaign the Germans had organized a force of five hundred transport aircraft, a new thing in warfare up to that point, and worked out a detailed air transport plan. The Germans were only able to hold their isolated position at Trondheim because of a sturdy air bridge of supplies and reinforcements. This was what German air officers called the "operational air war" at its finest.[21]

The Germans made an even more dramatic airborne statement in May 1941. Having just finished a successful campaign in the Balkans, they had once again forced the British into a hurried evacuation, this time to the island of Crete.[22] Unlike their post-Dunkirk lull, the Germans this time decided to pursue. At the urging of General Kurt Student, commander of the XI Fliegerkorps, the Germans hastily assembled forces for an airborne drop onto the island. On the morning of May 20, Crete was the target of a German airborne assault, Operation Mercury. This was another milestone in military history, the first operation planned for, and executed solely by, parachute troops. This operation was much larger than anything the Germans had previously tried. Making the landing would be an entire paratroop division, the 7th Flieger Division under General William Süssmann. Assisting it would be a special "Assault Detachment" of four battalions: three consisting of parachute troops and one of glider-borne infantry. Two regiments of the 5th Mountain Division were in Greece, ready to be airlifted onto Crete once the paratroopers had seized an airfield. Air support, in the form of General Wolfram Freiherr von Richthofen's VIII Fliegerkorps, would be lavish: almost 300 medium bombers, 150 Ju-87 *Stuka* dive bombers, 100 ME-109 fighters, and about the same number of the two-engine ME-110 fighter-bombers.[23]

At first light, the skies over Crete were suddenly filled with German transport aircraft. Paratroopers landed up and down the 140-mile length of the island, both by parachute and glider. The three principal targets were ranged up and down seventy miles of the northern coast of Crete. From west to east, the targets were the sector between Maleme and Canea, then the port of Retimo, and finally Heraklion. Student's troopers were landing everywhere, relying heavily on the disruptive effect of airborne landings. Student called it a "spreading oil spot": small groups of German forces inundating the countryside and then eventually forming up into a larger mass.[24] As in Denmark and Norway, the Germans once again demonstrated their gift for solid staff work, and all these widely dispersed landings were on time and on target.

This was not to be the pushover that Exercise Weser had been, however. First, since the airdrop on Crete was an improvised, rushed affair, the Germans made no real effort to disguise the buildup of their air assets in Greece. Using information gleaned from Ultra intercepts, Commonwealth planners knew every detail of the German airborne plan well before it began.[25] When the Germans landed, the defenders were ready. Every German landing was made under fire and suffered heavy losses. By contrast, German intelligence regarding what they would encounter on Crete — everything from the number and composition of the defending forces to the lay of the land itself — was extremely inadequate.[26] Enemy positions appeared on German maps as "artesian wells"; a position marked as "a British ration supply depot" on the road between Alikaneos and Khania, a perfect target for paratroopers, turned out to be a walled prison.[27] The first wave of landings also suffered from command problems from the outset. General Süssmann never made it to Crete; the wings tore off the glider in which he was riding while still in Greek airspace, and he was killed. Likewise, hostile fire seriously wounded the commander of German forces in the Maleme sector, General Eugen Meindl. The German effort between Maleme and Canea was leaderless.

A second problem was the lack of transport aircraft, once again a factor of the short lead time involved. The German force had to land in two waves: the Maleme-Canea sector in the morning, and then widely separated jumps at Retimo and Heraklion in the afternoon. By the time of the later landings, the fully alerted defenders had a turkey shoot, slaughtering the paratroopers as they floated down helplessly. The Black Watch Regimental History describes the mess that followed: "Every soldier picked his swaying target and fired and picked another and fired again. Many Germans landed dead, many were riddled as they hung in trees and telephone wires, some tangled with each other and fell like stones, one was cut up by another aircraft."[28] At both the later drops, the surviving paratroopers made a mad scramble off their landing zones and headed for the mountains.

Even after landing, the situation of the airborne forces at all four sites was precarious. It was imperative that they seize control of an airfield. Paratroopers are not regular infantry; they pay for their extraordinary mobility by a lack of heavy weapons, and they cannot stand up to sustained combat with regulars. In fact, these paratroopers did not even have access to their regular light support weapons. They came down in separate canisters for retrieval after landing; most troopers jumped with only a pistol, four hand grenades, and a knife.[29] The landings had been under such heavy fire that the Germans never did get to most of their canisters. By the end of the first day, none of the three airfields on Crete was anywhere close to being in German hands.

Ultimately it was the tangled nature of the Commonwealth command on Crete that rescued Operation Mercury. In charge of the forces defending Crete (or "Creforce") was General Bernard Freyberg, commander of the 2nd New Zealand Division. He had received his appointment on April 30 and must have wondered what he had gotten himself in for. The ragged remnants of a force that had been dismantled by the Germans in Greece, and once again forced into a hasty evacuation, Creforce was a disparate grouping of units: seventeen thousand British, more than six thousand Australians, some eight thousand New Zealanders, and a large number of Greeks (perhaps ten to twelve thousand).[30] Given enough time to drill and work out acceptable command procedures, and with a victory or two under its belt, such a force might have become a well-oiled machine. That was not the case on Crete. One officer put it this way: "We were a motley collection. We didn't know where our own people were;

we didn't know where the enemy were; many people had no rifles and no ammunition. If anyone fired at you, he might be (a) an enemy (b) a friend (c) a friend or an enemy who didn't know who the hell you were (d) someone not firing at you at all."[31] Making the command situation even more chaotic were Cretan irregular forces fighting on the side of the Allies, spearing wounded Germans they came across or mutilating the dead. Some sixteen thousand Italian prisoners taken by the Greeks were also on Crete, adding to Freyberg's responsibilities, as was the King of the Hellenes, George II. The result of having so many forces tasked with so many missions was a complete lack of any coordinated response to the landings. Creforce units that observed German air landings did their best and in many cases shot them to pieces. But far too many units on Crete simply stayed in place and waited for orders that never came.[32]

Creforce had more manpower than the Germans, but the imbalance of airpower more than offset the advantage. It is incredible, at this stage of the war, that Prime Minister Winston Churchill could tell Freyberg to hold Crete to the last man and to turn the port of Suda into "a second Scapa"[33] and then expect him to do that with three dozen aircraft, only half of which were serviceable at any one time. The British needed their frontline aircraft for service in Egypt. Freyberg had a reputation from World War I as a fighter and had a Victoria's Cross to prove it, but he could see that the situation here was probably irretrievable, especially after London informed him not to expect any air reinforcements. So Freyberg spent most of May attempting to turn his ragged force into an army, all the while observing the depressing spectacle of repeated and uncontested sorties by the Luftwaffe turning the ports and airfields of northern Crete into an inferno. Once the battle started, Creforce reserves found that road movement came at a price: the sudden appearance overhead of German aircraft.

The depressing situation regarding air cover probably had a lot to do with the most famous event in the battle for Crete. The airfield at Maleme quickly became the focus of the fighting. As the paratroopers formed up and headed for the field, they had come under heavy fire from a dominant height to the south, Hill 107.[34] A full Commonwealth infantry battalion, the 22nd New Zealand, held it firmly. May 20 saw a day-long, back-and-forth struggle for Hill 107. It was a confusing fight, without clear front lines, and with heavy losses on both sides. In the course of the day, there was an increasing sense of desperation on the part of the Germans — the campaign, and the very survival of 7th Flieger Division, hung in the balance. The commander of the 22nd New Zealand, Lieutenant Colonel L. W. Andrew, felt that he was nearing the end of his rope, as well. Casualties were heavy, communications with his subordinate companies were intermittent, and a counterattack late in the afternoon, spearheaded by two Matilda infantry tanks, had broken down as soon as it began. The struggle for Hill 107 was a classic example of an information-poor battle for both sides, and typically, both felt that they were losing it.

It certainly seemed that way to Student, as bad news poured into his headquarters at the Grande Bretagne Hotel in Athens. Not only hadn't an airfield fallen, it wasn't even possible to say that any of his forces had a secure airhead. Maleme, where German forces held about half the field, was the only place on the map where they were even close to success. Student now made a bold, and risky, decision. Tomorrow, 5th Mountain Division would begin landing at Maleme, even though the field was sure to be under British artillery fire. Original plans had called for the first reinforcements to land at Heraklion, since it was centrally located on the island's north coast. He now scrapped those plans in favor of ramming everything he could find into Maleme. He also decided to land airborne reinforcements to assist the Assault Regiment in their fight for Maleme airfield.[35]

Fortunately for Student, the enemy around Maleme was having its own troubles. Believing the German force to be much larger than it actually was, and fearing the long arm of the Luftwaffe, Lieutenant Colonel Andrew made a fateful decision. He decided to withdraw from Hill 107. As we survey the situation today, we can say that it was a disastrous decision, yet not incomprehensible. The New Zealand official history comments, fairly, on the "hard conditions in which he had to make his choice."

> He [Andrew] had spent a most exacting day trying to control a battle where all the circumstances were inimical to control. Communications within his battalion had failed him almost completely; and outside it they had proved extremely bad. He and his HQ had been severely harassed by bombing and strafing throughout the day to an extent for which neither training nor experience had prepared them. The enemy attack itself was of a kind still novel and from the start induced the feeling — and the reality as well — of enemy all round the perimeter and inside it also. The battle had begun with an enemy breach in the defence. The support he had expected and counted on from 21 and 23 Battalions had failed to materialise and this meant a radical departure from the original battle plan. His own counterattack with the treasured tanks and 14 Platoon, all that he had to call reserve, had completely failed.[36]

Indeed, he had spent much of the day sending messages to his commander, Brigadier James Hargest of the 5th New Zealand Brigade, to the effect that if reinforcements did not show up soon, he would have to withdraw from Hill 107. Hargest had two other battalions that had more than held their own that day, but also had to be concerned about a seaborne landing east of Maleme, and indeed, of further airborne drops. The official history says, charitably perhaps, that he "misread the situation."[37] That evening, Andrew's 22nd New Zealand Battalion moved east, eventually linking up with its sister battalions, the 21st and 23rd New Zealand. Early on the morning of May 21, German probes onto Hill 107 discovered that the hill was empty of defenders.

Student's gamble was in the best traditions of German command: a flexible response to a changing and fluid situation, a bold and dangerous decision. On came the JU-52s, starting at sunrise. They had to run a true gauntlet of British fire, some being blown apart as they tried to land, others skidding off the short, two-thousand-foot runway, just a "postage stamp,"[38] as one German report called it. Soon, the blazing wrecks of aircraft and dead bodies littered the airfield. Planes landed, disgorged their cargo, and immediately took off again. Gradually, enough aircraft made it safely down, either on the airstrip or directly on the beach, to deliver a battalion of well-equipped mountain troops. By the afternoon, they were in action, with their organic light artillery, on and around the airfield. By evening they had slithered up the winding mule paths into the mountains and silenced the British guns. The campaign for Crete had reached its turning point. Although there was tough fighting left, the rest of the campaign was a mopping-up operation, as Commonwealth forces crossed Crete's mountainous spine under nearly constant air attack, made it to the southern port of Sfakia, and, once again, evacuated — this time to Egypt. Some of them did, at any rate. About thirteen thousand Commonwealth troops fell into German hands. It was all over by May 31.[39]

It is still common to see Crete discussed for its long-term effects. Friends of the airborne point argue that the campaign was a clear demonstration of the vast capabilities of the parachute arm. Student's *Fallschirmjägern* had attacked and taken an island surrounded by hostile waters, held by defenders who outnumbered them by about three to one, and who knew they were coming. Naysayers, however, point out how very high the cost had been. The Germans had lost some 4,000 men killed and 2,500 wounded out of a small division, just 12,000 men. These were elite soldiers, and very expensive ones with highly specialized skills and training who could not be easily replaced. Student himself called

Crete the "graveyard of the German airborne force."[40] The losses certainly seemed to convince Hitler that the age of the paratrooper was over, now that surprise had been lost.[41] Never again would the Wehrmacht launch a large-scale airborne operation. The Allies, however, apparently learned the exact opposite lesson. In the wake of Operation Mercury, they began to enlarge and upgrade their airborne forces and ready them for action.

What of Mercury itself, however? In many ways, it was a reflection of German operational skill. The split-second timing, the extremely close liaison between ground and air forces, the ease with which German infantry and gunners formed ad hoc task forces under fire, Student's leap into the breach opened by the evacuation of Hill 107 — such things had been seen before in German military history, and they would be seen again. The entire campaign was audacious, involving, as Student pointed out, "our one parachute division, our one glider regiment, and the 5th Mountain Division, which had no previous experience of being transported by air."[42] The victory on Crete was hard fought, certainly, but not undeserved.

However, there were problems here, warning signs for future German operations. Perhaps they were born of overconfidence. The duration of the war was now approaching two years, and German land forces had not yet failed in their quest for victory. Still, German intelligence before the drop had not been merely insufficient, it had been completely abysmal. The Germans estimated the size of the Commonwealth force on Crete at about one-third of its actual. Counterintelligence had been altogether absent. The Germans had made no effort to hide the buildup of air transport and airborne forces in Greece, and the British were able to paint a remarkably accurate picture of what was about to happen. These were problems that would bedevil the Germans for the rest of the war. The art of operations is about more than maneuvering troops on a battlefield; good planners investigate the enemy they are about to strike and also try to conceal their own intentions from the enemy. Operation Mercury did neither.

Bad intelligence about the exact situation on the island led to a second, more surprising problem. The drop itself was so dispersed and scattered that it is impossible to detect a *Schwerpunkt* to the operation, surely a break with the traditional German art of war. The chief of Luftflotte IV, General Alexander Löhr, criticized the operation on these grounds. "In conceiving any operation there has to be a clear *Schwerpunkt*. Dispersion should be avoided, if at all possible."[43] The Germans tried to be strong everywhere on Crete, and in consequence were strong nowhere.

The afternoon drops at Retimo and Heraklion, in particular, were unmitigated disasters. If not for the unfortunate Commonwealth decision on Hill 107, the mass of 7th Flieger Division might have had to sit out the war in Allied POW camps. Any operation that requires heavily laden transport aircraft to land on an airstrip under direct fire of enemy artillery has probably cut things just a bit too close.

German Operations in North Africa

German operations in the Western Desert display the same mix of surpassing excellence and shocking sloppiness.[44] In late 1940, the Italian position in North Africa had collapsed. British forces under General Richard O'Connor had hit the Italians hard and scattered them at Sidi Barrani, pursued them across the desert, and then ran them down and destroyed them at Beda Fomm in February 1941. Adolf Hitler decided that he had no choice but to send German troops to the theater to salvage his ally — not for the last time in this war. It was a small force, consisting at first of elements of the 5th Light Division. In command was General Erwin Rommel, little known outside Germany at this point but a highly decorated fighter of World War I and most recently the commander of the successful 7th Panzer Division (the "Ghost Division," as it became known) during Case Yellow.[45]

Rommel arrived in the theater, took stock of the forces under his command (which also included four Italian infantry divisions and an armored division, the Ariete), performed a personal aerial reconnaissance, and then did the characteristic thing: he attacked. Striking out from his base at El Agheila on March 31, Rommel hit the British with a series of blows that left them stunned. He first smashed their forward position at Mersa Brega, supported by heavy concentrations of *Stukas*. Once German forces penetrated their front, the British began to retreat up the road toward Agedabia. Now Rommel launched a general offensive, with three simultaneous thrusts. On his left, the Brescia Division and 3rd Reconnaissance Battalion drove along the coastal road, harrying the British retreat. On the far right, elements of 5th Light Division and the reconnaissance battalion of the Ariete armored division would make a wide sweep into the open desert, across the base of the great Cyrenaican bulge, heading toward Derna on the coastal road, attempting to cut off the British path of retreat. In between them, the main body of Rommel's armor (5th Panzer Regiment, plus units of 5th Light Division and Ariete) would head for Msus and Mechili.[46]

In the face of the onslaught, the British front crumbled. The advance began to read more like a travelogue of a Cyrenaican tour than a military campaign. The column on the left took Agedabia on April 2, Benghazi on April 4, and Derna on April 7. The central tank-heavy column reached Msus and Mechili on April 6. Here it captured a mountain of British supplies and stores of all types, including the gasoline that would fuel the rest of the German drive eastward, as well as the commander of the 2nd Armored Division and his entire headquarters; the next day, the head of the column reached Gazala. The British rear areas were in chaos. On April 6, a German motorcycle patrol stopped a car wandering in the dark, obviously lost, and found that it contained the British commander in Cyrenaica, General Philip Neame, as well as General O'Connor himself. Both now went into German captivity, heralding the complete collapse of the British command structure in Cyrenaica — just one week after Rommel had begun what he told his superiors was a "reconnaissance in force."[47]

Rommel was "fighting deep," driving far into the rear of the British strategic position in Libya. His lunge forward built up an incredible head of steam that carried all before it. It was the O'Connor offensive in reverse, but much faster. It helped that his enemy's defenses were hopelessly inadequate. The British had followed up their dramatic victory over the Italian army — a series of actions that ended with a vast battle of annihilation at Beda Fomm — by going over to the defensive, and then by stripping their front of armor and artillery for the badly bungled intervention in Greece. Rommel was not, therefore, defeating British armored formations; there were few of those in his way. By April 11, he had the great fortress of Tobruk surrounded, while smaller formations pressed on to the Egyptian border. Soon Bardia had fallen and the border reached at Sollum and Ft. Capuzzo. This was top-speed maneuver, and the distances involved far exceeded the European conditions in which Rommel was trained. He had come more than six hundred miles in less than two weeks.[48] Although Tobruk remained unconquered in his rear, he had made good all the stupendous Italian losses, and then some.

And so a legend was born. The secret to Rommel's success was not simply his aggressiveness — which, as we shall see, was a living embodiment of the clichéd "two-edged sword." Rather, this was a triumph for German combined arms: panzers working in close cooperation with tactical airpower, mobile infantry, artillery, and especially antitank guns. In the attack, Rommel deployed mobile reconnaissance units forward, followed by antitank guns, screened and protected by his infantry. Closely behind the forward screen came the main body: armor and motorized infantry, ready to engage enemy tanks. Often, its maneuvers were designed to lure the British forward, onto the waiting German antitank screen. The 88-mm gun, a high-velocity antiaircraft gun, still gets most of the notoriety, and in fact, Rommel made superb use of this weapon in the antitank role. By the end of 1941, the two antiaircraft battalions of the Afrika Korps had destroyed 264 tanks, compared to just 42 aircraft.[49] There were, however, far too few "88s" to cover Rommel's front in any meaningful way. In fact, it was the German 50-mm antitank gun that did most of the damage, inflicting punishing losses on the unsuspecting British.[50] Then, at the precise moment when the surviving British tanks began their retreat, German armor would move up to attack deep into the flank and rear of the enemy position. Once the panzers had gotten behind the British positions, the battle was over. The mobile troops now played havoc with the enemy's lines of communication and retreat. The momentum of the attack was sustained without pause, often fueled by captured enemy supplies.[51]

British tactics were very different and followed a depressingly similar pattern. Unsupported tank charges went forward into the German lines. Often, they broke through the initial crust of the German defenses — onto the waiting batteries of antitank guns and artillery. The Germans chose their firing positions to give them the vulnerable flank of the British armored column. From then on it was a shooting exercise and not a very long or difficult one at that. It invariably seemed to end with the battlefield being illuminated by the flames of burning British tanks. In his breezy memoir, *Brazen Chariots*, British tank commander Robert Crisp described one such battle involving the 3rd Royal Tank Regiment:

> The principal influence brought to bear on tank design and tactics was the cavalry school of thought. The strategists wanted to make a tank which was as much like a horse as possible, and which could be used in action in more or less the same way. The Charge of the Light Brigade was their idea of the proper way to fight a battle. They merely substituted tanks for horses. . . .
>
> The first action was very typical of a number of those early encounters involving cavalry regiments. They had incredible enthusiasm and dash, and sheer exciting courage which was only curbed by the rapidly decreasing stock of dashing officers and tanks.[52]

He had to learn to strike a balance, he observed, since it was "of very little use to yourself or your army to be very brave and very dead."

Rommel's first great lunge to the Egyptian border had one failing, however. Tobruk held out, with the tough 9th Australian Division as its garrison.[53] Lying as it did far to Rommel's rear, Tobruk represented a serious threat to his lines of communication and supply. It is a sign of the paucity of resources in this area that Rommel did not even have enough forces to invest Tobruk properly, let alone storm it. Still, with a typically aggressive spirit, he tried. In two battles, the so-called "Easter battle" (April 10–14) and the "battle of the Salient" (April 30–May 4), the defenders taught the Afrika Korps that the rules of positional warfare still applied. Columns of German armor, with infantry riding along, spearheaded the attempt to breach the Australian perimeter. The defending infantry deliberately allowed them to pass into the interior of the position. Here they became mired in extensive minefields. Once they were thoroughly enmeshed in the mines, and their ability to maneuver consequently reduced, they came under heavy fire from artillery, antitank guns, and supporting tanks, all firing directly. The German infantry, watching their tanks go up in flames one by one, suddenly looked quite mortal. The entire assault force was badly shot up, and the commander of 15th Panzer Division, General von Prittwitz, was among the dead. An Australian company commander described the chaotic scene:

> The crossing was badly churned up and the tanks raised clouds of dust as they went. In addition, there was the smoke of two tanks blazing just outside the wire. Into this cloud of dust and smoke we fired anti-tank weapons, Brens, rifles, and mortars, and the gunners sent hundreds of shells. We shot up a lot of infantry as they tried to get past, and many, who took refuge in the anti-tank ditch, were later captured. It was all I could do to stop the troops following them outside the wire. The Germans were a rabble.[54]

Losses were heavy, and Rommel had to call off the attacks.

He understood what had just happened. Like any German officer of his generation and training, he recognized two basic categories of war. At Tobruk, the preferred German variety of mobile warfare *(Bewegungskrieg)* had suddenly given way to the much more expensive type known as positional warfare *(Stellungskrieg)*:

> In this assault we lost more than 1,200 men killed, wounded and missing. This shows how sharply the curve of casualties rises when one reverts from mobile to position warfare. In a mobile action, what counts is material, as the essential complement to the soldier. The

finest fighting man has no value in mobile warfare without tanks, guns, and vehicles. Thus a mobile force can be rendered unfit for action by destruction of its tanks, without having suffered any serious casualties in manpower. This is not the case with position warfare, where the infantryman with rifle and hand grenade has lost little of his value, provided, of course, he is protected by antitank guns or obstacles against the enemy's armor. For him enemy number one is the attacking infantrymen. Hence, position warfare is always a struggle for the destruction of men — in contrast to mobile warfare, where everything turns on the destruction of enemy material.[55]

Of all the theaters of war, the distinction between the two types of war was starkest in North Africa. Both sides soon learned, in the words of a postwar German staff study undertaken for the U.S. Army, that "troops which are not motorized are valueless in desert warfare and can do nothing whatever against a motorized enemy." The fighting in the desert "took on such entirely new forms owing to the almost exclusive use of mobile troops by both sides," they felt, "that it was not possible in planning to make use of any examples taken from military history."[56] Despite his purposeful image and reputation for directness, Rommel was actually feeling his way forward, commanding into the unknown.

Although the failure at Tobruk had made mobile operations impossible for the time being, Rommel's first campaign had been quite a success. He had succeeded in humiliating the British forces in Africa, recapturing all of Cyrenaica and propping up Germany's faltering ally in the process. Most important, he had laid hands on an immense amount of matériel. This was a key factor, since his supply lines across the Mediterranean were by no means secure. Now in charge of an entire Afrika Korps of three German divisions (his original 5th Light Division, reorganized into 21st Panzer Division in October 1941, plus 15th Panzer Division and 90th Light Division), he felt that he could look with optimism to future operations in the theater. Both sides now paused to regroup, refit, and resupply — a crucial consideration in desert fighting.

It was the British who would strike first, establishing a pattern in this war. Time was on the side of Rommel's enemies, since they could use any pause in operations to build up supplies much more efficiently than he could. On November 18, 1941, the British launched their first offensive against Rommel: Operation Crusader.[57] The newly designated 8th Army, under General Alan Cunningham, planned a two-corps drive against the Germans. It was not, by this stage of the desert war, a very daring or imaginative plan. A heavy armored force (XXX Corps) would swing around Rommel's southern flank and occupy Gabr Saleh. There it would wait for Rommel to approach and thereby precipitate a great clash of the two armored fleets. Once the British had smashed the mass of German armor, another force (XIII Corps, consisting almost exclusively of infantry formations) would attack the Axis positions at Sollum frontally, breaking through and moving on to the relief of Tobruk.

The plan certainly did not breathe the spirit of mobile warfare. The tanks of XXX Corps (mainly the three brigades of 7th Armoured Division) would thrust forward boldly enough and then halt and wait for the Germans to come to them. The division into tank and infantry corps was also unfortunate. The Germans, of course, did just the opposite, grounding any advance firmly in combined arms. "I sometimes wondered it if were the right formation," Cunningham wrote at the time. "The alternative would have been mixed groups."[58] Nevertheless, armed with a great superiority in the number of men, tanks, and guns, Cunningham should have had more than enough to deal with Rommel.

The results were uneven and, in fact, highly unsettling to Cunningham. The flank drive by XXX Corps soon ran into trouble. The armored brigades rolled forward to Gabr Saleh and got no response. As a result, there was much milling about and confusion in the British ranks. Major Crisp captures the atmosphere:

> As soon as it got light enough to see, shells started falling among us from goodness knows where. Unseen shellfire can be very disconcerting and there is none of the psychological relief of retaliation. We had no sooner got dispersed when tanks were reported, attacking the battalion's right flank. We took up hull down positions to meet this threat, but within a half an hour they were reported attacking our left flank. This threat proved equally nebulous, and for two hours we sat gazing into space and sand. Away in the distance I spotted a column of vehicles replenishing with petrol, but could not be sure which side they belonged to. Neither could anybody else.[59]

When 22nd Armoured Brigade finally did contact tanks at Bir Gubi, on the extreme left of the British advance, they were not Germans at all but Italians of the Ariete Division. Soon a full-fledged tank melee was under way here, sucking in virtually all of 22nd Armoured. Reckless British tank charges were no more effective against the Italians than they had been against the Germans, and the brigade was soon reeling back.

In prewar planning, the commander of XIII Corps had demanded some armor as flank protection in case Rommel should try something daring, as he was wont to do. Cunningham therefore deployed 4th Armoured

Brigade in a protective role here. That left just one brigade, the 7th Armoured, as the remnant of the original armored corps.[60] It rolled on to Gabr Saleh and beyond, heading toward the airfield at Sidi Rezegh on November 20. The news heartened Cunningham. There had been armored clashes, and the Germans seemed to be running from them.

Events at Sidi Rezegh would soon disabuse him of that notion. Here, 7th Armoured Brigade made contact all right, with virtually the entire armored strength of the Afrika Korps. Rommel had at first refused to believe that Crusader was anything more than a diversion to forestall his intended attack on Tobruk. If the tale is not apocryphal, he first received word of an all-out British offensive by listening to a BBC report. Nevertheless, the size and scope of the operation took him by complete surprise. Finally, he put his panzers on the road, first toward Gabr Saleh. Here, 15th and 21st Panzer Divisions hit elements of 4th Armoured Brigade, which Cunningham had finally released from its nursemaid duties. After an inconclusive skirmish, both divisions turned north and northwest toward Sidi Rezegh and smashed into 7th Armoured Brigade from the rear on November 21. German tanks handled their British counterparts, mainly thin-skinned "cruiser tanks" and U.S. M-3 Stuart cavalry tanks (called "Honeys" by the British) very roughly, inflicting heavy casualties. On November 22, the other two British armored brigades arrived on the scene, and the carnage and confusion of battle rose even further. The airfield was an incredible scene of destroyed aircraft, burned-out tanks, and Commonwealth infantry formations milling about aimlessly, waiting for orders and unsure how to proceed.[61] By the end of the day, the remnants of all British brigades had retreated from the airfield. As darkness fell on this terrible day, there was a last blow, as 15th Panzer Division inadvertently overran the headquarters of the last relatively intact British armored formation, the 4th Armoured Brigade.[62]

The destruction of his armor unhinged Cunningham completely, and by the next morning he was well into the process of ordering a general withdrawal back to Egypt. His corps commanders, however, recommended continuing the offensive, and seconding their opinion was the commander in chief, Middle Eastern Command, General Claude Auchinleck. The frontal assault by XIII Corps, under way since November 20, was making good progress, overrunning much of the Axis line from Sollum to Halfaya Pass ("Hellfire," in the British vernacular). It was clear to them that Rommel, too, had lost heavily in the Sidi Rezegh battles. As part of the overall plan for Crusader, a simultaneous attack by the Tobruk garrison would threaten Rommel's rear. Surely he would be unable to deal with all these threats simultaneously. Crusader went on.

.3 in

1.1 in

2.7 in
(1.9 + .7 in, spaced)

1.0 in

1.9 in

1.1 in

1.9 in

.6 in

Pz. Kw. 3
WITH 75-MM GUN

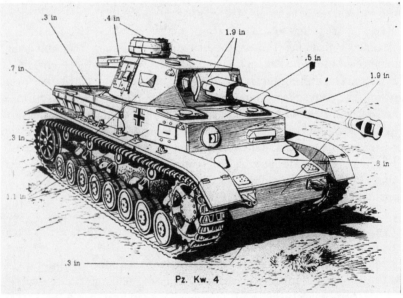

.3 in

.4 in

1.9 in

.7 in

.5 in

1.9 in

.3 in

.8 in

1.1 in

.3 in

Pz. Kw. 4

Schematic drawings detailing armor thicknesses of the Wehrmacht's two main battle tanks, ca. 1942, the Pzkw. III and Pzkw. IV, taken from the wartime files of the Detroit Arsenal. Note that the labeling of the Pzkw. III is in error; the gun should be a 50 mm. Courtesy of U.S. Army Tank-Automotive and Armaments Command (TACOM).

Rommel's position was certainly grave. By the morning of November 23 he was down to his last hundred tanks, both divisions having suffered almost as much punishment as they dished out in the previous day's fighting. Threats still faced them in every direction. It was at this point that Rommel decided on one of the boldest — and most controversial — moves of his entire career. On November 24, he ordered every vehicle he could scrounge up to begin a "dash to the wire," a daring raid far behind the British positions, up to the barbed wire entanglements on the Egyptian frontier. In the course of this wild ride he overran, in succession, the headquarters of XXX Corps, 7th Armoured Division, 1st South African Division, 7th Support Group, and 7th Armoured Brigade, unleashing panic as he went. Rommel came quite close to picking up another British commander for his collection, this time Cunningham, who was visiting XXX Corps. The drive finally stopped, unbeknownst to him, less than fifteen miles short of 8th Army headquarters and the entire store of water for four full divisions.

It is hard to read of the dash and not be caught up in the excitement. That is all the more reason to note that it was completely without effect. British transport had to scatter, and that certainly threw off 8th Army's timetable for relieving Tobruk. Otherwise, British fighting troops stayed where they were. The British had two forward supply dumps from which they were replenishing themselves, so his threat to their supply lines was nonexistent. German troops were now thoroughly disorganized and weary from a week of practically nonstop operations, and their supply situation was, once again, shaky, as the concentration of armor for the dash had uncovered virtually every Axis supply convoy in the region. Rommel's own headquarters, facing threats from inside and outside Tobruk, began placing ever more urgent calls for his return and the return of the fighting power he had led away from the thick of the fighting. The dash was over by November 27, with the troops back where they had started but now facing British formations that had used the three-day respite to rest and resupply.[63]

Even worse, the Tobruk garrison had succeeded in breaking out over the Duda escarpment to the south and linking up with New Zealand forces. Further confused battles at Sidi Rezegh were a stalemate, with heavy losses on both sides. By December 4, Rommel had no choice but to retreat back to the Gazala line, west of Tobruk, and after a none-too-vigorous British pursuit, with his supplies gone and his own losses heavy, he decided to go all the way back to the point at which his offensive had started in March, El Agheila. Operation Crusader had succeeded in mauling the Afrika Korps, as it now styled itself, and driving it out of Cyrenaica, but the victory had been a Pyrrhic one, with British losses significantly heavier than those of the Axis.

Even worse, it was soon obvious that Crusader was not at all a lasting victory. Rommel had been beaten, not destroyed. The desert war, perhaps more than any other, showed how unimportant was the possession of terrain compared to destroying enemy forces.[64] In January 1942, after only a few short weeks in El Agheila, Rommel was back on the offensive. Once again, he drove the British on before him, severely mauling their Armoured Division. By February, he was back at Gazala. Here exhaustion set in once again — the pace since the onset of Crusader had been simply grueling — and for the next four months, Axis and British forces faced each other across a position that came increasingly to resemble one from World War I, complete with trenches, barbed wire, and machine gun nests. On the British side, fortified "boxes," dense concentrations of tank obstacles and antipersonnel mines, came to dominate the front. In May, Rommel launched his offensive against the British lines at Gazala. The fighting here was quite confused. One phase actually saw Rommel's main force, which had as always driven around the main British line, actually attacking westward (that is, toward his own starting positions) to open a line of supply. He was simultaneously beating back British assaults from all points of the compass. Not for nothing did the battle become known as the "cauldron."[65] It is rare that a general willingly surrounds himself with enemy forces. Eventually, Rommel broke out of the Gazala stalemate. Continuing east, his troops stormed Tobruk, the fortress that had foiled him the previous year, on June 20–21.

Onward he plunged toward Egypt, and then over the border, finally stopping near a place called El Alamein. Here the salt marshes of the Qattara Depression lay to the south, impassable to panzers and thus preventing any flanking maneuver in that direction. If Rommel were to break through, he would have to do so with a frontal assault. Though his formations were understrength and tired after their pounding march across the desert, he ordered an immediate assault on July 1, called the First Battle of El Alamein, but in a month of seesaw fighting, the Afrika Korps failed to break through the British defenses. A second Axis assault, from August 31 to September 2, centered on the Alam Halfa ridge, protecting the rear of the British position at El Alamein. A combination of lack of fuel and the doggedness of the British defenders combined to foil Rommel again and took a heavy toll of attacking tanks. In both battles, U.S. Lend-Lease equipment played a major role in stiffening the British defenses, especially the arrival of more than two hundred M3 medium tanks of the Lee/Grant family. These carried both 37-mm and 75-mm guns, the former in the turret, the latter in a fixed mounting on the right front of the hull, and their armor was nearly impervious to anything the Germans could throw at them.[66]

Rommel's great lunge across the desert in 1942 had exhausted his men, worn out his equipment, and brought him one thousand miles from his own supply base. By the iron logic of this curious theater, he was now ripe for a counterstroke. In late October, the British 8th Army, heavily reinforced by U.S. equipment (especially tanks of the Lee/Grant family), launched a great offensive at El Alamein. Commanding it was General Bernard Law Montgomery. "Monty" was one of the war's most controversial figures, a military genius and the savior of his country to his many admirers, a pompous blowhard who was unable to back up his shameful self-promotion to his equally numerous detractors.[67]

The truth, as always, lies somewhere in between. That he was an obnoxious person was obvious to many, perhaps even to the man himself. As he once told a staff conference at Algiers as it discussed plans for the invasion of Sicily: "I know well that I am regarded by many people as a tiresome person. I think this is very probably true."[68] That he was a cautious commander is equally true. He once listed an "infinite capacity for taking pains and preparing for every foreseeable contingency" as "the foundation of all success in war."[69] However, in his defense, caution was a prerequisite for British command by late 1942. Another half-baked operational plan, like rushing an expeditionary force to the defense of Greece, a force that had to evacuate almost as soon as it arrived, or even Crusader, could have been disastrous for Britain at this juncture.

Although he enjoyed overwhelming superiority in men, tanks, planes, trucks, and artillery, his plan for battle at El Alamein was necessarily cautious.[70] Two factors were at play here. Not only was Montgomery in possession of one of Britain's precious field armies, but the terrain did not permit any other approach, in the initial stages, than a frontal assault that was bound to be bloody. The sea to the north, the Qattara Depression forty-five miles to the south, wall-to-wall Axis divisions in front of him — these were realities. The many analysts who criticize Montgomery for his handling of the Alamein battle have never come up with any better suggestions. Montgomery described the problem as follows:

First — to punch a hole in the enemy positions.
Second — to pass X Corps, strong in armour and mobile troops, through this hole into enemy territory.
Third — then to develop operations so as to destroy Rommel's forces.[71]

The infantry divisions of XXX Corps (9th Australian, 51st Highland, 2nd New Zealand, 1st South African, and 4th Indian) had the hard task. They would attack on an extremely narrow front, closely supported by tanks, and chew their way through Rommel's minefields and wire. Once they had succeeded, the tank divisions of X Corps (1st and 10th Armoured) would be unleashed as a pursuit corps *(corps de chasse)*, storming through the gaps and exploiting far into the German rear. The obvious critique (that the British were still wedded to a systematic view of battle that was tied to phase lines and strict timetables) goes beyond Montgomery's personal failings; it was the British way of war. A less obvious problem, perhaps, was the third aspect. Montgomery himself seems to have given little thought to just how those "operations so as to destroy Rommel's forces" were to proceed, where they were to take place, and what force levels they might involve. Punch a hole, enter it, chase Rommel — that was the sum total of his vision for this operation.

As it turned out, even this conservative plan might have been a bit too optimistic. From October 23 to November 2, Monty's infantry attacked, backed lavishly by airpower and artillery. The going was slow, however, and casualties extremely high. It was a battle of attrition, and in the end Monty had to call on the tank divisions of X Corps to assist the breakthrough, in Operation Supercharge on the night of November 1–2. Rommel's losses were also heavy, as they will be in any battle of attrition. By November 3, with his last reserves gone, he had no choice but to abandon the El Alamein position and retreat. This time he did not stop until he reached Tunisia. El Agheila, the former bottleneck, was no longer useful, since on November 8, U.S. and British forces had carried out amphibious landings on the North African coast from Casablanca to Algiers. Operation Torch moved swiftly forward against sporadic opposition from the Vichy French forces in the theater. Rommel was now trapped in a war on two fronts. Having already committed his armor to the breakthrough, however, Monty's pursuit was extremely leisurely. Rommel managed to evacuate Libya with the remnants of his command. The desert phase of his career was over.

El Alamein was a battle that fit perfectly well with British doctrine. It was controlled and self-contained, required limited forces, and began with the enemy prevented from maneuvering. Many have accused Montgomery of botching the pursuit or failing to prosecute it with sufficient vigor. But this was 8th Army's first real victory over an opponent who time and again in the past had come back from apparent defeats to launch savage counterattacks. Seen in that light, Montgomery's apparent lack of energy is more defensible.

It is not a simple thing to evaluate German performance in the desert theater, and even harder to evaluate Rommel as an operational commander. There are many factors to consider, many questions that need asking. The most pressing is, How important was this theater to German planners, from Hitler on down? They certainly did not lavish much in the way of matériel and supply. Judging what happens in a strategic backwater, which may well be how the Germans saw North Africa, is a very different thing from judging performance in a decisive theater. Rommel's command subordination to the Italian Supreme Headquarters in Africa *(Commando Supremo)* also formed a major part of the dynamic of operations, yet most who study these campaigns treat it as an afterthought. If, in fact, Hitler was simply trying to prop up his Italian ally, then the Afrika Korps achieved this limited goal, and more.

Rommel himself was one of history's great battlefield commanders. His virtues were many. He had the charisma of all of history's great captains. He led from the front. He was unfailingly aggressive, launching vigorous attacks even from a position of weakness. He had a penchant for bold maneuver and a classic sense of timing, an intuitive feeling for the ebb and flow of battle.

However, he also had several weaknesses as a commander, especially as an army commander. His spirit of aggression could often turn into impetuosity, even recklessness, in the heat of battle. The "dash to the wire" is proof of that. The areas of logistics and supply bored him, as he was quite willing to admit. Supply was the central problem of the desert war, however. Lack of it kept him from taking Tobruk on his first try, and lack of it again probably kept him from breaking through at Alamein and Alam Halfa. His opposition to an Axis landing on Malta — which might have guaranteed the security of his supplies from Europe — turned out to be a disastrous mistake. German officers, writing after the war, recognized the centrality of logistics to the North African War:

> The German-Italian forces operating in Africa therefore could not be adequately reinforced or supplied. This lack of any possibility of maintaining supply traffic was not due to any failure on the part of the German or Italian headquarters responsible for the movement of supplies, but solely to the fact that the German-Italian operational command did not succeed in keeping the supply routes to Africa open.[72]

True enough, and the end result was El Alamein, the battle of matériel.

But let us go deeper. In North Africa, once again, "nonbattlefield" factors crucial to operational-level warmaking, like intelligence, counterintelligence, supply, and logistics, reared their heads to the detriment of the German war effort. The Germans had evolved their concept of *Bewegungskrieg* — highly mobile operations leading to a swift and decisive victory — in a European environment, gauged to European distances and a temperate climate. When transplanted to a very different theater with harsh desert conditions, it proved to be a narrow, inadequate way of looking at war. It would prove its inadequacy even more dramatically in the Soviet Union. Seen in this way, Rommel's virtues and defects were quintessential reflections of the German way of war. Pity the enemy commander, particularly a commander of armor, who came within five miles of him in battle. In terms of style points, Rommel would certainly have to be declared the victor in North Africa. In the course of his two lunges across the desert, he had performed the "drive to the Channel" across northern France many times over. But this theater demanded more.

Failure: German Operations in the East

Operation Barbarossa, the invasion of the Soviet Union, would bring the German army its most glorious victories and its most catastrophic defeats.[73] By any standards, it was the greatest campaign in military history, involving some three million German and Axis troops. Fighting alongside the Wehrmacht in the initial invasion were two Romanian armies under Marshal Ion Antonescu and the Finns under Marshal Karl von Mannerheim; eventually, there would be participation by Hungarian, Italian, Slovak, and Croatian units, even an elite Spanish unit, the Blue Division, as well as volunteer contingents from the various occupied countries (France, Denmark, Norway, and others) in the Waffen-SS. It was also one of the most brutal campaigns of all time. Its strategic goal was nothing less than the destruction of the Red Army and what Hitler called the "liquidation of the USSR." In operational terms, Barbarossa called for the Wehrmacht, in a single, grandiose campaign, to occupy all European Russia up to the line Archangel–Astrakhan, something that appears only slightly less crazy today than it did at the time. With all due apologies to the fighting in the Pacific, this was "war without mercy" on both sides, prosecuted by two of the most barbarous regimes in human history.[74] When it was over, the destruction would stretch from Moscow to Berlin, and some twenty-five million people would be dead.

The opening of Barbarossa was a stunning success. Opening early on the morning of June 22, 1941, it achieved near total surprise. Powerful air strikes in the first hours wiped out much of the Red Air Force on the ground, with Soviet losses topping two thousand planes. The Wehrmacht advanced in a great three-pronged drive. Army Group North, under General von Leeb, moved on Leningrad. Army Group Center (General Fedor von Bock), along with most of the armored formations in the German order of battle, drove on Moscow. Army Group South (General Gerd von Rundstedt) thrust into Ukraine. Four huge *Panzergruppen* (tank armies) formed the spearheads: one with Army Group North (the 4th Panzergruppe, under General Erich Hoepner); two with Army Group Center (the 3rd under General Hermann Hoth and the 2nd under General Heinz Guderian); and one with Army Group South (the 1st, under General Ewald Kleist). Unlike recent German campaigns, from Crete to North Africa, this at least had a recognizable *Schwerpunkt:* the Moscow sector of the front, along the axis Bialystok–Minks–Smolensk. One principal criticism that might be levied was the large dispersion of armor. After all, half of it, two full *Panzergruppen*, was deployed in nondecisive sectors to the north and south. The arrangement betrays the fact that there had already been serious disagreements between Hitler and the General Staff over the objectives of Barbarossa: the General Staff arguing for Moscow and Hitler arguing for targets on the flanks, especially the economic resources of Ukraine.

In the north, German forces quickly overran the Baltic States, which had only been incorporated into Soviet territory in 1940. Hoepner's *Panzergruppe* covered half the distance to Leningrad in the first five days. Leading his charge was LVI Panzer Corps (General Erich von Manstein, the author of the plan for Case Yellow). Manstein drove some 50 miles on the first day alone, and 185 in the first four days.[75] In cooperation with a Finnish attack from the north, part of what the Finns called their "Continuation War," Leningrad was soon surrounded.

Army Group Center's progress was simply astounding, with Hoth and Guderian's *Panzergruppen* operating on the flanks, turning inward to form the encirclements. By June 26, a huge *Kessel* had been formed at Bialystok, followed by a second at Minsk, and then a third at Smolensk in July. Soviet losses in these encirclement battles were appalling: the Germans took 330,000 prisoners at Minsk, for example. In the first seven days of Barbarossa, "*Panzergruppe* Guderian" advanced an incredible 270 miles. This was not simply maneuver, either. It included a great deal of hard fighting.

Only in the south was the progress slower, although the holdup here was due mainly to the conformation of the border. Rundstedt's advancing forces had to pass through a choke point, the narrow gateway between the Carpathian Mountains to the southwest and the impassable Pripet Marshes to the northeast; in fact, the marshes forced any invader from the west to split forces north and south of it. As he advanced, Rundstedt would therefore be fighting a more or less private war. Still, by late July the panzers had broken into the open here as well, encircling Soviet forces at Uman in August, while the Romanian army drove on Odessa, the USSR's major port in the south.

It had to have been a satisfying month in German headquarters. Not only was the army winning great victories, but victories that proved the validity of the established German doctrine for the conduct of war: short, mobile campaigns leading to huge encirclements. If we may say that the German General Staff had a "Cannae-complex," then this was Cannae being repeated over and over. It was *Bewegungskrieg*'s finest hour, a true culmination of two hundred years of training. On July 3, General Franz Halder, commander of the German army staff (*Oberkommando des Heeres*, or OKH), wrote the famous comment in his diary that "the campaign against Russia was won in fourteen days," since the Wehrmacht had smashed the bulk of the Red Army west of the Dvina and Dnepr. Interestingly enough, he went on to add that "of course, it is not at an end yet. Owing to the extent of the territory and the stubborn resistance of the enemy, who is using everything he has got, that will take us many weeks yet."[76]

How prescient he was. As the panzer columns drove deeper into the USSR, problems began to arise. The first was the nature of the enemy. Although the Red Army was getting hammered as hard as any army in the history of war, it defended tenaciously, and it never stopped counterattacking. These were often improvised, clumsy affairs, but they took their toll on the Wehrmacht. In Ukraine, for example, the commander of the Kiev Military District, General M. P. Kirponos, hurled no less than four infantry armies and six mechanized corps against the invaders in the opening weeks of Barbarossa.[77] The sheer size of the forces involved was beyond anything the Wehrmacht had yet faced. German intelligence had failed utterly to recognize the enormity of the force that the Soviets could mobilize — just as it had failed utterly on Crete and in the desert. The Soviet regime, for example, called more than *five million* reservists to the colors by the end of June. Prewar German estimates envisioned some three hundred Soviet divisions; by December the Soviets had fielded six hundred. No other army on earth could have lost one hundred divisions, as the Soviets did, and still remain in the field.[78]

Not only was the Soviet manpower pool starting to look limitless, but Soviet equipment was much better than the Germans had been led to believe. Soviet tanks, in particular, were more than a match for anything the Wehrmacht had. The medium T-34, with its distinctive sloped armor, came as a great shock to the Germans when they first encountered it along the road to Moscow. The heavy KV-1 was a behemoth whose armor was impervious to German antitank guns. Thus, even in victory, German casualties were very high, and the huge distances involved led to much worse wear and tear on the panzers than previous campaigns. This was not Case Yellow, where a simple one-hundred-mile advance had sealed the victory.

Hitler's meddling, always a controversial topic in this war, also came into play. In August, with Soviet forces decimated and the road to Moscow open, he developed a concern about the slower progress on the northern and southern flanks. Certainly, on a situation map, Army Group Center's progress had far outstripped its partners. He ordered a corps from Hoth's *Panzergruppe* to the north to aid in storming Leningrad. Even more dislocating to the original plan for Barbarossa, he ordered *Panzergruppe* Guderian in its entirety to the south to help encircle Red Army forces in Ukraine. With Kleist coming in from the west, and Guderian swooping down from the north, the Germans formed a huge *Kessel* at Kiev. It trapped four full Soviet armies, the 5th, 37th, 26th, and 21st, and took some 665,000 prisoners in all.[79] Some of the responsibility, ironically enough, lay with Stalin's meddling, in particular his orders that anyone caught retreating from Kiev would be shot.

Kiev was a stunning German victory, perhaps the greatest single operational achievement of all time. It, too, requires careful evaluation. On the one hand, one cannot simply dismiss as a "mistake" any victory this grand, the virtual annihilation of forces in an entire theater. It is not simply a German tradition, but the shared wisdom of military history down through the ages, that the hostile army, not territory, is the real target of military operations. Kill the army, and you can do what you like, at your leisure, to the territory you desire. Nevertheless, the Germans did lose something in the Kiev diversion, and they would never get it back: time. Moscow could, perhaps, have been Guderian's for the taking in September. The situation would be quite different in December.

Above all, the halt on the road to Moscow and the stripping of armor from Army Group Center violated the cardinal principle of German operations since Frederick the Great. All operations must have a *Schwerpunkt*. In the words of Field Marshal Paul von Hindenburg, "A battle without a *Schwerpunkt* is like a man without character, who leaves everything to chance."[80] The Moscow axis was the *Schwerpunkt* of this operation when it began in late June. It is a sign of either poor initial planning or an unseemly impulsiveness on the part of Hitler and the German commanders that it was no longer so important in August. It is worth mentioning in this context that the diversion to the north, to aid in the seizure of Leningrad, was an absolute waste of forces. An attempt to break into the city on September 9 was a disaster, as the tanks became enmeshed in a network of antitank ditches and obstacles thrown up by the city's civilian population.

It wasn't until October that Army Group Center got back its armor and thus was once again ready to begin its drive on Moscow. This was no longer Barbarossa, but Operation Typhoon. It included three *Panzergruppen* (4th, 3rd, and 2nd) in a series of concentric drives toward the Soviet capital. Once again, in a phrase that occurs repeatedly in the course of both world wars, things began well for the Germans. At Vyazma, the panzers encircled remnants of six Soviet armies and then trapped another three at Bryansk. In these two battles, more than 750,000 prisoners, 1,200 vehicles, and 5,400 guns fell into German hands. The Soviets threw up defense line after defense line, but the panzers pierced each one. Once again, as in early July, victory seemed to be within Germany's grasp. "Campaign in the East Decided!" ran the October 10 headline in the Nazi party daily, the *Völkischer Beobachter*.

But once again, victory suddenly became elusive. On October 8 it began to rain, and by midmonth, the weight of millions of men and thousands of tanks had transformed Russia's dirt roads into muddy swamps. By October 22, Hoth's 3rd Panzergruppe was stuck in a sea of mud outside Kalinin; Bock, commanding Army Group Center, wrote in his diary on October 21 that "the Russians are less of a hindrance than the mud and the wetness." The mechanized German army was actually having to haul its equipment and guns forward the old-fashioned way, by teams of horses. On October 25, Bock complained in his dairy of being "stuck fast" in the mud.[81]

On November 6, the freeze hit, announcing the onset of the Russian winter. The good news for the Germans was that they could recommence their forward drive, as the cold froze the mud solid. Of course, the bad news was that temperatures plunged as low as −40 degrees Fahrenheit. Winter supplies were available but were piled up at depots far to the rear. Geared for a quick victory, and possessing inadequate transport, German planners had decided to give priority to fuel and ammunition, not winter supplies for the troops. Once again, the inadequacy of German doctrine was evident, at least when that doctrine had to conduct a war outside the cozy confines of central and western Europe. Lacking winter clothing and equipment, thousands of German soldiers froze to death. Equally hard on *Bewegungskrieg* was the problem of getting tanks and trucks to run in the intense cold. German scientists were at work on the problem, but they would not have a solution until 1942, when ethylene glycol, or "antifreeze," would make its appearance. Still, Typhoon inched forward, a last sign of the tremendous momentum that the operation had built up in its first days. By December reconnaissance patrols could actually spot the spires of the Kremlin in the distance.

Despite the short distance separating it from disaster, the Red Army never ceased its resistance. Officers and men alike had learned some hard lessons about fighting the Germans since June. The gravest threat came in the south, where *Panzergruppe* Guderian formed the southern end of the great German pincer aimed at Moscow. Here, at the important railroad town of Tula, the Red Army succeeded in braking German momentum. Guderian's panzers overlapped Tula on both sides but never did take the city itself.[82] With his own losses, both to the Russians and to the cold, at a crippling level, Guderian was unable to continue the assault on Moscow.

Both sides were now staggering. Despite the victory at Tula, the Soviet situation was grave. The Red Army's losses defy description, probably topping four million men. Foreign embassies had evacuated the capital. The government itself was making preparations to follow, and the smoke of burning government files could be seen for miles around. The Germans, too, were in horrible shape. The army was down to its last reserves, its front-line divisions were operating at a fraction of their regular strength, and many front-line Luftwaffe units were operating at just 25 percent, as the logistics for fuel, spare parts, and maintenance had all but collapsed. Nevertheless, Hitler and his generals remained sure that the Red Army was finished.

Their surprise was total when, early in the morning of December 5, the Soviets launched a great counteroffensive in front of Moscow. The forces involved were massive: a grand total of fourteen armies grouped into two army groups, or "fronts" in Russian parlance (Kalinin and Western). Spearheading the attack were troops of the Siberian Reserve, trained in winter combat, equipped with skis and parkas, who had been shipped from the Far East more than eight thousand kilometers in conditions of great secrecy. In overall command was the brilliant young Chief of the Soviet General Staff, General G. K. Zhukov.[83] Many other young Soviet generals would make their names in front of Moscow, as well: General K. K. Rokossovsky of the 16th Army and General I. S. Konev of the Kalinin Front, for example. It wasn't simply an exercise in brute force. Zhukov proved his own mastery of operational-level warfare. Kalinin and Western Front would seek an encirclement of the German forces in front of Moscow. Kalinin Front was responsible for destroying the northern pincer threatening Moscow, the Klin salient. The 29th and 31st Armies attacked the northern side of the salient; 30th Army and 1st Shock Army attacked the point; and three more armies (20th, 16th, and 5th) hit its southern face. Mobile units (cavalry corps and tank brigades, for the most part) charged into the gaps created by the infantry assaults. There was a second major thrust to the south, against Guderian's *Panzergruppe* at Tula. Here 50th Army and a "Cavalry-Mechanized Group" rudely pushed back Guderian's force, once irresistible, now utterly fought out.[84] Under this inconceivable onslaught, the German line gave everywhere and broke altogether in several places. For a time it seemed that Army Group Center was about to dissolve.

All through December the Red Army pushed the cold, demoralized Germans back from Moscow, inflicting heavy losses. Stalin evidently saw that the time had come to deliver a coup de grâce to Army Group Center, an absurdly premature notion. He ordered the offensive expanded to include the forces of Northwestern Front. They sought the far left flank and rear of the Germans, driving deep into the enemy position at Velikiye Luki and Smolensk. He also ordered a vain offensive to relieve Leningrad in the north and equally ill-fated ones to retake Orel and Kharkov to the south.[85]

Of course, it could have been worse. Many German generals panicked; this seemed like some sort of replay of 1812, with the Wehrmacht cast as the *Grande Armée*. A large number of them wanted to retreat out of the USSR altogether and have another shot in 1942, an absurd notion. Hitler, as is by now well known, resisted the advice of all the experts and gave orders that each man hold his position and defend it to the last. It was a correct assessment of the situation. By January, Soviet momentum wore down. Neither the Red Army's logistical ability nor its command and control mechanisms were sufficient to keep it moving forward forever, and the winter conditions were hardly less harsh on Zhukov's men than they were on the Germans. The Germans held the advantageous positions, the towns and communications arteries, and the Red Army the forests. Hitler's "stand-fast order" had saved the day. Vindicated versus his generals, he now fired them en masse. All three army group commanders (Leeb, Bock, and Rundstedt) were soon gone, and so was Guderian, one of the great media stars of the German war effort up to now. It was as if Kaiser Wilhelm II had dismissed Hindenburg and Ludendorff, and it shows how much more total the Hitler dictatorship was than the Wilhelmine monarchy. The replacements for this "Who's

Militär-Wochenblatt

UNABHÄNGIGE ZEITSCHRIFT FÜR DIE DEUTSCHE WEHRMACHT

| _126. Jahrgang_ | **Berlin, 26. Dezember 1941** | _Nummer 26_ |

Inhaltsübersicht:

In sämtlichen Aufsätzen handelt es sich um private Ansichten einzelner Persönlichkeiten, keinesfalls um Anschauungen maßgebender militärischer Dienststellen.

Großdeutschlands Freiheitskrieg.

124. Bulgarien, Kroatien, Slowakei, Ungarn und Rumänien erklären England und Nordamerika den Krieg. Neue Kaminrede Roosevelts. Der Stellungskrieg im Osten. Abwehr der britischen Nordafrika-Offensive. Luft- und Seekrieg.
Die militärischen und politischen Ereignisse vom 12. bis 17. Dezember 1941.

Japan im Angriff auf Hongkong und Singapur, Vorrücken japanischer Truppen auf den Philippinen, Landung auf Borneo, Kalifornien im Belagerungszustand, New York verdunkelt: diese Feststellungen bedeuten nur eine kleine Auswahl der Ereignisse, die in der vergangenen Woche die Lage im Osten schlagartig erhellten. Als Roosevelt bei den Verhandlungen mit Japan sein frevelhaftes Spiel mit dem Inselreich trieb, hoffte er, durch geschickte Winkelzüge die endgültige Entscheidung über das Verhältnis zwischen Japan und den Vereinigten Staaten so lange hinauszuzögern zu können, bis die englisch-amerikanischen Vorbereitungen zum Vernichtungskriege abgeschlossen waren. Das schnelle Zuschlagen der japanischen Wehrmacht riß ihm und die Kriegshetzer in USA. und England unsanft aus jenen Illusionen und enthüllte mit einem Schlage das Bild einer Lage, die für Amerikas und Englands Position in Ostasien und im Stillen Ozean alles andere als rosig ist. Dazu kommt, daß die Frage, wer an der Ausweitung des Krieges zu einem neuen Weltbrand von ungleich tieferer Wirkung als der Kampf der Jahre 1914 bis 1918 Schuld trägt, selbst für die Augen der daran nicht oder noch nicht beteiligten Teile der Welt klar liegt. Roosevelt hat sich gegenüber den Achsenmächten in den letzten Monaten, ja im Grunde schon vor Beginn des europäischen Krieges so viele Neutralitätsverletzungen und offene Kampfhandlungen zu Schulden kommen lassen, daß niemals mit größerem Rechte von angegriffenen Staaten das Eintreten des Kriegszustandes mit dem Angreifer festgestellt worden ist. Dasselbe gilt von der Haltung der Vereinigten Staaten und Englands gegenüber Japan, dem zuletzt nicht weniger als die Preisgabe seiner Existenz als Großmacht zugemutet wurde. Roosevelt und Churchill haben es also zu verantworten, wenn der Krieg nunmehr zu einer Auseinandersetzung zwischen Europa und dem unter der Führung Japans stehenden Ostasien und dem britisch-amerikanischen Empire geworden ist. Dieser Charakter des großen Krieges wird auch dadurch unterstrichen, daß in der Berichtswoche Bulgarien, Kroatien, die Slowakei, Ungarn und Rumänien an England und Amerika den Krieg erklärt haben. Gewiß war, formal gesehen, der Schritt dieser Staaten zunächst eine Folge der Verpflichtungen, die sie bei ihrem Anschluß an die Achsenmächte übernommen hatten. Zugleich aber spricht daraus die sich in Europa verstärkende Erkenntnis, daß in einer kriegerischen Auseinandersetzung, die über das Schicksal des europäischen Kontinents für Jahrhunderte entscheidet, kein selbstbewußter Staat tatenlos beiseite stehen kann, der auf die Berücksichtigung seiner

eigenen Wünsche Wert legt. Wer in diesem Kriege nicht Amboß werden will, muß Hammer sein.

Beachtlich ist die Reaktion, die die Ereignisse im Pazifik beim nordamerikanischen Volk und insbesondere bei Roosevelt ausgelöst haben. In den Vereinigten Staaten herrschte in den ersten Tagen des Kriegsausbruchs unter dem vernichtenden Eindruck der Katastrophe von Hawai eine ausgesprochene Panikstimmung, der USA.-Präsident selbst aber ist aus dem siegesicheren Schwätzer, der vorher nicht genug mit Nordamerikas Macht und Stärke und mit der Unerschöpflichkeit seiner Lieferungen zu prahlen wußte, plötzlich zu einem — stillen Philosophen geworden, der in seiner letzten „Kaminrede" elegische Betrachtungen über die angeblich durch die französische Revolution entdeckten „Menschenrechte" und ihre Verteidigung durch England und Amerika anstellte. Seine nachdenklichen Erörterungen paßten besonders gut für einen Augenblick, da die Vereinigten Staaten den widerstrebenden Ländern Mittel- und Südamerikas ihren Willen aufzuzwingen versuchen und den Wert dieser Menschenrechte nachdrücklich vor Augen führen, indem sie auch ihnen die Segnungen des amerikanisch-englischen Krieges zuteil werden lassen möchten. Man braucht nicht daran zu zweifeln, daß Roosevelt seine Selbstsicherheit wieder finden wird. Churchill, der ja öfter in ähnlicher Lage war, bietet dafür ein treffliches Vorbild, und die in England bewährten Methoden der Schönfärberei sind denn auch in New York bereits im Gange. Es ist allerdings anzunehmen, daß auf die Dauer die Ereignisse stärker sein werden als alle Versuche, sie hinwegzuinterpretieren.

Neben den Ereignissen in Ostasien stehen die Kämpfe auf dem Kriegsschauplatz der Achsenmächte natürlich weiterhin im Mittelpunkt des militärischen Interesses. Die Operationen in der Sowjetunion werden, da der deutschen Ankündigung entsprechend dort strategische Ziele während der Wintermonate nicht verfolgt werden sollen, ausschließlich von taktischen Erwägungen diktiert. Während die deutschen Stellungen, die auf dem Vormarsche erreicht worden waren, bisher nach dem Gesichtspunkt beurteilt wurden, ob sie sich als Basis für die Fortsetzung der Angriffsmaßnahmen eigneten, wird jetzt die Frage entscheidend, welche Geländeabschnitte den besten Erfolg bei der Abwehr feindlicher Vorstöße verheißen. Dieser durch den Übergang zur Abwehr bedingte Gesichtspunkt kann im einzelnen sowohl eine planmäßige Zurücknahme vorgetriebener Angriffsteile wie auch Angriffsoperationen taktischen Charakters verlangen, die auf die Einnahme beherrschender Geländepunkte ab-

2

Who of Blitzkrieg" were, for the most part, younger officers unquestioningly loyal to Hitler. For better or worse, it was now Hitler's war.

Evaluating Barbarossa and Typhoon

The move into the Soviet Union was the acid test of *Bewegungskrieg*. Despite all the impressive operational victories, the main German conception of warmaking since the days of Frederick the Great failed the test. Barbarossa presented the German army with a task for which it was not suited. The operation aimed at a six-week campaign to liquidate the Soviet Union. An army designed, trained, and equipped for short campaigns in central and western Europe, with an officer corps and General Staff trained to think almost purely in such terms, it was out of its depth fighting six-month campaigns in the heart of European Russia — just as it had been out of its depth in the logistics-dominated war in the desert. More than one thousand miles from its bases of supply, fighting an enemy who was falling back on its own, the Wehrmacht was fighting the wrong war. The same question always arises in analyzing the German army's campaigns: what if the short victory proved elusive? What was the contingency plan in such a case?

It is instructive to peruse the summer 1941 issues of the *Militär-Wochenblatt*, the semiofficial magazine of the German army. Its weekly appearance, with a summary of the events at the front under the series heading "Grossdeutschlands Freiheitskrieg," gives it a "you are there" quality that imparts the high hopes generated by the incredible victories, as well as the gradual disillusionment as the campaign dragged on. The July 4 issue described the early fighting and heralds the fall of Grodno (June 23), Brest-Litovsk, Vilna, and Kovno (all on June 24), and Dünaburg (Dvinsk, June 26). It noted the destruction of 4,107 Soviet aircraft and 2,233 tanks, including "numerous giant tanks, in which the Soviet army had placed special hopes." German forces had reached the area of Minsk, and a concentric advance from here and from East Prussia had already created a *Kessel* at Bialystok. Already, German forces had taken forty thousand prisoners.[86] The next issue (July 11) continues the saga of Bialystok, describing the "battle of annihilation" that had taken place there, a word with special connotations in German military tradition — the ultimate achievement. "It lasted ten days, and as of now the amount of prisoners and captured materiel are still uncounted." It was as great a victory as the annihilation of the Polish forces in the Vistula bend (also ten days in length) or "the battle of Flanders and Artois" in

1940 (the name the Germans almost invariably used for Case Yellow). It heralded the "collapse of enemy forces" and was therefore "a victory of world historical significance."[87]

And so it goes, through the issues of July and August. Each battle is larger than the last; each victory more impressive, with more prisoners, more booty captured, more tanks and aircraft destroyed. Each campaign heralds the final collapse of Soviet resistance. The *Kessel* at Minsk marked "the start of the Soviet catastrophe," with the "complete collapse of the Russian center" opening the way to Vitebsk and Smolensk. Soviet prisoners now numbered 324,000. "Even those who argue that enemy reserves in tanks, guns, and aircraft are inexhaustible has to admit that such losses are catastrophic, and make the final defeat unavoidable."[88] Next came the breakthrough of the "Stalin Line,"[89] the great annihilation battle at Smolensk, "the last great city before Moscow."[90]

By August 1, however, the *Militär-Wochenblatt* was losing its triumphalist note. As it summarized the course of the campaign, a new note was evident:

> In consequence of the vast forces involved, a huge "battle of materiel" is developing. The materiel battles of the previous war led only to the exhaustion of both sides, without achieving any sort of decision. In the east, it has restored the conditions for *Bewegungskrieg*, similar to the situation in France after the breakthrough of the Weygand line at the start of June 1940. There are stark similarities between the just-concluded fifth week of the struggle in the East and the week of June 7th–14th, 1940 in the west. That campaign took place between the Meuse and the Channel on a front of only about 400 kilometers. The present battles of decision against the Soviet army are spread across a front whose total length comprises almost 2,500 kilometers. The time it takes will naturally correspond to the distances that we must overcome.[91]

Apparently, events had postponed "the Soviet catastrophe." Now the talk was of the "hard, tough, and bitter" nature of the struggle; the Soviets "fought stubbornly," throwing their men again and again into fire. There was "strong resistance" everywhere, despite the report in the August 15 issue that the Soviet prisoner total now stood at 895,000, a number that rose to 1,800,000 by September 26. Those numbers were large enough that the reader might not even notice two discordant notes: first, that "the decision is now evidently being sought on the flanks," after weeks of discussing Moscow as the primary objective; and second, the first mention of German losses in the same issue, a little over 102,000, far more than any previous campaign.[92]

There was another flash of confidence at the time of the massive encirclement at Kiev:

> While our enemies chatter and bluff, the German Wehrmacht acts. In the east, the past week brought to an end the colossal battle that sealed the fate of Army Group Budenny east and southeast of Kiev. Up to now, we have become used to the success of our troops in this war. What has happened here, though, exceeds the scale of imagination and represents a victory unlike anything world history has ever seen. Six hundred and sixty-five thousand prisoners: that was Germany's entire army at the start of the world wars.[93]

Even now, however, there seems to be doubt. Even with 2,500,000 Soviet prisoners in German hands by October 10, the "annihilation blow" only makes possible "new operations with far-reaching goals."[94] Although the doctrine of *Bewegungskrieg* had clearly succeeded, the Soviet army was apparently not getting the message. The sense of disorientation and confusion is palpable, as the "continuing attack on Moscow"[95] suddenly changes to "the *Stellungskrieg* in the east"[96] and then to "tough defensive battles on the eastern front."[97] It simply seemed to be beyond the mentality of the trained German staff officer. After all, a series of "annihilation battles" had already taken place. The phrase "*Stellungskrieg* in the east" must have held particular terror for them — that is not, after all, why the Wehrmacht had come to the Soviet Union.

This is the key to understanding German operations in the east, more so than repeating the same old arguments between Hitler and his generals. They achieved unheard of victories in the opening weeks of Barbarossa. The same can be said for Operation Typhoon. But in both cases they failed, not surprisingly, since they were designed for smaller theaters and cozier conditions. The response of General Guderian, usually regarded as one of the great practitioners of armored war in the twentieth century and thus someone who presumably should have known better, was to fight until he had been whittled down to the last tank, almost literally, in and around Tula. He had a growing pile of reconnaissance reports detailing the growth of Soviet strength in his sector and could clearly tell that fresh enemy forces were arriving in Tula daily. Interestingly enough, this is almost exactly what Rommel was doing, at virtually the same time, in response to Operation Crusader: fighting down to his last tank and shell. Apparently, this is what happened when *Bewegungskrieg* failed to deliver what it promised.

Hitler's purge of his generals was a drastic move. It was also not undeserved.

Evaluating German Operations in World War II

The German General Staff had entered the war with a vision of a rapid victory, achieved through a war of movement on the operational level. There would be a series of rapid, highly mobile campaigns spearheaded by tanks and aircraft that would lead to great battles of annihilation. Underlying this operational preference was the assumption, not arguable in any real sense, that this was the only kind of war Germany could win. Inability to win quickly meant a war of attrition, a struggle of resources and manpower for which Germany was uniquely unsuited. German officers were convinced of the correctness of their doctrine. They had worked it out laboriously in operational exercises during the interwar years, exercises that revolved around the theme of cooperation and coordination between air and ground forces. Their confidence grew after the victory over Poland, and even more so after the incredible triumph of Case Yellow. It is that self-confidence, that swagger, that continues to recommend them to historians and military officers in search of models to emulate.

Certainly, many of those in the upper ranks of the German army were well-trained professionals, dedicated and sober analysts of the art of war. Many of them were brilliant operational commanders. A few, like Guderian and Manstein, were both. There are lessons to be learned from the German army. One is that officers should take the study of war seriously. War is not just a job. Nor, frankly, is it an adventure. Like medicine, law, and scholarship, it is a profession, and it requires a single-minded and selfless devotion from its practitioners. Another lesson is the importance of institutional culture. The German army allowed lower ranks to question and make suggestions to their superiors, within limits, of course. Finally, there was a decentralized method of command that left many operational decisions to the officer on the spot. This concept, which we call *Auftragstaktik*, dates back to Frederick the Great and served German military operations quite well over the years.

Despite the worth of these German concepts, modern armies must beware of any simplistic attempt to copy them. German warmaking grew out of Germany's history, culture, and geographic situation. Not only is it incapable of being transplanted, but the question arises: why would anyone want to? The war of movement on the operational level is a gamble. It is an inherently risky venture, one that stakes all on a single throw of the dice. To ask the most obvious question, what happens when the rapid victory of annihilation eludes an army that is trained only to achieve one? This is the real problem of the German General Staff, far more serious than the usual criticism about preferring the glamorous realm of maneuver to the mundane and plodding world of logistics. It planned to win both world wars quickly, it failed, and it then presided, for *years*, over the prosecution of highly destructive wars that it knew it had already lost.

3

The Allies in Search of
Decisive Victory

No less than the Germans, the Allied armies facing them were searching for the quick and decisive battlefield victory that would bring a timely end to the war. On the surface, there was no good reason why it should not have been attainable. The "Grand Alliance" of the Soviet Union, Great Britain, and the United States was, collectively, far richer than its German adversary. It controlled an immense resource base. All three were giants in the field of heavy industry and, as a result, were able to churn out thousands of tanks, aircraft, and naval vessels per month. The western democracies, in particular, were the most prosperous nations in the world, with a highly educated and motivated citizenry endowed with a great deal of technological savvy. The United States was the first "motorized" society on earth. If war was now a job for "armies on wheels," as S. L. A. Marshall described it in his 1941 book, there is no good reason that the U.S. Army should not have been in the forefront.[1] As for Great Britain, it was, after all, the country that had introduced the tank to the modern battlefield. If warfare had now become tank warfare, Britain should have been a master.

And yet, it was not to be. The Allies would win the war, certainly, but they took their time about it. The Germans hit their high-water mark — the moment in which they were closest to winning the war — in early December 1941, outside Moscow. From there, it would be three and a half years until the ultimate Allied victory. When it came, it came through superior numbers and resources of all sorts. It came, in other words, through attrition. It was not the result of the superiority of Allied operations. In fact, the German army remained, at least until 1944, the most operationally proficient force in the field.[2]

The last two years of the conflict show a mixed picture. On one hand, the great military debate of the 1930s over mechanization was over. All the contending armies were mechanized, relying on vehicles of all sorts for tactical, administrative, and logistical purposes. On the other hand, the age of bold armored thrusts, great encirclements, and decisive victory seemed to be gone. Despite the machines, the rules of "mechanized warfare" seemed not all that different from the principles of war as they had been known before 1939.[3] A certain equilibrium had returned, as the defenders learned to deal with armored attack, to avoid panic and collapse. Even the impressive Soviet victories on the eastern front were as much the result of a numerically superior enemy bludgeoning a less well equipped foe to death as they were the cut and thrust of penetration and encirclement. Put more simply, at no time in 1943 or 1944 did the Red Army threaten to break through into the clear and gallop for Berlin — in the way that the Germans had threatened Moscow in 1941. Soviet forces slashed their way through successive German positions but always outran their logistics. Likewise, Allied victories in the West after the Normandy invasion featured lavishly equipped mechanized armies with total control of the air pounding their way forward against German opposition of decidedly mixed quality. Although battlefield conditions never returned to those of World War I,[4] the war never again saw those swift, relatively painless victories that the Germans had achieved from 1939 to 1941.

Since the war, it has become common for historians to rate the various armies. Although most analysts would grant the German army operational superiority until quite late in the war, there has been great controversy over the relative merits of the Allied armies involved. British historians have tended to point out the shortcomings of U.S. forces, both tactical and operational, especially in the early fighting in North Africa and Sicily; American historians can still, sixty years after the fact, get exercised over the perceived failings of British general Bernard Law Montgomery. Until quite recently, virtually all western historians would rate the Red Army as the absolute bottom of the barrel tactically and operationally, and portray its victories as the inevitable product of a mindless steamroller. Today, there are many who rate it the finest army in the Allied camp, the originator of "operational art."

In fact, such ratings are meaningless. First, all three Allied armies were winners in the only statistic worth recording in any war. Each Allied army also conducted operations according to its own history, traditions, and culture. The U.S. Army, for example, fought within the context of a doctrine that emphasized applying massive military might against the enemy's main field force and that disdained risky operational maneuvers. The U.S. Army's 1923 Field Service Regulations stated the goal succinctly: "The *ultimate objective* of all military operations is the destruction of the enemy's armed forces in battle."[5]

The British, having at great cost devised a workable tactical approach on the modern battlefield in World War I, kept to it in this war. It fea-

The uneven quality of Allied armor. Top: the Soviet T-34/76 tank, more than a match for any contemporary German model at the start of the war in the East, and a shock to the Wehrmacht on the road to Moscow. Courtesy of U.S. Army TACOM). Bottom: U.S. M-4 Sherman tanks on line. Intended for the pursuit role, rather than for tank-to-tank battle, they found themselves outgunned throughout the fighting in Europe. From Notebook-Tanks-Book 1, U.S. Army Military History Institute.

tured set-piece battles, sensible short-term operational objectives, timetables, and phase lines. British commanders would first assemble waves of aircraft, masses of supporting tanks, and heavy artillery bombardment against the objective, and only then order the infantry advance. It was a reasonable policy for the most population-poor member of the Grand Alliance, and the one most determined to avoid a repeat of World War I disasters like the battle of the Somme.

In the end, the only way to judge the Allied armies is to compare them to their own doctrine. How closely did their doctrine fit the conditions in which they had to fight? How well did they follow their own doctrine? Perhaps most important, how did these armies react in times when objective conditions at the front forced them, temporarily, to discard their doctrine, to think and fight "outside the box"? We shall see British forces having to fight a mobile battle in Sicily and at Falaise; the U.S. army unable to bring its overwhelming power to bear in Italy and Normandy; and the Red Army struck with surprise blows again and again as they faced a wily German enemy who refused to admit defeat, even after its entire front had been ruptured. As we shall see, their records in this key area were decidedly mixed.

The Red Army and "Operational Art"

There has of late been a great deal of interest in the Soviet concept of "operational art," so much so that the phrase threatens to become a slogan without objective content. There is no doubt that, during the interwar era, the Soviet Union was the site of a great deal of interesting theoretical work on modern warfare. In fact, the entire notion that there is an "operational level" of war, clearly distinct from higher levels of strategy and lower levels of tactics, comes to us from czarist, and later Soviet, theoreticians. The concept of the "deep battle," associated with the writings of Marshal M. N. Tukhachevsky and G. S. Isserson as early as 1929, the formation of the first "mechanized corps" in the fall of 1932, the codification of the new doctrine in the Provisional Field Regulations of 1936, and the great emphasis on airborne formations are all proof, if such is still needed, that the Red Army was a fascinating test bed for new doctrine and equipment during the interwar period. The Germans themselves, evaluating the Soviet fall maneuvers of 1936, had this to say:

> Tanks were used in a meeting engagement, in a breakthrough, in a
> fight for an advanced position, in breaking off a combat, in a coun-

terattack, in pursuit, in a powerful river crossing assault, they were used tactically, in immediate cooperation with the infantry, they were also assembled into mechanized formations and given strategic assignments. Everything that could be asked of the tanks was demanded. We see a grand breadth of vision, a radical exhaustion of all possibilities, an almost boundless trust in the strength of armor.[6]

As is always the case, Soviet doctrine had its roots in the past. The Red Army drew many of its first wave of commanders from the ranks of the old czarist army. It had inherited a tradition of massed infantry formations carrying out broad-front offensives, in the Brusilov style, on separate operational sectors known as "fronts," as well as a heritage of more mobile strikes, using the cavalry as a *corps volant*.[7] Overlaid on this legacy, however, were new lessons derived from the Bolshevik experience in the Russian Civil War. These included an emphasis on offensive operations as opposed to defensive ones; a preference for new technology; and, perhaps most important, a theory of "consecutive operations."

Modern armies had grown so large, and possessed such strong recuperative powers, that it was impossible to destroy them in a single great battle, in the manner of a Napoleon or Helmuth von Moltke the Elder. Rather, it was necessary to launch repeated large-scale offensive operations, a series of consecutive blows that would not permit the enemy to recuperate.[8] In Tukhachevsky's vision, mixed groups of infantry, tanks, and artillery would make the breakthrough. Highly mobile groups of armor and cavalry in second and third echelons would then exploit far into the enemy's rear areas, constantly feeding fresh, new units along the breakthrough axis, aided by airpower and airborne troops. It was a new doctrine — mobile, yet tightly choreographed — known as "deep battle."

Unfortunately, that impressive Soviet doctrinal achievement was a dead letter by September 1939, quite literally. Tukhachevsky was gone, yet another victim of Stalin's ongoing purges of the Red Army. It is, even today, difficult to find words to describe their impact on the army. Bare statistics tell only part of the story, but they tell enough. Among the casualties were all sixteen military district commanders, 80 percent of the Red Army's corps and division commanders, and practically all the regimental commanders and their staffs. What was left was an officer corps cowed into inertia and almost pathologically afraid of making a mistake in battle.[9]

Paradoxically, while he was murdering the command and staff element of the army, Stalin was also overseeing a tremendous military expansion, a reaction to the increasingly perilous international situation. From 1.5 million men in 1937, the Red Army had grown to 5 million men by the time of the German invasion in June 1941. The deleterious impact on Soviet readiness for war cannot be overstated. The Red Army of the day consisted of huge masses of men being poorly trained and indifferently led by newly appointed officers who were often little more than political hacks.[10]

Another casualty of the purges was Tukhachevsky's brainchild, deep battle. Not only had it become "politically incorrect" and even dangerous, since it was associated with the now disgraced Marshal, but by now Soviet military planners had gained considerable experience with tanks in the Spanish Civil War. Their performance there had done much to erase that "boundless trust" that the Germans had noticed. In place of deep battle was a cautious, conservative doctrinal approach that doled out the tanks in small brigades for the purpose of infantry support — in other words, something not unlike the French system.

The story of the Red Army in World War II, then, is the discord between its progressive theories about how modern operations should be conducted and the grim realities of a war against the most adept and sophisticated military force ever assembled. The Red Army learned some hard lessons as it reeled backward in that horrible summer and fall of 1941, with the Wehrmacht carving chunks out of it almost at will. It would eventually work out a synthesis between theory and practice that would begin to bear fruit as early as that first winter. In the end, of course, it would triumph. Victory came at such a cost, however, that it is inconceivable that anyone should wish to emulate it.

Disaster in Finland

For the Soviet Union, the war opened with an act of shocking ineptitude. On November 30, 1939, the Red Army invaded Finland, the start of the so-called "Winter War" (*Talvisota* in Finnish).[11] It is clear today that Stalin expected an easy blitzkrieg-style victory in Finland. Despite massive numerical superiority, vastly superior equipment, and control of the air, however, the first month of the war was a disaster for the invaders. The Red Army was badly trained, and with so many of its higher officers recently murdered in Stalin's purges, very badly led. There was also that bane of any well-conducted operation: haste. Stalin ordered the invasion with almost no preparation period, and the army staff had to redeploy divisions from the Ukrainian Military District, with its relatively temperate conditions, to the frigid north.[12] Local commanders had scanty intelligence about the Finnish forces or their defensive preparations and, in fact, often had little knowledge of the terrain over which they had to fight.

The Finnish commander, Marshal Karl von Mannerheim, skillfully waged two wars at once. He deployed most of the regular army, six of its nine regular divisions, in the south, along the ninety-mile front of the Karelian Isthmus. Here he built a strongly fortified position, the "Mannerheim Line," an interlocking system of tank traps, trenches, reinforced concrete bunkers, and machine gun nests, and dared the Soviets to attack. They did, with the Soviet 7th Army of General K. Meretskov lumbering forward in clumsy frontal assaults that were shot to pieces. A modern historian describes the "organizational incompetence at every level of 7th Army's command hierarchy."[13] In the north, along the immense seven-hundred-mile border, Mannerheim waged a guerrilla war. Carrying the burden was the Home Guard, hardy citizen soldiers, dead shots who knew every inch of the land and who could handle the cold.[14] They fought as ski troops, coming up silently out of the forests to rake the ponderous Soviet columns with machine gun fire, then vanish back into the forest. Field kitchens and supply wagons were their special targets. They also used crude homemade gasoline bombs that proved effective against Soviet tanks. These "Molotov cocktails," a true poor man's weapon, were the one lasting legacy of this war.

The Home Guard was a fierce adversary. At Suomussalmi, they ambushed, trapped, and destroyed two whole Soviet divisions, the 44th and the 163rd. They did the same to two more, the 75th and 139th, at Tolvajärvi. By Christmas, the Finns had broken up most of the invading Soviet columns outside the Karelian isthmus into isolated, immobile fragments: starving, freezing, surrounded, and under constant attack by the Finns. The Finns called them *motti* (bundles of firewood stacked in the forest, meant to be picked up at a later time). Soviet losses were already in the hundreds of thousands, and Stalin had a general or two summarily executed for incompetence. The only useful historical precedent is what happened to British troops in the opening months of the Boer War. This was far worse, however, and was transformed into a true ordeal for all concerned by the weather. One Red Army man wrote of the importance of alcohol in these conditions: "They started giving us 100 grams of vodka a day. It warmed and cheered us during frosts, and it made us not care in combat."[15]

Like the Boer War, however, the result of this conflict could not be in doubt in the long term. The force disparity was simply too great. The

New Year saw the turning of the tide, as Stalin named one of his brighter young officers, General S. K. Timoshenko (just forty-four years old) to supreme command of the war. Timoshenko did the obvious: a coordinated frontal assault by two entire armies, the 7th and 13th, against the Mannerheim Line.[16] Some 600,000 men in all were involved, arrayed in four assault echelons, lavishly supported by air and artillery. Although Soviet losses were stupendous, the Finns were no match for such numbers. This was not deep battle, but brutal and immediate. Timoshenko also showed finesse, however, with the 28th Rifle Corps turning the Finnish right by attacking across the ice of the frozen Gulf of Finland toward the key port of Viipuri. The assault opened on February 1 and cracked the main Finnish positions by February 11. By February 25, Viipuri had fallen, and the main road from Viipuri to Helsinki was in Soviet hands. Finland, having taken thirty thousand casualties out of a total population of just four million, had no choice but to surrender. The Soviets had won the Winter War, taking the territories they had demanded and more: Viipuri, the northern port of Petsamo, about twenty thousand square miles of Karelia. The cost had been nearly unbelievable. Estimates of Soviet casualties vary widely. Later, Soviet leader Nikita Khrushchev, pointing out the criminal incompetence of the Stalinist dictatorship, would place the casualty list at one million Soviet dead, although that is surely an exaggeration. More sober estimates are nearly as bad, running to some 380,000 casualties, far more men than were in the entire Finnish army at the start of hostilities.

Since the creation of the General Staff system in nineteenth-century Europe, armies all over the world watch contemporary conflicts quite carefully to distill their lessons. It is a highly problematic venture, one that resists any kind of scientific or objective standards. Contemporary analysis of the Winter War made the common error of emphasizing the war's opening and ignoring its close. Phase one of the Winter War featured the Red Army carrying out some of the clumsiest, most inept frontal assaults that one could possibly imagine: "They chose to throw people chest first into the machine-gun and artillery fire of pillboxes, in bright sunny days with clear views."[17] Phase two offered an entirely contrary image: youthful and gifted Soviet commanders showing a solid grasp of modern military operations, skillfully employing a huge, well-supplied force and quickly crushing an enemy that had, a short time ago, seemed invulnerable. Only time would tell which was the real Red Army.

To their credit, the Soviets themselves realized that the war had been a fiasco. To their debit, they made the common mistake of overreacting. Deep battle was now a distant memory. The Red Army was concerned with the basics: the importance of reconnaissance, march security and concealment, and carefully phased attacks. Contemporary Soviet military literature shows a force obsessed with the minutiae of winter battle: which gear a tank should use in crossing deep snow, the importance of rapid first aid in extreme cold, the preparation of ski trails.[18] Command training now emphasized "overcoming the enemy's long term defenses by gradually accumulating forces and patiently 'gnawing through' breaches in the enemy's fortifications." According to one young commander, it was more like "engineering science" than the art of operations or maneuver. It was the worst possible time, that spring of 1940, to be developing a Maginot complex.[19]

German Invasion and Its Effects

We have already analyzed the first campaigning season of the German invasion. The real challenge to the Red Army in this period had little to do with operational art. Rather, it was simple survival. The Red Army's battle honors in this phase of the fighting consisted of repeatedly being on the wrong side of the greatest encirclement battles in history. The horrors of Bialystok, Minsk, Smolensk, and Kiev in the Barbarossa phase, followed by Bryansk and Vyazma at the outset of Typhoon, have no parallel in military history.

Even with these shocking events as a backdrop, however, certain verities still applied. The Germans, operating on a logistical shoestring, as was their wont, were advancing hundreds of miles from their bases; the Soviets were falling back on theirs. German strength was thus waning, inexorably, while the Soviets were gaining. The crucial moment, called by Clausewitz the "culmination point" of the campaign, occurred in front of Moscow.[20] The Soviet army had, in Marshal G. K. Zhukov, a young (also just forty-four), energetic, and brilliant chief of staff, who coolly determined the precise moment to launch his counterstroke. He concentrated "shock groups," essentially infantry units heavily reinforced by artillery and closely supported by tanks, against extremely narrow weak spots that reconnaissance had identified in the German line, and then blasted through them and opened up holes for the mobile units, echeloned to the rear, to exploit. The Soviet army was not ready to go deep; neither its command system nor its logistics network would permit it. But these short, sharp blows not only drove the German army away from Moscow permanently, but also shattered the command system, and temporarily the morale, of the entire Wehrmacht.

The Moscow counterstroke ended disappointingly from the Soviet perspective. Inadequate provision for bringing up supplies to the forward troops, as well as a system of command and control relying heavily on central direction, conspired to bring the offensive to a halt. Zhukov himself wrote that "we were particularly hard up for ammunition. . . . It probably takes some believing, but we had to fix a firing rate for each gun at 1–2 shots in twenty-four hours. And this, mark you, during an offensive!"[21] Stalin's decision to turn the Moscow counteroffensive into a general offensive all along the front, from relief attempts of Leningrad in the north to a thrust back into the Crimea from the Caucasus region in the south, was therefore highly premature. The Soviet military system was simply not ready for such operations on such a grand scale — yet. Perhaps the greatest waste in the winter fighting was Stalin's insistence on inserting airborne forces, with large, multiregiment drops into the German rear at Medyn, the Ugra River bend, and, most important, a series of operations to the west of Vyazma, none of which achieved anything commensurate with the cost.

The counteroffensive, nevertheless, was a watershed in Soviet military history. With national survival assured, the Soviet high command could devote more thought to the way it conducted operations. Two leading American experts on the Soviet army in World War II speak of a "resurgence of Soviet doctrine" in this period.[22] On January 10, 1942, Zhukov issued Stavka Directive No. 03, a document that would define Soviet operational methods for the rest of the war. It emphasized the role of the shock group as the spearhead of offensive action on the army or front (army group) level. Commanders were to concentrate their strength on an extremely narrow frontage to achieve overwhelming superiority against a single German unit. A front-level attack would have a width of just thirty kilometers, an army only fifteen. Artillery offensives were to precede each attack, with a density of up to eighty guns per kilometer. Targeting first the prepared defensives, they were then to shift to deeper targets to support the penetration, and then deeper still to support the exploitation. Ground support aircraft were to do likewise.

The directive indicates the direction in which the two armies would be heading for the rest of the war. The Red Army would be fighting from a position of tremendous matériel superiority. A German commander in 1942 or 1943 asked to concentrate an entire army on an attack frontage of fifteen kilometers would have simply laughed at the notion. Who would be holding the other fifty miles on either flank? Likewise, assembling eighty gun tubes per kilometer of front was beyond the wildest imagination of the Wehrmacht. Even taking into account the highly successful deception efforts of the Red Army, used to mask weakness in one spot to build up strength in the chosen sector, the Red Army was fighting a kind of war that was beyond German ability to match. One adversary spanned two continents; most of its heavy industry and resources were in invulnerable positions over the Ural Mountains; and it had incredibly wealthy allies who functioned as a sort of "second national economy," providing it with whatever it could not produce on its own. The other was crammed into central Europe, with its factories and mines being bombed around the clock by the western Allies. War is not fair. This conflict saw the Red Army marrying progressive mobile doctrine with the battle of matériel in a highly potent combination.

Case Blue and the Soviet Response

Germany had failed in its goal of a quick victory over the Soviet Union. It had gratuitously, and almost thoughtlessly, added the United States to the enemy coalition facing it, and as of 1942, it faced a war of attrition on two fronts. This was a war that, according to history and tradition, Germany could not win. Yet, in the Wehrmacht, the Germans still held an operational sword of great swiftness and power — perhaps the finest pure fighting machine in the world, however weak it might have been in terms of strategy, resources, and manpower. Despite the resurgence in Soviet doctrine, the German army was still a dangerous opponent. It still outclassed the Soviets in maneuver, in improvisation and flexibility, and above all in the close integration of the combined arms. Its administrative services and staff work were second to none in the world. For the next two years of the war, then, Zhukov would have to limit himself to counterpunching.

Convinced that it was winter that had beaten him, Hitler ordered another great offensive in summer 1942. Because Germany no longer had the strength for an advance in all three sectors, he had to make a decision. Apparently he had had enough of the heavily forested terrain in front of Moscow and Leningrad, and so had most of his staff officers. Case Blue would, therefore, aim at the southern sector of the front.[23] Army Group South would be split into two parts: Army Group A would drive for the oil fields of Baku, Maikop, and Grozny, deep in the Caucasus Mountains. Army Group B would aim at the industrial city of Stalingrad on the Volga River. This was not only the heart of the USSR's tank and tractor industry, it would also serve to protect the extremely long northern flank of Army Group A's drive into the Caucasus.

It is easy to find fault with Blue's operational conception. Getting to Baku would entail nearly insurmountable logistics difficulties — an area of warfare that had already begun to bedevil the Germans. A diversion of forces to clear the Crimea needlessly delayed the start of the offensive at a moment when every day and week was critical. Moreover, against all previous doctrinal and historical practice, these twin drives would be divergent. German staff officers had written widely on "operations with separated forces" in the past. A recent study by General Waldemar Erfurth, for example, had dealt with that very concept. Appearing first in serial form in the journal of the General Staff, *Militärwissenschaftliche Rundschau*, and then in book form, it had compared the classic Napoleonic conception of "operations on interior lines" with those of Moltke's "concentric operations on exterior lines."[24] There were cases in which both types succeeded in bringing about battle under favorable conditions. But in no case was there ever a doctrinal approach that called for separated army groups to march off away from one another. As the two great forces separated, there were bound to be huge gaps between them that the Soviets would surely notice. Hitler's expedient, to plug these gaps with allied troops of indifferent quality, mainly Romanians, was a recipe for disaster.

Even before it could begin, however, the Red Army launched its first great offensive of the war. General Timoshenko's Southwest Front would undertake concentric operations aiming at a double envelopment of Wehrmacht forces at Kharkov.[25] The northern wing of the encirclement would consist of 28th Army (General D. I. Riabyshev) and 21st Army (General V. N. Gordov) concentrating on a fifteen-kilometer front against German XVII Corps, part of the 6th Army under General Friedrich von Paulus. Once Riabyshev was through the line, 3rd Guards Cavalry Corps would exploit through the gap, encircling Kharkov from the north. In the south, Soviet 6th Army (General A. M. Gorodniansky) and an ad-hoc army-sized unit named "Group Bobkin" (for its commander) would crash through the positions of the German VIII Corps. As in the north, mobile units would exploit, in this case the 21st and 23rd Tank Corps, through the gap created by Soviet 6th Army. They were to link up with 3rd Guards Cavalry Corps and complete the encirclement. Exploiting the hole punched by Group Bobkin would be 6th Cavalry Corps, its mission to defend the newly formed "Kharkov pocket" against German relief attacks from the outside.

It couldn't have looked prettier on the map. Moreover, when it started on May 12, the attack achieved complete surprise, with four armies and more than one thousand tanks slamming into the German lines. It was

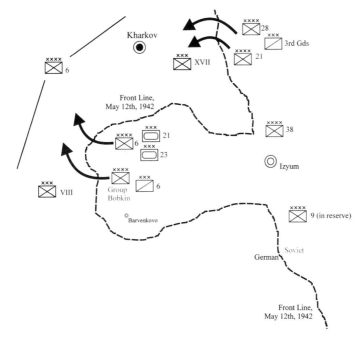

Learning the operational art: The Soviet drive on Kharkov, May 12–17, 1942.

soon clear, however, that in terms of mobile operations the Soviets still had quite a distance to travel to equal the Germans. This was not the frozen, exhausted, and paralyzed Wehrmacht of the previous December. The Germans quite masterfully parried both Soviet thrusts in the north and south, and then launched a well-planned counterattack of their own deep into the Soviet flank.

This was Operation Fredericus, beginning on May 17. The Germans had originally planned the operation as a double envelopment to pinch off the Izyum salient, and that is precisely what it did, only now there was a veritable mass of Soviet men and equipment inside: the entire southern arm of the intended Kharkov pincer, two armies and three corps. With 6th Army attacking the northern shoulder of the bulge, and 17th Army and 1st Panzer Army attacking the southern, the Germans achieved perhaps the neatest and easiest *Kesselschlacht* in their history by May 22. It must have seemed to both sides that it was back to business as usual, as several hundred thousand prisoners fell into German hands.

It was, therefore, a weakened Red Army that bore the brunt of Case Blue. The German offensive began on June 28 and at first achieved great

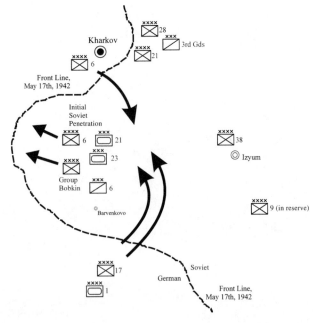

German counterstroke at Kharkov: Operation Fredericus, May 17–22, 1942.

success, slashing through the Soviet lines and covering one hundred miles the first week, hurtling across the main barrier in the region, the mighty Don River. Southern Ukraine is ideal tank country, as flat and as open as Kansas, and as the spearheads rolled forward, they must have been feeling invincible. One historian has described it as "the Wehrmacht at high tide."[26]

There was one ominous sign. The Germans achieved no great encirclements, proof that the Red Army had learned some lessons about mobile warfare in the past year, or at least the lesson of making itself scarce at the start of a German offensive. Even Hitler wondered openly about the lack of prisoners of war. Still, Blue rolled on in impressive fashion. By August 9, 1st Panzer Army (General Ewald von Kleist) had taken Maikop, although the Soviets had set fire to its oil fields before retreating. By September, the 4th Panzer Army (General Hermann von Hoth) and 6th Army (General Friedrich von Paulus) stood on the outskirts of Stalingrad.

Defending the city was Soviet 62nd Army, under the command of General V. I. Chuikov. His orders from Chief of Staff Zhukov were simple to relate, much more difficult to execute: he was to hold the city at all costs and to expect minimal reinforcement.[27] From September through mid-November, a brutal street battle took place in Stalingrad as 6th Army tried to clear the city block by block. This was no longer "operational level" warfare; it was a battle not of corps or divisions, but of squads, of point blank machine-gun fire, even that rare commodity in twentieth-century warfare, hand-to-hand combat. Stalingrad was an environment in which a German army trained and conditioned to fight battles of maneuver now found itself in an environment where simply crossing the street might mean instant death in a hail of machine-gun fire. Individual buildings were the focus: at the Dzerzhinsky tractor works, Soviet tanks rolled directly off the assembly line into combat. Men died trying to secure the grain elevator, the vodka works, a structure that became known as "Pavlov's House," for the commander of the company holding it, and the railroad loop called the "Tennis Racket." It was essentially a kind of siege warfare, with the Soviets turning each structure into a miniature fortress, and the Germans employing specialist troops (combat engineers well supplied with demolition charges) to storm them. Both sides bled in the streets and factories of the dying city. As ordered, however, Chuikov held on — to an ever-narrower strip of the city along the Volga, protecting the ferry sites across the river on which his reinforcements and supplies depended.

The battle in Stalingrad was only a prelude, however, to something much larger. The Soviet command was planning a classic battle of encirclement, Operation Uranus. Soviet planners must have been shocked at the situation that greeted them on the map. The great Swiss military analyst, the Baron Henri de Jomini, once described the geometrical form of a typical battle as a rectangle.[28] The two adversaries faced each other in parallel lines; a third side often consisted of a barrier of some sort, a river, forest, or national boundary. The struggle to control the fourth side, then, the open flank, was often decisive in the outcome. He would have been baffled by the "shape" of Case Blue. Two arrows, widely diverging, emerged from the starting point. At the tips of these arrows stood powerful fighting groups trained for highly mobile operations, yet for all practical purposes completely immobilized. For Army Group A, it was 1st Panzer Army, a tank-heavy unit being asked to operate in the Caucasus Mountains, a type of environment for which it was uniquely unsuited. For Army Group B, it was 6th Army and 4th Panzer Army, heavy mechanized units, stuck fast in urban fighting in Stalingrad.

On either side of the Stalingrad point were hopelessly extended flanks, with nary a terrain feature to strengthen them. The unlucky forces deployed to protect these long flanks were two Romanian armies, the 3rd in the north and the 4th in the south. Badly trained, poorly equipped, and almost completely lacking in antitank weapons, they could offer little resistance to any determined Soviet thrust. Between Army Groups A and B there stood a 190-mile gap, patrolled — and one must use the term loosely — by a single German division, the 16th Motorized, at Elista. Both of these Army Groups depended for their very survival on a single crossing over the Dnepr River far to the rear, the railway bridge at Dnepropetrovsk. Deep in the Caucasus, Army Group A's communications had to run another gauntlet through the gateway city of Rostov. There were literally no reserves anywhere on this front, a fact that had undoubtedly recommended it to the Soviets as a suitable place for an offensive. The chain of command was "utterly grotesque," in the words of General Erich von Manstein. Army Group A had no commander of its own; Hitler commanded it "in what might be called a part-time capacity."[29]

Much of the blame for these inane dispositions rests with Hitler, who was now issuing detailed directives in virtually every area of operational planning. The age of German *Auftragstaktik*, allowing flexibility and latitude to the individual army commanders, was long gone. As one modern scholar — no friend of the German General Staff — has written, "as flawed as the General Staff's performance sometimes was, Hitler's was even worse."[30] In fact, Hitler's conception for Case Blue cut against the grain of the entire Prussian-German military tradition. It aimed not at the destruction of enemy forces, but at an economic target — the Caucasian oil fields.[31] Hitler was forever declaring that Germany could not possibly continue the war unless some key mining or industrial region was seized and held: the oil fields of Maikop, the coal of the Donets Basin, the manganese mines of Nikopol, the nickel of Petsamo, and many more.[32] It was a way for this former corporal to assert his superiority to the generals. They simply made war; he, by contrast, had larger issues on his mind. Army Group A duly marched on Maikop in the face of increasing Soviet opposition that eventually rendered any German presence in the Caucasus untenable. Maikop fell into German hands in August, but Soviet forces had wrecked its oil wells and refineries. Germany managed to limp on for another three years without its oil.

There is some disagreement today about just who was responsible for conceiving the Soviet counteroffensive. Zhukov will always have his supporters; a great deal of evidence also points to the young (forty-one) and aggressive commander of the Southwest Front, General N. F. Vatutin.[33]

Victory will always have many fathers. At any rate, it does appear that Stalin was now more willing to leave the planning of large-scale operations in the hands of professionally trained subordinates. The disaster of the Kharkov offensive had apparently affected him deeply. In that way, his character arc ran entirely contrary to that of Hitler, who came to play a more important role in compiling detailed orders for units at all levels.

Whoever drew it up, the plan was a sound one. The Soviets were able to concentrate enough combat power on both flanks to simply vaporize the unfortunate Romanians.[34] The Southwest Front, Vatutin's command, would form the northern pincer. Two armies (5th Tank and 21st), deployed abreast, would crash through the thin screen of Romanian 3rd Army. Mobile units would then pass through the infantry that had made the breach. The 1st and 26th Tank Corps (from 5th Tank Army) and the 4th Tank Corps and 3rd Guards Cavalry Corps (from 21st Army) would wheel to the southeast, encircling Stalingrad from the north. Once again, a final mobile unit (8th Cavalry Corps, from 5th Tank Army) was to peel off to the southwest, to protect against relief attempts. Units of Stalingrad Front formed the southern pincer. Soviet 51st and 57th Armies were to blow through the Romanians, while mobile units (13th Tank Corps and 4th Mechanized Corps) linked up with those of the 5th Tank Army coming down from the north. The rendezvous point was to be the town of Kalach on the Don River. A last cavalry corps, the 4th, would provide the outer layer of the encirclement in this sector.

This time all went as planned. Operation Uranus opened on November 19. The Romanian armies on the flanks simply evaporated under strong Soviet attacks. By November 23, the spearheads of the two pincers had met at Kalach, trapping German 6th Army inside a thirty-by-twenty-five-mile pocket in and around Stalingrad. Those who argue that German commander von Paulus could have broken out if only Hitler had given him permission ignore the bleak supply situation he was facing after his long trek from Blue's start line. Such arguments are another attempt to shift all blame for every disaster onto Hitler's shoulders. But there was blame enough to go around here.

The Germans were not finished yet, of course. They had made a gross error in holding out an army to the Soviets, and Zhukov had snatched it in a classic Cannae maneuver. It was a brilliant example of operational art. Yet, another Soviet offensive in the north, Operation Mars, had as its goal the encirclement of German forces in their highly vulnerable position in the Rzhev salient. It failed utterly, with Soviet forces hammering away at German fortifications; it probably cost more than 400,000 Soviet casualties.[35]

Even worse was to come when the Soviets attempted to extend their operations in the south into the winter. With the German order of battle now light by a whole army, the great prospects beckoned. At the moment that the Red Army surrounded Stalingrad, its spearheads were only about 185 miles from the gateway city of Rostov, the key to Army Group A's communications.[36] The main body of Army Group A, by contrast, stood some 375 miles away from Rostov. The first Soviet attempt to drive south toward Rostov began life as Operation Saturn, a concentric drive by the three armies of Southwest Front (right to left, 1st Guards Army, 3rd Guards Army, and 5th Tank Army) against the 8th Italian Army and the ad-hoc German formation known as "Army Detachment Hollidt." Once those formations had pierced the Axis front on the Chir and reached Kamensk, a second echelon (consisting essentially of the 2nd Guards Army) would drive on Rostov, choking off Army Group A's line of retreat. The incredible size of the pocket they had surrounded in Stalingrad, estimated first at 90,000 men and then rapidly revised upward to some 200,000, forced the Soviets to drop the second echelon and commit 2nd Army toward the reduction of the Stalingrad pocket. Saturn now became "Little Saturn," a much shallower envelopment of the Italian 8th Army and Army Detachment Hollidt.[37] It succeeded in crushing those two unfortunate formations, as well it should have, given the gross numerical superiority it enjoyed. Even more important, by robbing General Erich von Manstein's Army Group Don of the reserves he intended to use for the relief of Stalingrad, Little Saturn doomed the Germans in the pocket.[38] Two further Soviet offensives in February–March 1943, Operation Gallop (Southwest Front) and Operation Star (Voronezh Front), both drove far to the west, steadily lengthening the German northern flank, and then ended in operational disaster in the face of counterstrokes from the wily Manstein.

Manstein was "at his best when the situation was worst,"[39] and he managed to weather Operation Little Saturn by shuttling units hither and yon, an operational juggling act that few other commanders of the war could rival. German divisional commanders and manpower alike also fought with their typical skill, with small encirclements often holding up the advance of huge Soviet forces long enough for a line to be formed behind them. Soviet inability to master the science of logistics also played a role. In Little Saturn, for example, Soviet mobile groups had to operate for up to twelve days at a time without systematic resupply. They attempted to do so, and again and again in the winter offensives, Manstein made them pay the price by launching bold counterstrokes once they were at the end of their strength, worn down and literally out of gasoline and ammunition.

Most important, once the reduction of the Stalingrad pocket had restored mobile conditions on the front, freeing both Soviet and German forces' attention, Manstein could launch coordinated, multicorps assaults at times and places of his choosing: against Operation Gallop it was the SS Panzer Corps, IIL Panzer Corps, and XL Panzer Corps, slicing through the extended Soviet front between Krasnograd and Krasnoarmeiskoye.[40] Against Operation Star, after the Soviet 3rd Tank Army had attacked to the south and been annihilated by the onrushing SS Panzers Corps, a "shock group"[41] of Panzer Grenadier Division "Grossdeutschland," SS Panzer Corps, and IIL Panzer Corps cut apart the Soviet Voronezh Front and retook the city of Kharkov. A thoroughly rattled Red Army had to flee behind the Donets. Manstein had restored the front to approximately where it had stood the previous summer, before Case Blue had even begun. It was an impressive result, given the relative size of the two forces involved and the German disaster at Stalingrad that kicked off the campaign. "As a withdrawal operation, it must inevitably be devoid of glory," he would write.[42] He could not have been more wrong.

Soviet Operations in World War II

Despite the incomplete nature of the victory, the Soviet army had just achieved one of the most remarkable recoveries of all time. Nearly "liquidated" in the previous year's fighting, it had now seized the initiative in the Ukraine. More important, the Germans now knew they were fighting a foe that had a firm understanding of highly mobile, operational-level warfare. The Germans found that their concept of *Bewegungskrieg,* something they considered uniquely their own, had now gone international. The Soviets, however, added their own twist, introducing the battle of matériel to the mix. When mobile warfare could take place on this scale and with this lavish level of support, it meant one thing: trouble for the Wehrmacht.

The years 1943–1945 would see almost nonstop action on the eastern front. There would be the battle of Kursk in the summer of 1943, the matériel battle par excellence.[43] Operation Citadel was a German attempt to pinch off the Kursk salient. Unfortunately for them, Kursk was a completely obvious target, and the offensive against it marked a bankruptcy of sorts for German operational thinking. Zhukov could read a map as well as any officer and better than most. Soviet air and ground reconnaissance, as well as partisan groups active in the German rear, were able to draw a remarkably accurate portrait of the German buildup and intentions. Zhukov built no less than eight concentric fortified lines in front of Kursk, with more than 1.3 million men ready for the German blow. Two complete fronts — Central Front under General K. K. Rokossovsky in the northern face of the salient and Voronezh Front under Vatutin in the southern face — manned the bulge. These two comprised a bit over one million men, and their mission was to hold off a German assault by less than half that number. The result was predictable.

In June 1944 the Soviets would launch a great offensive in Byelorussia (Operation Bagration).[44] The Red Army concentrated four complete fronts around the now increasingly beleaguered German Army Group Center, headquartered at Minsk. All told, some 116 infantry divisions and 43 tank divisions, numbering five thousand tanks, would form the strike force. The Wehrmacht was outnumbered by at least four to one; partisans were active in its rear areas; the Red Air Force ruled the skies. The Soviet IL-2 *Shturmovik* had by now replaced the German *Stuka* as the dominant ground attack aircraft in this war. Bagration would begin with the greatest artillery barrage in military history (some four hundred guns per mile of front). It is no wonder that Soviet planners counted on achieving no less than six breakthroughs in the initial stages. As always, large mobile groupings would then exploit through the hole created by the infantry, artillery, and tank regiments. By now, the Soviets had this down to a routine. The initial attacks tore open a 250-mile gap in the German lines. Army Group Center was destroyed, simply flattened by superior firepower and mass, with its losses topping 500,000 men.

We have mercifully arrived at a point where we need no longer adhere to stereotypes about the Soviet army in World War II. The common image for cold-war-era American readers was that of a faceless "Asiatic" horde, overcoming their better trained, more civilized German adversary with sheer numbers and masses of equipment.[45] That the writers painting this picture were often Germans, sometimes even former employees of the German Ministry of Public Enlightenment and Propaganda like Paul Karl Schmidt (who wrote as Paul Carell),[46] seemed to bother few people in the West. After all, the Germans were allies now, against these same Soviets, in the worldwide struggle against communism. An almost imperceptible process of identification with the Germans took place among western readers. One need think only of the tendency of Americans to refer to the "eastern front."[47]

Today, scholars have so thoroughly revised the old image that it is as dead as the cold war itself. The Soviet army in World War II was a formidable combination of mass and skill. The hordes of men and mountains of equipment were not figments of anyone's imagination. But what the West had completely ignored was the considerable operational skill with which the Soviet command fought the Germans. Officers like Zhukov, Konev, Rokossovsky, and Vatutin came up with well-planned operations and prepared them thoroughly, often deceiving the Germans completely as to the time and place of the next blow. Then they executed them ruthlessly, launching highly concentrated thrusts involving waves of armor, men, shells, and ground-support aircraft, smashing whatever unlucky German (or German allied) formation happened to be in the breakthrough sector.[48]

Once again, we observe the main dynamic of doctrine. It arises from specific circumstances and traditions that are unique to each army and the society from which the army emerges. The Russian, and later the Soviet, army had developed a theoretical basis for operational-level warfare that arose from the country's geographical position, vulnerability, size, and social structure. Stalin's industrialization of the country, an inhumane, even murderous policy, allowed his military commanders to pursue that doctrine to a degree previously undreamed. The Soviet army could mass more artillery per kilometer than any army in military history. General Konev was correct when he identified "a well organized artillery attack" as "the embodiment of our army's power."[49] Although we think of the Soviet army as a practitioner of "deep battle," it dished out the harshest punishment to units in the German tactical zone, as well as the closest operational reserves, in other words, about eighteen to twenty kilometers deep.

On the negative side, there is still a huge body of uncontested evidence that paints the Soviet army as an inflexible behemoth. Success came only in carefully planned, tightly choreographed operations. Once the initial stages of an advance had taken place — and after 1943 they rarely failed, so great was Soviet matériel superiority — its formations typically hammered away on the chosen axis long after chances for further gain had vanished. A report from the German 9th Army discussed this tendency after the Soviet debacle in Operation Mars:

The enemy leadership, which demonstrated skill and adaptability in the preparation and initial implementation of the offensive, once again displayed its old weaknesses as the operation progressed. Indeed, the enemy has learned much, but he has again shown himself unable to exploit critical unfavorable situations. The picture repeats itself when operations which began with great intent and local successes degenerated into senseless, wild hammering at fixed front-line positions once they encounter initial heavy losses and unforeseen situations.[50]

"Senseless, wild hammering." Indeed, flexibility was not one of the Soviet army's virtues. When the operational situation changed suddenly, it hardly ever reacted well. General Chuikov, the hero of Stalingrad, wrote about how much difficulty his forces had dealing with the German elastic defense, which consisted of "a planned withdrawal" followed by "a surprise counterattack backed up by mobile reserves."[51] He was describing action in 1944, by which time these methods should no longer have been news; the Germans had been using them for two years. Put another way, the German invasion caught the Red Army by surprise and forced it onto the defensive, overrunning most of European Russia in a few months. The Red Army would take almost three and a half years to cover the same distance in the opposite direction. Even in their victorious operations, Soviet commanders tended to exhibit a complete lack of scruples about their own losses, and the result was a casualty figure that should stagger the imagination even of its admirers. Such was the price, Zhukov and the others felt, of victory.

No other country can copy this model, or should want to. Starting in the 1980s, many officers in the U.S. Army became increasingly enamored of Soviet "operational art." Indeed, the term soon became a cliché in U.S. military circles. Staff officers should study the successes of Soviet operational planning, but they would also do well to consider the human cost. No U.S. commander will ever be able to incur the kind of losses Soviet armies and fronts achieved in their victories; public opinion would never stand for it. No U.S. commander will ever be able to point to an officer in action under his command and, on the spot, order him to a penal battalion, as Zhukov did on more than one occasion.[52] There is only one law regarding operational doctrine: in the end, each army must work out its own doctrine for itself, based on its national values, traditions, and culture.

The Odd Couple: U.S. and British Operations in World War II

It is difficult to treat British and U.S. operations in isolation. The two nations, linked by close ties of language, culture, and history, formed one of the closest military alliances of all time. Their staffs worked out strategy, operational planning, even tactics, together. The finest fighter aircraft in Western Europe was the P-51 Mustang. An American design, it did not really soar until designers outfitted it with a British engine, a Rolls-Royce. It was the perfect symbol of the Anglo-American war effort.

The strategic background of the two, though, could not have been less similar. Great Britain had faced Germany alone for the first two years of the war. Its army had failed against the Germans early, and failed again later. It had performed a hurried evacuation from the continent at Dunkirk in 1940; from Greece in April 1941; and then again from Crete in May. In fact, it's not unkind to say that up until 1942, the Dunkirk evacuation (Operation Dynamo) had been the high point of the war for the British. Already, by the time the Americans entered the war in December 1941, Britain was feeling the pinch: lack of energy, lack of resources, and above all, lack of men. Britain fought the last three years of the war under one major constraint: if it lost an army, it probably wouldn't be able to replace it.

The United States, by contrast, was awash in wealth, with huge economic and financial reserves and an industrial base that was immune from bombing. The uniquely American worldview, with its positive side (a "can-do" attitude)[53] and its negative (an often simplistic view of the complexity of a given issue), was much in evidence from the first days of U.S. involvement in the war. America flexed its industrial muscles, funneling a tremendous amount of aid into its allies via the Lend-Lease Program (seven thousand aircraft, fifteen thousand tanks, and fifty thousand trucks to the Soviet Union alone); constructing a great fleet of strategic bombers to pound German cities from the air; and training a mass army to reinvade Europe. More than ten million men and women would be under arms by 1945. It is also worth recalling that the United States managed to find the naval resources to fight Japan, even though Churchill and Roosevelt agreed that defeating Germany had to be the priority. The scope of the American war effort, even before it had sent a single man into combat in Europe, was unprecedented.

Reflecting these different strategic factors were the military doctrines of the two armies. To U.S. planners, especially the Chief of Staff, General George Marshall, strategy was a fairly simple problem. U.S. forces had to gear up for the main event: a cross-Channel invasion of Western Europe. Only there could the Allies get at the mass of the German army and destroy it. Staff work began almost immediately on an invasion plan for 1942 (Operation Sledgehammer) and then for 1943 (Operation Roundup), both to be used in case of a sudden Soviet collapse against Germany. These studies showed, however, that a direct invasion of Western Europe would be a difficult, costly, and incredibly complex undertaking.

To be frank, the British were not all that enthusiastic about the idea anyway. A cross-Channel invasion meant a direct confrontation with the weight of the German army, in positions that it had had a chance to fortify since 1940. That, in turn, meant losses. In the 1930s, there had been a great strategic debate in Britain over the use of the British army in a future war. There were those, military commentator and journalist Basil Liddell Hart foremost among them, who argued that Britain should "limit its liability" to air and naval assets in a future conflict. This was the traditional "British way of warfare," and discarding it had involved Britain in the greatest bloodletting of all time: the trenches of World War I.[54] There were others, and Liddell Hart was among them as well from time to time, who argued for the creation of an expeditionary force armed with modern weapons, tanks, and aircraft for use on the continent. In 1939, the second position had prevailed. A British Expeditionary Force had duly sailed off to France. Less than a year later, it had returned to Britain, without most of its weapons and equipment, in the greatest evacuation operation of all times. Britain was in no hurry to repeat the experience.

There is one thing these two powers shared, however. Both entered the war deeply divided over the question of battlefield doctrine. This was particularly true with regard to the crucial question of how best to employ armored forces. Great Britain had pioneered the tank in 1916 and spearheaded the examination of armor in the interwar period by forming an Experimental Mechanized Force in 1927. During the 1930s, it would lose its lead in mechanization to its once and future adversary, Germany. There are many reasons for this shift in the "armored balance of power." The decade of the Great Depression was hardly conducive to the kind of large research and development costs required to mechanize the army. There was no national consensus for higher defense spending. There was also a vigorous debate in Britain about the shape of the future army. Was it primarily intended as a heavy strike force for warfare on the continent? Or was it to be a light "gendarmerie" or "constabulary" to police the empire? Obviously, the former would need a much heavier configuration, and more tanks, than the latter.[55]

Along with these problems came a great deal of tactical confusion. It was one of those times, periodic in the history of armor, in which it appeared that antitank weapons had eclipsed the power of the tank. Liddell Hart, again, reflected the enthusiasm of the moment, arguing that modern defensive weapons had become strong enough to ward off attacks by even the heaviest tanks. Heavy tanks had other liabilities, as well.

They were too heavy for most bridges and roads, their size made them huge targets for enemy fire, and they were too expensive to produce in quantity. He argued that the trend of the future was the miniature tank, or "tankette," the Carden-Lloyds and Morris-Martels. Speed, not weight of armor or fire, was the essential attribute of the armored unit. The British became enamored of the light tank, the lighter and faster the better. Such vehicles, crewed by one or two men, formed a major portion of British tank forces at the outbreak of war. They would prove to be nearly worthless when the shooting started.

This conceptual argument foiled attempts to enunciate a British armored doctrine. Cavalry officers favored the light tank, to ensure the survival of their regiments in their traditional roles of exploitation and pursuit. General Hugh Elles, who had commanded the Tank Corps at Cambrai and became Master General of Ordnance in 1934, was now a supporter of the so-called "infantry tank."[56] He wanted a vehicle that was heavily armored (immune to the then-standard 37-mm antitank weapon), with minimal speed requirements, not much faster than the infantry. The Infantry (or "I") Tank Mark I was the result — weighing eleven tons, with a crew of two, a single machine gun, and a maximum speed of eight miles per hour. Its strength lay in its armor protection, some 60–65 mm. Later, an improved model, the Mark II (the "Matilda" of Western Desert fame) came on line, even more heavily armored (75 mm) and armed with a 40-mm gun. At the same time, under the influence of "Q" Martel, there appeared a new line of "cruiser" tanks, starting with the A.9, or Cruiser Tank Mark I. Designed for higher speed (the later Cruiser Tank Mark III could reach thirty miles per hour), it was equipped with the same 40-mm gun as the Matilda.[57]

The division of the tanks into two categories, cruiser and infantry tanks, plus light tanks besides, was an unfortunate development. The British separated the tank's two chief attributes: mobility and armor. It would have been a better use of scarce resources to design one rugged, all-purpose tank. What appeared instead were two vehicle types armed with the same gun. Suitable for the infantry tank, the 40-mm gun would prove wholly inadequate for the cruisers that had to deal with German armor.

An even more serious tactical weakness was an emphasis on the power of the tank at the expense of the other arms. It originated with officers of the Royal Tank Corps and spread to the rest of the army. The fire-breathing commander of the 7th Armoured Division, General Percy Hobart, was a perfect example. He was a tank man through and through, the spiritual successor of Fuller.[58] Such ideas tended to filter down to many of those taking part in the debate over mechanization in the 1930s. The "Armoured Division" was the result: a disastrously tank-heavy force of six tank battalions, some 321 tanks in all, both cruiser and light. Supporting them was precisely one motorized infantry battalion. The British performance in the Western Desert in 1941, when the Germans watched in amazement as British armor, unsupported by infantry or artillery, charged cavalry-style into the teeth of their 88-mm antitank guns, bears stark witness to the lack of combined arms in the British tank formations.

There is much less to say in the interwar period about American military doctrine. In fact, to say that the United States had a doctrine before 1940 would probably be a mistake. A "Superior Board" had met in 1919 to evaluate the lessons of World War I. In what can only be called a spectacular misreading of events, it argued that the American Expeditionary Force's success had validated the U.S. concept of "open warfare" (a term that had no existence before the war).[59] "Decisive results are obtained only by the offensive," the Board maintained. "The stabilized trench warfare which prevailed in France in 1917 was due in great measure to the lack of aggressiveness of both sides. Infantry must be self-reliant. Too much reliance was placed by the infantry on the auxiliary arms and not enough on the means within the infantry itself. This tended to destroy the initiative."[60]

With the National Defense Act of 1920 authorizing a strength of just 17,000 officers and 280,000 men for the army, and the Tank Corps abolished and its functions transferred to the infantry, the U.S. Army was hardly in the doctrinal forefront of the interwar period.[61] There was little evolution between the army's two sets of Field Service Regulations, in 1923 and 1939. The former saw one purpose for both air power and armor: to support infantry on the ground. The 1939 version still prescribed armor's mission as supporting the infantry, although there was some hedging: "as a rule," tanks were "to assist the advance of infantry foot troops." Aviation's principal mission was still to assist "the accomplishment of the mission of the field forces."[62] By 1939, as German army groups and panzer corps were overrunning Poland, there were still few mechanized units larger than battalion size in the U.S. Army.

The year 1940 changed many things, and one of them was the U.S. military. In July 1940, following the dramatic German victory in France, U.S. Army Chief of Staff George Marshall created the "Armored Force" under General Adna R. Chaffee, Jr. He had precisely one unit under his command, the 7th Cavalry Brigade (Mechanized), but soon expanded it into two full armored divisions, the 1st and the 2nd. Chaffee was a cav-

Two men waiting for the call of destiny. Left: Captain Dwight D. Eisenhower at Camp Meade, Maryland, Tank Center, 1919 or 1920. From Dwight D. Eisenhower Collection, 1919–1930, RG199S, U.S. Army Military History Institute. Below: Lt. Col. George S. Patton, Jr., in command of the 1st Tank Center in France, Tank Corps School near Langres, July 1918. Courtesy of U.S. Army Military History Institute (George S. Patton Collection, RG 689S).

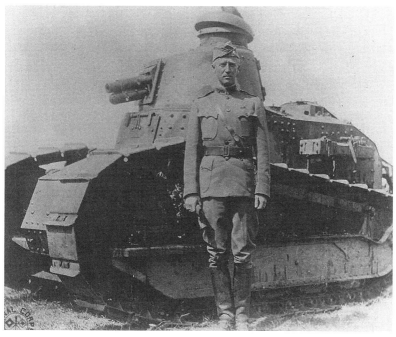

alryman and brought the horse arm's view to armored warfare. The "primary role" of the tank "is in offensive operations against hostile rear areas."[63] At the same time, however, the army kept separate tank battalions intended for direct support of the infantry.

Further complicating this nascent doctrine were the views of General Lesley McNair, chief of the U.S. Army Ground Forces (AGF).[64] An artilleryman, he did not believe that the purpose of the tank was to fight another tank. The conception of the tank versus tank duel, he later wrote, was "unsound and unnecessary." The tank helped the infantry break through enemy defenses, and then it exploited rapidly into the enemy's rear. It was not intended to take on enemy tanks. That was the task of a different family of vehicle, the "tank destroyer." It was a mobile, lightly armored vehicle mounting an antitank gun. The job of the tank destroyer was to go hunting German tanks, thus freeing U.S. armor for the cavalry role of exploitation and pursuit. It would prove to be one of the great doctrinal wrong turns of the century. The principal problem was that tank destroyers were totally unsuited for offensive operations. Their light armor made them easy prey for the German tanks they were stalking. One modern scholar has called the tank destroyer "McNair's pocket battleship solution — an armored fighting vehicle that could run away from trouble."[65] No other country copied the concept, and for good reason. As the U.S. Army was stuck fast in the Normandy hedgerows, wondering how it had gotten into such a mess, it might have considered the forty-five tank destroyer battalions in its order of battle. They included enough vehicles to have formed fifteen additional armored divisions.

U.S. doctrine also had a profound effect on the tank that the army would ride into combat in Europe. Armor and firepower were not essential for the intended cavalry exploitation role. Speed was. Although a heavy gun would certainly have come in handy against the current generation of German tanks, the Mark V Panther and the Mark VI Tiger, U.S. tanks were not supposed to go Tiger hunting. Tank destroyers were. The result was the M-4 Sherman medium tank. It was a versatile, sturdy, reliable design and capable of almost infinite variation. Its gyrostabilized gun was a true conceptual breakthrough, allowing for continuous target acquisition even while the tank was moving. But it was also completely incapable of penetrating the frontal armor of a Panther or Tiger; it would have to achieve most of its kills by engaging single German tanks in groups. It was hardly a sophisticated armored doctrine, but it was the only doctrine that such a tank could support.

Preparing for the real thing. Crew abandons a disabled M-3 tank during maneuvers of the 3rd Army at Camp Polk, Louisiana, February 1943. Signal Corps Photo, 165-L1-43-330, U.S. Army Center of Military History.

Sicily: Operations and Doctrine

On July 10, two armies (British 8th under Montgomery and U.S. 7th under Patton) landed in Sicily.[66] Although Operation Husky managed to secure the island after five weeks of hard fighting, it had its problems. Airborne troops, dropped at night, scattered badly. A large number fell into the sea and drowned, and losses included some 47 out of 144 gliders. Others flew over the Allied invasion fleet and fell victim to friendly antiaircraft fire. The operational plan, drawn up by the Supreme Allied Commander in the theater, General Sir Harold Alexander, was no work of art, either. Lacking trust in his allies, he had Montgomery land on the eastern side of the island. Its mission was to seize the port of Syracuse and then move on to Messina, cutting off the Germans from evacuation. Patton's job was merely to protect Monty's flank.

The Allies could not have made a worse choice. It fell to the British to make the hardest slog against the toughest opposition. In the back of

General Alexander's mind had to be his perceived weakness of the Americans. Just months ago they had nearly fallen apart under the German onslaught at the Kasserine Pass. An entire corps, the II under General Lloyd Fredendall, had suffered a terrible mauling. There were some British staff officers who referred to the men in olive drab as "our Italians." Montgomery's army hesitated after landing, however, at the time when the Germans were most disorganized and vulnerable. Paying meticulous attention to his battle array, he seemed loath to push inland. He did take Syracuse, the closest objective, but four weeks later he was only halfway to Messina, hung up in front of the German defenses at Catania and Mt. Etna.

Patton, who had succeeded Fredendall as II Corps commander after Kasserine and had distinguished himself in the fighting in Tunisia, fought well and aggressively. Alexander's operational plan, however, took him on a long and unnecessary drive around the periphery of the island against scant opposition. Patton actually got to Messina before Montgomery, a shocking thing if you know the map of Sicily. The most serious problems encountered in the American drive were mines, booby traps, and demolitions of various sorts left behind by the Germans, particularly in the last stages of their retreat through northeastern Sicily. The great American war correspondent Ernie Pyle wrote that the Germans "blew almost every bridge they crossed," nearly 160 in the American zone alone. "They mined the bypasses around the bridges, they mined the beaches, they even mined orchards and groves of trees that would be logical bivouacs for our troops." One sergeant told him, "This has been a bulldozer campaign."[67] By the time Patton's engineers had cleared paths through the mines and restored the bridges, most of the Germans were gone. The Allies followed up the surrender with landings on the Italian mainland, an even more problematic campaign that turned into a long, hard slog indeed.

The Mediterranean theater presented difficulties to both Allies. The British were forced to make amphibious landings in Sicily and Italy. These operations required dash, speed, and the ability to improvise upon landing. Montgomery's cautious and systematic approach caused grave problems both times, although it was fully in keeping with the British system. Likewise, the U.S. Army found that its doctrines did not necessarily match the situation in which it found itself. In contrast to its tradition of concentrating overwhelming force against the enemy, Patton's army essentially struck air in Sicily. The pointless "race for Messina" was the result.[68] In the Italian campaign, at both Salerno and Anzio, it found itself fighting against superior forces and almost perished both times. For the rest of the Italian campaign, the U.S. theater of operations was a narrow corridor up the western side of the Italian boot between the high Apennines and the sea, a corridor that nature had designed for a smaller foe to hold off a larger one. That is just what the Germans managed to do. The Mediterranean campaign is what happens when doctrine, formulated and inculcated into the troops well before the war, clashes with a mission that may only have occurred to policymakers a week ago.

Allied Operations in Western Europe

THE LANDING

The day after General Mark Clark's famous Jeep ride past the Roman Coliseum, on June 6, the Allies had made their long-awaited landing in northwestern France. Operation Overlord, so long in the making, was an epic undertaking, a massive and complex operation involving three million Allied troops, five thousand naval vessels, and more than eleven thousand aircraft, an amphibious Barbarossa. Given the complexity, the landings themselves went smoothly. At Utah beach, a well-coordinated assault by the U.S. 4th Infantry Division, along with the 82nd and 101st Airborne, overcame sparse resistance and penetrated inland. At Gold, Juno, and Sword beaches, British and Canadian forces landed without incident, aided by the specialized tanks of the 79th Armoured Division. These included a number of "DD" (duplex drive) amphibious tanks that literally swam ashore, as well as the "Crocodile," a tank outfitted with a flamethrower and useful in reducing German strong points and pillboxes — "Funnies," the British called them. Only at Omaha beach was there real opposition.[69] Here, the landing by the U.S. 1st Infantry and 29th Infantry Divisions coincided with a beach defense exercise by a full-strength German infantry division, the 352nd. All day long, U.S. forces lay pinned to the beach under heavy fire, dependent on their own fire and the light guns of offshore destroyers. The commander of U.S. 1st Army, General Omar Bradley, gave serious consideration to withdrawing them. "It was a nightmare," he later wrote. Finally, a few local commanders rallied the men around them and began to lead them up off the beach. They were still in danger, but by evening, they had won a foothold at Omaha. Behind them lay the bodies of more than two thousand dead.

The near-disaster of U.S. forces at Omaha stemmed above all from a lack of interservice cooperation. By now, there was a branch of the service with a great deal of experience in amphibious landings: the U.S. Marine Corps. The marines had learned some hard lessons in the Pacific, and their amphibious doctrine reflected that fact. The necessity of operating in full daylight, the incredible size and lethality of the force laying on the preparatory bombardment (including aircraft carriers, battleships, cruisers, and destroyers), as well as the ever-increasing length of the shelling (three full days on Iwo Jima, seven on Okinawa) — all these were outgrowths of marine experience. Surprise and concealment were much less important factors. Plastering the enemy with fire for days before the landing and then bringing the fire to a crescendo during the landing itself were essential. The Omaha planners' decision to land at "half-light" (at least in part a compromise between the U.S. preference for daylight and the British preference for night) and to rely almost exclusively on air support left the 1st Division dangerously exposed on a killing ground, with little to call upon except its own courage.

The men at Omaha also had the bad luck to run into tougher opposition than at the other four beaches. Once they had landed, however, and disaster stared them in the face, the U.S. Army — general officers, field-grade leaders, and men alike — had the flexibility and mental resourcefulness (not to mention the reserves of courage) to do something that sounds simple, but is in practice very, very hard. They stood up under fire and tried to press inland. It was one of the infantry's finest hours.

NORMANDY: BRITISH DIFFICULTIES

Once ashore, the Allies faced the same general problem that had hindered operations in Italy. By now, the U.S. Army was clearly the main Allied force, with a large manpower pool and nearly unlimited industrial resources. But once again, the British were in the spot that called for the most aggressive posture, the hardest fighting, and the heaviest losses. The U.S. Army, arrayed on the right, had to grind its way through the hedgerows (*bocage*) of Normandy, a situation, once again, in which it could not bring to bear the overwhelming industrial might that supported it. Assigning the beaches in Normandy was a simple function of the fact that British units were in eastern Britain and the Americans were in the west. It placed the British in front of the city of Caen, however, and presented them with an obstacle that they would not take for a full month.[70]

Montgomery had promised to take Caen on the first day. Facing the spearhead of a German panzer division (the 21st), he failed. A week later, on June 13, an attempt by 7th Armoured Division, the "Desert Rats," to flank Caen's defenses with a right hook far to the west led to disaster at Villers-Bocage. Here, the division's 22nd Armoured Brigade, equipped mainly with the mediocre Cromwell tank, fell into a skillfully laid ambush by Waffen-SS Obersturmführer Michael Wittman and a section of Tiger tanks, part of the 501st SS Heavy Panzer Battalion. Within minutes, much of the brigade was a flaming wreck. At one point, Wittman and the rest of his section actually broke cover, driving up and down the column, from which they had nothing to fear, and drilling tanks and personnel carriers at leisure. There was a third attempt at Caen on June 25, Operation Epsom. This was a shorter right hook to the west of Caen by much of British 2nd Army (Dempsey). The goal was to cross the Odon River and encircle the city from the southwest. It also came to grief at a rise just over the Odon, Hill 112. Not until Operation Charnwood on July 8 did Montgomery succeed in taking the northern half of Caen. The unique feature of this operation was Allied carpet bombing (the use of heavy strategic bombers in the tactical role) to help pave the way for the advance. But even here, enough German forces survived the maelstrom of bombing to limit the British advance to the northern bank of the river Orne.

The low point of this record of futility was, without a doubt, the disastrous breakout attempt on July 18, Operation Goodwood. A classic set-piece battle gone wrong, Goodwood was a huge operation, carried out by Montgomery's entire 21st Army Group (the 2nd British Army under Dempsey and the 1st Canadian Army under General H. D. G. Crerar). Despite heavy carpet bombing that, once again, smashed the German front, killing thousands and driving equal numbers deaf and mad, Montgomery got stuck in front of German positions on the Bourguébus Ridge. Despite everything, the air support, the vast forces at his command, and constant claims that a breakthrough was just around the corner, Montgomery had failed again. Goodwood, Eisenhower said angrily, had cost seven thousand tons of bombs to gain seven miles. There were many, and not just in the American command, who felt that it was time for Montgomery to go.

Much of this anger was simply a case of personalizing institutional failure. There were many reasons for the mediocre British performance in Normandy. The army was fighting with a shrinking replacement pool. It was suffering heavy losses in irreplaceable infantry. Its veteran units, such as the 7th Armoured and 51st Highland Divisions, victors in half a dozen battles, were tired and apathetic. Perhaps the entire British army was experiencing fatigue; some men had been fighting now for five years. It didn't help that British armored doctrine still relied too heavily on the supposedly irresistible nature of the tank. Most of these attacks featured inferior British tanks, unsupported by the infantry or the other arms, launching repeated charges into the teeth of prepared German defenses.

But on closer inspection, there is more going on here than a bad commander and a tired army. The real link between D-Day, Villers-Bocage, Epsom, and Goodwood is that none of them was carried out within the spirit of mobile warfare. All were tightly controlled, planned down to the last detail, and left little room for maneuver. Each one featured numerous opportunities to outmaneuver and outflank the Germans and, perhaps, break through into open ground. What the British army lacked were officers who could recognize such momentary opportunities when they arose and a military culture that encouraged them to seize those golden moments. Montgomery will never be known as a daring "panzer leader," but it is difficult to identify an officer in the British or Canadian command structure in Normandy who would have done much better.

THE U.S. ARMY STEPS UP: COBRA

Since its landing in June, the U.S. Army had had moderate success in Normandy. It had expanded from its bridgeheads, including the problematic Omaha, in a series of tough, infantry-dominated battles through difficult hedgerow country. It had overrun the Cotentin Peninsula and taken the port of Cherbourg, crucial to Allied logistics — all this at a cost of some 100,000 casualties.[71] Since then, it had watched Montgomery's flailing attempts at a breakthrough in the east with increasing impatience and even contempt. It seemed to U.S. commanders that Montgomery's greatest priority was not a breakout per se, but a breakout in his sector, with U.S. forces playing the role of flank guard. "I was always suspicious of Monty's plans," wrote U.S. general Omar Bradley, "because they were so often tied in with what will this do for Monty. . . . He always wanted to make headlines."[72] By mid-July, with the Allies well and truly bogged down in Normandy, however, the situation was becoming intolerable. Virtually every Allied memoir, in fact, mentions pressure from the media, which was expressing increasing impatience with the deadlock.

Around July 10, Bradley conceived an operation that would change the course of the war. His 1st Army would launch a great offensive in the west: Operation Cobra.[73] It was to be something different in the history of the U.S. Army, a breakthrough attempt on a very narrow, carefully selected front. The sector was a short stretch of the east-west road running from St. Lô to Périers, just about seven thousand yards. Concentrated along this short front, Stavka-style, would be all of U.S. VII Corps under General Joseph Collins. He would smash through the German line, assisted by what had now become the Allied calling card in these offensives, carpet bombing. Bradley marked off a rectangle on the road, three and a half miles wide, one and a half deep. He felt that the road, an easily identifiable landmark from the sky, would reduce the chances of inaccurate bombing striking U.S. troops: "The bombers, I reasoned, could fly parallel to it without danger of mistaking our front line."[74]

Once the bombers had paralyzed the German defenders, U.S. forces would break through, holding open the shoulders of the penetration for a large mobile force to exploit. At first, the force levels for Cobra were relatively unassuming: two divisions in the initial assault and two in the exploitation. As planning proceeded and Bradley began to gain confidence in its potential, he expanded both the breakthrough and the exploitation to three divisions. Performing the former would be three infantry divisions of the VII Corps (the 9th, 4th, and 30th); the exploitation would be the mission of the 1st Infantry Division (motorized) under General Clarence Huebner, the 2nd Armored Division (General Edward Brooks), and the 3rd Armored Division (General Leroy Watson), driving southwest toward Coutances.[75] As the size of the offensive grew, Bradley began to consider having VIII Corps (General Troy Middleton), to the immediate right of VII Corps, join in on the second or third day. Middleton would drive due south, trapping whatever German forces lay between him and VII Corps. It is unclear just how much Bradley expected from Cobra, but it was probably not much more than a breakout from the *bocage* into more open country to the south.

Facing this large and well-supported force was German 7th Army, under the command of SS General Paul Hausser. It included just two understrength corps, the LXXXIV and the II Parachute, the former in the Cobra zone, the latter to the east, toward Caumont. Hausser could also call upon the services of the recently arrived Panzer Lehr Division. His principal problem was that the U.S. Army had launched a series of savage drives toward St. Lô in previous weeks, and he had used most of his reserves to stop them. Hausser was commanding not a defensive position in depth, but a thin crust of forward positions with little backup. The Germans had the troops to reinforce him: the entire 15th Army. Hitler was still holding it out of the fray, however, to oppose what he felt was to be the real Allied strike against Fortress Europe: a landing on the Pas de Calais — an incredible example of his own blundering and a successful Allied disinformation campaign.

Cobra began inauspiciously on July 25, with a series of carpet-bombing mishaps. Disagreement between army and air force about the exact path of the bomb runs (whether they should be perpendicular or parallel to the road) led to serious incidents of fratricide. In fact, such incidents are endemic to saturation bombing. Heavy bombers are area weapons, no matter how good their bomb sights or crews. Two of Collins's divisions, the 9th and the 30th Infantry, suffered heavy casualties. One of the 9th's assault battalions had to be replaced, and the 30th Division had the unhappy distinction of being hit by its own bombers on two separate occasions. The bombing also killed General McNair, by now Commander of Army Ground Forces — the highest ranking Allied officer killed in Western Europe.

They also did what Bradley intended them to do, however. The repeated waves of fighter-bombers from the 9th Air Force began the job, followed by 1,500 heavy B-17 and B-24 bombers of the 8th Air Force. They pulverized the front-line German positions, killing thousands and stunning the survivors. According to Bradley, "though air had pummeled us, it had pulverized the enemy in the carpet to litter the torn field and roads with the black hulls of burned-out tanks, the mutilated bodies of soldiers, and the carcasses of bloated, stiff-legged cattle." The Panzer Lehr Division, in particular, holding the front just west of St. Lô, all but vanished in the storm. Its commander, General Fritz Bayerlein, described it best: "The planes kept coming overhead like a conveyor belt." As the bombs continued to rain down, "my front lines looked like a landscape on the moon, and at least seventy percent of my personnel were out of action — dead, wounded, crazed, or numbed."[76]

The first day found Collins's infantry divisions probing into the rubble against sporadic German resistance. The second saw VIII Corps joining the attack; still, progress was slow. On the third day, an increasingly impatient Collins inserted his 2nd Armored Division on his left flank. It advanced into air. Soon, both VII and VIII Corps were moving forward. The Americans had what the Allies had been seeking since June: a breakout. With most of the German armor still arrayed against the British, U.S. armored forces quickly blasted their way through the front line toward Coutances. Aiding their progress through the difficult terrain (this was still very much the hedgerow country) was an ingenious invention, the Culin hedgerow cutter tank, or "Rhinoceros." With VII Corps coming over from the northeast and VIII Corps moving almost due south, the U.S. Army formed its first encirclement of the war, at Roncey. The armored divisions of VIII Corps (4th and 6th) now took center stage, hustling down south toward Avranches under a nearly irresistible umbrella of tactical air power provided by the 9th Air Force. They passed through the Avranches bottleneck and finally broke out of Normandy. By this time, these divisions, and the VIII Corps to which they belonged, had a new boss: General George Patton. He was the commander of the newly activated 3rd Army, to which VIII Corps belonged.

Although the new command was not officially scheduled to become operational until August 1, Bradley had told him to follow VIII Corps closely and help work out any bottlenecks it might encounter on the way to Avranches. Bradley moved upstairs to command the all-American 12th Army Group and handed over 1st Army to General Courtney Hodges.

What happened next has continued to excite controversy to the present day. On August 1, the 4th and 6th Armored Divisions left Normandy and then promptly turned away from German forces, entering the Brittany Peninsula. The objective here was to seize the ports of the peninsula, Brest and St. Malo, along with the Quiberon Bay area. This was not an improvisation on Patton's part. Bradley had intended a move into Brittany as part of the original conception for Cobra. He was a general with a good understanding of the Allies' supply problems. The ports of Brittany would ease the situation considerably.

Unfortunately, this was exactly the wrong time to be thinking of long-term planning. The Americans had blown a hole in the German line, and there was, for the foreseeable future, nothing left to plug it. Now, the two lead armored divisions had turned away from the breakthrough, and the high command was not even sure where they were over the next few

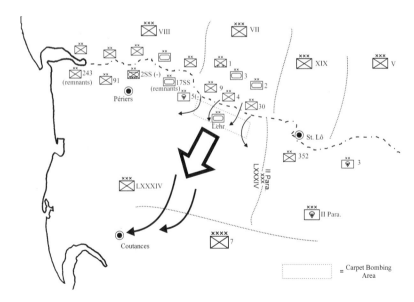

General Omar Bradley's operational art: The Cobra Breakthrough, July 25, 1944.

days. So rapid was their pace that they had outrun their communications. Bradley soon realized that there were more important missions for such a large concentration of armor, and on August 3 he ordered Patton to leave "a minimum of forces" in Brittany and turn the rest of his army toward the east, aiming for the Seine.

As Cobra "uncoiled" itself, a long line of corps began to sneak around the southern flank of those German forces still engaged with Montgomery. A sensible reaction would have been a phased but rapid retreat to form some sort of defensible line. Instead, Hitler's response to Cobra, and by now it is entirely appropriate to speak of "Hitler's response," rather than that of the German General Staff, was to order a counterattack by all his armor toward Mortain and thence to the coast. This was Operation Lüttich, intended to cut off those American divisions in Brittany and south of Avranches. "All available Panzer units," Hitler ordered, "regardless of their present commitment, are to be taken from other parts of the Normandy front, joined together under one specially qualified Panzer operations staff, and sent into a concentrated attack as soon as possible."[77] Apparently dumbfounded by the orders, which he knew meant the collapse of the entire German position in Normandy, General Gunther von Kluge nevertheless launched Lüttich on August 7. It was a dismal affair. As one analyst has pointed out, by the time Lüttich started, it already "lagged significantly behind the rapidly evolving operational situation." Motorized artillery didn't arrive where it was supposed to; divisions hurrying to take part became snarled with one another in traffic jams; the Luftwaffe failed utterly in providing aerial cover to the ground forces. The Germans did make progress toward Mortain with 1st SS, 2nd SS, and 2nd and 116th Panzer Divisions, but there ran into a stalwart defense by elements of the newly arrived U.S. 30th Division, which had had only a few hours to prepare defensive positions after a fatiguing march from Tessy,[78] and by a punishing cloud of Allied fighter-bombers. The situation for the Germans was now grave. Patton's drive to the east continued to gain speed. With his 3rd Army already far to the east of Mortain, the best mobile formations left to the German army in the west had slipped into an Allied noose near Falaise. The stage was set for a great *Kesselschlacht*, a battle of annihilation of all German forces in Normandy.

THE CANADIAN ARMY: OPERATION TOTALIZE

The annihilation did not happen, however.[79] To seal off the Falaise pocket, all Montgomery's forces had to do was perform a short drive down from the north and join hands with Patton. With U.S. forces running amok toward the east, the wall of armor that had faced Montgomery's army group was now gone. Now it was his turn for a breakout. The spearhead would be Crerar's Canadian 1st Army. A short advance from Canadian II Corps south of Caen would seal the deal: an encirclement of the Germans.

Operation Totalize began on the evening of August 8. General G. G. Simonds, commanding II Corps, knew that the ground over which he would have to advance was good tank country, ideal for the long-range fire of superior German tanks. He therefore decided on a night advance. Always risky in terms of cohesion, it was safer than trying to advance in broad daylight against a Tiger tank. Once again, in a battle array that would have made Soviet *Stavka* proud, he crammed two complete armored divisions (1st Polish under General Stanislav Maczek and 4th Canadian under General George Kitching) into attack frontages of just one thousand meters apiece, a solid mass of armor. One Canadian crewman wrote of leaving his tank and returning to the regimental column: "We were closed so tight that my feet never touched the ground, I just stepped from tank to tank."[80] This immense phalanx rolled forward on the night of August 8 and soon passed through the German front line. That morning, the commander of the unit in the immediate path of the offensive, 12th SS Panzer Division's Kurt Meyer, was astounded when he spotted the massed armor: "Seeing these concentrations of tanks almost took our breath away."[81]

But now something puzzling happened. "We could not comprehend the behavior of the Canadians," Meyer wrote. "Why did those overwhelming tank forces not push on their attack?" With a huge armored force in hand, and sparse German opposition in front of him, General Simonds halted. Phase two of Totalize called for the attacking formations to stop and wait while a huge force of U.S. B-17 bombers from the 8th Air Force laid down carpet bombing on the German positions in front of him. The Canadians, no less than the British, were wedded to the phase line and the rigid schedule in their operational planning. The eminent Canadian historian John A. English argues that "Crerar essentially harbored a trench warfare mentality" and that Simonds's preference for the narrow attack frontage "typified the proclivity of an artillerist." It was no accident, English maintains, that the Canadians launched Totalize on August 8, the anniversary of the great assault on Amiens in 1918 — the "black day" for the German army in World War I.[82]

Some 479 bombers duly showed up overhead after several hours and plastered the Normandy countryside. By the time they arrived, Meyer had already begun a counterattack with two armored battle groups that had rattled the Canadians. Rattling them further was yet another carpet-bombing mistake, as a couple of U.S. squadrons dropped their bombs short, inflicting more than three hundred casualties, including the commander of the Canadian 3rd Infantry Division, General R. F. L. Keller. Totalize went on another day, with unsupported Canadian tank attacks going in against small groups of German Panthers and Tigers, and paying the price. The operation did gain eight miles and managed to maul a pair of German infantry divisions, but it did not break out. Montgomery would not seal the Falaise pocket until August 19, by which time a good portion of the German manpower nearly trapped there — perhaps some forty thousand men — would find a way to escape. In addition, headquarters formations at all operational echelons (two army headquarters, three of four corps, and twelve of fourteen divisions) escaped the trap.[83] Along with troops of the 15th Army (relatively unmolested in the Pas de Calais) and forces from southern France, these command elements would form the restored German army that halted the Allies in the fall.

Western Allied Operations in World War II

The Western Allies, operating from a vastly superior base of resources and matériel, faced the German army in North Africa, Sicily, Italy, and Western Europe. On just one occasion, Operation Cobra, did they achieve a true operational breakthrough. The British army had proven tenacious and skilled enough in previous set-piece battles like El Alamein. In Normandy it proved nowhere near mobile enough to handle encounter or pursuit battles with the Wehrmacht. In General Montgomery it had a supreme commander who planned carefully and seemed to leave nothing to chance but who failed to prosecute any of his attacks with enough vigor to get them through the considerable German forces that he faced. Only when the Germans stripped their armor away from his front was he able to get moving again, but even then he failed to move swiftly enough to achieve decisive victory at Falaise.

The U.S. Army, in both Italy and Normandy, found itself fighting under grave disadvantages. In neither place could it bring to bear the superior force that American industry was capable of producing. Its armored doctrine was a disaster by any rational standard, with its tanks intended for a pursuit role in the style of the old cavalry and with hybrid "tank destroyers" handling the heavy duty of standing up to superior German armor like the Panther and Tiger. It managed to overcome these deficiencies through trial and error, improvisation, and a peculiarly American mental flexibility. In the course of the Normandy campaign, it reinvented itself, conceiving its situation in new ways and devising solutions that were novel to its own heritage. Cobra was the spectacular result.

There were some problems with Cobra, obviously. General Bradley's shuffle into and out of Brittany was the most obvious. Bradley has become an American hero, and much of the literature on the campaign is an encomium to his skillful handling of it. He was, certainly, a gifted but modest man who cared deeply for the welfare of his troops. In the course of Cobra, however, he first ordered Patton into Brittany, and then ordered him out. After the battle of the Falaise pocket, he ordered him back in to assault Brest. U.S. forces took the port but suffered heavy casualties in the process. It is impossible to argue, to be polite, that all three of these postures regarding the importance of Brittany were correct. With the fall of Antwerp, the possession of Brest became meaningless, anyway; not a single pound of supply ever came through it. In addition, the U.S. command shuffle during Cobra was a curious thing indeed in the midst of a potentially decisive operation. Having the soon-to-be appointed higher commander of the breakthrough forces (4th and 6th Armored Divisions) tagging along behind them in an unofficial capacity for the first few days was a unique occurrence in the annals of modern war. Command troubles were bound to arise, and did, as 4th and 6th Armored went careening through Brittany.

Still, the U.S. Army deserves high credit for this signal moment in its history. Its largely green troops had barely managed to get ashore at the principal assault beach on June 6[84] and then had spent nearly two months attempting to beat the Germans in Normandy in its traditional way: amassing a huge force and then driving forward everywhere. That had failed, and the casualties had piled up since June 6. Then, in Operation Cobra, one of its most traditional-minded commanders — a man who landed in France "still in the process of learning the ropes"[85] as an army commander — came up with a solution. It was nothing less than an American version of German or Soviet operational-level warfare. General Bradley identified and isolated a weak spot in the German line, crashed through it on a narrow front with the support of masses of tanks and aircraft, and then passed a huge mobile force through the breach and into the German rear. One historian has recently written that it was this hard-won "ability to understand and exploit the full capabilities of the U.S. army"[86] that was the key to the campaign. Cobra was something new for the U.S. Army, a conceptual breakthrough from broad-front advance into maneuver-based operational warfare, made infinitely more effective by wedding it to the battle of matériel. It was a new "American way of war."

Forgotten No Longer:
The War in Korea

A number of military campaigns seem destined to be forgotten. Perhaps they were so short as to barely register on the consciousness of contemporaries (the U.S. invasion of Grenada comes to mind, even the recent NATO war in Kosovo[1]) or were fought over such obscure origins that they seem barely worth explaining to later generations. Perhaps it is simply a matter of timing. This is the argument frequently put forth for the Korean War. Trapped between two of the most dramatic conflicts in the history of the U.S. Army — World War II and Vietnam — it seems doomed never to garner the attention from scholars or the public that it deserves. Add to that the fact that it ended in a messy stalemate, and you have a war that Americans, in particular, will supposedly never take to heart in the way they have the glorious victory of World War II, or devote their passion to in the way that they have to the controversial defeat in Vietnam.[2] A 1986 book on the conflict called it "the war before Vietnam," and that seems to sum it up neatly.

Virtually everyone agrees that Korea is the "forgotten war." And they say so — again and again — as they publish yet another book on it. A recent bibliographic survey identifies some two thousand items available on the Korean conflict. There is something for everyone, from you-are-there evocations of the fighting on Porkchop Hill or the Chosin Reservoir (the stock-in-trade of S. L. A. Marshall[3]) to a series of challenging ideological debates over the origins of the war (the works of professor Bruce Cumings[4]) to coffee table photo books, and virtually every stop in between. Recently, the Chinese view of the fighting, a topic virtually unknown in the West, has been the subject of two scholarly works,[5] and another major work deals with U.S. airpower strategy in Korea.[6] A key part of America's "civic religion" is the observation of this or that anniversary, and the fiftieth anniversary of the outbreak of the Korean War was the opportunity for an avalanche of official literature.[7] Korea may never be as much of an American obsession as the Civil War or World War II, but neither is it the twentieth-century equivalent of the "War of Jenkins's Ear." It is time to retire the "forgotten war" rhetoric.[8]

In operational terms, Korea was a very important war, a bridge between the immense conventional battles of World War II, with their clear-cut sense of winning and losing, and the long twilight struggle that the United States had recently decided to undertake as a result of the Truman Doctrine. It was the first battle in the American war on communism; it would not be the last. The first portion of the war featured a series of highly mobile offensive operations by the North Korean People's Army, the United Nations forces spearheaded by the U.S. Army, and the badly named Chinese People's Volunteers (CPV). The second phase of the war was far different: a static positional struggle, a *Stellungskrieg* of firepower and attrition. This "war of posts," repeated and bloody battles over certain key pieces of terrain such as "Old Baldy" or "Pork Chop Hill," lasted two full years. As men went to their deaths in this meat grinder, truce talks were going on in the background the entire time. Whatever bad reputation Korea has had among military historians probably stems from this second period.[9]

The first year was a war of rapid, often catastrophic retreats: a U.S. and South Korean rush down the peninsula with the North Koreans in hot pursuit; an even more rapid North Korean rush up the peninsula, with a victorious U.S. force having just pulled off one of the greatest operational maneuvers in its history, the Inchon landing; and then, finally, one more U.S. skedaddle back down, this time running in fear from a series of devastating blows by the Chinese, the "great bug-out." The U.S. military, in particular, went from disaster to decisive victory to disaster — all in the short space of five months. Military history knows no other war quite like it.

The NKPA Victorious: From Invasion to the Pusan Perimeter

Starting just five years after the end of World War II, the "police action" in Korea began at a time when postwar demobilization and cutbacks had gutted the American military.[10] There were just ten divisions in the army, five in the continental United States, one in Germany, and four in Japan—all seriously understrength, with divisions short one of three regiments or regiments short one of three battalions. It was a skeleton force suddenly having to confront President Truman's commitment to fight communism on a worldwide basis, surely the most widespread, open-ended mission any army has ever undertaken. That disconnect between mission and means would be one of the principal themes in the war's very active first year. Given U.S. force levels at the time, Korea was fundamentally going to have to be war on the cheap. It would be a "war in peacetime."[11]

The war would be problematic for U.S. forces in another way, as well; for the first time in U.S. history, its armed forces would be engaged in a limited war. For this was, by definition, a limited conflict: limited geographically to the self-contained Korean Peninsula, limited in terms of how many resources and lives the U.S. government (reflecting public opinion) was willing to spend; and limited in the sense that the United States had to be highly conscious of world opinion, especially that of the United Nations organization, in formulating its wartime strategy.[12] This would require a wrenching adjustment on the part of U.S. commanders, virtually all of whom had recently taken part in the humbling of the Wehrmacht in 1944–1945. Not all of them would make the adjustment. The most celebrated casualty of the new limited-war outlook would be the Supreme Commander in the Far East, General Douglas MacArthur. His decline and fall was a symbol for a military force that had traditionally aimed at the utter destruction and overthrow of the enemy, now having to beg permission of the civilian government to bomb this or that target.

Despite its limited character, the Korean conflict might have looked like total war if you were in the middle of it. It opened with a powerful thrust by the North Korean People's Army (NKPA) across the thirty-eighth parallel into South Korea. The NKPA would be a fierce adversary in the early fighting. It would prove itself far superior to the forces of South Korea (Republic of Korea, or ROK) it faced, and it was more than the U.S. Army could handle, as well.[13] It possessed seven front-line divisions (numbered one through seven, consecutively), which formed the heart of its strike force. Equipped by the Soviet Union and trained by Soviet advisers, the divisions also had a fair number of communist veterans of the Chinese Civil War. This was not an army marching to war for the first time. Traditionally configured in the triangular manner, with three regiments of three battalions each, an NKPA division contained about eleven thousand men. Each one also had a full complement of supporting arms. One analyst described it as closely resembling an early Soviet division of World War II. An NKPA division had twelve 122-mm howitzers, twenty-four 76-mm guns, twelve SU-76 self-propelled guns, twelve 45-mm antitank guns, and thirty-six 14.5-mm antitank rifles.[14] The remaining three divisions (numbered 10th, 13th, and 15th) were new units, formed just before the outbreak of the war and consisting largely of conscripted members of the North Korean communist youth organization. Nondivisional units included a separate infantry regiment (the 766th); a motorcycle reconnaissance regiment (the 17th); and the elite unit of the NKPA: the 105th Tank Brigade, equipped with 120 Soviet T-34/85 tanks, divided evenly between three regiments (the 107th, 109th, and 203rd). The brigade also had a regiment of mechanized infantry attached, for a total manpower of six thousand.[15] Another 30 T-34s would take part in the early fighting, for a total of 150 tanks in the NKPA arsenal.[16] Finally, there was a substantial border constabulary of five brigades, totaling some eighteen thousand men. A small tactical air force rounds out the picture. The NKPA had some 180 Soviet-produced aircraft, about a third of which were trainers.[17] With a highly motivated staff and manpower, and well equipped for modern war in difficult terrain, the 135,000 men of the NKPA were about to give a very good account of themselves.[18]

Facing the initial onslaught from the north was a completely inadequate ROK force. Consisting of eight small divisions (1st, 2nd, 3rd, 5th, 6th, 7th, 8th, and Capital), it was a force configured almost purely for border protection and internal security duties.[19] Although the authorized strength of a division was ten thousand men, only four divisions were even near it. Organization was nonstandard: some divisions had three regiments, others two, and one (the 5th) had two regiments and a battalion. There were no tanks, no medium artillery, no fighter aircraft or bombers. The ROK's air force included just twenty-two aircraft, split between liaison and training duties. Its mobile forces consisted almost entirely of twenty-seven armored cars. There had been American assistance in training the force. An American "Korean Military Assistance Group" (KMAG) was in South Korea, under General William L. Roberts, and it must bear some responsibility for what was about to transpire. The ROK army had requested 189 M-26 Pershing tanks from KMAG in late 1949, but Roberts had turned down the request because of the tough Korean terrain and the poor conditions of the country's roads and bridges. In general, the U.S. government wanted to walk a fine line here. It supported South Korean independence and wanted to arm the country to defend itself, without needlessly antagonizing the Soviet Union and China. There was also distrust that South Korean president Syngman Rhee might use any modern weaponry he got from the United States against his domestic political opponents.[20]

Given the balance of forces, the opening campaign was inevitably a decisive victory for the NKPA. On Sunday morning, June 25, 1950, NKPA columns crossed the thirty-eighth parallel in force, from coast to coast.[21] On the surface, this was a simple, two-army advance: 1st Army in the west would move on Seoul and Taejon, while 2nd Army, to the east, would move down the center of the peninsula through Ch'unch'on and Wonju, headed eventually for the port of Pusan in the southeastern corner of the country. In fact, as befitting the extremely broken terrain, there were no less than six major thrusts, covering each of the principal north-south corridors through the mountains. On the 1st Army front, the 14th Infantry Regiment (of the 6th Division) plus a Border Constabulary Brigade attacked the Ongjin Peninsula, while two separate heavy columns, including four infantry divisions and the 105th Armor Brigade, drove on Seoul from the northwest and northeast. On the 2nd Army front, two more columns (one division apiece, the 2nd and the 7th) would attack in the center, the former directly against Ch'unch'on, the latter bypassing it for Hongch'on; one more thrust would move down Korea's eastern coast, separated from the main action by the Taebaek mountains. This attack group consisted of the 5th Infantry Division, the 766th Independent Regiment, and the 17th Motorcycle Reconnaissance Regiment. There were even a pair of small amphibious landings in 1st Army sector, against Kangnung and Samchok, carried out by elements of the 766th Independent Regiment and an indeterminate number of guerrilla fighters, who soon took to the hills to harass ROK defenders in the area.[22]

The attack on Seoul was clearly, and appropriately, the *Schwerpunkt* of the operation. The northwestern group included two infantry divisions, the 1st and the 6th (the latter missing its 14th Regiment, then taking part in the Ongjin operation), plus the 203rd Armored Regiment (105th Brigade). Anchored on the Pyongyang-Seoul rail line, its route of march took it through the ancient capital city of Kaesong, then to Munsan-ni, and, finally, marching roughly parallel to the Han River, on to Seoul. The converging column approaching from the northeast consisted of the 3rd and 4th Infantry Divisions, plus the rest of the 105th Armored Brigade. They would drive down separate roads for Uijongbu, and through this "Uijongbu corridor" to Seoul. All told, four of the NKPA's veteran divisions, and virtually all its armor, were heading for Seoul. Even though this was a broad front offensive, designed to smash as much of the weak ROK army as possible in the opening days of the operation, it was still well conceived and well planned. This was taken, in the cold war atmosphere of the day, as prima facie evidence of Soviet direction, but we need no longer believe that today. The history of the twentieth century was filled with small or Third World nations devising elegant operational solutions to their political problems — Bulgaria in the First Balkan War of 1912, India in its 1971 war against Pakistan, Israel in a series of wars against its Arab neighbors. Whatever amount of military assistance it may have received from Moscow, North Korea belongs to the list.[23]

The invasion caught South Korean forces, and the KMAG advising them, completely flat footed. Beginning at Ongjin in the west at 4:00 A.M. and then proceeding to the eastern coast, the attacks succeeded virtually everywhere.[24] At Ongjin, cut off from the ROK mainland by the Yellow Sea, the NKPA 6th Regiment made short work of the ROK defenders (17th Regiment, Capital Division). By nightfall of the second day, the 17th evacuated by sea, abandoning its battalion of 105-mm guns. The 6th Regiment then handed over the peninsula to the 3rd Border Constabulary Brigade and rejoined its parent division for the drive on Seoul. The first of the drives on the capital, through Kaesong, featured elements of the NKPA 6th Division railing directly into the town, located just two miles south of the 38th parallel. The North Koreans had repaired a section of track in secret the night before. This brought them into Kaesong behind the ROK defenders (the 12th Regiment, 1st Infantry Division). In concert with a frontal attack by the rest of the 6th Division, Kaesong was in North Korean hands within five hours. One Western military analyst identified this as a favorite NKPA tactic:

> The North Koreans repeated time after time one technique which was marvelously effective: they engaged fixed enemy positions with direct frontal attacks or fire, then sent forces around both flanks, if possible, in an envelopment movement designed either to surround the enemy and then squeeze him into a small perimeter to destroy him or force him to surrender, or, if this failed, to cut off his retreat or reinforcements by means of roadblocks in his rear.[25]

It worked nearly everywhere against the ROK army. Even when it didn't — a supporting attack by the NKPA 1st Division and the 203rd Tank Regiment directly against Korangp'o-ri that failed to break through, for example — it hardly mattered. With the rest of the front in headlong retreat, no ROK unit could make a stand even if it wanted to. In general, the ROK 1st Division had been spread far too thin, holding the line Yonan-Kaesong-Korangp'o-ri, a distance of about thirty-five miles, with just two regiments.

The decisive breakthrough came in the Uijongbu corridor. Here, two columns (4th Division, with the 107th Tank Regiment in support, and 3rd Division, with 109th Tank Regiment in support) hurtled down on two separate roads that converged on Uijongbu. In their way was the

ROK 7th Infantry Division. Punished heavily by armor and artillery to which it could not respond, it fell back. A counterattack ordered for June 26 by the ROK army Chief of Staff, General Chae, was a fiasco.[26] He planned to push 7th Division up the Tongduch'on-ni road and the newly arriving 2nd Division up Poch'non road. The latter unit, however, was barely present in strength. Two of its battalions could move up from Seoul, just twenty miles away, but the rest of the division was still at Tae-jon and was only then in the process of transporting by rail to the north. Chae ordered the attack anyway. His 7th Division did make some progress, but the 2nd Division refused to attack at all, simply defending in place with its two battalions. It is difficult to fault the divisional commander; attacking would have been suicide. As it was, a vigorous thrust by the NKPA 3rd Division with strong tank support simply crashed through his defensive cordon in front of Uijongbu. Now threatened with encirclement, the ROK 7th Division had to beat a hurried retreat toward Seoul. The road to the South Korean capital was open.

Although there had been some checks on the NKPA, the opening two days were as successful as a military operation could be. Everywhere the ROK army had suffered a severe mauling. Its counterattacks had been uncoordinated and abortive. Individual ROK units had given a good accounting of themselves. At Ch'unch'on, the 7th Regiment (6th Division) had held off an assault by the NKPA 2nd Division, fighting from prepared bunkers and inflicting heavy losses. The arrival of a second NKPA Division (the 7th) supported by a handful of T-34s sealed the ROK defenders' fate, however. In general, where ROK army units came under attack by infantry alone, they managed to hang fairly tough. The first appearance of NKPA armor, however, was usually enough to send them running in panic. General Paik Sun Yup of the 1st ROK Division admits as much in his memoirs, speaking of the "T-34 disease" that seemed to afflict his men: "The symptoms of the disease were straightforward. As soon as the men heard the word 'tank,' they fell into a state of terror."[27]

Over the next few days, a panic gripped Seoul. Much of the population took to the roads south, clogging the few good roads for reinforcing troops. Skillful NKPA attacks had dismantled the ROK army divisions to the north of the city, although some ROK elements were still fighting uncoordinated actions against the invaders. But a powerful arc of North Korean units, 1st, 3rd, and 4th Divisions, plus the 105th Armored Brigade, was now converging on Seoul. This was operational-level warfare as it had been known since the days of Moltke the elder: forces from widely separated bases of operation conducting convergent maneuvers, linking up only on the decisive battlefield.

As it turned out, the ROK army was already in the process of melting away. As defeated units retreated into Seoul, command and control — not this army's strong suit, as the early fighting would attest — began to dissolve. The ROK government decided to abandon the city, as did the ROK army headquarters, the latter leaving on June 27 without bothering to inform its KMAG advisers. The army high command and KMAG had previously worked out a detailed program of demolitions, roadblocks, and obstacles in the event the city came under attack, but in the pandemonium of the moment, it went undone.

By the evening of June 27, NKPA units had reached the outskirts and were clearly preparing for the assault. The climax of Seoul's emotional meltdown came in the early hours of June 28, when sappers detonated charges under the Han River highway bridge to the immediate south of the city while it was crammed full of fleeing civilians and soldiers, destroying it and cutting off the retreat of virtually the entire ROK army still in Seoul.[28] There is still controversy over who ordered the bridge blown, with all the competent authorities denying it. At any rate, what was to have been a retreat now turned into the dissolution of an army. Individual soldiers had to make their escape by twos and threes, swimming over the Han. Virtually all their equipment, transport, and heavy weapons fell into the hands of the NKPA when it occupied Seoul later that morning. Although commanders of the defeated divisions managed to reform their remnants on the south bank of the Han over the next few days, the impact of these three days of war on the ROK army was catastrophic. Of a ninety thousand man force on June 25, the ROK command could account for only twenty-two thousand at the end of June. It had been a North Korean blitzkrieg and, within the narrow limits of operational-level warfare offered by the Korean Peninsula, a masterpiece of its type.[29]

After a short respite to resupply themselves, the NKPA divisions in Seoul struck south, plunging across the Han toward the city of Taejon. All across the front, the ROK was in flight. But that war — the civil war of the North versus the South — was already over. By the end of the month, the world was coming to Korea. The United Nations voted to condemn North Korean aggression against South Korea. President Truman then authorized the use of U.S. ground forces in the peninsula. General MacArthur, in turn, had ordered 8th Army, under the command of General Walton H. Walker, to Korea. Walker, finally, ordered the U.S. 24th Division (General William Dean) into action from its peacetime garrison on the island of Kyushu, in Japan.

What happened next was one of the most notorious moments in the history of the U.S. Army. The advance guard of the 24th Division arrived in Pusan by airlift on July 1. It consisted of two rifle companies of the 1st Infantry Battalion, 21st Regiment, commanded by Lieutenant Colonel Charles ("Brad") Smith, reinforced by mortars and a recoilless rifle platoon.[30] After landing at Pusan in the southeastern corner of the peninsula, "Task Force Smith" had orders to cross Korea along the main road through Taegu to Taejon "and beyond, if you can." The goal was to stop the North Koreans as far north of Pusan as possible. Cheered by friendly crowds as they rode through Pusan, Task Force Smith arrived in Taejon by rail on July 2.

By July 5, after a harrowing journey on roads packed with South Korean civilian refugees streaming south and jittery combat engineers preparing for demolition the very bridges over which the Americans were marching, Task Force Smith was in a blocking position three miles north of Osan, a spot that Lieutenant Colonel Smith had reconnoitered personally. No more than 540 men, fresh out of their comfortable billets in Japan, they were about to face an assault by a full NKPA division with armor support.

No one has ever been able to fault Smith's defensive dispositions. They seemed more than adequate. He had his men holding the high ground on either side of the road. He had a great deal of firepower up in the front line: rifles, machine guns, 4.2-inch mortars, bazookas, and 75-mm recoilless rifles. Behind the line in good firing positions were four 105-mm howitzers, elements of the 52nd Field Artillery Battalion that had been ordered up to Osan to support his task force.

His weakness, one that would prove to be decisive, was in the antitank department. Without a real antitank gun, Smith had to rely on a fifth 105-mm howitzer, deployed forward. For this first encounter with enemy tanks since 1945, Smith had only a half-dozen high explosive antitank (HEAT) rounds, the only type in the American arsenal capable of penetrating the frontal armor of a T-34/85. In fact, when the 52nd Field Artillery had loaded out at Sasebo, Japan, there had been only eighteen HEAT rounds available to the entire unit.

Early on the morning of July 5, a column of thirty-three North Korean tanks led the assault on Task Force Smith. His howitzers opened up with an impressive display of gunnery, but the ordinary high-explosive (HE) shells simply bounced off the sloped armor of the T-34s. Neither the recoilless rifle nor the bazookas (with their small 2.36-inch rockets) had any effect at all. The forward howitzer did manage to disable the two lead tanks, but the rest drove straight on through the American position, rolling into Osan and cutting off Task Force Smith's rear. From that point on, Task Force Smith was on its way to destruction.

Following the tank penetration, around noon, elements of the NKPA Division began to work their way around Smith's flanks, a series of knoblike hills and finger ridges. Hit hard by North Korean infantry assault, outflanked to both right and left, with enemy tanks in his rear, Smith gave the order to retreat. Retreat soon turned into rout, however, as the North Koreans caught the withdrawing force in a withering crossfire. The unit lost discipline, abandoning much of its equipment, and even its wounded (save for one brave corpsman who refused to leave them). Task Force Smith essentially dissolved, losing about half the force, although individual members of the task force would wander, dazed and confused, about the countryside for days, drifting into towns to the south.

The destruction of Task Force Smith at Osan was an object lesson in the costs of unpreparedness. It was a humiliating defeat for the United States at the hands of a tiny Asian nation. "Everyone thought the enemy would turn around and go back when they found out who was fighting," said a surviving artilleryman.[31] Even General MacArthur later spoke of Task Force Smith as "an arrogant display of strength." Yet the real lesson of Osan was not a new one: tanks were still capable of easily overrunning an infantry position that did not possess antitank weapons, whether it was the Americans at Osan in 1950 or the men in the German front line at Cambrai in 1917.

It is also important not to make the Task Force Smith episode something it wasn't: the defeat of a substantial American force. More troops were arriving in Korea every day as the 8th Army began to take shape. The arrival of the rest of the 24th Division helped salvage the situation, and the hurried shipment of the new, larger 3.5-inch bazooka gave the troops a much-needed weapon capable of dealing with the T-34. The 24th Division certainly did not cover itself with glory, but in its fifteen-day retreat down the peninsula, it did carry over a "delaying action" of sorts, and it gave the rest of the U.S. forces time to get into a defensive position in front of Pusan. Still, the NKPA kicked it from one position to the other, almost always combining a frontal assault with a well-executed flanking maneuver, and inflicted heavy losses on it. It happened to the division's 19th Infantry Regiment at the Kum River from July 13 to 16, and it happened again to the 34th Regiment at Taejon. In the disastrous fighting for Taejon, the division commander, General Dean, ran into a North Korean roadblock and had to flee into the countryside. He subsequently fell down a steep slope and suffered a severe head injury. He would wander through the mountains for over a month before falling into North Korean hands. By this time, the 24th Division's morale had collapsed, understandable given the events of the past few weeks. Repeatedly, units of the 24th Division panicked and ran when faced with assault by North Korean armor, throwing down their equipment and often even abandoning their wounded in their headlong flight to the south.[32]

Nevertheless, other divisions were coming into the theater. The U.S. 25th Division (General William Kean) arrived at Pusan between July 10 and 15. The commander of the 8th Army, General Walker, immediately ordered it to central Korea, to bolster ROK units there. The 1st Cavalry Division landed at P'ohang-dong, north of Pusan, between July 15 and 22. Its mission was to protect the northwestern approaches to Pusan from what was looking to be the main NKPA thrust and, incidentally, to relieve the 24th Division, by now thoroughly fought out. The 24th pulled back to Taegu for rest and recuperation. But the new divisions experienced more of the same. Both of them advanced to contact, and both soon had to fall back. Once again, the cause was skillful NKPA attacks that pinned U.S. units frontally, and then worked around their southeastern flank, threatening to separate them from Pusan.[33]

In addition, ROK commanders had re-formed their divisions from remnants of the units lost in Seoul, replacements, and new conscripts. The I Corps (Capital and 8th Divisions) and II Corps (1st and 6th Division) were holding the central front, while 3rd Division, under direct control of ROK army headquarters, was on the eastern coast. Thus, by late July, a line had been formed, from left to right: 24th Division, 1st Cavalry Division, 25th Division, II ROK Corps, I ROK Corps, and on the extreme right of the line, 3rd Division. ROK units were falling back almost due south, while U.S. divisions were swinging their line of retreat from the south to the east.

Already the talk was of defending a "Pusan perimeter." There seemed little hope of stopping the NKPA much farther north. With the north-south course of the Naktong River forming a natural barrier to the west of Pusan, the problem of defending would be considerably simpler than fighting maneuver warfare in the heart of Korea with lone divisions out of contact with one another. Still, the situation was very much in flux as the front moved steadily to the south. U.S. forces, even with full control of the air, had still not gotten the situation under control. The intelligence situation was nothing less than abysmal, with U.S. forces seemingly unaware of just which units they happened to be facing at any given time.[34]

In fact, an entire NKPA division, the 6th, was off the situation maps altogether. Eighth Army intelligence had lost contact with it after the fall of Seoul. It suddenly showed up again in late July, along with 4th Division, spearheading a drive around the left flank of 8th Army. Skirting the southern coast of Korea, the NKPA divisions were heading for

Chinju, driving for Pusan from the west. General Walker had to quickly take a regiment of the 24th Division out of reserve and rush it to Chinju, although that expedient cannot have given him much confidence. After the NKA 6th Division pushed it back at Chinju, he rushed in another regiment, this time the 27th (of the 25th Division) from the reserve. This timely reinforcement stabilized the situation. It was the NKPA's last, best chance to drive on Pusan, strand the 8th Army in Korea, and win a strategic victory. It was as close as any American army has ever come to disaster.

Pusan, Inchon, Pyongyang: The U.S. Victorious

By August 4, U.S. and ROK army forces were inside the Pusan perimeter.[35] It was not as secure a defensive position as it might appear on a map. Forming a rectangle one hundred miles from north to south and roughly fifty from east to west, its garrison was hardly large enough to secure a defense line, at least as one was commonly conceived in the West. For example, three American divisions held about ninety miles of front on the western face. The situation looked better in the north. Here, five ROK divisions held a fifty-mile front. These units, however, were filled with a combination of new recruits and men who had fled in terror from this same enemy a little more than a month ago. The NKPA still held a decisive moral advantage over its ROK adversary.

Although it was not immediately apparent, however, the war had reached a turning point. The crisis for the United States and the ROK army had passed. The NKPA had fought its way to the very southern tip of Korea in impressive fashion, winning victory after victory. At Pusan, however, it reached what Clausewitz had referred to as the "culmination point." Exhaustion was starting to set in as its losses mounted, and in fact it appears that it had by now conscripted a large number of reluctant South Koreans into its ranks. Eventually they constituted almost a third of the total NKPA force around Pusan, though it is doubtful that they were employed in front-line assault units. The NKPA's supply lines were stretched across all of mountainous South Korea, and they were taking a daily pounding from U.S. air power, both air force and naval air assets. This was a serious problem since virtually every NKPA supply convoy had to pass through the narrow corridor south of Seoul, a situation made to order for U.S. air power.

Meanwhile, every day that passed saw the arrival of more U.S. forces in the theater. The 5th Regimental Combat Team, units of the 2nd Division,

A pause in the midst of some hard fighting on the Pusan perimeter. PFC
Harold R. Bates and PFC Richard N. Martin, U.S. Marine Corps looking
out over the Naktong River, August 19, 1950. Photographed by
Sgt. Frank C. Kerr, USMC. "All Hands" collection, NH 96991, Naval
Historical Center.

as well as the 1st Provisional Marine Brigade were all inside the perimeter as well. One estimate has U.S. and ROK forces outnumbering their attackers by this point, ninety-two thousand (about half of whom were American) to seventy thousand. Most important, the war of movement and maneuver had ended for the time being. There was no more maneuver room in any real sense. Instead, the NKPA would now, if it were to penetrate the perimeter, have to launch a series of frontal assaults from a standing start. This was a classic example of a *Stellungskrieg* (the war of position), in which NKPA forces had sacrificed the one advantage they had held: the ability to outmaneuver U.S. forces in Korea's mountainous terrain.

But, in fact, this was a kind of war that the U.S. Army could fight better than any army in the world. With ability to maneuver no longer at a premium, the contest became much more one of firepower and logistics. No longer did U.S. or ROK forces need to worry about their flanks while warding off a frontal assault. Air power could play an increasingly important role, too, as U.S. air assets could concentrate on a relatively small corner of Korea, rather than try to cover the entire peninsula. Until now, the lack of decent airfields, the rainy weather, and air force emphasis on raids deep into North Korea had all reduced the impact of tactical air power in the fighting. For all intents and purposes, U.S. forces had been fighting without air cover. That had already led to bad blood between army and air force. A particularly heated argument raged over jet versus propeller-driven aircraft. Air force F-80s had to fly from Japan and often had little flying time over tactical targets in South Korea. Many ground commanders actually preferred slower piston aircraft, F-51 Mustangs, because of their longer "loiter time" over the target, although their liquid-cooled engines were very vulnerable to ground fire.[36] Moreover, there was a major shortage of air–ground coordination teams, an area in which U.S. forces had excelled just a few short years ago, and there were several notorious friendly fire incidents in the early weeks. The arrival of the marines, with their own dedicated air wing, did nothing to soothe ruffled army feelings that their men were having to fight at a disadvantage while the air force targeted enemy industry and infrastructure to the north.

That was no longer the case within the perimeter. In this relatively small rectangle, air force, naval air, and marine air assets all played a role. In a moment that hearkened back to Operation Cobra in World War II, ninety-eight B-29s even carried out a massive carpet bombing mission against NKPA forces massing for a drive across the Naktong on August 16, pulverizing them with nine hundred tons of bombs.[37] Heavy naval gunfire could also come into play, punishing any NKPA force trying to press into the extreme flanks of the perimeter in the southwest or north-east. It is tempting to say that a modern U.S. force defending a limited perimeter, backed with sufficient artillery, enjoying control of the air, and holding a secure port at its back, can hold any spot on earth almost indefinitely.

Nevertheless, there was hard fighting along the edge of the perimeter. The North Koreans launched attacks toward Masan in the southwest; against the so-called "Naktong bulge" about halfway up the western face; toward Taegu, the "corner" of the rectangle; and, most significantly, against ROK forces holding the northern face in front of Kyongju.

For six weeks, the NKPA kept up the pressure on the Pusan perimeter. One attack in the south, on August 7, crashed head-on into a U.S. attack out of the southwestern corner of the perimeter, led by "Task Force Kean" (most of the 25th Division, with 5th RCT and 1st Provisional Marine Brigade attached).[38] Bloody fighting resulted that ended in mutual exhaustion. In the north, repeated successes against the ROK divisions led General Walker to commit the entire U.S. 24th Division to the fighting sector. Now under the command of General John Church, and fighting in very different circumstances than in the weeks when it was out on a limb with open flanks, constituting the only U.S. force in the entire peninsula, it gave a good accounting of itself in the defensive battles that followed.[39]

Armor also made an appearance. After the initial assaults on the ROK army, tanks had played a peripheral role in the fighting. The difficulty of the terrain, as well as defense commitments in Europe, precluded the deployment of entire armored divisions in the theater. Nevertheless, the U.S. Army built up its armored forces rapidly after the debacle at Osan. Three medium tank battalions arrived in Pusan on August 7. These were the 6th (equipped with the M-46 tank), the 70th (with the M-26 and M-4A3), and the 73rd (with the M-26). The 6th Medium Tank Battalion served as 8th Army reserve near Taegu in August, the 70th joined the 1st Cavalry Division, and companies of the 73rd served in dispersed positions on the Pusan perimeter. Eighty more tanks arrived as reinforcements in mid-August, along with another medium tank battalion, the 72nd, which was organic to the 2nd Infantry Division. All told, six medium tank battalions, averaging sixty-nine tanks apiece, were in Korea by the end of the summer. In addition, four regimental tank companies and about thirty light tanks were available for duty. There were more than five hundred U.S. tanks within the Pusan perimeter by late August, outnumbering NKPA tanks by at least five to one. During August, there were a series of engagements at Obong-ni ("No-Name Ridge") behind the Naktong bulge, and along the Sangju-Taegu corridor (the "Bowling Alley"). At the latter, U.S. M-26 tanks of the 73rd Tank Battalion, infantry with 3.5-inch bazookas, and continuous sorties by ground attack aircraft accounted for a number of T-34/85s, proving that although the Soviet tank was an effective weapon, it was not invincible.[40] Characterizing the Pusan perimeter fighting in general, the NKPA was able to make local penetrations at virtually any point it chose. Widening those tactical successes into any sort of operational breach proved to be far beyond its capabilities, however. In attempting to do just that, the NKPA — like the German 6th Army at Stalingrad — essentially fought itself out, rendering it dangerously vulnerable to any sudden change in the operational situation.

General MacArthur did not take long to exploit his newfound superiority. He had decided early that his counterstroke, when it came, would not be a hard slog back up the peninsula. Instead, he would take advantage of U.S. amphibious mobility, much as he had done in the Southwest Pacific during World War II, to launch a strike deep into the North Korean flank and rear. In planning Operation Chromite, MacArthur and his staff examined several potential landing sites on both coasts of Korea, including Chumunjin on the east coast and Kunsan on the west coast. The latter, at the mouth of the Kum River, would be a safe bet — lightly defended by the North Koreans and difficult for them to reinforce. MacArthur, characteristically, settled on a much more dramatic, and risky, plan: an amphibious landing at Inchon, the port that serves Seoul.[41] Such a strike into the very heart of occupied Korea would place a U.S. force astride the NKPA's supply lines and render their entire position south of Seoul untenable. The effect on morale of a sudden liberation of the capital would be tremendous, and the operation would also bring Kimpo airfield, the best in Korea, back into U.S. hands.

It seems from the documentary record that not a single responsible U.S. planner or policymaker thought that an Inchon landing was a good idea. General Omar Bradley, for example, now Chairman of the Joint Chiefs of Staff, thought the age of such large-scale amphibious landings was past.[42] There were several less flashy, but far safer alternatives. If extra troops were available, why not simply feed them into the Pusan perimeter? Or use them in a short "end run" around the enemy's flanks near the perimeter? General Joseph Collins, then Army Chief of Staff, was in favor of a landing at Kunsan. In a July 23 meeting in Tokyo between MacArthur, Collins, and the Chief of Naval Operations, Admiral Forrest P. Sherman, MacArthur argued that a Kunsan operation would be too shallow of an envelopment and that it wouldn't cut NKPA lines of communication to Seoul. Yes, Inchon was a risky undertaking, but the very risk would ensure surprise: "The enemy commander will reason that no one would be so brash as to make such an attempt,"[43] he argued. In the end he had his way.

There were major difficulties in staging a landing at Inchon. Admiral James H. Doyle, asked to give his opinion on the feasibility of such an operation, described it as "not impossible," and that is apt.[44] The principal problem was the tides. The difference between high and low tide at Inchon is an incredible thirty-five feet, and when the tide has receded the result is six thousand yards of mud flats. The landing, therefore, would have to take place at high tide, a period of only about six hours per day. The islands in the channel funnel the tides at relatively high speeds, especially through "Flying Fish Channel," making navigation perilous. Once disembarked, a landing force would have to scramble over a twelve-foot stone seawall, using ladders. Never before had an amphibious operation targeted a built-up area like Inchon. After Inchon was secure, the force would still have a twenty-mile slog to get to their real objective: Seoul. These factors also dictated the time of the landing. Low tides were common from May through August; from October onward, rough water would be a serious problem. Thus, the landing would have to take place in mid-September.

Once he got approval of the plan, MacArthur had to assemble his force. His chief of staff, General Edward M. Almond, would head the newly formed X Corps. Getting units to fill it was the problem. MacArthur requested, and got, the rest of the 1st Marine Division. Its elements from the United States would join the 1st Provisional Marine Brigade, by now a veteran unit of the Pusan perimeter battles. He also received the 7th Infantry Division from Japan. It was seriously understrength, as it had contributed manpower to the other units that had already shipped out for Korea, and MacArthur had to fill it back up with replacements from the United States, as well as 8,600 South Korean recruits, part of the KATUSA effort (Korean Augmentation to the United States Army Program).[45] Serving as the X Corps reserve would be an ROK Marine Corps regiment. It was something of a motley crew, on a shoestring budget for such an ambitious undertaking.

On the morning of September 15, Operation Chromite went into action. An assault force of 3rd Battalion, 5th Marine Regiment, reinforced with armor, assaulted Wolmi Island protecting the harbor. After a pause forced by the receding tide, the 1st and 5th Marine Regiments assaulted beaches labeled Red and Blue, respectively, directly into Inchon. Some troops scaled the seawall with ladders, others passed through holes in the wall created by naval bombardment. U.S. airpower completely iso-lated Inchon from the interior, although there were few North Korean troops in the vicinity. The 7th Division would join the beachhead over the next few days, while the marines had already begun to push inland.[46]

The approach to Seoul was not without incident. On September 20, the 5th Marine Regiment carried out a difficult crossing of the Han River at Haengju, under fire the entire time, and then had to fight a determined NKPA defense for the possession of Hill 125. Once over the river, they had to lever the better part of an NKPA brigade off their main line of resistance at Hill 296, a jumbled collection of finger ridges that the Japanese had used as a tactical training ground during the years of their occupation of Korea. Meanwhile, to its right, the 1st Marines under "Chesty" Puller met tough resistance in the industrial suburb of Yongdungpo. The NKPA employed five T-34s, but the marines made short work of them with their 3.5-inch bazookas. Fire from two battal-ions of supporting artillery, plus air strikes from marine Corsairs flying from the escort carrier *Badoeng Strait*, softened up the resistance. Still, the 1st Marines had to clamber over the dikes and the high banks of the Kalchon Canal, literally going "over the top," and losses were heavy.[47]

The battle for Seoul proper began on September 22. Although Mac-Arthur had assured the marines that they would be fighting rear-echelon troops, that was plainly not the case. The X Corps commander, General Almond, reflecting MacArthur's increasing impatience with the slow progress toward the city, wanted the two marine regiments split up for a concentric advance into Seoul: 5th Marines from the west and 1st Marines from the southeast, well beyond Yongdungpo. The commander of the 1st Marine Division, General Oliver Smith, disagreed; Almond's plan meant that the marines would enter battle with their major components divided by the Han River and then having them attack toward each other. Almond finally decided to commit an army regiment, the 32nd (of the newly landed 7th Division), to attack the city from the southeast, while the marines pushed in from the west. There would be some hard feelings between Smith and Almond, and between the army and marines, for some time.

Still, breaking into the city and clearing it were two different things. This was a sprawling city of more than a million people, and the NKPA defenders built sandbag barricades in most of the principal intersections. The marines had to root them out position by position. NKPA snipers also did a great deal of damage from buildings and rooftops. The marines had invaluable help from their M-26 Pershing tanks, as well as from the Corsairs, which did less and less bombing, and more and more strafing and rocketing as the fighting proceeded. They also learned that their

The iconic photograph of U.S. Marines scaling the seawall at Inchon, September 15, 1950. In the lead is First Lieutenant Baldomero Lopez, leading 3rd Platoon, Company A, 1st Battalion, 5th Marines on the northern side of Red Beach. Lopez was killed in action a few moments later and received the Congressional Medal of Honor posthumously. U.S. Marine Corps photograph, Naval Historical Center, NH 96876.

3.5-inch bazooka was not only a useful antitank weapon, but an extremely effective building and wall buster. There was pressure from on high to finish the job quickly, the men could tell. "Who knows?" said one company commander of the 1st Marines; "Puller was being pushed by somebody in division. The division was being pushed by someone in X Corps, and the corps was being pushed by the man himself, or someone speaking for him, in Tokyo."[48] Both the X Corps commander, General Almond, and "the man himself" announced the fall of the city prematurely, a matter of grievance to those who were still fighting to take it. With two marine regiments driving into the city from the west, another (the 7th) moving to cut off the Uijongbu-Seoul road to the north of the city, and 32nd Regiment coming in from the southeast, U.S. forces took Seoul by September 29. Much of the city was a mass of smoldering ruins. In *This Kind of War*, a book that had enormous influence on U.S. military intellectuals when it first appeared in 1963, T. R. Fehrenbach justified the destruction:

> The American way of street and town fighting did not resemble that of other armies. To Americans, flesh and blood and lives have always been more precious than sticks and stones, however assembled. An American commander, faced with taking the Louvre from a defending enemy, unquestionably would blow it apart or burn it down without hesitation if such would save the life of one of his men. And he would be acting in complete accord with American ideals and ethics in doing so.[49]

It was something that would be seen again, in Vietnam.

The crucial factor in the fall of Seoul, beyond the strength and firepower of the attacking force, was that the North Koreans were unable to reinforce it. MacArthur had achieved strategic surprise, it is true, but the city was still being contested ten days later. Josef Stalin, supposedly, recommended that the NKPA send four divisions from Pusan to Seoul immediately, and from time to time, analysts have wondered why that did not occur. There is no mystery, however. The NKPA had pinned itself outside the Pusan perimeter. Disengaging four main force units and suddenly sending them to the north would have been impossible for several reasons. They were already engaged, all along the line, with U.S. and ROK forces. Their own losses were approaching catastrophic levels, and morale was suffering apace. Finally, getting north would have meant running a gauntlet of U.S. air power, which by this time may be safely described as impenetrable.

The Inchon landing, at first, had little impact on fighting around Pusan. General Walker's 8th Army was now ready to begin its breakout operation from the perimeter. From the dark days of July, his force was now bulging with four U.S. divisions, plus their supporting units. Far East Command had already decided to establish corps organization within the army, an important step for future operations. I Corps became operational in mid-August. It included the 24th Infantry Division, 1st Cavalry Division, 5th Regimental Combat Team, British 27th Infantry Brigade, and the ROK 1st Division. Orders were drawn up to establish a second corps, the IX, but a lack of communications personnel and equipment forced its postponement until later in September. As a result, 2nd and 25th Divisions fought under Walker's direct command in the upcoming battle. It was a curious command feature on the eve of such an important offensive.

The breakout began on September 16, as the marines were still securing Inchon. The *Schwerpunkt* would be in the corner of the rectangle, toward Waegwan and Sangju. Here, NKPA resistance promised to be fiercest but, at the same time, the rewards were potentially the greatest. This was the closest point to the newly landed X Corps. Although it wasn't exactly close — 180 miles as the crow flies, but much longer as the soldier marches through Korea's winding mountain roads — it did offer the quickest path to a linkup between X Corps and 8th Army.

As things turned out, that linkup came more rapidly than either Walker or MacArthur could have guessed. On September 16, I Corps, with 5th RCT in the lead, struck near Waegwan. Over the course of the next five days, 5th RCT shattered the right flank of the 3rd NKPA division. An attack by 1st Cavalry Division on the right then broke through altogether. The 3rd Division was the first NKPA unit simply to fall apart under the pressure, men fleeing in a rout or surrendering en masse. In the west, 2nd Division attacked toward the Naktong, and by September 18 its 38th Regiment was over the river against weakening opposition. Here, too, U.S. forces began taking large numbers of prisoners. Finally, on the right flank, the two reconstituted corps of the ROK both made breakthroughs of their own. The II Corps conformed to the breakout of the U.S. forces to its left, heading north into central Korea. The I Corps, holding the extreme right flank up to the eastern coast, drove straight north toward P'ohang-dong, supported by naval gunfire. From its own dark days in the opening battles of the war, the ROK, too, had made an impressive recovery.

The reasons for the NKPA collapse are easy to identify. First, all these attacks enjoyed a truly impressive level of tactical air support, as the air force relearned the trade that had broken the Wehrmacht in 1944. Both propeller F-51s and jet F-80s were the terror of anything that moved on the NKPA side of the fighting, employing machine guns, rockets, and a great deal of napalm. Second, the continuing senseless attacks ordered by the NKPA command along the perimeter, attacks that had in fact lasted right up until the U.S. counteroffensive, had literally destroyed their own forces. Units were down to skeleton strength, were under- or unsupplied, and had lost all fighting spirit. Interdiction of supplies and replacements to the NKPA also played a crucial role; once plopped down in front of Pusan, units were receiving a tiny fraction of the supplies they needed.[50] There are numerous tales, too many to be discounted, of NKPA veterans shooting new recruits, many of whom were South Koreans, who showed too little spirit in the attack. Word of the Inchon landings also seems to have filtered down to the troops, despite the efforts of their commanders to keep them in the dark. In general, that moment had arrived, typical of attrition warfare, in which one side simply collapses. The NKPA reached that point at Pusan, with or without the Inchon landings.

Still, with the NKPA in the process of dissolution in the south, 8th Army after it in full pursuit mode, and X Corps standing unopposed at Seoul, MacArthur was master of all that he could survey. He had now deployed a powerful force — large and well equipped — far in the strategic depth of the enemy position. Operation Chromite marked an operational breakthrough of the first magnitude and reminds us that it is not necessary to have many tanks to carry out a blitzkrieg. Its men and commanders had the confidence that comes with carrying out a tough and complex task successfully. There were few units to speak of in its immediate vicinity. Its possibilities were virtually endless. It could strike south, to trap the NKPA force against the Pusan perimeter in a battle of annihilation; it could move east to establish passive blocking positions and cut off NKPA supply lines; finally, it could lunge to the north across the thirty-eighth parallel and into North Korea. The last course could only take place on the assumption that the NKPA units around Pusan were no longer a threat, which was exactly the case by the end of September.

In the end, MacArthur decided on none of these. Elements of the 1st Cavalry Division from Pusan made contact with 7th Division out of Inchon after a wild ride on September 26. The remainder of 8th Army would soon be approaching Seoul and could take over operations in this crucial sector. MacArthur now planned to reembark X Corps at Inchon and launch another amphibious operation. Operation Tailboard would be a right hook, complementary to the blow struck at Inchon. The target was the important industrial city of Wonsan on the northeastern coast of Korea. Once again, virtually everyone in the U.S. military hierarchy thought it was a ridiculous idea. With more than 100,000 troops streaming north at top speed, and transport needed desperately to get their supplies to Seoul, a reembarkation now would be highly disruptive. This time the critics were right. The 1st Marine Division went by sea, the 7th Division first by rail to Pusan, then by sea — both units literally swimming against the tide of soldiers and equipment moving in the opposite direction.[51]

In the end, the entire affair was completely unnecessary. So rapid was the advance of U.N. forces out of Pusan that ROK army troops actually got to Wonsan first. When the transports of X Corps finally did arrive offshore, they found that thick belts of mines in the harbor blocked their passage. A motley collection of minesweepers — always low on the navy's priority list in peacetime — had to go in and clear channels through them while the transports floated offshore, laden with matériel and a batch of increasingly filthy, sick, and demoralized marines. From October 19 on, the entire flotilla had orders to reverse course every twelve hours from south to north, as a precaution in potentially hostile waters. "Operation Yo-Yo," the men called it.[52] It was not until October 26 that the marines landed at Wonsan, greeted by sarcastic ROK troops who had already been there for sixteen days. The 7th Division began to land several days later, at Iwon up the coast. The embarkation of X Corps at Inchon for a pointless foray to the northeast was the first in a series of indefensible decisions by MacArthur that would eventually wreck this campaign.

The liberation of South Korea would not be the end of the war. MacArthur decided, with Washington's backing, to cross the thirty-eighth parallel, invade North Korea, finish the job of destroying the NKPA, and reunite the country, presumably under the leadership of Syngman Rhee. The campaign that followed began as a triumphant victory parade, with loosely organized U.N. columns moving at top speed, rounding up demoralized NKPA prisoners as they drove north. Occasionally, some small remnant would turn and fight, and U.N. forces would crush it. An enormous haul of war booty fell into the hands of 8th Army: fifty boxcars loaded with ammunition here, twenty T-34 tanks there, and, unfortunately, the bodies of numerous U.S. prisoners of war murdered by their captors. But there was seemingly nothing that could stop the momentum. Pyongyang fell to 8th Army on October 19, and on October 20, the 187th Regimental Combat Team (Airborne) staged a drop to block the roads leading north out of the North Korean capital, landing at Sukchon and Sunchon. The plan was to close up to the

Yalu River, crushing whatever elements of the NKPA had managed to survive the onslaught.

But anyone following these operations on a situation map could clearly see one trouble spot. When X Corps had landed at Wonsan, MacArthur, for reasons that will never be adequately understood, kept it organizationally separate from 8th Army. General Walker's command consisted of I Corps (24th Division, 1st Cavalry Division) and IX Corps (2nd Division, 25th Division). The X Corps remained under Far East Command, that is, under MacArthur's personal direction. Perhaps he still wanted to retain some vestige of a field command, but the result was a ridiculous arrangement in which X Corps had to report back to Tokyo. Walker seemed to realize this early on — there are few professional officers who wouldn't — and asked MacArthur repeatedly to be kept informed of the plans and dispositions of X Corps. For the pursuit up the Yalu, then, X Corps would be operating in a private theater of war, a virtual vacuum, with one hundred miles of mountains between it and 8th Army's main body.

Chinese Intervention: The Triumph of Light Infantry

Starting in late October, U.N. forces began to encounter heavier resistance. As 8th Army pushed over the Chongchon River, the last natural barrier before the Chinese border, it fought a series of sharp scraps with units that had evidently avoided the morale breakdown that had beset the NKPA after Pusan. It was soon clear that they were Chinese forces, "People's Volunteers," as the government in Beijing began to call them. On November 1, the 8th Cavalry Regiment (1st Cavalry Division) fell victim to a well-coordinated attack near Unsan. Enemy forces infiltrated its positions overnight, establishing blocking positions, and then launched a frontal attack in the morning. It cut the regiment to pieces.[53]

This is not the place to rejoin the heated controversy over this massive failure of U.S. intelligence, but we can make a few comments. It was clear to MacArthur by October that Chinese forces were present in North Korea. They had somehow infiltrated their way across the Yalu River bridges without being spotted by U.S. reconnaissance flights, which were, by this point in the war, being conducted only half-heartedly. It is equally clear that the directive of the Joint Chiefs authorizing MacArthur to cross the thirty-eighth parallel into North Korea had specified that he was not to employ U.S. forces in operations along the Yalu and that he had no intention of following those orders. To be fair to the army as a whole, several of his subordinate commanders could see what was happening. After the debacle at Unsan, Walker immediately pulled his 8th Army forces back, south of the Chongchon River, maintaining only a bridgehead on the northern bank. In the east, the commander of the 1st Marine Division, General Oliver Smith, edgy at the increase in enemy activity to his front, had concentrated his own division for battle, near a frozen reservoir at Chosin (Changjin). In doing so he repeatedly risked the wrath of X Corps commander, General Almond, who was constantly urging the units of his command to continue their advance. By mid-November, Almond had dispersed his forces so widely that there was no hope of the Corps operating as any kind of cohesive formation.

MacArthur's worst blunder in this campaign, however, was ordering the advance continued on November 24. The 8th Army would drive north, X Corps would swing almost due west, and the two pincers would catch the rest of the NKPA between them. This "Home by Christmas" offensive would result in one of the worst disasters in U.S. military history. The plan had, literally, to ignore piles of intelligence reports now flowing into headquarters at all levels — MacArthur's, Walker's, and Almond's — that trouble was brewing. It was a remarkable example of a Supreme Commander's ability to believe what he wants to believe and ignore intelligence to the contrary. MacArthur's successor, the outspoken airborne general Matthew Ridgway, later critiqued X Corps dispositions:

> I find it amazing that highly trained professionals with extensive combat experience could have approved and tried to execute the tactical plan of operations for the X Corps in northeast Korea in November 1950. It appears like a pure Map Exercise put on by amateurs, appealing in theory, but utterly ignoring the reality of a huge mountainous terrain, largely devoid of terrestrial communications, and ordered for execution in the face of a fast approaching, sub-arctic winter.[54]

He might just as well have been speaking of MacArthur's entire conduct of the Yalu campaign by this point.

The Chinese achievement in getting into position to oppose the U.N. advance deserves special mention. They had to carry out virtually all movements by night. During the day, they proved to be masters of camouflage, disguising their positions, men, animals, and equipment from the hostile eye of Allied aircraft. Their march discipline was nearly complete, enforced by the occasional execution. One Chinese army had marched nearly three hundred miles from Antung in Manchuria to its assembly areas in sixteen to nineteen days; one of its divisions, following a more tortuous route over the mountains, had averaged eighteen miles per day for eighteen days, traveling exclusively between 7 P.M. and 3 A.M. A modern authority on the Korean conflict compares their achievements in this campaign with the best march accomplishments of antiquity: Xenophon's *anabasis* out of Persia, for example.[55] Lacking the impedimenta of more modern forces, this was an army that could travel fast, travel light, and travel off road much more effectively than could the U.N. force it faced.

By late November, more than 200,000 Chinese troops had filtered south of the Yalu. Six armies faced Walker across the Chongchon. Even allowing for the fact that a Chinese army was roughly the size of a western corps, Chinese commander Peng Te-huai had 8th Army handily outnumbered in this sector. Moving in an arc from west to east, he had the 50th, 66th, 39th, 40th, 38th, and 42nd Armies, forming the 13th Army Group. They were poised for a concentric advance on the 8th Army formations that had just crossed the Chongchon. They included, again moving from west to east: I Corps (24th Infantry Division, ROK 1st Infantry Division, and 27th Commonwealth Brigade); IX Corps (25th Infantry Division, 2nd Infantry Division, and the recently arrived Turkish Brigade), and functioning as the right flank guard of the army, II ROK Army Corps (7th and 8th ROK Divisions). Walker also had the 1st Cavalry Division, the British 29th Brigade, and the 187th RCT (Airborne) in reserve.

The opening Chinese attacks saw 38th Army and 42nd Army attacking the ROK II Corps in the mountains and shredding them almost effortlessly. The Chinese were able to find the boundary between the two divisions and slam into it with a substantial force — most of the 112th Division, on the night of November 25–26. Within minutes, there was a hole half a mile wide in the center of ROK II Corps, through which poured a mass of men, the main body of 38th Division, penetrating the ten miles toward Tokchon. The Corps commander didn't receive news until nearly midnight, about five hours after disaster had occurred; ROK officers rarely rushed bad news to higher echelons. His attempt to close the gap by rushing a reserve regiment up into the breach had no effect. Chinese advance forces were already established in blocking positions. The next evening, an all-out offensive against the two ROK divisions essentially destroyed them in a single blow, uncovering the entire right flank of 8th Army. A simple swing to the west by these Chinese forces would place 8th Army in mortal danger. The unit immediately threatened was 2nd Division. Walker reacted by bringing 1st Cavalry Division and the Turkish Brigade out of reserve to shore up the flank to the right of 2nd Division. They were under fire almost immediately from an enemy who seemed to be everywhere, the Turks suffering particularly heavy casualties.

At the same time, Chinese forces were across 8th Army's entire front in strength. Chinese 39th and 40th Armies hit the 2nd and 25th Divisions hard, with one regiment of the latter, the 24th, melting away in panic. Nor did many other units do much better. Finally, in the west, Chinese 55th and 60th Armies struck the 1st ROK Division, sending it reeling back. The "battle of the Chongchon" (November 25–28), therefore, ended with 8th Army mauled and forced into headlong retreat. Two full Chinese armies, 38th and 42nd, were driving toward its line of retreat. The 2nd Division, in particular, had to hold the flank for the rest of the army and then attempt its own retreat down "the gauntlet" from Kuni-ri to Sunchon.[56] Only a massive commitment of Allied tactical airpower was able to hold open enough of a path for a remnant of the shattered division to survive.

The stage was set for the longest retreat in U.S. military history. The "bug-out," as it became known to the men, would not stop until it had passed back through Pyongyang and recrossed the thirty-eighth parallel. An official history, never prone to exaggerate U.S. losses, describes 8th Army's plight:

> After the defeat at the Chongchon river, General Walker realized that it was necessary to withdraw his 8th Army from its positions before the Chinese could move around its still open right flank. He ordered an immediate retreat to create an enclave around Pyongyang. However, even as troops occupied their new positions, he realized that he lacked the forces to maintain a cohesive defensive line. Three of his ROK divisions (6th, 7th, and 8th Infantry Divisions) had disintegrated; the U.S. 2nd Infantry Division was in shambles; and all the other units had taken heavy losses in men, materiel, and morale.[57]

One officer said his men had "retrograde movement fever," and that is as good a way to put it as one can find. In their haste, they destroyed ammunition dumps and wrecked much-needed equipment. Accidents of all sorts — from untimely demolitions to jittery examples of friendly fire — took many lives among the U.N. forces. Self-inflicted wounds as a path to discharge from the army also made their appearance. There was talk in the ranks that the army was headed for new defensive lines around Pusan. Others claimed to have heard that 8th Army was evacuating Korea altogether. Such news usually got a warm response from the men. By the time the worst of the "fever" had passed, 8th Army was three hundred miles away from its starting point north of the Chongchon River.

What had happened to the Chinese? For all their virtues as light infantrymen, these forces lacked the logistical tail to conduct anything more than short operations. They could assemble in secret and carry enough supplies for four or five days. Once they had launched their attacks, however, they were out in the open and took a fierce beating from U.S. airpower. As their supply lines lengthened, they became ever more vulnerable to it. Despite the fears of many in the 8th Army, there was little chance that the Chinese were going to push them into the sea.

The situation was potentially even more disastrous for X Corps. Separated from the main body of 8th Army, and with its three divisions spread widely over mountainous northeastern Korea in the dead of winter, X Corps lay vulnerable to a well-executed strike. It was a chance for Peng to annihilate an American corps. Unfortunately, from his perspective, his initial attack slammed into the 1st Marine Division, already dug in around the Chosin Reservoir.[58] The defense put up by the 1st Marines was an epic, made more dramatic by the ungodly conditions. The marines were facing the better part of a Chinese Army Group (the 9th), with six Chinese divisions arrayed around them concentrically: the 60th, 58th, 59th, 89th, 79th, and 80th. Late on the evening of November 27, the Chinese attacked along both sides of the frozen reservoir. In the east, the 80th Division overran "Task Force Faith," containing elements of the 1st Battalion, 32nd Infantry Regiment. It had only just arrived in the region to relieve the 5th Marines and allow General Smith to concentrate his division on the southwestern side of the reservoir. The marines were hit hard, as well, with 79th and 89th Divisions attacking their positions at Yudam-ni, while three others worked around to their rear. The marines managed a fighting withdrawal to their divisional headquarters at Hagaruri. From here, they blasted their way through fifty miles of Chinese-controlled roads and hills over the next twelve days, heading for the nearest port, Hungnam. Marine patrols fought a nonstop battle to clear the ridges on either side of the road, allowing the main column (divisional headquarters, remnants of Task Force Faith, and an increasing number of civilian refugees) to pass. The marines, their divisional commander said, were not retreating, simply "attacking in another direction." They inflicted colossal losses on the Chinese. The climax of the withdrawal, at least in administrative terms, was the airdropping of eight massive segments of treadway bridge, 2,500 pounds apiece, to fill in a destroyed section of road near Funchilin Pass (December 7). Three days later, the marines made contact with Task Force Dog, elements of the 7th Infantry Division reinforced with artillery. The worst of the danger was over.[59]

MacArthur had already ordered X Corps to be evacuated from Hungnam and to rejoin 8th Army in western Korea. With the marines going first, the corps pulled out of Hungnam from December 9 through 24. In this American Dunkirk, more than 105,000 men and 18,000 vehicles were pulled safely offshore. The Chinese, who had by now learned that they would rather not tussle with the marines, watched the evacuation but did nothing to impede it. As a bonus — and it is almost enough to justify the entire sorry history of X Corps operations in northeastern Korea — U.S. transports also took away 91,000 Korean civilians who had decided to flee south for their liberty.

The Lessons of the Korean War

As Winston Churchill once observed, however, wars are not won by successful evacuations. The Chinese landed one last hammer blow on 8th Army in late December. This "Third Phase Offensive" opened on December 26 and once again threw 8th Army — by now having utterly lost its morale — into headlong retreat. Seoul fell once again to the enemy, changing hands for the third time in this short war, and U.N. forces retreated to "Line D," between Pyongtaek on the west coast and Samchok on the east, sixty-five miles south of where they had been at Christmas. The Chinese — their supplies and their energy spent, their logistics outrun — were not even pursuing by this point.

It was here that the bug-out ended. There was a new commander of the 8th Army, after an automobile accident had taken the life of General Walker. General Ridgway was an airborne officer, a fighter, and a charismatic personality. He was the right man at the right time. He rapidly restored the morale and fighting spirit of 8th Army. He understood, he wrote, that the Chinese "traveled light, traveled at night, and knew the terrain better than we did." He knew that they could move off the roads in a way that was no longer customary for the more advanced western armies. But that had to change. "There was nothing but our own love of comfort that bound us to the roads," he felt. It was time to forget about the roads, get out in the terrain, and fight.

His prescription was simplicity itself: "Find them! Fix them! Fight them! Finish them!"[60] That is precisely what happened. In a series of carefully planned assaults, classic set-piece battles supported by massive amounts of air and artillery, he drove the Chinese back, mile by mile, to

This kind of war: Pinned down by Chinese Communist fire, men of the
15th Regimental Combat Team, 3rd Infantry Division, take cover during the
drive toward the thirty-eighth parallel, March 23, 1951. Signal Corps, Korean
War Collection, Action #6, Box 8, U.S. Army Military History Institute.

the north. Here once again was the twentieth-century American way of
war: aiming not at territory but at the complete destruction of enemy
forces. Even the names of his operations are instructive: Operation
Thunderbolt, an advance back to the Han (February 1951); Operation
Killer (February–March), to destroy Chinese forces in the Chechon
salient in the central front; and, finally, Operation Ripper (March), which
featured, once again, the liberation of Seoul. By spring, U.N. forces again
stood on the thirty-eighth parallel. Ridgway had overseen one of the
most remarkable recoveries in military history.

The Korean War has left behind an ambiguous legacy. On one hand,
many officers in the U.S. military wanted nothing more than to forget
that it happened and to ensure that it never happened again. "No more
Koreas!" became a slogan of sorts, a demand that never again should U.S.
troops fight under the kind of constraints they had experienced in Korea.
They were fighting Chinese troops, yet China itself was off limits to a

U.S. attack. Virtually every day, U.S. airmen fought battles with enemy aircraft whose bases could not be touched. Finally, the last two years of the conflict had seen a "war of posts," with this ridge or that valley being the target of a back-and-forth struggle in the interests of winning a positional advantage on a limited sector of front, or simply to keep the troops sharp — but that had no appreciable impact on the outcome. In the end, many officers complained that they were asking their men to "die for a tie," a stalemate rather than the decisive victory U.S. forces had won in all previous wars. Right next to "No More Koreas!" was the slogan "No More Task Force Smiths." Never again should the United States go to war as hopelessly unprepared as it did in early July 1950. Peacetime illusions, and budget cuts, were the target here.

Today, the U.S. military claims to view Korea as a victory, if not for the United States, then at least for the United Nations. A veritable avalanche of government material on the war is currently available, from multiple, and even overlapping, volumes of the official history to literally dozens of commemorative booklets published in concert with the war's fiftieth anniversary in 2000. They paint a generally accurate picture of events at the front and by and large don't stint on the disasters of 1950. They also tend to lay responsibility for the problems at MacArthur's door, rather than explain them as systemic or institutional failings of the U.S. military. But for the most part, they express a "mission accomplished" tone. A recent characterization by a source within the military referred to Korea as "a genuine success" for the army that "caused a temporary increase in its size and budget."[61] That tone has echoed in numerous popular works that emphasize the heroism of U.S. troops in small unit actions throughout all phases of the war. It is a deserved homage to the brave men who fought in Korea and a reminder that there were, and will continue to be, many "great generations" of American soldiers.

Frankly, it is difficult to harmonize "No More Koreas!" with the view that the United States won the war. After all, why would one be so dead set against repeating a conflict that turned out to be a victory? In fact, the war can be viewed as a success only in the fact that South Korea remained in existence at the end and by conveniently forgetting MacArthur's invasion of North Korea that ended in disaster. The roots of that disaster were not "communist human wave assaults," or "Asiatic disrespect for human life," or some of the other phrases that were still being trotted out decades later. Chinese light infantry, moving quickly and silently, was able again and again to outmaneuver a much more technologically sophisticated and better-equipped force. It fought better,

Stellungskrieg in Korea: The 68th Battalion, Division Artillery attached to the 1st ROK Division, fires its 90-mm antiaircraft guns. Box 4, Korean War SC Collection, RG6S-KWP .474, U.S. Army Military History Institute.

operationally speaking, than the forces it engaged. It was not capable of carrying out consecutive operations, but so shocking was the first blow it landed that the U.S. forces retreated some three hundred miles before they stopped. For a large part of that distance, they were completely out of contact with the Chinese. Once the new commander, General Ridgway, had reestablished the morale of his force, and the U.N. force had once again formed a cohesive line, backed by artillery and armor and covered by air power, there was little chance that the Chinese would be able to crash through it. The Chinese army and its light weapons were most assuredly not capable of slamming it out toe-to-toe with the U.N. forces, with the possible exception of the South Koreans.

Interestingly enough, the Chinese exhibit the same sort of ambivalence toward the war. During the entire period of negotiations and the years immediately after the end of the war, Mao Tse-tung trumpeted China's "victory" to the world. After centuries of humiliation at the hands of the imperialists, China had finally stood up. "The imperialist aggressors ought to bear this in mind," he said. "The Chinese people are now organized, they are not to be trifled with. Once they are provoked to anger, things can get very tough." Peng agreed. "After three years of fierce fighting, the first-rate armed forces of the greatest industrial power of the capitalist world were forced [by the Chinese troops] to stop at where they began [their invasion of North Korea]." A new age had begun, he warned: "Gone forever is the time when the western powers have been able to conquer a country in the [Far] East merely by mounting several cannons along the coast [as they had] in the past hundred years."[62]

Not everyone in China agreed. To many in the Chinese Communist Party, the heavy casualties suffered by the Chinese People's Volunteers, especially during the last two years of positional fighting, had proved that Mao was nothing but a "military romantic." His ideas about modern war, that a well-motivated infantryman was superior to all the modern weaponry and technology of the industrialized capitalist powers, his idea that "it is people, not things, that are decisive," were nothing but dangerous illusions under modern conditions. There is strong evidence that Chinese commanders were starting to experience difficulties keeping morale up and grumbling down among their troops toward the end of the fighting. The men had come to realize that they were being asked to shoulder an unfair burden in their battles with American troops.

The principal lesson of this war was the continuing importance of the infantry.[63] With modern armies the world over emphasizing their mechanized-heavy components to a greater and greater degree, and with many theorists the world over announcing that atomic weaponry had made infantry armies obsolete, the foot soldier had stood up, wearing Chinese khaki or olive drab, and had made a convincing case for his own continued relevancy. The NKPA in the war's early days, the U.S. Army and Marines within the Pusan perimeter and again at Inchon and Seoul, and finally and most emphatically the Chinese in the winter offensives of 1950 had dominated the fighting. Armor and air power had played a purely subordinate role, supporting infantry in the attack or defense. It was as if the great military debate of the 1920s over the role of these new "machine weapons" had never taken place or had been stood on its head.

The U.S. Air Force, to be sure, had carried out a strategic campaign against North Korea almost from the outset of the fighting. After dispatching the small North Korean air force, it had enjoyed the enticing sight of an entire country laid out at its feet, open to whatever mayhem it wanted to cause. During this long war, it left no target of any economic or strategic worth untouched. Targets included Pyongyang, first firebombed in January 1951; the Fusan hydroelectric plant, destroyed in

July 1952; the Toksan and Chasan Dams in May 1953, and many, many more.[64] Bombing also destroyed virtually every bridge in North Korea. The North Korean economy has, perhaps, still not recovered today. But this destruction did little to end the war, which was largely being fought, of course, by the Chinese. Perhaps more immediate to them was this unusual statistic: with supply convoys a main priority of the U.S. air effort, casualties among Chinese truck drivers were about 20 percent — far higher than the front-line fighters.

Despite what is being said today, no one in U.S. military circles should have been very happy with the army's overall performance in the Korean War. On the operational level, in particular, there was very little to see on the positive side. The rapidity with which U.S. forces responded to the NKPA invasion had been truly impressive. The unhappy fact of Task Force Smith's demise has often served to mask the fact that it took place on just the eleventh day of the conflict and that Smith and his troops had been involved in nothing more hazardous than the routine of peacetime garrison duty less than two weeks before. Their arrival at Pusan via airlift would become a model for subsequent U.S. military interventions.

After the defeat at Osan, things went from bad to worse. The 24th Division arrived, again, it must be said, with impressive dispatch. One of its component regiments was already in combat on July 13, just the nineteenth day of the war, at the Kum River. Once again, the NKPA blew it away. Disaster followed at Taejon on July 20, when most of the division and its commanding general met their demise. The mission of the 24th Division was a hopeless one in an operational sense. Divisions of the NKPA — their men well trained, well armed, and very highly motivated by their communist and nationalist ideals — were swarming all over South Korea. MacArthur's orders had sent the division up the road to Taejon with no flank protection, with its ROK army allies already in an advanced state of dissolution, to fight a hardy enemy with an already demonstrated penchant for flanking operations. The cry "No More Task Force Smiths" should, with justice, be extended to "No more sacrificed divisions!" The usual explanation — that MacArthur and the U.S. command somewhat arrogantly believed that a simple show of force would make the NKPA back down — is no explanation at all. It is not even a sufficient excuse.

Once they had retreated to Pusan, U.S. forces fought a very strong positional battle in the defense of the perimeter. They broke out of the perimeter once they had well and truly attrited the NKPA divisions attacking Pusan, and then they carried out the bold amphibious stroke at Inchon. Inchon, a bold gamble on MacArthur's part, seemingly played a secondary role in the rapid reconquest of South Korea. The Pusan break-out almost certainly would have taken place without it. Yet the lightning fall of the South Korean capital was a great moral fillip to the U.N. side and had to have been a crushing blow to the North Koreans. It turned what might have been a clear defeat down in Pusan into a rout — the virtual destruction of the North Korean army as it tried to beat a hasty retreat to the north.

From here, things fell apart. The almost immediate reembarkation at Inchon — the 1st Marine Division by sea, the 7th Division by rail to Pusan — was highly disruptive to supply and communications for the 8th Army as it advanced on Seoul and beyond. The complete waste of the entire corps in Operation Yo-Yo was simply foolish. The vaunted advantages of amphibious mobility seemed somewhat overstated when the ROK army actually beat X Corps to Wonsan. So did marine air units. So did the X Corps commander, General Almond, who got tired of wait-ing for minesweepers to clear the port and flew in by helicopter. So did Bob Hope. Once they had landed, Almond dispersed his divisions over an immense and primitive hinterland, with a completely inadequate road net, to perform a mission that many of his own men could not even ex-plain to themselves. MacArthur had taken a substantial portion of his army — three complete divisions in a war in which the U.S. commit-ment was seven — and separated it from his main body. Those troops would have come in quite handy on the Chongchon in November, as 8th Army was fighting for its life. The X Corps itself was saved from destruc-tion only by the fortunate fact that the Chinese struck the marines, the most tenacious infantry in the U.S. order of battle. One marine lieu-tenant described the sarcastic greeting his company got from the ROK troops when it landed at Wonsan: "They had learned the middle finger salute, which they tendered to us with great enthusiasm."[65] It was a per-fect judgment on this entire inept operation.

As for 8th Army itself, it performed well at Pusan, fighting from static positions. After going over to a very impressive offensive, it carried out the advance from Pusan on the southern tip of the peninsula virtually to the Chinese border in a single month. But once the Chinese entered the war, their attacks exposed grave operational weaknesses. Admittedly, the Chinese had achieved surprise, and that must be admitted as a part of the equation. The reasons *why* they achieved surprise have filled vol-umes since 1950, and MacArthur will always have his supporters and detractors (rather more of the latter than the former today, it seems). Even after the Chinese had announced their presence in dramatic terms, hammering the 8th Cavalry Regiment (1st Cavalry Division) at Unsan in late October in their "First Stage Offensive," 8th Army took no reactive or protective steps, or better yet, considered an attack on them with the incredible firepower at its disposal. Thus, the massive offensive in late November, the "Second Stage," caught it completely, but inexcusably, unprepared even to defend itself. Individual units fought well here and there, and, of course, the tales of valor on the part of individual U.S., Commonwealth, Turkish, and ROK troops are legion. Their bravery is not the point here. The 8th Army met defeat on the operational level. Hit frontally, in the flank, and even in the rear by forces that had infiltrated to their positions by night, the command of 8th Army lacked the flexibility to respond to repeated Chinese flanking moves. Then, once the army started running, its commanders lacked the determination and strength of will to stop it. It is a sign of how badly the troops of 8th Army wanted to be led that they responded so quickly to General Ridgway, who whipped it back into fighting shape in no time.

And what of the Chinese? They had certainly shown that they were a force to be reckoned with in any future conflict in East Asia. Tactically they were quite proficient. Troops carried out prodigious marches under difficult conditions almost completely by night. In the attack they seemed to be without fear, and their system of communications — a mix of whistles, rattles, drums, and trumpets — was effective if primitive. It was also, if the huge amount of memoir literature is to be believed, highly unnerving to U.S. troops in the dark of night in unfamiliar Korea.[66] Their supporting weapons, almost exclusively mortars in the early days, were, likewise, quite simple, but again were handled with a deadly efficiency. Their motivation — equal parts communism and Chinese nationalism — was strong. They mauled a number of U.N. units and gave an entire division of U.S. Marines premature gray hairs at Chosin. Not everyone can say that. All this was achieved, moreover, against an enemy who enjoyed a clear firepower advantage, not to mention air support.

Operationally, the verdict is mixed. They were able to achieve surprise in their initial assaults on 8th Army and X Corps, and they were able to maintain the momentum of their initial victories for weeks. What they were not able to do — lacking the modern systems of supply, replacement, and administration — was to sustain their advance deep into South Korea. Someone versed in Soviet operational theory of World War II might have said that they lacked the ability to carry out "consecutive operations," designed to land a series of blows that harry the enemy to his complete and final destruction. Then again, the Soviet army was only able to achieve that after amassing a huge numerical superiority over the Germans. The Chinese fought the U.N. forces in Korea with a rough numerical parity. The firepower disparity between the Chinese and U.N. troops prevented the Chinese from winning anything more than local successes. They found out very soon that they could not destroy entire U.N. units in a single action. In only one case in the entire war did they destroy a U.S. regiment (the 32nd Regiment, 7th Division at the Chosin Reservoir), and they never came close to getting a division, despite actually having them surrounded on occasion. The Chinese could break through their front, place roadblocks in their rear, and force them to run a gauntlet of fire in the retreat. U.N. firepower, however, delivered by artillery or from the air, almost always saved the beleaguered forces in the end.[67]

Today scholars still debate the impact of the Korean War on the Chinese army. Some argue that Mao's military romanticism remained in place for years after Korea, with a continued belief that all that was needed for modern warfare was a company of infantrymen, a handful of mortars, and a sound indoctrination in the principles of communism. Others, however, note that the Chinese commander in Korea, Peng, became a staunch advocate for modernization of Chinese forces along western lines. As defense minister in the 1950s, he encouraged professionalization of the officer corps, insisted on standardized troop training in place of indoctrination, and argued for the acquisition of new, modern weaponry. His purge in 1959, on charges of being part of a "right opportunist clique" and conducting "unprincipled factional activity," was a temporary victory for Mao's views. Given the current Chinese force modernization programs, however, perhaps Peng won in the end.[68]

5

The Arab-Israeli Wars

The real proving ground for operational-level warfare since the end of World War II has been the Middle East. There is no state in the world for which a rapid operational victory is more important than Israel. The state is so tiny that it lacks all strategic depth. Enemy aircraft can literally overfly every inch of Israel in minutes. In 1967, an Egyptian fighter plane taking off from El Arish in the Sinai could be over Tel Aviv in twelve minutes. There was no safe hinterland, where defeated Israeli forces could regroup and industries could relocate. Nor, in the Arab-Israeli Wars, has there even really been such a thing as a "frontier battle." Any serious operational defeat — one that mauls a substantial portion of the Israeli Defense Force (IDF) or forces it into retreat — would automatically have the gravest strategic consequences for the country. Even today, it is a basic part of Israeli security doctrine that "Israel cannot afford to lose a single war."[1] Since the foes in these conflicts have promised, repeatedly and publicly, that their war aims involved the dismantling of the Jewish state, it has also been impossible to speak of a "limited war" in the series of Arab-Israeli conflicts, or at least the major ones of 1948, 1956, 1967, and 1973.

In other words, the military history of Israel is an extreme case of what we might call the "German syndrome." Neither country, historically, believes that it can win a long war. Crucial factors of geography, manpower, and resources always tilt in favor of their enemies. Battlefield victory, rapid and decisive with minimal friendly losses, is not simply desirable. It is essential. Just as Prussian-German armies since the age of Moltke traditionally sought the battle of annihilation, so too has the IDF. In every way — officer and troop training, operational planning, the logistics net — seeking rapid victory has permeated the very fiber of the IDF from its inception. The results have been truly impressive. The IDF will never be the largest army in the world. Pound-for-pound, however, it just may be the best.

The War for Independence

Israel's first war was much different than its later ones. First of all, it was an infantry struggle, an unusual start for a military force that would ride its tanks to victory in subsequent conflicts. This war belonged to "the lightly armed, hard hitting, fast moving foot soldier," in the words of one observer.[2] Also unlike later wars, Israeli casualties were extremely heavy, numbering some six thousand, or about 1 percent of the population of the Yishuv, the Jewish community in Palestine. Finally, although the IDF would soon become known as the conventional force par excellence, this war was much more of an unconventional struggle by small bands of guerrillas, at least in its earliest phases. Nevertheless, this war formed the IDF and left an indelible mark on its later operations.

From the moment that the United Nations announced the partition in November 1947, battles erupted between Jew and Arab in Palestine.[3] Each side aimed to position itself as favorably as possible for the British departure in May 1948. The combatants were a menagerie of armed defense groups on both sides. For the Arabs, they included the Arab Liberation Army under Fauzi el Kaukji and the Arab Army of Salvation led by Abd el Kader el Husseini (the cousin of the mufti of Jerusalem). For the Jews, there was the Haganah and its elite mobile units, the Palmach, both under the control of the elected leadership of the Yishuv. Other groups, like the Lehi (also known as the "Stern Gang," for its leader) and the Irgun, operated independently, sometime at cross-purposes from the Haganah. Neither side was particularly well armed or organized for a sustained conflict, and both spent their energy carrying out ambushes, attacks, and reprisals on each other's communities and villages. Even in this irregular phase, with its sporadic combat, the Haganah leadership had to view the war as total. Yigal Allon, one of the founding figures of the IDF and Israel's leading field commander in the war, described Haganah strategy in this period as defending every Jewish settlement, no matter how remote it happened to be or how many problems its defense posed.[4]

The Israelis describe this first phase of the fighting as the "battle of the roads." Arab guerrillas controlled the roads between the principal Jewish settlements, effectively laying siege to them. Jewish supply columns had to shuttle from settlement to settlement under guard, suffering heavy casualties from Arab fire and ambush. A typical convoy might include twenty to thirty buses guarded by makeshift armored buses or armored cars, plus its Haganah escort. Although the coastal plain between Haifa and Tel Aviv held most of the population of the Yishuv, the operational key to the fighting was the city of Jerusalem. Home to about 100,000 Jews, Jerusalem relied on convoys from the coastal regions for food and arms. Much of the thirty miles of bad road from Tel Aviv, however, were in Arab hands. In April 1947, the Haganah command decided to launch its first offensive of the fighting. It was the largest Jewish operation to date, code-named "Nachson."[5] A full Haganah "brigade" (actually 1,500 men, organized into three battalions) was involved, armed with weapons purchased from Czechoslovakia. It succeeded in clearing enough of the road from Tel Aviv to Jerusalem to rush three convoys of arms, ammunition, and supplies to the beleaguered Jewish population of the Holy City.

On May 14, 1948, the partition of Palestine came into effect. Israel declared its independence, and its Arab neighbors — Egypt, Lebanon, Syria, Transjordan, and Iraq — invaded it. The tiny state seemed helpless to anyone looking at a map, and the general expectation, from Arab leaders to the White House, was that the Arab armies would overrun Israel in a matter of weeks and perhaps slaughter all the inhabitants. Nevertheless, Israel had a few key advantages. Its enemies formed only the loosest of coalitions. The five powers, plus the Palestinian guerrilla groups, opposed the establishment of a Jewish state in Palestine, but they could agree on little else. Although the population of the Arab states was fifty times that of Israel (30,000,000 to 600,000, to be precise), they were not yet modern societies in any real sense. Having just emerged from colonial rule, they lacked the systems of administration that modern war requires, as well as the political stability to impose conscription.

The Israelis actually mobilized more men in the course of war. By the end of 1948, twelve Israeli brigades faced fourteen on the Arab side, hardly indicative of the vast disparity in manpower between the two sides.[6] Like the old Boers of South Africa, the Israelis were an entire people in arms and, despite their civilian appearance and behavior and their tendency to argue with orders they didn't like, highly proficient in the basic military skills of fire and movement. In fact, a considerable number of them were veterans of the western or Soviet armies in World War II. Allon described his soldiers as "a modern version of the laborers of Nehemiah who worked with one hand and held a weapon in the other."[7] A modern force with a unified command structure could probably have made short work of them in 1948 — but a unified command was the very thing the Arabs lacked.

The Israelis, by contrast, had just that. On May 28, the Haganah, the Irgun, and other Jewish defense groups merged to become the IDF.

Although its appearance was still irregular, it now had a chief of staff, Ya'acov Dori (formerly chief of staff of the Haganah), responsible to a tough-minded prime minister, David Ben-Gurion, and a state to defend.

Finally, geography and the divided nature of the opposition allowed Israel to exploit the strategy of the central position, smashing whichever enemy grouping happened to appear most threatening at the time, while holding off the others with token forces. It was a strategic defense, but it had to be pursued in the context of an aggressive tactical and operational offensive. Allon described the IDF's priorities this way:

> The first, most urgent tasks seemed to be the following: to eliminate the danger to Tel-Aviv and its immediate surroundings by liberating Lydda and Ramla and penetrating the hilly country east of the coastal plain; to lift the siege of Jerusalem; to outflank the Transjordanian-held Old City from the north. The second task was to secure the Haifa region by liberating Nazareth and the remaining parts of Lower Galilee. At the same time, the Egyptians in the south, the Iraqis in the east, and the Syrians in the north had to be checked by tactics of active defense, based on settlements and mobile forces, until offensive action could be undertaken against them.[8]

This was the IDF at war in its earliest days. Note the words that Allon uses: "eliminate, liberate, penetrate, and outflank." Note also that the IDF pursues the defensive only until offensive action could proceed against Israel's enemies. The IDF is the world's most aggressive military force. If it is true that events in infancy and childhood are decisive in the formation of the adult personality, then the 1948 war was truly the IDF's formative experience. That, more than particular operational successes or failures, is the true legacy of Israel's War for Independence.

A good example is Operation Horev, the IDF's last major operation in the war (December 1948), intended to secure Israeli possession of the Negev against Egypt.[9] By IDF standards in this war, Allon commanded a huge force of five brigades, including the 8th (Armored). He employed it with a great deal of finesse, however, infiltrating small mobile parties into the Egyptian rear, feinting a frontal attack, and then moving his main body along an older track through the desert to outflank the enemy. Allon described it, in a good encapsulation of IDF doctrine, as "a combination of guerrilla actions and rapid advances by large bodies."[10] It showed how far the IDF had come from its militia origins and was a harbinger of things to come.

The Sinai Campaign of 1956

The history of the IDF in the early 1950s is intertwined with the career of General Moshe Dayan, who became Israeli Chief of Staff in 1953. His entire life was spent in Palestine. Born in Degania in 1915, he was the first baby born in an Israeli *kibbutz*. He handled a gun for the first time at the age of ten and joined the Haganah at age fourteen, after the Arab assault against Jewish worshipers at the Western Wall in Jerusalem in August 1929 and the massacre of Jewish settlers at Hebron a few days later. In 1937, during the heart of the "Arab revolt," he began to serve as a guide for British army units stationed in Palestine. A series of failed British attempts to defend the Iraq Petroleum Company pipeline against Arab attacks led young Dayan to the first stirrings of his own military doctrine: "It became clear to me that the only way to fight them was to seize the initiative, attack them in their bases, and surprise them when they were on the move." In a sentence, he had outlined the strategy he would use with such success in the later Arab-Israeli Wars. Imprisoned by the British in 1939 for membership in the Haganah, he was released in 1941 and served as a guide with the British force invading Syria. In the fighting there, he lost an eye to a French bullet. The eye patch that he henceforth wore in public would make him one of the truly unmistakable figures on the world scene. He served as a commando leader in the War of Independence and in May 1948 halted a Syrian attack by tanks and armored cars against Degania with little more than infantry, Molotov cocktails, and bazookas.

In July, he traveled to New York to accompany the body of an American Jewish army officer who had been killed while serving with the IDF. Here he met Abraham Baum, who had served in the U.S. 37th Tank Battalion under General Creighton Abrams. According to a recent biographer, Baum fired Dayan's imagination with his story of the attempt to liberate the American POW camp at Hammelburg, some forty miles behind the lines. Baum described how his task force had traveled light, just armored cars, half-tracks, and light tanks. Lacking heavy weapons support, he ordered his men to "open up with everything we have" if they saw any Germans. Task Force Baum made it to the camp but was attacked on the way back and lost half its vehicles. Baum was taken prisoner. Still, he told Dayan, the essence of modern combat was unleashing all possible firepower on an unsuspecting enemy. "You wouldn't believe it," he said, "it worked. I don't know what you're doing in Israel, but I suggest that the moment you come to an obstacle, you open fire in all directions with whatever you have, machine guns, mortars. You should shoot and drive, shoot and drive."

Following Baum's advice, Dayan drew up a list of "dos and don'ts" that became the basis of Israeli strategy in the next three decades. Do not precede attacks with reconnaissance patrols a day or two in advance of the battle; the information they gleaned was often insignificant and their activity destroyed any chance of surprise. Go straight to the attack, with reconnaissance forces out in front of the main body, reporting back constantly. Keep moving at all times. Command from the front and never rely on second-hand reports. If there is a road in the area, use it. Use a large force, even for a small mission, and always give the enemy the impression that your force is larger than it is. Attack on a narrow front, even from a single column. Use a constant barrage of firepower as much to frighten and scatter the opponent as to kill him. After the assault, immediately regroup the armor and ready it for mobile operations. Use infantry to occupy ground once it has been taken.[11]

Surrounding himself with a group of talented young officers, such as Major Ariel Sharon, Dayan instilled these principles into the IDF, along with a spirit of aggressiveness that was second to none. He also oversaw a rapid expansion in the IDF's arsenal. When he took over the leadership of the army, it had just one armored brigade, consisting of one battalion of M-4 Shermans, one infantry battalion on half-tracks, and two battalions on trucks. By 1954, some 100 French AMX-13 light tanks with a high-velocity 75-mm gun, had arrived, with some 150 extra guns and 150 renovated U.S. M-3 half-tracks. All told, it was enough for two new brigades. Dayan now established an Armored Corps Headquarters. In 1955, another sixty Shermans arrived from France, which the Israelis upgraded with the 75-mm gun from the AMX-13. The French sent another shipment of M-4A3 E8s just before the 1956 war, upgraded Shermans with wider treads and improved suspensions, mounting the 76.2-mm long tank gun. Thus, the IDF's armored forces included no less than four types of Shermans: the French modification (designated M-50); the Israeli modification (M-51), M-4s with their original short 75-mm guns and others with the short 76-mm cannon; plus about one hundred AMX-13s and some four hundred half-tracks.[12] Dayan was not a "tank man," as such. He had faith, above all, in mobile infantry from his commando days. Nevertheless, he now commanded a sizable armored force.

Arab strength was growing as well. Since the military coup of 1952, Egypt had become the most powerful "front line" Arab state. President Gamal Abdel Nasser repeatedly proclaimed his intention to destroy Israel, and he began to receive arms in abundance from the Soviet Union (through Czechoslovakia). By 1956, Egypt had a force of about three hundred medium tanks (T-34/85s and JS-3s), two hundred armored personnel carriers, one hundred SU-100 assault guns, two hundred 57-mm antitank guns, and a large number of field guns, howitzers, recoilless rifles, and scout cars. It was a formidable arsenal by any standards.[13]

Based on a simple balance of forces, then, Israel's 1956 offensive into Sinai should have failed outright or at the most led to a stalemate. Instead, Operation Kadesh was a lopsided victory for Israel's new armored force. The plan bore all the marks of Dayan's daring, aggressive character. In a precampaign briefing on October 8, Dayan stressed to his commanders the need to advance as far and as fast as they could. There was no reason, he told them, "to fear that Egyptian units who will be bypassed will launch a counter-attack or cut our supply lines. We should avoid analogies whereby Egyptian units would be expected to behave as European armies would in similar circumstances." Instead, he believed that once isolated, the entire Egyptian front would simply collapse. His priorities, he said, were "first, paratroop drops or landings; second, advance through by-passing the enemy positions; third, breakthrough." It was better to use airborne forces to capture the deepest objectives right away rather than "to reach them by frontal and gradual advance after head-on attacks on every Egyptian position starting from the Israeli border and slogging it out all the way to Suez." In the same way, infantry and armor were simply to bypass enemy positions and keep heading west. Assault and breakthrough were last resorts, only where bypassing the Egyptians was impossible. Carrying this line of thought to its logical conclusion, Dayan stressed that the first task of Kadesh would be to capture the Egyptian positions near the canal; the IDF would leave Gaza, directly on Israel's border, for last.[14]

Interestingly, Operation Kadesh aimed at neither of the two usual objectives of military planning: the destruction of the enemy's field force or the occupation of its territory. The former would require hard fighting and high Israeli casualties, and the latter simply was not in the political cards at this time. Kadesh's goals, therefore, were "to confound the organization of the Egyptian forces in Sinai and bring about their collapse."[15] The IDF could best achieve its aims, he told Ben-Gurion, by seizing "the crossroads and key military positions which will give us control of the area and force their surrender."[16] Low Egyptian troop morale would do the rest.

The entire operation took only one hundred hours. On the afternoon of October 29, a weak battalion of Israeli paratroopers, part of Sharon's 202nd Paratroop Brigade, dropped at Parker Memorial just east of the

Mitla Pass. This was the event that "triggered" British and French intervention. The battalion now dug in and waited for relief. It was not long in coming. With his men mounted on jeeps and half-tracks and supported by a company of AMX-13 tanks, Sharon now embarked on a wild 190-mile ride across the Sinai in relief. He overran defended positions at Kuntilla, where he skillfully maneuvered tanks so that they approached the fortification out of the setting sun; Thamad, where he used the rising sun to achieve the same effect; and Nakhl, before linking up with the battalion on October 30 after just thirty hours.

The paradrop and linkup was a spectacular way to place an Israeli threat close to the Suez Canal, but it was only the prelude to the main assault. Nine brigades of tanks and mechanized infantry were to drive through Sinai in two major columns: one to the north, along the Rafah-El Arish-Kantara axis, and a more or less parallel one to the south, through Abu Agheila and thence on to Ismailia, starting on D+2. The principal obstruction was the main Egyptian defensive position, the triangle between Rafah, El Arish, and Abu Agheila. Ignoring his German advisers, who had recommended that the weight of Egyptian deployment be in the western Sinai where it could react to any attack, Nasser had deployed almost all his strength in the forward positions of the triangle. This forward deployment of most of the Egyptian strength played into Dayan's hands, giving him the opportunity for the lightning victory that the situation demanded.

No one could say it all went according to plan. The 7th Armored Brigade, part of the central column, had the most eventful time of any Israeli unit. Its commander, General Uri Ben Ari, advanced into the Sinai a full day before his orders allowed, nearly giving Dayan a heart attack in the process.[17] Dayan had wanted the armored units to move only on D+2, after the paradrop and after the infantry had breached the defenses in the triangle. In this way, he believed the Egyptians would interpret IDF moves as simply part of a raid, perhaps a raid gone bad: paratroopers dropping far into the rear being rescued via a linkup with a mobile infantry column. At first Dayan was furious with Ben Ari but then learned that the southern front commander, General Assaf Simchoni, had actually ordered Ben Ari into action. Simchoni felt that not a moment should be wasted after the airborne drop and that Dayan's schedule risked losing the chance of surprise.

Ben Ari's brigade now attacked the Um Katef position directly and failed to make much headway, coming under accurate antitank fire. It was at this point that Dayan arrived on the scene, first at Southern Command headquarters and then at 7th Brigade. He considered ordering Ben Ari to turn around and go back to his start line; military discipline and an orderly chain of command demanded it. Instead, he ordered 7th Brigade to bypass Um Katef and continue its advance to the west. "I could not," he wrote, "avoid a sympathetic feeling over the hastening of the brigade into combat even before they were required." He summed up his feelings on the matter in a proverb: "Better to be engaged in restraining the noble stallion than in prodding the reluctant mule."[18]

That evening, the noble stallion had a stroke of luck. Sliding to the west around Um Katef, Ben Ari discovered an undefended pass, the Deika defile. The next morning, he fell on the Abu Agheila position from the rear, thus driving into the triangle from the west and shattering a large number of the Egyptian units defending inside. It should be said that the IDF's 10th and 37th Infantry Brigades, tasked with breaching the defenses of Um Katef from the east, were having little success. It no longer mattered, however. Hardly pausing for breath, Ben Ari's 7th Brigade had turned to the west, sending out small combat teams that overran most of central Sinai in a single day. It was D+2. Ben Ari was, at this point, supposed to be crossing the border. Instead, he had won the war.

Another breach of discipline had a much more unfortunate result. After Sharon's brigade had linked up with the airborne drop near Mitla, he requested and got permission (again, from Simchoni) to carry out a "reconnaissance patrol." This reconnaissance patrol included two full companies of infantry on half-tracks, three tanks, the brigade's truck-borne reconnaissance unit, and a troop of heavy (120 mm) mortars. As this "patrol," including a major portion of the brigade's fighting strength approached the pass, however, it came under heavy and accurate Egyptian fire that took a heavy toll on the mounted column. It was not a token Egyptian force here, but a reinforced battalion, five full companies of Egyptian infantry, well protected in hillside caves and supported by artillery and antitank guns. In the opening moments, the column's fuel truck, ammunition truck, and three other vehicles went up in flames. The paratroopers had to scamper up the hillside and take on the Egyptians in hand-to-hand combat, which they did. By the end, Sharon had seized Mitla Pass. Then, since the brigade was still based at Parker Memorial, he promptly abandoned it. The cost, by Israeli standards, had been extremely high, "unprecedentedly heavy," in Dayan's words. The elite formation in the IDF had lost 38 killed and 120 wounded.

Once again, in any other army on the planet, Sharon's career would have been in serious jeopardy. There were those in the IDF who felt that it should have been. Once again, Dayan wasn't among them. In a long discussion of the issue in his *Diary of the Sinai Campaign*, he concedes that "there was no vital need to attack the Egyptian unit defending the approaches to the canal." Nevertheless, "the valor, daring, and fighting spirit of the paratroop commanders" deserved praise. The paratroopers made tactical errors that cost them a great deal of blood. "The truth is that I regard the problem as grave when a unit fails to fulfill its battle task, not when it goes beyond the bounds of duty and does more than is demanded of it." One thing about Sharon's Mitla adventure did bother him, however:

> There is no need to say how much we all deplore their heavy casualties; but my complaint, a grave complaint, against the paratroop command is not over the battle itself so much as over their resort to terming their operation a "patrol" in order to "satisfy" the General Staff. I am saddened that they should do this, and I regret that I did not succeed in molding such relations of mutual trust between us that if they wished to act contrary to my orders, they would do so directly and openly.[19]

The IDF was an unusual army, and Dayan a highly unusual commander.

His handling of the infantry attack on Um Katef is also highly instructive, standing in stark contrast to his attitude toward Simchoni, Ben Ari, and Sharon. They had disobeyed direct orders in order to get into the fight; Dayan sympathized and eventually confirmed their insubordination. When 10th and 37th Brigades seemed reluctant to press home their attacks against Um Katef, however, Dayan had a testy meeting with their commanders in which he impressed upon them the necessity of vigorous attacks. The 7th Brigade, as well as the 202nd Paratroop Brigade, would soon be running out of supplies, as they used up what they were carrying with them, and Um Katef stood on one of the few paved roads in Sinai. "They had a thousand and one good and understandable reasons why they were unable to storm the Egyptian positions, with their minefields and well-laid defenses," he wrote.

> But I was impatient with them. I had no ear for the complaints, problems, and difficulties raised by the brigade command. Their men are tired, supplies do not reach them on time, the nights are cold, the days are hot, their dust-clogged rifles don't fire, their vehicles get stuck in the sand. I know that all this is true, but I have no solutions to such problems. The Negev I cannot change, and the new axis *must* be opened.[20]

Late in the day on October 31, the British and French began their air assault on the Egyptian air force. Egyptian forces in the Sinai, receiving orders to pull back, now simply came apart. Abu Agheila, Um Katef, and Rafah — the three apexes of the triangle — were soon in Israeli hands. Both northern and central routes across the Sinai toward Kantara and Ismailia were jam-packed with fast-moving Israeli columns. So intent on movement were they that they usually disdained to pick up Egyptians trying to surrender. The Egyptians were no longer a threat as a fighting force. It was a classic of mechanized exploitation, lasting from November 2 to 5. It ended, as agreed with the French and British, with Israeli columns just ten miles from the Suez Canal. In less than a week, the IDF had conquered the Sinai Peninsula, taken more than five thousand Egyptian prisoners, and captured enormous quantities of stores and war matériel.[21] The IDF's losses were remarkably light, just 172 killed and 700 wounded. The high standard of Israeli leadership did not come cheap, however. Over half of all IDF casualties were officers.

Operation Kadesh showed that the IDF could handle mobile forces like few other armies in the world. The main assault dispensed with orthodox operational considerations altogether, avoiding frontal attack, driving on without consideration for flanks or communications, heading for the Egyptian rear while much of the enemy's front-line units were barely engaged. It demonstrated conclusively that an army of conscripts and hastily summoned reservists could handle modern weaponry and operate in an environment of modern firepower. Some of the Israeli solders had been in their uniforms for a matter of hours as they were driving into Sinai. It proved that an army did not need to have strict barracks discipline or present a spit-and-polish appearance to launch destructive and decisive operations. This was a matter of some consternation to foreign military observers:

> Officers are often called by their first names amongst their men, as amongst their colleagues; there is very little saluting; there are a lot of unshaven chins; there are no outward signs of respect for superiors; there is no word in Hebrew for "sir." All my own experience in the British and American Armies had taught me that first-class discipline in battle depends on good discipline in barracks. Israel's army seems to refute that notion.[22]

Finally, Kadesh showed that the concept of *Auftragstaktik*, allowing initiative to lower ranking commanders to act as the situation dictated, even if it meant disregarding higher orders, was still alive and well, in often extreme form, in the IDF.

After their great victory at Suez, the Israeli commanders engaged in a great deal of often heated debate, discussing what had gone wrong and what had gone right. Dayan's plan — to use infantry to open a path through the fortified triangle, had not worked. Instead, it was the armored formations that did it all: not just the glamorous job of exploiting across the desert, but the grunt work of chewing through the wire. The tanks of the 7th Brigade were the classic example. In less than two days, they had

1. *Attacked* Um Katef frontally
2. *Slid around to its rear* after being repulsed, luckily running across the Deika defile
3. *Attacked* and made the decisive breach in the triangle's defenses at Abu Agheila
4. *Turned to the west,* launching one of the most dazzling performances of all time in the exploitation.

Even though Dayan was a mobile infantryman himself, he could not deny the incredible accomplishment of his armored forces. In the aftermath of the Suez War, the development of air and armor received the highest priority in the Israeli armed forces. They alone were capable of the sort of rapid, decisive campaigns that Israel's small size and the international political situation required.

Finally, a word about IDF command and control in 1956. There was none, or hardly any. Dayan had given independent task forces their objectives and set them loose. They didn't always follow their orders. Rarely did they refuse to march. Typically, they left their start lines early or attacked when they had explicit orders not to do so. It is hard to disagree with Martin van Creveld's description of the IDF as "substituting morale for proper organization" in 1956. Those who disobeyed not only went unpunished, but in fact earned the sneaking admiration of their Chief of Staff. If problems arose, even ones that led to the death of men under his overall command, he dismissed them as "misfortunes."[23] Dayan's own command style was to fly or to drive from headquarters to headquarters in the field for face-to-face meetings with his commanders, often to hear their explanations of why they had disobeyed his orders. Sometimes he was in radio contact with Tel Aviv on these jaunts, and sometimes he wasn't. It is true that fighting the war of movement requires decentralized systems of command and control. The more extreme the preference for the former, the more extreme the demand for the latter. Against an inferior enemy who did not maneuver and who was expected to give up the moment Israeli troops got into his rear, this system worked perfectly. Later wars would put it to the test again.

And what of the Egyptian force? Caught absolutely flat-footed by an aggressive young army, it was beaten before it could even bring many of its units to battle. On paper, the Egyptians commanded a formidable force. Two complete divisions stood ready in Sinai: the 2nd Infantry Division defending the canal, and the 3rd Infantry Division defending northern and central Sinai. The 3rd Division was manning the triangle, with reinforced brigades at Rafah (5th Infantry Brigade) and Um Katef/Abu Agheila (6th Infantry Brigade). A battalion of the 4th Brigade and two squadrons of tanks formed the divisional reserves, ready to reinforce or counterattack as necessary. Once the shooting started, however, these units came under attack from the front, the flanks, and the rear. The pace of the action was so rapid that it does not appear the various brigades of 3rd Infantry Division even communicated with one another, let alone cooperated. The Egyptians did not maneuver and did little else in this campaign than shoot at whatever Israeli force happened to be in front of them. Sometimes their fire was effective, as we have seen. More often it was sporadic and without central direction. They did not "operate" in any real sense. Once Israeli forces got into their rear, they simply abandoned their positions and tried to get back home.

The Six Day War

A rapid battlefield victory has traditionally been the aim of the war of movement. From the German army in 1914, with its objective of a six-week victory over France, through the German blitzkrieg and Soviet "deep battle" in World War II, the goal of mobile warfare has been the quick victory of annihilation. In 1956, Dayan had worked overtime to make sure that his forces had surprise on their side, a prerequisite, he believed, to a decisive victory. Despite some gaffes, he had largely achieved his aim. In 1967, however, the IDF went itself one better. In a conflict that would become characterized above all by its brevity, immortalized as a "Six Day War," the IDF showed that it could achieve decisive victory even before a conflict had actually begun.[24]

Although this might seem like a paradox, it is by definition the goal of a preemptive strike. The side feeling threatened by superior forces lashes out and crushes them before they even realize that they are at war. Ideally, a preemptive war is fought by one side only; the other side is simply destroyed. The attacking side goes beyond the current notion of "getting inside the opponent's decision cycle."[25] In a preemptive war, the "defending" side doesn't have a decision cycle. This is precisely what happened in 1967. The IDF victory in this conflict broke new ground in the totality of its surprise, rapidity, and destructiveness. One former IDF officer labeled it "a counter-attack in anticipation,"[26] a modern analyst "the apogee of Blitzkrieg."[27] Another sympathetic observer wrote that, in 1967, the IDF "did unto the Egyptians before it could be done unto them."[28] No doubt the Egyptian soldiers who were the hapless victims of this preemptive strike would have chosen different words.

In what would become the traditional pattern of these wars, the 1956 victory left Israel as vulnerable as ever. France and England had to abandon the canal, and Israel had to evacuate the Sinai. Over the next decade, both Israel and the Arab states armed feverishly on land and in the air. Although Israel had created an air force (IAF) back in the War for Independence, and it had done some good work in 1956, it now became a full-fledged partner of the land forces. By 1967, the IAF was armed with French planes, twenty Super Mystère B-2s and seventy-two Mirage IIICs, the first supersonic aircraft in the IAF inventory.[29] They had a great deal to contend with. The Soviet Union supplied its Arab clients liberally: an IL-28 bomber squadron in 1955, MiG-17s in 1957, the SA-2 surface-to-air missile in 1960. By 1967, there were some two hundred first-line MiG-21 fighters in Arab hands.

On land, Arab armies had the T-34/85 before 1956. During the 1960s large numbers of T-54s and T-55s replaced them. These were the first generation of postwar Soviet tanks, recognizable by their low profile and hemispheric turret. By 1967, Egypt had about 1,200 armored fighting vehicles: 350 T-34s, 500 T-54s and T-55s, 100 heavy JS-3s, and 150 SU-100 assault guns. Israeli tanks, American M-48 Pattons, British Centurions, up-gunned "Super-Shermans," and AMX-13s were for the most part superior in quality — with better fire control systems, larger ammunition-carrying capacity, and more space for the crew. Israel also did a great deal of redesign work, replacing the Patton 90-mm gun with the greatly superior 105-mm gun from the Centurion.[30] The resulting hybrid "Patturion" became one of the most effective tanks of the 1967 war. Whether those advantages were enough to make up for a tremendous numerical inferiority was open to question, however. The combined tank forces of Syria and Egypt outnumbered the Israelis by at least two to one.

In a lesson learned from 1956, this time the Israeli high command eschewed any detailed or prescriptive plan. In fact, the 1967 operation didn't even have a name, although IDF officers tried hard to think one up after the fact. As the IDF's director of operations, General Ezer Weizmann, put it, "We've got a plan for everything — even for capturing the

North Pole. The plans are like bricks. They can be used one by one to build up for a structure as the situation develops. We don't go in for preconceived, and therefore inflexible, master plans."[31] One is tempted to add that even if the General Staff drew one up, there was no guarantee that the field commanders would follow it. Instead, the 1967 war grew out of seven years of exercises, maneuvers, and war games that had familiarized every IDF officer with the key terrain in Sinai — and here, too, the 1956 experience proved invaluable.

When war did come, in June 1967, it was air power and armor — and nearly absolute surprise — that again paved the way to an Israeli victory. Hostilities opened with a surprise Israeli air attack directed against the Arab air forces. Within a few hours on June 5, the IAF completely wrecked Egyptian and Syrian air power. Nearly two hundred aircraft lay destroyed on the ground in the initial raid. When those planes that did survive went aloft, they found Israeli pilots to be among the most skilled in the world. Total losses for this "Six Day War" were 452 Arab planes, against just 46 Israeli.

Denuded of air cover, the Arab armies found themselves helpless against the Israeli ground assault. This time, there was no fudging or clever compromise language about "confounding the organization of the Egyptian forces" or "bringing about their collapse." The aim this time was annihilation. The Sinai front commander, General Yeshayahu Gavish, had three divisional task force organizations (ugdot in the plural) at his disposal. At 8:15 A.M. on June 5, all three were to cross the border into Sinai simultaneously. Starting on the Israeli right, the ugdah of General Israel Tal, commanding officer of the IDF's Armoured Corps, was to strike the Egyptian 7th Division, entrenched along the coast. Tal was to break through the fortifications at Rafah and reach El Arish, thus unhinging the Egyptian defenses in the north. To Tal's left, a smaller ugdah consisting almost exclusively of reservists under General Avraham Yoffe would cross over ground that the Egyptians had long considered impassable north of Abu Agheila, with the mission of destroying Egyptian armor riding to the rescue of the 7th Division at El Arish. Finally, General Sharon's ugdah in the south had the difficult task of blasting through the principal fortified Egyptian position at the Abu Agheila-Um Katef crossroads. Once those objectives had been achieved, all three ugdot would drive forward relentlessly, heading for the Mitla and Jiddi Passes, the only two routes out of the Sinai for the defeated Egyptian forces.[32]

The Egyptian order of battle in the Sinai was, once again, formidable. It included seven divisions. Even granting that one of them, the 20th Palestinian, was tied to the positional defense of the Gaza Strip, that still left six maneuver divisions facing just three Israeli divisions. The front line consisted of 7th Infantry Division at Rafah with 2nd Infantry Division up on its right, manning the Um Katef-Abu Agheila complex. Behind them was a second line: 3rd Infantry Division between El Arish and Jebel Libni and, to its right, 6th Infantry Division, from Kuntilla to Nakhl. Finally, two armored divisions stood ready to counterattack: the 4th Armored Division around Bir Gifgafa, and the "Shazly Force," named for its commander, the future Chief of Staff of the Egyptian army, deployed between the 3rd and 6th Infantry Divisions. It was an utterly sound deployment of "shield and sword": once the Israelis had gotten themselves mired in the fortifications of the forward divisions, the armor could be sent in for the killing blow.[33]

But that would be true only if the Egyptian army were ready to fight. Once again, as in 1956, Israeli success was swift and complete. Although an hour-by-hour, battalion-by-battalion account would describe some hard fighting here and there, the three Israeli divisions had broken through everywhere by the second day. In the north, Tal's *ugdah* overran Rafah, combining a frontal assault by tanks of the 7th Armored Brigade (Colonel Shmuel Gonen), with a turning movement by a mixed force of Patton tanks and paratroopers mounted on half-tracks. Hitting an entire reinforced infantry division in entrenched positions, even with the benefit of surprise, Tal had to chew his way through. By the end of the first day, he had made little progress. Nevertheless, he was able to call on the IAF for devastating levels of ground support, a decisive element in all three Israeli divisional areas. Once again, Tal's division operated on all levels with a very light command touch. One of his staff officers testified that "It is hard to find even one commander in Tal's *ugdah* who operated according to plan. Almost all the plans were foiled during the fighting, but all objectives were attained in full — and faster than expected."[34]

Things were different in the south. Sharon's *ugdah* had the most difficult task of all: breaking through the Abu Agheila/Um Katef defensive complex — the same one that had held up the Israeli infantry assault in 1956. Here, Sharon planned and executed a complex and tightly choreographed assault, the only way to overcome a position of this strength, he felt. His goal, he said, was "to attack the entire depth of the Egyptian position simultaneously." He began by inserting a small force of paratroopers, under Danny Mat, a few miles to the north of the Egyptian trenches; they crossed the sand dunes and in a deadly midnight attack silenced the Egyptian artillery. Simultaneously, a massed bombardment by Israeli batteries — a true rarity in these wars — opened up on the

Egyptian trenches, followed immediately by an infantry assault. Working their way into the three lines of trenches, they carried colored lights so that their own artillery could employ a creeping barrage to lead them forward. Finally, once the northern sector of trenches had fallen, sappers moved in to clear a path through the mines in front of the trench system. A battalion of Sherman tanks now crashed through the outer perimeter, engaging the Egyptian armor within the position. The latter defended themselves ably enough, but then met destruction as another battalion of Israeli Centurions moved in from the rear (that is, the west). Although the IDF was nonpareil in mobile operations, Sharon's assault on Um Katef proved that its hastily assembled citizen soldiers could also carry out a magnificent set-piece battle. Above all, the assault depended on what Sharon called *tahboulah*, a shock to unnerve the defenders:

> It was a complex plan. But the elements that went into it were ones that I had been developing and teaching for many years, starting back in 1953 with the paratroopers — the idea of close combat, nightfighting, surprise paratroop assault, attack from the rear, attack on a narrow front, meticulous planning, the concept of the "tahboulah," the relationship between headquarters and field command. This would be the first time I commanded a division in battle. But all the ideas had matured already; there was nothing new in them. It was simply a matter of putting all the elements together and making them work.[35]

Within hours, Sharon had taken the crucial Abu Agheila-Um Katef complex and shattered the defending Egyptian 2nd Infantry Division, at a cost of just 40 killed and 140 wounded. The path to Sinai was open.

Between them, Yoffe's *ugdah* struggled as much against the terrain as against the Egyptians. Crossing a series of soft sand ridges, one of his brigades, under Colonel Issachar "Yiska" Shadmi, managed to get through, drive off an Egyptian National Guard company reinforced with antitank guns, and take up an ambush position just south of Bir Lahfan. Here, as day one ended, a single battalion of Israeli tanks faced the better part of two Egyptian armored brigades. The Egyptians came up in column, with their running lights on, since it was impossible for Israeli tanks to be at Bir Lahfan. Yiska allowed them to come within range and then ordered his lead platoon to open fire, one round apiece. Each round destroyed its target. A brief exchange of fire destroyed four more T-55s, at the expense of one Israeli Centurion. Thus chastened, the Egyptians halted, and there the two forces sat for the first night. The next morning, the Egyptians made the acquaintance of the IAF, which destroyed four tanks, and numerous personnel carriers and trucks. In the course of the morning, the battalion continued to kill Egyptian tanks with accurate long-range fire. The arrival of another battalion from the south, where it had been assisting Sharon's struggle for Abu Agheila, delivered the final blow, slamming into the Egyptians from the flank. Yiska's brigade had shattered the main fighting strength of the Egyptian 4th Armored Division. It is worth noting that Yoffe's *ugdah* consisted almost exclusively of reservists. His brigade commander, Yiska, was a hotel manager a few short days before, and Yoffe himself ran Israel's Nature Conservancy.[36]

Having broken through everywhere, Israeli tanks now set out for another high-speed drive across the Sinai. The Egyptians were caught up in the headlong charge of an elite armored formation in full stride and were simply overwhelmed, hit frontally, from the flanks, and continually pounded from the air. Shadmi's brigade reached the Mitla and Jiddi passes on June 7 after a great lunge across the desert that saw tank after tank run out of fuel. A token force of just nine tanks reached the objective, with four of them having to be towed. But they, along with a small force of infantry and a few mortars, were enough to hold the pass against the first columns of Egyptian vehicles desperately trying to get out of Sinai. The cream of the Egyptian army was now trapped.

There were moments of confusion, to be sure, but by now they no longer mattered. One of them was a brief armored clash between columns from Yoffe's and Sharon's *ugdot*. Yoffe's tanks came on in a rush, firing as they moved, and Sharon was unable to raise them by radio. He had to send his operations officer, Yitzhak Ben-Ari, toward the attacking tanks in a jeep to let them know their mistake — which must have been quite a ride. At Nakhl, Sharon heard that the Egyptian 6th Infantry Division was approaching, being pursued from Kuntilla by an Israeli brigade that had been screening the Negev border. Employing a tank brigade, a reinforced battalion of half-tracks, and the divisional reconnaissance unit, he laid a trap for the fleeing enemy force:

> But just as the battle was joined, my command half-track with all the communications equipment in it broke down. We quickly cabled it behind one of the tanks, and I had the unique experience of being towed into battle. Between the tank brigade in front, the half-tracks on the flank, and the pursuing Israeli force behind, the Egyptian 6th Division entered a terrible killing field. The scene in front of Nakhl was like a valley of death. For miles the desert was covered by ruined tanks and burned-out armored personnel carriers. Bodies littered the

ground, and here and there across the scene groups of Egyptians were standing with their hands on their heads. It wasn't until evening that the destruction came to an end. By then the 6th Division had ceased to exist.[37]

One of the biggest Israeli problems was how to keep up the incredible momentum on roads choked with fleeing Egyptian units. The improvised solution was simply to stay on the roads and advance along with the retreating forces. Many times during this campaign, IDF and Egyptian units were intermingled on the same road, heading west together.[38]

All that remained was the "battle of the passes," although that is an inaccurate name for what was a slaughter of Egypt's mechanized army. Pushed back to the passes and realizing its way home was blocked, what was left of it collapsed. The scene at the passes — Mitla to the south and Jiddi to the north — was incredible. Individual tanks tried to run the gauntlet of Israeli armor at the passes. The carnage in men and vehicles was terrible. Hundreds of burning vehicles blocked the road; piles of twisted wreckage mounted up on both sides of it, pushed off the road by the next tank willing to try for home. This was warfare much as the armor prophets had imagined it in the 1920s. What had been an impressive armored force just a few days ago had disintegrated into a disorganized mob. Egyptian tank losses in this short war topped eight hundred, a great number of them abandoned in working condition.[39]

Evaluating the Six Day War is more complex than it first appears. On the one hand, the IDF had won one of the most stunning victories in military history. Outnumbered against the Egyptians alone, it had shredded them in less than a week of high-intensity combat and then had reserves of strength and energy to deal punishing blows to Jordan and Syria as well. It did so not with superior weaponry — virtually every source is clear on that point. Israeli commanders carried out many operations in this war on a logistical shoestring. Sharon describes with some amusement the ice cream wagons, hot dog vans, milk trucks, and civilian buses that he used to ferry much of his force out to Abu Agheila in the opening hours.[40] Rather, the IDF succeeded because of "soft factors": superior training, morale, and initiative.

Once again, although the victory had been total, it is important to keep in mind the low military qualities of the opposition. The IDF caught the Egyptians flat-footed in 1956 and did so even more dramatically in 1967. This, of course, begs the question of why an army with so much modern equipment — not to mention a horde of Soviet advisers — was constantly being caught flat-footed. There was a regrettable tendency all over the

Arab world to attribute the defeat to Jewish treachery, or to intervention by the great powers — the United States and Great Britain — on Israel's behalf. U.S. warplanes, flying from carriers in the eastern Mediterranean, were said to have assisted Israel in the opening air strikes. This is patently untrue, but hundreds of articles in the Arab press in the months after the war "substantiated" such allegations.[41] Other Arab scholars, more promisingly, pointed to a "technological and scientific gap" between Arab and Israeli societies that left the Egyptian army unable to assimilate its masses of new equipment and matériel.[42] For their part, many Israelis were willing to argue that there was a "civilization gap" in the Mideast and that they would always be able to inflict punishing defeats on their less-advanced, or even primitive, neighbors.[43]

Yehoshafat Harkabi, former head of Israeli military intelligence and later a scholar of some repute, offers a sociological explanation. "The weakness of the social links which join Arab to Arab," he argues, left the Egyptian army without the cohesion necessary on the modern battlefield. Although he cautions against generalizing on the always tricky issue of national character, "in discussing social groups and peoples, there is no escape from assigning a collective personality to the group under discussion." Although Israeli soldiers fought as a "brotherhood of warriors," risking danger to self to advance the goals of the unit to which they belonged, the Egyptian soldier fought alone. It was a cyclical process. In the Sinai, Egyptian officers abandoned their men, whom they rarely knew by name and toward whom they felt no real responsibility. Egyptian soldiers broke at the first sign of trouble, out of a feeling that their officers were preparing to abandon them to their fate anyway. Neither felt the bonds of the unit, or the team, in any real sense.

Harkabi also sees the tendency of the Arab governments to broadcast the most fantastic lies during the war as one more manifestation of the lack of any true social contract in the Arab world.

> Throughout the Six-Day War the most amazing false announcements were issued. For example, if official Arab claims of Israeli air losses had been true, every plane in the Israeli Air Force would have been shot down — not once, but several times. Apparently Arab pilots and anti-aircraft gunners gave false reports of their exploits, to which their boastful commanders added their exaggerated accounts.

Since this penchant toward falsehood, this "tendency to lie," was deep rooted, he argued, it would not be easy to change. It was certainly resistant to orders from above. One cannot, Harkabi pointed out, simply publish an edict, "As from tomorrow, no more lies!"[44]

As the world would soon see, these explanations do not really explain much at all. Conspiracy theories out of the Arab press notwithstanding, U.S. planes had not bombed Egyptian air bases. The "scientific and technological gap," while at least being a serious attempt to discuss the Arab defeat, did not prevent the North Vietnamese from doing pretty well against their French and U.S. adversaries, to give just one example. The sociological explanation, blaming deep-rooted problems of social integration, language, and culture in the Arab world, might have seemed convincing in the wake of the 1967 war. Just six years later, it would ring quite hollow.

In the end, the triumphs of 1956 and 1967 are part of an old, old story. On one side, the IDF had combined guile and surprise, drive and aggression, ability to formulate plans in advance and then to improvise better ones on the battlefield, into a package of mobile warfare unmatched since the Wehrmacht's performance in the early years of World War II. It maneuvered when it could, crashed through in bloody assault when it had to, and never lost sight of the objective: the passes at the western edge of the Sinai. When the IDF is operating under an irresistible air umbrella, it is hard to imagine many armies in the world defeating it in the Sinai, whatever the state of their social contract. The Egyptians joined a long list of other armies in other times and places: the Russians at Tannenberg in 1914, the French in 1940, the U.S. 8th Army on the Chongchon River in 1950: outmaneuvered, outfought, and routed.

The Yom Kippur/Ramadan War

Analysts usually portray the period between 1967 and 1973 as one in which the IDF took its first doctrinal wrong turn. As the IDF performed its customary battle postmortem, it was clear that it owed its improbable victory in 1967, above all, to the combination of tank and aircraft. The tanks had won the war on the ground, and the IAF played the air superiority and interdiction roles nearly to perfection. This led, most observers agree, to a dangerous deemphasis on infantry training. In fact, that emphasis predates 1967 by a good while. As early as 1960, no less an authority than Sir Basil Liddell Hart visited Israel and warned against the dangers of complacency in general and overreliance on tanks and aircraft alone, to the detriment of the foot soldier.[45]

A certain amount of self-satisfaction was probably bound to arise in the IDF, given the course of the 1956 and 1967 wars. The army had developed its doctrine against weak and poorly trained enemies, even if they were often lavishly equipped with Soviet equipment. The blitzkrieg across the Sinai in 1956 saw much more maneuver than actual fighting, as Egyptian forces threw up their hands in surrender. The same can be said for the Six Day War. Repeatedly, unsupported charges by tanks were enough to break the will of even strongly fortified Egyptian units. In some areas, to be sure (the storming of the Golan Heights, for example, or Sharon's battle for Um Katef), the IDF showed a tremendous amount of skill at combined arms, with tanks, mechanized infantry, and paratroopers all working together. Nevertheless, the IDF had evolved into a mech-heavy force that relied almost exclusively on its armor.

Once again, although the Six Day War was over, there was no peace between Israel and its Arab neighbors. A "war of attrition" ensued from 1969 to 1970, with cross-canal raids on both sides, sometimes quite deep. In October 1968, Israeli heliborne forces launched a raid on the Nag Hamadi power station, far into upper Egypt and hundreds of miles away from the canal. Egyptian artillery regularly bombarded Israeli supply columns servicing front-line troops on the canal. The IDF responded by building a series of fixed fortifications along the canal, the Bar Lev line (named for IDF Chief of Staff Chaim Bar Lev). The Soviet Union soon replaced Egypt's lost weaponry — its own prestige was on the line, after all — and sent a great deal of advanced new equipment as well, especially in the crucial area of air defense. Israeli pilots soon learned to avoid areas covered by Egypt's surface-to-air missile (SAM) sites.[46]

It was clear soon after June 1967 that another great war in the region was inevitable. Arabs had taken to referring to the 1967 war as the "Third Round," not decisive in any real sense. Planning for the "Fourth Round" began almost immediately. It came in 1973, the "Yom Kippur War" to the Israelis and the "Ramadan War" to the Arabs. It featured some of history's great armored engagements — at the so-called "Chinese Farm" during Israel's counterattack against the Egyptian bridgehead in the Sinai Peninsula, and in the Golan Heights against Syria, where outnumbered Israeli tank crews stopped an enormous Syrian tank assault dead in its tracks.[47]

In Egypt, the Chief of Staff, General Saad El Shazly, began formulating plans for a cross-canal offensive into Sinai as early as 1971. No military romantic, he based his plans for Operation The High Minarets on a sober estimate of his own force's strengths and weaknesses. Although every Egyptian dreamed of landing a blow deep into the Sinai, engaging and destroying Israel's main armored forces there, he knew that such a bold stroke was not possible at that time. Egypt's air force, despite the influx of new equipment from the Soviet Union, was not ready to take on the IAF. "Twice," he wrote, "it had been destroyed on the ground."[48] Without control of the air, the Egyptian army could not compete on anything like even terms with the Israelis. Thus, the operation he envisioned called for a crossing of the Suez Canal on a broad front, followed by a limited advance into Sinai. With Egyptian SAMs rushed right up to the water's edge, they would be able to provide an umbrella under which the army could consolidate its bridgeheads. Then, the land forces across the Suez would wait for the inevitable Israeli armored counterattack. Armed with antitank guns, rockets, and new generation antitank guided missiles (ATGMs), Egyptian infantry would do what it had always done fairly well: defend itself in fixed positions. The Egyptians knew the IDF's weak point: an extremely low tolerance for casualties. The Suez operation would thus force the Israelis with two unacceptable choices: leave the Egyptian army in the Sinai, and thus shatter their myth of invincibility, or attack a carefully prepared and strongly defended position and take heavy losses. Under pressure from the Egyptian defense minister, General Ahmed Ismail Ali, Shazly also did preliminary work on an advance from the bridgeheads toward the Mitla and Jiddi passes (Operation 41, later renamed Operation Granite Two), but he considered such an operation to be too risky, as it would take his forces out of SAM range. In the end, they reached compromise language in the operational orders: "After an operational pause, we will develop our attack to the passes."[49] The ambiguity on this point would come back to haunt the Egyptians.

In one dramatic way, the 1973 war broke the pattern of its predecessors. This time, it was the Arabs who struck first and who achieved near-total surprise. It was not until the morning of October 6 that the Israeli intelligence services reported to the government that the Arab states were going to launch a war that very afternoon. Israel's carefully laid and thoroughly rehearsed plans to call up the reservists simply fell apart. In particular, there was no time to assemble the regular brigades. Instead, the IDF formed temporary units of whatever manpower was available and sent them off to the front. The joint Egyptian-Syrian offensive, now code-named Operation Badr, caught the Israelis nearly as flat-footed as the Arabs had been in previous wars — a unique experience for the IDF and thus a good test of its vaunted capability to improvise.

In Sinai, the Egyptians threw two whole armies across the Suez Canal on the afternoon of October 6, destroying the Bar Lev line and establishing formidable bridgeheads on the eastern side. The 456 men and seven tanks of the line fought bravely but were no match for their attackers. Within five hours, five reinforced infantry divisions were across the canal; joining them by midnight were eight hundred tanks. Egyptian 2nd Army held a bridgehead from Port Fuad to Matzmed. To its right (south), 3rd Army held one between Botzer and Nissan. In keeping with the original conception, both bridgeheads were incredibly shallow, just six to nine miles, sheltering under the Egyptian SAM umbrella on the west bank. The crossing was a well-managed operation indeed, as fine as any modern army has ever carried out. The engineering aspects alone were formidable, with assault teams having to blast through the huge Israeli sand barrier on the far side of the canal with specially designed water cannon. Engineers also built eight heavy bridges and four light bridges, and assembled some thirty-one ferries on the first day alone.

The initial Israeli response nearly transformed this admittedly serious setback into a disaster. Success in previous wars had bred in the IDF a faith in the tank that recalls that of Great Britain before World War II (though, it should be said, without the obstinacy that would continue to characterize the British *during* the war). Thus, the IDF's first move was to launch an immediate series of counterattacks with their tank units as soon as they arrived. Leading the way was General Avraham Mendler's three-brigade tank division. This sort of thing had worked before, and most Israeli tank commanders seemed confident that it would work again. But much had changed since 1967, especially in the way of antitank defenses. Egyptian infantry was equipped with a variety of manportable antitank weaponry, such as the Soviet-made RPG-7, a simple handheld rocket launcher, and the "Sagger" wire-guided missile. These weapons proved capable of penetrating Israel's M-48s and Centurions, and the first few days of combat saw catastrophic Israeli tank losses in Sinai, several hundred at least.

The IDF learned a hard lesson that day, a very old one: the value of combined arms. The attacks had gone in without adequate air coverage, as Soviet-supplied SAMs and air defense guns like the ZSU-23-4 and the ZSU-57-2 formed a sort of "Maginot line in the sky," keeping the Israeli air force well away from the action.[50] Likewise, the attacks had proceeded with almost no infantry support, and heavy fire from Egyptian missiles had wreaked havoc on Israeli tanks. Although reports at the time credited much of the damage to the RPG-7, the Sagger was the true success story of this phase of the fighting: a sophisticated weapon, quite simple to operate and effective at well over a kilometer. The best way to neutralize these newfangled man-portable antitank systems, ironically, would have been to employ old-fashioned tactics, with tanks and infantry cooperating closely in the advance. But this was just the sort of traditional thinking that had fallen by the wayside in the IDF since the easy victory of 1967. By October 7, Mendler's division had only about ninety tanks still operational.[51] The first wave of Israeli attacks had ground to a halt.

There is some controversy today about Egyptian intentions in the Sinai. As we have seen, the original plan for Badr was a limited offensive into Sinai. Arab historians writing since the war agree on that point. However, some in the Egyptian high command, the defense minister General Ismail, for example, were interested in a further advance — at least to the passes, and perhaps from there into central Sinai. It appears that Egyptian probes were going forward as early as October 8 but met determined Israeli resistance. Having advanced only ten miles, the Egyptians now dug in and waited for another round of Israeli counterattacks. Elements of two more Israeli armored divisions arrived in Sinai, led by General Avraham (Bren) Adan and General Sharon, and for all intents and purposes the crisis in this sector had passed.

The situation on the Syrian front was at first even more desperate. On the Golan Heights, the Syrians launched the kind of offensive taught by their Soviet advisers: great waves of tanks in three echelons lumbering forward on a very narrow front, about forty miles wide. In this constricted space, the Syrians deployed no less than three complete mechanized divisions (from north to south, 7th, 9th, and 6th), with one tank and two mechanized brigades each, in the first echelon; two tank divisions (the 3rd and the 1st) in the second echelon; and two tank and two mechanized brigades in the third. Altogether, about 1,600 Syrian tanks took part in the assault, supported by 1,000 guns. Israeli forces on this front included a grand total of 177 tanks of the 7th Armored Brigade in the north; 77 tanks of the 188th Brigade in the south; and about 60 artillery pieces. Overall, the IDF commander in Golan, General Rafael (Raful) Eytan, was outnumbered by at least six to one in armor. In given breakthrough sectors, however, the Syrian ratio was even higher.[52]

On the northern edge of the Golan, the superior gunnery of the IDF's 7th Armored Brigade tore great holes in the ranks of the attacking Syrian phalanx. By nightfall of October 6, Syrian tank losses in its sector had topped three hundred. In the south, the balance of forces was much more lopsided, with the Barak Brigade facing an assault by at least 450 Syrian tanks, with RPG-7 teams and heavy artillery support. Israeli tank crews had to call on every ounce of their superiority in training and initiative, getting around the flanks of their adversary, laying traps, springing ambushes, delaying the Syrian advance, retiring to the rear for refueling and resupply, and then motoring straight back into combat. But the Barak Brigade was gradually ground down by Syrian numbers and by October 7 was down to some fifteen tanks. All three of its senior commanders were dead.

Saving the day on the Golan front was the Israeli air force, diverted north from Sinai to meet the crisis. With fighter-bombers clearing a path, flying in the teeth of heavy antiaircraft and missile fire, elements of two hastily deployed armored divisions entered the fray, halting the Syrians after an advance of six miles. By the evening of October 7, IDF defenses in the Golan had increased to two divisions: Raful's in the northern sector, and a division under reserve officer Dan Laner to his right. By the early morning of October 8, a third Israeli division began to arrive, and here too the crisis was over. Israeli tanks now readied themselves for the counterattack, to prove in the words of General Moshe Dayan that "the road from Damascus to Tel-Aviv also runs from Tel-Aviv to Damascus."[53] Nevertheless, this had not been a typical battle for the IDF. According to one IDF commander, it had not been "our sort of war." Rather than a lightning victory of maneuver, this had been a grinding battle of attrition. Martin van Creveld characterized it as "a *Materialschlacht* on a huge scale that left both sides bruised and bleeding."[54]

Although the IDF had sustained serious losses in the first two days of fighting — at least three hundred tanks — the situation on both fronts was stabilized. It was now time for the IDF, remaining true to its successful tradition, to seize the initiative. Once again, however, the Israelis were forced to realize that they were facing a skilled and tenacious enemy in the Sinai. A new round of IDF counterattacks between October 8 and 10, spearheaded by the armored divisions of Adan and Sharon, failed completely. There were heavy losses, with one brigade, the 190th under General Nathan "Natke" Nir, almost completely destroyed in the fighting, and one of his forward battalion commanders, Lieutenant Colonel Assaf Yagouri, actually taken prisoner. Yagouri's battalion, with the brigade commander accompanying, had driven to within 1,500 yards of the canal.

> They suddenly found themselves almost on top of enemy trenches from which infantry opened fire on them with machine guns and anti-tank RPGs. At the same time, scores of enemy tanks opened fire from the ramparts and barriers on both sides of the canal, and Sagger missiles were also directed at them. Tanks were hit one after another and crewmen could be seen jumping out of the burning vehicles. Natke ordered a retreat, but within minutes fourteen tanks were hit.[55]

The sources indicate little disagreement between the adversaries on this round of engagements. In the words of Israeli Chaim Herzog, "Israel armor attacking with the *élan* of cavalry charges, without infantry support, and with inadequate artillery support, made no sense whatsoever in the face of masses of anti-tank weapons which the Egyptians had concentrated, and which were by now known to all the Israeli commanders."[56] His description echoes closely that of Egyptian General Shazly, who wrote in his diary on October 9:

> The enemy has persisted in throwing away the lives of their tank crews. They have assaulted in "penny packet" groupings and their sole tactic remains the cavalry charge. In the latest manifestation, two brigades have driven against the 16th Division. Once again, the attack has been stopped with heavy losses. In the past two days the enemy has lost another 260 tanks. Our strategy always has been to force the enemy to fight on our terms; but we never expected them to cooperate.[57]

In fact, IDF operational command, in the hands of the G.O.C. for the southern front, Shmuel Gonen, was completely out of touch with conditions at the front. At first ordering Adan to undertake a limited offensive in the north to seize the initiative, he then changed his mind on the eve of battle. He consulted neither his divisional commanders nor General David "Dado" Elazar, the IDF Chief of Staff, of his change. Almost at the last second, Adan received orders that spoke of a breakthrough to the canal, followed by a crossing — both of which seemed like fantasies to the hard-pressed divisional commander. During the battle itself, Gonen issued a constantly changing set of operational orders, uncovering Adan's left flank by ordering Sharon far to the south, and then calling on both divisions to "roll up" the Egyptian bridgehead, when neither one had even made a dent in it. Adan's bitter postwar assessment was that "it was my impression that Gonen behaved in this matter as if we were conducting some kind of war game, an exercise involving no troops — neither ours nor the enemy's — and in which there was no battlefield reality."[58]

Once again, it seemed that momentum had shifted to the Egyptians. Since the crossing, they had sat still, the "operational pause," mentioned in the plans for Operation Badr. After internal debate, the Egyptian command finally decided to push inland. It came on October 13, with a series of probing attacks against Israeli positions, and was followed by a full-scale assault the next day by some one thousand tanks. Egypt employed virtually its entire armored reserve: the 21st Armored Division, in reserve behind 2nd Army, and the 4th Armored Division, in reserve be-hind the 3rd Army. But Israeli reinforcements had arrived, bringing up Israeli tank strength to seven hundred. They were rested and fully ready for the assault. By now, Israel was the beneficiary of U.S. aid — TOW missiles, to be exact (for *t*ube-launched, *o*ptically tracked, *w*ire-guided), a two-man weapon that would prove devastatingly effective.[59] Moreover, the Egyptians were advancing beyond the range of their SAM network, leaving them vulnerable to Israeli air power. The Egyptians came on, and came on again, only to be slaughtered by the combined effect of Israeli tank fire, TOW missiles, and air attack. By the end of the day on October 14, the offensive power of the Egyptian forces was gone; tank casualties amounted to at least 50 percent; and the commander of 2nd Army, General Saad Mamoun, was in bed following a breakdown. Chief of Staff Shazly, who argued strenuously against launching the attacks but had to bow before the will of General Ismail and President Anwar Sadat, called it "our most calamitous day."[60]

The IDF was winning a similar victory in the north. Here, skillful as-saults by Israeli armor on October 11 and 13 mauled not only the Syrians, but also Iraqi and Jordanian units that had entered the fighting. The ambush of an Iraqi tank brigade, in particular, was a masterpiece, destroy-ing eighty Iraqi tanks with no Israeli losses. By October 13, the IDF was well over the 1967 cease-fire line and actually within long artillery range of the outskirts of Damascus. At this point, political exigencies forced the Israelis to halt their advance. A march on Damascus almost certainly would have brought Soviet intervention.

All that remained was to break the will of the Egyptians in the Sinai. To do this, it was necessary to restore mobility to the front. The IDF had now tried two frontal assaults on the dug-in Egyptians, and no one showed much enthusiasm for a third. The solution to the problem was not the tank. The IDF had to think outside the "armor box" in which it had lived since 1967. The answer it came up with was a surprise cross-ing of the canal at Deversoir, just north of the Great Bitter Lake, on the night of October 15–16. Leading the way were elements of a paratroop brigade, crossing on rubber rafts, and a few light amphibious vehicles (the *Gilowas*). They formed a tentative bridgehead on the west bank. But it was no easy matter to reinforce it. Israeli engineers had already built an 80-ton, 190-yard-long bridge before the war, and now they began the laborious and dangerous task of wheeling it into place.

The Suez crossing was Ariel Sharon's finest hour. In the years after the 1967 war, Sharon served as the chief of the Southern Command. Always outspoken, he objected bitterly to Bar Lev's policy of building a fortified line along the Suez Canal. "Committing ourselves to a static defense" was a mistake, he believed. "We would be making fixed targets of ourselves three hundred yards from the Egyptian lines. Our positions and movements would be under constant surveillance, our procedures would become common knowledge." Sharon believed that in the event of a renewed war, the IDF had to be ready to cross the canal into Africa, to take the war into Egypt as soon as possible. In the last few months before his scheduled retirement in 1973, he actually prepared three crossing sites: at Kantara in the north, Ismailia in the center, and at Deversoir in the south. At Deversoir, the thickness of the Israeli barrier wall posed a problem, so Sharon changed the structure of the wall at one particular spot. Its outward appearance remained the same, but it would be much easier to blast through. Facing the problem of how to remember the exact spot, Sharon spotted some piles of red brick in the vicinity and built a "yard" near the spot, with a hardened floor almost a thousand yards long. A quick glance would reveal a perhaps-unfinished Israeli construction project. But in a crossing battle, it would serve as a "protected staging area for troops, tanks, and other bridging equipment."[61] The IDF also started work on a great preconstructed steel rolling bridge, which would have to be dragged into place before any crossing.

Sharon reacted to the Egyptian attack in 1973 with immediate and loud calls for a crossing operation. He had always been a difficult subordinate, but never so difficult as now. Branded a madman by some in those first few desperate days, when the very survival of Israel seemed at stake, he persisted, constantly reassuring the chief of Southern Command, Shmuel Gonen, that "the Egyptians are not heading for Tel-Aviv. That's beyond them." Concentration of force was the key, he told Gonen, and the IDF could achieve it faster than the Egyptians. During one testy exchange, when Gonen had tired of his constant suggestions, Sharon told him, "You don't have to deal with me at all. Just deal with the Egyptians!"

The fighting on October 8, called by Sharon "the black day of the Israeli Defense Forces," made a deep impression on him. "We had sent in one of our renowned armored charges, and the Egyptians had not only stood up to it, they had destroyed it." On October 9, he gave orders to his three armored brigade commanders to conduct a holding operation. But he also ordered probes by his reconnaissance forces, which that evening managed to penetrate to the Lexicon Road, just a few hundred yards from the shore of the Great Bitter Lake. Sharon saw a great opportunity. His tanks had uncovered an "open seam" between the Egyptian 2nd and 3rd Armies — and the Egyptians had not even seemed to notice.

He contacted Gonen and asked for permission to begin preparations for a crossing. The reception was chilly, and he eventually had to hear through Gonen's deputy that the commander had rejected his plan. He spent the night trying to get through to General Israel Tal, the deputy commander in chief, who was "out." Again, he found himself presenting the plan to one of Tal's staff officers. He felt, he said, like "a voice crying in the wilderness."[62] The situation changed only on October 14, after the IDF had shattered the massive Egyptian armored attack in the Sinai. Bar Lev gave Sharon permission to cross the canal on the night of October 15–16. His division broke through the Egyptian lines, secured a corridor to the canal, and then established a crossing point at Deversoir. Rubber assault boats were brought forward to ferry commander Danny Mat's paratroop brigade to the west bank. By 1 A.M. on the morning of October 16, the first paratroopers were starting to cross the canal. They found the west bank nearly deserted, and radioed back the code word "Acapulco": success. Sharon's crossing had achieved total surprise. Soon joining the initial force was the rest of the paratroop brigade, reinforced by several armored personnel carriers and twenty-eight tanks. General Avraham Adan's armored division crossed over and launched a strike down the western shore of the Great Bitter Lake toward Suez City.

At this point, a new problem arose. Realizing what had happened in their rear, the Egyptians decided to contest the crossing site. On October 16, they launched a three-pronged counterattack: south from the position known as the Chinese Farm (actually a Japanese agricultural station in the Sinai), which stood just northeast of the roads leading to the canal; north from the 3rd Army bridgehead, with 25th Independent Armored Brigade driving up along the Great Bitter Lake; and from the west, with 116th Infantry Brigade attacking out of its reserve positions on the Egyptian side of the canal. The latter two formations were shot to pieces, but over the next few days, the largest tank battle since Kursk would take place in the vicinity of the Chinese Farm. But again, "tank battle" was what the IDF was all about. Losses were heavy on both sides, but far heavier on the Egyptian. Israeli tanks and infantry gradually forced the Egyptians back from their irrigation ditches and buildings, widening the path to the crossing site, and by October 18, Israeli engineers had completed two bridges over the canal.

The Egyptian attack at the Chinese Farm seriously upset Sharon's timetable, and it is tempting to speculate what might have happened if the Egyptian high command had not wasted two entire armored divisions in their hasty attacks of October 13–14. On October 16, the IDF high command refused to authorize any more troops across the canal while bitter fighting was raging in Sinai, although Sharon did order his engineers to assemble the assault rafts into a bridge over the canal. Meeting with Gonen, Bar Lev, Dayan, and Adan that day, Sharon was shocked to hear himself being upbraided by Bar Lev: "The distance between what you promised to do and what you have done is very great." It was only with difficulty, Sharon later wrote, that he restrained himself from smacking Bar Lev in the face. But the command had legitimate concerns. Sharon's bridgehead was tenuous, facing forces of unknown size on the western bank of the canal and dependent for supply on a single road, the Akavish. The paved Tirtur road was the only one along which the giant rolling bridge could pass — but running as it did through the Chinese Farm, it was still shut tight. Nevertheless, this improvised command meeting now "decided to what they should have done two days earlier."[63] Once a pontoon bridge was completed, the IDF would cross the canal in force. Sharon's division would hold the yard, secure the crossings, and then cross over and proceed north to Ismailia and west twenty-five to thirty kilometers toward Cairo. The divisions of Adan and Kalman Magen would cross, and then drive south into the rear of the Egyptian 3rd Army.

Three armored divisions were soon across the canal into Africa, with Adan and Magen rushing south to the Gulf of Suez and Sharon moving north toward Ismailia, all three overrunning and destroying SAM sites as they went, shooting up Egyptian facilities and transport, and generally wreaking as much havoc as they could. With a hole torn in the SAM umbrella, the IAF could now intervene in devastating direct support missions of the armor divisions. By October 22, the Suez-Cairo road had been cut and the entire 3rd Army encircled. Cut off from supply, with its water supply running low, pounded from the air by the IAF, it found its salvation only in an internationally brokered cease-fire.

It is a paradox that the war that represented the high point of Israeli military achievement, and particularly of Israeli tanks, led so many observers to depressing conclusions regarding the future of armor. In the immediate aftermath of the war, it was said that the day of the tank was finished, that the foot soldier with his RPG-7 or TOW missile had sealed its doom, that technology had finally provided a solution to the dominance of armor.[64] Certainly, Israeli tank losses in the first few days had been heavy, and the primary culprit had been the man-portable anti-tank devices. But any reasonable analysis (and perhaps that is always hard to come by so soon after the heat of battle) would have to say that Israeli armor had achieved its greatest successes of all in 1973. It had fought successfully on two fronts. In Sinai, after the first difficult days, it had stopped a greatly superior enemy and then broke through at its chosen

Schwerpunkt near the Chinese Farm, crossed the canal, and carried out a bold strategic penetration of the Egyptian interior. Equally impressive was the achievement in the Golan, which was nothing short of an epic: vastly outnumbered, and with hordes of Syrian tanks bearing down on them, the Israelis managed not only to stop the enemy's advance but to launch a devastating counterattack that, but for the international political situation, might well have ended with Israeli tanks entering Damascus. On both fronts, but especially in Golan, the Israelis "fought outnumbered and won." In the annals of armored combat, only the Germans in 1940 match the performance of Israeli armor in 1973.

One individual action sums up the fighting. General Adan's ambush and destruction of the Egyptian 25th Armored Brigade on October 17 was a classic of the type. The brigade was advancing northward toward Lakekan with the Great Bitter Lake on its left, part of the general counterattack toward the Israeli crossing point. At 12:30 P.M., a company of four Israeli tanks opened fire on the lead tanks of the Egyptian column. The Egyptians halted on the road and did not resume their advance until 2:45 P.M. Now an entire Israeli tank brigade, under General Nathan ("Natke") Nir, hidden in the hills to the east, went into action.

> They dashed forward on the Egyptians' flank and opened fire. Within minutes many Egyptian tanks were ablaze and Natke's tanks began rushing forward to narrow the range. In the midst of the confusion that rapidly developed among the Egyptians who began moving about every which way, a few tanks launched a hopeless attack toward Natke. Even though Natke's brigade was deployed in dominating positions on Grafit, and the Egyptians were exposed on lower flat terrain, there was some excitement among the men in Natke's tanks, who radioed: "They are charging us!"
>
> More and more fires appeared in the plain before us. The Egyptians, moving in an unsecured column, were caught on the killing ground in the worst possible situation. On one flank Israeli armor was operating against them from good positions, while on their other flank was the lake, and adjacent to it was a huge minefield that we had laid back during the War of Attrition. In front of them were Israeli tanks, and more tanks were moving to close off any possible escape route to their rear.

By 4:00 P.M. the 25th Brigade had been virtually annihilated. Israeli losses had been negligible. Natke radioed Adan, "I think we can cross off this brigade."[65]

Conclusions

The IDF has achieved a series of incredible victories since the birth of Israel in 1948. It owes some of its success to good equipment, some of it supplied by the United States, some of it home grown. Officers of the IDF bristle when it is suggested that all their victories have been "made in the U.S.A."[66] Israel itself has made numerous improvements to the tanks it has bought from abroad. Innovations over the years included larger and more accurate guns and fire control systems, better armor, and new engines designed to handle the stresses of Israel's desert environment. Such improvements have given Israel a battlefield edge against the Arabs' largely Soviet-produced inventory. Israel's own tank design, the Merkava (Chariot), has shown that Israeli tank designers have come into their own, and it showed its mettle in the fighting in Lebanon in 1982.[67] The same might be said of Israeli U.S.-produced aircraft — already the world's finest when they leave their American factories, then improved by the Israelis to better suit their conditions and demands. And once again, the IAF has its own domestically produced fighter, the Kfir.

Far more important than the material factor, however, has been Israeli morale. Israel knows that a single operational defeat would mean the end of its national existence. The IDF has some of the world's most highly motivated soldiers. Its training program is surpassed by none in its rigor. The annual swearing-in ceremony for cadets of the armored corps actually takes place on the mountaintop of Masada (Metzada), site of the Jewish rebels' last stand against the Romans in 70 A.D. This and similar rituals succeed in inculcating an esprit de corps into these black-bereted tank crews that has saved Israel from extinction in the war for independence and again in 1973 and that was the basis for stunning victories in both 1956 and 1967. One Israeli officer, speaking in 1967, declared that if the Egyptians ever did defeat the IDF and drove into Israel itself, "this would have been a second Masada. When the Egyptians got here they would have found no one alive. I would have killed my wife and daughter rather than let them fall into their hands. And I don't know anyone who wouldn't have done the same."[68] It is a feeling deeply rooted in Jewish and Israeli history, and no other country can possibly duplicate it — or should want to.

It is a truism to observe that, after three of the greatest operational victories of all time, Israel still finds no peace. The subsequent history of Israel since the 1973 war, pundits argue, has demonstrated the limits of operational prowess. Israel can fight a conventional war against its neighbors whenever it wishes, crush their land and air forces, and win decisive victories, as it did against the completely outclassed Syrians in southern Lebanon in 1982. Such triumphs, however, seem to many to be increasingly meaningless in terms of Israeli national security. In a sense, the IDF is back where it started, before the great Arab invasion of May 1948, fighting Palestinian rebels. The Haganah found that phase of the war much more difficult than the later conventional struggle, and the IDF seems to be reliving that experience. To which we should add one last observation: nothing Israel faces today, the *intifada* and suicide bombings and international opprobrium notwithstanding, is as terrible as a defeat in a conventional war would have been.

Finally, what of the Arab armies? Unable to impose their will on the new state of Israel in 1948, their armies flicked away almost contemptuously by the IDF in 1956 and 1967, the Arab states had at last joined the ranks of the world's competent military forces in 1973. The plan for war was sound, based firmly on the Egyptian soldier's strengths and weaknesses. A simultaneous crossing of the Suez Canal into the face of an Israeli fortified line by two complete armies is nothing to underestimate. Once over the canal, they took the best that the initial Israeli armored counterattacks could deal out, and shattered them. They did not maneuver, and in fact the plan was based on the notion that they could not maneuver on equal terms with the IDF.

Even after their enemy had crossed the Suez Canal into their rear, Egyptian forces on both sides of the canal kept up their fighting spirit. In Golan, Syrian tank crews may have displayed little tactical finesse as they came on in their rigid version of Soviet operational art, but no one can ever fault their courage or determination. Neither side maneuvered on this front. In the end, the Syrian tanks wound up in a shooting match with some of the best shots in the world — and lost. Yes, both the Egyptians and Syrians were outmaneuvered and outfought by the end. But they were never truly routed. In the process, they put to rest dubious notions of some sort of flaw in the "Arab national character" or social contract that prevented them from fighting modern war.

Operational Success and Failure:
The Indo-Pakistani War of
1971 and the Iran-Iraq War

The great powers of the world have not had a monopoly on operational excellence in the twentieth century. In the First Balkan War of 1912, the Bulgarian army carried out a campaign in Thrace against the Turks that still stands as a model of operational planning and execution, even if it did fall short of its ultimate goal, Constantinople. In a series of wars since 1945, the tiny Israeli Defense Force succeeded again and again against a coalition of armies many times its own size. The North Vietnamese army, during the long years of conflict with the French and Americans, proved to be a thoroughly professional outfit, led by as fine an operational mind as the century had to offer, General Vo Nyugen Giap. Indeed, as in so many other fields, we might say that the twentieth century has witnessed the "globalization" of operational military excellence.

The implications for those interested in the operational art, professional soldiers and scholar alike, are clear. One must "get out more," go beyond reading the histories and professional journals of one's own country or military establishment. *Military Review*, *Parameters*, and the *Journal of Military History* might be a solid "trinity" for American readers, for example, but perhaps a perusal of the foreign literature is in order: the *Army Doctrine and Training Bulletin (Le Bulletin de Doctrine et d'Instruction de l'Armée de Terre)* of Canada, the *Journal of the United Service Institution of India*, or Pakistan's *Defence Journal*, to give just three English-language examples. There, as in the American journals, one will find trained professionals at work, incisive minds debating weighty issues of doctrine, armament, and strategy. The same problems that trouble western officers — the role of information, fighting deep, the correct employment of armor in a firepower-intensive battle, problems of command and control under modern conditions — are currently grist for the mill of their colleagues in dozens of foreign nations.[1] Encountering the military thought of different cultures on these and other questions can be an instructive experience.

The Indo-Pakistani War of 1971: Origins and Planning

A sterling example of operational excellence was the Indian army's decisive victory in 1971 over Pakistan.[2] It was a blitzkrieg, integrated into South Asian conditions, that totally altered the balance of power in the subcontinent and dismembered India's principal rival, Pakistan. Its origins are to be found in the curious dual nature of the Pakistani state, in which sources of power, political influence, and social advancement were largely concentrated in the western wing, while the population of East Pakistan increasingly came to see themselves as second-class citizens, despite the fact that they were a majority of the total Pakistani population. A political movement, the Awami League, arose in the late 1960s, under the leadership of Sheikh Mujibur Rahman. In March 1971, revolt broke out in East Pakistan. Units of the Pakistani army that were heavily Bengali in their ethnic makeup, five complete battalions of the East Bengal Regiment to be specific, joined the uprising, and soon there was a full-fledged civil war in the eastern wing. The response of the Pakistani government, under its dictator Yahya Khan, was a ruthless military crackdown. Two divisions from the west, the 9th and 16th Infantry Divisions, were airlifted by civilian jetliners into East Pakistan, joining the single reinforced division already there, the 14th.[3] Troops secured the capital, Dacca, and then fanned out into the provinces, subduing rebel forces, restoring government authority, and also brutalizing the civilian population. "Operation Searchlight" succeeded in crushing the revolt, but it also drove literally millions of refugees, perhaps as many as ten million, over the border into India.[4]

Having already fought two wars against Pakistan, India was not blind to the opportunities offered by the breakdown of civil order in East Pakistan. The arrival of the refugees, the intolerable burden placed on India in providing for them, the atrocities of the Pakistani army in East Pakistan — these became staples of the reportage in the Indian media. The Indian government of Indira Gandhi carried on a vigorous debate between the hawks, who wanted to use the crisis to dismember Pakistan now, and those who pointed out that Pakistan had allies in the form of both the United States and, of more immediate danger, China.[5] By April 1971, the balance was definitely in favor of war, although the Indian chief

of the Army Staff, General Sam Manekshaw, argued against an immediate opening of hostilities. He promised Gandhi total victory, however,
if he were allowed to choose the precise moment to strike. He would
make good on that promise.[6]

For Manekshaw, the problem of timing was crucial and extremely
complex. For several reasons, he was against unleashing the dogs of war
in April. Pakistan normally garrisoned the eastern wing with a single
division. Indian strength was about the same; planning in the east usually centered on keeping the narrow "Siliguri Corridor" open, as well as
screening the great city of Calcutta.[7] Now, however, the rebellion had
brought two more Pakistani divisions, and another (the 36th) was in the
process of arriving. Communications troops and a newly raised paramilitary force (the East Pakistan Civil Armed Force, or EPCAF) added
about another division. India faced a choice of fighting with insufficient
force in the east or gathering troops from the four corners of the subcontinent and rushing them into action with a newly reoriented operational plan. Both were unacceptable options, Manekshaw felt. The latter,
especially, would be a recipe for disaster.

Gathering the necessary force would therefore take time. But time
was running short. By mid-June, the monsoon season would turn much
of East Pakistan into a quagmire. Also, a strike in April or May would
open the possibility of Chinese intervention on Pakistan's behalf. This
was all the more difficult since India would have to draw the necessary
forces for a campaign in the East from the Chinese border. There was
much reading of the tea leaves in India over Chou En-Lai's April 13 pro-
nouncement that China promised to help Yahya Khan maintain the "territorial integrity of Pakistan."[8] China and India had fought in 1962, a
brief campaign that saw the Chinese shatter an entire Indian division in
short order. The Indians had greatly improved their readiness on the
Chinese border, but they were not eager to repeat the contest. For all
these reasons, Manekshaw preferred to fight when snow had closed the
Himalayan passes on which the Chinese relied.

These factors added up to a winter campaign: November or even
December. The Indian army did not, however, sit by passively as the
months passed. Manekshaw oversaw a myriad of activities in this period,
readying the army for a strike into East Pakistan. Engineers constructed
assembly areas for the thousands of men and mountains of equipment
that would be arriving, as well as roads in the traditionally communica-
tions-poor eastern provinces. The army topped off its stock of weapons,
ammunition, and spare parts. The high command canceled the "annual
changeover," in which a percentage of Indian units moved from opera-

tional to nonoperational status — a peacetime thrift measure.[9] From June to November, he also oversaw a comprehensive series of war games on the divisional, corps, and army level.[10] These were important to the genesis of the Indian operational plan and then helped to suggest significant changes to it.

From remnants of the East Pakistani rebel units, he oversaw the creation of an auxiliary military force, known as the Mukti Bahini.[11] Its three regular brigades, plus some seventy to eighty thousand irregulars, under the command of Colonel M. A. G. Osmani, were active in harassing the Pakistani army in the border regions. Indian Border Security Force (BSF) paramilitary units actively assisted the Mukti Bahini, offering logistical and artillery support, and even crossing over the border into East Pakistan in several places. By November, several regions in East Pakistan on the Indian border were under ostensible Mukti Bahini control, but in fact small Indian forces were in occupation as well. There were so-called lodgments, for example, near Garibpur (9th Indian Division) and Darsana (4th Indian Mountain Division) in the southwest, as well as near Thakurgaon and Kurigram in the north (71st Mountain Brigade and 9th Mountain Brigade, respectively).[12] In addition, India had helped arm and train nearly 100,000 refugees, sending them into East Pakistan to carry out guerrilla operations against the Pakistani army.

Most important, Manekshaw had an operational plan prepared, which was ready by June. Code-named "Windfall," it was largely the work of General K. K. Singh, then director of military operations at army headquarters. There would be many staff officers who would try to take the credit for it after its success, and indeed, the plan did undergo an evolution from Singh's original conception. He envisioned a rapid strike — the word *blitzkrieg* shows up repeatedly in Indian analyses and histories of the campaign — into East Pakistan, defeating hostile forces there and overrunning as much of the country as possible.[13] It had to occur rapidly, before the international community enforced some kind of ceasefire, as it surely would. Bearing the brunt of the mission would be units transferred from the Chinese front, specifically from the Uttar Pradesh-Tibet border and from the North East Frontier Agency (NEFA). Here, Manekshaw was relying on improvements made since 1962 in the border defenses, as well as the closing of the Himalayan passes.[14]

The question arose early in the planning as to exactly when the movement of these units should take place. Moving too soon would risk discovery by the Chinese or the Pakistanis, and thus a loss of surprise. There were some in the Indian General Staff who argued for bringing the assault troops to the East Pakistan border at the last possible

Architect of victory: The affable — and very able — General Sam Manekshaw (center), seen here exchanging a few words with an enlisted man. Bharat Rakshak, Consortium of Indian Military Websites.

moment. Manekshaw, who possessed the great virtue of understanding his force's weaknesses as well as its strengths, felt this would be disruptive and might jeopardize the entire operation. "I don't like this fancy stuff," he said. "You should realize that my formations are not the German Panzer divisions. They take their own time to move."[15] In the end, the troops moved up in plenty of time, and although the Pakistanis did detect most of their movements, Manekshaw's slower deployment meant better battle readiness when the shooting started.

In operational terms, geography offered both problems and opportunities. About as large as Arkansas, East Pakistan was as surrounded by the Indian army as Poland had been by the Germans in 1939. Like the German Wehrmacht, Indian forces would have their pick of axes of approach. Principal thrusts might emerge from the Indian state of West Bengal to the west, from Meghalaya in the north, or from Tripura and Nizoram in the east. From the start, geography would force a hard choice on the East Pakistani commander, General Amir Abdullah Khan Niazi. He could offer a linear defense of the entire length of the 2,100 kilometer border, or he could pull back his forces for a defense of some central position, perhaps a redoubt around the capital, the so-called "Dacca

Bowl."[16] He did not have to hold this position forever, only until the declaration of a cease-fire. It is never easy for a commander to abandon the vast majority of the territory entrusted to his defense, however, and it was apparently not easy for Niazi.

Balancing the geographical advantage for India was the terrain of the country. To say that East Pakistan was a land of rivers is understating the case considerably. Great rivers, where one cannot see the far shore from the near, as well as many smaller ones, divide the land into four great sectors: the northwestern sector, north of the Ganga River and west of the Brahmaputra; the southwestern, south and west of the Ganga and Padma Rivers; the northern, between the Jamuna and Meghna Rivers; and the eastern, lying east of the Meghna. The deltas of the various rivers reach far into the heart of the country. Thus, whichever axis of approach the Indians took, they would soon have to cross a Mississippi-like water barrier. An operational posture emphasizing a Dacca redoubt, in fact, might have offered Niazi some chance of success.[17]

A further hindrance to plans for an offensive was the fact that although India enjoyed a favorable balance of land forces, it was not a dramatic one. Once troops had been stripped from the Chinese sectors, India could place seven divisions into the fray in the east. Pakistan, as we have seen, had four and was in the process of assembling another one from various nondivisional elements in East Pakistan. Both sides, of course, had to leave the vast majority of their armed forces along the West Pakistan–India border, especially in disputed (and still disputed) Jammu-Kashmir. India did enjoy a clear superiority in armor, however, with three regiments, two independent squadrons and a battalion of armored personnel carriers; Pakistan could muster only one armored regiment and a few independent squadrons.[18] India also enjoyed a decisive superiority in the air. Pakistan had only a single squadron of F-86 Sabrejet fighters in East Pakistan. India, by contrast, mustered ten complete squadrons for this campaign, as well as twelve transport helicopters that would play an important role in the course of operations. Friendly air power, flying through virtually noncontested skies, was one of the keys to the success of the Indian plan. To increase their mobility, Indian forces would have to be as light as possible. Tactical air would take over many of the functions of artillery; and the helicopters, too, would do yeoman's work, resupplying forward units, evacuating the wounded, and carrying out a number of crucial airlifts.[19]

Singh's original plan called for several simultaneous thrusts into the heart of Bangladesh. In the southwest, II Corps (headquarters at Krishnagar) would strike from out of its Darsana lodgment toward Jhenida, Jessore, and Khulna. In the northwest, XXXIII Corps (headquartered at Siliguri) would move on Hilli and eventually Bogra. In the east, a completely new formation, IV Corps, based at Agartala, would launch a multipronged offensive. On its extreme right, it would target Sylhet; its central thrust would strike directly toward Dacca, passing through Comilla, Maynamati, Daudkandi, lunging to the banks of the Meghna River, with another column moving on Feni, Laksham, and Chandpur, threatening the capital from the south. The end result of these drives would be strong Indian forces arrayed concentrically around Dacca, ready for the final blow. The extreme left of IV Corps would be responsible for striking south, toward East Pakistan's major port of Chittagong, closing off any potential evacuation route for the enemy. Covering the tremendous gap between XXXIII and IV Corps was a smaller ad-hoc command, the 101 Communications Zone. Commanding a broad front in a remote area, it was to devote itself to defense and administrative tasks (hence, a "communications zone," rather than a corps). But once the Pakistani army was fully engaged in other sectors, a favorable opportunity might arise here. Commanding a lengthy, but direct, route to Dacca, it would drive south through Jamalpur and Tangail toward the capital. In all cases, Singh's plan called for securing crucial points that prevented intersector movement, such as bridges, ferries, and airfields, so that each Pakistani force would face defeat in detail without hope of reinforcement and so that forward-deployed Pakistani units would have no chance of retreating into the depths of the province toward Dacca. Once Indian forces had crushed the enemy's main strength near the border, any formation in a position to do so would strike out for Dacca.[20]

It was a solid plan, and in many ways a remarkable one. Characterized by a realistic assessment of both sides' forces and by a healthy degree of flexibility that recognized the role of uncertainty in war, it stands in the best tradition of modern operational-level planning. Its series of converging columns was a classic example of a war of movement, to be specific, an "operation on exterior lines" of the type practiced by the elder Helmuth von Moltke. Moreover, its emphasis on maneuver flew in the face of Indian tradition, which leaned heavily on firepower and the deliberate, set-piece battle in the British style. Its aim of total victory within two weeks, what one officer called "the lightning concept,"[21] marked a break with previous Indian war planning, which had emphasized territorial gains as postwar negotiating chips.

In its original incarnation, however, the plan failed to indicate a point of main effort, what the Germans call the *Schwerpunkt*. Further discussions among the staff, as well as the operational commander for the east, General Jagjit Singh ("Jaggy") Aurora, resulted in a decision to strike the main blow with IV Corps. Far isolated from its neighboring formations, connected to them by a primitive communications net (including large stretches of unpaved road in Pakistani artillery range), operating out of bases and depots that had only just been constructed, IV Corps was a risky choice. However, for that very reason, Manekshaw, Singh, and Aurora felt that the surprise element would work in their favor here. The Pakistanis could read a map as well as anyone and would never expect that the main thrust would come through such an underdeveloped region. All these Indian officers had served in the east and knew the terrain and the possibilities as well as anyone.[22]

The Pakistani plan of operations was, by contrast, much more confused. Niazi seemed unable to choose between the two obvious stratagems. On the one hand, he might pull back from the frontiers, concentrate and fortify himself around the "Dacca Bowl." This would take him out of the areas of major Mukti Bahini activity and present the Indians with a tough nut to crack at the end of what were sure to be extended and strained supply lines. On the other hand, he might defend along the borders with an eye to delaying the Indian advance as long as possible, and then pull back for a defense in depth. In the event, he chose to do both, adopting a "theater fortress" posture.[23]

Niazi did deploy well forward, hard along the border. He met the Indian invasion, essentially, with companies and battalions in isolated but heavily fortified positions, replete with bunkers, large stocks of supply and ammunition, and mortar or artillery support. In this way, he hoped to make India pay for any early gains, when, presumably, the attackers' morale would be the most fluid. A bloody nose, administered early, might set the tone for the whole campaign. He even exhorted his units to "fight to the last man," or at least until they had sustained 75 percent casualties. At the same time, however, he was planning for a defense of a central redoubt of ten fortresses. His border outposts, he said, were "like the extended fingers of an open hand. They will fight there as long as possible before they fold back to the fortress to form a fist to bash the enemy's head."[24] What sort of "fist" he could form with units that had previously been mauled in battle and then beat a hurried retreat was a question that he never addressed. In fact, what Niazi had done was to place the bulk of his army in tactically strong, but operationally and strategically hopeless, positions.

He now faced the problem of how to cover such an extended front with the limited troops at his disposal. He did so, literally, by taking a few men from this company and a few men from this mortar troop and a few more from the EPCAF, dub them a "company," place them under the command of an unfamiliar, and perhaps grossly inexperienced, officer and plunk them down in a border town. The Pakistani order of battle for the campaign is quite difficult to decipher, incredibly so when one realizes there were only four divisions. One analyst said that it was possible to use the word "cavalier" to describe Niazi's creation of ad-hoc formations and headquarters units, "if that word did not have the connotation of being at least stylish."[25] It is a valid critique. What is amazing, and a tribute to the qualities of the Pakistani soldier, is how well some of them fought under such adverse conditions.

Niazi's operational plan revealed itself to the Indians during the border skirmishes in November in support of the Mukti Bahini. The Pakistani garrison at Kamalpur in the northeastern sector of the country held out against the guerrillas, and then an Indian attack, for twenty-one days before surrendering. Likewise, in the town of Hilli, which guarded East Pakistan's pinched waist in the northwest, a single company of the Pakistani frontier force held out from late November to December 12. For this reason, as the Indian plan gradually evolved, it placed a premium on bypassing packets of resistance whenever possible. Indian forces were to move around both flanks of such obstacles to attack them from the rear, as well as to block their retreat toward Dacca. Again, it was a break with the systematic, carefully prepared set-piece assault in favor of a war of movement. General Sukhwant Singh wrote that as a result of Hilli, "the El Alamein concepts, so deeply ingrained in the old school of generals, met their doom."[26]

To Dacca: Indian Operations in East Pakistan

The war opened officially on the evening of December 3 with a dramatic but generally ineffective Pakistani air strike into India. Apparently feeling that such a bold gesture would force the hands of both Great Power patrons, the United States and China, and that time was running out on the possibility of Chinese intervention (a factor in Indian timing, as well) Pakistan had gone for broke. The air strike was the signal for the start of general hostilities. Within hours, both fronts had erupted into fighting. The Indo-Pakistani wars were unusual, perhaps unique, in that both sides were fighting a war on two fronts. Both sides concentrated their

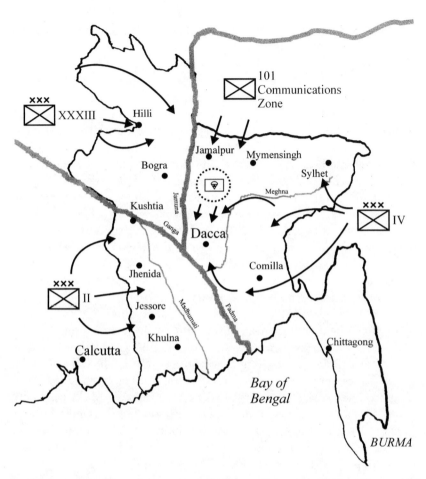

Decisive victory: The 1971 Indo-Pakistani War, Eastern Theater.

main strength in the west, where fighting took place all along the border from Kashmir in the north to Sind in the south. The fighting, especially in Kashmir, was tough, back and forth, and essentially without great strategic advantage to either side. In other words, it was a rerun of the previous Indo-Pakistani conflicts.

Things were different in the east, where Aurora sent his large and well-equipped force of more than 130,000 men into East Pakistan. In the southwest sector, Indian II Corps launched its offensive. It included the following units:[27]

Indian II Corps (General T. N. Raina)
    4th Mountain Division (General M. S. Barar)
        7th Mountain Brigade
        41st Mountain Brigade
        62nd Mountain Brigade
    9th Mountain Division (General Dalbir Singh)
        32nd Mountain Brigade
        42nd Mountain Brigade

Raina deployed his 4th Mountain Division (General Barar) on the left, driving toward Jhenida, and 9th Mountain Division (General Singh) to its right, moving on Jessore. Supporting the corps were two tank regiments equipped with T-55 and PT-76 Soviet tanks and a medium artillery regiment. Raina faced a single Pakistani division, the 9th, responsible for holding an impossible front six hundred kilometers long. As part of Niazi's linear deployment, its two brigades were abreast, headquartered at Jhenida (57th Brigade) to the north and at Jessore (107th Brigade, as well as divisional headquarters) to the south. To the left of these two brigades, at Khulna, sat a "brigade" of East Pakistani irregulars, which saw little action; in fact it dissolved as the fighting got under way. It was manifestly impossible for such a tiny force to offer an effective linear defense, and in fact its inadequacy calls into question Niazi's entire deployment. By breaking up already small units into even tinier ones and detailing them to defend in place, he had simply surrendered the initiative to General Raina.

Raina was a good commander, one of the few who had acquitted himself well in the 1962 debacle, and he took advantage of Niazi's immobility. The Indian divisions broke out of their lodgments, penetrating the irregular border defense units and pushing into East Pakistan between Jhenida and Jessore. Within three days, Jhenida had fallen to a surprise assault of 41st Mountain Brigade and Jessore had been evacuated. When the headquarters of 57th Brigade tried to retreat from Jhenida eastward to Magura, it found that Indian columns were already there ahead of it. It retreated to the north, to Kushtia. News of the rapid fall of Jhenida seemed to have cracked the morale of the Pakistani divisional commander, General Ansari. One Pakistani report has him spending far more time on his prayer mat than running his division,[28] and another Pakistani officer would later write that Ansari's operational rating was "zero multiplied by zero."[29] He now attempted to draw back his divisional headquarters, also in Jessore, but found that it had to run a gauntlet of Indian forces already in his rear areas. He and a few ragged and demoralized remnants of his division (nonbrigade infantry, support troops, and administrative personnel) finally made it across the Madhumati River toward Faridpur. To the south, the 107th Brigade defending Jessore had fended off attacks by the 9th Indian Division, with elements of the two units trading casualties. The Pakistani commander, General Malik Hayat Khan, followed his orders to retreat very reluctantly. Ironically, he had requested permission to retreat the very first day, and if he had been allowed, he would probably have arrived in the "Dacca Bowl" with a complete brigade in hand. As it was, Hayat Khan's retreat now had to be to the south, to Khulna.

These divergent retreats had completely dismembered the 9th Pakistani Division, chopping it into three pieces capable of little more than defending in place. The path to Dacca now lay virtually open to Raina's II Corps. At this point, Indian operations in the sector became temporarily unhinged. A small action at Kushtia on December 9, in which a tank squadron from the Pakistani 29th Cavalry successfully ambushed an Indian tank troop and lead units of the 22nd Rajput infantry battalion, suddenly seized Raina's attention. Rather than forge on ahead to Dacca, he now ordered Indian 4th Division commander, General Barar, to wheel

Blitzkrieg: A column of Indian Army T-55s from the Indian 7th Cavalry Regiment, on its way to Dacca, the capital of East Pakistan, soon to be the capital of independent Bangladesh. Bharat Rakshak, Consortium of Indian Military Websites.

to the north. Believing the entire 57th Brigade to be at Kushtia, Raina wanted 4th Division concentrated for an assault on the town. By December 12, he had to admit defeat, as 57th Brigade had already slipped over the Ganga River at Hardinge Bridge.[30] Not until December 14 was 4th Division ready to cross the Madhumati River. It did so skillfully, with 62nd Mountain Brigade crossing to the north and 7th Mountain Brigade crossing to the south of the main Pakistani position, including General Ansari's headquarters. The force used an assortment of light craft assembled by the Mukti Bahini, and by December 15 had encircled Ansari's headquarters and divisional remnant. He surrendered to the Indians on December 16, hours before the general Pakistani surrender in the east. The saga of II Corps was that of a successful offensive — it had dismembered its opposition, after all — but also of a missed opportunity.

The fighting in XXXIII Corps sector, which included the well-defended Pakistani strongpoint at Hilli, was the most difficult of the entire war. The corps consisted of the following units:[31]

Indian XXXIII Corps (General M. L. Thapan)
    20th Mountain Division (General L. S. Lehl)
        9th Mountain Brigade
        66th Mountain Brigade
        165th Mountain Brigade
        202nd Mountain Brigade
    71st Mountain Brigade Group
    340th Mountain Brigade Group

It is possible to attribute some of the difficulty in this region to the Indian corps commander, General M. L. Thapan. He was known as a cautious commander, according to one fellow officer, a "copybook general."[32] Of all the commanders, the new "lightning concept" seemed most foreign to him. He planned an attack along the obvious line, out of the Balurghat bulge toward Hilli. Manekshaw was apparently inclined to replace him with his chief of staff at the outset of the fighting but apparently felt that such a move would be more disruptive to operations than allowing him to stay on. At the conclusion of the war, his forces had overrun most of the territory in his sector, but a large number of fortified positions still remained in Pakistani hands.

Certainly, the Pakistani prosecution of operations in this area was no better than it had been in the southwest. Guarding this large sector of East Pakistan was, again, a single division, the 16th (General Nazir Hussain Shah). Its three brigades were well dispersed through the battle zone, and Niazi had performed a great deal of his usual shuffling and ad-hoc arranging of units, to the detriment of unit cohesion. Since the terrain is relatively flat here, 16th Division also had a tank regiment (29th Cavalry) assigned to it. Violating every principle of armored warfare put forth since the battle of Cambrai, however, Shah broke the regiments down into squadrons and dispersed them among his brigades, where they essentially served as weak artillery support for nonmaneuvering infantry. He also bragged, after the war, that he had increased the number of units under his command by reducing the manpower in each, hardly a path into the history books: "My concept is to split one company into two," he said, "thus stretching one battalion into two. I never used my staff as staff. They were commanding troops. I had three brigades, but I was able to make five out of them."[33] He was inept. But Thapan, by launching a direct attack against Hilli, simplified Shah's operational problem considerably.

The strike against Hilli was a grinding frontal assault, something the Indians largely managed to avoid in this war. There was nary a hint of maneuver and not much in the way of preparatory fire. It was the mission of 20th Mountain Division, and the entire division soon became entangled in a complex of fortified positions. The Pakistanis had been preparing their defenses since May, basing them on the numerous villages in the area. The 20th Division commander, General Lachman Singh, described the Hilli position:

> They had constructed two-layered bunkers in village houses and had coordinated mutual support with machine guns located in the neighboring villages. The roofs of the houses had been demolished and the construction material employed to arrange overhead protection. The light shells of mountain guns could not do much damage to these bunkers. The narrow lanes in the villages were covered by light machine gun fire. Strong tunneled bunkers had been developed on the banks of numerous ponds to direct enfilade fire on the assaulting troops. The defenses had been further strengthened by the use of wire and mines.[34]

In the end, it was the shape of the border that got things moving for XXXIII Corps. Even though Thapan's drive into Hilli was stuck fast, it did serve the purpose of fixing Shah's attention to the west. This allowed other formations of XXXIII Corps, attacking directly from the north, to make headway against only sporadic opposition. Particularly important here was the 71st Mountain Brigade Group, under the command of General P. N. Kathpalia.[35] Entering East Pakistan through the Tatalya salient in late November, it overran Pachagarh, threatening the town from the front with one battalion while another slipped around its rear. From there, Kathpalia took Boda from a single company of 48th Punjab Regiment and swept through Thakurgaon on December 3 after a single-day's advance of sixty kilometers.[36] Soon he was threatening the fortified town of Dinajpur from the north.

With 20th Mountain Division still banging its head painfully at the Hilli position, corps commander Thapan was now forced into maneuver.[37] The independent 340th Mountain Brigade Group, involved up to now in the siege of Dinajpur from the south, was ordered to abandon the siege and slip to the east, toward Pirganj. Commanded by an excellent officer, General Joginder "Jogi" Singh, 340th's advance was a model of modern operations. He never halted his advance, never stopped maneuvering, and never attacked a position frontally. He also skillfully used combat groups, consisting of tanks and tank-mounted infantry, to increase his mobility, repeatedly beating the Pakistanis to defensive lines they had intended to occupy, bypassing their frontal defenses, and attacking them from the flanks or rear. His drive on Pirganj, into the nearly undefended Pakistani security zone, nearly netted big game when he just missed a column of jeeps in which the Pakistani sector commander, General Shah, was riding. More to the point, he almost single-handedly forced the Pakistanis to thin out their forces in Hilli to deal with this new threat, a need that grew more urgent as he drove on Bogra far into the rear, the logistical hub for Pakistani forces in this sector. When Hilli finally did fall, on December 12, the mass of XXXIII Corps was able to wheel to the south and join him in his drive on Bogra. The corps failed to catch up with him. It was 340th Mountain Brigade Group that entered Bogra first, on December 16, ending the fighting in this sector. Sukhwant Singh paid tribute to the "highly unorthodox moves" that characterized Jogi's battlefield performance: "Whatever tangible gains were made in the way of developing the thrust line some 130 kilometers deep in Pakistan territory up to Bogra can be attributed to the decision of Joginder Singh to break away from typical Indian World War II concepts and restore the power of maneuver on the battlefield."[38]

With Bogra in Indian hands, continued hostilities would have certainly found the Pakistanis in supply difficulties. Still, five Pakistani fortified positions remained unreduced, including Rangpur astride the Indian lines of communication, so the same might be said of Indian supply difficulties had the war dragged on a few more weeks. Thapan had advanced against tenacious opposition and he had clearly triumphed, but his was a triumph of the old school: unimaginative, slow, and quite costly.

He took few chances and reaped few rewards. For most of the war, he had one brigade in motion and five besieging Pakistani fortified towns. His subordinate Joginder Singh won far higher honors.

It was in the east, in IV Corps sector, that India won the war. Here we see the boldest approach, and here too we see the most active role for Indian tactical air power. If any part of Operation Windfall deserved to be called a blitzkrieg, this was it. It was the operational *Schwerpunkt* in Indian planning, as the forces allotted to it indicate:[39]

Indian IV Corps (General Sagat Singh)
 8th Mountain Division
  59th Mountain Brigade
  81st Mountain Brigade
 23rd Mountain Division
  83rd Mountain Brigade
  "Kilo" Force (a six-battalion brigade)
 57th Mountain Division
  61st Mountain Brigade
  181st Mountain Brigade
  301st Mountain Brigade
  311th Mountain Brigade Group

In addition, General Sagat Singh commanded three independent armored squadrons, two mechanized infantry battalions, and nearly all the organized Mukti Bahini battalions formed in India. It was a formidable array of force by the standards of this war.

It had to be, given the missions that General Aurora entrusted to it. From his corps headquarters at Agartala, General Sagat Singh would be overseeing several widely separated thrusts: one between Akhaura and Comilla in the center, and from there a drive to the Meghna River at Daudkandi and Chandpur, the last water barrier before Dacca, which lay only seventy miles from the border; one toward Sylhet, far in the northeast, through Maulvi Bazaar; and, the situation permitting, a third to peel off almost due south, making for the key port of Chittagong and further on to Cox's Bazaar.[40] The capture of Chittagong would sever any potential escape routes to the sea for Pakistani troops. The operations of IV Corps were, as numerous Indian analysts have written, an application of B. H. Liddell Hart's concept of the "expanding torrent," with divergent, highly mobile columns exploiting the breakthrough at Akhaura-Comilla.[41] The end result would be a ring around Dacca to the south and southeast, preparatory to the final assault. Although no specific orders existed for the seizure of Dacca, Sagat Singh wanted no half-measures. "Leave it to me," he told one staff officer, "I will get there."[42]

Although Pakistani intelligence had noticed the Indian buildup since the summer and had ordered him to expect the main thrust to come from this direction, Niazi defended in the east no better than in any other sector. He deployed a single regular division, the 14th Infantry (General Abdul Majid Qazi), guarding the approaches to Sylhet, along with one of the ad-hoc units that proved so worthless in combat in this war, in this case the "39th Infantry Division," with its brigades posted at Comilla, Laksham, and Chittagong to the south, guarding the strategically most important route: the approaches to Dacca. Niazi may have been thinking, above all, of keeping open an evacuation route to Chittagong. But this is not the only explanation for his stress on the south. Before the opening of war, Sagat Singh had played a ruse, improving roads and bridges along the border, erecting a dummy supply dump for an entire division, not to mention a phantom radio network simulating brigade traffic, opposite Feni. The plan was to get Niazi worried about communications between Dacca and Chittagong.[43]

It appears, like so many other Indian stratagems of this war, to have had the intended effect. There were no prior lodgments for Indian troops on the eastern border, but, paradoxically, it meant that the size and scope of the Indian effort here came as much more of a surprise. Sagat Singh's IV Corps hit the foe with the entire package. A full-scale assault from north to south, well supported by tactical air, cracked open the Pakistani defenses within three days. Airmobility played a crucial role. To assist 8th Mountain Division's drive on Sylhet, the Indians airlifted a battalion (the 4/5 Gorkha Rifles of the 59th Mountain Brigade) into position south of the city, preventing a Pakistani retreat from Sylhet into the Dacca area.[44] Meanwhile, 23rd and 57th Mountain Divisions easily overran the frontier defenses between Akhaura and Comilla, reaching the Meghna River in one great lunge, completely isolating all Pakistani units still to the east, and with friendly forces now at Daudkandi and Chandpur, threatening Dacca from the south. Elements of the 14th Pakistani Infantry Division did manage to break contact and retreat across the Meghna to Bhairab Bazaar. Undaunted, the Indians carried out another airlift, this one completely improvised. It began on the night of December 9–10, and in the course of the next few days put the full 311th Mountain Brigade Group (57th Mountain Division) across the river. The brigade was well south of the Pakistani force and interspersed between it and Dacca.[45]

The buildup of the bridgehead over the Meghna to threaten Dacca from the north was a decisive element in the Indian victory. It is worth noting that it received inestimable help from the local civilian population, with hundreds of people eagerly jumping into the water to assist the light amphibious PT-76 tanks get across the river when their engines overheated under the strain, and many others feeding a constant stream of information to forward Indian troops.[46] With their assistance, the Indians had two full brigades across the Meghna by December 14, ready to drive down on Dacca from the north. Indian forces had breached the river barrier around the capital and entered the uncovered top of the "bowl."

The advance of Sagat Singh's IV Corps to and over the Meghna was a classic of the type. Strictly enjoining his units to bypass Pakistani defenses, he wanted them to concentrate on lapping around their flanks and into their rear. He especially emphasized the establishment of roadblocks to prevent forward units from retreating toward Dacca. Flanking and surrounding a Pakistani strong point, plastering it with artillery — high explosive and napalm — and then striking it a sharp frontal blow was usually enough to force a surrender. When opportunity knocked, as it did at the Meghna, he was willing and able to improvise, as with the air landing of the 311th Mountain Brigade Group. Although many Pakistani units, both regulars and border defense forces, fought quite bravely, their commanders were no match for the Indians on the operational level.

By this time, IV Corps was no longer fighting alone in the Dacca sector. Alongside it marched advancing units of the 101 Communications Zone. The tale of this force, operating in the northern sector of East Pakistan, is the most interesting of all. Commanded by General Gurbux Singh Gill, the zone's operational task was essentially defensive: to protect the extended communications between XXXIII Corps in the northeast and IV Corps in the southeast, and to serve related administrative tasks. Gurbux was an unusual character, however, and a most curious choice to command such a passive mission. He was brusque and aggressive, hardly the sort to content himself with administrative tasks while there was battlefield glory to be won.[47] His command was not large, originally consisting of a single brigade, the 95th Mountain, under an equally aggressive commander, General Hardev Singh Kler. As war approached, Aurora added a "brigade group" ("FJ Force," a nucleus of regular troops augmented by East Pakistani liberation forces) to Gurbux's zone. It appeared that Pakistani forces were so weak in this sector (a single brigade, the 93rd, for 180 kilometers of front) that an advance from 101 Communications Zone would be possible. In addition, the territory directly south of the zone was among the most active in terms of guerrillas, with large areas around the town of Tangail actually in the hands of rebel forces under Kader Siddiqui. These "Kaderites" would certainly be a help to any Indian drive to the south.[48] Gurbux saw his opportunity. It appears that he did a great deal of surreptitious stockpiling of supplies, arms, and weapons in the months leading up to the war, enough to sustain an offensive advance to the south, toward Dacca.

Cross-border attacks preceded the formal declaration of war, with Gurbux's forces taking the Pakistani frontier outpost of Kamalpur after a stiff fight and heavy bombardment. Riding toward the newly conquered post, the jeep in which Kler and Gurbux were riding struck a mine. Gurbux's wounds were serious, and his war was over. His replacement, General Gandharav Nagra, was less of a presence than Gurbux, but he benefited from the former commander's planning. From Kamalpur, Nagra launched a two-pronged drive: Kler's brigade toward Jamalpur and FJ Force toward Mymensingh. There was stiff fighting at the former, before mobile Indian columns bypassed it and got into the Pakistani rear. On December 10, the Pakistanis evacuated both towns. Although sitting in good defensive positions and quite capable of defending themselves, the Pakistani forces of the 93rd Brigade had already received their order to retreat. With Indian forces knocking on the door of Dacca, Niazi was trying to "close the fingers of the fist" far too late. During the brigade's retreat to Tangail, it was already under harassing attacks from the Kaderites.[19]

And now the state was set for the climax of the war. In the afternoon of December 11, the skies north of Tangail suddenly filled with transport aircraft of the Indian air force: Russian AN-12s, Canadian Caribous, American Fairchild Packets and Dakotas.[50] Within minutes, they had disgorged an entire battalion of Indian paratroopers. These were men of the 2nd Parachute Battalion, under the command of Lieutenant Colonel K. S. Pannu. This was not an improvisation. As part of prewar operational planning, General Aurora had drawn up a priority list of potential airborne operations. The Tangail sector attracted him from the start, and in fact was number one on the list:

Task No. 1. A Para Bn Gp to be dropped at Tangail to set up a block in that general area, with a view to drawing forces from Dacca, prevent any link up between Dacca and Mymensingh, and to operate in conjunction with guerrilla forces (SIDDIQUI FORCE). Time frame NOT before D + 5.[51]

The drop was not perfect — they never are. Strong winds blew some of the landings off target, with one Dakota missing the drop zone by a full seventeen kilometers. The civilian population was quite helpful in this context, helping troopers out of ponds and rivers and fetching stores and equipment that had blown off course. But once again, the Indians left little to chance in a particularly well run operation. There was even a "dummy drop" some twenty minutes before the real one. Consisting of sixty cloth dummies stuffed with pyrotechnics to simulate both paradrop and supporting fire, it landed a few miles away from the real drop zone to confuse Pakistani observers.

It was hardly necessary, by this point. The decomposition of Pakistani command and control on all levels was already well advanced. The commander of the force retreating from Mymensingh (93rd Brigade) was in Tangail and actually observed the drop. He sent out scouts to see what was happening. They returned with the happy news: "Sir, the locals say they're Chinese."[52] Soon after that bubble burst, despair set in when Niazi apparently received an exaggerated report (some blame CBS News) that five thousand Indian paratroopers had landed.[53]

The drop at Tangail was the last straw that destroyed an already overburdened Pakistani command system. First, much of 93rd Brigade, the last relatively whole unit in the Pakistani order of battle, was now cut off from Dacca — as it learned when it tried to continue its retreat toward Tangail. Coming on in some disorder and not even in tactical formation, it ran squarely into roadblocks at Poongli Bridge over the Turag River established by the tough troopers of the 2nd Parachute. The slaughter, from both Indian rocket launchers and small arms, was terrific, a terrifying climax to the fighting of this war. Other elements of the 93rd Brigade decided to leave the road network and try to move cross-country, where more often than not they fell into the not-so-gentle hands of the Kaderites.[54] Second, and more important, once the 95th Brigade had linked up with the paratroopers on December 12, Dacca was under assault from five separate columns, in a broad arc from northwest to southeast. Repeated air assaults on the capital reinforced the notion that it was only a matter of time.

The actual assault on Dacca never got very far beyond an exchange of fire in the suburbs. Early on the morning of December 16, General Nagra reached the outskirts of the capital — the paratroopers were already there, the first Indian troops to reach it. He had once been Indian military attaché in Karachi and knew General Niazi personally. He now sent his aide-de-camp, as well as an adjutant from the 2nd Parachute Battalion, into Dacca with a message: "My dear Abdullah, I am here. The game is up. I suggest you give yourself up to me and I'll look after you."[55] Niazi signed the surrender that afternoon, at the racetrack in Dacca, before a raucous crowd of Bengalis, estimated at one million, screaming themselves

The face of victory: A confident Indian enlisted man (*Jawan*) standing guard in newly liberated Dacca. Bharat Rakshak, Consortium of Indian Military Websites.

hoarse, toasting the independence of their new nation, Bangladesh. Over 100,000 Pakistani troops went into Indian captivity.

The 1971 War Evaluated

The Indian achievement was a notable one. The *Times* of London described the campaign in terms familiar to westerners: "It took only 12 days for the Indian Army to smash its way to Dacca, an achievement reminiscent of the German *blitzkrieg* across France in 1940. The strategy was the same: speed, ferocity, and flexibility."[56] As always after such events, it is easy to find a note of triumphalism among Indian analysts. This is especially true of military men who fought in the campaign and who published memoirs, and there are a lot of them. For Indian general D. K. Palit, victory in Bangladesh was a wake-up call for the rest of the world:

> From all these conflicts, the watching world formed an image of our military machine: the verdict — a good second-class British left-over, steadily declining in operational potential. Surprisingly self-sufficient in weapons and ammunition for a developing nation — it was nevertheless on the wane in actual combat capability. At best it could be considered comparable to the Pakistani armed forces — but, certainly in Western eyes, even that was debatable.

Now, he said, "it seems to have pulled a rabbit out of its hat." Operation Windfall, he said, was "the most decisive liberation campaign in military history — giving a nation of 75 million people its independence in one lightning strike."[57] The well-respected soldier–scholar, General Sukhwant Singh, also saw 1971 as an epochal event, India's first military victory in ten centuries, a turning point in its history that up to now had been "replete with repeated defeats, humiliations, and subjugation by more enterprising invaders."[58] General H. S. Sodhi (301st Mountain Brigade) called it "a stunning success."[59] To Major G. D. Bakshi, what India had done was nothing less than to destroy the postwar paradigm of limited wars, resurrecting the respectability of Clausewitz's concept of total war.[60] Nor were the soldiers alone. For scholar Pran Chopra, it was nothing less than "a second liberation" for India, and in operational terms "a swift and mobile war, rejecting the rigidities of copybook prescriptions."[61] The Pakistanis shared the notion that this had been an epochal event. It was, the official government report said, a defeat "without parallel in the history of Islam."[62]

Lieutenant General A. A. K. Niazi (center), Commander of the Pakistan Army in the East, signs the Instrument of Surrender. To his immediate right is the deservedly satisfied Lieutenant General Jagjit Singh Aurora, GOC of Indian forces in the Eastern Theater. Bharat Rakshak, Consortium of Indian Military Websites.

It certainly was one of the century's most complete and decisive victories, in which one country presided over the dismemberment of its long-time rival. It can be compared with what the Allies did to Germany after 1945, in a sense: turning it into two Germanies that were guaranteed to be mutually hostile. The rivalry between victorious India and rump-Pakistan remained, of course, and in fact became immeasurably more heated as a result of 1971. But Pakistan as a power on the western rim of the subcontinent could never present the kind of conventional military threat to India that the old two-wing state could.

In an operational sense, one is impressed with the completeness of the package that India threw at Pakistan in the east. The short campaign featured high-tempo maneuver warfare, as Indian commanders bypassed most large concentrations they encountered and drove deep into the flanks and rear of their foe. This was all the more impressive in that the Indian forces were not mechanized to any significant degree, and tanks played a significant role in only one sector, the northwest. It highlighted the increasing importance of air mobility, using both the helicopter and the parachute. The paradrop onto Tangail was the most spectacular moment of the entire campaign. It employed precision air strikes, used both tactically against Pakistani ground forces, operationally against their lines of supply, and strategically against Dacca and other government targets. The last played a definite role in cracking the morale of Niazi, the commander in East Pakistan. The campaign even contained a small amphibious assault, in support of the drive against Chittagong, on December 14.[63]

General Singh Aurora deserves special mention. Running the entire show from his command post at Fort William, with four corps spread over 1,500 miles, he bore a heavy burden but proved more than equal to the challenge. Counting Mukti Bahini troops under his command, as well as Indian troops still on the Chinese border, he commanded some 500,000 men. Virtually every Indian analyst who wrote about the war repeated the exaggerated claim that "No lieutenant general in military history has commanded so large an army," but his achievement was impressive enough.[64] His plan was not a detailed recipe for victory, but a series of overall guidelines whose application he left up to his subordinate commanders. Some were more deserving of such confidence than others, with IV Corps commander General Sagat Singh the standout. Most impressive was the flexibility of Aurora's plan, which allowed him to respond to favorable opportunities as they presented themselves. When an opportunity arose to cross the Meghna and threaten Dacca from the undefended north, he was able to improvise a complicated airmobile landing. When a vacuum suddenly opened in front of 101 Communications Zone's advance, he was ready with the dramatic airdrop at Tangail, having already done a great deal of preparatory work. His original *Schwerpunkt* had been IV Corps, and IV Corps had had a lot to do with the victory. He was, however, quite willing to improvise and alter the original plan in the interests of achieving a decisive victory.

In the years since 1971, Indian analysts have dropped the boasting tone and subjected the campaign to a much more critical evaluation. This is a reflection of India's status as an open democracy, a rare thing in this part of the world, and is greatly to its credit. The war's origins, the early maneuvers (that is, before the formal opening of hostilities on December 3), and the course of the operations themselves have all come in for a great deal of often heated discussion. The general line of argumentation may be stated simply: Pakistan, and especially the Pakistani commander in the east, lost the war; India did not win it. By focusing on the ineptness of Niazi and other Pakistani weaknesses, much of the alleged brilliance of the Indian victory seems to tarnish. Much of the "flash" of the campaign, for example, its heliborne transport missions and the airborne drop, would have suffered heavy losses if there had been any significant Pakistani air presence. Some criticized the amount of time it took India to prepare for this war, nine full months, and argued that future war scenarios — particularly a Pakistani-Chinese alliance — might not allow so much lead time. More specific self-criticisms of the execution of the campaign include the slow pace of operations in the northwest and southwest sectors, particularly the focus on a frontal assault against Hilli; the number of occasions that local commanders, despite all the lip service being paid to maneuver warfare, still seemed to be fighting the traditional set-piece battle, with its phase lines and timetables; and the totally inadequate measures taken in the area of transport and supply. This was a campaign in which it was entirely possible to see Indian troops flush with victory being supplied by rickshaw, bicycle, or oxcart, "hardly a point of pride for any professional force," to quote one brigadier.[65] Even the "magic moment" of the campaign for most Indian writers, the paradrop on Tangail, has come in for its share of criticism. Some point out that much of 93rd Brigade was already past the Poongli Bridge when the landing took place; others say that it would have been far more effective as part of a linkup with IV Corps, which was already much closer to Dacca, and might have ended the war a day sooner. The Indian chief of the Army Staff, General Manekshaw, probably said it best: "But to say that it was something like what Rommel did would be ridiculous. It had to happen."[66]

More than thirty years later, it is possible to put the 1971 war into perspective. To be sure, this was a war in which all the prewar circumstances were favorable for India, and all the breaks went India's way once the fighting started. The Indian army was not so much invading a foreign country as it was attacking a foreign occupation force: West Pakistani troops holding in thrall a hostile population of some seventy-two million. The Indians therefore had the assistance of liberation forces like the Mukti Bahini and the Kaderites. In the battle for information — a particular problem on the operational level — these forces kept the Indians informed as to where the Pakistanis were and, more important, where they were going. The opposite was not at all true. The Indians were facing a force that had deployed for internal security duties and that had, further, found itself dragged to the borders to suppress rebel activity. Niazi's mission called for him to fight internal rebellion and external invasion at the same time, with a mere four divisions. He may not have been the greatest general in the history of Asia, but there certainly were mitigating circumstances to the poor manner in which he conducted operations.

The Arjun, the Indian army's home-grown main battle tank. Although its design reflected the lessons of the 1971 war, the Arjun suffered from repeated delays and cost overruns and did not enter mass production until 1996. Main armament is a 120-mm rifled gun, with thermal sleeve and fume extractor. Bharat Rakshak, Consortium of Indian Military Websites.

Still, India fought the war with which it was faced. Given a specific set of highly favorable circumstances, the Indian army command, Manekshaw, Aurora Singh, and their staff officers, fashioned a sturdy plan that featured a high degree of flexibility. It was able to adapt to changing situations at the front, and, in the end, it achieved total mastery over its opponent in the chosen theater of war, in record time and with remarkably few casualties. Few armies in this century can make such a claim. Perhaps it wasn't like anything that Rommel had done. No. Manekshaw has something to his name that Rommel never had: a victorious war.

The Iran-Iraq War: Overview

One of the century's greatest armed conflicts — in terms of duration, scope, and casualties — was the war between Iran and Iraq.[67] It was a big, conventional war fought for the most part in good tank country. The front was huge, seven hundred kilometers long, with real opportunity for maneuver and decision. But rather than offer instructive examples of the operational art, the fighting in this war brought home with renewed emphasis a crucial lesson: tanks and other forms of modern equipment do not necessarily make a blitzkrieg. It was the same point that had become obvious in the last few years of World War II. A second lesson suggests itself, as well: it seems that exporting tanks and technology to the Third World is not necessarily the same as exporting doctrine and expertise.

Beginning with Iraq's invasion of Iran in September 1980, the war dragged on for eight years, in the course of which it passed through several distinct stages. In the first, Saddam Hussein's mechanized and armored units drove into Iran, apparently feeling that the chaos of the Islamic revolution would prevent Iran from mounting a strong defense. Of course, even a cursory reading of history — the French and Russian revolutions, for starters — would indicate otherwise. He did not, however, intend to crush the Iranian army. Rather, Saddam Hussein started the war with limited aims. He and his high command apparently envisioned a rapid campaign to seize border districts and towns that had long been in dispute between the two states: Khorramshahr, Abadan, Ahwaz, Dezful, and especially the Shatt al Arab, the mouth of the great Tigris-Euphrates river complex.[68] Once again, the notion of engaging a new revolutionary state in a limited war flies in the face of history and the dynamic of such regimes. Having only just established themselves, revolutionary leaders must treat every war as a test of their legitimacy, their very ability to rule.[69]

Although there is still a good amount of disagreement among analysts about how this war was fought on the operational level, it is possible to sketch a general picture. The war began in what has become a predictable way, with Iraq attempting an Israeli-style preemptive strike on the Iranian air force. Six Iranian air bases and four army bases were the targets. Involving virtually all Iraq's fighters and bombers, it did manage to drop a great deal of ordnance. Unfortunately, it did not cause commensurate damage. With Iraqi pilots poorly trained for this kind of precision strike, and with Soviet-built avionics more or less unhelpful, targeting was poor. The bombs designed to crater the runways had very little effect, and many bombs failed to explode at all. Most important, the Iranians had placed most of their fighters in bombproof shelters, and much of their munitions and matériel in concrete bunkers. There is another theory, that Saddam Hussein was interested in keeping his losses at a minimum and so ordered high-altitude bombing, which was naturally ineffective.

Although a few exposed transport aircraft were not so lucky, Iran's air force essentially survived the strike intact.[70]

The fighting on land, at first, went better for Iraq. The Iraqi army could muster some twelve divisions (including five armored and two mechanized) at the start of the war. It appears that seven took part in the initial invasion. The *Schwerpunkt* was in the south: five of the seven (a force of three armored and two mechanized divisions) drove into Khuzistan against sporadic opposition.[71] Two armored and one mechanized division attacked toward Dezful and Ahwaz. They advanced between Musian and Susangerd, taking the latter, undefended city, crossing the seasonably fordable Kharkeh River, and then advancing toward their two target cities. On September 25, the Iraqis announced that both Dezful and Ahwaz were under siege.[72] Farther south of this thrust, one armored and one mechanized division, plus special force and support units, attacked toward Khorramshahr and Abadan. There was not far to go; both of these cities are hard upon the international border. Most of the effective brigades in the Iraqi army, and apparently its best officers, were involved in the lunge toward Khorramshahr and Abadan — a strike at the heart of the Iranian oil industry. Within days, Iraqi forces had lapped around the two latter cities, isolating them from the north but not investing either one fully.[73] Both were still open to resupply from the Persian Gulf.

There were subsidiary thrusts in the center and north of the international boundary. In the north, Iraqi forces in division strength attacked through Qasr e-Shirin toward Kermanshah. In a week of fighting, they had seized a small patch of Iranian territory extending to the foothills of the Zagros mountains, about 125 square kilometers in all, as well as a handful of villages. The intention here seems to have been largely defensive, to secure the main Tehran-Baghdad route and protect the northeastern approaches to the Iraqi capital from the Iranian armored division headquartered at Kermanshah.[74] A final Iraqi thrust, also in division strength, struck through Mehran in the center. Once again, a militarily useful border adjustment seemed to be what Saddam Hussein had in mind here, rather than any sort of crushing blow against the Iranian army. In this case, it was the southeastern approaches to Baghdad.

At first, the Iranian army was hard pressed to resist any of these moves. Like the Red Army in 1939, it had recently been the victim of an ideological purge at the hands of the revolutionary Islamic regime. Gone — either shot or imprisoned — were a great chunk of the army's field grade officers, including half of those from the ranks of major to colonel. Like the Bourbons after 1789, the shah's once-prized army had

fallen on hard times. Those who had survived were under the close surveillance of "spiritual guidance officers," who, under a different system,
might have been called political commissars. The mullahs who ruled Iran
had no use for staff officers or modern equipment or professional armies.
Instead they relied on Koranic exhortations and promises that God would
provide victory to his people. The regime was in the process of constituting a new force, the Pasdaran (Revolutionary Guards), but the battle
worthiness of these units was a matter of some dispute. Iran thus faced
the Iraqi invasion with just four weak divisions (of nine total in the army).
Arranged in a line from north to south, there was an infantry division
at Urmiyeh, another at Sanandaj, and an armored division at Kermanshah. The crucial region of Khuzistan in the south had a single understrength armor division at Ahwaz.[75] There was no defensive *Schwerpunkt*,
no grouping of forces, no arrangement in depth, nothing that an observer
would recognize as a modern operational deployment.

Despite the great opportunity that beckoned, with well-equipped Iraqi
divisions in hand, moving against a force that seemed in the throes of
dissolution, the Iraqi invasion did not achieve all that much. The Iraqi
tactic of choice was the infantry assault, backed by massed artillery fire,
rather than bold armored thrusts. When Iraqi tanks did go forward, they
did so without adequate infantry support. Despite a great deal of confusion among the Iranian defenders and government, the initial Iraqi
attacks bogged down just a few dozen kilometers inside Iran. Again, the
notion has surfaced that some of this was due to Saddam Hussein's fear
of friendly casualties. Though the attackers had reached all of their four
principal objectives in the south (Khorramshahr, Abadan, Dezful, and
Ahwaz), they had failed to take any of them. Iraqi claims to have Dezful
and Ahwaz under siege proved to be inaccurate. Most of Khuzistan
remained in Iranian hands.

Khorramshahr, in particular, was the scene of heavy fighting. An Iraqi
armored division reached the city in the first days of the invasion and
then paused to allow its heavy artillery to catch up. When it finally did
enter the city on September 28, it met an inferno, regular Iranian forces,
Pasdaran, and, according to some reports, an aroused populace in full
revolutionary fervor, armed with Molotov cocktails and rocket launchers, willing to die as martyrs and equally willing to destroy their own
city rather than see it fall into the hands of the invader. All month they
fought. It was not until early November that the Iraqis managed to
secure the city, and their casualties had been catastrophic. Infantry losses
in this one engagement topped the total of all casualties sustained by
Israel and the Arab armies together in all their wars.[76] Iraq had also lost

more than one hundred tanks, and their loss stalled the Iraqi drive on the much larger oil city of Abadan for two crucial weeks. In a sense, even though the Iranians finally lost Khorramshahr, this battle was the Valmy of the Iranian revolution — the event that guaranteed its survival. It ended the first phase of the war.

The second phase saw a rejuvenated Iran attack the Iraqi invaders and drive them off Iranian soil. Beginning in January 1981, Iran launched a series of attacks all along the front. These early efforts failed, however, because of tactical mistakes, a lack of coordination among the various units involved, and the generally slow pace of the operations. An attack by the Iranian 16th Armored Division near Susangerd, for instance, featured each brigade of the division advancing separately, without any serious attempt at reconnaissance. On January 6, the division's 1st Brigade was ambushed by the Iraqis and destroyed. That was bad enough, but the next day the 2nd Brigade advanced into the same Iraqi defensive position, with the Iraqis even stronger in antitank weapons than they had been the previous day. The result was the same, followed by the 3rd Brigade on January 8. Though the Iraqis were the obvious victors, they had not dazzled with their tactics, either. Point-blank tank battles were the order of the day, and tank losses ran into the hundreds for each side.[77]

A second series of Iranian counterattacks beginning in September 1981 was much more successful. One of these operations, "Thamil ul'Aimma," featured a combined arms force of some thirty to forty thousand men and small tank units attacking in Khuzistan, infiltrating down the Karun River, and taking the Iraqi forces besieging the eastern side of Abadan in the rear.[78] Infiltrating Iraqi positions by night, they were able to penetrate much of the Iraqi front line. The Iraqis were caught by surprise, having failed to do elemental reconnaissance of the area. As the Iranian garrison in Abadan joined the attack, the Iraqi force, some five full brigades, melted away in panic. They left behind a considerable amount of equipment. It was a competent operation on the part of the Iranians, well prepared by artillery barrages and fire support from tanks, featuring simultaneous assaults in both the front and rear of the Iraqi positions.

Such occasions of tactical skill and combined arms were rare. Iran, enjoying a decisive superiority in manpower and with its traditional national feeling heightened by religious and revolutionary fervor, relied for the most part on something very different: human wave assaults. Carrying them out were the Pasdaran and its auxiliary volunteer force, the Basij-e Mustazafin (the Mobilization of the Oppressed), the latter having first been organized as a defense against a potential U.S. attack on revolutionary Iran. The new tactics made their first appearance in the Iranian March 1992 offensive in northern Khuzistan, near Dezful and Shush. Like something from a bygone age, massed waves of Pasdaran and Basij militia advanced in echelons of one thousand men, at intervals of two hundred to five hundred yards. "It's horrifying," one Iraqi officer said, "they swarm at you like roaches."[79] The only note of modernity here was their weaponry: shoulder-held RPG launchers. The shock of the assault drove the Iraqis back some forty kilometers and almost sent them out of Khuzistan altogether. The deputy commander of the Iranian 21st Division was moved to declare that "we are going to write our own manuals, with absolutely new tactics that the Americans, British and French can study at their staff colleges."[80]

Although we are still waiting for that to happen, these primitive tactics did have a great deal of success against Iraq in 1982. There was another Iranian offensive in May, again featuring human wave assaults by the Pasdaran. It succeeded in recovering Khorramshahr in a single day's attack. The Iranians took the surrender of two Iraqi army brigades, along with three brigades of the Popular Army (Ba'ath Party militia), some twenty thousand men in all. The Pasdaran took heavy casualties storming dug-in Iraqi tanks and artillery pieces but were eventually able to saturate and overrun the defenders, driving the Iraqis back over the international border in this sector.[81] It was the low point of the war for Iraq.

Iraq asked for a cease-fire, to which Iran responded by invading Iraq. The war now yielded a mirror image of its opening stages, though in much more extreme form. Beginning in July 1982, Iranian units drove into Iraq, with the declared goal of toppling Saddam Hussein's regime. The first major target of the offensive was the Iraqi oil city of Basra. Here, operational conditions resembled those of World War I. Iraqi defenses consisted of earthworks, trenches, machine gun nests, and fortified artillery positions; like the Basque stronghold of Bilbao in the Spanish Civil War, the fortifications here were known as the "Iron Ring." Once again, armor was subordinate in the Iranian tactical scheme to massed waves of infantry. A great assault by five divisions managed to break through the Iraqi line, however, penetrating about ten miles inside Iraq, some ten miles north of the city. Now four Iraqi divisions launched their own counterattack. It was the world's largest infantry battle since World War II. When it was over, Iran had lost about twenty thousand men, the Iraqis seven thousand. This established the basic pattern of the Iranian invasion. Again and again, superiority in firepower and tanks enabled Iraq to halt the Pasdaran drives. On occasions when Iranian armor did lead the attack, as at Shalamcheh, the Iranians learned the price they had paid for purging so many of the top officers from the shah's army. The attack came on without any reconnaissance. The Iraqis managed to outflank the attacking column on both sides and drive it back.[82]

By 1984, even Iran's seemingly inexhaustible supply of manpower began to run dry. It seemed content to fight a war of attrition, which it believed would eventually end in its favor. There was just one problem: the fear of Islamic fundamentalism as represented by revolutionary Iran had led much of the world to support Saddam Hussein in this war, which, after all, his own aggression had started. Just as Iranian strength slowly began to ebb, Iraq began to receive huge reinforcements of tanks, aircraft, and spare parts from a wide variety of sources, particularly France. Iran had begun the war with some 1,735 main battle tanks. They were a combination of American and British models, purchased in the days of the shah: 400 M-47s and M-48s, 460 M-60A1s, and 875 Chieftains. Against this, Iraq could call upon 2,750 main battle tanks. Virtually all, some 2,500, were of the early Soviet postwar generation, including T-54s, T-55s, and T-62s, although there were also about one hundred older T-34s and fifty of the newest Soviet model, the T-72.

By 1985, the number of Iranian tanks had probably shrunk to no more than 1,050. Partially offsetting the catastrophic losses to its own armored vehicles, which had suffered more than 50 percent casualties, was the capture of a significant amount of Iraqi equipment during the fighting. In the same period, however, Iraq saw its numbers rise to 4,820, nearly double the number with which it had started the war. For the most part, these were still Soviet imports, but to the overall figure must be added some 1,500 Chinese T-59s and T-69 IIs, as well as some captured Iranian Chieftains. Auxiliary arms also benefited greatly: a fleet of heavy Japanese-built earthmovers played a key role in Iraqi battlefield engineering, and German tank transporters greatly improved the strategic mobility of Iraqi armor. Saddam Hussein's military strength owed a great deal to the industrialized West. The balance sheet indicated that it was Iraq, not Iran, that was likely to a win a war of attrition.[83]

In this increasingly stalemated war, both sides continued to undertake large-scale operations that yielded little in terms of strategic results but kept the casualty list mounting. On February 9, 1986, an Iranian amphibious operation overran the Faw Peninsula on the Shatt al Arab. A flotilla of transport craft put nearly a division of Iranian infantry across the Shatt at six separate points on a roughly forty-mile front. They had perfected their landing techniques on the lakes and rivers of northern Iran. A feint attack to the north, against Iraqi III Corps in the Hawizah Marshes north of Basra, took place simultaneously. Defending Faw was

Iraq's VII Corps, and its commander has been described as "far too slow to react"[84] and "extraordinarily incompetent"[85] in his handling of the battle. He failed to attack the landing force when it was most vulnerable — just after disembarking. Then, apparently fearful that he would be punished for his failure, he sent dispatches to Baghdad to the effect that he had driven off the landing force. Soon, the Iranians had advanced from their beachheads and overrun the tip of the peninsula.

Predictably, Iraq reacted directly to the Iranian challenge and focused its entire operational effort on retaking the Faw. The VII Corps commander was gone, replaced by the fire-breathing commander of III Corps, General Abdul Maher al Rashid. Promising to retake Faw in three days, he began to counterattack almost immediately. First in were the Republican Guards, who had a reputation as Saddam Hussein's fire brigade, thrown in wherever an emergency demanded it. Their first foray into the Faw, however, was a disaster. Motoring down the northern road into the peninsula (one of three) in a driving rainstorm, they came under heavy Iranian artillery fire and suffered badly. Nevertheless, their arrival stiffened the Iraqi line, preventing the possibility of an Iranian breakout.

The Iranians now held some ten miles of the peninsula, and their presence there was a real danger to the Iraqi city of Basra to the north. In addition was the possibility of a second Iranian amphibious operation toward the west, directly against the important Iraqi port of Umm Qasr. Above all, Faw had pointed out the bankruptcy of Iraq's wartime strategy of passive defense. There seemed now to be no position that Iranian infantry could not seize, as long as the Iranians did not care about the number of casualties they took. It appears that the civilian authorities in Iraq from Saddam on down were stunned by the loss of Faw. Collapse of the regime now looked like a real possibility. Thus, it was imperative to retake Faw. Rashid kept up the pressure during February and March. Despite repeated attempts to evict them, supported by air, armor, and above all massive artillery barrages, the dug-in Iranian infantry proved to be a tough adversary.

Perhaps the main result of the Faw operations was that Saddam's Baath regime for the first time decided on a popular mobilization for war.[86] In particular, Saddam greatly expanded the Republican Guards, filling their ranks with college students whose universities the state had ordered closed for the duration of the war. In 1986, the Guards had consisted of seven brigades. That number now grew to twenty-five within nine months. Clearly the regime still had reserves of popularity upon which it could call. Mechanized infantry formations under Iraq's best professional officers, the new Guards brigades underwent rigorous combined arms training in 1986 and 1987. They would soon prove to be the dominant force on the battlefield — the difference between victory and defeat. Their rise to prominence also signaled a sea change in Iraqi military policy, with Saddam Hussein interfering less and less in operations, deferring instead to the advice of his officers. It would prove to be a wise choice on his part.

Nevertheless, the Iranians were still riding high. Their infantry had long ago established a moral dominance over the Iraqis. Now they had also managed to procure large numbers of air defense and antitank weapons from abroad. Success in procuring spare parts had doubled the size of their F-14 fleet to twenty-four. A mid-May Iraqi attack against the town of Mehran on the central front, undertaken for no other reason than to restore public confidence, had misfired badly. Although the Iraqis had taken the town, the result was a salient into Iranian lines that could not be held. An Iranian counterattack in July easily took it back, crushing two Iraqi brigades and killing one of the brigadiers. American TOW missiles, part of the "Irangate" shipment, might have played a role in Iran's victory here. The regime in Baghdad continued to teeter.

The Iranians began to plan for the war's endgame, the "final offensive." So confident were they that they even announced the date by which they expected to achieve the final victory over Iraq: January 21, 1987 (their New Year). True to their word, the Iranians launched a great offensive on January 9, 1987, an all-out effort to seize Basra. This offensive, code-named "Karbala-Five," involved four divisions of Iranian infantry attacking across Fish Lake, an artificial water barrier constructed by the Iraqis. It was part of the "Iron Ring" around Basra. The Iranians came by motorboat across the lake, having by now had some experience in amphibious operations. They landed on the southwest shore, formed up, and attacked toward the Shatt, just twelve kilometers away. Their first attack crashed into Republican Guard infantry, however, and was held in check. Attempts to flank the Iraqi position also came to naught, hung up in front of tough Iraqi opposition, both Republican Guard and Border Guard formations, as well as a series of earthen berms. With huge masses of Iranian infantry now crammed into a very narrow space, and with the berms hindering their movement, Iraqi artillery had a field day, inflicting ghastly losses. The Iranians had advanced to within seven miles of the giant city. They would get no closer.

Karbala-Five is a controversial operation today. Some analysts argue that the offensive was a clear sign to the international community that Iran had reestablished its superiority on land and that Iraq remained in great danger. Others, including at least one analyst for the U.S. Marine Corps, see Karbala-Five as a turning point in the war, in which an experienced and professional Iraqi army established such a clear superiority over the Iranian revolutionary levies that Iraq's eventual victory in the war was all but guaranteed. Certainly, the Iraqis had fought competently at Karbala-Five.[87] What might be their one real contribution to the art of war, the hastily constructed earthen berm, was the real star here. Not only did it offer Iraqi forces cover from which to fight, it also channeled Iranian attacks into killing grounds where Iraqi artillery could pulverize them. But even those who argue for the crucial nature of this battle admit that "there is not a lot of information" about it. In the absence of Iranian or Iraqi archival sources on Karbala-Five, it is impossible to say much more.

However we view Karbala-Five today, it seemed to contemporary observers that Iran was still on the offensive and that the pressure was still on Iraq. The result was the increasing internationalization of the conflict in Saddam Hussein's favor. Aid to Iraq, already a factor for years, continued to grow. In March 1987, the United States agreed to reflag Kuwaiti tankers against threatened Iranian attacks and sent a sizable naval presence to the Persian Gulf. This policy survived the accidental Iraqi missile attack on the USS *Stark*, which killed thirty-seven crew members. Incidents in which reflagged tankers hit Iranian mines only reinforced the image of Iran as international outlaw, a fact brought home to Tehran by the lack of international condemnation when the U.S. Navy accidentally shot down an Iranian airbus in July 1988 and killed 290 civilians.

Backed by virtually the entire international community, Iraq took the offensive in 1988. The Iraqi Tawakalna ala Allah ("on God we rely") offensive began in April 1988 and consisted of five major battles. By far the most impressive Iraqi achievement was a decisive victory over the Iranians in the Faw Peninsula. Here the Republican Guards spearheaded the assault.[88] An attack at Fish Lake in May was a straight-ahead drive by masses of Iraqi armor, which drove the exhausted Iranians away from Basra. In July, an Iraqi attack at Dehloran to the north led to an advance of some twenty-eight miles into Iran along an eighty-mile front and netted thousands of prisoners and massive amounts of equipment. Both of these operations were typical "scoop-ups" of the type that occur at the end of a long war of attrition, when one side is exhausted and cannot go on. The example of the German army at Amiens in 1918 comes to mind. The Iraqis then withdrew from Iran, a symbol of their renunciation of territorial ambitions. While the Republican Guards were reestablishing Iraqi strength on the ground, a flurry of missile attacks on Iranian cities in early 1988 terrified the civilian population. An estimated 1.5 million people fled Tehran during this period.

Increasingly isolated, with both superpowers arrayed against it, and with its manpower reserves finally running dry, Iran had to ask for a cease-fire in July 1988. It was a bitter pill for the Ayatollah Khomeini, who announced publicly that the decision was "more deadly than taking poison."[89] International pressure forced Saddam Hussein to accept in August. It wasn't the military situation, which was by now quite favorable to Iraq. The long war was over.

The "Lessons" of Iran-Iraq

Despite the epic nature of this conflict, which stretched over a front of 730 miles and which killed or wounded more than one million people, thousands of them in missile attacks on each other's cities, the Iran-Iraq War will probably not go down as a classic in the annals of conventional war. Saddam Hussein did win a victory of sorts, but it took him not fourteen days, as in the case of the Indo-Pakistani war of 1971, but eight full years. Both warring powers were bankrupted, drained of manpower, and generally exhausted. In fact, Saddam Hussein may have seen himself driven to invade Kuwait in 1990 simply as a way of paying his bills. If so, the Iran-Iraq War is still the driving force behind contemporary events in the Mideast. There is no such thing as a beneficial long war, and there never will be.

The only real lesson on the operational level was a negative one. It was also one that that the world already knew, at least since the experience of the French army in 1940: good equipment does not necessarily equal good operations. Tanks do not make a blitzkrieg. Both sides in this war used modern armored vehicles, tanks, antitank guided missiles, and helicopters — the full arsenal of modern land war. But neither side used any of it very effectively. The pace of operations was extremely slow, with tanks waiting in hull-down positions for artillery to saturate the front, and only then moving forward. On several occasions early in the war, Iraq allowed its armored forces to bog down in urban fighting, as at Khorramshahr, where it sustained serious losses. Even later, when it had real numerical superiority over the Iranians, Iraqi armor was often used as mobile artillery, a complete waste of the special fighting capabilities of the tank. Nor did the Iranians handle their armor any better. For Iran, the real problem was not doctrine or the correct employment of its armored formations, but scrounging enough spare parts to keep the tanks running. Both sides seemed at sea with regard to some of the more complex things their machines could do: the computer range finders on tank guns, for example, or sophisticated aircraft avionics. It was something like a modern computer owner who owns a state-of-the-art machine and can't get beyond word processing. When tank did meet tank on the battlefield, there tended to be an absence of long-range gunnery or maneuver. Neither "fire control" nor "target acquisition" was a high priority for either side. Both sides closed the range, blasted away with inaccurate fire, and hoped for the best. Although tank battles might go on for extended periods of time, with a great deal of fire, there were often minimal losses on both sides. In the end, victory or defeat rested on the shoulders of the infantry, which bore the brunt of the fighting and suffered conditions reminiscent of the Western Front in 1916, although neither army ever approached a western standard of professionalism.

Often, the passage of time softens initial impressions. Certainly in the scholarly community, this is the case. "Revisionist" views come to the fore; what was once thought ghastly receives a rational explanation; individuals once held to be incompetent are found to be undiscovered geniuses. In the case of the Iran-Iraq War, the opposite seems to be the case. This war was taken quite seriously as it was happening. Analysts weighed in with assessments of both armies, their tactics, operations, and strategies. Widely respected pundit Anthony Cordesman, who is perhaps the closest American equivalent to Liddell Hart, wrote books about the lessons of the war, as well as numerous articles in the professional literature, while it was still raging. There are a myriad of dangers to such instant analysis, of course, as in the case of a volume that he published in 1987, in which he predicted that there was "no clear end in sight" to the conflict. His volume on Iran-Iraq, coauthored with Abraham R. Wagner and part of their series, *The Lessons of Modern War*, runs to more than six hundred pages. It is suitably critical of both sides throughout but does conclude that the Iraqi army was able, finally, "to create a force capable of effective maneuver warfare."[90]

Others went much further. Historian and Marine Corps analyst Stephen C. Pelletiere, in his various works on the war, described the Iraqi army as "a first-class fighting institution,"[91] "formidable" in both positional and mobile defense.[92] Its general staff was excellent, he said, pointing out that it was "shaped by the traditions of the Prussian military";[93] its commanders, he wrote, were "excellent problem solvers."[94] James Blackwell, who became well known for his work as an analyst for

CNN, actually placed Saddam in the context of "Iraq's ancient martial heritage," the heir to Sargon, Tiglath-Pileser II, and Nebuchadnezzar. By the end of the war with Iran, he wrote, "the Iraqi army quickly gained a reputation for being on a level of tactical and operational proficiency equal to that of the best Western armies." It was, he wrote, "an incredible military machine," "well trained, battle-tested, and highly skilled at conducting combat operations."[95] Nor were they alone, as the often shrill American reportage — both print and electronic — about the Iraqi army on the verge of Operation Desert Storm would indicate.

None of this is new, nor is it evidence of special incompetence on anyone's part. From the Boer War to the present day, there is nothing riskier than the act of "punditry," attempting to explain the lessons of this or that conflict in its immediate wake. The analyst is asked, and often paid, to give an opinion. It often has to be done instantly, in front of various demanding audiences: policymakers, television viewers, or both. The stakes are therefore quite high, and giving an honest "I really don't know" does not seem like an acceptable option. One has to give one's best guess, and most analysts try to make it an educated one. More often than not, however, the pundits turn out to be wrong. No example in history better illustrates the problem of punditry more than these overblown assessments of the Iraqi army.

The historian is more fortunate. In retrospect, there were no lessons of the Iran-Iraq War. Both sides bled their own countries dry, one in the interests of revolutionary Islamic ideology, the other out of simple hunger for power. Saddam used oceans of poison gas in the course of the war, against both the enemy and against Kurdish rebels inside the country; Khomeini used young boys as shock troops and "mine clearers." Saddam had an embarrassing experience: he started a limited war, had to ask for peace terms two years later, and was actually turned down. Khomeini was even more unusual: a leader who showed his ideological mettle by boldly refusing to settle for victory. Both were able to rely on popular levies, the Iranians from the start, the Iraqis after the loss of the Faw Peninsula in 1986. Neither did much with them, except get them killed in large numbers. It was a typical war of attrition. First, Iraq teetered on the brink of defeat, like France in 1917, but recovered. Then, having shot its logistical and manpower bolt, Iran suddenly collapsed, like Germany in 1918.[96] It is difficult to argue with Chaim Herzog, who wrote in 1989 that "from a pure battlefield point of view there is little to learn from this senseless, dreadful conflict."[97]

It is true that the forces of both Iran and Iraq did get better over the course of the war. It is devoutly to be hoped that eight years of practice would make anyone better at anything. Both sides did manage to launch interesting operations from time to time. However, if operational skill means anything more than following a tightly scripted plan, if it includes, for example, the ability to react to changing situations and exploit them to win a decisive victory, then, in operational terms, both of these armies were terrible.

7

The U.S. Army: Collapse and Rebirth

American Operations in the Post-1945 Era

It is common to assume that each of the world's great powers has a "traditional way of war." For the Germans, it is the highly mobile campaign designed to win a quick, decisive victory, in the style of Frederick the Great or the elder Helmuth von Moltke. For the British, it is to avoid entangling commitments on the European continent in favor of a maritime strategy designed to expand the empire. In the case of the United States, however, it is much more difficult to make a generalized statement of this type. At various times in its history and in various places, the United States has emphasized a maritime strategy, a joint (naval-land) strategy, and a nuclear strategy based first on strategic bombers, then one based on a "triad" of bombers, submarines, and intercontinental ballistic missiles. In terms of land operations, it has a strong tradition of maneuver-based warfare dating back to the Revolutionary War and the Mexican War; it has an equally strong tradition of firepower-based attrition war. The country's formative military experience, the Civil War, saw a tremendous amount of both types. In fact, one might argue that it is precisely this flexibility of means that has been the principal characteristic of American war making over the years, rather than rigid adherence to any one specific operational doctrine.

That flexibility has not always won the recognition it deserved. In his enormously influential work *The American Way of War* (1973), U.S. military historian Russell Weigley identified the title concept with gathering overwhelming force, attacking the enemy's main field force, and flattening it. It was a strategy, he said, that grew as the young country grew. The land's wealth, resources, and power brought about a preference for a total victory, Weigley argued, the "destruction of the enemy's armed force" along with the "complete overthrow" of the foe himself, ending in his unconditional surrender.[1]

At the heart of this thesis was a particular interpretation of U. S.

Grant. Weigley's Grant was a commander noted not for his operational subtlety, but more for his imperviousness to casualties. Grant's calculus was simple: he could afford the losses, and General Robert E. Lee could not. It was Lee, commanding the forces of a state that would surely lose a prolonged war of attrition, who strove for what we might call the "German solution": offensive campaigns of elegant maneuver aiming at the quick operational victory. Grant realized that he had no need for such a risky posture. Why lose in an afternoon a war he was sure to win in two years? Hence the bloody slogging match through the Wilderness, Spottsylvania Courthouse, and Cold Harbor, on the way to Appomattox. Grant grabbed Lee, refused to let him maneuver, and eventually bled him to death, along with a large portion of the manpower in both armies. Hence Weigley's conclusion: "Grant never gained decisive results in any single battle, and he did not expect to. He returned decision to the war by prolonging battle through the whole campaign, inflicting casualties until he won not a dramatic Napoleonic victory but the peace of exhaustion."[2]

Weigley's argument contained a germ of truth, but it was also what a German officer would describe as *einseitig:* one-sided. The young republic had fought three wars before 1860 (the Revolutionary conflict, the War of 1812, and the Mexican War) with very small armies that had to maneuver against consistently larger and more powerful forces. It had managed to win two of those wars and to draw one. Scott's march on Mexico City, during which he actually abandoned his supply lines back to his coastal base at Veracruz, was a classic example of a smaller force out-maneuvering and out-fighting a much larger adversary fighting on his home turf and in defense of his capital. It struck many contemporaries as daring, even reckless, and there were many predictions of disaster, predictions that lasted until the very point that Scott entered Mexico City.

It is in his portrayal of Grant, however, that Weigley crosses the line into caricature. As a raft of more recent scholarship has pointed out, Grant could maneuver with the best of them. The Vicksburg campaign was his masterpiece. Slipping past Vicksburg on the western bank of the Mississippi, Grant carried out a surprise crossing of the river downriver from the fortress city on April 30, 1863. He then decided on what J. F. C. Fuller called "one of the boldest steps ever taken in war."[3] Cutting loose from his supply lines and living off the land, he launched a vigorous drive toward Jackson, Mississippi, and routed the Confederate forces there. His sudden turnabout toward Vicksburg against enemy forces commanded by a highly rattled General John Pemberton ended in the decisive victory at Champion Hill. These were some of the most elegant maneuvers in the history of the U.S. Army. Nor were his thrusts against Lee in northern Virginia based on a simple strategy of bludgeoning. He consistently tried to outflank Lee, which was why every engagement fought in the campaign wound up being just a bit closer to Richmond. Weigley has made the common error of confusing the worst moments in Grant's conduct of the war — let us say the first two hours at Cold Harbor — with his entire career. They were bad hours, but they did not lose the war.

Nevertheless, Weigley's "American way of war" is still useful in describing one principal aspect of U.S. operational doctrine, especially in the twentieth century. It did not stem from Grant but from the pervasive French influence that dominated U.S. thinking before, during, and after World War I: a doctrine that emphasized a systematic, set-piece approach of finding, pinning, and destroying the enemy with fire rather than clever operational maneuver. During World War I, the French served as mentors to the U.S. Army, and much of the equipment that the army used (tanks, artillery, and aircraft) was of French manufacture. The French doctrine of the "methodical battle" — carefully phased attacks based on overwhelming firepower — became U.S. doctrine as well, and it served the U.S. Army well enough to win the brief campaign against Imperial Germany in 1918. In the interwar period, the American F.S.R. *(Field Service Regulation)* of 1923 was essentially a translation of the French manual of 1921 *(Instruction provisoire sur l'emploi tactique des grande unites)*. It remained U.S. doctrine in the early days of World War II, until the army found itself stuck in the hedgerows of Normandy and had to resort, for the first time since the Civil War, to a more intense devotion to operational-level planning to get itself moving forward again. The result was Operation Cobra, the high point for American military operations in the war.

The postwar environment left the United States with a new global mission, as it replaced the fallen European empires as a guarantor of order and stability in such far-flung regions as Korea, the Southeast Asian littoral, and the Middle East. Suddenly, U.S. planners faced the same puzzle that the British Empire had faced between the two world wars. The by-now traditional U.S. force was a heavy mechanized force of big battalions, based around tanks, artillery, and air power, prepared to fight a great war against the Soviet Union on the "central front" in Europe. But was that truly what the United States needed now? Or, in its newly declared war on the shadowy forces of world communism, did it need something else entirely: an imperial police force (a "constabulary," in British parlance)? Such a force would need to be extremely light and have training in all sorts of activities that American armies have traditionally disdained (civilian crowd control, propaganda, political organization). Its need for tank forces, and even infantry for that matter, would be small, since its cutting edge would be air power, elevated in the minds of U.S. planners to almost mythical status by the American possession of the atomic and hydrogen bombs in the years immediately after World War II.

This was the great American military conundrum. On the one hand, there was a necessity, disputed by no sane person, to prepare for another *grande guerre*, already named "World War III" even before it had been fought. The American commitment to Europe and to the North Atlantic Treaty Organization (NATO) dictated the army's size, armaments, and doctrine. On the other hand, while the U.S. Army spent its energy, time, and treasure preparing for war with the Soviet Union, it never actually fought a war in Europe. In fact, it fought everywhere but Europe, carrying out a whole host of missions tied to the Truman Doctrine. We have already seen how ill prepared it was for a war in Korea. That lack of preparation was partly responsible for the alternating pattern of disaster and success that characterized its operations. The 1960s brought an even more intractable problem: the war in Vietnam. A muscular army formed to fight immense battles with fleets of tanks and aircraft found itself in a guerrilla struggle, a war requiring light infantry to patrol the bush, where the principal tactical unit was the squad, and where fire support was the light mortar.

To the Fulda Gap: The Phantom War

It is not easy to write a book about a war that never happened, but that did not stop some of the world's best minds from doing just that in the post-World War II era. The topic was the expected U.S.-Soviet conflict across the so-called central front in Germany. The "next war," as it was almost universally known, was the most intensely analyzed conflict of all time. An entire industry of writers and publishers, in and out of uniform and in and out of the academy, devoted their considerable talents to describing its opening battles and predicting its outcome. A mountain of books dealt with it, with titles such as *The Third World War, Not Over by Christmas*, and *First Clash*.[4] Numerous military simulations in game form were available on the market: the "The Next War" by Simulations Publications Inc., for example; "NATO" by Victory Games; or the multivolume "Third World War" by Game Designers Workshop.[5] The military establishments of both superpowers designed their armored vehicles and weapons systems according to its demands and bent their military doctrine to its peculiarities. And, in the end, both armies found themselves plunged into crisis when the wars that they had to fight were nothing like the huge European set-piece engagement that they had been expecting. For the United States, it was Vietnam; for the Soviets, Afghanistan.

Once the collapse of the Soviet Union removed the strategic basis for a great war in Central Europe, the mountain of literature dedicated to the topic has the faint aura of nostalgia about it. Basically, cold war analysts made two types of assessments. The first was quantitative, the simple act of "cannon counting"; the second was the trickier proposition of assessing quality. In the first, the advantages lay with the Soviets. According to U.S. Department of Defense figures for the mid-1980s, the Warsaw Pact outnumbered NATO in just about everything: 42,500 to 13,000 in main battle tanks; 31,500 to 10,750 in artillery and mortars; 78,800 to 30,000 in armored personnel carriers and infantry fighting vehicles; 24,300 to 8,100 in antitank guided weapon launchers (crew served, mounted, or both); and 7,240 to 2,975 in tactical aircraft.[6] Soviet forces stationed in Germany alone (the Group of Soviet Forces Germany, GSFG) added up to some nineteen divisions: nine tank divisions and ten mechanized divisions. Soviet forces in all of Eastern Europe amounted to thirty divisions (sixteen tank and fourteen mechanized). In addition, the USSR could call on 45 more divisions of non–Soviet Warsaw Pact troops plus 65 divisions in the European USSR (23 tank, 37 mechanized, and 5 airborne divisions), for a total of 140 divisions.

To counter this, there were sixteen divisions in the whole U.S. Army (four armored, six mechanized, three infantry, one light infantry, one air assault, and one airborne). Each was about twice as large as a Soviet division, but that still left a large numerical deficit for the United States, even after adding the NATO allies. If classical military analysis requires a three-to-one superiority in numbers to achieve a breakthrough of an enemy front, Pact forces would have had at least that in most areas. In designated breakthrough sectors, they would have had much more than that.[7]

Geography added to NATO's problem. Reinforcement would have been a much more difficult affair for the United States than for the USSR. Soviet reinforcements would have come by road or rail from the Eurasian landmass, from the Baltic, Byelorussian, Carpathian, Odessa, Kiev, and Northern Caucasus military districts. U.S. reinforcements (National Guard divisions, for the most part) would have had to come by sea or airlift from the continental United States to Europe. U.S. forces practiced this annually in their Return of Forces to Germany (REFORGER) exercises. But these exercises consistently showed that

Preparing for the war that never came: A column of M1A1 main battle tanks on maneuvers in central Europe. Courtesy of U.S. Army TACOM.

the Soviet surface fleet, submarine fleet, and air force would have severely tested U.S. REFORGER ability.[8]

The second kind of assessment was qualitative. Here the advantages lay with the United States and NATO, based on their clear technological lead on the battlefield. By the late 1980s, the principal NATO main battle tanks were the M-1 Abrams (U.S.), the Leopard II (Germany), and the Challenger (U.K.). All were more than a match for the Soviet T-80: more mobile, roomier for the crew, and with laser acquisition and targeting, far more accurate. In the air, likewise, U.S. F-15 and F-16 fighters clearly outclassed the Soviet MiG-25 Foxbat. Soviet aircraft generally lacked all-weather capability, carried smaller payloads, had shorter ranges, were tougher to fly, and needed more maintenance than U.S. planes. In terms of ground support, the U.S. A-10 Thunderbolt was the best around, a tank-killer extraordinaire, with bombs, air to surface missiles, and an awesome Gatling gun that can fire 4,200 tank-killing rounds per minute.[9] By the 1980s, virtually all U.S. tactical aircraft carried highly accurate precision-guided munitions (PGMs), or "smart bombs," using laser-guidance systems to direct bombs to their targets. Finally, there was "Stealth" technology, as embodied in the F-117 fighter-bomber. Nearly invisible to enemy radar, it proved its worth on the opening night of Operation Desert Storm by penetrating Iraqi airspace and destroying the Iraqi air defense headquarters in Baghdad.

Both sides in any NATO-Pact conflict would have been fighting within the constraints of coalition warfare, with unpredictable consequences. Although many in the West pointed to the higher degree of weapons and equipment standardization within the pact, there was also a great amount of tension between the Soviet Union and its East European satellite states. It is hard to imagine Polish or Slovak soldiers fighting hard for Soviet domination of Europe, even though the officer corps of the various national contingents might have been loyal. Dissent among the subject populations, the Poles, for example, would have posed a serious threat to the long supply line from the Soviet Union to the theater of war in Western Europe. On the NATO side, the French presented a sort of wild card, which no doubt pleased them immensely. Out of NATO but still a signatory to the North Atlantic Treaty, and with their own nuclear arsenal, the *force de frappe*, the French had gone their own way since the 1960s. It is difficult to imagine them staying out of a NATO-Pact conflict. Even after leaving the organization, they kept a full corps of two divisions in Germany and went on regular maneuvers with NATO. Nevertheless, their unusual status lent an air of uncertainty to Western planning.

NATO was an alliance of free democracies, and that would have spoken well for cohesion on one level. Still, there were differences between the national contingents. A huge gap existed between the big three (the U.S. Army, the British Army of the Rhine, and the West German Bundeswehr) and the smaller partners: the Dutch army, which was actually unionized; the Belgians, weak and underfunded; and the Greeks and Turks, whose own rivalry precluded much in the way of joint planning on NATO's southern, or Mediterranean, flank. All in all, the problem was a daunting one, even within particular U.S. Corps. When General Frederick M. Franks took over command of the U.S. VII Corps in Germany in August 1989, it included two U.S. divisions (1st Armored and 3rd Infantry), a German division (12th Panzer), and a Canadian brigade (4th Canadian Mechanized Brigade Group). Such a diverse grouping of forces might well have experienced command and coordination problems in combat.[10]

In terms of the individual soldier, the average U.S. infantryman or tanker was both better educated and better trained than his Soviet counterpart. U.S. troops were permitted more scope for personal initiative, while the Soviets still relied on a fierce discipline that discouraged individuals from making decisions on their own and that might have resulted

in missed opportunities in combat. Above all, a Western soldier repre-
sented a free society. On the eve of the battle of Issus, Alexander the
Great addressed his troops and steeled their nerve for the coming fight:
"Above all," he reminded them, "we are free men, and they are slaves."[11]
For all its apparent weaknesses, that benefit also accrued to NATO.
Whether it would have offset a gross numerical inferiority is a question
that thankfully remained unanswered.

The "Next War": Operations

A Warsaw Pact invasion of West Germany would have been able to call
upon vast numerical superiority at the point of contact. The five Soviet
armies within the GSFG (2nd Guards Tank, 3rd Shock, and 8th Guards
armies in the first echelon, 20th Guards and 1st Guards Tank armies in
the second) would be the spearhead of the fighting, of course, but joining them would be two East German armies (the 3rd and 5th) and forces
from the Polish Pomorze (Pomeranian) Military District. In addition,
two Czech armies (1st and 4th), supported by the Soviet Central Group
of Forces, would be immediately available for a drive into southern West
Germany.[12]

These massive forces would have had their choice of several attrac-
tive axes for the attack, but three stand out. The first and most obvious
was a drive across the North German plain. Here lay the best tank country, the most direct route to the Rhine River as well as the West German Ruhr district, the industrial heartland of Western Europe. Although
this was the traditional invasion route over the centuries, the region had
become far more built up since the end of World War II. In addition,
Pact forces would encounter a water crossing every six miles, either a
natural river or stream (the Elbe, Weser, Main, and Neckar, for example) or one of West Germany's numerous canals.[13] Still, the northern
approach offered the Pact the most promising hopes for a rapid victory.
An attack on Denmark to open the Baltic approaches would almost certainly have accompanied a Pact drive in the north. Forces for such an
operation would probably have included Polish airborne and marine
forces (6th Airborne and 7th Sea Landing Divisions), as well as a Soviet
airborne division. The defenders here would have been NATO's Northern Army Group (NORTHAG): the West German I Corps guarding
the approaches to Hamburg, and the British I Corps defending Hannover, with support from the Belgian I army (to the right of British I
Corps), and the Dutch I Corps. NATO had transferred a U.S. armored

brigade to the region in the 1980s, but by and large, American strength would not have been available to defend this crucial region.

Two other likely avenues of approach were the Fulda Gap in central Germany, a transition region between the relatively flat north and the mountainous south of West Germany, and the Hof Gap on the border between East Germany and Czechoslovakia. A Soviet thrust through Fulda would have posed a grave threat to NATO's integrity.[14] The gap led directly across West Germany's uncomfortably narrow waist. The major city of Frankfurt was less than a hundred kilometers away from the border at this point, and the Rhine River just forty more beyond it. Here lay NATO's Central Army Group (CENTAG), two contiguous U.S. Army corps flanked by two from West Germany: from north to south, the III West German Corps, V U.S., VII U.S., and II German. Though it did not garner as much attention as the two gaps to the north, some analysts have identified the II West German Corps sector as a potential problem spot for NATO. The corps had a large operational responsibility, including the defense of most of Bavaria and the approaches to Munich. A Soviet approach here, perhaps even passing through neutral and weakly defended Austria, might have caught NATO relatively unprepared. It would have required an "Ardennes gambit," however, in the style of the Wehrmacht's great success of 1940, a risky passage of a mech-heavy force through tough terrain generally regarded as unsuited for armored operations.[15] Of course, U.S. commanders had satellite intelligence unavailable to the French in 1940, assets that almost certainly would have picked up large Soviet troop concentrations and movements. Also important to this sector was the French attitude. A prompt French entry into the war would have brought the II French Corps into play to assist West German II Corps in defending the line of the Lech River, west of Munich, although preventing the fall of the city itself would have been difficult.

In retrospect, NATO was caught between two poles. A sensible, indeed orthodox, operational posture would have been a mobile or active defense. NATO forces, according to this response, would let the tremendous strength of the initial thrust be dissipated by covering forces along the border: U.S. armored cavalry regiments, for example, or the numerous West German border defense units. Then, when the momentum of the Pact advance began to lag, NATO could go over to the counteroffensive. The only problem, however, was that mobile defense posture meant abandoning most of the Federal Republic of Germany. For this very reason, by the 1980s, NATO had publicly committed itself to a posture of forward defense — alliance politics demanded it. Forward defense, however, ran the danger of enemy penetration at one or more places, leading to exploitation by second and third Pact echelons, and thus an early Soviet victory. There was no good answer to this problem.

A key factor governing the course of operations would be the lead time available to NATO forces. A rapid surprise blow from a "standing start," with front-line units literally launching the offensive out of the garrisons, offered risks for both sides. It certainly would have been a nightmare for NATO, its main force units still in the barracks, having to rush to the front without the supplies or the ammunition to fight a major engagement, its aircraft largely on the ground, its headquarters and supply services in a state of utter confusion. Use of chemical weapons as part of such a surprise offensive would only have increased the sense of panic on NATO's side. NATO's operational posture relied on the arrival of large-scale reinforcements from the continental United States, and in the case of a bolt out of the blue Pact offensive, those reinforcements would have been very far away, indeed. But although a surprise blow would have allowed the Pact to achieve strategic surprise, it also would have violated the long-standing Soviet doctrinal principle of having a second and third echelon in place to conduct continuous operations along a given axis. It would also have been a war by improvisation, a type in which NATO would presumably hold most of the advantages, that is, if it survived the initial blow.

An attack after a long buildup, perhaps in an atmosphere of international crisis or crises, would have sacrificed surprise. It would have given both sides time to mobilize, and in particular would have given U.S. forces time to prepare: reinforcements would have already arrived in the theater, drawn upon their stocks of pre-positioned material, and hustled to the border. Any extended prewar crisis would probably also have forced the French to opt into the conflict even before the shooting started. However, such a scenario would also have meant a fully mobilized Warsaw Pact, with its later echelons ready to go from the outset, and would have been an immeasurably more destructive conflict. In general, it might be said that if the "standing start" model might have offered both sides more room to maneuver, the long crisis model would have been a war of attrition from the beginning.

In between these two poles, of course, lay an entire spectrum of potential scenarios. The most likely, perhaps, would have been a Pact invasion launched by units already on military maneuvers near the border, or as part of the GSFG's semiannual rotation of troops in November or May. This scenario would have awarded the Pact at least tactical surprise and a better balance of forces, with NATO still walking into its fair share of walls as it attempted to shift to a war-fighting posture. NATO strategists also discussed several limited scenarios in the 1960s and 1970s, a seizure of Bornholm Island, for example, or the "Hamburg grab," in which a Pact coup de main seized that single West German city and then dared NATO to respond.[16] Hindering the likelihood of the latter scenario was the need for the Pact to force a crossing over the mighty Elbe River to get to Hamburg in the first place.

Numerous other factors would have affected the shape of operations. West Berlin held a truly anomalous position. Stuck far inside East Germany and thus surrounded by the Warsaw Pact, it held a garrison of three brigades (one French, one British, and one American), plus a police force of fifteen thousand Germans. The paramilitary branch of the police, the "Readiness Police" (Bereitschaftpolizei, or Bepos) was probably the best-equipped urban police force in the world, trained in the use of machine guns, armored cars, grenade launchers, and light anti-tank weapons.[17] Given a determined Warsaw Pact attempt to take Berlin, it is doubtful that the garrison could have held out, but it certainly could have inflicted losses on the attackers. Most analysts, in fact, believed that the Pact would simply screen Berlin in the event of an offensive to the west. If Soviet troops broke through NATO in the west and won the war, they could always deal with Berlin at their leisure.

Another factor would have been the almost certain Pact use of airborne forces in the opening stages of an invasion, perhaps working in cahoots with fifth columnists already smuggled into West Germany before the balloon went up. The Soviet Union maintained a massive force of paratroopers into the 1980s, at least eight divisions, a small number of airmobile brigades, and a considerable number of jump-trained special forces units. The opening of a Pact offensive would probably have seen jumps up to one hundred kilometers into the NATO rear in an attempt to seize strategic points, block NATO reinforcements from the breakthrough sector, and generally wreak as much havoc as possible. NATO planners expected Soviet special forces (Spetsnaz), speaking one or more NATO languages fluently and perhaps even wearing NATO uniforms, to engage in kidnapping, assassination, and acts of sabotage.[18] Their effectiveness depended to a large extent on how much warning NATO had of the impending invasion and how much success they had in penetrating NATO's air defenses.

In the end, this war would likely have come down to two factors. First, NATO could not hold a Pact offensive without the arrival of U.S. reinforcements from across the Atlantic. Their arrival or nonarrival, determined by a new "Battle of the Atlantic" on the sea, under the sea, and in the air, would therefore have been crucial. The second factor, which despite the mountains of studies parsing it from every conceivable angle remained absolutely unpredictable, was the use of nuclear weapons. Soviet doctrine, at least in its published form, generally accepted their use from the outset of the fighting. After all, why would any military establishment hold back any weapon it has when victory or defeat is in the balance? The United States envisioned a war that began with conventional weapons and then, at some point in the future, "went nuclear." The likeliest scenario is the United States being confronted with demands from battlefield commanders for authorization to use tactical nuclear weapons, particularly if some disaster had befallen NATO at one or more points in the Soviet assault.[19] Predicting the subsequent course of events once the bombs had fallen is difficult, if not impossible.

Vietnam: The Operational View

In the 1960s, U.S. forces found themselves involved in a very different war from the hypothetical one just discussed. Their failure to bring to an end a communist insurgency in South Vietnam is a well-known story, and there is no need to recount it in detail. It was a war in which, irony of ironies, the U.S. Army suddenly found itself transformed into the Redcoats, a foreign *Soldateska* patrolling a hostile countryside. It was a war in which virtually every movement, even in supposedly secure areas, had to be treated as a tactical redeployment. It was a war that left the armed forces confused, wracked by racial tension, and with a large part of the manpower experimenting with drugs — in other words, a war that left them a close reflection of the civil society out of which they came.

And yet, the failed antiguerrilla struggle was just one side of the Vietnam experience. In early 1968, the U.S. military fought three battles that indicate that, as badly as it mishandled the guerrilla side of the conflict, it was still quite skilled at conventional warfare. U.S. forces were completely mechanized and therefore enjoyed a vast advantage in mobility. Widening that advantage was the U.S. breakthrough into airmobility. The helicopter-borne assault force was the real doctrinal breakthrough of the war, able to go anywhere and hit anything in a war without flanks. Finally, the United States possessed far heavier weapons of all sorts and, in a tradition dating back to World War II, enjoyed extremely effective air support. All told, there had never been an army in the history of the world that could move faster or generate more firepower than the U.S. force in Vietnam.

KHE SANH

When the U.S. Marine firebase at Khe Sanh came under attack in early 1968, just before Tet, the Vietnamese New Year's holiday, it seemed to many American policymakers and journalists to be a disaster in the making.[20] Khe Sanh seemed in particular to be a ghastly rerun of the French disaster at Dien Bien Phu in 1954. And, in fact, the name "Dien Bien Phu" appeared repeatedly in the American media's coverage of the battle, not to mention government and army documents. There was a certain surface similarity between the two situations, to be sure. Like the unfortunate French in 1954, the men of the 26th Marine Regiment were surrounded at their small base out on Highway 9. They were under observation and almost constant artillery fire, including that of heavy 122-mm mortars; the marines were, more or less, unable to strike at their foe, who remained hidden from sight. They were under siege, and the United States Marine Corps (USMC) is not a force traditionally configured for siege warfare. Heightening the sense of urgency was the North Vietnamese army (NVA) success in overrunning the Special Forces Camp at Lang Vei on the night of February 6–7. The base, manned by twenty-four U.S. Green Berets and several hundred indigenous troops, sat some nine miles west of Khe Sanh. The NVA hit it with a murderous assault, even employing armor for the first time, eleven light amphibious PT-76 tanks, to be exact.[21] All things considered, Khe Sanh was a rotten and dangerous spot for the marines, made even worse by the single enemy shell that detonated the combat base's main ammunition dump during the opening bombardment on January 21. It was a hellish night.

Nevertheless, it should have been obvious that the situation did not justify the often hysterical reportage in the American media. U.S. forces at Khe Sanh were nowhere near as isolated as the French had been at their remote base in 1954. In fact, they weren't really isolated at all. Despite being under constant shelling in a remote and desolate region, Khe Sanh remained under the firm protection of the U.S. air umbrella throughout all three months of the siege. Dien Bien Phu had been 150 miles from the nearest French airfield; Khe Sanh sat just 30 miles away from the massive U.S. air base at Da Nang. The 834th Air Division, in particular, was a full operational partner of the forces on the ground.[22] There were hourly resupply missions and speedy evacuation of the wounded. Even after NVA shelling closed the base runway to the huge C-130 transport aircraft on February 10, supplies continued to come in via paradrop. Heavier equipment and supplies used the "Low Altitude Parachute Extraction System" (LAPES). The pilot of the transport

Peering toward Dien Bien Phu? Forward observers of the 26th Marines try to spot North Vietnamese army mortars from the front lines at Khe Sanh, February 1968. Brigadier General Edwin H. Simmons Collection, VA020893, the Vietnam Center Archive, Texas Tech University.

opened the tailgate of his aircraft as he approached the drop zone. The cargo was mounted on a pallet, which passed over a roller system mounted on the floor of the aircraft.[23] It wasn't a perfect system, and it worked best for bulk items like ammunition and rations. Nevertheless, it certainly proved sufficient to keep a large and powerful complement of marine artillery well supplied with ammunition. During the siege, the artillery battalion at Khe Sanh would fire nearly 160,000 rounds in direct support of marine ground forces.

One problem that was potentially more serious than North Vietnamese opposition was the natural confusion resulting from marine, navy, and air force aircraft all using the same restricted airspace. Interservice friction eventually led General Westmoreland to appoint a "Single Manager for Tactical Air." He gave General William Momyer, his deputy for air and the commander of the 7th Air Force, authority to oversee all tactical air missions in South Vietnam. It didn't make everyone happy, and the marines, fiercely protective of their "air-ground team," liked it least of all. One analyst declared that Westmoreland was trying to "reconcile the irreconcilable," and that seems a fair assessment.[24] In fact, the "Single Manager" concept simply added another layer of bureaucracy to an already confusing situation.

Although the U.S. media and public focused on the danger to the 26th Marines, the force to be pitied was the NVA. Communist forces took a fierce pounding at Khe Sanh. From January to April 1968, enemy units ringing the base were under nearly continuous bombardment not only from marine and navy tactical air power, but also from B-52 Stratofortresses. Flying in from Andersen Air Force Base on Guam; U-Tapao, Thailand; or Kadena, Okinawa, these raids were part of the "Arc Light" effort, the name given generally to B-52 missions in Southeast Asia. Westmoreland dubbed the B-52 bombing at Khe Sanh Operation Niagara, and it truly was a nonstop cascade of bombs. On one level, it was simply a repeat of the kind of carpet bombing that had broken open the German position in Normandy in 1944. The bombers were much heavier by now, and, in addition, the procedures had grown much more scientific. Bombers attacked using a grid system, in which several B-52s plastered an assigned one- by two-kilometer box at regular intervals, employing both high explosive and napalm. At first, the pace was three aircraft every ninety minutes. After a single day of operation, February 15, General Selmon Wells (3rd Air Division, Guam) ordered a change to six B-52s every three hours.[25] Although regulations stated that B-52 targets could be no closer than three thousand meters to friendly positions, the urgency of the situation at Khe Sanh soon saw that safety interval reduced to one thousand meters. Since the NVA already knew from experience that close proximity to U.S. positions meant immunity from B-52 strikes, these new close-in strikes were all the more effective. On the night of February 29–March 1, for example, B-52s hit a major NVA attack being prepared along a double axis: the Poilane plantation along Highway 9 and east of Hill 881 South. The results were devastating; marines on the front line, their noses bleeding from the concussion of the bombs, could see bodies being tossed in the air. Colonel David Lownds, commander of the 26th Marines, believed that "those strikes caught at least two battalions. We were already in contact on the perimeter . . . with a battalion, so I feel we had a regiment." An early morning patrol uncovered a total of seventy-eight bodies.[26]

Statistics often lie, but here is one that doesn't: the "Arc Light" raids delivered the equivalent of a 1.3 kiloton blast — in other words, a small nuclear weapon — on NVA positions every single day of the siege. Put another way, each of the approximately thirty thousand NVA soldiers at Khe Sanh got his own personal five tons of high explosive. West-moreland himself believes that the B-52 bombing was "the thing that broke their backs." Enemy casualties were enormous. Even sober esti-mates put the NVA casualty figure between ten and fifteen thousand dead. American dead in the fighting for Khe Sanh itself were just 205, although the figure jumps considerably if losses at Lang Vei, the relief operation known as "Pegasus," and the period of mobile operations after the siege are included (to some 1,000 dead and 4,500 wounded). It is often mentioned, with some surprise, that the North Vietnamese never did launch a full-scale infantry assault against the base. It's no wonder.

The NVA's operational conduct of the battle still puzzles, however. General Vo Nyugen Giap, the NVA commander, assembled a huge force by the standards of this war, marched them up within artillery range of the 26th Marines, and then had them sit there. He may not have been interested in an immediate assault on Khe Sanh, but instead in threat-ening it to see how the Americans reacted. If their reaction was sluggish, then he might have a real opportunity to overrun the base with the siz-able force at his disposal. This would constitute a major operational vic-tory, to be sure. However, Giap's conduct of Khe Sanh makes the case for his brilliance on the operational level — a case made many, many times over the years — much weaker.[27] By concentrating his men in static positions around Khe Sanh, he had finally offered U.S. forces a target worth shooting at. They did, making him pay for his blunder with a casualty list that only American firepower could generate. Whatever they may have thought they were doing at Khe Sanh, the soldiers of the NVA were actually going to school in the "American way of war."

CITY FIGHT AT HUE

The fighting around Khe Sanh blended smoothly into the great North Vietnamese offensive of 1968, timed to coincide with Tet, the Viet-namese New Year. NVA and National Liberation Front (NLF) forces struck targets all over South Vietnam, a dispersed assault that would cost them dearly. North Vietnamese planners expected that such a grandiose gesture would provoke a popular uprising in the south in favor of reunification with the north, as well as large-scale desertions among the "puppet troops" of the South Vietnamese army (ARVN, for the Army of the Republic of Vietnam). Such romantic notions proved to be false. Nevertheless, the Tet offensive generated some of the most dramatic moments in the entire history of the war, many of them watched with horror by shocked television audiences in the United States. From Ca Mau in the deep south to Quang Tri city just below the Demilitarized

Zone, there was no spot in the country immune from Tet. Most disturbing to U.S. planners was the way that city after city, safely in the hands of ARVN or U.S. forces, came under attack by a force that was supposedly incapable of doing such a thing.

Early in the morning of January 31, NVA and NLF forces launched an assault against the city of Hue.[28] A former imperial capital and now South Vietnam's third largest city, with a population of 140,000, it was one of the most unusual sites imaginable for a twentieth-century battle. The older portions of Hue were actually a square, walled city. The Citadel, as it was called, lay north of the Huong (Perfume) River, comprising some two thirds of Hue's total area. Its earth-filled masonry walls stood 6 meters high and stretched 2,500 meters per side. Additions to the ramparts over the years had made the walls some 75 meters thick in places. During their occupation of Indochina, the Japanese had excavated passageways and constructed bunkers throughout its length. To complete this unusual picture, each of the Citadel's four corners was aligned with the points of the compass, and the entire structure was actually surrounded by a zigzag moat, a terrain feature that has not figured prominently in the training of the modern U.S. military. Within the Citadel lay another walled city, the Imperial Palace itself, with walls measuring seven hundred meters on a side, and two to five meters high. There was more to Hue than the Citadel, however. About a third of the city lay to the south, across the Huong and outside the walls.

Like the Tet offensive itself, the attack on Hue tried to hit everywhere, all at once. The NVA made no attempt to concentrate its strength for a decisive strike, and the forces involved hardly seem adequate to assault and hold a sizable urban center. Three battalions of the NVA 6th Regiment hit the Citadel, approaching from the west, while another three battalions of the 4th Regiment assaulted portions of the town south of the Huong. Another whole regiment, the 5th, remained hidden in the hills and bamboo thickets to the west, ready to reinforce as needed. Fire from mortars and 122-mm rockets supported the land assault, as did an entire NVA sapper battalion (the 12th), absolutely necessary in a city marked by as many watercourses as Hue. A number of NVA and NLF soldiers had infiltrated into the city before the attack, and in the confusion of preparations for the holiday, they had been able to smuggle in a large amount of matériel: weapons, ammunition, and explosives. The communist plan was to seize as much of the city as possible as rapidly as possible, sowing confusion among the defenders and civilian population. The list of objectives, in fact, ran to 314 items — municipal and provincial police stations, government offices, the Imperial Palace, the treasury, and

Hue: Aerial view of the amazing walled city, showing the built-up area on the southern bank of the Perfume River and the southern point of the Citadel. John F. Abel Collection, Personal Papers Collection, Marine Corps University Research Archives, Gray Research Center, Quantico, Va.

Aerial view of Hue, showing the bastions and moat along the
southeastern wall. John F. Abel Collection, Personal Papers Collection,
Marine Corps University Research Archives, Gray Research Center,
Quantico, Va.

many more. The weather also helped the attackers. The northeast monsoon produced enough rain, wind, and fog to ground U.S. aircraft and to help the attackers infiltrate their way into the city. Finally, since it was the Tet holiday, many South Vietnamese soldiers were home on leave, visiting family and friends.

Defense of Hue was in the hands of the 1st Infantry Division of the South Vietnamese army. The divisional commander, General Ngo Quang Truong, had taken note of an increased level of NVA and NLF activity in the area in recent months, including the discovery of a new and well-equipped five-hundred-bed military hospital during a recent ARVN sweep in the mountains west of Hue, as well as the presence of two crack NVA regiments and a large cache of weapons in the immediate neighborhood. He had reacted by placing his headquarters in the northeastern quarter of Hue in a state of increased alert, canceling leaves for his officers, and summoning his men back to duty. Although this heightened state of readiness had not been communicated to his entire rank and file, his divisional command post became the nerve center for the defense of Hue.[29]

Hue fell to the attackers within hours. By daybreak, 90 percent of the Citadel was in NVA/NLF hands, the two notable exceptions being Tay Loc airfield and the 1st Division command post. The ARVN "Black Panther" (Hac Bao) company played a conspicuous role in this early portion of the fighting, taking up a blocking position near Tay Loc in the western portion of the Citadel, stopping the 800th Battalion of the 6th NVA Regiment there, then being ordered back to the compound to drive out elements of the 802nd Battalion that had succeeded in breaking into it. The commander of the Black Panthers, Captain Tran Ngoc Hue, was a native of Hue; his mother had named him, in the traditional fashion, after the city of his birth. Knowing every nook and cranny of the city, Captain Hue was an invaluable asset to the U.S./ ARVN side, and the Black Panthers would prove to be a crucial fire brigade during the fighting inside the Citadel, thrown in wherever the situation was most dire.[30]

Likewise, 4th Regiment overran most of the city outside the Citadel, on the southern bank of the Huong. Here, the U.S. Military Assistance Command Vietnam (MACV) headquarters defended itself against a series of uncoordinated attacks.[31] Perhaps because of the confusion of the night assault, the attackers had missed a number of important military targets in this district, especially the 7th ARVN Armored Cavalry battalion and the 1st ARVN Engineer Battalion cantonments. Still, by sunrise on January 31, communist forces controlled all of Hue except for a number of widely separated pockets of resistance. There were immediate signs of the new order. The flag of the NLF now fluttered over the Citadel. More to the point, using a list obviously drawn up beforehand, NLF and NVA cadres began to round up thousands of "enemies of the people," individuals suspected of supporting the South Vietnamese regime, and shooting them.[32]

The existence of the besieged garrisons was both a help and a hindrance to U.S./ARVN efforts to retake Hue. On one hand, they stuck into the occupiers' positions like a thorn, offering sally points from which ARVN or U.S. forces could bring the communists under attack from the flank or rear, while main force units engaged them frontally. The NVA/NLF could not set up any sort of coordinated defense of Hue while these heavily armed enclaves sat in their midst. On the other hand, they dictated the direction of U.S./ARVN efforts from the start. Rather than simply launch an attack to retake Hue, the Allies first had to relieve the MACV and 1st ARVN headquarters compounds. Only when they had opened corridors to these and other isolated posts could they launch a comprehensive campaign to clear the city, and in the process hopefully inflict maximum casualties on the NVA/NLF forces who had seized it.

First, however, U.S. and ARVN forces had to get to Hue. The NVA/NLF posted forces outside the city in a cordon, closely watching the northern and southern approaches along Highway 1. In the opening days of the battle, as the NVA regiments tried to secure the city and wrest away the various enemy holdings inside the Citadel, several battles were fought between approaching U.S./ARVN reinforcements and communist blocking forces. A series of operational donuts was the result, with U.S./ARVN forces on the outside ring, at spots like PK 17 ("*Poste Kilometre*," in French, giving the distance away from Hue), Camp Evans, and Phu Bai; NVA/NLF forces constituted a smaller ring, forming a cordon around the city; their comrades in Hue formed the third circle, occupying the vast majority of both the Citadel and the south bank of the Huong; finally, at the center lay scattered areas still held by the U.S. or ARVN military. The forces involved were relatively small, only about a division total on each side, and so each of the donuts was relatively permeable. No one was really "under siege" in Hue.

The salient feature of Hue was that U.S. and ARVN forces now had something rare in this war: a legitimate target at which to shoot. And over the course of the next month, they slowly retook the city from the NVA and Viet Cong. The NVA had done a very indifferent job of cordoning off the city. Reinforcements arrived at MACV from Phu Bai in the south, a company at a time. They had to fight their way through communist sniper fire and occasional roadblocks, but they usually managed to get through. U.S. Marines of the 2/5 and 1/1 battalions arrived first, and others were to follow. To the west, a battalion of the 1st Cavalry division (2/12 of the 3rd Brigade), recently staged into the area and without use of its helicopters, launched an attack to close off the western approaches to the city.[33] Near the so-called "T-T woods" (for Thon Que Chu–Thon La Chu), it crashed unknowingly into a full NVA regiment deployed around the NVA Tri-Thien Hue Front headquarters at Thon Que Chu. The commander of 2/12, Lieutenant Colonel Bob Sweet, showed a great deal of grit as well as tactical finesse. He "withdrew his unit forward" from the engagement to a piece of high ground to the southwest. From here, 2/12 could call in highly accurate fire on any NVA units approaching Hue from the west.[34] A second cavalry regiment, the 5/7, would later assault into the same woods and clear them. This latter victory, achieved once again by a force fighting in the old-fashioned way (that is, without its helicopters), effectively isolated Hue from outside reinforcement on February 21, an event that would trigger the collapse of NVA resistance in the Citadel.[35]

On the operational level, the American effort deserves high praise. The speed with which the U.S. forces (and ARVN within the city) regained the initiative was impressive and in fact was the decisive factor in the battle. With the U.S./ARVN higher command trying to plug holes in literally dozens of dikes all over South Vietnam in the opening days of Tet, the achievement at Hue was all the more satisfying.

On the tactical level, however, the battle was a slow, agonizing struggle. In southern Hue, south of the Huong River, a handful of companies, mainly U.S. Marines of the 2/5 and 1/1 Battalions, bore the brunt of the fighting. Assaulting an enemy who outnumbered them and who occupied tough, entrenched positions in a built-up area, the marines nevertheless made steady progress. From what looked like their hopelessly surrounded enclave at MACV, the marines began to attack outward almost immediately, a result of orders from their higher command (Task Force X-Ray in Phu Bai). The orders looked too bold and out of touch at the time, typical perhaps of rear echelon who do not understand the true gravity of events at the front, but they proved to be entirely correct. The marines, with three companies of 2/5 (Fox, Golf, and Hotel) in the lead, retook Hue University on February 2, the treasury complex on February 4, the hospital on February 5, and the prison and the provincial administration complex two days later, essentially shattering

War in a residential neighborhood. A Marine of A Company, 1st Battalion, 1st Marine Regiment (A/1/1), uses a tree for cover as he returns fire at a North Vietnamese position during street fighting in Hue. Brigadier General Edwin H. Simmons Collection, VA020953, the Vietnam Center Archive, Texas Tech University.

an entire NVA Regiment with a handful of companies. The marines completely liberated southern Hue by February 10.

The action then shifted to the Citadel itself. On February 10, the U.S. command airlifted another marine battalion, 1/5, directly into the Citadel. Fighting alongside ARVN 1st Division but not under its command, the marine companies of 1/5 ground forward block by block into the southeastern corner of Hue. Much larger ARVN forces, several whole battalions of the Vietnamese Marine Corps, reduced the southwestern corner. The Citadel, befitting its name, was a tough nut, and both Allies suffered heavy losses. With the center of the city occupied by the Imperial Palace, which for political reasons the marines were not allowed to bombard, and the outside wall itself honeycombed with bunkers and firing positions, there was much less room for maneuver than there had been in southern Hue. In the Citadel, there was no such

Every building a fortress: U.S. Marines draw a bead on the elusive enemy inside the Citadel. Vets with a Mission website: www.vwam.com.

thing as a truly safe approach march. The Palace also forced the marine and ARVN thrusts away from one another, as they passed to either side of it. Mutual support was therefore impossible.

Not that the marines would have gotten any. A serious problem within the Citadel was the poor state of relations between the marines and ARVN. One mission of 1/5, to relieve positions in eastern Hue held by the 1st ARVN Airborne Task Force on February 13, ended in disaster when the ARVN units withdrew prematurely from Phase Line Green, allowing NVA to reoccupy supposedly secure areas. As a result, Alpha Company of 1/5 walked into a blizzard of NVA fire completely unawares; the unit was not even in tactical formation yet. Two men killed and thirty-three wounded was the result. Charlie Company followed, walking into the same blizzard of fire. The fiasco at Phase Line Green is still, like every other aspect of this war, controversial. Many argue ARVN's brief and blame a marine communications foul-up rather than ARVN incompetence.[36] General Truong, in particular, has many fervent defenders. Others blame rules of engagement that limited marine preparatory fire within the Citadel out of deference to Vietnamese sensibilities.[37] In fact, it is difficult to write of the battle without expressing admiration for the men who fought there, and that includes ARVN troops, as well as NVA. The former usually appear in American histories of the battle as incompetent at best and cowardly at worst,[38] but they carried the brunt of the battle throughout; the latter battled on bravely after the hopelessness of their strategic position became clear.

The marines, however, whether inside the Citadel or south of the river, made hardly a false step. The men of the assault companies had no real tradition of urban warfare and had received little training in it. The last time marines had been engaged in a city fight was Seoul in 1950, but that was nothing compared to this. They showed an impressive ability to improvise tactics on the fly, weaving a complex and effective web of combined arms, which in Hue meant mortar fire, 3.5-inch rockets, grenades, 106-mm recoilless rifles, and above all great billowing clouds of CS tear gas. Kicking open the door, tossing in a grenade, and then spraying the inside of the room with fire — that was the distinctly nonsubtle approach at Hue. Some of the marines' most dangerous fighting occurred for the sole purpose of retrieving their dead and wounded in the streets. They even staged a dramatic flag-raising ceremony over the Provincial Administration building in southern Hue on February 6. A handful of marines struck the NLF flag that had been flying there since the communist assault and, violating regulations that forbade such things, raised Old

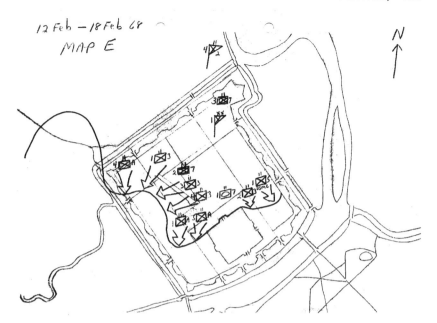

Battle for the Citadel: Hand-drawn "situation map" for the Battle of Hue, showing the combined USMC-ARVN drive against communist positions inside Hue. Papers of former MACV adviser Colonel Peter E. Kelley, U.S. Army Military History Institute.

Glory. It sounded an overtly heroic, but entirely appropriate, note. From top to bottom, there was no finer hour in the history of the Corps.

PEGASUS

To bring down the curtain on this trio of conventional battles, U.S. Army forces finally had their moment in the sun. Operation Pegasus aimed at reopening Highway 9 and reestablishing land communications with the marines at Khe Sanh.[39] It was a complex plan, involving many elements. Two marine battalions would launch a ground attack to the west along the highway, with 2/1 advancing just to the north of the road and 2/3 moving alongside to the south. A third battalion, 1/1, was in reserve, ready to be committed as needed. Utilizing the protection on either flank, the 11th Marine Engineer Battalion was to proceed directly along the road, filling in shell craters, repairing bridges, and in general opening up Highway 9 as a valid supply route again. The main event of Pegasus, however, and the aspect of the operation that generated its name, was to be a series of airmobile assaults by the 3rd Brigade, 1st Cavalry Division, into the terrain along both sides of the road. Assembling just to the north of Ca Lu at the newly prepared Landing Zone (LZ) Stud — in reality a huge airfield staging complex larger than many bases — the cavalry would clear a path for the marines to proceed toward Khe Sanh, attacking and destroying whatever NVA forces they encountered along the way. Following up would be forces of the 2nd Brigade, 1st Cavalry, to be inserted into the battle on the fourth day (D+3) and the 1st Brigade the day after that. And, not to be forgotten, there was a third element of Pegasus besides the marine relief column and the airmobile landings: the 26th Marines themselves, still hunkered down at Khe Sanh. They would launch a series of attacks against NVA forces ringing the base, reaching out toward the relieving force. A combined airmobile-ground operation requires far more careful planning than a simple ground assault. "A lot of things were going to be moving through the same air space," 1st Cavalry Division commander General John Tolson wrote, "bombs, rockets, artillery shells, helicopters, and airplanes. We had to assure ourselves that none got together inadvertently."[40]

The actual attack went about as smoothly as any operation in the entire war. The marines led off at 7:00 A.M. on April 1, the Huey-borne cavalry a bit later, due to weather, at 1:00 P.M. Both forces made good progress. The 1st Battalion, 7th Cavalry regiment (1/7) air assaulted into LZ Mike south of the highway, well ahead of the marines; 2/7 followed. North of Highway 9, 5/7 air assaulted into LZ Cates, along with the 3rd Brigade command post. Opposition was minimal, a result of both surprise and also of the fact that the NVA had been drawing down their forces, removing them from the hammering they had been taking in front of Khe Sanh. There were probably no more than ten thousand NVA still in the area, down from a high of thirty thousand. The first day went so well, covering half the distance to Khe Sanh, that Tolson at that point decided to introduce the 2nd Brigade into the battle a day ahead of schedule.

The next days continued the pattern. Airmobile assaults continued along both sides of the road on April 2: 2/7 to LZ Thor; 2nd Brigade moved up to LZ Stud, ready for action the next day, if needed. Two marine companies airlifted into LZ Robin, in direct support of the land drive. The marines continued to slash their way through the jungle up Highway 9, through mountainous and heavily wooded terrain. The 2nd Brigade arrived on April 3, air assaulting south of the highway into landing zones to the south and west of LZ Thor. The 1st Battalion of the 5th Cavalry (1/5), along with 2/12, fresh from the difficult fighting at Hue, and 2nd Brigade headquarters took off from LZ Stud and air as-

The new cavalry: The Vietnam War saw the U.S. Army's pioneering new
airmobile tactics that would later form an integral part of AirLand Battle
doctrine. Vietnam Photos, RG123S, U.S. Army Military History Institute.

saulted LZ Wharton, just south of the old French fort near Khe Sanh,
while 2/5 did the same to LZ Tom. It was time to introduce the fourth
ingredient to the mix. On April 4, Tolson ordered the marines in Khe
Sanh, who were under his operational control for Pegasus, to strike
against the NVA encircling them. Although many of the marines had
been in underground bunkers for the better part of three months, they
unfolded themselves and marched off, finally, to come to grips with their
foe. These were tough fights against a still-entrenched adversary. The
first target, Hill 471, fell to the 1st Battalion, 9th Marines after a stiff
fight and heavy losses to NVA 122-mm mortar fire. The next day, April
5, elements of another brigade of the 1st Cavalry Division (the 1st) made
their appearance, with 1/8, 1/12, and 1st Brigade headquarters opening
up LZ Snapper, due south of Khe Sanh.

By now, the two U.S. forces were within a stone's throw of each other.
There were so many battalions engaged, however, that it is actually

difficult to identify the "magic moment" when Khe Sanh was relieved. One such moment might be April 6, when elements of the 2/12 airlifted onto Hill 471, relieving the marines who had recently taken it; General Tolson called it "the first relief." It might be the arrival of 2/7 at the Khe Sanh wire at 8:00 A.M. on April 8. "The 1st Cavalry Division became the new landlord" of Khe Sanh at that moment, he wrote.[41] It most assuredly was *not* the April 6 linkup of the ARVN 3rd Airborne Task Force with their countrymen of the 37th Rangers who were inside the Khe Sanh perimeter, a senseless publicity stunt that General Westmoreland recommended as being "beneficial to the image of the Vietnamese."[42]

Pegasus was a well-conceived and well-executed operation that succeeded in reopening the supply lines to Khe Sanh in record time and with remarkably low casualties. Although there was some stiff fighting here and there (for the French fort, for example, and in the marine breakout battles), Pegasus seems to have caught the NVA at the start of its pullout from the Khe Sanh engagement. Whether that be true or not, the 1st Cavalry Division certainly played a role in accelerating that pullout. Operation Pegasus has to stand as one of the most successful U.S. operations of the war, as well as an important harbinger of things to come in terms of U.S. military doctrine. And, of course, this being the Vietnam conflict, two months after Operation Pegasus relieved Khe Sanh in such dramatic fashion, the U.S. military decided to abandon the base altogether.

Rebirth: The Development of U.S. Operational Doctrine

Anyone who tries to draw conclusions from the Vietnam War will almost certainly anger the legions of Americans who have already made up their minds about it. The preceding discussion has not been an attempt at a revisionist view on the basic issue of the war. Rather, the purpose of focusing on Khe Sanh, Hue, and Pegasus is simply to point out that, on basic issues of military doctrine and skill at planning and carrying out complex military operations, there was much more for the armed services to keep from their Vietnam experience than to jettison. The U.S. Marines and Army fought Vietnam quite skillfully on the operational level. Any military establishment that can lay down a wall of firepower like the air and ground forces at Khe Sanh, that can assault like the marines at Hue, and that can maneuver like the army's airmobile units in Pegasus has little to apologize for in the area of operations.

Nevertheless, they lost. The defeat in Vietnam left the U.S. Army, in particular, shaken and unsure of itself. It is not surprising that it was a time of soul searching. A strongly self-critical body of literature appeared, including Douglas Kinnard's *The War Managers* (1977);[43] Richard A. Gabriel and Paul L. Savage's *Crisis in Command: Mismanagement in the Army* (1978);[44] and the pseudonymous work by "Cincinnatus," *Self-Destruction: The Disintegration and Decay of the United States Army During the Vietnam Era* (1981),[45] although the author's eventual unmasking as Professor Cecil B. Currey (a U.S. Air Force reservist who had not seen actual duty in Southeast Asia) would dull the edge of his critique.[46] All these works presented the same essential argument. Starting in the late 1950s, the army had endorsed an administrative model taken from the corporate business world. The entrepreneurial concept of "management" had supplanted older warrior traditions like leadership and loyalty. Not surprisingly, in such an environment, self-interest and careerism had taken hold among the officer corps. And just like the business world it aped, the army had come to rely increasingly on systems analysts, with their graphs and pie charts and statistical indicators of success, for its planning. Hence the obsession with what the commandant of the U.S. Army War College, General DeWitt C. Smith, Jr., called that "odious phrase," the body count.[47] Out of this period of introspection would come intellectual rebirth, doctrinal reform, and the creation of a high-quality combined arms force that would be the best in the world: the heir to the French and German armies of the nineteenth and twentieth centuries.

The first real sign that the army was serious about reforming itself was the formation of the U.S. Army Training and Doctrine Command (TRADOC) in 1973. Under its first commander, General William E. DePuy, an internal conversation began that is still going on thirty years later. At issue was the most effective way to apply the tremendous power of the United States on the modern battlefield. One result of this discussion — the one that lay down the groundwork for all those to follow — was to recognize the importance of operational-level warfare. For the first time in many years, U.S. military planners had to admit that there was more to military success than simply assembling an overwhelming force, shipping it to the theater of war, and grinding down an adversary, as in previous U.S. conflicts. Now they admitted that there was an art to handling "echelons above division."[48]

Within months of DePuy's taking the helm at TRADOC, the 1973 Arab-Israeli War broke out. Its short, violent course came as quite a shock to military observers the world over and hit the U.S. Army very hard. The salient characteristic of the modern battlefield seemed to be that it had become an increasingly lethal place. Modern antitank weaponry, as

well as the effectiveness of antiaircraft guns and missiles in denying airspace to ground support aircraft, seemed to signal an end to the tank-
aircraft blitzkrieg. Only a balanced team of combined arms had any hope
of success.[49]

These considerations formed the basis for the new edition of Army
Field Manual 100-5, *Operations* (FM 100-5) that appeared in July 1976.
Written largely by DePuy himself, it confronted the key problem for the
U.S. Army at the time: how to fight and win on an armor-dominated bat-
tlefield against an enemy who enjoyed vast quantitative superiority in both
men and equipment. The introduction stated the problem succinctly:

> Because the lethality of modern weapons continues to increase sharply,
> we can expect very high losses to occur in short periods of time. En-
> tire forces could be destroyed quickly if they are improperly em-
> ployed. Therefore, the first battle of our next war could well be its
> last battle. . . . This circumstance is unprecedented: we are an army
> historically unprepared for its first battle. We are accustomed to vic-
> tory wrought with the weight of materiel and population brought to
> bear after the onset of hostilities. Today the U.S. Army must above
> all else, *prepare to win the first battle of the next war.*[50]

The chapter on modern weaponry pointed out that the 1973 clash
between massed formations of Arab and Israeli armor had ended with
losses of 50 percent in less than two weeks of combat. It had been a war
of high-intensity firepower unlike any previous conflict, characterized
most of all by a "new lethality."

A conflict with the Warsaw Pact in Central Europe, likewise, would
be swift and bloody, with manpower and matériel losses occurring on a
previously unimaginable scale. If they were to survive, U.S. and NATO
forces would have to exploit all the traditional advantages of the defense:
skillful use of cover and concealment; choosing the ground on which to
fight; sighting weapons for maximum effectiveness; mines and obstacles;
and the advantage of first fire. Maneuver was nowhere near as important to DePuy's scheme as was firepower.

The killing power of the new weapons meant that a defending force
could be outnumbered three-to-one and still expect to win; an attacker
now needed a six-to-one ratio in his favor. But commanders had to remember to substitute firepower for manpower, relying on the potential
of U.S. weapons (self-propelled artillery, tank and mechanized infantry,
airmobile antitank weapons, helicopters, and close air support) for quick
massing of firepower at selected spots on the battlefield. Strong covering

forces would engage the enemy forward, not only to slow him down and force him to reveal the main thrust of his attack, but to begin his destruction. Logistical units had to be ready to "arm, fuel, fix, and feed forward."[51]

There can be no doubt that the manual emphasized the defense. Offensives were to be undertaken only if the commander "expects the outcome to result in decisively greater enemy losses than his own, or result in the capture of objectives crucial to the outcome of the larger battle."[52] In fact, movement was hardly necessary at all, except to get units into better defensive terrain from which they could fire. Even on the defensive, U.S. forces had to concentrate forward, abandoning the traditional two brigades forward/one in reserve deployment. In the words of one U.S. Army historian, "divisional commanders had to be willing to concentrate six to eight of their maneuver battalions on one-fifth of their front to meet breakthrough forces of twenty to twenty-five battalions." Air and ground cavalry would have to suffice for holding the rest of the line. It would be what FM 100-5 called an "active defense," using the extremely high mobility of mechanized forces to concentrate at the decisive spot and halt the Warsaw Pact advance with defensive fire. Since the old dichotomy of line and reserve was now gone, such concentration would consist of a series of tricky lateral maneuvers by units already deployed in forward positions on the battlefield, rushing to the point of the Soviet breakthrough. Once concentrated, the defenders had to be ready to open fire quickly. Given the high lethality of the new weaponry, particularly tank guns and antitank guided missiles, firing first had taken on an even greater importance than in previous years; in fact, it was now absolutely essential. The defenders had to be ready to engage the assault force at ranges of up to three thousand meters, forcing the enemy to reveal his intentions and beginning his destruction.[53]

The new manual received decidedly mixed reviews, which seem to have gotten worse over time. One analyst praised it for rediscovering the "timeless principle" of the superiority of the defense.[54] Numerous others criticized it for the same reason, arguing that it deemphasized maneuver, gave insufficient attention to the role of the offensive, and therefore signaled the acceptance of a more passive orientation for U.S. forces. It seemed to many in the force that there was very little that was "active" about active defense.[55]

One of the most heated critiques came from outside the army. William S. Lind, at that time a legislative aide to Senator Gary Hart, argued that the "new lethality" might offer just as many advantages to the offense as to the defense.[56] He pointed to the Egyptian army in 1973, which had used its new defensive weaponry, both antitank and antiaircraft, as a shield for offensive operations across the Sinai. One of the oldest lessons in military history is the effectiveness of combining a strategic offensive (the Egyptian thrust across the canal) with a tactical defensive (forcing the Israelis to attack the bridgehead). Thus, the possession of weapons that aid the tactical defense was likely to strengthen Soviet offensive capabilities. Lind also focused closely on the new manual's bias toward attrition and firepower.

> Doctrine for mechanized and armored forces may be divided into two basic types which could be characterized as the attrition/firepower and maneuver doctrines. The Germans developed the maneuver doctrine before and during World War II; the Soviets in many ways have adopted it. . . .
>
> Both doctrines employ fire and maneuver. However, in the attrition/firepower doctrine, maneuver is primarily for the purpose of bringing firepower to bear on the opponent to cause attrition. The objective of military action is the physical reduction of the opposing force. In the maneuver doctrine, maneuver is the ultimate tactical, operational, and strategic goal while firepower is used primarily to create opportunities for maneuver. The primary objective is to break the spirit and will of the opposing high command by creating unexpected and unfavorable operational or strategic situations, not to kill enemy troops or destroy enemy equipment.[57]

Maneuver versus attrition. The two terms soon became watchwords for competing visions of what the U.S. military should become. As always in such debates, there was a tendency to caricature the opposition. "Maneuverists" picture "attritionists" as blind reactionaries, devoid of any feeling for the operational art, the intellectual progeny of those who fought to the last ditch to keep horsed cavalry in the army. "Attritionists" (and most would object to the very name) see "maneuverists" as full of ideas that are as half-baked as they are newfangled, forever chasing the illusion of a cheap battlefield victory without fighting or killing, "dislocating" the foe's "center of gravity," rather than killing the enemy; forever seeking to re-create their favorite German campaign of World War II.[58] The battle continues to rage in the "Letters" section of *Armor* magazine, right up to the present day.

In fact, Lind's argument rested on faulty assumptions. First, the notion that the German army never intended to physically destroy its adversaries in battle, but rather break their spirit, is simply false. It flies in the face of two hundred years of German military history and would certainly have come as a surprise to whole generations of German staff officers from the elder Moltke through World War II; even a passing acquaintance with the original German sources disproves it utterly. Second, his belief that the Soviet art of war drew from German sources for its inspiration ignores a great deal of Russian theoretical work in the early portion of the twentieth century. In fact, there were clear differences between German and Soviet operational war making. They were quite obvious from 1941 to 1945, and lumping them together makes for strange conceptual bedfellows. Finally, Lind drew some very dubious conclusions from his analysis. He was one of a group of military "reformers" advising the U.S. Army to retire its complicated, high-tech weaponry and recast itself into a low-tech mode with more easily replaceable equipment. The army, thankfully, ignored that advice.

Another of his criticisms was more to the point: A real weakness of the new doctrine — one that would eventually lead to its rejection by the army — was that it was too preoccupied with the "first battle." What if the defenders did indeed crush the first Warsaw Pact attacks? Wasn't the whole point of Soviet doctrine that the attack would proceed with second, third, and perhaps even fourth echelons? Even if the Pact lost the first battle of the next war, it might very well go on to win the second. The army's response was that it had to lay emphasis on the "first battle," to overturn the traditional notion of American war making — that even if the opening battles of a war were lost, time and matériel would eventually make things right. One officer admitted to Lind, however, that there was no doctrine for a second battle. It was, he said, "something of a Chinese fire drill at that point."[59]

Lind was by no means alone in his attacks on "active defense." There was criticism aplenty within the ranks as well. Ironically, DePuy was the first victim of the sharper intellectual climate he had fostered within the force. Many criticized the manual for being idiosyncratic and for ignoring military history. It was as if the current situation in Central Europe was so novel that it necessitated discarding all the lessons of the past, including the traditional principles of war. The maintenance of a battlefield reserve was gone, for example, replaced by a never-before-attempted doctrine of lateral movement of troops in the combat area. To many critics, DePuy had committed the sin — all too typical in the modern period — of overemphasizing the lessons of the most recent war, in this case the Arab-Israeli clash of 1973. One modern analyst, writing in 2001, speaks of DePuy having used the 1973 war "as a lever to impose his own view" of how the U.S. Army should fight in the future.[60] But even here, DePuy seemed to take a one-sided view, looking at the Golan Heights battle as normative, rather than the Israeli maneuver across the Suez that eventually won the war.

A last serious criticism was the assumption that the Soviet Union intended to fight according to its traditional plan of tank formations massed on a very narrow front in great depth, with a first echelon of six hundred tanks being launched against a single U.S. division, followed by a second echelon of six hundred more. By 1977, it seemed that something of a revolution was taking place in Soviet doctrine as well. Soviet literature began to deemphasize the "narrow and deep" approach in favor of multiple thrusts by mechanized infantry regiments, reinforced by armor. In October 1981, Warsaw Pact forces staged an exercise on the Baltic coast entitled "Zapad 81." It was here that "operational maneuver groups" made their first appearance.[61] These were smaller formations, mainly mechanized infantry, intended to launch a series of assaults at selected points in the enemy line, seeking weak spots or gaps, at which point a heavy armored reserve would be inserted.

The implication for DePuy's "active defense" was that the Soviets did not simply intend to pick a spot for the assault and then hammer away blindly regardless of the level of NATO firepower and their own casualties. In addition, any Soviet search for weak spots was almost guaranteed to find them, given the new U.S. doctrine's insistence on covering much of the frontage covered by a division with patrols of air cavalry. There would be weak spots aplenty in any such arrangement. Simply put, perhaps the 1976 FM 100-5 assumed too much about Soviet behavior. In the words of one leading NATO analyst, the Soviets were "not going to line up so they can be bombed by NATO one sunny Friday afternoon."[62]

All these criticisms from within the army, which even today strike the reader as startlingly frank, were signs of a larger development. By the late 1970s, a full-fledged intellectual renaissance was under way within the American armed forces. The formation of TRADOC was only one example. The army also began to encourage a wide range of vigorous and open debate within its service journals and to tolerate a level of disagreement and criticism that would have been unthinkable just a few years before. The journal of the army's Command and General Staff College at Ft. Leavenworth, *Military Review*, became an indispensable guide to the current state of doctrinal debates. In intellectual tone and breadth of interests it was fully the equal of the interwar German journal, the *Militär-Wochenblatt*. Another crucial part of the revival was the opening of new operational-level schools: SAMS (School of Advanced Military Studies) for the army; SAW (School of Advanced

Warfighting) for the marines; and SAAS (School of Advanced Airpower Studies) for the air force. It was, in a sense, a "German" solution to the problem of formulating doctrine: training an elite corps of strategists and planners in the style of the German General Staff. At these schools, and throughout the services, there was an eruption of scholarly military history written by both active and reserve officers that even now shows few signs of slowing down. David M. Glantz, founder of the U.S. Army's Foreign Military Studies Office and the author of dozens of works on the doctrine, organization, and operations of the Soviet army, stands out as the most prolific example of this new type of soldier-scholar.

In this atmosphere of intellectual ferment, dissatisfaction with the active defense eventually coalesced into a new version of FM 100-5, which appeared in August 1982. "Active defense," therefore, was a short-lived concept, being army doctrine for just a little over six years. Leading the charge against it was the new TRADOC commander after 1977, General Donn A. Starry. He had assisted DePuy in the development of active defense, but commanding a corps in Germany had led him to think in terms of the opportunities beckoning at the operational level of war. Starry also brought a keen interest in military history to his new post, an invaluable asset. Surrounding himself with an elite corps of military intellectuals, he set about crystallizing doubts about the active defense — now generally shared within the army — into a completely new doctrine. Starry was a classic example of the right man in the right post at the right time, but his writing team deserves recognition as well. Lieutenant Colonel Huba Wass de Czege, Lieutenant Colonel L. D. Holder, and Lieutenant Colonel Richmond B. Henriques wrote the new manual, with Lieutenant General William R. Richardson (TRADOC deputy commander) and Lieutenant General Richard E. Cavazos (then commander of U.S. III Corps) playing a strong advisory role.

Under Starry's guidance, these officers gave a great deal of thought to the very thing the active defense seemed to ignore: how to hit the Pact's later echelons. Starry was convinced that it would be necessary to integrate all the vast forces in the U.S. arsenal — conventional ordnance, chemical munitions, and even nuclear weapons — to crush the second and later echelons of a Warsaw Pact offensive in Central Europe. The key was to do it long before they could even arrive on the battlefield. "Seeing deep" became the new slogan: using tactical air power, missiles, and artillery in attacks far behind enemy lines.[63] It was not a completely new idea; World War II commanders would have called it "interdiction." Improved target acquisition, however, and long-range strike capability had extended the traditional concept of interdiction from a somewhat random process of delaying and disrupting enemy supply and movement to something far more deadly. "Seeing deep" meant hitting rear-area targets with the full arsenal, and that included chemicals and tactical nuclear weapons. "Integrated battle planning" would omit no weapon likely to be of use against the Warsaw Pact second and third echelons.

At first army planners used the term "extended battlefield" to describe the new doctrine but by March 1981 had settled on "AirLand Battle" instead. It marked a departure from the traditional U.S. Army doctrine of a main battle area. The military art was now entering a "new dimension" that allowed for "the simultaneous engagement of forces throughout the corps and division areas of influence." Besides fighting the traditional main battle, U.S. commanders had to be ready to fight the deep battle against enemy reserves, as well as the rear battle against Soviet airborne landings or special operations. The extension of the battlefield away from a matching set of lines, in a sense, brought some depth to a NATO alliance that was constrained politically from surrendering territory in West Germany.[64] It helped solve one of NATO's essential problems: how to square "flexible response" with "forward defense."

But there was more to the new FM 100-5 than simply hitting the enemy's second echelon. As a reaction to the previous manual's emphasis on defensive fire and attrition — sort of a high-technology World War I — the new doctrine emphasized the offensive. Augmenting the traditional massive firepower of the U.S. Army was a new stress on rapid and aggressive battlefield maneuver. In fact, more than twice as many pages were devoted to offense than to defense in the 1982 manual.

AirLand Battle had four basic tenets: Initiative, Agility, Depth, and Synchronization. The commander was to seize the initiative, shocking the enemy with the initial assault and not allowing him to recover. He was to think and act more rapidly than the foe, "getting inside his decision cycle," forcing him away from his own plans and causing him to break down.[65] He was to bring every part of the enemy force under attack at once: bold armored thrusts in the front or flanks, cruise missiles deep in the rear, air interdiction to isolate the battlefield from friendly reinforcement, airmobile assaults against sensitive command or communications installations — forcing the enemy to defend everywhere at once, never knowing which blow was the killing one. Such a complex series of interlocking operations required split-second timing, of course. Synchronization, with the attacker orchestrating fire, movement, and assault into one grand symphony of destruction, was the key to the new doctrine.

This concept was heavily influenced by military history, with particular reference to the successes of the German and Israeli armies. The

writers of the manual, well versed in military history and theory, borrowed freely from Clausewitz and Liddell Hart, especially the latter's
notion of the "indirect approach," as well as from the writings of a diverse group including Marshal Maurice de Saxe, Ardant du Picq, John
Keegan, Martin van Creveld, and S. L. A. Marshall. There were allu-
sions to "friction" in battle, to the ancient Chinese writings of Sun Tzu,
to the battle of Tannenberg, to Stalingrad and Tobruk, as well as to Civil
War campaigns like Grant's maneuver on Vicksburg.

The German influence was clearest. The new manual adopted the traditional German notion of *Auftragstaktik*, a decentralized command system with the commander devising a mission and then leaving the
methods and means of achieving it to his subordinate officers. In the
high-complexity, high-velocity extended battlefield of the future, such
a flexible system would be essential to success. The manual also adopted the German concept of the *Schwerpunkt*, where the attacker would
make the decisive effort. In fact, it is not an exaggeration to say that the
AirLand Battle was nothing less than a call for U.S. ground forces, working in close cooperation with air power, to re-create the German blitzkrieg. Even if forced temporarily onto the defense, U.S. forces would
launch devastating and unexpected blows against the enemy's front lines,
penetrating and overrunning his assembly areas, while long-range air,
artillery, and missile strikes against follow-on and reserve forces turned
his supposedly secure rear area into an inferno.

In the years after 1982, it became difficult to pick up any professional
military journal without reading something about the German army.
There were occasional complaints that one needed a German-English
dictionary to read a typical issue of *Military Review*.[66] There were discussions of the 1940 campaign as a forerunner of the AirLand Battle,
citations from Rommel and Guderian (and also from the great armored
prophets of the interwar period who were alleged to have inspired them:
Liddell Hart and Fuller), and above all, discussions of Clausewitz. The
truths first formulated by this philosopher of war — that it is the province
of violence and uncertainty and friction, that it is, like all human activities, "intimately bound up with chance," that it resists any attempt to
reduce it to a system of rules and regulations — now became part of the
intellectual heritage of the U.S. Army.

Of course, the beauty of an intellectual renaissance is that it soon chal-
lenges the new consensus. There was something of a reaction to the mania
for things German by the late 1980s, as many officers began to imbibe
more deeply of the sources of Soviet operational and tactical theory. The
fall of the Soviet Union and the opening of the Russian archives made

possible a new appreciation for the "operational art" as envisioned and practiced by Tukhachevsky, Zhukov, Konev, and others. A kind of intellectual version of the Great Patriotic War got under way, and each side scored its points. But however strong those disagreements became, the intellectual atmosphere in the U.S. Army before 1991 was certainly a welcome change from the period before the American entry into World War II, when U.S. doctrine was seemingly formed in a vacuum, oblivious to what was actually happening on the battlefields of Europe. The most important achievement in the army was that, in the words of one officer-scholar, "no longer was doctrine to be whatever the highest ranking man in the room said it was."[67] And that was no minor accomplishment.

Conclusion

Officers in the army took to AirLand Battle in a way that they never did to the "active defense." The old doctrine had been particularly unsatisfying, described by one irritated Pentagon officer as "how slowly do you want to me to lose?"[68] The new doctrine was exciting, maneuver oriented, and aggressive in character. The army was to seize the initiative in battle, and "with deep attack and decisive maneuver, destroy its opponent's abilities to fight and to organize in depth."[69] Officers and men had to be ready to use the principle of surprise (another glaring omission from the 1976 manual), "throwing the enemy off balance with powerful initial blows from unexpected directions and then following up rapidly to prevent his recovery." The entire operation had to be "rapid, unpredictable, violent, and disorienting to the enemy."[70]

The 1986 revision of FM 100-5 showed further refinement. Now for the first time, the army explicitly recognized the operational level of warfare between tactics and strategy, and introduced the now-ubiquitous term "operational art" into the American military vocabulary. The manual stressed the importance of encirclement and annihilation of enemy forces, introduced Clausewitzian concepts like "culmination point" and "center of gravity" ("the hub of all power and movement, on which everything depends"), and grounded the discussion even more firmly in military history than did its 1982 predecessor. It praised Grant as "a master of maneuver, speed, and the indirect approach," included a detailed account of the Vicksburg campaign (pp. 91–94), and also offered an analysis of the great German victory at Tannenberg, complete with campaign map (pp. 130–131). Indeed, knowledge of military history was a prerequisite to reading the 1986 manual. Here, for example, was its discussion of Clausewitz's "culminating point," taken from Appendix B ("Key Concepts of Operational Design"):

> Classic operational examples of the same phenomenon just in WWII were Rommel's drive into Egypt which culminated at El Alamein, the Japanese drive from Burma into India which culminated at Imphal-Kohima, Patton's rapid advance across France which bogged down for lack of supplies in Lorraine, the December 1944 German counterof-fensive through the Ardennes which resulted in the Battle of the Bulge, the advance of General Paulus' 6th German Army to Stalingrad, and the combined penetration of the Russian 6th Army and Popov's Tank Corps Group into the Ukraine which precipitated the third battle of Kharkov.

What was most impressive about this passage, beyond the authors' breadth of knowledge of historical campaigns, was the fact that the army could, by 1986, reasonably expect most of its operational-level officers to understand a reference to Group Popov. The 1986 FM 100-5, in fact, would represent for the army a kind of intellectual culmination point.

It had all started with the disaster in Vietnam. It has become a truism to argue that the end of U.S. involvement in Southeast Asia allowed the army to return to a mission with which it was more comfortable: preparing for large-scale continental warfare with the Soviet Union. There is some truth to it, although it would be glib and unfair to say that army planners "breathed a sigh of relief" after Vietnam. It is hard to deny, however, that the U.S. Army never did come to grips with the problems of guerrilla warfare, never reformed itself into a force that could successfully prosecute a guerrilla war, and outside its Special Forces components, never regarded irregular warfare as normative in any way. After closing the chapter on Vietnam, the army shifted its emphasis back to armored warfare in central Europe. It was, in the words of Robert A. Doughty, "a return to the conventional," in more ways than one. After the uncertainties of the Vietnamese bush, it was a much more comfort-able place to be for a mechanized western army.[71]

As seductive as this line of argumentation is, there is still one prob-lem with it. The final product of the army's new focus on doctrine, the refined version of AirLand Battle found in the 1986 FM 100-5, bore strong and consistent marks of its origins in the Vietnam experience. The aggressive spirit of U.S. ground forces in Hue, attacking even from a position of weakness to seize the initiative from the enemy; the over-whelming firepower delivered into the very depth of the NVA positions around Khe Sanh, hitting them front, rear, and center without cease until they were ready to break; the agility and synchronization of Operation Pegasus, with ground, airborne, and air units describing an extremely complex arc of destruction against a thoroughly bewildered opponent — all are the hallmarks of AirLand Battle. It shouldn't come as a surprise. Virtually all the officers who shaped AirLand Battle — General Starry among them[72] — had passed through the crucible of Southeast Asia. Far from being a war best forgotten and barren of lessons for the future, Vietnam was the spiritual and intellectual birthplace of the army's new operational doctrine.

8

The U.S. Army at War: Desert Storm

The National Training Center and OPFOR

The U.S. military did more than simply write new theoretical doctrine in the 1980s. It improved itself in every way. It raised personnel standards steadily throughout the decade — a reflection of increased funding and higher pay made possible by the gigantic increase in the military budget under President Ronald Reagan. New equipment left the drawing board and began to come into use with the troops. Analysts usually speak of the era's "big five": the M-1 Abrams main battle tank; the M-2 Bradley, a third-generation armored personnel carrier that with its 25-mm chain gun was more properly called an "infantry fighting vehicle"; the AH-64A Apache attack helicopter carrying a massive complement of weaponry (HELLFIRE antitank missiles, 70-mm Hydra 70 folding-fin rockets, and a 30-mm single-barrel chain gun); the UH-60A Black Hawk utility helicopter, capable of carrying an entire infantry squad or a 105-mm howitzer, plus its crew and ammunition); and, finally, the Patriot air defense missile.[1] Interestingly enough, the media had pilloried every one of these weapons systems while they were in development, especially the M-1. Sensational reports had declared it to be both over budget and under its advertised performance standards. The controversy would last until 1991, and Operation Desert Storm.

A last aspect of the intellectual rebirth in the military was the great deal of thought given to the problem of training. The increased lethality of the battlefield required ever more intense and realistic forms of training. A U.S.-Soviet war in central Europe would have featured tank-heavy forces on both sides, a fully mechanized complement of infantry equipped with handheld antitank guided missile systems, and the full panoply of modern war — sophisticated tactical air, aided immensely in its effectiveness by modern electronic systems for target acquisition; helicopters, the tank's nemesis on the contemporary battlefield; and perhaps even nuclear, biological, and chemical weapons. There was no doubt

Dueling prototypes: the GM (top) and Chrysler (bottom) designs for the XM-1, forerunner to the turbine-driven Abrams MBT. Chrysler eventually won the contract. Courtesy of U.S. Army TACOM.

that the fighting would be unprecedented in terms of its violence and intensity.

During the 1970s and 1980s, western analysts drew up a sobering picture of the Soviet army at war — drawn in part from its performance in World War II but also from a great deal of contemporary study and intelligence by organizations such as the Soviet Studies Group at Ft. Leavenworth. The Soviets would pound on a given operational axis with overwhelming force: hordes of tanks, mechanized infantry loaded in BMP armored personnel carriers, and massive concentrations of artillery. The frontage of the attack would be exceedingly narrow by western standards, a mechanized phalanx so narrow that it was virtually guaranteed to break through what was in front of it — "flatten" is more like it. Then, to exploit the gap created by the assault force, a second echelon of fresh armored and mechanized divisions would come up on the very same axis. When it had engaged NATO reserves or reinforcements, and bludgeoned them, a third echelon of fresh divisions would do the same. In this way, a tactical breakthrough would soon be expanded into a great operational-level gash in NATO's defensive positions. The attack would be brutal, relentless, and the Soviets would drive it home without regard to casualties.

A typical evocation of such views is *The Third World War*, a book published in 1978 by General Sir John Hackett, onetime commander of the Northern Army Group (NORTHAG) in NATO.[2] Assisting him were "other top-ranking NATO generals and advisors," including Air Chief Marshal Sir John Barraclough, the chairman of the Royal United Services Institute for Defence Studies. In the book, written as an "after-action account," the Warsaw Pact has launched a conventional assault in 1985. It is, in a sense, a limited war in that Soviet war aims include the neutralization of West Germany, the dissolution of NATO that will result inevitably from the first aim, and the removal of U.S. influence from the continent. Nevertheless, the scenes of the initial Pact assault give a good idea of what western analysts expected from the Soviet army. The commander of C Squadron, 8th Royal Tank Regiment in I British Corps, has just received orders to move to the regiment's emergency deployment position:

> His tank topped the crest on the last words, and there opened up before him the most frightening sight he had ever seen. The open ground below, stretching to a faintly seen line of trees about two kilometers away, was swarming with menacing black shapes coming fast towards him. They were tanks, moving in rough line-abreast about

200 meters apart, less than 1,000 meters off and closing the range quickly. Another line was following behind and a third just coming out of the trees. The world seemed full of Soviet tanks.

"You might have told me," he said into the microphone: "Am engaging now. Out!"[3]

Likewise, a Soviet defector writing under the alias of "Viktor Suvorov" painted a portrait, highly influential with civilian policymakers and the public at large, of a fierce fighting machine, a combination of both mass and guile, using masses of tanks, aircraft, and men in direct assault, but also airborne units, diversionary forces (Spetsnaz), and campaigns of strategic deception.[4] In battle it would be relentless and have no compunction whatsoever about using every weapon in its arsenal from the outset. He described what he said was the philosophy of the Soviet General Staff:

"If you want to stay alive, kill your enemy. The quicker you finish him off, the less chance he will have to use his own gun." In essence, this is the whole theoretical basis on which their plans for a third world war have been drawn up. The theory is known unofficially in the General Staff as the "axe theory." It is stupid, say the Soviet generals, to start a fistfight if your opponent may use a knife. It is just as stupid to attack him with a knife if he may use an axe. The more terrible the weapon which your opponent may use, the more decisively you must attack him, and the more quickly you must finish him off.[5]

He went on to describe a typical Soviet "strategic offensive," unfolding in five stages, beginning with an initial nuclear strike, a mass air attack by Soviet aircraft, and a mass rocket (missile) attack. Stage Four would be "offensive operations by individual fronts."

Each Front concentrates all its efforts on ensuring success for its Tank Army. To achieve this the All-Arms Army attacks the enemy's defenses and the Front Commander directs the Tank Army to the point at which the breakthrough has been achieved. At the same time, the entire resources of the Front's artillery division are used to clear a path for the Tank Army. The rocket brigades lay down a nuclear carpet ahead of the Tank Army, and the Air Army covers its breakthrough operation. The Front's antitank brigades cover the Tank Army's flanks, the airborne assault brigade seizes bridges and crossing points for its use, and the diversionary brigade, operating ahead of and on the flanks of the Tank Army, does everything possible to provide it with favorable operating conditions. . . . A Tank Army is like a rushing flood, tearing its way through a gap in a dyke, smashing and destroying everything in its path.[6]

Stage Five was the climax, as the second echelon of Soviet forces pushed forward into the breakthrough sector. "Towards the end of the action there may be five or even six Tank Armies in the Group, bringing its establishment up to as much as 10,000 tanks."[7] This was the hypothetical assault that the U.S. Army spent the entire postwar period preparing to stop. The army might have to fight light, well-trained Chinese infantry in Korea; it might find itself up against stealthy and skillful guerrillas in Southeast Asia. But as those conflicts ended, it always came back to its real mission: fighting the Russians.

In 1981, the army opened up its National Training Center (NTC), in Ft. Irwin, California, in the Mojave Desert.[8] Its purpose was to give U.S. forces experience in fighting against "the Threat," the Soviet army under central European conditions. It came complete with an "opposing force," or OPFOR, an armored cavalry regiment (roughly a reinforced brigade in size) of American personnel with training, equipment, and even uniforms approximating those of the Soviet army. A laser-based engagement system determined hits and kills. Most important, a corps of "observer-controllers" (OCs) blanketed the unit undergoing training — advising, criticizing, and in general making life as miserable as possible for the friendlies ("Blue Force"). Finally, each maneuver ended with an "after-action review," a final discussion in which the OC pointed out mistakes in judgment and action and how they impacted the course of the exercise.

According to the testimony of virtually every U.S. soldier who has fought against them, the OPFOR were a worthy adversary. They rarely lost an engagement. The NTC was their turf, "every valley, pass, crest, wadi, and crevice," in the words of Colonel James R. McDonough, an officer intimately familiar with Ft. Irwin. He described OPFOR as an enemy

who knows the line of sight of every weapon's emplacement, who can register the fires of his artillery and mortars by memory; an enemy who has seen a score of times the blunders of his foes led astray by the deceptive terrain as they followed wadis into disastrous death traps or tried to scramble up seemingly gently sloping paths that suddenly turn into unclimbable cliffs; an enemy who knows every hidden crack in every cliff face, who can dig in his vehicles and men so expertly that they cannot be seen within spitting distance, but who can see out to the limits of their ranges and beyond.[9]

OPFOR was more than just a tough adversary. They were actually an eerily close facsimile of a Soviet motorized rifle regiment, the "32nd Guards." Consisting of elements of the 6th Battalion, 31st Infantry (Mechanized) and the 1st Battalion, 73rd Armor, wearing specially designed uniforms (dark green fatigues, red epaulets, and black berets with a red star), they drove M-551 Sheridan armored reconnaissance vehicles visually modified to look like Soviet T-72s, Dodge trucks modified to look like Soviet BRDM reconnaissance vehicles, as well as Soviet vehicles captured by the IDF during the Arab-Israeli Wars. Personnel took part in a variety of role-playing simulations to indoctrinate them into Soviet ideology and propaganda. Finally, to simulate central European conditions, the "32nd Guards" usually enjoyed numerical superiority against the unit undergoing training (Blue Force).[10]

OPFOR's stock in trade, worked out a thousand times over ground that it had come to know intimately, was the massed charge by armored vehicles, coming up suddenly and unexpectedly. In her official history, *The Origins and Development of the National Training Center*, historian Anne W. Chapman describes OPFOR at work:

> A favorite scenario . . . was to arrange the three task forces of the motorized rifle regiment in a column. As the column approached the Blue Force position, the three OPFOR task forces came on line in three echelons. As the OPFOR moved still closer, the companies that made up each task force came line abreast, forming nine fingers. As the distance between the BLUFOR and OPFOR narrowed, the OPFOR companies fanned out to present a sort of rolling front. That mode of operations was designed to take advantage of the OPFOR's numerical superiority and to cause panic and confusion in the ranks of the Blue Force.[11]

Using such tactics, OPFOR has, over the years, whipped a good portion of the U.S. Army. It is easy to summarize a typical reaction by units of Blue Force when suddenly confronted by 150 armored vehicles seemingly coming up out of nowhere, heading straight for them: panic. Likewise, the use of CS tear gas, air assault, and AH-64 Apache attack helicopters has ensured swift punishment for Blue's missteps.[12] Chapman lists the stunned reaction of a typical Army National Guard Unit: "They use brute force to overcome us. . . . They're damn good. They'll send ten tanks to destroy one of ours. They don't care if they die."[13] There has even been, not surprisingly, a steady diet of complaints that the OPFOR holds an unfair "home field advantage" and that training at the NTC is therefore unrealistic. One defeated company commander summed up the attitude thusly: "The OPFOR are the Russians as they wish they were."[14]

This is simply whining. It should be axiomatic by now that no war game can ever simulate the kill-or-be-killed atmosphere of war, no matter how realistic it may seem to be. National Guard officers who complained about the unfair nature of the NTC were missing the point. This was tough training, and it set the bar extremely high. OPFOR knew the terrain, it fought very cleverly, and it made sure to punish any opponent who performed slipshod maneuvers on its simulated battlefield. To complain about OPFOR is essentially to complain about competence.

Deserving of special mention are the observer-controllers, the equivalent to the "umpires" in the old German system. They did much more than observe; they evaluated, judged, and rendered the final report. In his book *The Defense of Hill 781: An Allegory of Modern Mechanized Combat*, Colonel McDonough describes an unfortunate officer ("Lieutenant Colonel A. Tack Always"), a light infantryman, who has died and has to pass through the "purgatory" of the NTC to work off his sins of service parochialism. He meets a Command Sergeant Major who introduces him to the delights of life at the NTC. Here the CSM explains the role of the observers:

> They kind of watch you and help to point out the error of your ways. You'll meet them soon enough. Nasty bunch, if I do say so myself. Must have been particularly rotten in life. They'll show up en masse as soon as you get your operations orders, follow you everywhere you go, say disparaging things to you, talk badly about you over their radios, and render a report as to how you did.[15]

Throughout the Lieutenant Colonel's adventures, the observers are there, smirking when he has just given some particularly absurd order or gloating as they point out his errors in the after-action review. Here is the Lieutenant Colonel's description:

> Like so many jackals, the dreaded observers descended upon the headquarters, each one seeking his counterpart, with a sneer upon his lips and an air of contemptuous disdain for the hapless victims. A harder bitten lot would be difficult to imagine — faces seared by the desert

sun, eyes glaring with sadistic eagerness, hands calloused and chapped from the writing of so many long and derogatory reports.[16]

Another form of observation at the NTC — quite unforgiving in the shortcomings that it revealed in commanders and men — was the un-blinking electronic eye. Again, the Command Sergeant Major explains:

> They have a superb electronic setup down here. Everything you say over the radio will be recorded so you can't deny you said it later, and everything you do will be filmed so that your most ridiculous moments can be played back for all to see. At any time you can expect everybody and his brother to be eavesdropping on you, offering their views as to how incompetent you are, spreading disparaging rumors, and unequivocally stating they could do it better.[17]

The simulation of an actual enemy was something new, a conceptual step forward that linked doctrine and training. Traditionally, the typi-cal war game or maneuver had been a face-off between a hypothetical Red Team and Blue Team. The NTC, by contrast, grounded U.S. train-ing in a real-world context and made sure that war-fighting doctrine did not emerge out of some sort of intellectual or theoretical vacuum. It has continued to do so up until the present day, simulating terrorism, the presence of media, civilians on the battlefield, and much, much more. There is even a guerrilla force, the People's Pahrumphian Guerrillas. It operates a forty-person "cell," targeting lucrative targets like helicop-ters, radar installations, and headquarters. It even tries to recruit dis-gruntled or mistreated civilians into its ranks. The world has changed, and OPFOR has changed with it:

> Today's OPFOR formations have various flexible entities that include infantry forces; small, independent reconnaissance elements; raiding detachments; flank threats from adjacent friendly unit sectors; decep-tion elements; and unpredictable formations that attack based on con-ditions, not on predetermined timetables. While still highly competitive, the OPFOR is now a freethinking enemy that exploits every weakness in the blue force's plan.[18]

The NTC is not the only advanced training method the army has. Firing ranges have continued to improve their sophistication, present-ing much more of a challenge to participants. A Joint Readiness Training Center for training light forces opened in 1987. Established first at Ft.

Chaffee, Arkansas, it eventually moved to Ft. Polk, Louisiana. For upper echelons, there is a command exercise without troops, the "Battle Command Training Program" (BCTP), strongly reminiscent of the German army's *Rahmenübung* (or skeleton exercise). Combining a five-day seminar with a five-day computer-driven command-post exercise ("Warfighter"), it presents the commanders of large units and their staffs with the same operational problems they might face in real life.[19] During General Carl E. Vuono's tenure as TRADOC chief, a capstone training document appeared, FM 25-100, "Training the Force" (November 1988), followed by an implementation document, FM-25-101, "Battle-Focused Training."[20] These and other advances placed the U.S. Army in the forefront of modern training techniques, the heir to the previous champions: the Germans. From the birth of the *Kriegsspiel* in the nineteenth century, no other armies have made a more profound attempt at simulating war in peacetime.

Desert Storm

Iraqi dictator Saddam Hussein could not have picked a worse time for his invasion of Kuwait. Soon after the Iraqi thrust across the Kuwaiti border early in the morning of August 2, 1990, it was clear that he was facing a coalition of the industrial West and most of the states in his own region. Not only that, but his adventurist policy now meant that his army — which had shown no great talent either operationally or tactically in the war with Iran — would inevitably have to square off against the best-trained, best-equipped, and best-led U.S. Army in history.[21] Although the American military never fought the battle for which it had prepared so long — defending Western Europe from the Soviet army — it now got its chance to cross swords with a large, heavy mechanized force organized and trained more or less on the Soviet model. The outcome could not be in doubt. The only question was how much time and how many Coalition casualties it would take. That Iraq's casualties would be enormous was never in question. One great irony of the conflict about to unfold was that the U.S. Army entered it with far more desert training than the Iraqis. In the end, it had more trouble fighting the OPFOR at Ft. Irwin.

The Iraqis conducted their invasion competently enough, although calling it a "textbook *Blitzkrieg*," as one analyst did, is yet another example of the absurdly overblown rhetoric of the pundits regarding the Iraqi army.[22] At 1:00 A.M. on August 2, two Iraqi Republican Guards armored divisions, the Hammurabi and the Al-Madinah, crossed the border from the north and headed directly for Kuwait City, supported by a Special Forces Division landing directly in the city and heliborne landings along the divisional march routes. The Kuwaiti army, just twenty thousand men strong, offered sporadic but ineffective resistance. The second day saw the entry of the Tawakalna Mechanized Division, which along with the two armored divisions drove south to the Kuwaiti border with Saudi Arabia. Hard on their heels followed the remainder of the Republican Guard (six motorized infantry divisions) and three divisions from the regular Iraqi army. It was a huge force, ideal for stamping out any potential resistance in a smaller neighbor, which it now proceeded to do with alacrity. Its size, however, also represented a clear threat to the great oilfields of eastern Arabia and virtually forced the West — led by the United States — to react.

In many ways, the coalition war to free Kuwait was unique, the product of a conjunction of events that is unlikely to occur in the future.[23] In the days of the cold war, the United States would have been hard pressed to assemble such a formidable coalition for war in the Middle East. Sparing troops and assets from Germany would have been a calculated risk, and Soviet diplomacy would no doubt have been active among the Middle Eastern regimes. But with the cold war winding down, even the Soviet Union voted "yes" on U.N. Resolution 660, condemning the Iraqi invasion and demanding withdrawal. One result was that the United States was able to pull nearly nine hundred M1-A1 tanks out of their pre-positioned sites in Europe and send them to Saudi Arabia. Eventually, it brought the entire VII Corps out of Europe and into the Middle East — a development that would have been unthinkable during the old cold war days — just two years earlier.

Saddam thus found himself isolated diplomatically. Had he intended an assault on Saudi Arabia, it would only have been possible as a lightning strike immediately following the occupation of Kuwait. Simulations run by western think tanks were never able to come up with a good reason why he didn't. Even after the arrival of the first U.S. units, mainly light infantry and paratroopers, there would have been little to stop Iraqi forces from crossing the Saudi border. But the Iraqi army had never shown itself capable of consecutive or continuous operations in the war with Iran. Its logistics and support network would not permit them. True to form, it now halted. Even if Saddam had wanted to lunge toward the Saudi oilfields, it would have taken a great deal of time to relieve the Republican Guards and then resupply and replenish them for another advance. As a result, the Iraqis entered Kuwait and sat, until they were destroyed.

The first operational objective of U.S. forces was to protect Saudi Arabia, hence the defensive code name, "Desert Shield." The U.S. Central Command (CENTCOM) had, only one month earlier, war-gamed an attack by "Country Red" on Kuwait and Saudi Arabia. The exercise, "Internal Look 90," gave Red large armored forces, including some four thousand tanks, as well as a powerful air force, and nuclear, biological, and chemical capability.[24] Some of its provisions proved to be optimistic: the United States would have ample warning of such an invasion and would have already begun mobilizing forces and shipping them to the region eighteen days before the actual attack. In addition, the force originally designated for the operation was a mix of seven heavy and seven light brigades, and it was soon clear to the CENTCOM chief, General H. Norman Schwarzkopf, and the 3rd Army commander, Lieutenant General John Yeosock, that such a force was inadequate to deal with the kind of heavy Iraqi force likely to be encountered. "Internal Look 90" dealt not with the tactical situation on the ground, but with the ability of the United States to get a credible force in place in Saudi Arabia in a timely manner. When the game suddenly turned into reality the very next month, U.S. planners were quite familiar with the myriad of issues involved: available strategic sealift, port capacity, and the amount of support required from the host nation, to name just a few.

Not surprisingly, then, American response to the Iraqi invasion was swift. President George Bush ordered U.S. forces to Saudi Arabia on August 6. The first U.S. air squadron was in Saudi Arabia within thirty-four hours of its deployment order: forty-eight F-15C air superiority fighters of the 1st Tactical Fighter Wing.[25] Although the lack of air-refueling facilities limited the number of craft that could fly into the theater at any one time, by the end of September 1990, there were 437 U.S. Air Force fighter aircraft in Saudi Arabia, a powerful deterrent against any Iraqi move south.[26] The road from the border to Dhahran — the Iraqi invasion route — is three hundred kilometers of exposed desert, and it is quite doubtful that an Iraqi force of any consequence could have survived the gauntlet of U.S. air power it would have had to run.

The actual arrival of ground forces was, of course, slower, given the seven thousand mile journey involved. Nevertheless, the lead elements of the 2nd Brigade, 82nd Airborne Division, the divisional "ready brigade," were in the air by the afternoon of August 8 (U.S. time) and landed in Saudi Arabia the next day. Although many on the American side, apparently including General Schwarzkopf, saw them as little more than "speed bumps" in the event of an Iraqi invasion of Saudi Arabia, the men and commanders didn't necessarily share that view.[27] They were, after all, lavishly equipped with Humvees armed with TOW missiles that far outranged the Iraqi tanks they'd be facing, and also had a light armor battalion and a helicopter gunship battalion in support. It was not a negligible force.

With the Iraqis making no move, U.S. forces and supplies continued to arrive in the theater, mostly at the gigantic Saudi port of Dammam. It was a colossal job:

By August 21 a billion pounds equivalent of material had arrived or was on its way aboard a ship or an airplane. By the beginning of the war in January, over two and a half million tons of dry cargo had been delivered to the Persian Gulf. The effort required some unusual requests for desert supplies. By the end of 1990, the military had ordered a million and a half sticks of lip balm, three million desert camouflage suits, a million atropine anti-nerve gas auto-injectors, 425,000 bottles of sunscreen, a quarter of a million pairs of sun goggles, a million desert boots, and 130,000 bullet-proof vests.[28]

By the end, the Desert Shield effort would move "500,000 passengers and nearly 3,700,000 tons of cargo — roughly the equivalent of the population of Denver, Colorado, with their possessions — a third of the way around the world."[29] The arrival of heavy U.S. forces by the end of October definitely precluded any Iraqi thrust across the Saudi border. Desert Shield had been a stunning logistical achievement, and one that only the U.S. military could have pulled off successfully.

The American theater commander, General Schwarzkopf, could now begin planning the counterattack that would evict the Iraqis from Kuwait. Aiding him immeasurably was the Iraqi army's reaction to the arrival of huge U.S. reinforcements. It had begun to dig itself in, fortifying its positions on the Saudi border with Kuwait. From the operational perspective, this was a disastrous decision that placed Iraq's front-line formations at the mercy of U.S. firepower, both ground and air. Other armies in other times and places — the Germans in Normandy during Operation Cobra, the NVA at Khe Sanh, the Chinese in the latter years of the Korean War — could have told the Iraqis what that meant. This would be a battle of maneuver, but only by one side.

The forces upon which Schwarzkopf could call were overwhelming. By November, he had XVIII Airborne Corps in the theater, with its 82nd Airborne and 101st Air Assault Divisions; the 12th Combat Aviation Brigade; and three heavy formations — the 24th Mechanized Division, the 1st Cavalry Division, and the 3rd Armored Cavalry Regiment.

In a meeting with the chairman of the Joint Chiefs of Staff, General Colin Powell, in late October, Schwarzkopf requested, and got, an even bigger gun: the VII Corps from Germany, under Lieutenant General Frederick M. Franks. After some shifting of its component units, it included two complete armored divisions, the 1st and 3rd, plus the 1st Infantry (mechanized) Division from the United States. Later, Franks would receive 1st Cavalry Division, as well, making VII Corps the most powerful armored corps in the history of the U.S. Army. Its equipment was top of the line, as well, its tanks consisting exclusively of M1-A1 Abrams main battle tanks, their 120-mm guns firing new depleted uranium rounds for added penetration. Their infantry fought from M-2 Bradley armored personnel carriers, with their 25-mm chain guns. It was clear that U.S. planners were thinking of offensive action against Iraq. Desert Shield was about to become Desert Storm.

Allied forces added dramatically to U.S. strength. The VII Corps, for instance, had the British 1st Armored Division, and XVIII Airborne Corps had the services of the French 6th Light Armored Division. There were enough Arab-Islamic units to form two corps, as well: a Joint Forces Command North (JFC-N) and a Joint Forces Command East (JFC-E). They included an entire corps from Egypt (one armored and one mechanized division, along with a Ranger Regiment) and an armored division and Special Forces Regiment from Syria (these being somewhat of an unknown quantity, and the only Coalition formations to be equipped largely with Soviet equipment). There were also fairly sizable contingents from the Royal Saudi Land Forces, National Guard, and Marines; remnants of the Kuwaiti army that had managed to slip Saddam's noose; the other four members of the Gulf Cooperation Council (Bahrain, Qatar, Oman, and the United Arab Emirates); small forces from Morocco (6th Mechanized Infantry Regiment), Pakistan, and Bangladesh (1st East Bengal Infantry Battalion); three hundred mujahideen from Afghanistan (who served largely as military police); and infantry battalions from Niger and Senegal.[30]

Operational planning was in the hands of General Schwarzkopf as CENTCOM chief and commander of the army component of CENTCOM (ARCENT); the 3rd Army commander, General John Yeosock; and General Franks, whose VII Corps was obviously going to be the Coalition's sledgehammer. Victory has many fathers, and there is some debate — never to be fully resolved — over the genesis of the operation.[31] Suffice it to say that, from the start, U.S. planners envisioned a single-wing envelopment of the Iraqi right (west) flank and that, as more U.S. forces became available, the envelopment stretched out farther and farther to the left, growing wider and deeper. There was general agreement on the necessity of strategic deception, as well, and as the U.S. force grew, the number of feints increased. Eventually there were three: one directly from the south, a frontal attack into the Iraqi fortifications along the border; the second a marine amphibious landing into or around Kuwait City; and the third a drive along the Wadi al Batin, a dry riverbed that ran along the western border of Kuwait, a kind of highway into the Iraqi positions. It was clear from Iraqi dispositions that these were the three attacks that Saddam's high command was expecting, especially the last. Iraqi planners clearly intended some sort of flank strike against Coalition forces as they emerged from the wadi. Uppermost in the minds of U.S. planners was the necessity of striking the Iraqis a hard blow with the concentrated fist of Coalition armor. They hadn't brought all those tanks along for nothing. Schwarzkopf set the tone from the first staff meeting, telling his commanders that he wanted the Republican Guards, Saddam's "center of gravity," destroyed, not simply pushed back or beaten or mauled.[32] The question was how best to achieve it.

Again, it seems that all three principal commanders — Schwarzkopf, Yeosock, and Franks — had much the same idea: an approach through the "Southern Desert" west of the Wadi al Batin, a deep and desolate quarter virtually devoid of terrain features or roads. In fact, at least one civilian analyst, James F. Dunnigan, was in print before the campaign began with just that suggestion.[33] On December 21, 1990, Franks presented a corps operational plan to General Powell and Secretary of Defense Richard Cheney that called for a last-minute shift of the entire VII Corps — 145,000 men and some 60,000 vehicles — to the left (or west) of the wadi. Franks likened it to a quarterback "calling an audible" at the line of scrimmage, and later, General Schwarzkopf would go him one better in the football-metaphor department by referring to the maneuver as a "Hail Mary" play.[34] West of the wadi, the prepared fortifications guarding the Saudi-Kuwaiti border known as the "Saddam Line" trailed off, with just a few weak infantry divisions strung out to provide security in what the Iraq command viewed as a quiet sector of the line. After all, no sensible commander of a huge armored force would want to operate in such desolate country.

The new arrangement would force VII Corps into two separate operational postures. On its right, the 1st Infantry Division would carry out a systematic breaching operation of the Iraqi fortifications, through which would follow the U.K. 1st Armored Division and eventually the corps's entire massive supply train. The corps's left wing, by contrast, would form a great maneuver mass, swinging around the Iraqi positions altogether into the rear. Its powerful armored divisions would form the operational *Schwerpunkt*. Once through the Iraqi lines, they would head north, wheel rapidly to the right, and smash into the right flank of the Iraqi Republican Guard division. If all went right, the Iraqis would not even know they were there until it was too late.[35]

Even farther to the left of VII Corps, XVIII Airborne Corps also had two missions. First, it would act as a flank guard for VII Corps's great wheel, screening it from any Iraqi forces that happened to be lurking in the vicinity. Second, the entire corps, using its great heliborne mobility, would lunge deep inside Iraq. There it would establish a series of forward bases, closing up to the Euphrates River along Highway 8, the principal north-south route in the area, and blocking off the escape route of the Republican Guards. Its 24th Mechanized Division would also turn east at the same time as VII Corps and participate in the final destruction of the Republican Guards.[36]

Although the plan had enough brute force to satisfy even the die-hard, it also included subterfuge. To mask VII Corps intentions until the last possible moment, 1st Cavalry Division would launch a feint up the Wadi al Batin. It would confirm Iraqi commanders in their mistaken impression that this was the main axis of attack and fix their attention to the south, while the hammer was actually about to strike them from the west. Its work done, 1st Cavalry would then rejoin the main body of VII Corps for the climactic battle against the Republican Guards.

Meanwhile, the center and right of the Allied line would be doing much the same thing — convincing the Iraqis that the main Coalition thrust was going to be a direct strike into Kuwait. To the immediate right of VII Corps lay JFC-N (Egyptian 4th Armored Division, Egyptian 3rd Mechanized Division, Syrian 9th Armored Division, and Saudi task forces "Khalid" and "Sa'ad"). They were to advance, more or less frontally, directly along and to the east of the wadi, while U.S. signal detachments filled the airwaves with fraudulent radio traffic simulating an attack by multiple corps. Still moving to the east, the 1st Marine Expeditionary Force (1st and 2nd Marine Division, supported by the 1st Marine Air Wing) would do the real thing, slamming into the Iraqi fortifications before first light. Their presence was also to be an indication to the Iraqi command that the main Coalition effort was going to be a direct blow from the south. In fact, the U.S. command had made sure to announce loudly and clearly that another Marine Expeditionary Force, the 2nd, was on its way to the Gulf. Their fear of the marines led the Iraqi command to station at least three divisions (two infantry and one armored) in or near the city. Finally, JFC-E occupied the coastline (a

Coalition army all its own, with contingents from nine separate Arab-Islamic nations).

Preceding the offensive was the most punishing air assault in military history. As in Korea, the air force once again had the favorable situation of an entire country prostrate at its feet. This time, the Central Air Force (CENTAF) commander, Lieutenant General Charles A. Horner, had both the technology to target the bombing much more precisely than in any previous air campaign and the muscle to pound virtually any target that he, or General Schwarzkopf, wished.[37] Analysts usually describe a four-phase air campaign: (1) destruction of strategic targets in Iraq; (2) suppression of Iraqi air defenses; (3) operations in the Kuwaiti theater against Iraqi ground forces; and (4) close air support for the ground campaign. In fact, from its opening in the early morning hours of January 17, the campaign moved repeatedly from one phase to the other and then back again. General Horner would later say the "four phase" talk was mainly for civilian consumption, including that of the president of the United States: "You had to have [phases]," Horner later said, "because you knew you've got to brief it up to the president, so it's got to be understandable, it's got to make sense, and it's got to be complete."[38] He was also quite unimpressed with the sharp distinction, so common to ground force officers, between the tactical, operational, and strategic levels of war. The words, he argued, had become "meaningless and dysfunctional" and were "more often used to divide people" than to illuminate objective truths about war.

> To an airman this is meaningless. My tactical fighter (tactical), flying to Baghdad (operational), kills Saddam Hussein (strategic). . . . So finally, in talking about air plans and air operations, I keep as far from these words as I can. Airpower is essentially very simple: aircraft can range very quickly over very wide areas and accurately hit targets very close to home or very far away. Nothing more. Nothing less.[39]

And range and hit they did. The initial attacks, spearheaded by stealth F-117s and Navy Tomahawk cruise missiles, dealt the Iraqi command a blow from which it never recovered. Targets in the first few minutes of the campaign included command and control facilities and power plants in and around Baghdad, as well as the presidential palace and the Baath Party headquarters. The most serious casualty was the National Air Defense Center in the capital, destroyed by a precision-guided bomb dropped from an F-117.[40] The pilot apparently managed to deliver his bomb directly down one of the building's ventilation shafts, an incredible scene that American television audiences would see over and over. With Iraqi defenses now blinded, a massive force of strike aircraft roamed at will over the country. Airmen called this aerial behemoth "the gorilla," and as it trampled Iraq's war-making capability beneath it, it seemed an apt metaphor.[41] Containing F-111s, F-4Gs, F-15Es, B-52s, navy F-18 Hornets, all supported by radar-jamming EF-111 Ravens, the attacking waves hit air defense facilities, airfields, fixed and mobile SCUD missile launchers, suspected chemical munitions storage areas, and much more. Within the first hour of the bombing, the Coalition had won absolute control of the air.

By the end of day one, any sense of a phased air attack on Iraq had gone out the window. The Coalition had achieved phases one and two almost simultaneously. And although attacks on targets in Iraq continued, U.S. B-52 bombers were already hitting Republican Guard units in Kuwait by the end of the day — the beginning of a relentless schedule of bombing that would see them hit the Guards every hour, twenty-four hours a day, for the entire war. Meanwhile, F-15s and F-111s were destroying highway and railroad bridges over the Euphrates River, the Guards' main escape routes should retreat become necessary. More than 150 tankers were also airborne, flying an intricate set of patterns, each one responsible for refueling four to six aircraft. Air power was hitting the Iraqi front-line troops, their rear area bases, and the lines of communication and supply between them — all at once. This was the "operational air war," a term first coined by the German Luftwaffe in 1925, carried out to perfection.[42]

There were one or two hitches in the air campaign. The first was the weather — after its promising opening, the air war had to contend with ten days of fog, low cloud cover, and rain. More serious was the sudden diversion of massive air assets to hunt for mobile SCUD missile launchers in the desert. It became necessary when Saddam Hussein launched seven SCUD attacks on Israel on the second day of the air war (January 18). The launchers were small — modified eight-wheel trucks essentially — and even with Coalition technology proved to be a tough target to locate. One factor that did not come into play was the Iraqi air force. The few planes that challenged Coalition aircraft paid the price. Within a week, much of the Iraqi air force was destroyed, and the aircraft that survived did so by escaping to Iran.

For the next four weeks, the Iraqi forces in the Kuwaiti Theater of Operations (KTO) sat and were bombed, taking a fierce pounding day and night. The B-52s hit them with area bombing, while Coalition fighter-bombers took them out vehicle by vehicle and gun by gun, "tankplinking," Horner called it.[43] During that entire period, it is hardly an exaggeration to say that for five weeks, Iraqi forces witnessed the incineration of every convoy of trucks that tried to bring them supplies and replacements. And eventually, of course, the trucks simply stopped coming. The effect that this necessarily had on Iraqi troop morale is one key to understanding the rapid course of the land campaign.

As is well known, the campaign itself ran only one hundred hours and went as well as any American commander could have hoped. The diversions kicked off first, early on the morning of February 24, 1991. At 4:00 A.M., 1st Cavalry Division advanced up the Wadi al Batin, while the marines assaulted the "Saddam Line" directly, with the two Arab commands on either side. There was progress virtually everywhere. The marine thrust north seemed foolhardy to some marines when they first heard it, a blatant frontal assault after ten years of discussion about the benefits of "maneuver warfare."[44] Nevertheless, with two marine divisions attacking abreast (2nd to the left, 1st to the right), it made good progress, easily breaching the minefields, sand berms, and fire trenches of the Iraqi position, and allowing the passage of the U.S. Army Tiger Brigade as an exploitation force. The Arabs to either side made slower progress, and by the end of the first day, the marines were on the point of a fairly deep salient into the Iraqi lines. It might have meant something in a different context, but not here. Already the first Iraqi troops were surrendering.

Meanwhile, far to the west, the real storm was brewing. Also at 4:00 A.M., lead units of XVIII Airborne Corps were across the border. On the Corps's far left, the French 6th Light Armored Division ("Division Daguet"), supported by a brigade of the 82nd Airborne Division, crossed the border and headed for the first-day objective, labeled "Rochambeau," against light opposition from the Iraqi 45th Infantry Division.[45] An American soldier attached to the French was one of the first to witness a sight that would become commonplace over the next four days:

> There was something wrong with this division, a division that had seen action inside Iraq and, as we could tell from the debris of the battlefield, was well-fed, equipped, armed, and dug in. Prior to the seizure of the Escarpment and its passes, photo imagery had revealed those positions, and we thought that the fight for the critical high ground could be severe and costly. What we found was basically an uncontested crossing and lots of abandoned equipment. Some of the weapons and uniforms were brand-new, never fired or worn, just thrown away by the retreating Iraqis.[46]

Three hours later, most of the 101st Airborne Division (1st Brigade and 1st Battalion, 2nd Brigade) lifted off via helicopter to Forward Operating Base Cobra, a full ninety-three miles into Iraq, halfway to the Euphrates River that was the corps's operational objective. More than three hundred helicopters took part in ferrying the troops forward, the largest air assault operation in history.[47] Cobra became the base for operations farther into Iraq by the entire corps. Within two days, for example, there were almost 400,000 gallons of fuel there, brought forward in gigantic bladders.

With 101st Division holding the corps center at Cobra, 24th Mechanized Division and 3rd Armored Cavalry Regiment on its right, and French 6th Light Armored Division and 82nd Airborne on its left, the corps had the most ground to cover. It was equivalent to the position of the German 1st Army in the opening battles of World War I, only here the wheel was to the right rather than to the left, and the mobility was that of the tank and the helicopter. Crucial to the overall plan was the 24th Division. Along with 3rd Armored Cavalry, it was to drive due north to Highway 8 (running parallel to the Euphrates) and then wheel right for the great Iraqi city of Basra, cutting the Iraqi line of communications to the KTO. Once the French and the 101st were in place, 24th Division pushed over the border at 3:00 P.M. in a blinding sandstorm. Advanced units encountered little opposition, and by evening the division's main body was more than twenty-five miles into Iraq, apparently still undetected.

Although the original plan called for VII Corps to attack on the second day of the ground campaign, the early success won everywhere led Schwarzkopf to accelerate the pace. At 3:00 P.M. on February 24, General Franks ordered the most powerful armored formation in U.S. history across the border. With 1st Cavalry Division (still under CENTCOM control) tying up some six Iraqi divisions in the Wadi al Batin to the right of the corps, 1st Infantry Division had to make a series of breaches in the Iraqi positions (wire and land mines, mainly) in the center. It would then hold open the breach, allowing 1st U.K. Armored Division to follow (containing the 7th Armored Brigade, the "Desert Rats" of World War II fame). This process took all day, the minefields being far more troubling than the minimal Iraqi resistance this far west. Even the insistently enthusiastic *Final Report to Congress* from the U.S. Department of Defense described 1st Division's operations as "deliberate."[48] Meanwhile, on the corps's left, the 2nd Armored Cavalry Regiment advanced northward, clearing a path for two armored divisions to advance abreast behind it (1st Armored on the left, 3rd Armored on the right). They made good progress, but the slow start in front of the Iraqi minefield led General Franks to call a halt to the entire corps for the evening, an "operational pause" that nearly drove Schwarzkopf to apoplexy and that continues to be controversial.[49] Here, too, this might have mattered in the different context of a different war, but VII Corps, too, was already starting to accept the surrender of Iraqi infantry in front of it.

On day two of the campaign, XVIII Airborne Corps continued its progress virtually unopposed. The 3rd Brigade of the 101st Airborne air assaulted 175 miles north from its assembly on the border to the very banks of the Euphrates, just west of An-Nasiriyah.[50] It was the deepest air assault in history, and already the corps was wrestling with a problem: how to handle the thousands of prisoners of war falling into its hands. The advance of the 24th Division, moving in a great "battle-box" formation, continued apace on the right wing of the corps. In the east, the marines and their two Arab command escorts continued to work their way north toward Kuwait City, and in fact U.S. intelligence, gathered and transmitted to commanders almost instantaneously by the new Joint Surveillance Target Attack Radar System (JSTARS), already detected the start of massive Iraqi exodus from Kuwait, moving north along the two roads out of Kuwait City. The VII Corps resumed its advance to the north, resembling a great battering ram: a front line of 1st Armored Division, 2nd Armored Cavalry Regiment, and 3rd Armored Division, with 1st U.K. Armored directly behind 2nd Armored Cavalry, and 1st Division directly behind the British. Franks was already beginning to receive incoming fire — not from the Iraqis, but from Schwarzkopf — about his tardiness, but he had his corps well in hand and prepared for action.

The VII Corps would make contact with the Iraqis on day three (February 26), and it did so in style. Franks spent the morning crossing Phase Line "Smash" and completing his wheel. He now faced almost directly east, with the full combat strength of three divisions and an armored cavalry regiment: 1st Armored to the north, 3rd Armored to its immediate right, and then 2nd Armored Cavalry Regiment and 1st Infantry Division. In the afternoon, 2nd Armored Cavalry Regiment made first contact, at a spot on the map designated as "73 Easting."[51] Driving in between two Iraqi divisions (12th Armored and Tawakalna) in the midst of a dust storm, the 2nd relied on its thermal imaging system to wreak a fair bit of havoc, supported by the fire of Apache attack helicopters. They inflicted heavy casualties on Iraqi tanks and armored personnel carriers. That same evening, 3rd Armored Division blasted into the flank of the Tawakalna Division and essentially destroyed it with minimal loss. The next day, Franks went back to work. By now, three more armored formations were on line: the 1st Infantry Division in the south, which had reassembled since opening the breaches, hurried to the north, and passed through the 2nd Armored Cavalry Regiment after the scrap at 73 Easting; the 24th Infantry Division (mechanized), still part of XVIII Airborne Corps, which had made the longest drive of all, some 250 miles, and which had nearly outrun its own fuel tankers; and the 1st Cavalry Division, back from its feint into the Wadi al Batin.

Day four found Franks bringing down his hammer: a coordinated, multidivision assault against the Republican Guard divisions in front of him that lasted most of the night.[52] The Guards, forced into a hasty reorientation of their front from the south to the west, never did establish a cohesive defense. Enjoying mastery of the air, with the support of a huge complement of attack helicopters and with absolute superiority in men, equipment, and ammunition, the U.S. attack was irresistible. The depleted uranium sabot fired by M1-A1 tanks not only killed the opposing tank, it typically blew their turrets off the ring, then sometimes passed into a second tank, and killed it, too. It even blasted through the characteristic Iraqi defensive position, the berm, with ease. The principal problem for U.S. forces proved to be staying aligned and avoiding friendly-fire incidents. Here, too, technology helped, with Global Positioning System (GPS) receivers called into play. The remnants of the Tawakalna and 12th Armored Divisions cracked first, followed in rapid succession by the Al-Madinah and Adnan Divisions. On the extreme north end of the battle, 24th Infantry (Mechanized) Division ended its long trek from the border by engaging and shattering the Hammurabi Division. Morning brought the cease-fire.

In this campaign, the U.S.-led coalition fought the battle of maneuver nearly to perfection. Heavy U.N. forces avoided a frontal attack against the main Iraqi positions in Kuwait, opting instead for a classic example of the operational art, the envelopment by one wing, leading to a *manoeuvre sur les derrières* of which Napoleon would have been proud. The business end of this wide sweep was the left wing, specifically the U.S. VII Corps and XVIII Airborne Corps. Exploiting their speed, both mechanized and airmobile, driving deep into the flank of the Iraqi positions, catching the defenders unprepared and literally facing the wrong way, the two left wing corps managed to destroy a good part of the Iraqi strength in western Kuwait. Supported by devastating levels of air power, these two corps managed to engage and shatter the enemy reserve, the much-touted Republican Guard formations, while the destruction of the Iraqi front line was still going on. Of seven Republican Guard divisions, the Tawakalna and Al-Madinah were destroyed outright. Two others, the Hammurabi and the Adnan, were crippled in the fighting. In its showdown with Hammurabi, the 24th Infantry suffered a casualty list of precisely one man wounded.[53] The remainder of the Republican Guard formations managed to escape to the north. They would be instrumental in putting down civil disturbances over the next few weeks and maintaining Saddam in power.

The Storm Evaluated

Desert Storm was the most successful campaign in U.S. military history. It liberated Kuwait in record time and shattered Saddam Hussein's warmaking capability, although the man himself — as well as his regime — would show surprising staying power. Although the Iraqis fought badly and were ineptly led, Desert Storm did manage to evict a huge mechanized army out of its heavily fortified positions and then destroy it at an almost nonexistent cost. Coalition forces destroyed more than thirty divisions, captured or destroyed nearly four thousand tanks, and took almost ninety thousand prisoners in less than four days of fighting. It ranks with the great annihilation battles of all time. U.S. deaths were less than 300, and even that total was inflated by a Scud missile strike on a barracks at Dhahran that killed 27 and wounded 98. Another 35 dead — both army and marines — fell to friendly fire. Prewar casualty estimates had run into the tens of thousands.

In the immediate wake of the war, hyperbole filled the air, calling the victory "a defining moment in military history," likening it to Hannibal's triumph at Cannae or the Allied victory over the Wehrmacht.[54] Even after the initial rush had faded, there was still a sense that the U.S. Army had reached a milestone, the culmination of a long, twenty-year rebuilding process, the end of "the long road back" from Vietnam. American forces, it was said, had finally gotten it right. This was an army, after all, that had gone through eight divisional reorganizations in the twentieth century, from the World War I "square" to the disastrous "pentomic" model of the late 1950s,[55] an army that has had a historical tendency to form "task forces" for their own sake rather than for anything they might achieve in battle. The new doctrine of AirLand Battle got especially good reviews. In its *Final Report to Congress*, the Defense Department declared that "the basis for ARCENT (Army Component Central Command) operations was Air-Land Battle doctrine. The essence of AirLand Battle is to defeat the enemy by conducting simultaneous offensive operations over the full breadth and depth of the battlefield. It is the intellectual road map for operations conducted at corps and above, and tactics, conducted below corps."[56]

How new was any of it? A better trained, better equipped, and more powerful army, enjoying absolute control of the air, launched an enveloping attack on its hapless adversary, catching him out of position and facing the wrong way, and routed him. Seen on a situation map, it looks very much like the Schlieffen Plan of 1914, in fact. A German staff officer of that era would have understood the principles that governed the actions of Powell, Schwarzkopf, and Franks. Decisive victory can come about only through *Bewegungskrieg*, the war of movement on the operational level. Maneuver, well supported by fire, is the key to victory. A well-planned campaign should always have a clearly defined *Schwerpunkt*. None of these things was particularly new — at least to the Germans.

There was even a certain amount of Clausewitz's friction in the campaign, just enough to allow a considerable portion of the Iraqi Republican Guard to escape. Schwarzkopf had, from the beginning, placed destruction of the Guards at the top of his priority list. In his memoir, he "names names," as it were, blaming General Franks for failing to prosecute the campaign with enough energy. His feeling that Franks was moving too slowly, never far below the surface, exploded on the campaign's last day, in what appears now as a meaningless dispute over the occupation of the airfield at As Safwan, the site Schwarzkopf had picked for the armistice talks with the Iraqis. Schwarzkopf raged at Yeosock, Yeosock had to pass it on to Franks, Franks gave Major General John Rhame of the 1st Infantry Division some undeserved grief. The historian of the 3rd Army referred to it as a "who shot John?" affair, an exercise in meaningless blame fixing, and that is probably as good a description as one can find.[57]

Despite claims at the time, it is particularly difficult to see the hand of "AirLand Battle" in this conflict. Rather, it would be more accurate to say that it was an air-land battle. That is, it had opened with a long, immense, and tremendously successful air campaign that destroyed the Iraqi command net, a large part of the Iraqi army in Kuwait, and the logistics and communications lines that linked the two. It was a bombardment, the most successful bombardment of all time, perhaps, but still a bombardment. Following it was a well-designed land operation, with the business end (the envelopment from the left wing carried out by XVIII Airborne and VII Corps) advancing nearly unopposed into the Iraqi flank and rear, supported by a huge armada of close air support — equally unopposed. The attack by the left, particularly that of

VII Corps, at times seemed more concerned with dressing its ranks like a great wheel of nineteenth-century cavalry than it did with modern mechanized maneuver.[58] It was not a series of armored columns, but a great line, stretching as far as the eye could see from north to south. It slammed into the Iraqis with earthshaking force as a result, but both Schwarzkopf and Powell were wondering what took it so long.[59] One perceptive young tanker of the 1st Armored Division said, "it was like a movie from World War II — you look to your left and to your right and everybody is firing in line."[60] And this in a campaign that pundits commonly praised for its "non-linearity."[61]

It may have been linear, firepower-drenched warfare, but it was still very, very good. For the first time in its history, the army had conceived, planned, and executed an entire campaign on the operational level. The decision to shift to the left the two corps in the sector west of the Wadi al Batin, transferring some 250,000 soldiers into a barren desert wasteland, was the most audacious decision in U.S. military history. This was not simply a tactical shift: XVIII Airborne Corps moved about 250 miles to the left, VII Corps about 150. The fact that Iraq apparently did not know of the shift until their Republican Guard formations were in the process of getting acquainted with VII Corps shows how skilled the army had become at strategic deception and disinformation. Constant battering by U.S. airpower also kept the redeployment hidden from the Iraqis. Feints by the 1st Cavalry Division into the wadi, as well as the marines into the teeth of the Iraqi defenses from the south (not to mention the constant threat of a marine landing on the coast) were something very new in U.S. war making. The constant updating of real-time intelligence from JSTARS, as well as satellite surveillance and GPS, was a quantum leap in the quick flow of information, always the thorniest command and control issue. Above all, the plan aimed at a quick and decisive victory, combining maneuver, firepower, attrition, and destruction into one potent and distinctly American package. And that was new.

The Day the World Changed? September 11, 2001

Is there a future for operational-level warfare? Will nations continue to call on divisions, corps, and armies in the future to fight and win decisive victories? Military analysts in the 1960s warned that the future belonged to the guerrilla and that conventional, large-unit warfare had become a dangerous anachronism. So too there are voices today, surveying the emptiness where the World Trade Center once stood, who warn that the future belongs to the terrorist, and who prophesy that next time the attack may involve nuclear, biological, or chemical weapons. Since September 11, 2001, the U.S. military has some very serious security problems with which it must deal. It is highly unlikely, so the argument runs, that an ability to restage Case Yellow will help to solve them.

In fact, this is an extremely narrow view. There is little in the world more secure than this prediction: as long as there are borders, and nation-states, there will be those who will have recourse to the sword to settle their differences. There are a good half-dozen spots on the globe today that could see a major war tomorrow: the Indo-Pakistani subcontinent is one, and the Korean Peninsula is another. The proliferation of modern weaponry — another unfortunate by-product of the cold war — has continued apace, and does not look like it is about to cease. The U.S. invasion of Iraq in March 2003, an event that had its roots in the terrorist strike on New York, might be just the first of several "regime changes" in the region. We have not yet reached the end of history.

What of the United States Army, however? The victory in Desert Storm, like the victories in World War I and World War II, resulted in a tremendous drawdown in the size of the force. Many of the units that performed so well against the Iraqis are no more: the 1st Infantry Division, for example. Military activity since 1991 has consisted of a variety of open-ended peacekeeping missions in places like Bosnia and Macedonia; a war (with NATO allies) against rump-Yugoslavia from March to June 1999 that took place completely in the air and that ended in success when Serbian forces withdrew from Kosovo;[62] and Afghanistan, where a massive commitment of U.S. airpower and modest-sized land forces assisted the Northern Alliance in overthrowing the Taliban regime linked to the September 11 terrorist attack by Al-Qaeda. None of these were operational-level campaigns, defined as involving corps-level command and above.

With Afghanistan, the U.S. Army and Marines must feel as if they have come full circle. After the debacle in Vietnam, the U.S. military had undergone what General Franks calls an "enormous and profound transformation"[63] — new doctrine, new training, sophisticated new weaponry — that marked a culmination in the history of modern operational-level warfare. It was an army that could match unparalleled mobility with unrivaled firepower, a force that could run rings around its opposition and blast it into the hereafter as it wished. It fought in a manner that combined the flexibility of German *Bewegungskrieg* and the relentless pressure of Soviet operational art. It was a tool almost perfectly configured for the battle of annihilation.

Like all modern armies, the U.S. Army has often debated the relative virtues of going heavy and going light. Top: the heaviest American tank design of World War II. Originally designated the T-28 heavy tank, the lack of a turret led the army to reclassify it as Gun Motor Carriage T-95. The 105-mm gun was set in a ball-shaped mantlet covered by no less than 12 inches of armor, and the vehicle required an eight-man crew. Bottom: the XM808 Twister from 1970, an experimental "articulated" vehicle consisting of two four-wheeled bodies joined by a yoke. It still holds virtually every course speed record at Aberdeen Proving Ground and Ft. Knox. Courtesy of U.S. Army TACOM.

292

And now, of course, it is fighting a war in small squads, based on imperfect information provided by the various hill tribesmen in Afghanistan. It has already walked into its fair share of problems, as in the poorly planned and coordinated Operation Anaconda in February 2002, which inserted units of the 10th Mountain Division directly into a hail of hostile gunfire.[64] Even the B-52s overhead are an eerie reminder of Vietnam (although that may simply be a reflection of how old these aircraft really are). Fighting has been going on in Afghanistan for two years now, and although the Taliban leaders are gone, the country's political system remains unstable, to put it politely. There is no threat of U.S. forces suffering any sort of major defeat, just as there is little hope of any sort of decisive victory.

Why, then, should the U.S. military continue to train for operational warfare? One reason is that the tenets of war enunciated in U.S. Air-Land Battle doctrine (initiative, agility, depth, and synchronization) are as valid for small-scale guerrilla fighting as they are for big-unit slugfests. A second is that the process that produced AirLand Battle, the intellectual rebirth of the army that actually began with General DePuy's unfairly maligned 1976 FM 100-5 and culminated in the 1982 and 1986 revisions, may still have much to offer in terms of the kind of fighting now going on in Afghanistan. Military intellectuals in the United States designed AirLand Battle, and they may yet succeed in devising similar solutions — firmly based in U.S. traditions of military culture — for guerrilla warfare. There has been a promising start with the introduction of guerrilla and irregular warfare to the National Training Center, as well as the addition of a "fifth tenet" of war to the previous four: versatility.

Since 1991, most trends in the U.S. Army seemed to be leading away from large-scale operational warfare. Several highly dubious notions surfaced within the army: the idea that American military might was so absolute that no adversary would dare to challenge it in any sort of conventional conflict; a belief that concepts like the "fog of war" and the Clausewitzian notion of "friction" had become obsolete because of new intelligence and information technology; a belief, in sum, that technology had changed the very essence of war and that only a highly theoretical "systems logic" approach could understand it.[65] While theoreticians were undertaking these flights of fancy, moreover, the Clinton administration was funding the peacekeeping deployments and limited wars of the 1990s at the expense of fundamentals like training. TRADOC, which had spearheaded the operational and intellectual revolution within the army, found itself consistently short of funds, some $360 million by

March 2001.[66] Training programs for large-scale operations fell by the wayside, and by 2000, many TRADOC schools and installations were at half-strength.

Perhaps the most ridiculous development of the era was the appearance, in the 1993 FM 100-5, of a concept for "operations other than war," a bizarre thing indeed to find in the army's capstone doctrinal manual. Here, the army would do well to heed its own admonition, included in the 1986 version of the manual: "The whole of military activity must relate directly or indirectly to the engagement. The end for which a soldier is recruited, clothed, armed, and trained, the whole object of his sleeping, eating, drinking, and marching, is simply that he should fight at the right place and the right time."[67] Indeed. The words are those of Karl von Clausewitz. As useful as the concept of "operations other than war" might have been in designing a post–cold war raison d'être for the army or in guaranteeing continued funding from Congress, there is absolutely no place in FM 100-5 for the intricacies of hurricane relief or the details of the 1991 antimeningitis campaign in the Cameroons. There are plenty of other organizations that do that sort of work, and probably do it better than the army. The most recent rewrite of "Operations," FM 3-0, goes one better, introducing the term "full spectrum operations." It includes everything from the Lewis and Clark expedition to relief efforts during the San Francisco earthquake to the army's work with the Civilian Conservation Corps during the Depression.

There were other signs of a post-1991 wrong turn. With General Erik Shinseki's appointment as U.S. Army Chief of Staff in 1999, the army began a process of "Transformation," a move toward what he called the "Objective Force." It would be a medium-weight configuration that wouldn't have to worry about being a "speed bump" in the manner of the 82nd Airborne early in Desert Shield, but would be nimble enough to avoid the embarrassment of Task Force Hawk in the Kosovo War, when the army's M-1 tanks and Bradley infantry vehicles proved too heavy for the region's poor roads and light bridges. The Objective Force, supposedly, will be more deployable and thus more suited to the kind of low-intensity/peacekeeping missions that increasingly seem to dominate the army's agenda.[68]

In fact, the U.S. Army seemed unconsciously to be treading a road that interwar theoreticians would have found familiar. In peacetime, planners are often enamored of speed and lightness in vehicles and weaponry. "Light," however, is often nothing more than a euphemism for "smaller," which, in turn, is often a euphemism for "cheaper." Then a war starts, and light vehicles prove their unsuitability for modern combat. The British

The U.S. Army is currently moving away from its traditional mech-heavy configuration into the realm of "Transformation." Left: the U.S. Army's proven commodity, and more trouble than any contemporary army can handle. Eleven M-1 main battle tanks on line during desert maneuvers. Below: today's question mark. The new LAV (Light Armored Vehicle): lighter, highly mobile, and more easily deployable to remote troublespots. Courtesy of U.S. Army TACOM.

army's experience in the early days of World War II, when the masses of light armor and "tankettes" that formed so much a part of its armored strength went to their doom, would seem to be worth recalling in this context. It is nearly inconceivable that a proven high-quality force of unparalleled mobility and destructive power, such as the U.S. Army in 1991, would decide to transform itself completely based on the size of the bridges in Albania, but nevertheless it seems to be happening.

There is one last reason for the army to keep its heavy metal, however, and it trumps any of the others. The world is an unpredictable place. What may seem like a "new world order" or "the end of history" today may appear to be something very different tomorrow. Think of the history of the twentieth century. A prediction in 1945 that "within five years, U.S. forces will be launching an invasion of North Korea" would have puzzled contemporaries; North Korea didn't even exist yet. A prediction that, as a result of that invasion, U.S. forces would be at war with China would have been likewise puzzling. China was an American ally at the time. What of a prediction, when NATO was formed, that it would see virtually no military action at all until a bombing campaign against Yugoslavia — definitely not the raison d'être of the alliance — far in the future? Finally, the one war that U.S. planners felt certain would break out at some point, a great conflagration involving the Soviet Union, never did take place. Large-scale conventional operations will continue to be with us, however.[69] It would be foolish, indeed, for the U.S. Army to throw out the hammer prematurely. It is best kept in the toolbox for that moment in the future, which will surely come, when circumstances once again demand a decisive operational victory.

"Shock and Awe": The Iraq War, 2003

The U.S.-led invasion of Iraq in 2003 demonstrated the continued relevance of operational-level warfare. Although it is too early to draw definitive conclusions from the military victory, several points do suggest themselves. First, no war in history better illustrated the dangers of "punditry" — instant analysis, delivered nowadays by twenty-four-hour cable news networks. The opening days of the campaign saw a stream of untrammeled and often ridiculous declarations. The pundits, both within and outside the defense establishment, began by declaring the campaign to have been an absolute victory, over almost as soon as it had started, a lightning blast that had apparently killed Saddam Hussein and unhinged his regime with virtually no Coalition casualties and with

Light, but still packing a punch: Another view of the LAV (Light Armored Vehicle), this one equipped with a 105-mm gun. Courtesy of U.S. Army TACOM.

Iraq's infrastructure completely intact. A grand total of two days later, many of these same commentators, including a large number of present and retired officers — General Barry McCaffrey being the most egregious example — had changed their tune completely. The campaign was badly flawed, they now agreed. It had relied on too few troops, who were now operating at the end of an untenable supply line; moreover, it appeared that the Pentagon had based the entire operation on expectations of an anti-Saddam civilian uprising that showed no signs of materializing. The news media, as has always been its wont, soon reduced Operation Iraqi Freedom to two clichés. The campaign, conceived as a rapid, third-wave information- and technology-based blitzkrieg of "shock and awe," had instead placed too few "boots on the ground."

At the start of the fighting, the chief of U.S. Central Command, General Tommy Franks, predicted "a campaign unlike any other in history." Featuring a damn-the-flanks-and-supply-lines, full-speed-ahead thrust toward Baghdad on the part of the 3rd Infantry Division, "embedded reporters" broadcasting footage of firefights as they were transpiring, and even specially trained dophins to clear mines from the harbor at Umm Qasr, Iraqi Freedom seemed to indicate that the long-promised future had finally arrived: technology had lived up to its promise and had changed the very nature of war. Indeed, it was difficult to watch the footage out of Baghdad the night of the first great bombardment, as a seemingly inexhaustible wave of cruise missiles slammed again and again with pinpoint precision into the buildings and symbols of Saddam's rule, and not come to the conclusion that this was war according to an entirely new set of rules and assumptions.

On closer inspection, however, much of the novelty vanishes. In fact, the campaign fits snugly into a traditional scheme of analysis. An elite but small coalition force, consisting of not much more than one U.S. division for the first week, barged into Iraq from neighboring Kuwait. It drove forward faster than any large mechanized unit in the history of warfare, without concern to its flanks or to the security of its supply lines. An irresistible air umbrella covered it from above, capable of destroying with precision weapons every single Iraqi vehicle or position that it spotted.

Unfortunately, this lightning drive on Baghdad left behind it not "oc-cupied territory," but a yawning void, a vacuum into which irregular forces like the "Fedayeen Saddam" soon filtered. Essentially flying columns consisting of a few truck-mounted machine guns, the Feday-een shot up a column here, took a few prisoners there, and generally made a nuisance of themselves. They hit not front-line, main-force U.S. units, of course, but rear echelon troops, including one unfortunate U.S. supply and maintenance company that apparently took a wrong turn outside An Nasiriyah and paid the price. The forces tasked with open-ing up and securing a supply line behind 3rd Infantry Division, mean-while, found the going a bit tougher than expected. Prewar intelligence had apparently gambled that the long-suffering Shia population of south-ern Iraq would rise up immediately against their Saddamite oppressors. Such predictions proved to be illusory, as the locals either would not or could not challenge Iraq's internal security forces. The war plan may here have fallen prey to the U.S. military's current obsession with the-ories of systems logic, with their dubious claims to be able to predict the behavior of enemy armies and governments.

In the end, it hardly mattered, but that was due mainly to the Iraqi army's utterly inept performance on the operational level. The Iraqi com-mand, whether it still included Saddam or not, threw a unit or two in the American path, but not much more. U.S. tactical superiority and precision air strikes reduced those unlucky defenders to speedbumps. Once the 3rd Division arrived on the outskirts of Baghdad, it carried out the one legitimate innovation of this campaign: the "thunder run" into the capital — a bold raid by heavy armored units into the heart of the enemy's power. It was proof positive to the population that Saddam had indeed fallen and the trigger, finally, for the civilian uprising that had been so late in coming. It also gave the lie to all the talk of "Transformation" in the U.S. military. Apparently, there is still a great deal of utility in massed formations of heavy M-1 tanks.

Every now and then, a conflict comes along that seems to answer fundamental questions of military doctrine. World War I demonstrated the supremacy of firepower under modern conditions; World War II, the importance of armor and mechanization. In March 2003, Operation Iraqi Freedom answered the question, "Can a single U.S. infantry division pulverize the entire Iraqi army?" with a bold affirmative. The combination of brute force on the ground and precision in the air rendered the enemy helpless. Beyond that, it is far too early to say what, if anything, the victory meant. The uncertainty multiplies when one considers the fact that this might not be the last such campaign in the U.S. war on terrorism.

Conclusion

Drawing up a list of characteristics for decisive victory — a taxonomy — is quite simple. A decisive victory is rapid, it is complete, and it comes at relatively small cost. Achieving one is another story, and the military history of the past century demonstrates how truly rare it is. Nevertheless, it is possible to survey the numerous wars since 1899 and make some general comments about victory and defeat.

First, there is no "one size fits all" prescription for decisive victory on the operational level. It is appropriate to recall the German admonition, *Kein Schema*, here. Indeed, there is "no formula" for success. Buzzwords and fads come and go, such as the U.S. Army's current obsessions with systems analysis, the "information society," and "asymmetric warfare," but the true military intellectual should know enough by now to disdain them. Rather than seek an overarching theory of war, military planners should steep themselves in a "relentless empiricism," in the words of two contemporary scholars.[1]

One may certainly observe, for example, that an analysis of twentieth-century campaigns has made it clear that the force that strives for mobility, that seeks to fight *Bewegungskrieg*, the war of movement on the operational level, has a clear advantage. Seen from the opposite perspective, there is no more secure guarantee of operational defeat than passively defending in place. From the Bulgarian army in the opening campaign of the First Balkan War through the German army at Tannenberg, the Soviet army at Stalingrad, and the Indian army in East Pakistan, the side that maneuvered more effectively won the campaign.

However, is it really possible to say that mobility is more important than firepower? Each of these victorious armies listed earlier also fought the battle of combined arms quite skillfully, coordinating fire from a number of sources: infantry, artillery, and, in the later examples, aircraft. In fact, mobility might be useful only insofar as it allows the force to place fire more effectively from more points on the compass (including directly overhead). Effective fire also serves to increase the friendly force's mobility, by forcing the enemy to keep its collective head down and suppressing its fire.

In other words, on closer examination of actual campaigns of the period, hard and fast distinctions between mobility and firepower disappear. So, too, do other seemingly intractable opposites, buzzwords like "maneuver" and "attrition" warfare. Forces maneuver to place themselves in an advantageous position to wear down the enemy at the greatest possible speed, in other words to destroy him, and to do so with as little friendly loss as possible. In 1940, the elegant German maneuver through the Ardennes allowed the Wehrmacht to inflict more than 1.2 million casualties and take the surrender of three enemy armies in a six-week campaign, for minimal losses. The Israelis utterly destroyed the adversaries facing them in just six fateful days in 1967, first through a series of assaults cracking the Egyptian fortified positions in the Sinai, then through lightning maneuver that carried the IDF to the banks of the Suez. Likewise, it might be necessary in some cases to wear down the enemy first, to restore conditions in which maneuver is possible. The Allied campaign in Normandy in 1944 offers just such an example. Maneuver should have one end in mind: destruction of the enemy force. The two concepts are not separable, and good armies should be able to maneuver and coordinate their fire equally well. Specifically, fire support and the maneuver arms must train together, understand each other, and work in close cooperation on the battlefield. Categorical or *einseitig* (one-sided) sloganeering about the relative merits of "firepower" and "maneuver warfare" betrays a certain ignorance about the true nature of military operations.[2] In fact, if there is one simple link between victorious armies over the past one hundred years, it has been that they were equally adept at both. In the end, what is absolutely essential is that armies perceive the importance of the operational level of war, for it is only here that they can achieve decisive victory.

The same might be said for the relationship between doctrine and practice. Every successful army in the last century, the Bulgarians in the First Balkan War, the Germans in both world wars, the Red Army, the Israel Defense Force, or the U.S. Army in Desert Storm, has given careful thought to its doctrine and formulated one based on its geography, available resources, and political situation. No matter how well grounded it is intellectually, however, a doctrine that lacks intense, rigorous, and realistic training is a bit like faith without works: dead. For an army to realize its doctrine to the fullest possible extent, and to minimize friction during wartime, it must drill, drill, and drill — at every level.[3] Successful prosecution of warfare on the operational level has always been highly complex, and today it is even more complex than ever, with engagements taking place simultaneously short and deep, on the ground, in the air, and in the "nap of the earth," with electronic measures and countermeasures doing their invisible but deadly work, and a nearly constant, almost overwhelming amount of information pouring into headquarters. It cannot be improvised, nor is there any room for a concept like "beginner's luck." It requires that both officers and manpower be fully educated in its demands. Operational-level exercises are, therefore, an irreplaceable component of modern training. Exercises without troops can be quite helpful in presenting commanders and their staffs with the same sort of problems they might face in wartime, but there is no substitute for large, operational-scale field maneuvers. From the Wehrmacht's first test of a full panzer division in the German Fall Maneuvers of 1937 to the repeated honing of NATO's transport and war-fighting capabilities in REFORGER to one of the toughest training regimens ever established, at the Ft. Irwin NTC, the maneuver ground has been, and will always be, crucial to the development of the operational art. Unfortunately, large-scale operational maneuvers have typically been among the first casualties of tight budgets, in Germany in the 1920s and the United States more recently. History would indicate that it is a bad place to save money.

Finally, as much as operational success depends on training and doctrine and weaponry, it also depends on a deep knowledge of the campaigns of the past. It would be the highest imaginable folly for the present-day U.S. Army to believe that its technology (which in some cases has yet to be invented) has somehow invalidated all the lessons of past wars. The "book called Military History"[4] to which General von Schlieffen referred in 1910 is still open to the commander. Now, more than ever, it demands to be read.

Notes

Introduction

1. The primary source for the German panzer drive from Sedan to the sea is Heinz Guderian, *Panzer Leader* (New York: Ballantine Books, 1957), pp. 79–91.

2. For Kleist's testimony, see B. H. Liddell Hart, *The German Generals Talk* (New York: Quill, 1979), p. 130.

3. Lieutenant Colonel Guse, "Ein modernes Austerlitz," *Militär-Wochenblatt* 125, no. 20, November 15, 1940, pp. 947–949. Guse argues that Case Yellow and Austerlitz were also similar in operational terms. Both feature a counterstroke after an enemy had committed itself to an attack, and in each case the *Schwerpunkt* was the spot that linked the enemy's attack wing with its stationary forces. In 1805, this was the Pratzen Heights; in 1940, Sedan.

4. Carlo d'Este, *Fatal Decision: Anzio and the Battle for Rome* (New York: Harper-Collins, 1986), p. 70.

5. See Robert M. Citino, *Quest for Decisive Victory: From Stalemate to Blitzkrieg in Europe, 1899–1940* (Lawrence: University Press of Kansas, 2002).

6. See the excruciating ways in which army planners continue to parse this word in John L. Romjue, *American Army Doctrine for the Post-Cold War* (Ft. Monroe, Va.: TRADOC, 1997), with distinctions between "near-deep" and "far-deep" (p. 99), rather than just "near" and "far," and the definition of "depth" as "the extension of operations in time, space, resources, and purpose" (p. 117).

7. Quoted in Eberhard Kessel, "Moltke und die Kriegsgeschichte: Zur Erinnerung an Moltkes Todestag vor 50 Jahren (24 April 1891)," *Militärwissenschaftliche Rundschau* 6, no. 2, 1941, p. 96.

1. Toward World War II

1. See Gerhard Weinberg, *A World at Arms: A Global History of World War II* (Cambridge: Cambridge University Press, 1994), pp. 894–899, for the human and material costs of the war. Referring to the tendency to refer to World War I as the "Great War," Weinberg has this to say about World War II: "Both by comparison with that terrible event, and when set against all other wars of which we have any knowledge, the second world-wide conflagration of this century deserves to be called 'The Greatest War'" (p. 4).

2. The phrases are the titles of, respectively, Dwight D. Eisenhower, *Crusade in Europe* (Garden City, N.Y.: Doubleday, 1948); Charles B. MacDonald, *The Mighty Endeavor: The American War in Europe* (New York: Da Capo, 1992); and Studs Terkel, *"The Good War": An Oral History of World War Two* (New York: Pantheon Books, 1984).

3. The classic exception, a book that generated a great deal of discussion when it was published, is A. J. P. Taylor, *The Origins of the Second World War* (London: H. Hamilton, 1961). Taylor's thesis, that Britain and France share a great deal of the guilt for the war and that Hitler was yet another in a long line of nationalists at the helm of the Reich, has not won adherents. For a particularly good demolition, see Weinberg, *World at Arms*, pp. 6–47.

4. For *Bewegungskrieg*, see Robert M. Citino, *Quest for Decisive Victory: From Stalemate to Blitzkrieg in Europe, 1899–1940* (Lawrence: University Press of Kansas, 2002), p. 195.

5. Dennis E. Showalter's body of work is essential to our understanding of the nineteenth-century "railroad and rifle revolution." See, especially, his monograph, *Railroads and Rifles: Soldiers, Technology, and the Unification of Germany* (Hamden, Conn.: Archon Books, 1976). It continues to serve as a model for the incorporation of operational history with broader trends in society, politics, and technology. See, also, Steven S. Ross, *From Flintlock to Rifle: Infantry Tactics, 1740–1866* (London: Frank Cass, 1996).

6. The discussion of the importance of information in this era is summarized from Robert M. Citino, "Beyond Fire and Movement: Command, Control, and Information in the German *Blitzkrieg,*" an unpublished paper prepared for a conference held under the auspices of the Center for Strategic and Budgetary Assessment, in Washington, D.C., March 2002.

7. For Moltke, see Daniel J. Hughes, ed., *Moltke on the Art of War: Selected Writings,* (Novato, Calif.: Presidio, 1993), combining a selection of Moltke's most important works and incisive commentary. The professional journals of the German army are the source of literally hundreds of articles on Moltke. See, for example, General of Artillery Ludwig, "Moltke als Erzieher" and the unsigned article, "Generalfeldmarschall Graf von Schlieffen über den großen Feldherrn der preußisch-deutschen Armee," both in *Militär-Wochenblatt* 125, no. 17, October 25, 1940, pp. 802–804 and pp. 805–807, as well as Lieutenant Colonel Obkircher, "Moltke, der 'unbekannte' General von Königgrätz: Zur Erinnerung an den 75. Gedenktag der Schlacht bei Königgrätz am 3. Juli 1866," *Militär-Wochenblatt* 125, no. 52, June 27, 1941, pp. 1994–1997.

8. For Königgrätz, see Geoffrey Wawro, *The Austro-Prussian War: Austria's War with Prussia and Italy in 1866* (Cambridge: Cambridge University Press, 1996), a meticulously researched account that presents the Austrian view of the conflict, and Gordon A. Craig, *The Battle of Königgrätz* (Philadelphia: Lippincott, 1964), still the standard work on the battle and on the campaign that led up to it.

9. There is a huge literature on the war in South Africa. Start with Fred R. van Hartesveldt, *The Boer War: Historiography and Annotated Bibliography* (Westport, Conn.: Greenwood Press, 2000), and Bill Nasson, *The South African War, 1899–1902* (Oxford: Oxford University Press, 2000). Useful in part are Thomas Pakenham,

The Boer War (New York: Random House, 1979), which makes more claims to originality than it can sustain, and Byron Farwell, *The Great Anglo-Boer War* (New York: Norton, 1976), which has all the advantages and disadvantages of popular history. The best account of operations in the war is W. Baring Pemberton, *Battles of the Boer War* (London: Batsford, 1964). In general, all these works focus on the British role in the fighting, British doctrine, and British problems in employing the new technology of war, to the general detriment of the Afrikaner view. There is a large literature in Afrikaans, of course, but the language barrier makes it unavailable to most western scholars. There is a need for a synthesis: a general history of the war incorporating both English and Afrikaans sources.

10. For the Russo-Japanese War, see two recent scholarly works: Bruce Menning, *Bayonets Before Bullets: The Imperial Russian Army, 1861–1914* (Bloomington: Indiana University Press, 1992) includes a solid history of the war (pp. 152–199) in the context of an analysis of doctrine, training, and organization in the Russian army throughout the period. Richard W. Harrison, *The Russian Way of War: Operational Art, 1904–1940* (Lawrence: University Press of Kansas, 2001), pp. 7–23, looks carefully at operations and is extremely hard on Kuropatkin, who for much of the war "behaved like a division commander" preoccupied with "the minutiae of battle," rather than a theater commander seeking an operational decision (p. 23). The new edition of Tadayoshi Sakurai, *Human Bullets: A Soldier's Story of the Russo-Japanese War* (Lincoln: University of Nebraska Press, 1999) is indispensable for the experience of the Japanese foot soldier. For the pursuit after Liaoyang and the "who put those mountains there" reaction, see Sir Ian Hamilton, *A Staff Officer's Scrap-Book* (London: Edward Arnold, 1912), p. 317.

11. For the role of the millet during the first Japanese assault on Port Arthur, see Citino, *Quest for Decisive Victory*, p. 81; for its effect at Liaoyang, see ibid., p. 86.

12. For the battle of the Modder River, see Pemberton, *Battles*, pp. 55–78; Pakenham, *Boer War*, pp. 197–207; Farwell, *Anglo-Boer War*, pp. 91–101. See also Stephen M. Miller, *Lord Methuen and the British Army* (London: Frank Cass, 1999) for a game attempt to rehabilitate Methuen's generalship.

13. There is no monograph in English on operations in the Balkan Wars. Any historical inquiry into the conflicts must still rest on the primary sources and period accounts. Lieutenant Hermenegild Wagner, *With the Victorious Bulgarians* (Boston: Houghton Mifflin, 1913) is a very useful analysis of the Bulgarian war effort by the German correspondent of the *Reichspost*, although rival correspondents often attacked his veracity. The other side of the hill receives attention in Ellis Ashmead-Bartlett, *With the Turks in Thrace* (New York: George H. Doran, 1913), an account by the special correspondent of the *London Daily Telegraph*. Philip Gibbs and Bernard Grant cover both sides in *The Balkan War: Adventures of War with Cross and Crescent* (Boston: Small, Maynard, and Company, 1913). Two extremely useful works are A. Kutschbach, *Die Serben im Balkankrieg 1912–1913 und im Kriege gegen die Bulgaren* (Stuttgart: Frank'sche Verlagshandlung, 1913), and the German translation of the memoirs of Turkish III Corps commander Mahmud Mukhtar Pasha, *Meine Führung im Balkankriege 1912* (Berlin: Ernst Siegfried Mittler und Sohn, 1913).

14. The Hentsch mission remains the most controversial aspect of the opening campaign in the West. See B. H. Liddell Hart, *The Real War, 1914–1918* (Boston: Little, Brown, 1930), pp. 83–84; C. R. M. F. Crutwell, *A History of the Great War, 1914–1918* (Chicago: Academy Chicago, 1991), p. 34; Cyril Falls, *The Great War* (New York: Capricorn, 1959) pp. 68–69; and John Keegan, *The First World War* (London: Hutchinson, 1998), pp. 130–133.

15. Brian Bond, *Liddell Hart: A Study of His Military Thought* (New Brunswick, N.J.: Rutgers University Press, 1977), p. 38.

16. For the latest word on Gallipoli, see Tim Travers, *Gallipoli 1915* (Charleston, S.C.: Tempus, 2001), a highly detailed account, unlikely to be superseded for some time. Edward J. Erickson, *Ordered to Die: A History of the Ottoman Army in the First World War* (Westport, Conn.: Greenwood Press, 2001), has the tremendous attraction of being based on heretofore untapped Turkish sources.

17. Martin Middlebrook, *The First Day on the Somme: 1 July 1916* (New York: W. W. Norton, 1972) is still the standard work on the Somme, although it is by necessity restricted in its treatment. Tim Travers's *The Killing Ground: The British Army, the Western Front, and the Emergence of Modern Warfare, 1900–1918* (London: Allen & Unwin, 1987), uses the Somme as a "case study," in "how to apply the traditional principles to what was seen as a new and puzzling form of warfare" (p. 127). Peter H. Liddle, *The 1916 Battle of the Somme: A Reappraisal* (London: Leo Cooper, 1992) argues, unconvincingly, "that in 1916–17 terms, a British victory was won on the Somme, not one to be greeted with bell-ringing and bunting, indeed one more appropriately honoured by the draperies of mourning, but a victory nonetheless" (p. 156). He points to the German withdrawal to a new defensive position in early 1917 as proof. Much of the book is a tedious attack on other historians of the Somme, including Travers, but especially Denis Winter, *Haig's Command: A Reassessment* (London: Viking, 1991), accusing the latter of conducting ad hominem attacks on Haig and of using "selective evidence."

18. The interwar period has attracted intense study of late, analyzed by both scholars and military operators alike. See the two essential works: Williamson Murray and Allan R. Millett, eds., *Military Innovation in the Interwar Period* (Cambridge: Cambridge University Press, 1996) and Harold R. Winton and David R. Mets, *The Challenge of Change: Military Institutions and New Realities, 1918–1941* (Lincoln: University of Nebraska Press, 2000). The Murray/Millett volume is arranged topically; the Winton/Mets volume by nation. The list of monographs on the era is large and getting larger. See, among others, Robert M. Citino, *Quest for Decisive Victory* and *The Path to Blitzkrieg: Doctrine and Training in the German Army, 1920–1939* (Boulder, Colo.: Lynne Rienner, 1999); James S. Corum, *The Roots of Blitzkrieg: Hans von Seeckt and German Military Reform* (Lawrence: University Press of Kansas, 1992); Eugenia C. Kiesling, *Arming Against Hitler: France and the Limits of Military Planning* (Lawrence: University Press of Kansas, 1996); David E. Johnson, *Fast Tanks and Heavy Bombers: Innovation in the U.S. Army, 1917–1945* (Ithaca, N.Y.: Cornell University Press, 1998); William O. Odom, *After the Trenches: The Transformation of U.S. Army Doctrine, 1918–1939* (College Station: Texas A&M University Press, 1999);

Harold R. Winton, *To Change an Army: General Sir John Burnett-Stuart and British Armored Doctrine, 1927–1938* (Lawrence: University Press of Kansas, 1988).

19. See, for example, Lieutenant Colonel Köhn, "Die Infanterie im 'Blitzkrieg,' " *Militär-Wochenblatt* 125, no. 5, August 2, 1940, pp. 165–166, in which "blitzkrieg" is used only in quotation marks and is described as a "catch-phrase" *(Schlagwort)*, as well as Colonel Rudolf Theiss, "Der Panzer in der Weltgeschichte," *Militär-Wochenblatt* 125, no. 15, October 11, 1940, pp. 705–708, which likewise uses the term in quotes. By 1941, German usage in the professional literature had dropped the quotes, although the word was still not being used in any sort of precise technical sense. See Lieutenant Colonel Gaul, "Der Blitzkrieg in Frankreich," *Militär-Wochenblatt* 125, no. 35, February 28, 1941, pp. 1513–1517.

20. For a German analysis of the Experimental Mechanized Force, see the unsigned series of articles entitled "Englische motorisierte Versuchsbrigade," *Militär-Wochenblatt* 122, no. 14, October 11, 1927, pp. 501–507; no. 15, October 18, 1927, pp. 540–543; and no. 16, October 25, 1927, pp. 570–571.

21. Quoted in General Ernst Kabisch, "Systemlose Strategie," *Militär-Wochenblatt* 125, no. 26, December 27, 1940, p. 1235.

22. See, for example, the unsigned article "Zentralisation und Dezentralisation," *Militär-Wochenblatt* 115, no. 27, January 18, 1931, pp. 1038–1039, which discusses in some detail the issues of centralized and decentralized command without ever using the term *Auftragstaktik*. It is interesting to speculate what the Germans would think of the use of German terms like *blitzkrieg* or *Auftragstaktik* in the U.S. Army. A contemporary German officer would never have used foreign terms with such frequency. See the unsigned article "Fremdwort und Heeressprache," *Militär-Wochenblatt* 113, no. 2, July 11, 1928, pp. 48–50, as well as the article by the editor of the *Militär-Wochenblatt*, General Konstantin von Altrock, entitled "Sprach- und Schreib-dummheiten," *Militär-Wochenblatt* 113, no. 2, July 11, 1928, pp. 50–52. For a strongly worded essay on the way in which German terms and concepts can be misused within the contemporary U.S. Army, see Daniel J. Hughes, "Abuses of German Military History," *Military Review* 65, no. 12, December 1986, pp. 66–76.

23. For discussion of *Auftragstaktik*, see Antulio J. Echevarria II, *After Clausewitz: German Military Thinkers Before the Great War* (Lawrence: University Press of Kansas, 2000), pp. 32–42 and pp. 94–103. See also Daniel J. Hughes, "Schlichting, Schlieffen, and the Prussian Theory of War in 1914," *Journal of Military History* 59, no. 2, April 1995, pp. 257–277.

24. "Zentralisation und Dezentralisation," p. 1038.

25. A point made in the unsigned article, "Der Angriffsschlacht von Cambrai vom 30. November bis 6. Dezember 1917," *Militär-Wochenblatt* 112, no. 22, December 11, 1927, pp. 803–804.

26. For a more complete expression of this argument, see Robert M. Citino, " 'Die Gedanken sind frei': The Intellectual Culture of the Interwar German Army," *The Army Doctrine and Training Bulletin* (Canada) 4, no. 3, Fall 2001.

27. The phrase is General Erich von Ludendorff's, describing German operations in the Warsaw-Lodz campaign in the fall of 1914. Quoted in Colonel von Schäfer,

"Die Enstehung des Entschlusses zur Offensive auf Lods: Zum Gedenken an General Ludendorff," *Militärwissenschaftliche Rundschau* 3, no. 1, 1938, p. 25.

28. For the *Funkübung*, see Citino, *Path to Blitzkrieg*, pp. 208–212.

29. "Neugestaltung der Kriegführung," *Militär-Wochenblatt* 120, no. 18, November 11, 1935, pp. 747–750; and no. 19, November 18, 1935, pp. 787–792.

30. Heinz Guderian, "Die Panzertruppen und ihr Zusammenwirken mit den anderen Waffen," *Militärwissenschaftliche Rundschau* 1, no. 5, 1936, pp. 607–626.

31. Colonel Fuppe, "Neuzeitliches Nachrichtenverbindungswesen als Führungsmittel im Kriege," *Militärwissenschaftliche Rundschau* 3, no. 6, 1938, pp. 750–758.

32. See the article by General of Artillery Ludwig, "Gedanken über den Angriff im Bewegungskriege," *Militärwissenschaftliche Rundschau* 1, no. 2, 1936, pp. 153–164.

33. Major Friedrich Bertkau, "Die nachrichtentechnische Führung mechanisierter Verbände," *Militär-Wochenblatt* 120, no. 15, October 18, 1935, p. 612.

34. See, for example, Rolf Bathe, *Der Feldzug der 18 Tage: Die Chronik des polnischen Dramas* (Oldenburg: Gerhard Stalling, 1939). Steven J. Zaloga and Victor Madej, *The Polish Campaign* (New York: Hippocrene, 1991), p. 158, address the "myth of the 'eighteen-day war,' " pointing out that Army Group South "lost more men killed in the final half of the war than in the first two weeks."

35. For the role of the Luftwaffe in the Polish campaign, see James S. Corum, *The Luftwaffe: Creating the Operational Air War, 1918–1940* (Lawrence: University Press of Kansas, 1997), pp. 272–275. For a detailed operational account of the fighting around Modlin, see Major Wim Brandt, "Bilder aus der Belagerung von Modlin," *Militär-Wochenblatt* 124, no. 30, January 19, 1940, pp. 1451–1454.

36. Hans von Luck, *Panzer Commander* (Westport, Conn.: Praeger, 1989), p. 26.

37. For the fight on the Bzura, see Zaloga and Madej, *Polish Campaign*, pp. 131–138.

38. James Lucas, *Battle Group! German Kampfgruppen Action of World War Two* (London: Arms and Armour, 1993), pp. 10–24, focuses on the operations of 4th Panzer Division in Warsaw and on the Bzura.

39. For Case Yellow, see Jeffrey A. Gunsburg, *Divided and Conquered: The French High Command and the Defeat in the West, 1940* (Westport, Conn.: Greenwood Press, 1979), and Robert A. Doughty, *The Breaking Point: Sedan and the Fall of France, 1940* (Hamden, Conn.: Archon Books, 1990). A particularly worthy popular treatment is Alistair Horne, *To Lose a Battle: France 1940* (Boston: Little, Brown, 1969). For the role of Guderian's panzers in the campaign, see Florian K. Rothbrust, *Guderian's XIXth Panzer Corps and the Battle of France: Breakthrough in the Ardennes, May 1940* (Westport, Conn.: Praeger, 1990), essentially an essay (running to just ninety-five pages of text) extended by maps and documents.

40. Guderian, *Panzer Leader*, p. 79; Doughty, *Breaking Point*, p. 133; Rothbrust, *Guderian's XIXth Panzer Corps*, p. 69.

41. For the Allied attacks at Montcornet, Crécy, and Arras, see Horne, *To Lose a Battle*, pp. 425–430, 498–509; Gunsburg, *Divided and Conquered*, pp. 231–234, 245–246, 249–250. Kenneth Macksey, *Tank Versus Tank: The Illustrated Story of Armored Battlefield Conflict in the Twentieth Century* (New York: Barnes & Noble, 1999), pp. 74–80, is especially good on Arras.

42. See Robert M. Citino, "The Weimar Roots of German Military Planning," in *Military Planning and the Origins of the Second World War in Europe*, ed. B. J. C. McKercher and Roch Legault (Westport, Conn.: Praeger, 2001), pp. 59–87.

43. Major Allen Kimberly, acting U.S. military attaché to War Department, Berlin, 23 September 1924, "German Army Maneuvers, September 4th to 19th, 1924." See Citino, *Path to Blitzkrieg*, pp. 120–123.

44. Paul Johnston, "Doctrine Is Not Enough: The Effect of Doctrine on the Behavior of Armies," *Parameters* 30, no. 3, Autumn 2000, pp. 30ff., contains an argument to this effect.

45. See Colonel Mantey, "Praktische Winke für das Anfassen kriegsgeschichtlicher Studien," *Militär-Wochenblatt* 116, no. 24, December 25, 1931, pp. 867–870.

2. In Search of the Impossible

1. See "Grossdeutschlands Freiheitskrieg 1940," part 44, "Der Abschluss der Vernichtungsschlacht in Flandern und im Artois sowie der Beginn der neuen deutschen Offensive über die Somme und den Oise — Aisne-Kanal in der Woche vom 2. bis 8.6.1940," *Militär-Wochenblatt* 124, no. 50, June 14, 1940, p. 2241–2248. The phrase is used in successive paragraphs (pp. 2245–2246); so too is "the most successful battle of all time" (p. 2245).

2. See Williamson Murray, "May 1940: Contingency and Fragility of the German RMA," in *The Dynamics of Military Revolution, 1300–2050*, ed. MacGregor Knox and Williamson Murray (Cambridge: Cambridge University Press, 2001), pp. 154–174.

3. For a summary of the rise and development of the German airborne forces, see F. Stuhlmann, "Fallschirmjäger," *Militär-Wochenblatt* 125, no. 25, December 20, 1940, pp. 1191–1192. An inquiry into the Scandinavian campaign must begin with a recent work: Adam R. A. Claasen, *Hitler's Northern War: The Luftwaffe's Ill-Fated Campaign, 1940–1945* (Lawrence: University Press of Kansas, 2001). Claasen has combined a voracious appetite for the secondary literature on the campaign with a great deal of archival research, and the result is a much more detailed — and nuanced — portrait of German combined operations in the north than has heretofore been available. The book ranges far beyond Luftwaffe activity to include land and naval combat, as well as the interplay of all three arms.

Another important work by a contemporary scholar is James S. Corum, "The German Campaign in Norway as a Joint Operation," *Journal of Strategic Studies* 21, no. 4, December 1998, pp. 50–77, which not only looks carefully at the successes of German interservice cooperation in the campaign but also at Allied failures in the same area. "In Norway, it was less a question of German brilliant planning and mastery of the operational art than it was of a mediocre plan executed energetically versus a bad plan executed poorly," he concludes (p. 74). Still a worthy primary source, recently rereleased in a new edition, is Erich Raeder's memoir, *Grand Admiral* (New York: Da Capo Press, 2001), especially pp. 300–318. See also Chris Smith, "Strike North: Germany Invades Scandinavia, 1940," *Command* 39, September 1996, pp. 18–

27, for sound analysis and the trademark of this now defunct military history and war-game magazine, excellent maps.

4. For the political background to the Norwegian campaign, see "Grossdeutsch-lands Freiheitskrieg 1940," part 36, "Deutschlands Antwort auf die Kriegserklärung der Weltmächte an die Neutralität: Die Besetzung Dänemarks und Norwegens durch deutsche Truppen," *Militär-Wochenblatt* 124, no. 42, April 19, 1940, pp. 1923–1926.

5. A good summary of the Danish campaign is to be found in Major Macher, "Die Besetzung Dänemarks," *Militär-Wochenblatt* 125, no. 45, May 9, 1941, p. 1793, writ-ten on the occasion of the campaign's first anniversary.

6. See Claasen, *Hitler's Northern War*, pp. 62–65.

7. Macher, "Die Besetzung Dänemarks," p. 1793.

8. Still useful as summaries of the initial German landings and the Norwegian response to them, see two articles in the *History of the Second World War (HSWW)* series: J. L. Moulton, "Hitler Strikes North," *HSWW*, no. 3, 1978, pp. 68–74, and Leif Bohn, "The Norwegian View," ibid., pp. 77–78.

9. Claasen, *Hitler's Northern War*, pp. 43–44, discusses the immense difficulty of coordinating these various bodies — the "Export Group," the "1st Naval Transport Group," and a group of three tankers — and getting them to their destinations on time. For the German naval order of battle, see Tom Dworschak, "Operation Weser Exer-cise: The German Navy in Norway, 1940," *Command* 39, September 1996, pp. 28–33.

10. Claasen, *Hitler's Northern War*, p. 70.

11. For the sinking of the *Blücher*, see Carl O. Schuster, "Coastal Defense Victory: Blücher at Oslo," *Command* 39, September 1996, pp. 30–31, a sidebar to Dworschak, "Operation Weser Exercise." Again, as in all issues of *Command*, the maps are superb. Schuster argues for either a landward thrust against the fortress by assault troops landed that same day (which is what eventually happened) or, failing that, a damn-the-torpedoes run by a "lighter, faster and more expendable ship," instead of a "ves-sel with VIPs aboard." See also Claasen, *Hitler's Northern War*, p. 66. Richard D. Hooker, Jr., and Christopher Coglianese, "Operation *Weserübung*: A Case Study in the Operational Art," in *Maneuver Warfare: An Anthology*, ed. Richard D. Hooker, Jr. (Novato, Calif.: Presidio, 1993), point out that, as disastrous as the loss of the ship was, it only held up the capture of Oslo by half a day (p. 380).

12. For Fornebu, see Claasen, *Hitler's Northern War*, pp. 68–69. Timothy J. Kutta, "The Capture of Fornebu Airfield," *Command* 39, September 1996, pp. 20–21, a sidebar to Smith, "Strike North," contains a detailed description of the aerial jock-eying of all concerned.

13. For the details of this little known aspect of the Norwegian campaign, see "Aus dem Feldzuge in Norwegen," parts 1 and 2, "Die Kämpfe um die Landverbindung nach Drontheim im April 1940," *Militärwissenschaftliche Rundschau* 6, nos. 2 and 3, 1941, pp. 185–192 and 232–241, and "Aus dem Feldzuge in Norwegen," part 3, "Von Drontheim bis Namsos," *Militärwissenschaftliche Rundschau* 6, no. 4, 1941, pp. 323–331.

14. For the Namsos-Aandalsnes landings and the devastating impact of Luftwaffe bombing, see Claasen, *Hitler's Northern War*, pp. 100–117, as well as J. L. Moulton, "Conquest of Norway," *HSWW*, no. 4, 1978, pp. 85–94.

15. David G. Thompson, "Norwegian Military Policy, 1905–1940: A Critical Appraisal and Review of the Literature," *Journal of Military History* 61, no. 3, July 1997, pp. 503–520, has done the great service of investigating the campaign from the Norwegian perspective. For the Norwegian view of the Allied forces in Norway, see pp. 518–519.

16. For Hitler's decree, see Claasen, *Hitler's Northern War*, pp. 108–109.

17. See "Grossdeutschlands Freiheitskrieg 1940," pt. 39, "Englands diplomatische und militärische Niederlage in Norwegen," *Militär-Wochenblatt* 124, no. 45, May 10, 1940, pp. 2041–2044.

18. Some three thousand sailors survived the sinking of their vessels and joined General Dietl's land force in the defense of Narvik (Raeder, *Grand Admiral*, p. 310).

19. For a discussion of how Hitler handled the bad news out of Narvik, see the memoirs of General Walter Warlimont of the High Command of the Wehrmacht (OKW), *Inside Hitler's Headquarters 1939–45* (Novato, Calif.: Presidio, 1964), pp. 76–81. Warlimont describes "Hitler hunched on a chair in a corner, unnoticed and staring in front of him, a picture of brooding gloom…. I turned away in order not to look at so undignified a picture" (pp. 79–80). He could not help but make a comparison to "Moltke's imperturbable calm and self-assurance on the battlefields of Bohemia and France."

20. There is a fine account of the Narvik fighting in Chris Smith, "Strike North," pp. 24–26.

21. For a discussion of "operational air war," see James S. Corum, *Luftwaffe: Creating the Operational Air War, 1918–1940* (Lawrence: University Press of Kansas, 1997).

22. There is a great deal of literature on the Crete campaign, much of it from Great Britain or New Zealand. The best scholarly account is still Ian McDougall Guthrie Stewart, *The Struggle for Crete 20 May–1 June 1941: A Story of Lost Opportunity* (London: Oxford University Press, 1966), a book that has aged quite well. The text is lucid, and the criticism — of both the German attacker and the Commonwealth defenders — judicious. See, in particular, the discussion on pp. 481–483. A good short introduction, probably still the most widely read account of the campaign, is found in Hanson Baldwin, *Battles Lost and Won: Great Campaigns of World War II* (New York: Harper and Row, 1966), pp. 57–113 ("Crete — The Winged Invasion"). See also John Aikman Hetherington, *Airborne Invasion: The Story of the Battle of Crete* (New York: Duell, Sloan and Pearce, 1943), a period journalistic account; George Forty, *The Battle for Crete* (Hersham, Surrey: Ian Allan, 2001), combining a fine selection of photographs with a great deal of unedited testimony from participants on both sides; D. M. Davin, *Crete: Official History of New Zealand in the Second World War, 1939–45* (Wellington, N.Z.: War History Branch, 1953), still an authoritative voice, and particularly so when discussing the unfortunate role of the 5th New Zealand Brigade during the Maleme fighting; and Baron Friedrich August von der Heydte, *Daedalus Returned: Crete 1941* (London: Hutchinson, 1958), the account by a German airborne battalion commander. Alan Clark, *The Fall of Crete* (London: A. Blond, 1962) is a typically fine work by this popular author. See also Christopher Buckley, *Greece and Crete, 1941* (London: H. M. Stationery Office, 1952), part of the series

The Second World War, 1939–1945, "a popular military history by various authors in eight volumes," which has the attraction of offering a comparative discussion of both the failed intervention in Greece and the fighting on Crete; Geoffrey Cox, *A Tale of Two Battles: A Personal Memoir of Crete and the Western Desert, 1941* (London: William Kimber, 1987), a memoir by a soldier of the New Zealand 23rd Battalion, that offers the same sort of comparative analysis for Crete and North Africa; Franz Kurowski, *Der Kampf um Kreta* (Herford, Bonn: Maximilian-Verlag, 1965), which had much new to offer when it appeared, particularly in terms of the size of the German force landed on Crete; Hans-Otto Muhleisen, *Kreta 1941: Das Unternehemen Merkur, 20. Mai–1. Juni 1941* (Freiburg: Rombach, 1968), a trenchant account published by the Federal Republic of Germany's *Militärgeschichtliches Forschungsamt,* including a great deal of primary documentation from the German side; and Callum A. MacDonald, *The Lost Battle — Crete, 1941* (New York: Free Press, 1993), which not only traces the rise of German airborne forces up to 1941 but offers a great deal of biographical information on General Kurt Student. Anthony Beevor, *Crete: The Battle and the Resistance* (London: John Murray, 1991) not only takes the story up to 1945 — something new in the literature — but includes several of the Ultra dispatches that General Freyberg had at his disposal before and during the campaign. Tony Simpson, *Operation Mercury: The Battle for Crete* (London: Hodder and Stoughton, 1981) is a solid operational and tactical history. Finally, for a postwar analysis by German officers (part of the *German Report Series*), see "Airborne Operations: A German Appraisal" (Washington, D.C.: Center of Military History, 1989). For the German report series and its impact on the postwar U.S. Army, see Kevin Soutor, "To Stem the Red Tide: The German Report Series and Its Effect on American Defense Doctrine, 1948–1954," *Journal of Military History* 57, no. 4, October 1993, pp. 653–688. One still little-used German primary source is the unpublished manuscript by Conrad Seibt, "Einsatz Kreta Mai 1941," part of the *German Report Series,* B-641, by the quartermaster of the XI Fleigerkorps during the campaign. A copy of the report, along with the rest of this immense series, is on file in the U.S. Army Military History Institute at Carlisle Barracks in Carlisle, Pennsylvania. It is a rich source, still largely untapped by scholars.

23. Baldwin, *Battles Lost and Won,* p. 69, quoting the British official history. See also Davin, *Crete,* p. 79.

24. For Student's briefing to his officers, see von der Heydte, *Daedalus Returned,* pp. 40–43.

25. German Field Marshal Albert Kesselring, referring to the difficulties in prosecuting an air landing in the absence of surprise, went so far as to say that "Crete is the classic example of how this should not be done." See "Airborne Operations: A German Appraisal," pp. 3–4. Both MacDonald, *Lost Battle,* and Beevor, *Crete: The Battle and the Resistance,* especially the latter, are thorough in their treatment of Ultra. See the book review of these two works by Raymond Callahan, *Journal of Military History* 58, no. 4, October 1994, pp. 759–761.

26. Von der Heydte recalls that the corps intelligence officer informed officers at the predrop briefing that "on the island were the remnants of two or three Greek

divisions, much weakened by the battles on the mainland, and a British force of divisional strength." In addition, "a portion of the population would be sympathetic towards a German attack" (*Daedelus Returned*, p. 43).

27. "Airborne Operations: A German Appraisal," pp. 4–5.

28. Quoted in Stewart, *Struggle for Crete*, pp. 205–206. For the testimony of numerous New Zealanders who were there on that first day, see also Simpson, *Operation Mercury*, pp. 152–186.

29. See "Invasion and Battle for Crete," online, www.feldgrau.com/cretewar.html. See also Baron Friedrich August von der Heydte, "Notes on German Airborne Operations," appendix to "Airborne Operations: A German Appraisal," pp. 45–56.

30. The numbers vary widely, a sign of the chaotic Commonwealth command arrangements on Crete. See Baldwin, *Battles Lost and Won*, pp. 66 and 410 n. 17.

31. Quoted in MacDonald, *Lost Battle*, p. 173.

32. Such was the case as 22nd New Zealand Battalion fought for its life on Hill 107, while its two fresh sister battalions (21st and 23rd) stood by. For discussion, see Davin, *Crete*, p. 135.

33. Stewart, *Struggle for Crete*, p. 27.

34. The fateful events on Hill 107 form the heart of the New Zealand Official History. See Davin, *Crete*, especially pp. 114–116, which examine the motives and actions of the commander of the 22nd New Zealand Battalion, Lieutenant Colonel Andrew, and pp. 131–138, which do the same thing for his commander, Brigadier Hargest (5th New Zealand Brigade). The general comes out much the worse, a verdict that has survived to the present day in the literature. See Stewart, *Struggle for Crete*, pp. 480–482, for a nuanced discussion.

35. For Student's decision, see the unsigned article, "Die Eroberung von Kreta," *Militär-Wochenblatt* 126, no. 6, August 8, 1941, pp. 147–150, especially p. 149.

36. Davin, *Crete*, pp. 115–116.

37. Ibid., p. 138.

38. Quoted in Baldwin, *Battles Lost and Won*, p. 83.

39. For the role of the 5th Mountain Division in overrunning the island, see "Schilderungen aus den Kämpfen der Gebirgsjäger bei der Eroberung von Kreta im Mai 1941," *Militärwissenschaftliche Rundschau* 6, no. 3, 1941, pp. 262–273.

40. Quoted in Stewart, *Struggle for Crete*, p. 478.

41. For Student's account of his conversations with Hitler, see B. H. Liddell Hart, *The German Generals Talk* (New York: Quill, 1979), pp. 159–161, still, for all its faults, a useful book. See also Stewart, *Struggle for Crete*, p. 477.

42. Liddell Hart, *German Generals Talk*, p. 159.

43. See Mühleisen, *Kreta 1941*, p. 25, for discussion of Löhr's role.

44. Perhaps no area of World War II has had so many books written about it as the Desert War. The books are aging, however, and little new is coming up to replace them. Perhaps this is that rare creature: a tapped-out field. For a rare exception, and a good overview of the entire campaign, see George Forty, *The Armies of Rommel* (London: Arms and Armour, 1997). See also W. G. F. Jackson, *The Battle for North Africa, 1940–43* (New York: Mason, Charter, 1975) and Ronald Lewin, *The Life and*

Death of the Afrika Korps (London: Batsford, 1977). In the historiography of the field, the military biography, with all its traditional faults and virtues, still holds sway. See, for example, Correlli Barnett, *The Desert Generals* (Bloomington: Indiana University Press, 1982); Nigel Hamilton, *Monty*, 3 volumes (London: Hamish Hamilton, 1981–1986); John Keegan, ed., *Churchill's Generals* (New York: Grove Weidenfeld, 1991); Ronald Lewin, *Montgomery as Military Commander* (London: Batsford, 1971) and *Rommel as Military Commander* (London: Batsford, 1968); and Kenneth Macksey, *Rommel: Battles and Campaigns* (London: Arms and Armour, 1979). The best among them manage to raise enough questions about their subject to make them worth reading. Often, however, they lapse into hagiography, and their format often prevents them from going beyond the issue of personalities. Other works worthy of consultation include the vast number of memoirs, by figures both great and small. See R. L. Crimp, *The Diary of a Desert Rat* (London: Leo Cooper, 1971); Robert Crisp, *Brazen Chariots* (New York: Ballantine, 1961), perhaps the finest book to come out of the war; B. H. Liddell Hart, ed., *The Rommel Papers* (London: Collins, 1953); Bernard Law Montgomery's *El Alamein to the River Sangro; Normandy to the Baltic* (London: Barrie and Jenkins, 1973) and *Memoirs of Field-Marshal the Viscount Montgomery of Alamein* (Cleveland: World, 1968); and Heinz Werner Schmidt's *With Rommel in the Desert* (New York: Bantam, 1977) by Rommel's aide-de-camp. Among the secondary literature, Michael Carver's books are essential: *Tobruk* (London: Batsford, 1964); *El Alamein* (London: Batsford, 1962); and *Dilemmas of the Desert War* (London: Batsford, 1986). And for two well-done pictorial works among the hundred available, see A. J. Barber, *Afrika Korps* (London: Bison, 1977) and George Forty, *Desert Rats at War: North Africa* (London: Ian Allan, 1975). Finally, three books deserve special mention: Wolf Heckmann, *Rommel's War in Africa* (Garden City, N.Y.: Doubleday, 1981), for being the first to dare to puncture the Rommel bubble, pointing out the general's numerous personal and operational faults; Hans-Otto Behrendt, *Rommel's Intelligence in the Desert Campaign, 1941–43* (London: William Kimber, 1985), for being the only book to deal exclusively with this crucial problem; and Bruce Gudmundsson, ed., *Inside the Afrika Korps* (London: Greenhill Books, 1999), an edited version of the report drawn up for the U.S. Army by German Colonel Rainer Kriebel, simply for showing that there is still something new to say, and to read, about these campaigns.

45. For how Rommel first came to Hitler's attention, see Schmidt, *With Rommel in the Desert*, pp. 90–94. For a biographical sketch of the general, see Robert M. Citino, *Armored Forces: History and Sourcebook* (Westport, Conn.: Greenwood, 1994), pp. 266–269.

46. A standard account of Rommel's opening offensive out of El Agheila is F. W. von Mellenthin, *Panzer Battles: A Study of the Employment of Armor in the Second World War* (New York: Ballantine, 1956), pp. 52–65. For more recent works, see Forty, *Armies of Rommel*, pp. 115–119, and Bruce Allen Watson, *Desert Battle: Comparative Perspectives* (Westport, Conn.: Praeger, 1995), pp. 1–13.

47. Forty, *Armies of Rommel*, p. 117. See also Liddell Hart, ed., *Rommel Papers*, p. 101.

48. And he was more than nine hundred miles from his supply base in Tripoli. See Ward A. Miller, *The 9th Australian Division Versus the Africa Corps: An Infantry Divi-*

sion Against Tanks — Tobruk, Libya, 1941 (Ft. Leavenworth, Kans.: U.S. Army Command and General Staff College, 1986), pp. 5–6.

49. Edward B. Westermann, *Flak: German Anti-Aircraft Defenses, 1914–1945* (Lawrence: University Press of Kansas, 2001), p. 121.

50. For the 88mm gun, see John Weeks, *Men Against Tanks: A History of Antitank Warfare* (New York: Mason/Charter, 1975), pp. 64–65. For German antitank guns in general, see W. J. K. Davies, *German Army Handbook 1939–1945* (New York: Arco, 1973), pp. 100–107. See also Crisp, *Brazen Chariots:* "The word 'eighty-eight' was invading the tank-crew vocabulary as a symbol of shattering mutilation . . . during the entire campaign we were to find no effective answer to the enemy's use of antitank weapons well forward with his Panzers" (p. 33). On another occasion, leading a column with towed antitank guns into battle, he despaired: "Nor could I foresee any possible situation, unless we were completely surrounded, in which the antitank guns could be properly brought into action" (p. 167). The Germans managed — repeatedly.

51. See Paddy Griffith, "British Armoured Warfare in the Western Desert," in *Armoured Warfare*, ed. J. P. Harris and F. H. Toase (London: Batsford, 1990), pp. 70–87. See also *German Methods of Warfare in the Libyan Desert* (Washington, D.C.: Military Intelligence Service, 1942). Rommel was one of the favorites of the war-gaming community for many years. See A. A. Nofi's fine article, "The Desert Fox: Rommel's Campaign for North Africa, April 1941–December 1942," *Strategy and Tactics* 87, July–August 1981, pp. 4–15, for a tactical analysis of a typical desert battle.

52. Crisp, *Brazen Chariots*, pp. 13, 31.

53. Miller, *9th Australian Division*, covers the First Battle of Tobruk in detail. See also Heckman, *Rommel's War*, pp. 69–86.

54. Miller, *9th Australian Division*, p. 31.

55. Ibid., p. 4.

56. *German Experiences in Desert Warfare During World War II*, volume I, originally part of the *German Reports Series*, most recently issued as Fleet Marine Force Reference Publication (FMFRP) 12-96-I (Quantico, Va.: United States Marine Corps, 1990), pp. 3–4. The writing team included German generals Fritz Bayerlein, Albert Kesselring, Siegfried Westphal, and others.

57. The best short account of Operation Crusader — cogent and clear throughout, no mean feat for such a confused operation — is still Barnett, *Desert Generals*, pp. 83–120, seen through the experience of General Alan Cunningham. No account communicates the chaos of the battle better than Crisp, *Brazen Chariots*. See especially the friendly fire incident on pp. 147–148, and the hilarious discussion of the difference between a "demonstration" and a "reconnaissance in force," pp. 141–142. Finally, Gudmundsson, ed., *Inside the Afrika Korps*, offers the most detailed account yet from the German side.

58. Barnett, *Desert Generals*, p. 88.

59. Crisp, *Brazen Chariots*, p. 33.

60. Barnett, *Desert Generals*, pp. 88–89.

61. Crisp, *Brazen Chariots*, pp. 41–42, describes the chaos, and on p. 49 labels the situation a "balls-up."

62. Barnett, *Desert Generals*, p. 101–102.

63. Crisp, *Brazen Chariots*, pp. 82–84. There is a frank passage: "We heard of the panic in the headquarters and supply areas, and were unpatriotically delighted at the thought of generals and staff officers fleeing for Alexandria or wetting themselves in slit trenches" (p. 82). See also Barnett, *Desert Generals*, p. 114.

64. Crisp, *Brazen Chariots*, p. 128.

65. Actually, the "witches cauldron" *(Hexenkessel)*. For Gazala, see Barnett, *Desert Generals*, pp. 123–158, and Mellenthin, *Panzer Battles*, pp. 107–137.

66. For the Lee/Grant tanks, see Eric Grove, Christopher Chant, David Lyon, and Hugh Lyon, *The Military Hardware of World War II: Tanks, Aircraft, and Naval Vessels* (New York: Military Press, 1984), pp. 52–54. For their impact on the fighting, see Schmidt, *With Rommel in the Desert*, pp. 147–148.

67. For a short biography of Montgomery, see Citino, *Armored Forces*, pp. 258–261.

68. Montgomery, *Memoirs*, p. 178.

69. Ibid., p. 352.

70. A recent, very helpful volume on "Al-Alamein" (as it is now transliterated) is Jill Edwards, ed., *Al-Alamein Revisited: The Battle of al-Alamein and Its Historical Implications* (Cairo: American University in Cairo, 2000). In the proceedings of a symposium held on May 2, 1998, at the American University, the contributions include an introductory article by Michael Howard ("The Battle of al-Alamein") and a well-crafted analysis of the German perspective on the battle by Thomas Scheben ("The German Perspective of War in North Africa, 1940–42: Three-dimensional, Intercontinental Warfare"). See also Fred Majdalany, *The Battle of El Alamein: Fortress in the Sand* (Philadelphia: Lippincott, 1965), another installment in the old, but still useful *Great Battles of History* series, and Carver, *El Alamein*.

71. Montgomery, *Memoirs*, p. 116.

72. *German Experiences in Desert Warfare*, p. 14.

73. Since the fall of communism, there has been a veritable "revolution in historical affairs," as once-closed archives are now open to researchers. The result has been a much more detailed portrait of the Red Army than was heretofore possible. The point man in this development has been David M. Glantz, the leading authority in the west on the Soviet military. His entire oeuvre may be described thus: a Soviet-centered, yet fair, perspective; crisp, even laconic, writing; and a true mountain of documents that no English-language scholar has ever seen. It is a formidable combination. Start with two books: for the buildup to Barbarossa, see David M. Glantz, *Stumbling Colossus: The Red Army on the Eve of World War II* (Lawrence: University Press of Kansas, 1998); for the Russo-German war itself, see David M. Glantz and Jonathan M. House, *When Titans Clash: How the Red Army Stopped Hitler* (Lawrence: University Press of Kansas, 1995), a welcome change from traditional analysis that saw Barbarossa strictly in terms of how the Wehrmacht lost it. Other scholars whose investigation of the Russian sources has borne fruit include Richard W. Harrison, *The Russian Way of War: Operational Art, 1904–1940* (Lawrence: University Press of Kansas, 2001) and Carl van Dyke, *The Soviet Invasion of Finland* (London: Frank Cass, 1997). Another recent and influential work placing Soviet operational art at the cen-

ter of twentieth-century military history is Shimon Naveh, *In Pursuit of Military Excellence: The Evolution of Operational Theory* (London: Frank Cass, 1997). Naveh is not a historian, but a theoretician. The work is steeped in the language and concepts of systems logic, and the result can be extremely opaque. Phrases like "the amplitudes of the deviating manoeuvre," (p. 146), "the precondition of suppressing operational cognition," (p. 112), and "the abstract and holistic nature of the operational aim," (p. 132) pile on top of one another, and so do tortured passages like the following: "By preventing the essential synergy within the defending system from materializing, the fragmenting strike reflects the negative aspect of accomplishing the operation's objectives, while the flowing of the manoeuvring mass into depth by means of the same fragmentation strike, expresses the positive aspect in the evolution of the operational strike manoeuvre" (p. 215). Still worthy among the older works is Alan Clark, *Barbarossa: The Russian-German Conflict, 1941–1945* (New York: Quill, 1985). Although previous works had tended to lay all the blame for the disaster that befell the Wehrmacht in 1941 on Hitler, a view encouraged by the surviving German generals and best expressed in Liddell Hart's *German Generals Talk*, Clark argued persuasively that the German field commanders and General Staff shared a great deal of the responsibility. The culminating development of that thesis is Geoffrey P. Megargee, *Inside Hitler's High Command* (Lawrence: University Press of Kansas, 2000), a demolition of the notion of an infallible German General Staff. Also useful are John Erickson, *The Road to Stalingrad* (New York: Harper and Row, 1975) and *The Road to Berlin* (London: Wiedenfeld and Nicolson, 1983), forming a fine, two-volume history of the entire war. A number of commanders have left their memoirs. Heinz Guderian, *Panzer Leader* (New York: Ballantine, 1957) is still essential, as is Erich von Manstein, *Lost Victories* (Novato, Calif.: Presidio, 1982). From the Soviet side, see G. K. Zhukov, *Marshal Zhukov's Greatest Battles* (New York: Harper and Row, 1969) and *The Memoirs of Marshal Zhukov* (New York: Delacorte, 1971); V. I. Chuikov, *The Battle for Stalingrad* (New York: Holt, Rinehart and Winston, 1964) and *The End of the Third Reich* (Moscow: Progress Publishers, 1978); and Ivan Konev, *Year of Victory* (Moscow: Progress Publishers, 1969). The collection *Battles Hitler Lost: First Person Accounts of World War II by Russian Generals on the Eastern Front* (New York: Richardson & Steirman, 1986) is indispensable. It includes, among others, G. K. Zhukov, "The War Begins" and V. D. Sokolovsky, "The Battle of Moscow." For the battle of Moscow, see Janusz Piekalkiewicz, *Moscow 1941* (Novato, Calif.: Presidio, 1981). Finally, for a critical bibliography of all this literature and more, see Rolf-Dieter Müller and Gerd R. Uberschär, *Hitler's War in the East, 1941–1945: A Critical Assessment* (Providence, R.I.: Berghahn Books, 1997). The use of German transliteration of Russian names in the entries, however, may leave some English-language readers puzzled (for example, "Suworow" and "Wolkogonow").

74. John W. Dower, *War Without Mercy: Race and Power in the Pacific War* (New York: Pantheon Books, 1986).

75. For the drive of LVI Panzer Corps, see Manstein, *Lost Victories*, pp. 175–188.

76. Quoted in Warlimont, *Inside Hitler's Headquarters*, p. 179.

77. Five of those mechanized corps (8th, 9th, 15th, 19th, 22nd) saw heavy action

in the opening days. See Glantz and House, *When Titans Clashed*, pp. 53–55, as well as an article that deserved broader distribution: Vance von Borries, "Operation Barbarossa: The Southern Wing," *Schwerpunkt* 1 (September 1993), pp. 6–10, apparently the only issue ever published of this magazine. See also Clark, *Barbarossa*, pp. 53–54.

78. Glantz and House, *When Titans Clashed*, p. 68.

79. Ibid., pp. 75–78. For a vivid account, see also Alexander Werth, *Russia at War* (New York: Carroll and Graf, 1992), pp. 202–212.

80. Quoted in Heinz-Ludger Borgert, "Grundzüge der Landkriegführung von Schlieffen bis Guderian," *Handbuch zur deutschen Militärgeschichte 1648–1939*, volume 9, *Grundzüge der militärischen Kriegführung* (München: Bernard & Graefe Verlag, 1979), p. 543.

81. See Piekalkiewicz, *Moscow 1941*, pp. 113, 160, 163.

82. The primary source on Tula from the German side is Guderian, *Panzer Leader*, pp. 185–203; see also Glantz and House, *When Titans Clashed*, pp. 83–87.

83. For a biographical sketch of Zhukov, see Citino, *Armored Forces*, pp. 279–280. For the Moscow counteroffensive, see Sokolovsky, "The Battle of Moscow," in *Battles Hitler Lost*, pp. 51–61. See also Piekalkiewicz, *Moscow 1941*, pp. 208–237.

84. See Glantz and House, *When Titans Clashed*, pp. 87–94.

85. For Soviet attempts to widen the offensive, see ibid., pp. 91–97.

86. "Grossdeutschlands Freiheitskrieg," pt. 99, "Kreuzzug gegen den Bolschewismus," *Militär-Wochenblatt* 126, no. 1, July 4, 1941, p. 6.

87. "Grossdeutschlands Freiheitskrieg," pt. 100, "Die Vernichtungsschlacht von Bialystok," *Militär-Wochenblatt* 126, no. 2, July 11, 1941, pp. 29–30.

88. "Grossdeutschlands Freiheitskrieg," pt. 101, "Die Doppelschlacht von Bialystok und Minsk," *Militär-Wochenblatt* 126, no. 3, July 18, 1941, pp. 57–58.

89. See also General of Artillery Ludwig, "Der Durchbruch durch die Stalin-Linie," *Militär-Wochenblatt* 126, no. 5, August 1, 1941, pp. 123–125.

90. "Grossdeutschlands Freiheitskrieg," pt. 102, "Katastrophenanzeichen in der Sowjetunion," *Militär-Wochenblatt* 126, no. 4, July 25, 1941, p. 87.

91. "Grossdeutschlands Freiheitskrieg," pt. 103, "Vor der Entscheidung im Osten," *Militär-Wochenblatt* 126, no. 5, August 1, 1941, p. 113.

92. "Grossdeutschlands Freiheitskrieg," pt. 105, "Die 7. Woche des Ostkampfes," *Militär-Wochenblatt* 126, no. 7, August 15, 1941, p. 171; pt. 111, "Einschnürung Leningrads schreitet fort," *Militär-Wochenblatt* 126, no. 13, September 26, 1941, p. 341.

93. "Grossdeutschlands Freiheitskrieg," pt. 112, "Verlauf und Abschluss der Riesenschlacht von Kiew," *Militär-Wochenblatt* 126, no. 14, October 3, 1941, p. 368.

94. "Grossdeutschlands Freiheitskrieg," pt. 113, "Der Führer kündigt den Zusammenbruch der Sowjets an," *Militär-Wochenblatt* 126, no. 15, October 10, 1941, 395–397.

95. "Grossdeutschlands Freiheitskrieg," pt. 121, "Fortschreidender Angriff auf Moskau," *Militär-Wochenblatt* 126, no. 23, December 5, 1941, p. 625.

96. "Grossdeutschlands Freiheitskrieg," pt. 124, "Der Stellungskrieg im Osten," *Militär-Wochenblatt* 126, no. 26, December 26, 1941, p. 715.

97. "Grossdeutschlands Freiheitskrieg," pt. 125, "Harte Abwehrkämpfe an der Ostfront," *Militär-Wochenblatt* 126, no. 27, January 2, 1942, p. 755.

3. The Allies in Search of Decisive Victory

1. See S. L. A. Marshall, *Armies on Wheels* (New York: Morrow, 1941), especially Chapter 8, "Machines and Men," pp. 207–242.

2. See Robert M. Citino, "Was the Reputation of the Wehrmacht for Military Superiority Deserved?" in *History in Dispute* 4, *World War II, 1939–1945*, ed. Dennis E. Showalter (Detroit: St. James Press, 2000).

3. See Paddy Griffith, *Forward into Battle: Fighting Tactics from Waterloo to the Near Future* (Novato, Calif.: Presidio, 1990), especially the chapter in which the author calls into question "the alleged triumph of armor over infantry" (pp. 95–135).

4. Ibid. Griffith quotes Soviet marshal V. I. Chuikov describing a position on the Magnuszew bridgehead in 1944. It is a scene of trenches, barbed wire entanglements, machine gun nests, underground dugouts, incessant bombardment, and lice. The entire passage is highly reminiscent of Erich Maria Remarque's *All Quiet on the Western Front*. See also V. I. Chuikov, *The End of the Third Reich* (Moscow: Progress Publishers, 1978), pp. 60–68.

5. Quoted in David E. Johnson, "From Frontier Constabulary to Modern Army: The U.S. Army Between the World Wars," in *The Challenge of Change: Military Institutions and New Realities, 1918–1841*, ed. Harold R. Winton and David R. Mets (Lincoln: University of Nebraska Press, 2000), p. 180. See also Johnson's *Fast Tanks and Heavy Bombers: Innovation in the U.S. Army, 1917–1945* (Ithaca, N.Y.: Cornell University Press, 1998).

6. Major M. Braun, "Gedanken über Kampfwagen- und Fliegerverwendung bei den russischen Herbstmanövern 1936," *Militär-Wochenblatt* 121, no. 28, January 22, 1937, pp. 1589–1592. See also the report on the U.S. military attaché in Moscow, Lieutenant Colonel Philip R. Faymonville, on the 1935 Kiev maneuvers, which featured an airborne landing by five hundred men and an attack on the paratroopers by a "strong detachment of fast tanks," in David M. Glantz, "Observing the Soviets: U.S. Army Attachés in Eastern Europe During the 1930s," *Journal of Military History* 55, no. 2, April 1991, pp. 153–183.

7. See, for example, Bruce Menning, "The Deep Strike in Russian and Soviet Military History," *Journal of Soviet Military Studies* 1, no. 1, April 1988, pp. 9–28. One of the more extreme advocates for the notion of Russian and Soviet military prowess is Bryan Fugate. See his *Operation Barbarossa* (Novato, Calif.: Presidio, 1984) and *Thunder on the Dnepr: Zhukov-Stalin and the Defeat of Hitler's Blitzkrieg* (Novato, Calif.: Presidio, 1997). The latter book contains the startling, perhaps absurd, claim that "there was a history of fighting spirit and doctrinal coherency dating back much earlier, to the time of the Tatar occupation and the rise of the Muscovite principality," which stretches the term "doctrine" about as far as it can possibly go. For a deservedly skeptical review of Fugate's work, see the review of *Thunder on the Dnepr* by Earl F. Ziemke, *Journal of Military History* 62, no. 2, April 1998, pp. 423–433.

8. See Richard W. Harrison, *The Russian Way of War: Operational Art, 1904–1940* (Lawrence: University Press of Kansas, 2001), pp. 34–35, 157–168.

9. David M. Glantz, *Stumbling Colossus: The Red Army on the Eve of World War II* (Lawrence: University Press of Kansas, 1998), p. 30.

10. For the impact of the purges on efficiency, see Glantz, "Observing the Soviets." See also Glantz, *Stumbling Colossus*, p. 33.

11. The best book currently available on the Winter War, incorporating newly available Russian sources, is Carl van Dyke, *The Soviet Invasion of Finland, 1939–40* (London: Frank Cass, 1997). Still useful, and for years the unchallenged standard work on the topic, is Allen F. Chew, *The White Death: The Epic of the Soviet-Finnish Winter War* (East Lansing: Michigan State University Press, 1971). For a period account by the commander of the Finnish II Army Corps in Karelia, see General Öhquist, "Ein finnischer Armeeführer über den Finnish-Russischen Krieg," *Militär-Wochenblatt* 125, no. 40, April 4, 1941, pp. 1660–1663. Finally, there is a significant body of popular literature on the conflict. See, for example, Eloise Engle and Lauri Paananen, *The Winter War: The Soviet Attack on Finland* (Harrisburg, Pa.: Stackpole Books, 1973). Thoroughly nonscholarly, it nonetheless conveys the flavor of the conflict.

12. David M. Glantz and Jonathan M. House, *When Titans Clashed: How the Red Army Stopped Hitler* (Lawrence: University Press of Kansas, 1995), pp. 19–20.

13. Van Dyke, *Soviet Invasion of Finland*, p. 74.

14. Engle and Paananen describe the "uniform" of the Home Guard: "knitted bibs, headwarmers, neckwarmers, gloves, and socks, not necessarily matching" (p. 44).

15. M. I. Lukinov, "Notes on the Polish Campaign (1939) and the War with Finland (1939–1940)," *Journal of Slavic Military Studies* 14, no. 3, September 2001, pp. 120–149. Lukinov's regiment was heavily engaged in the assault on the Mannerheim line. See pp. 134–145.

16. See van Dyke, *Soviet Invasion of Finland*, pp. 135–187, for the Timoshenko offensive. For the general's views on the continued utility of frontal assault, see pp. 127–128 n. 6.

17. Lukinov, "Notes on the Polish Campaign and the War with Finland," p. 147.

18. See, for example, the following articles from the Soviet military journal *Krasnaya Zvesda*, translated into English by the Translation Section of the U.S. Army War College and on file in the U.S. Army Military History Institute at Carlisle Barracks in Carlisle, Pennsylvania (hereafter, MHI): "Troop Training for Winter Operations," December 11, 1939; P. Channow, "Conduct of Tanks in Deep Snow," December 30, 1939; I. Kolesnikov, "Winter Operations," January 12, 1940; and P. Mikhailov, "Tactical Employment of Ski Troops in Forest Areas," January 18, 1940.

19. Harrison, *Russian Way of War*, p. 246.

20. For Moscow, see Glantz and House, *When Titans Clashed*, pp. 87–97.

21. G. K. Zhukov, "The Battle of Moscow," in *Moscow 1941 Stalingrad 1942: Recollections, Stories, Reports*, ed. Vladimir Sevruk (Moscow: Progress Publishers, 1974), pp. 67–68.

22. The name of a section in Glantz and House, *When Titans Clashed*, p. 99–101. For Soviet views of the Kharkov offensive, see David M. Glantz, *Kharkov 1942: Anatomy of a Military Disaster Through Soviet Eyes* (Shepperton, Surrey: Ian Allan,

1998). For an overview of operations on both sides, see Stephen B. Patrick, "Kharkov: The Soviet Spring Offensive," *Strategy and Tactics* 68, June 1978, pp. 4–14.

23. A suitable departure point for any investigation into the dramatic events of 1942 is Lewis C. Rotundo, *Battle for Stalingrad: The 1943 Soviet General Staff Study* (Washington, D.C.: Pergamon-Brassey's, 1989), not only a fine study of operations, but a good example of the frankness with which the Red Army analyzed its recent combat experiences. The best scholarly work on the campaign from the German side is the recent work by Joel S. A. Hayward, *Stopped at Stalingrad: The Luftwaffe and Hitler's Defeat in the East, 1942–1943* (Lawrence: University Press of Kansas, 1998). Although ostensibly about the air campaign, it is actually a comprehensive account of Case Blue both in the air and on land, based on an impressive collection of both primary and secondary materials, refreshingly free of the myths and anecdotes on which most of the history of the Stalingrad campaign has heretofore been based. Still useful is Andrei Yeremenko, "Battle of Stalingrad," in *Battles Hitler Lost: First Person Accounts of World War II by Russian Generals on the Eastern Front* (New York: Richardson & Steirman, 1986), pp. 62–75.

24. See Waldemar Erfurth, "Das Zusammenwirken getrennter Heeresteile" *Militärwissenschaftliche Rundschau* 4, no. 1, 1939, pp. 14–41; no. 2, pp. 156–178; no. 3, pp. 290–314; and no. 4, pp. 472–499.

25. See Glantz and House, *When Titans Clashed*, pp. 111–116.

26. Alan Clark, *Barbarossa: The Russian-German Conflict, 1941–1945* (New York: Quill, 1985), pp. 205–219.

27. For a recent, and quite powerful, evocation of the ordeal at Stalingrad — intended for a general audience, but solidly researched — see Anthony Beevor, *Stalingrad* (New York: Viking, 1998).

28. Baron Henri Antoine de Jomini, *The Art of War* (Westport, Conn.: Greenwood, 1971; reprint of the 1862 edition), pp. 71–72.

29. Erich von Manstein, *Lost Victories* (Novato, Calif.: Presidio, 1982), pp. 291–293.

30. Geoffrey P. Megargee, *Inside Hitler's High Command* (Lawrence: University Press of Kansas, 2000), p. 178.

31. See Hayward, *Stopped at Stalingrad*, pp. 1–13, for the German war economy's urgent need for Caucasian oil.

32. See, for example, Manstein, *Lost Victories*, p. 199, for the Donetz and Nikopol references.

33. Glantz and House, *When Titans Clashed*, p .130.

34. There is an immense literature on Operation Uranus, much of it reading exactly the same, since it was based on the same German accounts. Two worthy entries today are Glantz and House, *When Titans Clashed*, pp. 129–147, for the Soviet documents, and the chapter in Clark, *Barbarossa* (entitled, "The Entombment of the 6th Army"), pp. 239–248, for the crisp writing.

35. Operation Mars was little known in the West (or the former Soviet Union, for that matter) until recently. See David M. Glantz, "Counterpoint to Stalingrad: Operation Mars (November–December 1942): Marshal Zhukov's Greatest Defeat" (Ft. Leavenworth, Kans.: Foreign Military Studies Office, 1997). The article is also avail-

able online at http://rhino.shef.ac.uk:3001/mr-home/rzhev/rzhev3.html. For the complete treatment, see David M. Glantz, *Zhukov's Greatest Defeat: The Red Army's Epic Disaster in Operation Mars, 1942* (Lawrence: University Press of Kansas, 1999).

36. For German concern over Rostov, see Manstein, *Lost Victories*, p. 369. For the winter battles from the Soviet perspective, see David M. Glantz, *From the Don to the Dnepr: Soviet Offensive Operations, December 1942–August 1943* (London: Frank Cass, 1991).

37. For the Saturn/Little Saturn transformation, see Glantz, *From the Don to the Dnepr*, pp. 10–18.

38. Manstein has been castigated for denying any responsibility for the disaster, laying the blame on Hitler above and Paulus below. See Joachim Wieder and Heinrich Graf von Einsiedl (editors), *Stalingrad: Memories and Reassessments* (London: Arms and Armour, 1995), a vastly expanded version of Wieder's original 1962 edition, mainly the work of editor Einsiedl, which blame Manstein's "unsure and indecisive conduct" upon taking over Army Group Don. See also Manfred Kehrig, *Stalingrad: Analyse und Dokumentation einer Schlacht* (Stuttgart: Deutsche-Verlags Anstalt, 1974), published under the auspices of the *Militärgeschichtliches Forschungsamt*.

39. Glantz, *From the Don to the Dnepr*, pp. 80–81.

40. Manstein, *Lost Victories*, pp. 428–433; Glantz, *From the Don to the Dnepr*, pp. 121–125.

41. Manstein, *Lost Victories*, pp. 433–437; the term "shock group" is used by Glantz, *From the Don to the Dnepr*, p. 213.

42. Manstein, *Lost Victories*, pp. 367–368.

43. David M. Glantz and Harold S. Orenstein have recently translated and edited the primary Soviet planning documents for Kursk. See *The Battle for Kursk, 1943: The Soviet General Staff Study* (London: Frank Cass, 1999). See also Glantz and Jonathan M. House, *The Battle of Kursk* (Lawrence: University Press of Kansas, 1999), which offers a detailed narrative down to regimental level, as well as a veritable reference library of information in the appendixes. Niklas Zettering and Anders Frankson, *Kursk 1943: A Statistical Analysis* (London: Frank Cass, 2000) is just what it says it is. It continues the trend of lowering the number of tanks destroyed in this "greatest tank battle of all time," not to mention manpower losses. For example, German losses at Kursk amounted to only 3 percent of the total German casualties during 1943. Suffering particularly in the reassessment is the mythic status of the battle of Prokhorovka. It seems that tank losses on both sides there were relatively slight. See Robin Cross, *Citadel: The Battle of Kursk* (New York: Barnes & Noble, 1994), pp. 229–231. Despite the lurid title of the article, Stephen K. Rothwell with John Desch and Timothy Kutta, "SS Panzer: Bloodbath at Kursk," *Command* 36, March 1996, pp. 16–34, offers much the same argument as Cross. See especially pp. 32–33. Rothwell also defends the much-maligned "Elefant" tank destroyer (see pp. 28–29).

44. A recent, and quite informative, work on the 1944 offensive in Byelorussia is Walter S. Dunn, *Soviet Blitzkrieg: The Battle for White Russia, 1944* (Boulder, Colo.: Lynne Rienner, 2000). Among Dunn's sources is a personally constructed "Russian order of battle" database of 9,100 Soviet units, "compiled from published Soviet order of battle data and German intelligence reports" (p. xii).

45. The classic example is chapter 19 of F. W. von Mellenthin, *Panzer Battles: A Study of the Employment of Armor in the Second World War* (New York: Ballantine, 1956), entitled the "The Red Army," pp. 349–367. The section entitled "Psychology of the Russian Soldier" begins: "No one belonging to the cultural circle of the West is ever likely to fathom the character and soul of these Asiatics, born and bred on the other side of the European frontiers" p. 349.

46. A representative sample of his work is Paul Carell, *Scorched Earth: The Russian-German War, 1943–1944* (Boston: Little, Brown, 1970).

47. See the article by Kevin Soutor on the German Military History Program, "To Stem the Red Tide: The German Report Series and Its Effect on American Defense Doctrine, 1948–1954," *Journal of Military History* 57, no. 4, October 1993, pp. 653–688.

48. For representative examples of Soviet writing on operational art, especially its emphasis on "the massing of men and materiel on decisive axes," see A. A. Grechko, *The Armed Forces of the Soviet State: A Soviet View* (Moscow: Voennoe Izdatel'stvo, 1975), translated and published under the auspices of the U.S. Air Force (*Soviet Military Thought* series, no. 12), especially pp. 204–207; V. Ye Savkin, *The Basic Principles of Operational Art and Tactics: A Soviet View* (Moscow: Voennoe Izdatel'tsvo, 1972), also issued by the U.S. Air Force (*Soviet Military Thought* series, no. 4), especially pp. 201–240; V. G. Reznichenko, "Evolution of Tactics in the Great Patriotic War," *Military Thought* 10, no. 5, September–October 2001, pp. 74–77; and Ivan Vorobyov, "Evolution of Tactics in Wars and Armed Conflicts of the 20th Century," *Military Thought* 11, no. 1, January 2002, pp. 84–95.

49. Ivan Konev, *Year of Victory* (Moscow: Progress Publishers, 1969), p. 10.

50. Quoted in Glantz, "Counterpoint to Stalingrad," p. 24.

51. V. I. Chuikov, *The End of the Third Reich* (Moscow: Progress Publishers, 1978), pp. 20–21.

52. For one Zhukov penal battalion story, see Robert M. Citino, *Armored Forces: History and Sourcebook* (Westport, Conn.: Greenwood, 1994), p. 280. And behind Zhukov, of course, stood Josef Stalin. The recent and justly celebrated biography of Stalin by Soviet general Dmitri Volkogonov, *Stalin: Triumph and Tragedy* (New York: Grove Weidenfeld, 1991) offers chapter and verse on Stalin's wartime brutality, including measures taken against the families of officers who had surrendered. See especially the author's discussion of the "cruel time" at the start of the war, pp. 415–424.

53. For a warning of the effect of the "can-do" attitude on U.S. military performance, see the article by William S. Lind, "Some Doctrinal Questions for the United States Army," *Military Review* 57, no. 3, March 1977, pp. 54–65, and especially pp. 56–57.

54. See B. H. Liddell Hart, *The British Way in Warfare* (London: Faber and Faber, 1932).

55. The best scholarly discussion of this entire problem is Harold R. Winton, *To Change an Army: General Sir John Burnett-Stuart and British Armored Doctrine, 1927–1938* (Lawrence: University Press of Kansas, 1988).

56. For a biographical sketch of Elles, see Citino, *Armored Forces*, p. 232.

57. For a biographical sketch of Martel, see ibid., p. 256.

58. J. P. Harris, "British Armour 1918–1949: Doctrine and Development," in *Armoured Warfare*, ed. J. P. Harris and F. H. Toase (London: Batsford, 1990), p. 48, calls Hobart "one of the rudest men in the Army, a fanatic for his own conception of armoured forces." The standard biography is still Kenneth Macksey, *Armoured Crusader: A Biography of Major-General Sir Percy Hobart* (London: Hutchinson, 1967). For a biographical sketch, see Citino, *Armored Forces*, pp. 243–244.

59. See Robert L. Bateman's review of William O. Odom, *After the Trenches: The Transformation of U.S. Army Doctrine, 1918–1939* (College Station: Texas A&M University Press, 1999) in *Parameters* 29, 4, Winter 1999/2000, pp. 141–142.

60. Johnson, "From Frontier Constabulary to Modern Army," p. 167.

61. Ibid., p. 170.

62. Ibid., pp. 180–181.

63. Ibid., pp. 191–192.

64. For a biographical sketch of McNair, see Citino, *Armored Forces*, pp. 256–257.

65. Roman Johann Jarymowycz, *Tank Tactics: From Normandy to Lorraine* (Boulder, Colo.: Lynne Rienner, 2001), p. 92.

66. For Operation Husky, the U.S. Army official history is still useful. Albert N. Garland and Howard McGaw Smyth, assisted by Martin Blumenson, *Sicily and the Surrender of Italy: United States Army in World War II, the Mediterranean Theater of Operations* (Washington, D.C.: Center of Military History, 1993). Originally published in 1965, it was reissued to commemorate the fiftieth anniversary of World War II. Like all official histories, it does not focus on the operational level (corps, armies) as such; rather, it ranges freely from squad-level combat to grand strategy. For the German perspective, see the unpublished manuscript by Paul Conrath, "Der Kampf um Sizilien," a 1951 contribution to the *German Report Series*, C-087, by the commander of the Hermann Goering Parachute Panzer Division during the campaign. A copy of the report is on file at the MHI. The standard work on the Sicilian campaign is Carlo W. D'Este, *Bitter Victory: The Battle for Sicily, 1943* (New York: Dutton, 1988). Like all his works, this one contains a good deal of primary and secondary research woven into a smooth and readable narrative. He also spends a great deal of time on personalities, not only assessing individual commanders and quite often taking sides in their feuds, but including a boatload of often irrelevant biographical detail aimed at the popular reader. In the process he often personalizes highly complex events. His work, for all its many virtues, is a sign of how far military history remains from the mainstream of scholarly historiography.

67. Ernie Pyle, *Brave Men* (New York: Grosset & Dunlap, 1943), p. 40.

68. Called by Patton, with typical bombast, "a glorious chapter to the history of war." See George S. Patton, *War as I Knew It* (New York: Bantam Books, 1979), p. 62.

69. For the landing at Omaha, see Adrian R. Lewis, *Omaha Beach: A Flawed Victory* (Chapel Hill: University of North Carolina Press, 2001), a work strongly critical of preinvasion planning; for "Operation Neptune," the landing of U.S. 1st Army at Omaha and Utah, see Steven T. Ross, ed., *U.S. War Plans, 1938–1945* (Boulder, Colo.: Lynne Rienner, 2002), pp. 187–224. Ross reproduces the operational plan — complete with exact numbers of men and vehicles for the assault, follow-up, and

build-up forces (pp. 201–224). The best accounts of the D-Day landings are Carlo D'Este, *Decision in Normandy* (New York: Harper, 1994), pp. 107–150, and, still, Charles B. MacDonald, *The Mighty Endeavor: The American War in Europe* (New York: Da Capo, 1992), pp. 285–309.

70. The Normandy campaign has been the subject of a huge mass of literature, nearly all of which spends too much time on the personalities of the campaign: American historians almost unanimously condemning Montgomery for his lack of drive, his arrogance, and sometimes even his dress; British historians largely arguing Montgomery's brief and making snide points about their allegedly amateurish Allies. It is a tiresome argument that falls apart when one looks at more systemic problems of the fighting in Normandy: the terrain; the Allied inability to field a tank that could take on the German armor in Normandy; the elite nature of the German panzer formations in the theater; and, above all, doctrine in the U.S., British, and Canadian armies. For details of this apparently unstoppable controversy, see the studies of the literature in G. E. Patrick Murray, *Eisenhower Versus Montgomery: The Continuing Debate* (Westport, Conn.: Praeger, 1996), and Stephen T. Powers, "The Battle of Normandy: The Lingering Controversy," *Journal of Military History* 56, no. 3, July 1992, pp. 455–471. D'Este, *Decision in Normandy*, for example, is a fine book with a great deal of operational detail, marred by sounding the same anti-Montgomery note throughout. D'Este centers his indictment on the question of whether Montgomery claimed too much credit after the war for the breakout plan — hardly a matter of earth-shaking import. Jarymowycz, *Tank Tactics*, is a recent and interesting addition to the literature: a Canadian author highly critical of Allied armored doctrine in general, the U.S. tank destroyer concept in particular, and the British and Canadian preference for the "set piece battle." Two other recent works that set a new standard in the literature are James Jay Carafano, *After D-Day: Operation Cobra and the Normandy Breakout* (Boulder, Colo.: Lynne Rienner, 2000), which looks at the campaign through the lens of the "combat command, regimental and battalion commanders, the 'field-grade' leaders" (p. 4) and argues that "the ability to understand and exploit the full capabilities of the U.S. Army" was the key to the eventual breakout, rather than a magic technological bullet like the Culin hedgerow cutter or the brute firepower or carpet bombing (p. 260); and Russell A. Hart's exhaustive and meticulously researched *Clash of Arms: How the Allies Won in Normandy* (Boulder, Colo.: Lynne Rienner, 2001), which stresses the "institutional flexibility" and adaptability of the U.S. Army in Normandy compared to its allies; offers controversial argumentation that "the tenacity of the German defense of Normandy must also be explained in ideological terms"; and, a sine qua non for future research into the Normandy campaign, offers full coverage of the Canadian experience. Another type of literature — now swamping all others — is the "greatest generation" genre. Best exemplified in the writings of the late Stephen Ambrose, it is an outgrowth of Seymour Lipset's "American exceptionalism," embodying the sense that Americans are somehow unique, touched by fate in a direct way, and endowed with a special mission. It is not scholarly history. Consider the following passage from Ambrose, *Citizen Soldiers: The U.S. Army from the Normandy Beaches to the Bulge to the Surrender of*

Germany, June 7, 1944–May 7, 1944 (New York: Touchstone, 1997), p. 159: "There were hundreds of young officers like Fussell, lieutenants who came into Europe in the fall of 1944 to take up the fighting. Rich kids. Bright kids. The quarterback on the championship high school football team. The president of his class. The chess champion. The lead in the class play. The solo in the spring concert. The wizard in the chemistry class. America was throwing her finest young men at the Germans." Of course, every line in this passage could have been written about the soldiers of the Wehrmacht, or the British army, or the Romanians for that matter.

71. The finest book on the "learning curve" of the United States in Europe is Michael D. Doubler, *Closing with the Enemy: How GIs Fought the War in Europe, 1944–1945* (Lawrence: University Press of Kansas, 1994). The 100,000 figure is on p. 60.

72. Murray, *Eisenhower Versus Montgomery*, p. 72. See also Omar N. Bradley, *A Soldier's Story* (New York: Henry Holt and Company, 1951).

73. For Cobra, see Carafano, *After D-Day*; Hart, *Clash of Arms*, especially "A Campaign Overview," pp. 247–264; and Jarymowycz, *Tank Tactics*, pp. 107–202. An extremely interesting account, better known in Canada and the United Kingdom than in the United States, is Milton Shulman, *Defeat in the West* (Waldenbury, East Sussex: Masquerade, 1986). At the time, Shulman was a Canadian intelligence officer who conducted interviews with twenty-six captured senior officers of the Wehrmacht, including Gerd von Rundstedt, Josef ("Sepp") Dietrich, and Kurt Student. In many ways, this is a superior work to B. H. Liddell Hart, *The German Generals Talk* (New York: Quill, 1979), since there was none of the fishing for compliments or toadying that went into the preparation of the latter volume.

74. Bradley, *A Soldier's Story*, p. 330.

75. The official history, Martin Blumenson, *Breakout and Pursuit: United States Army in World War II, the European Theater of Operations* (Washington, D.C.: Office of the Chief of Military History, 1961) is still extremely useful for order of battle information and for its use of the primary sources. For a distillation, see Blumenson, *The Duel for France, 1944: The Men and Battles That Changed the Fate of Europe* (New York: Da Capo, 2000).

76. Bradley, *A Soldier's Story*, p. 358; the Bayerlein quote is found in MacDonald, *Mighty Endeavor*, p. 334.

77. Quoted in D'Este, *Decision in Normandy*, p. 414.

78. For a splendidly researched account of the saga of Mortain, see the new work by Mark J. Reardon, *Victory at Mortain: Stopping Hitler's Panzer Counteroffensive* (Lawrence: University Press of Kansas, 2002); Alwyn Featherston, *Saving the Breakout: The 30th Division's Heroic Stand at Mortain, August 7–12, 1944* (Novato, Calif.: Presidio, 1993) is useful, albeit much more of a narrowly focused popular history.

79. The two best accounts of the travails of Canadian II Corps in Operation Totalize are in John A. English, *The Canadian Army and the Normandy Campaign: A Study of Failure in High Command* (Westport, Conn.: Praeger, 1991), especially pp. 263–288, and Jarymowycz, *Tank Tactics*, pp. 163–183.

80. Jarymowycz, *Tank Tactics*, p. 166.

81. See Hubert Meyer, *The History of the 12. SS-Panzerdivision "Hitlerjugend"* (Winnipeg: J. J. Fedorowicz, 1994), p. 173. And for an in-depth look at *Auftragstaktik* in action, see Meyer's orders to his various *Kampfgruppen* for the counterattack (p. 172).

82. English, *The Canadian Army and the Normandy Campaign*, pp. 267–268, 271.

83. Joachim Ludewig, *Der deutsche Rückzug aus Frankreich 1944* (Freiburg: Rombach, 1995), p. 116.

84. See Lewis, *Omaha Beach*, pp. 291–307, for a cogent, incisive attack on planning and doctrine for the Omaha landing. His discussion of "greenness" is on pp. 301–303.

85. Reardon, *Victory at Mortain*, p. 14.

86. Carafano, *After D-Day*, p. 260.

4. Forgotten No Longer

1. The Kosovo War of 1999, the first military conflict in the history of NATO, has thus far generated one book, by the NATO commander, Wesley K. Clark, *Waging Modern War: Bosnia, Kosovo, and the Future of Combat* (New York: Public Affairs, 2001).

2. The classic example of this line of argumentation is Clay Blair, *The Forgotten War: America in Korea, 1950–1953* (New York: Times Books, 1987). A weighty book in every sense, its size alone does much to belie the thesis in its title. See also Callum A. MacDonald, *Korea: The War Before Vietnam* (New York: Free Press, 1986).

3. See, for example, S. L. A. Marshall, *The River and the Gauntlet: Defeat of the 8th Army by the Chinese Communist Forces November, 1950 in the Battle of the Chongchon River, Korea* (Alexandria, Va.: Time-Life Books, 1982), a reprint of the 1953 edition.

4. See Bruce Cumings's two-volume, meticulously documented work, which has generated a great deal of controversy: *The Origins of the Korean War*, volume 1, *Liberation and the Emergence of Separate Regimes, 1945–1947* (Princeton, N.J.: Princeton University Press, 1981) and volume 2, *The Roaring of the Cataract* (Princeton, N.J.: Princeton University Press, 1990). He has also presented his main argument — that the Korean War began as a Korean Civil War that was arrested by the massive U.S. intervention of 1950 — in Jon Halliday and Bruce Cumings, *The Unknown War* (New York: Pantheon, 1988), and most recently, in Cumings, *Korea's Place in the Sun: A Modern History* (New York: W. W. Norton, 1997). The accusation that Cumings is as much of an ideologue as a historian continues to arise. See Allan R. Millett, "A Reader's Guide to the Korean War," *Journal of Military History* 61, no. 3, July 1997, pp. 583–597.

5. See Shu Guang Zhang, *Mao's Military Romanticism: China and the Korean War, 1950–1953* (Lawrence: University Press of Kansas, 1995) and Xiaobing Li, Allan R. Millett, and Bin Yu, eds., *Mao's Generals Remember Korea* (Lawrence: University Press of Kansas, 2001).

6. Conrad C. Crane, *American Airpower Strategy in Korea, 1950–1953* (Lawrence: University Press of Kansas, 2000).

7. The Department of the Army's Center of Military History has, for example,

reprinted all the currently extant volumes of the official histories: Roy E. Appleman, *South to the Naktong, North to the Yalu* (Washington, D.C.: Center of Military History, 1961), one of the most controversial volumes ever to appear under the rubric of official history; Walter G. Hermes, *Truce Tent and Fighting Front* (Washington, D.C.: Center of Military History, 1966); James F. Schnabel, *Policy and Direction: The First Year* (Washington, D.C.: Center of Military History, 1972); and Billy C. Mossman, *Ebb and Flow: November 1950–July 1951* (Washington, D.C.: Center of Military History, 1990). Save for the "Korean War 50th Anniversary" stamp on the cover, all are unchanged from earlier editions. See also the series *The Korean War*. Consisting of five short works labeled "brochures," they contain good short operational-level accounts of the fighting — division and above — as well as the always alluring attraction of superb maps: William J. Webb, "The Outbreak 27 June–15 September 1950"; Stephen L. Y. Gammons, "The UN Offensive 16 September–2 November 1950"; Richard W. Stewart, "The Chinese Intervention, 3 November 1950–24 January 1951"; John J. McGrath, "Restoring the Balance, 25 January–8 July 1951"; and Andrew J. Birtle, "Years of Stalemate, July 1951–July 1953." They are undated, although the introduction by Brigadier General John S. Brown, Chief of Military History, refers to "fiftieth anniversary activities." The air force has published several commemorative works as well. See Wayne Thompson and Bernard C. Nalty, "Within Limits: The U.S. Air Force and the Korean War" (Maxwell Air Force Base: Air University Library, 1996); William M. Leary, "Anything, Anywhere, Anytime: Combat Cargo in the Korean War" (Maxwell Air Force Base: Air University Library, 2000); William T. Y'Blood, "MiG Alley: The Fight for Air Superiority" (Maxwell Air Force Base: Air University Library, 2000); and the companion volumes A. Timothy Warnock, ed., *The USAF in Korea: A Chronology 1950–1953* (Maxwell Air Force Base: Air University Library, 2000) and Judy G. Endicott, ed., *The USAF in Korea: Campaigns, Units and Stations, 1950–1953* (Maxwell Air Force Base: Air University Library, 2001). The navy has reissued Curtis A. Utz, "Assault from the Sea: The Amphibious Landing at Inchon" (Washington, D.C.: Naval Historical Center, 2000), originally published in 1994, as well as two new works: Joseph H. Alexander, "Fleet Operations in a Mobile War, September 1950–June 1951" (Washington, D.C.: Naval Historical Center, 2001) and Thomas B. Buell, "Naval Leadership in Korea: The First Six Months" (Washington, D.C.: Naval Historical Center, 2002), the latter two being part of the series *The U.S. Navy and the Korean War*, edited by Edward J. Marolda. Leading the way, however, has been the U.S. Marine Corps. The *Marines in the Korean War Commemorative Series* has high production values, an excellent selection of photographs, and lucid text, and is an altogether worthy addition to the historiography. See John C. Chapin, "Fire Brigade: U.S. Marines in the Pusan Perimeter" (Washington, D.C.: U.S. Marine Corps Historical Center, 2000); Edwin H. Simmons, "Over the Seawall: U.S. Marines at Inchon" (Washington, D.C.: U.S. Marine Corps Historical Center, 2000); Joseph H. Alexander, "Battle of the Barricades: U.S. Marines in the Recapture of Seoul" (Washington, D.C.: U.S. Marine Corps Historical Center, 2000); Ronald J. Brown, "Counteroffensive: U.S. Marines from Pohang to No Name Line" (Washington,

D.C.: U.S. Marine Corps Historical Center, 2001); Allan R. Millett, "Drive North: U.S. Marines at the Punchbowl" (Washington, D.C.: U.S. Marine Corps Historical Center, 2001); Bernard C. Nalty, "Stalemate: U.S. Marines from Bunker Hill to the Hook" (Washington, D.C.: U.S. Marine Corps Historical Center, 2001); and John P. Condon (supplemented by Peter B. Mersky), "Corsairs to Panthers: U.S. Marine Aviation in Korea" (Washington, D.C.: U.S. Marine Corps Historical Center, 2002).

8. See, for example, Lester H. Brune, ed., *The Korean War: Handbook of the Literature and Research* (Westport, Conn.: Greenwood Press, 1996), an exhaustive set of twenty-three scholarly articles examining the historiography of the war from every conceivable angle, including Kim Chull Baum, "The Korean Scholars on the Korean War" (pp. 157–174); Chen Jian, "Chinese Policy and the Korean War" (pp. 189–205); Jack J. Gifford, "The U.S. Army in the Korean War" (pp. 223–249); Warren A. Trest, "Air Force Sources: Rethinking the Air War" (pp. 250–265); and Lester H. Brune, "The U.S. Navy and Marines in the Korean War" (pp. 266–284). See, likewise, no less than three review essays in the *Journal of Military History:* John Edward Wilz, "Korea: The Forgotten War," *Journal of Military History* 53, no. 1, January 1989, pp. 95–100; Glen Steven Cook, "Korea: No Longer the Forgotten War," *Journal of Military History* 56, no. 3, July 1992, pp. 489–494; and Allan R. Millett, "A Reader's Guide to the Korean War," *Journal of Military History* 61, no. 3, July 1997. Finally, a special word of commendation is in order to the U.S. Naval Institute, which in 2000 released *The Sea Services in the Korean War, 1950–1953* (Annapolis, Md.: U.S. Naval Institute, 2000), a CD containing the two volumes of the official history of the U.S. Navy, the five of the marine official history, the official history of the U.S. Coast Guard, and a comprehensive navy-marine photo-essay. It is, literally, a library that you can hold in the palm of your hand.

9. Blair, *Forgotten War*, for example, devotes nearly nine hundred pages to the first year of the war and less than one hundred to the final two. See the review essay by Wilz, "Korea: The Forgotten War." Gifford, "The U.S. Army in the Korean War," p. 235, makes this point explicitly, complaining of the lack of attention paid to the last two years of the war. He faults Hermes's official history *(Truce Tent and Fighting Front)* for neglecting the war of posts: "Hermes never examines the strategic significance of the battles or their effect on the U.S. army because a war of posts was contrary to the principles of war taught and believed in by the U.S. Army."

10. See Robert L. Bateman, "What We Haven't Learned," *Military Review* 80, no. 1, January–February 2000, pp. 49–55, who suggests that disarmament after a great war is such a part of American tradition that U.S. Army doctrine should take into account "the realities of congressionally imposed force structure."

11. See J. Lawton Collins, *War in Peacetime: The History and Lessons of Korea* (Boston: Houghton Mifflin, 1969), the memoir of the U.S. Army Chief of Staff.

12. See David Rees, *Korea: The Limited War* (New York: St. Martin's, 1964), who argued that, just as Great Britain had to fight numerous little wars as a price of its world power status, so too would the United States. One of the most influential books written on the war, but one whose prose increasingly seems fevered, is T. R. Fehr-

enbach, *This Kind of War: A Study in Unpreparedness* (New York: Macmillan, 1963) argued that liberal democracies like the United States would always have a difficult time with limited conflicts like Korea, since "any kind of war short of jihad was, is, and will be unpopular with the people." A conscript army would never fight such a war effectively; something different was required: "However repugnant the idea is to liberal societies, the man who will willingly defend the free world in the fringe areas is not the responsible citizen-soldier. The man who will go where his colors go, without asking, who will fight a phantom foe in jungle and mountain range, without counting, and who will suffer and die in the midst of incredible hardship, without complaint, is still what he has always been, from Imperial Rome to sceptered Britain to democratic America. He is the stuff of which legions are made" (p. 658).

13. For the NKPA's order of battle, see Appleman, *South to the Naktong*, pp. 8–12; Schnabel, *Policy and Direction*, pp. 36–39; Webb, "The Outbreak," p. 7; Bevin Alexander, *Korea: The First War We Lost* (New York: Hippocrene, 2000), pp. 1–4; and David J. Ritchie, "Korea: The Forgotten War," *Strategy and Tactics* 111, May 1987, pp. 12–24.

14. Appleman, *South to the Naktong*, p. 11.

15. Ritchie, "Forgotten War," p. 24.

16. Appleman, *South to the Naktong*, p. 10.

17. Ibid., p. 12.

18. See Fehrenbach, *This Kind of War*, pp. 12–14, and James L. Stokesbury, *A Short History of the Korean War* (New York: William Morrow, 1988), pp. 38–39, which, like his entire *Short History* series, matches a thorough grounding in the subject with deft writing.

19. Appleman, *South to the Naktong*, pp. 12–18, including the very helpful ROK Army order of battle chart on p. 15; Schnabel, *Policy and Direction*, pp. 31–36; Webb, "The Outbreak," pp. 6–7, and Ritchie, "Forgotten War," pp. 14–15.

20. Collins, *War in Peacetime*, p. 17; Michael Carver, *War Since 1945* (New York: G. P. Putnam, 1981), p. 154. It is interesting to note how little trust Rhee elicited in some U.S. quarters. The 8th Army would actually have a plan on the books, "Operation Everready," in case Rhee ever failed to respond to U.N. directives. See Paul M. Edwards, *To Acknowledge a War: The Korean War in Historical Memory* (Westport, Conn.: Greenwood, 2000), p. 93.

21. The initial stages of the fighting — the NKPA assault on the ROK army — is still somewhat of a stepchild in the field. Most authors, especially American ones, seem to want to get through it so they can discuss "the main event," the arrival of the U.S. Army. As always, Appleman, *South to the Naktong* (pp. 19–35), is the exception to the rule. Schnabel, *Policy and Direction*, by contrast, hardly treats it at all — giving it a single paragraph (p. 61). Likewise, Fehrenbach, *This Kind of War*, gives it just eleven pages (pp. 54–64), and Blair's massive *Forgotten War* just five (pp. 57–61). Stokesbury, *Short History of the Korean War*, belying its title, actually gives over a good section to the opening NKPA moves (pp. 33–49). In all these accounts, information for the NKPA beyond division numbers is extremely vague; there is not a single mention of a specific divisional commander, for instance, although here the fault lies with North Korea's closed archives and mania for secrecy.

22. Appleman, *South to the Naktong*, pp. 27–28; Fehrenbach, *This Kind of War*, pp. 59–60.

23. Schnabel, *Policy and Direction*, pp. 36–37, speaks of the NKPA being "under the close control of the Russians" but admits that, although there were 150 Russian advisers per NKPA division in 1948, the number had dwindled to between three and eight by 1950.

24. It is unclear who fired the first shots at Ongjin. The fighting here — perhaps starting as a cross-border raid by the ROK army — is the key to the claims of Cumings and other revisionists that the Rhee regime provoked the north to spark massive U.S. intervention in the Korean Civil War.

25. Bevin Alexander, *Korea: The First War We Lost* (New York: Hippocrene, 2000), p. 4. It is a good point that Alexander spoils by going on to claim that the NKPA "followed the model of the greatest of all armies at envelopment, the Mongols of the thirteenth century under Genghis Khan and his successors" (p. 5), continuing a disturbing trend among modern students of war to see the hand of the Great Khan still at work among modern armies. For a German example during World War II, see Lieutenant Colonel Völkel, "Tchingis-Chan als Vorbild und Lehrmeister des modernen Pz.-Kavalleristen," *Militär-Wochenblatt* 126, no. 12, September 19, 1941, p. 322.

26. Appleman, *South to the Naktong*, pp. 63–64; Fehrenbach, *This Kind of War*, pp. 63–64; Alexander, *The First War We Lost*, p. 28.

27. See Paik Sun Yup, *From Pusan to Panmunjom* (Dulles, Va.: Brassey's, 1992), an interesting memoir by one of the ROK army's leading commanders, although it is silent on Paik's "past in the Japanese army" and his "dogged pursuit of the communist guerrillas in the south, 1948–50" (Millett, "A Reader's Guide to the Korean War," p. 590).

28. Appleman, *South to the Naktong*, pp. 30–35.

29. Webb, "The Outbreak," p. 9.

30. For the destruction of "Task Force Smith," see Appleman, *South to the Naktong*, pp. 59–76, the account on which all others are based, including Robert M. Citino, *Armored Forces: History and Sourcebook* (Westport, Conn.: Greenwood, 1994), pp. 110–111, and Jonathan M. House, *Combined Arms Warfare in the Twentieth Century* (Lawrence: University Press of Kansas, 2001), pp. 185–187. The events at Osan — a tiny engagement in what was about to become a huge war — have taken on a life of their own in the scholarship, becoming a blank slate on which the writer can draw almost any lesson desired. To Fehrenbach, *This Kind of War*, Task Force Smith was an object lesson in the dangers of indiscipline: "The young men of Task Force Smith carried Regular Army serial numbers, but they were the new breed of American regular, who, not liking the service, had insisted, with public support, that the Army be made as much like civilian life and home as possible. Discipline had galled them, and their congressmen had seen to it that it did not become too onerous. They had grown fat" (100).

Likewise, House views the Osan engagement as demonstrating the importance of his theme: combined arms. Blair, *Forgotten War*, exonerates Smith, and blames the defeat on the tactical dispositions of the 24th Division commander, General William Dean. Edwin L. Kennedy, Jr., "Force Protection Implications: TF Smith and the 24th Infantry Division, Korea 1950," *Military Review* 81, no. 3, May/June 2001, pp. 87–92, sees Osan as pregnant with implications for today's army: "With reductions in unit strengths, training readiness, and capabilities of current U.S. forces, the Army would do well to reexamine historical precedents regarding incremental application of force to a conflict." Finally, Task Force Smith also seems to bring out a tendency to hyperbole. Stanley Sandler, *The Korean War: No Victors, No Vanquished* (Lexington: University Press of Kentucky, 1999), p. 56, calls Osan "a rude awakening almost on the order of Pearl Harbor." Bevin Alexander, *Korea* (p. 61), contra Fehrenbach, states that "in all American history, no group of soldiers had displayed greater bravery and dedication than the mostly untried young men of Task Force Smith."

31. Appleman, *South to the Naktong*, p. 70.

32. Max Hastings, *The Korean War* (New York: Simon and Schuster, 1987), as is his wont, spares no criticism of the performance of U.S. infantry in Korea. "Through the wretched weeks that followed, among the gloomiest in the history of the United States Army," the 24th Division failed again and again to inflict any punishment at all on the advancing NKPA. "Terrain, logistics, poor communications, and refugees did more to delay the North Korean advance in the first weeks of July than the American infantry in their path." For more of the same in a different context, see his *Overlord: D-Day, June 6, 1944* (New York: Simon and Schuster, 1984). For details of the 24th Division's disastrous performance, see Appleman, *South to the Naktong*, pp. 121–181.

33. Appleman, *South to the Naktong*, pp. 190–200.

34. The ever-critical Hastings, *Korean War*, attributes the poor intelligence, at least in part, to American racism (pp. 69–70).

35. It is doubtful that anyone will ever surpass the official histories for details of the Pusan fighting. See Appleman, *South to the Naktong*, pp. 235–487, 542–572, and, for the marine role, Lynn Montross and Nicholas A. Canzona, *The Pusan Perimeter: U.S. Marine Operations in Korea, 1950–1953*, vol. 1 (Washington, D.C.: Historical Branch, HQMC, 1954).

36. Crane, *American Airpower Strategy in Korea*, pp. 7–8.

37. Ibid., p. 36.

38. Chapin, "Fire Brigade," pp. 18–20.

39. Webb, "The Outbreak," pp. 22–24.

40. See Appleman, *South to the Naktong*, pp. 353–363. Confirmed North Korean losses from August 18–25 were thirteen T-34/85 tanks, five self-propelled gins, and twenty-three other vehicles (p. 362).

41. The Inchon landing continues to elicit several different responses, mainly in terms of its relation to the Pusan breakout. Did Inchon enable the breakout? Was it even necessary, since the forces at Pusan would have broken out anyway? Was Inchon the "anvil" upon which 8th Army could "hammer" the Koreans? There are no obvious answers. Even the normally reliable Appleman, *South to the Naktong*, p. 542, seems unsure. He argues that 8th Army "was to launch a general attack all along its front to

fix and hold the enemy's main combat strength and prevent movement of units from the Pusan Perimeter to reinforce the threatened area in his rear." However, he then states that "this attack would also strive to break the enemy cordon that for six weeks held 8th Army within a shrinking Pusan Perimeter." He also goes on to use the hammer (8th Army) and anvil (X Corps) metaphor. Schnabel, *Policy and Direction*, pp. 176–177, argues that X Corps landing at Inchon precipitated a "general withdrawal" of the NKPA from the Pusan perimeter, which for unspecified reasons then turned into a "rout." The schizoid nature of Inchon and Pusan has continued up to the present. See Stanley Sandler, *No Victors, No Vanquished*, who argues, at one and the same time, that the Inchon landing was probably unnecessary (pp. 92–93) and that the presence of U.S. forces on its lines of communication was what led to the collapse of the NKPA before Pusan (pp. 103–104).

42. Blair, *Forgotten War*, p. 227.

43. Collins, *War in Peacetime*, p. 125.

44. Appleman, *South to the Naktong*, p. 493.

45. See the official U.S. history of the KATUSA program, Richard Weinert, "The KATUSA Experience: The Integration of Korean Nationals into the U.S. Army, 1950–1965," *Military Affairs* 38, no. 2, April 1974, pp. 53–58.

46. For the most recent account of the marine landing, with helpful maps, see Simmons, "Over the Seawall."

47. For the tough fighting in Seoul, see Alexander, "Battle of the Barricades." For a more comprehensive account, see Lynn Montross and Nicholas A. Canzona, *The Inchon-Seoul Operations: U.S. Marine Operations in Korea, 1950–1953*, vol. 2 (Washington, D.C.: Historical Branch, HQMC, 1955).

48. Alexander, "Battle of the Barricades," pp. 29–30.

49. Fehrenbach, *This Kind of War*, pp. 223–224. Virtually every writer on the war mentions the horrible devastation of Seoul in the course of its liberation. See, for example, Hastings, *Korean War*, p. 112.

50. See the chart, "Average Supplies Received by a Representative North Korean Division, June–September 1950," in Eduard Mark, *Aerial Interdiction in Three Wars* (Washington, D.C.: Center for Air Force History, 1994), p. 281.

51. MacArthur's conception for Tailboard has brought forth a storm of criticism since the war. Appleman, *South to the Naktong*, pp. 609–612, was as critical as an official history was allowed to be at the time, especially on X Corps being a separate command. Blair, *Forgotten War*, pp. 331–333, is extremely critical, as is Hastings, *Korean War*, pp. 119–120. Fehrenbach, *This Kind of War*, p. 285, demurs. The iron laws of geography meant that any troops in eastern Korea would be separated from the main body. "Whatever the order of battle, X Corps and Eighth Army were forced to live, advance, and fight in virtual isolation from each other. No matter who had been given command, the mountains would have remained."

52. For the Wonsan landing, see Alexander, "Battle of the Barricades," pp. 50–64; Appleman, *South to the Naktong*, pp. 631–637.

53. For Unsan, see Appleman, *South to the Naktong*, pp. 689–708, as well as his *Disaster in Korea: The Chinese Confront MacArthur* (College Station: Texas A&M Uni-

versity Press, 1989). Like all of Appleman's works, this is not operational-level history. It deals mainly with battalion-level actions and sometimes goes even below that. The level of detail can be intimidating for a casual reader, and attempting to draw the larger picture is not always easy. A good, short introduction to the ordeal of 8th Army at the hands of the Chinese is to be found in Eliot A. Cohen and John Gooch, *Military Misfortunes: The Anatomy of Failure in War* (New York: Free Press, 1990), pp. 165–195, "Aggregate Failure: The Defeat of the American Eighth Army in Korea, November–December 1950."

54. Quoted in Mossman, *Ebb and Flow*, p. 47 n.

55. Appleman, *Disaster in Korea*, p. 14.

56. Ibid., pp. 227–293.

57. Stewart, "Chinese Intervention," p. 20.

58. For the Chosin (Changjin) reservoir, begin with the Marine Corps official history: Lynn Montross and Nicholas A. Canzona, *The Chosin Reservoir Campaign: U.S. Marine Operations in Korea, 1950–1953*, vol. 3 (Washington, D.C.: Historical Branch, HQMC, 1957). Then see two more works by Appleman, *East of Chosin: Entrapment and Breakout in Korea, 1950* (College Station: Texas A&M University Press, 1987) and *Escaping the Trap: The U.S. Army X Corps in Northeast Korea, 1950* (College Station: Texas A&M University Press, 1990). Shelby Stanton, *America's Tenth Legion: X Corps in Korea, 1950* (Novato, Calif.: Presidio, 1989) is solid operational history, yet also spends a great deal of time wrestling with General Almond's personality, his southern background, and his racism.

59. For operational-level analysis of the ordeal of X Corps, see Richard W. Stewart, *Staff Operations: The X Corps in Korea, December 1950* (Ft. Leavenworth, Kans.: Combat Studies Institute, 1991).

60. Matthew B. Ridgway, *The Korean War* (New York: Da Capo, 1967), p. 89.

61. House, *Combined Arms Warfare*, p. 206.

62. Zhang, *Mao's Military Romanticism*, pp. 248, 253.

63. For small-unit infantry actions in Korea, see two works by S. L. A. Marshall, *Commentary on Infantry Operations and Weapons Usage in Korea, Winter of 1950–51* (Chevy Chase, Md.: Operations Research Office, Johns Hopkins University, 1951), and *The River and the Gauntlet*. See also the blistering review of the latter by Appleman in *Military Affairs* 17, no. 2, Summer 1953, pp. 95–97. See also Russell A. Gugeler, *Combat Actions in Korea* (Washington, D.C.: Office of the Chief of Military History, 1970).

64. Crane, *American Airpower Strategy in Korea*, pp. 120, 160.

65. Alexander, "Battle of the Barricades," pp. 53–55.

66. Marshall, *Infantry Operations and Weapons Usage*, p. 134.

67. Li, Millett, and Yu, *Mao's Generals*, p. 23.

68. Ibid., pp. 30–31. For an introduction to the complex problems of the People's Liberation Army's force modernization programs, see Larry M. Wortzel, ed., *The Chinese Armed Forces in the 21st Century* (Carlisle, Pa.: U.S. Army War College, Strategic Studies Institute, 1999), a collection of papers presented at the eighth PLA conference held at the Wye Plantation in Virginia in 1998.

5. The Arab-Israeli Wars

1. See the very informative website for the IDF at www.idf.il. The three standard works in English on the IDF are still Edward Luttwak and Dan Horowitz, *The Israeli Army* (New York: Harper and Row, 1975), Gunther E. Rothenberg, *The Anatomy of the Israeli Army: The Israel Defence Force, 1948–1978* (New York: Hippocrene, 1979), and Martin van Creveld, *The Sword and the Olive: A Critical History of the Israeli Defense Force* (New York: Public Affairs, 1998). The first two works are quite similar: the "Introduction" to Luttwak and Horowitz and the "Preface" to Rothenberg both emphasize the necessity for Israel — a land without a military tradition — to devise its own unique doctrine in the course of virtually nonstop fighting. Luttwak and Horowitz write, "Though chronological, this book is neither a history of the Israeli Army nor a history of Israel's wars" (p. xi); Rothenberg writes, "Though organized in chronological form, this book is not a history of the wars and campaigns which historians have dissected and about which journalists have written colorful accounts" (p. 10). Luttwak and Horowitz are more influenced by the "new military history" of the 1970s, in particular their inclusion of a rather lengthy discussion of the sociology of the Arab armies and their "amoral familism" that rendered them unfit to wage modern war (pp. 282–287). Their book was finished just before the 1973 war; Rothenberg had the luxury of writing well after that war had ended, and his work is more useful as a result. On that basis alone, Creveld's work is a major achievement. He wrote in 1998, in the wake of the long and unwinnable "Lebanese morass" (pp. 285–306) and the even more intractable military problem of suppressing the Palestinian Intifada. As a result, his work is, as advertised, a "critical history" without a trace of the triumphalism of earlier works on the IDF. In trying to crush civilian unrest, he argued, "the IDF was caught in moral dilemmas with which it could not cope and which continue to haunt it day and night" (pp. 361–362). As a result, "by the mid-nineties, the faith of Israeli society in its military had been broken." He also has extremely harsh things to say about the increased role of Israeli women in combat roles (p. 361), criticism he developed further in his article, "Armed but Not Dangerous: Women in the Israeli Military," *War in History* 7, no. 1, 2000, pp. 82–98. See Eugenia C. Kiesling's tightly argued rejoinder to Creveld in "Debate: Armed but Not Dangerous: Women in the Israeli Military," *War in History* 8, no. 1, 2001, pp. 99–100.

2. James S. Metcalfe, "Foot Soldiers War," *Infantry Journal* 64, March 1949, pp. 25–28. Quoted in Rothenberg, *The Anatomy of the Israeli Army*, pp. 65–66.

3. The body of literature on operations in Israel's War of Independence is much smaller than that of later wars. One work stands out, by virtue of its size and comprehensive nature: Uri Milstein, *History of the War of Independence*, vols. 1–4 (Lanham, Md.: University Press of America, 1996). Written by one of Israel's leading military historians and projected to twelve volumes, it is a revisionist account — highly critical of Israel's military and political leadership and of the amateurishness of the military forces — that has made him "Israel's most cherished and hated" military historian. See the review of the first American volume of Milstein's work in the Jewish *Post*. It is avail-

able online at www.jewishpost.com/jp0209/jpn0209a.htm. Milstein's fourth volume, *Out of Crisis Came Decision* (1998), brings the narrative only up to the time of the Deir-Yassin massacre in April 1948, so there is much work yet to be done. Once again, the IDF website has a great deal of material. See www.idf.il/english/history/indepen-dence.stm. There is no revisionist, or indeed recent, Arab account of operations in this war, still referred to throughout the Arab world as *al-Nakba* ("the disaster"). The archives on the war in Egypt, Jordan, Iraq, Syria, and Lebanon are still closed, and there is little prospect that they will be open anytime soon. See Eugene L. Rogan and Avi Shlaim, eds., *The War for Palestine: Rewriting the History of 1948* (Cambridge: Cambridge University Press, 2001), especially the editors' introduction, p. 6. There is, however, a huge Palestinian presence on the Web. See, for example, the Nakba page, a presenta-tion of the Khalil Sakakini Cultural Center, at www.alnakba.org.

4. Yigal Allon, *The Making of Israel's Army* (New York: Universe Books, 1970), p. 31.

5. There is a detailed discussion of the "battle of the roads" as well as Operation Nachson at the IDF website. On Nachson, see Milstein, *Out of Crisis Came Decision*, pp. 287–296, for a typically critical account, arguing that Nachson "squandered" Israeli strength "in a relatively quiet sector," while the Israeli defenders of Kastel were neglected.

6. See Joseph Miranda, "The First Arab-Israeli War, 1947–49," *Strategy and Tactics* 185, May–June 1997, p. 14.

7. See Yigal Allon, "The Making of Israel's Army: The Development of Military Concepts of Liberation and Defence," in *The Theory and Practice of War*, ed. Michael Howard (Bloomington: Indiana University Press, 1975), pp. 335–371 — an expanded version of the chapter in Allon's book (also titled *The Making of Israel's Army*, see note 4) on the War of Independence. The quote is from p. 343.

8. Allon, *The Making of Israel's Army*, pp. 37–38.

9. For discussion of Horev, along with a helpful map, see Luttwak and Horowitz, *Israeli Army*, pp. 48–50, as well as the second revised edition of B. H. Liddell Hart, *Strategy* (New York: Meridian, 1991), pp. 390–391 and 397–400, called here "Oper-ation Ayin" and offered to the reader, naturally, as an example of the success of the "indirect approach."

10. Allon, *The Making of Israel's Army*, pp. 41–42.

11. For a biographical sketch of Dayan, see Robert M. Citino, *Armored Forces: History and Sourcebook* (Westport, Conn.: Greenwood Press, 1994), pp. 228–230. The best biography of Dayan is Robert Slater, *Warrior Statesman: The Life of Moshe Dayan* (New York: St. Martin's Press, 1991); see especially pp. 89–92.

12. See Rothenberg, *Anatomy of the Israeli Army*, pp. 98–100, and David Eshel, *Israel's Armor in Action* (Masada: Eshel Drasmit, 1978), pp. 22–25.

13. Bryan Perrett, *Soviet Armor Since 1945* (London: Blandford, 1987), p. 137, gives a total figure for the Egyptians of 430 tanks and 300 tank destroyers.

14. The Israeli primary source for the 1956 war is Moshe Dayan, *Diary of the Sinai Campaign* (New York: Schocken, 1967). See p. 39. The Egyptian side of the war is missing in action, at least in English-language sources.

15. For the operational order for Kadesh, see ibid., pp. 210–219.

16. Ibid., p. 39.

17. Luttwak and Horowitz, *The Israeli Army*, pp. 151–155.

18. Dayan, *Diary of the Sinai Campaign*, p. 96.

19. Ibid., pp. 100–102.

20. Ibid., p. 116.

21. Rothenberg, *Anatomy of the Israeli Army*, p. 109.

22. The English observer is Robert Henriques, *A Hundred Hours to Suez* (New York: Viking, 1957), p. 12. See Allon, "The Making of Israel's Army," p. 371 n. 14.

23. Creveld, *The Sword and the Olive*, p. 149.

24. A blizzard of material on the Six Day War emerged in its immediate wake, including Randolph S. Churchill and Winston S. Churchill, *The Six Day War* (Boston: Houghton Mifflin, 1967), an account enlivened by their travels and contacts within the Middle East, and Peter Young, *The Israeli Campaign 1967* (London: William Kimber, 1967). Edgar O'Ballance, *The Third Arab-Israeli War* (Hamden, Conn.: Archon Books, 1972) is a typically readable account; O'Ballance has to bend over backward to lend excitement to such a lopsided war, and he does so, often turning a one- or two-hour delay in an IDF breakthrough into a crisis ("Brigadier Sharon, now realizing the true strength of the Um Katif position, was compelled to admit that his quick, 'regardless of cost' plan had failed," p. 123). The pertinent sections in Rothenberg, *Anatomy of the Israeli Army* (pp. 135–152) and Luttwak and Horowitz, *The Israeli Army* (pp. 209–298) are both useful, with the latter having pride of place due to the fact that 1967 was the war around which the entire book is shaped. Unfortunately, the 1973 war soon stole thunder away from 1967, and there has been almost no new research into the earlier war until the recent release of Michael B. Oren, *Six Days of War: June 1967 and the Making of the Modern Middle East* (Oxford: Oxford University Press, 2002). Essentially a diplomatic and political history, the author's comprehensive, multilingual research into the archives yields much of interest on the operational level, as well, including the Egyptian intentions for "Operation Dawn," a combined air-land strike against Israel's nuclear reactor facility at Dimona. Once again, there is no satisfactory account in English from the Arab side.

25. For the "decision cycle," a loop of "observation-orientation-decision-action" (often referred to in the U.S. military as the "Boyd cycle"), see Robert R. Leonhard's excruciatingly theoretical *The Art of Maneuver: Maneuver-Warfare Theory and Air-Land Battle* (Novato, Calif.: Presidio, 1991), pp. 51, 87–88, 277. Colonel John Boyd delivered numerous oral briefings on the topic, entitled "Patterns of Conflict," but never in fact consigned it to print. See Richard M. Swain, *"Lucky War": Third Army in Desert Storm* (Ft. Leavenworth, Kans.: U.S. Army Command and General Staff College Press, 1997), p. 97 n. 3.

26. The phrase is Yigal Allon's. See *Making of Israel's Army*, pp. 73–74.

27. Creveld, *The Sword and the Olive*, pp. 179–199.

28. Samuel M. Katz, *Israel's Army* (Novato, Calif.: Presidio, 1990), p. 4.

29. Young, *The Israeli Campaign 1967*, p. 46; see also Rothenberg, *Anatomy of the Israeli Army*, pp. 126–130.

30. Young, *Israeli Campaign*, p. 26; Rothenberg, *Anatomy of the Israeli Army*, pp. 122–123; Edgar O'Ballance, *The Third Arab-Israeli War*, pp. 44–47.

31. Churchill and Churchill, *Six Day War*, p. 65.

32. For the IDF's operational plan, see Luttwak and Horowitz, *Israeli Army*, pp. 231–234; F. H. Toase, "The Israeli Experience of Armoured Warfare," in *Armoured Warfare*, ed. J. P. Harris and F. H. Toase (London: Batsford, 1990), pp. 171–172; Rothenberg, *Anatomy of the Israeli Army*, pp. 140–141; Young, *Israeli Campaign*, pp. 99–103.

33. Luttwak and Horowitz offer the best account of Egyptian defensive plans (*Israeli Army*, pp. 234–237).

34. Ibid., p. 241. For discussion of Tal's command at Rafah, and the revisionism within Israel about it, see Martin van Creveld, "Military Lessons of the Yom Kippur War: Historical Perspectives," *Washington Papers* 3, no. 24 (Beverly Hills: Sage, 1975), pp. 1–4.

35. Ariel Sharon, with David Chanoff, *Warrior: The Autobiography of Ariel Sharon* (New York: Touchstone, 1989), pp. 190–191. See also Luttwak and Horowitz, pp. 246–247.

36. Eric Hammel, *Six Days in June: How Israel Won the 1967 Arab-Israeli War* (New York: Charles Scribner's Sons, 1992), pp. 219, 221.

37. Sharon, *Warrior*, p. 201.

38. See Luttwak and Horowitz, *Israeli Army*, pp. 249–253, for this novel tactic.

39. Rothenberg, *Anatomy of the Israeli Army*, p. 143.

40. Churchill and Churchill, *Six Day War*, pp. 118–119.

41. First mentioned, at least publicly, by President Nasser in his June 9 resignation speech (Churchill and Churchill, *Six Day War*, pp. 89–91). See also Yehoshaphat Harkabi, "Basic Factors in the Arab Collapse During the Six-Day War," in *Arab-Israeli Relations: A Collection of Contending Perspectives and Recent Research*, vol. 3, *From War to War: Israel and the Arabs, 1948–1967*, ed. Ian S. Lustick (New York: Garland, 1994), pp. 111–112.

42. Harkabi, "Basic Factors in the Arab Collapse," p. 112.

43. Hassan el Badri, Taha el Magdoub, and Mohammed Dia el Din Zohdy, *The Ramadan War, 1973* (Dunn Loring, Va.: T. N. Dupuy Associates, 1974), p. 22.

44. Harkabi, "Basic Factors in the Arab Collapse," pp. 112–113, 122, 124.

45. For Liddell Hart's visit to Israel, see Brian Bond, *Liddell Hart: A Study of His Military Thought* (New Brunswick, N.J.: Rutgers University Press, 1977), pp. 260–261. The Israeli press hailed Liddell Hart as "the Clausewitz of the 20th Century."

46. The best work on the topic is still Yaacov Bar-Siman-Tov, *The Israeli-Arab War of Attrition, 1969–70* (New York: Columbia University Press, 1980).

47. The literature on the 1973 war dwarfs that of the others and is greatly improved by the addition of works from the Arab world that have been translated into English. For an excellent primary source, see Lt. General Saad el Shazly, *The Crossing of the Suez* (San Francisco: American Mideast Research, 1980), the memoir by the Chief of Staff of the Egyptian Armed Forces in 1973. He left Egypt after a falling-out with President Anwar Sadat and was part of an anti-Sadat political movement in exile, so much of the work deals with the political situation in Egypt and its effect on the army.

Nevertheless, it also includes a great deal of detail on planning, operations, and the way in which the latter diverged from the former in the course of the fighting. For a work that will challenge western notions throughout, including the notion that the IDF won any sort of victory at all, see Badri, Magdoub, and Zohdy, *Ramadan War.* The triumphalist tone of the work, written by three senior officers of the Egyptian army, is insistent: "Thus our armed forces in less than six hours destroyed the greater part of the Bar Lev line. They had reversed the Six Day War defeat and shattered the myth of the undefeatable Israeli army" (p. 66). Standard western works are Rothenberg, *Anatomy of the Israeli Army*, pp. 177–202; Luttwak and Horowitz, *Israeli Army*, pp. 337–397; and Chaim Herzog, *The War of Atonement, October 1973* (Boston: Little, Brown, 1975), a good operational history by the former chief of Israeli military intelligence. Edgar O'Ballance, *No Victor, No Vanquished: The Yom Kippur War* (San Rafael, Calif.: Presidio, 1978) offers his typically useful journalistic account and also takes pains to minimize every Israeli achievement and maximize every Arab; Peter Allen, *The Yom Kippur War* (New York: Charles Scribner's Sons, 1982), does just the opposite. Memoirs from the Israeli side include Moshe Dayan, *Moshe Dayan: The Story of My Life* (New York: William Morrow, 1975); Sharon, *Warrior*; and Avraham (Bren) Adan, *On the Banks of the Suez: An Israeli General's Personal Account of the Yom Kippur War* (Novato, Calif.: Presidio, 1991), written by the commander of one of the IDF's armored divisions that was in the thick of the fighting and ended the war across the canal in Africa. Finally, as a sign of the nonaligned world's intense interest in this war, see Brigadier Mohammad Ibrahim Nagaty, "Lessons of Ramadan War," *Defence Journal* (India) 1, nos. 9 and 10, 1975, pp. 5–9; and Sultan Ahmad Geelani, "The Fourth Arab-Israel War: A Recapitulation," in the same issue, as well as K. Subrahmanyam, "The Lessons of the 1973 Arab-Israeli War," *Institute for Defence Studies and Analyses Journal* (India) 6, no. 3, January 1974, pp. 416–442. For the war's lessons, see Anthony H. Cordesman and Abraham R. Wagner, *The Lessons of Modern War*, vol. 1, *The Arab Israeli-Conflicts, 1973–1989* (Boulder, Colo.: Westview, 1990), like the entire series, a book largely aimed at technicians.

48. Shazly, *Crossing of the Suez*, p. 19.

49. Ibid., p. 37.

50. Luttwak and Horowitz, *Israeli Army*, p. 352.

51. Rothenberg, *Anatomy of the Israeli Army*, p. 186; Cordesman and Wagner, *Arab-Israeli Wars*, pp. 57–60.

52. For Soviet doctrine and its impact on the Arab armies, see Michael Eisenstadt and Kenneth M. Pollack, "Armies of Snow and Armies of Sand: The Impact of Soviet Military Doctrine on the Arab Militaries," *Middle East Journal* 55, no. 4, Autumn 2002, pp. 549–578. The best work on the epic nature of the Golan fighting is still Herzog, *War of Atonement*, pp. 56–145; see also Luttwak and Horowitz, *Israeli Army*, pp. 372–378.

53. Quoted in Frank Aker, *October 1973: The Arab-Israeli War* (Hamden, Conn.: Archon Books, 1985), p. 89.

54. Creveld, "Military Lessons of the Yom Kippur War," p. 15.

55. Adan, *On the Banks of the Suez*, p. 140.

56. Herzog, *War of Atonement*, p. 191. He, for one, is highly critical of Adan for attacking east to west into the teeth of the Egyptian defenses, rather than against the weaker northern flank of the Egyptian bridgehead.

57. Shazly, *Crossing of the Suez*, p. 240 — a widely quoted passage. See Cordesman and Wagner, *Arab-Israeli Wars*, p. 57.

58. Adan, *On the Banks of the Suez*, p. 130.

59. Toase, "Israeli Experience of Armoured Warfare," p. 178. By the end of the day on October 14, with the fortunes of war clearly running in the IDF's favor, Chaim Bar Lev is reputed to have said to Prime Minister Golda Meir, "It has been a good day. Our forces are themselves again, and so are the Egyptians."

60. Shazly, *Crossing of the Suez*, pp. 249–250.

61. See Sharon, *Warrior*, pp. 220, 235–236, 269–270.

62. For a defense of Gonen and a criticism of Sharon, see Luttwak and Horowitz, *Israeli Army*, pp. 381–384, which accuses Sharon of failing to see the big picture, specifically the serious vulnerability of the Israeli line of communications to the crossing point. See Sharon, *Warrior*, pp. 299, 300, 303, 306, 308.

63. Sharon, *Warrior*, pp. 326–328.

64. Adan, *On the Banks of the Suez*, pp. 301–302.

65. For a good evocation of the era's mood, see Creveld, "Military Lessons of the Yom Kippur War." A generally sober account avoiding the hyperbole of so much of the period literature, it nonetheless speculates about the end of the "Third Armoured Period" (starting in 1917), extrapolates from material losses on both sides to a prediction that the days of "victory through limited liability" may indeed be over, and predicts that future wars "will become more, rather than less, total, subjecting the resources of the societies waging them to an ever increasing drain and strain." It would be a new "totalization of war" (p. 50), a long leap of logic indeed from a conflict that had lasted a bit over two weeks.

66. After the 1967 war, Major General Yitzhak Rabin observed that "all this has been done by the IDF alone, with what we have, without anybody or anything." Rothenberg, *Anatomy of the Israeli Army*, p. 152.

67. For photographs and discussion of the Merkava, see Eshel, *Israel's Armor*, pp. 78–80.

68. Churchill and Churchill, *Six Day War*, p. 67.

6. Operational Success and Failure

1. To give just a few examples of doctrinal debate within professional military circles in India, see G. D. Bakshi, "Land Warfare in the Subcontinent: The Indian Quest for Doctrine," *Indian Defence Review Digest* 4, 1992, pp. 12–20, as well as "The Sino-Vietnam War — 1979: Case Studies in Limited War," by the same author, *Indian Defence Review* 15, no. 3, July–September 2000, pp. 95–107; Ajay Singh, "Developing an Information Warfare Strategy," *Indian Defence Review* 13, no. 1, January–March 1998, pp. 37–39; R. K. Singh, "Tank Is Aging — What Next?" *Journal of the United*

Service Institution of India 57, no. 450, January–March 1978, pp. 63–68; J. K. Dutt, "Deep Thrust," *Journal of the United Service Institution of India* 57, no. 450, January–March 1978, pp. 69–75; Anjani Kumar Sinha, "Covering the Last 200 Metres and Fighting on the Objective," *Journal of the United Service Institution of India,* 54, no. 437, October–December 1974, pp. 393–402; O. S. Kalkat, "Strike Hard and Deep," *Journal of the United Service Institution of India* 53, no. 432, July–September 1973, pp. 268–271.

2. There is an immense Indian literature on the 1971 war, much less from the Pakistani side, and almost none in the West. For the Indian side, begin with the operational history by D. K. Palit, *The Lightning Campaign: The Indo-Pakistan War* (Salisbury: Compton, 1972), and then, for comparison, consult the magisterial work by Sukhwant Singh, *India's Wars Since Independence,* vol. 1, *The Liberation of Bangladesh* (New Delhi: Vikas, 1980). Both written by retired Indian officers, the first reflects the initial triumphalist wave of works written in the immediate wake of the war, the second is judicious and critical throughout, unsparing in its criticism of failings on the Indian side as well as the Pakistani. The third and final volume of Sukhwant Singh's *India's Wars Since Independence, General Trends* is also useful in integrating the experience of 1971 into broader themes in Indian military history. See also Major K. C. Praval, *Indian Army After Independence* (New Delhi: Lancer International, 1990), especially pp. 317–360. For other good overviews of the war, complete with its political background and implications, see Pran Chopra, *India's Second Liberation* (Delhi: Vikas, 1973) and Krishna Chandra Sagar, *The War of the Twins* (New Delhi: Northern Book Centre, 1997). The memoir literature alone is massive: Jagdev Singh, *Dismemberment of Pakistan: 1971 Indo-Pak War* (New Delhi: Lancer International, 1988), an account by a brigadier attached to IV Corps as chief engineer; Lachman Singh, *Victory in Bangladesh* (Dehra Dun: Natraj Publishers, 1981), the commander of 20th Mountain Division; a work by the commander of the 71st Mountain Brigade, P. N. Kathpalia, *Mission with a Difference: The Exploits of 71 Mountain Brigade* (New Delhi: Lancer International, 1986); and by the outspoken commander of the 301st Mountain Brigade, H. S. Sodhi, *Operation Windfall: Emergence of Bangladesh* (New Delhi: Allied Publishers, 1980). For the battalion level, see Ashok Kalyan Verma, *Rivers of Silence: Disaster on River Nam Ka Chu, 1962 and the Dash to Dhaka Across River Meghna During 1971* (New Delhi: Lancer Publishers, 1998), by the commander of the 18th Battalion of the Rajput Regiment. For the Pakistani side, see the report of the official governmental inquiry, *Report of the Hamoodur Rehman Commission of Inquiry in the 1971 War: As Declassified by the Government of Pakistan* (Lahore: Vanguard, 2000). The report, as massive as it is, offers little that is new on the campaign. It condemns the commander in East Pakistan, General Amir Abdullah Khan Niazi, on grounds of faulty strategy and also immoral and corrupt behavior. More intriguing is the report's condemnation of the "moral degeneration which set in among senior army commanders as a result of their continued involvement in Martial Law duties, lust for wine and women, and greed for land and houses" (p. 285). See also two works by Attiqur Rahman, Mohammed, *Our Defence Cause: An Analysis of Pakistan's Past and Future Military Role* (London: White Lion, 1976), and *Leadership: Senior Commanders* (Lahore: Ferozsons Book Corp., 1973)

for the effects of the war on the Pakistani army. Brian Cloughley, *A History of the Pakistan Army: Wars and Insurrections; with a New Chapter on the Kargil Issue*, 2d ed. (Oxford: Oxford University Press, 2000), is a fine scholarly account, sympathetic to the Pakistanis but also quite fair in dealing with the army's failings in 1971. Without doubt, however, the best Pakistani book on the war is Siddiq Salik, *Witness to Surrender* (Karachi: Oxford University Press, 1977), a public relations officer with the Pakistani forces in Bangladesh, Salik was a perceptive observer of the chaos swirling around him who managed to keep his humanity — and his sense of humor — in the maelstrom. His portraits of the Pakistani commanders, in particular, are unforgettable. Other worthwhile items are *The 14 Day War* (New Delhi: Publications Division, Government of India, 1972), an annotated collection of press releases and speeches from the war; Deendayal Dinesh, *Indira Wins the War* (Delhi: Oriental Publishers, 1972); Ravi Rikhey's idiosyncratic *The War That Never Was* (Delhi: Chanakaya, 1988); Gautam Sharma, *Our Armed Forces* (New Delhi: National Book Trust, India, 2000); Ashok Krishna, *India's Armed Forces: Fifty Years of War and Peace* (New Delhi: Lancer Publishers, 1998); John Gaylor, *Sons of John Company: The Indian and Pakistan Armies 1903–91* (Tunbridge Wells, Kent: Spellmount, 1992); and Michael Carver, *War Since 1945* (New York: G. P. Putnam's Sons, 1981), pp. 227–233. Finally, any researcher into the conflict should consult the journal literature, which is copious. A good place to start is the *Journal of the United Service Institution of India*, the Indian *Institute of Defence Studies and Analyses*, the *Indian Defence Review*, and the *Defence Journal* of Pakistan. Within American journals, the pickings are unfortunately slim and often written by Indian officers. See, for example, Maharaj K. Chopra, "Military Operations in Bangladesh," *Military Review* 52, no. 5, May 1972, pp. 51–60; K. Brahma Singh, "Lest We Forget," *Military Review* 53, no. 1, January 1973, pp. 77–86; and Cyril N. Barclay, "A Soldier Looks at the Indo-Pakistani War," *Army* 22, no. 5, May 1972, pp. 20–26.

3. Sukhwant Singh, *The Liberation of Bangladesh*, pp. 11–13.

4. For the ten million figure, see the exchange of letters between General Lachman Singh and Indira Gandhi, reprinted in Lachman Singh, *Victory in Bangladesh*, pp. 296–298. Sukhwant Singh, *The Liberation of Bangladesh*, mentions the admittedly hard-to-fathom number no less than three times (pp. 8–9, 15, 96).

5. China's intentions in 1971 will have to remain a mystery. Pakistani leaders professed to believe in the possibility of Chinese intervention — right up to the surrender of their army in Bangladesh. For an overview of the consideration given to China in Indian military planning, see Sukhwant Singh, *The Liberation of Bangladesh*, pp. 18–23; Praval, *Indian Army After Independence*, p. 317. Pakistani dictator Yahya Khan declared outright that "China would intervene if India attacks Pakistan" (Chopra, *India's Second Liberation*, p. 106). And yet it was clear to Indians from Chinese troop movements (or lack thereof) that there was a very small possibility of intervention during a winter campaign in East Pakistan. For the Pakistani perspective, see Cloughley, *History of the Pakistan Army*, pp. 162, 180–181.

6. H. S. Sodhi, *Top Brass: A Critical Appraisal of the Indian Military Leadership* (Noida: Trishul, 1993), p. 92; Praval, *Indian Army After Independence*, p. 317.

7. For the "Siliguri Corridor" and the potential for various Pakistani thrusts, see Chopra, *India's Second Liberation*, pp. 35–36, 118–120.

8. Sukhwant Singh, *The Liberation of Bangladesh*, p. 23.

9. For Manekshaw's vigorous reforms, see Cloughley, *History of the Pakistan Army*, pp. 179–180, and Sukhwant Singh, *The Liberation of Bangladesh*, pp. 43–44.

10. For the importance of war games in shaping the Indian operational plan, see Sodhi, *Operation Windfall*, pp. 153–154, and Sukhwant Singh, *The Liberation of Bangladesh*, pp. 79, 91–92.

11. Sagar, *War of the Twins*, pp. 243–247; Lachman Singh, *Victory in Bangladesh*, pp. 50–64; and Sukhwant Singh, *The Liberation of Bangladesh*, pp. 30–37.

12. Palit, *Lightning Campaign*, 71; Sukhwant Singh, *The Liberation of Bangladesh*, pp. 125–126; Cloughley, *History of the Pakistan Army*, p. 208.

13. To give just a few examples among hundreds, Sukhwant Singh, *The Liberation of Bangladesh*, calls his chapter on the fighting (pp. 130–160) "The Blitzkrieg"; Dinesh, *Indira Wins the War*, references blitzkrieg on p. 166; Palit, *Lightning Campaign*, references blitzkrieg in the title, of course, and also on p. 16; he then goes one better than that on pp. 101 and 106, using (no doubt unconsciously) the correct German doctrinal term, "the war of movement."

14. Sukhwant Singh, *The Liberation of Bangladesh*, pp. 65–66.

15. Ibid., p. 49.

16. For the "Dacca bowl," see Palit, *Lightning Campaign*, pp. 101–103, especially the map on p. 102, and Lachman Singh, *Victory in Bangladesh*, p. 49.

17. For a military geography of East Pakistan, see Lachman Singh, *Victory in Bangladesh*, pp. 1–13, as well as Palit, *Lightning Campaign*, pp. 164–166.

18. Pakistani armor amounted to fifty-two American Chaffee tanks of 1950s vintage and twelve PT-76 models captured from India during the 1965 fighting (Cloughley, *History of the Pakistan Army*, p. 191).

19. For a discussion of the missions entrusted to the Indian air force, see Chopra, *India's Second Liberation*, pp. 126–127.

20. Sukhwant Singh, *Liberation of Bangladesh*, pp. 68–72.

21. The title of Palit, *Lightning Campaign*, chapter 6, pp. 94–105. Much of the chapter is online at the Bharat Rakshak Consortium on Indian Military Websites (www.bharat-rakshak.com).

22. Chopra, *India's Second Liberation*, pp. 123–125.

23. For a good discussion of Niazi's operational options, see Salik, *Witness to Surrender*, pp. 123–128. Salik likened Niazi's preference for a theater fortress concept to a "Tobruk strategy" and a "deployment for defeat." See also Cloughley, *History of the Pakistan Army*, pp. 187–189.

24. Salik, *Witness to Surrender*, p. 128.

25. Cloughley, *History of the Pakistan Army*, p. 189.

26. Sukhwant Singh, *The Liberation of Bangladesh*, p. 169.

27. From Cloughley, *History of the Pakistan Army*, pp. 186–187; Palit, *Lightning Campaign*, pp. 103–104.

28. Salik, *Witness to Surrender*, p. 145.

29. Agha Humayun Amin, "Tank Ambush at Kushtia," *Defence Journal* (Pakistan) 4, no. 4, November 2000, p. 50.

30. Ibid., pp. 46–50.

31. From Cloughley, *History of the Pakistan Army*, p. 196.

32. Sukhwant Singh, *The Liberation of Bangladesh*, p. 80; Cloughley, *History of the Pakistan Army*, p. 191.

33. Sukhwant Singh, *The Liberation of Bangladesh*, pp. 164–165.

34. Lachman Singh, *Victory in Bangladesh*, p. 76; see also the detailed map on p. 77. Lachman Singh was commander of the 20th Mountain Division tasked to take Hilli.

35. See General Kathpalia's own, quite self-congratulatory memoir, *Mission with a Difference*, including descriptions of the "relentless pressure" his brigade put on the Pakistanis (p. 84). For a dissenting voice about just how relentless his pressure really was, see Sukhwant Singh, *The Liberation of Bangladesh*, p. 165; for commentary on the controversy, see Cloughley, *History of the Pakistan Army*, pp. 193–194.

36. For the advance to Thurkagaon, see Kathpalia, *Mission with a Difference*, pp. 84–89 and 114–115; the sixty kilometer figure is mentioned in Sukhwant Singh, *The Liberation of Bangladesh*, p. 165.

37. For the operations of 20th Division in the Hilli battle, see Lachman Singh, *Victory in Bangladesh*, pp. 65–94.

38. Sukhwant Singh, *The Liberation of Bangladesh*, p. 180.

39. Cloughley, *History of the Pakistan Army*, p. 186.

40. For a discussion of IV Corps and its mission, see Chopra, *India's Second Liberation*, pp. 123–124.

41. Sukhwant Singh, *The Liberation of Bangladesh*, refers to Liddell Hart by name on p. 92, references the "expanding torrent" on pp. 92 and 128, as well as the "indirect approach" on p. 128.

42. Cloughley, *History of the Pakistan Army*, pp. 213–214; Sukhwant Singh, *The Liberation of Bangladesh*, p. 151, claims to have first put the idea of seizing Dacca into Sagat Singh's mind.

43. Sukhwant Singh, *The Liberation of Bangladesh*, p. 152.

44. Cloughley, *History of the Pakistan Army*, p. 215; Chopra, *India's Second Liberation*, p. 179.

45. Cloughley, *History of the Pakistan Army*, p. 216; Chopra, *India's Second Liberation*, p. 181.

46. Palit, *Lightning Campaign*, pp. 123–125; Lachman Singh, *Victory in Bangladesh*, pp. 228–229.

47. For Gurbux Singh Gill, see Sukhwant Singh, *The Liberation of Bangladesh*, pp. 85, 184; Cloughley, *History of the Pakistan Army*, p. 201, and Lachman Singh, *Victory in Bangladesh*, p. 137.

48. For the "Kaderites," see Chopra, *India's Second Liberation*, pp. 181–182; Palit, *Lightning Campaign*, pp. 57, 128–129; and Sukhwant Singh, *The Liberation of Bangladesh*, pp. 205–208.

49. Cloughley, *History of the Pakistan Army*, pp. 199–206; Sukhwant Singh, *The Liberation of Bangladesh*, pp. 183–201. During the tough fight for Kamalpur, one of

the war's most famous episodes, quoted in every book on the campaign, took place. Brigadier Hardev Singh Kler, commanding 95th Mountain Brigade Group, sent a message to the Pakistani commander in Kamalpur, Lieutenant Colonel Sultan Mahmood, demanding his surrender. Sultan sent back a note enclosing a bullet and saying that "he hoped to find you (Kler) with a sten in your hand next time instead of the pen you seem to have so much mastery over." See Cloughley, *History of the Pakistan Army*, p. 204, and Sukhwant Singh, *The Liberation of Bangladesh*, pp. 194–195. Salik, *Witness to Surrender*, p. 188, offers a slight variant of the note.

50. Palit, *Lightning Campaign*, p. 127. For the paradrop, see Matthew Thomas, "The Airborne Assault Operations in Tangail: Indo-Pak Conflict 1971," *Indian Defence Review Digest* 2, 1992, pp. 16–24.

51. Ibid., p. 20.

52. Cloughley, *History of the Pakistan Army*, p. 199; Salik, *Witness to Surrender*, p. 190.

53. Maroof Raza, "The 1971 War in Retrospect," *Indian Defence Review* 12, no. 1, January–March 1997, pp. 127–128.

54. Thomas, "Airborne Assault Operations," pp. 23–24; Palit, *Lightning Campaign*, pp. 129–130.

55. Once again, one of the most often described moments of the entire war. See Palit, *Lightning Campaign*, p. 134; Sukhwant Singh, *The Liberation of Bangladesh*, p. 213; and Chopra, *India's Second Liberation*, p. 182. Again, Salik, *Witness to Surrender*, p. 210, offers a slight variation to the wording.

56. Quoted in Palit, *Lighting Campaign*, p. 16. See also Mohammed Akbar Khan, "The East Pakistan Crisis — An Analysis," *Defence Journal* (Pakistan) 2, no. 12, 1976, pp. 31–40. The author, a major in the Pakistani army, describes the operation in slightly more sinister tones, saying it resembled "Hitler's blitzkrieg against France" (p. 37).

57. Palit, *Lightning Campaign*, p. 15.

58. Sukhwant Singh, *General Trends*, p. 34.

59. Sodhi, *Top Brass*, p. 248.

60. G. D. Bakshi, *The Indian Military Revival: The Saga of the Fateh Shibji* (New Delhi: Lancer International, 1987), p. 89.

61. Chopra, *India's Second Liberation*, p. 187.

62. *Hamoodur Rehman Commission*, p. 281.

63. Lachman Singh, *Victory in Bangladesh*, p. 280; Sukhwant Singh, *The Liberation of Bangladesh*, pp. 159–160.

64. Palit, *Lightning Campaign*, p. 105; Chopra, *India's Second Liberation*, p. 129; Cloughley, *History of the Pakistan Army*, pp. 185–186.

65. For a criticism of the Indian army's maneuver doctrine in 1971, see B. N. Sharma, *What They Don't Teach You at Army School: A Critique of Indian Military Thought* (Delhi: Shipra, 1996), pp. 71–72, as well as Sodhi, *Operation Windfall*, pp. 282–284. For the primitive logistics, see Sodhi, *Top Brass*, p. 116, as well as Jagdev Singh, *Dismemberment of Pakistan*, p. 142. Brigadier Sodhi is an interesting writer, highly critical in the best way, but also evidently nursing some grudges over his treatment by superior officers (see his description of the precampaign war game

in *Operation Windfall*, pp. 153–154), as well as about who did or did not get decorations or promotions or both after the campaign (see *Top Brass*, p. 117; and *Operation Windfall*, pp. 233–234, 286–288).

66. Quoted in Sodhi, *Top Brass*, p. 185.

67. There is a large body of literature on the Iran-Iraq War. Start with the works of Anthony H. Cordesman: *The Iran-Iraq War and Western Security, 1984–1987: Strategic Implications and Policy Options* (London: Janes, 1987), written while the conflict was still raging, and (with Abraham R. Wagner), *The Lessons of Modern War*, vol. 2, *The Iran-Iraq War* (Boulder, Colo.: Westview, 1990). Stephen C. Pelletiere, *The Iran-Iraq War: Chaos in a Vacuum* (Westport, Conn.: Praeger, 1992) is a worthy history of the entire war focusing on operations, by a professor of national security at the United States Army War College in Carlisle, Pennsylvania. The book is noteworthy for its pro-Iraqi tone, constructing the conflict as a clash between Iranian "religious zealots" (xiii) and Iraqi "military professionalism" (xiv). See also Stephen C. Pelletiere and Douglas V. Johnson II, *Lessons Learned: The Iran-Iraq War*, vol. 1, a study later issued by the U.S. Marine Corps as FMFRP 3-203 (Washington, D.C.: U.S. Marine Corps, 1990). Three collections of scholarly articles should be consulted: Shirin Tahir-Kheli and Shaheen Ayubi, eds., *The Iran-Iraq War: New Weapons, Old Conflicts* (Westport, Conn.: Praeger, 1983); Efraim Karsh, ed., *The Iran-Iraq War: Impact and Implications* (Tel Aviv: Jaffee Center for Strategic Studies, 1987); and R. C. Sharma, ed., *Perspectives on Iran-Iraq Conflict* (New Delhi: Rajesh, 1984). Two journalistic accounts are worthwhile. The ubiquitous Edgar O'Ballance (this was his twenty-second book), *The Gulf War* (London: Brassey's, 1988); and Dilip Hiro, *The Longest War: The Iran-Iraq Military Conflict* (New York: Routledge, 1991). Richard Jupa and Jim Dingeman, "How Iran Lost/Iraq Won the Gulf War," *Strategy and Tactics* 133, March/April 1990, pp. 49–55, is a typically good operational analysis from the leading war-gaming journal of the day. For a firsthand view at Iranian revolutionary fervor in the early period of the war, see *Two Years of War* (Teheran: Islamic Revolution's Guards Corps Political Office, 1982), with its declaration of the "triumph of the spiritual man" (p. 24) and its warnings of "plots and treasons" (p. 33) against the revolutionary government on the part of "compromisers" (p. 37). For an opposite view by an anti-Khomeini Iranian exile, see Behrouz Souresrafil, *The Iran-Iraq War* (London: C. C. Press, 1989).

68. Pelletiere, *Iran-Iraq War*, p. 34.

69. Cordesman, *Iran-Iraq War and Western Security*, p. 3; Cordesman and Wagner, *Iran-Iraq War*, p. 78.

70. The best analysis of the Iraqi air strike is Cordesman and Wagner, *Iran-Iraq War*, pp. 81–84.

71. There is disagreement on the basic issue of how many Iraqi divisions attacked, and where they attacked. Pelletiere says "the Iraqis committed six divisions in their initial assault" (*Iran-Iraq War*, p. 36); Cordesman and Wagner, *Iran-Iraq War*, p. 87, say that "three armored and two mechanized divisions attacked along a broad front" in the south; Hiro, *Longest War*, p. 41, gives a figure of four ("three armored and one mechanized Iraqi divisions penetrated Khuzistan"). As Pelletiere and Johnson point

out in *Lessons Learned*, p. 4, since "Iraq and Iran are probably two of the world's most closed societies," getting precise information on the war continues to be difficult.

72. Hiro, *Longest War*, p. 41. A good synopsis of the opening phase of the war is found in K. R. Singh, "Iraq-Iran Conflict: Military Dimensions," in *Perspectives on Iran-Iraq Conflict*, ed. R. C. Sharma, pp. 51–54.

73. Pelletiere, *Iran-Iraq War*, pp. 36–37.

74. Cordesman and Wagner, *Iran-Iraq War*, p. 85.

75. William O. Staudenmaier, "A Strategic Analysis," in Tahir-Kheli and Ayubi, *Iran-Iraq War*, pp. 34–35.

76. Chaim Herzog, "A Military-Strategic Overview," in *Iran-Iraq War*, ed. Efraim Karsh, p. 260.

77. Cordesman and Wagner, *Iran-Iraq War*, pp. 113–114.

78. Ibid., pp. 123–125; Staudenmaier, "Strategic Analysis," p. 40; O'Ballance, *Iran-Iraq War*, pp. 66–67. Other sources place the start of the Iranian counteroffensive in November 1981. See Pelletiere and Johnson, *Lessons Learned*, p. 10, and Hiro, *Longest War*, p. 55.

79. For the Iranian human wave, see Cordesman and Wagner, *Iran-Iraq War*, p. 130; Pelletiere and Johnson, *Lessons Learned*, p. 52.

80. Hiro, *Longest War*, p. 56.

81. For Khoramshahr, see Pelletiere, *Iran-Iraq War*, pp. 40–42; Cordesman and Wagner, *Iran-Iraq War*, pp. 130–131; and O'Ballance, *Iran-Iraq War*, pp. 82–85.

82. See O'Ballance, *Iran-Iraq War*, pp. 93–95, for a description of Operation Ramadan al-Mubarak.

83. Cordesman and Wagner, *Iran-Iraq War*, pp. 435–442.

84. Cordesman, *Iran-Iraq War and Western Security*, p. 93.

85. Pelletiere, *Iran-Iraq War*, p. 96.

86. Seen by Pelletiere as the turning point of the war, *Iran-Iraq War*, pp. 105–110.

87. Pelletiere, *Iran-Iraq War*, pp. 117–126, and Pelletiere and Johnson, *Lessons Learned*, pp. 85–97, both argue that Karbala-Five was in fact a tremendous Iranian defeat, involving perhaps more than seventy thousand casualties, where Iraq found the antidote to the human wave attacks by the Pasdaran in the combined arms tactics of the new Iraqi Republican Guard formations. For a contrary view, see Dilip Hiro, *Longest War*, pp. 183–184.

88. For Tawakalna, see Pelletiere, *Iran-Iraq War*, pp. 141–149.

89. Quoted in Herzog, "Military-Strategic Overview," p. 266, and Cordesman and Wagner, *Iran-Iraq War*, p. 397.

90. Cordesman, *Iran-Iraq War and Western Security*, pp. 144–156; Cordesman and Wagner, *Iran-Iraq War*, p. 413.

91. Pelletiere, *Iran-Iraq War*, p. xiv.

92. Pelletiere and Johnson, *Lessons Learned*, p. 61.

93. Pelletiere, *Iran-Iraq War*, p. xiv.

94. Pelletiere and Johnson, *Lessons Learned*, p. 62.

95. James A. Blackwell, *Thunder in the Desert: The Strategy and Tactics of the Persian Gulf War* (New York: Bantam, 1991), pp. xxxiii, 2, 27, 213.

96. Cordesman, *Iran-Iraq War and Western Security*, pp. 148–149; Jupa and Dingeman, "How Iran Lost/Iraq Won the Gulf War," p. 49.

97. Herzog, "Military-Strategic Overview," p. 268.

7. The U.S. Army

1. Russell F. Weigley, *The American Way of War: A History of United States Military Strategy and Policy* (Bloomington: Indiana University Press, 1973), p. xxii.

2. Ibid., Chapter 7, "A Strategy of Annihilation: U. S. Grant and the Union," pp. 128–152. The extract is from page 145.

3. J. F. C. Fuller, *Grant and Lee: A Study in Personality and Generalship* (Bloomington: Indiana University Press, 1957), p. 182.

4. The prospect of a U.S.-Soviet confrontation produced a characteristic literary form: the future history novel. See, for example, General Sir John Hackett et al., *The Third World War: August 1985* (New York: Macmillan, 1978), a strategic, operational, and tactical analysis of a future U.S.-Soviet conflict in novel form, written by one of the twentieth century's foremost soldier-scholars and "other top-ranking NATO generals and advisors"; Kenneth Macksey, *First Clash: Combat Close-up in World War III* (Toronto: Stoddart, 1984), describing the trials of the 4th Canadian Mechanized Brigade in the event of a war in Europe; Harold Coyle, *Team Yankee: A Novel of World War III* (Novato, Calif.: Presidio, 1987), about the battlefield experience of an American tank-heavy combat team in West Germany in the context of the future universe first created by Hackett's *Third World War*; and, first in sales if not necessarily in literary grace, Tom Clancy, *Red Storm Rising* (New York: Putnam, 1986). All these novels feature detailed accounts of hardware and much inadvertently hilarious dialog. For nonfictional discussions of the "next war," see Laurence Martin, *Before the Day After: Can NATO Defend Europe* (Feltham, Middlesex: Newnes Books, 1985), and Elmar Dinter and Paddy Griffith, *Not Over by Christmas: NATO's Central Front in World War III* (New York: Hippocrene, 1983), an analysis that, like all Griffith's work, is highly idiosyncratic, alternately brilliant and infuriating.

5. One could fashion a history of thinking about World War III by analyzing the hundreds of war games ("conflict simulations" to many of their owners) that were produced from the 1970s to the early 1990s. There were three major companies through much of the period: Avalon Hill (AH) in Baltimore, Maryland; Simulations Publications, Inc. (SPI) in New York; and Game Designers Workshop (GDW) in Bloomington, Illinois. The latter two companies, SPI in particular, led the way in designing games on NATO-Pact conflict, many of them distributed through SPI's magazine *Strategy and Tactics (S&T)*, a bimonthly journal that included a simulation game. It had among its staff a number of individuals who have gone on to establish themselves as respected military analysts, working for both civilian and government think tanks: James F. Dunnigan, David C. Isby, Albert A. Nofi, and many others. See in particular the games of the "Central Front" series starting in *S&T* 82, Septem-

ber–October 1980 ("Fifth Corps: The Soviet Breakthrough at Fulda," designed by Dunnigan); *S&T* 88, September–October 1981 ("BAOR: The Thin Red Line in the 1980s," designed by Charles T. Kamps, Jr.); *S&T* 117, February 1988 ("North German Plain," by Kamps), and *S&T* 131, November–December 1989 ("Donau Front," by Kamps); *S&T* 79, March–April 1980, contains a game dealing with the fighting in Berlin in the context of World War III, "Berlin '85: Enemy at the Gates," designed by Dunnigan, David Ritchie, and Redmond A. Simonsen.

6. For these figures, see the *Soviet Military Power* booklets, issued by the U.S. Department of Defense in September 1981 and March 1983. Glossy, fully illustrated, and free to the public, they played a part in publicizing the Reagan administration's case for a military buildup. See, specifically, *Soviet Military Power* 1983, pp. 62–63. Critics at the time, not least the Soviet government, accused them of exaggeration. It issued a rejoinder in the form of the booklet *Whence the Threat to Peace?* (Moscow: Military Publishing House, 1982). *Soviet Military Power 1982*, for example, contained what proved to be a highly inaccurate artist's rendering of the new Soviet T-80 tank; the real thing was little more than a slightly tweaked T-72.

7. Dinter and Griffith, *Not Home by Christmas*, pp. 45–46, discuss the "three-to-one" ratio. Borrowing from the work of F. W. Lanchester, they argue that a true ratio of combat forces is the square of their strength. Thus a Pact quantitative superiority over NATO of 7:3, for instance, is actually a force ratio of 49:9, a much greater advantage to the Pact.

8. For the problems of NATO reinforcement of Germany, see Martin, *Before the Day After*, pp. 51–56. For the 1983 REFORGER, see the account from General Frederick Franks, then-commander of the 11th Armored Cavalry Regiment, Blackhorse, in Tom Clancy, with General Fred Franks, *Into the Storm: A Study in Command* (New York: Putnam, 1997), pp. 110–112. Clancy and Franks have produced a useful book, particularly in those sections in which Franks is speaking directly.

9. The cannon was the GAU8/A, which fires 30mm depleted-uranium armor-piercing shells, twice as heavy as lead. See Jon Connell, *The New Maginot Line* (London: Secker and Warburg, 1986), pp. 49–50.

10. Clancy and Franks, *Into the Storm*, p. 166.

11. Arrian, *The Campaigns of Alexander* (New York: Penguin, 1982), p. 112.

12. For a good analysis of the opening moves of a Warsaw Pact invasion, see Charles T. Kamps, Jr., "The Central Front: The Status of Forces in Europe and the Potential for Conflict," *Strategy and Tactics* 82, September–October 1980, pp. 4–14, especially pp. 10–11. See also Hackett et al., *Third World War*, pp. 101–103, for a hypothetical Soviet operational plan, and pp. 148–173 for the first eight days of operations.

13. See Charles T. Kamps, Jr., "The Next War: Modern Conflict in Europe," *Strategy and Tactics* 69, July–August 1978, pp. 15–20, 25–35, including extremely detailed orders of battle for NATO and the Pact.

14. For the Fulda Gap, see Kamps, "The Central Front," pp. 4–10, including a "skeleton order of battle, Fulda Gap battle area" (p. 8). See also the war-gaming journal *Counterattack* 1, October 1987: Bill Gibbs, "Modern Combat Doctrine," pp. 5–18; Henry Cord Meyer III with John Burtt, "The Bundeswehr: Mission, Organization,

Doctrine," pp. 19–24; Owen Stanley, "Soviet Conventional Combat Philosophy," pp. 52–62; and Michael Bennighof, "Wiedervereinigungskrieg" pp. 63–64.

15. For an analysis of a possible Soviet thrust into southern Germany, see Charles T. Kamps, Jr., "Ardennes of the '90s: The Bavarian Option in the Next War," *Strategy and Tactics* 131, November–December 1989, pp. 17–24, 42–46.

16. For a Bornholm or Hamburg grab, see Dinter and Griffith, *Not Over by Christmas*, p. 17.

17. See Kerry Pendergast and David Ritchie, "Berlin '85: The Enemy at the Gates," *Strategy and Tactics* 79, March–April 1980, p. 8.

18. The main peddler of Spetsnaz fear in the west was Soviet defector Viktor Rezun, who wrote under the pseudonym "Viktor Suvorov." See his *Inside the Soviet Army* (New York: Macmillan, 1982), pp. 75–77, and "Spetsnaz: The Soviet Union's Special Forces," *Military Review* 64, no. 3, March 1984, pp. 30–46.

19. This is the line taken by Hackett et al., *Third World War*, in which the U.S. refusal to use nuclear weapons, even in the face of demands from the "men on the spot," is crucial to the final NATO victory. Nuclear weapons do play a role in Hackett's universe. Once they are forced to the defensive, and NATO is approaching the East German border, the Soviets destroy Birmingham, England, with a single "warning shot"; Hackett and team then have the United States and Great Britain even up the score by incinerating Minsk, of all places, as a way to loosen the bonds of loyalty among the subject nationalities to Moscow. Minsk, of course, is the historic capital of the Byelorussian people and is today the capital of independent Belarus. See *Third World War*, Chapter 25, "The Destruction of Birmingham" (pp. 287–303) and Chapter 28, "A Devastating Response" (pp. 304–309).

20. No one will ever accuse the Vietnam conflict of being a "forgotten war." The literature on the war as a whole is enormous, and its major battles are beginning to accumulate impressive canons of their own. Begin by consulting The Edwin E. Moïse Vietnam War Bibliography, a comprehensive online resource located at http://hub cap.clemson.edu/~eemoise/bibliography.html. Moïse is a leading scholar on the war and most recently the editor of *Historical Dictionary of the Vietnam War* (Lanham, Md.: Scarecrow Press [Rowman & Littlefield], 2001). For Khe Sanh, start with the exhaustive work by John Prados and Ray W. Stubbe, *Valley of Decision: The Siege of Khe Sanh* (Boston: Houghton Mifflin, 1991). The authors are somewhat of an odd couple, Prados a well-respected military analyst who knows operations as well as anyone, Stubbe a veteran of the Khe Sanh fighting and the Lutheran chaplain of the 1st Battalion, 26th Marines. The result is a unique book that alternates between hardcore operational details and a haunting search to derive some spiritual meaning from the chaos. It even ends with an "Amen." The book also contains new maps, the most accurate yet drawn of the battlefield. It is hard to argue with the review by Douglas Porch, *Journal of Military History* 57, no. 1, January 1993, pp. 180–181, which compares the book to Bernard Fall's classic account of the battle of Dien Bien Phu, *Hell in a Very Small Place* (Philadelphia: Lippincott, 1967). Still useful, and still the most widely read book on the battle, is Robert Pisor, *The End of the Line: The Siege of Khe Sanh* (New York: Ballantine, 1982); it is popular history, with long, rambling excur-

sions into the life of General Westmoreland, General Giap, the "dark-skinned, prim-itive" montagnard peoples (p. 85), and the trials of Felix Poilane, French planter in the Khe Sanh region. Like all books on Khe Sanh, Pisor's has to work around the fact that the "main event," as it were, a North Vietnamese army assault on the base, never happened; the excursions pad the work to book length. For a short survey of issues related to the siege, see Peter Brush, "The Battle of Khe Sanh, 1968," in *The Tet Offensive*, ed. Marc Jason Gilbert and William Head (Westport, Conn.: Praeger, 1996), pp. 191–213. General William C. Westmoreland has told his side of the story in *A Soldier Reports* (Garden City, N.Y.: Doubleday, 1976). Official U.S. military publications contain a great deal of useful information as well as huge blind spots. See General Willard Pearson, *The War in the Northern Provinces, 1966–1968* (Wash-ington, D.C.: Department of the Army, 1975); General John J. Tolson, *Airmobility, 1961–1971* (Washington, D.C.: Department of the Army, 1973), both part of the *Vietnam Studies* series. Most of the series is available online at the Center of Mili-tary History website, located at www.army.mil/cmh-pg. For the crucial role played by airpower, see Bernard C. Nalty, *Air Power and the Fight for Khe Sanh* (Washing-ton, D.C.: Office of Air Force History, 1973).

21. For Lang Vei, see William R. Philips, *Night of the Silver Stars: The Battle of Lang Vei* (Annapolis, Md.: Naval Institute Press, 1997). For the tank attack, see pp. 73–96.

22. Nalty, *Air Power and the Fight for Khe Sanh*, pp. 42–59.

23. For LAPES and its related "Ground Proximity Extraction System" (GPES), see Prados and Stubbe, *Valley of Decision*, pp. 376–379; Pearson, *The War in the North-ern Provinces*, pp. 75–76; Nalty, *Air Power and the Fight for Khe Sanh*, pp. 51–53.

24. For the argument over appointing a single manager, see Prados and Stubbe, *Valley of Decision*, pp. 383–386; Nalty, *Air Power and the Fight for Khe Sanh*, pp. 68–81. See also Faris R. Kirkland, "The Attack on Cap Mui Lay, Vietnam, July 1968," *Jour-nal of Military History* 61, no. 4, October 1997, pp. 738–739.

25. Nalty, *Air Power and the Fight for Khe Sanh*, pp. 82–88. The details of the grid system are discussed on pp. 82–83.

26. Quoted in Prados and Stubbe, *Valley of Decision*, p. 409.

27. Most recently, in Cecil B. Currey, *Victory at Any Cost: The Genius of Viet Nam's General Vo Nguyen Giap* (McLean, Va.: Brassey's, 1997). According to Currey, Giap opposed the 1968 Tet offensive, believing that NVA forces were not ready for large-scale offensive operations, but was overruled by other senior party members. But see the judgments on Giap's handling of Khe Sanh in Pisor, *End of the Line*, pp. 264–267. One extremely important development is the start of investigation into the heretofore unavailable North Vietnamese sources. See Ang Cheng Guan, "Khe Sanh — From the Perspective of the North Vietnamese Communists," *War in His-tory* 8, no. 1, January 2001, pp. 87–98.

28. Hue has gotten a fair amount of attention in the literature, but not as much as it deserves. Start with two works: Keith Nolan, *Battle for Hue, Tet 1968* (Novato, Calif.: Presidio, 1978), and Eric Hammel, *Fire in the Streets: The Battle for Hue, Tet 1968* (Chicago: Contemporary Books, 1991). Both are popular works that are also grounded thoroughly in the documents, as well as in numerous interviews with par-

ticipants in the battle, and both focus on the "grunt's-eye" view of the fight. Nolan bases his work on interviews with thirty-six participants. Hammel goes even further. Like all his numerous books (he has written more than a dozen on topics as varied as the Chosin reservoir campaign in the Korean War to the Golan Heights in the 1973 Arab-Israeli War), *Fire in the Streets* is based on "voluminous taped and written exchanges between the author and ninety-one survivors of the Hue fighting" (p. 356). Although a scholar can wish that Hammel had attributed every quote in his book with a careful citation, his work reminds us that military historians ignore popular history at their peril. The historiography of Hue has also benefited from having one of the few historical monographs devoted to the role of ARVN. See George W. Smith, *The Siege at Hue* (Boulder, Colo.: Lynne Rienner, 1999). Smith was a U.S. Army information officer attached to the ARVN 1st Infantry Division. He worked closely with divisional commander General Ngo Quang Truong and Captain Tran Ngoc Hue (the latter commanding the Hac Bao, or "Black Panther" company, ARVN's elite fighting unit), and maintained his relationship with both until the present. He arranged a visit with both men in March 1997, a truly poignant moment in the book. See also issues 2–7 of *The First and the Finest*, the newsletter of the U.S. Advisory Team, MACV, which contain a serialized article by Smith, "The Battle of Hue." Copies of the newsletter are on file in the U.S. Army Military History Institute at Carlisle Barracks in Carlisle, Pennsylvania. See the other pertinent official sources, especially Pearson, *The War in the Northern Provinces, 1966–1968*, pp. 39–48. Shorter pieces include Frederick F. Irving, "The Battle of Hue," *Military Review* 49, no. 1, January 1969, pp. 56–63; Jon E. Tellier, "The Battle for Hue," *Infantry* 85, no. 4, July–August 1995, pp. 21–26; and James J. Wirtz, "The Battles for Saigon and Hue: Tet 1968," in *Soldiers in Cities: Military Operations on Urban Terrain*, ed. Michael C. Desch (Carlisle, Pa.: Strategic Studies Institute, 2001), pp. 75–87. Finally, Nicholas Warr, *Phase Line Green* (Annapolis, Md.: Naval Institute Press, 1998), although containing some interesting information on the battle, is a strange book, written by a still-troubled platoon commander who fought with the 1st Battalion, 5th Marines, and who years later realized that his wartime experience was "haunting" him and that he had "to write it all down as a form of therapy" (p. x); like any such book, it is difficult to read. Warr feels that his unit was let down by virtually every officer above company level in the course of the fighting. See the review, shockingly ad hominem, by Merrill Bartlett in *Journal of Military History* 62, no. 1, January 1998, pp. 228–231, who describes the book as being "loaded with carping invective" against all and sundry, and who says that the author "should have been 'relieved for cause' and sent to the rear with an unsatisfactory fitness report" (p. 229). For a more sympathetic reading, see Smith, *Siege at Hue*, pp. 136–137.

29. Hammel, *Fire in the Streets*, pp. 17–18, Smith, *Siege at Hue*, pp. 19–20, and Pearson, *The War in the Northern Provinces*, pp. 40–41, all identify Truong's decision as a key factor in the eventual victory of U.S./ARVN forces in Hue. Holding onto the compound was crucial for the later battle to take the Citadel. As Warr, *Phase Line Green*, points out, possession of the compound meant that the marines were already inside the Citadel: "If we had been forced to attack the enemy from the outside of the

Citadel, we would have paid a terrible price just to get inside" (p. 211). General Schwarzkopf knew Truong in Vietnam and calls him "the most brilliant tactical commander" he had ever known. See H. Norman Schwarzkopf (with Peter Petre), *It Doesn't Take a Hero: The Autobiography* (New York: Bantam, 1992), p. 122.

30. See Smith, *Siege at Hue*, pp. 23–28, for the adventures of the Hac Bao in the early hours of the fighting in Hue.

31. For MACV's travails, see Hammel, *Fire in the Streets*, pp. 39–41 and 59–60, and Smith, *Siege at Hue*, pp. 31–42.

32. Pearson, *The War in the Northern Provinces*, p. 48; Smith, *Siege at Hue*, pp. ix–x, describes the exhumation of a mass grave.

33. A constant problem for the 1st Cavalry Division in Vietnam. See the review by James L. Collins, Jr., of Shelby Stanton, *Anatomy of a Division: The 1st Cav in Vietnam* (Novato, Calif.: Presidio, 1987) in *Military Affairs* 52, no. 3, July 1988, p. 162. Collins points out that "the helicopter authorization of the 1st Cavalry Division was sufficient to move only a third of the fighting men at one time."

34. For Lieutenant Colonel Sweet and the 2/12, see Hammel, *Fire in the Streets*, pp. 192–204; Smith, *Siege at Hue*, pp. 91–94; as well as Charles A. Krohn, *The Lost Battalion: Controversy and Casualties in the Battle of Hue* (Westport, Conn.: Praeger, 1993).

35. The best account of 5/7 in the T-T woods is Hammel, *Fire in the Streets*, pp. 308–334.

36. Smith, *Siege at Hue*, pp. 134–137.

37. This is Warr's point of view, expressed strongly in *Phase Line Green;* he was the commander of Charlie Company, 1/5.

38. Nolan, *Battle for Hue*, for example, rarely mentions ARVN at all, and when he does, he usually portrays them in a derogatory way: looting (pp. 86–88, 172), "sitting and watching" while the marines had to "do the ARVN's job for them" (p. 163), "spectators" in the battle to deliver their own city (p. 172). A notable exception is his portrayal of the Black Panthers (p. 171).

39. Operation Pegasus has, as yet, no exclusively dedicated monograph; it deserves one. The genesis and course of the operation is ably described in Prados and Stubbe, *Valley of Decision*, pp. 417–449. The primary source, and a highly useful one, is Tolson, *Airmobility*, written by the commander of the 1st Cavalry Division in Pegasus; see also Pearson, *The War in the Northern Provinces*, pp. 73–92. Two other works help inform on Pegasus: Stanton, *Anatomy of a Division*, and J. D. Coleman, *Pleiku: The Dawn of Helicopter Warfare in Vietnam* (New York: St. Martin's, 1988). The latter analyzes the operations of 1st Cavalry Division at Pleiku (or the "Ia Drang campaign"); although it is a good operational history of a particular campaign, much of the book is written in a style so enthusiastically breathless that it skirts the line between history and cheerleading on numerous occasions; the prologue (pp. 1–11) and the opening chapter (pp. 12–13) are particularly egregious. The Ia Drang was a particularly hard fought campaign in which 1st Cavalry Division took very heavy losses; the fact that the division won a Presidential Unit Citation for the fight is not evidence that it was a victory. Nevertheless, it offers much food for thought on the concept of airmobility and its legacy on later army doctrine; see especially "In the

Final Analysis," pp. 267–273. The author was in the division and wrote the combat operations after-action report for Pleiku, as well as the recommendation for the presidential citation. Also worthy of consulting is the unpublished dissertation by Robert L. Towles, "The Tears of Autumn: Air Assault Operations and Infantry Combat in the Ia Drang Valley, Vietnam, November 1965" (Kent, Ohio: Kent State University, 2000), and the monograph by Peter J. Schifferle, "The Ia Drang Campaign 1965: A Successful Operational Campaign or Mere Tactical Failure?" (Ft. Leavenworth, Kans.: School of Advanced Military Studies, 1994).

40. Tolson, *Airmobility*, p. 170.

41. Ibid., pp. 176–177.

42. Quoted in Prados and Stubbe, *Valley of Decision*, p. 437.

43. Douglas Kinnard, *The War Managers* (Hanover, N.H.: University Press of New England, 1977).

44. Richard A. Gabriel and Paul L. Savage, *Crisis in Command: Mismanagement in the Army* (New York: Hill and Wang, 1978).

45. "Cincinnatus," *Self-Destruction: The Disintegration and Decay of the United States Army During the Vietnam Era* (New York: Norton, 1981).

46. See the contending reviews on Cincinnatus's work in Richard A. Gabriel and Alan Gropman, "Cincinnatus Inside Out: Parts I and II," in *Air University Review*, July–August 1981, available online at www.airpower.au.af.mil/airchronicles/aureview/1981/jul-aug/gropman.htm.

47. "Cincinnatus," *Self-Destruction*, p. 71.

48. See, for example, Paul Cate, "Large-Unit Operational Doctrine," *Military Review* 58, no. 12, December 1978, pp. 40–47.

49. See John L. Romjue, *From Active Defense to AirLand Battle: The Development of Army Doctrine, 1973–1982* (Ft. Monroe, Va.: TRADOC, 1984), especially the February 1976 note from General DePuy to General Fred Weyand, U.S. Army Chief of Staff (pp. 82–86).

50. *Field Manual (FM) 100-5*, "Operations" (Washington, D.C.: Department of the Army, 1976), pp. i and 1-1.

51. Ibid., pp. 3-5 to 3-9.

52. Ibid., p. 4-3.

53. Romjue, *From Active Defense to AirLand Battle*, pp. 9–10.

54. Archer Jones, "The New FM 100-5: A View from the Ivory Tower," *Military Review* 58, no. 2, February 1978, p. 27.

55. For the hostile reception of DePuy's manual, see Romjue, *From Active Defense to AirLand Battle*, pp. 13–21.

56. William S. Lind, "Some Doctrinal Questions for the U.S. Army," *Military Review* 57, no. 3, March 1977, pp. 54–65.

57. Ibid., pp. 57–58.

58. See, for example, the hilarious recent article by Steven Eden, a lieutenant colonel, a respected military historian, and the commander of the 3rd Battalion, 81st Armor, "Three Cheers for Attrition Warfare," *Armor* 111, no. 2, March–April 2002, pp. 29–31, the correspondence it generated in the *Armor* 111, no. 4, July–August

2002 issue, and the response by Lieutenant Colonel Ernest A. Szabo, "Attrition vs. Maneuver and the Future of War," *Armor* 111, no. 5, September–October 2002, pp. 39–41. See John F. Antal, "Maneuver Versus Attrition: A Historical Perspective," *Military Review* 72, No. 10, October 1992, pp. 21–33, for a good discussion of the issues involved, as well as William S. Lind, who started it all, "The Theory and Practice of Maneuver Warfare," in *Maneuver Warfare, an Anthology*, ed. Richard D. Hooker, Jr. (Novato, Calif.: Presidio, 1993), pp. 3–18. Ten years later, the terms are still controversial, what the Germans call *Schlagworte* (slogans). For a sensible alternative — one that thoughtful officers suggested when the argument first began — see James R. McDonough, "The Operational Art: Quo Vadis?" in Hooker, *Maneuver Warfare*, especially pp. 110–112. He argues the "false dichotomy" of fire versus maneuver and the way that maneuver warfare has become for many the "Holy Grail" of land warfare, "distinguished in some circles by its capitalization as 'Maneuver Warfare,' an almost mystical beknighting (via English grammar) of an otherwise common — and useful — concept" (p. 111). In this he echoes one of AirLand Battle's original doctrinal writers. See Huba Wass de Czege, "Army Doctrinal Reform," in *The Defense Reform Debate*, ed. Asa Clark (Baltimore, Md.: Johns Hopkins University Press, 1984), pp. 101–120. For more on maneuver and its new importance to the U.S. Army in the early 1980s, see also Anthony M. Coroalles, "Maneuver to Win: A Realistic Alternative," *Military Review* 61, no. 9, September 1981, pp. 35–46; and by the same author, "Implementing a Maneuver Style of War," *Military Review* 62, no. 12, December 1982, pp. 20–25; as well as L. D. Holder, "Maneuver in the Deep Battle," *Military Review* 62, no. 5, May 1982, pp. 54–61.

59. Lind, "Some Doctrinal Questions," p. 57.

60. Jonathan M. House, *Combined Arms Warfare in the Twentieth Century* (Lawrence: University Press of Kansas, 2001), p. 239. This is very much the point of view taken by Paul H. Herbert, "Deciding What Has to Be Done: General William E. DePuy and the 1976 Edition of FM 100-5, Operations," *Leavenworth Paper* no. 16 (Ft. Leavenworth, Kans.: Combat Studies Institute, 1988). Herbert is the only thinker to examine closely the influence of the German Bundeswehr, with its insistence on a forward defense and its proscriptions against "aggressive" warfare, on DePuy's doctrinal line. See pp. 61–68.

61. See Connell, *The New Maginot Line*, pp. 103–104, and Romjue, *From Active Defense to AirLand Battle*, pp. 16–17. See also the two-part article by Philip A. Karber, "The Tactical Revolution in Soviet Military Doctrine," *Military Review* 57, nos. 11–12, November–December 1977, pp. 83–85, 33–34.

62. Connell, *The New Maginot Line*, p. 104.

63. For the evolution of "seeing deep," see, among others, Donn A. Starry, "Extending the Battlefield," *Military Review* 61, no. 3, March 1981, pp. 31–50; C. Lanier Deal, Jr., "BAI: The Key to the Deep Battle," *Military Review* 62, no. 3, March 1982, pp. 51–54; and Holder, "Maneuver in the Deep Battle." For the impact of new technology, see Michael Clarke, "AirLand Battle and the Application of New Technology," in *New Conventional Weapons and Western Defence*, ed. Ian Bellamy and Tim Huxley (London: Frank Cass, 1987), pp. 151–161.

64. See House, *Combined Arms Warfare*, p. 251.

65. An idea associated with Colonel John Boyd of the U.S. Army, who coined the concept of an "OODA (*O*bserve, *O*rient, *D*ecide, *A*ct) loop" as the basis for combat interaction. Boyd delivered his 327-slide briefing, named "Patterns of Conflict," more than 1,500 times during his career. It was highly influential on maneuver warfare advocates like William S. Lind. See Ricky L. Waddell, "Maneuver Warfare and Low-Intensity Conflict," in *Maneuver Warfare: An Anthology*, pp. 121–122, and William S. Lind, *Maneuver Warfare Handbook* (Boulder, Colo.: Westview Press, 1985), pp. 4–6. See Grant T. Hammond, *The Mind of War: John Boyd and American Security* (Washington, D.C.: Smithsonian Institution Press, 2001).

66. A representative example is Stephen W. Richey, "Auftragstaktik, Schwerpunkt, Aufrollen: The Philosophical Basis of the AirLand Battle," *Military Review* 64, no. 5, May 1984, pp. 48–53.

67. See James S. Corum, "Evolution of US Army Doctrine and Current Trends: A Return to Doctrinal Roots," *New Zealand Army Journal*, no. 23, July 2000.

68. Quoted in Clarke, "AirLand Battle and the Application of New Technology," p. 4. See also Jones, "FM 100-5: A View from the Ivory Tower," pp. 17–22.

69. *Field Manual (FM) 100-5*, "Operations" (Washington, D.C.: Department of the Army, 1982), pp. 1-5, 4-1; quoted in Romjue, *From Active Defense to AirLand Battle*, p. 67.

70. *FM 100-5*, "Operations" (1982), p. 2-1; quoted in Romjue, *From Active Defense to AirLand Battle*, p. 68.

71. See Robert A. Doughty, "The Evolution of U.S. Army Tactical Doctrine, 1946–76," *Leavenworth Paper* no. 1 (Ft. Leavenworth, Kans.: Combat Studies Institute, 1979). See also the very perceptive article, published just after Vietnam, by Ravi Rikhye, "U.S. Army Shifts to Armour Warfare," *Journal of the Royal United Service Institution of India* 105, no. 439, April–June 1975, pp. 147–158.

72. Starry was the author of *Mounted Combat in Vietnam* (Washington, D.C.: Department of the Army, 1978), part of the *Vietnam Studies* series, a fascinating monograph in light of later doctrinal developments and Starry's key role in generating them.

8. The U.S. Army at War

1. For the "big five," see Frank N. Schubert and Theresa L. Krauss, eds., *The Whirlwind War: The United States Army in Operations Desert Shield and Desert Storm* (Washington, D.C.: Center of Military History, 1995), pp. 28–33.

2. General Sir John Hackett et al., *The Third World War: August 1985* (New York: Macmillan, 1978).

3. Hackett, *Third World War*, pp. 21–22.

4. "Viktor Suvorov," *Inside the Soviet Army* (New York: Macmillan, 1982). Suvorov's actual name is Viktor Rezun. See David M. Glantz, *Stumbling Colossus: The Red Army on the Eve of World War* (Lawrence: University Press of Kansas, 1998), pp. 3–8.

5. "Suvorov," *Inside the Soviet Army*, p. 161.

6. Ibid., pp. 165–166.

7. Ibid., p. 167.

8. See two works by TRADOC historian Anne W. Chapman, *The Army's Training Revolution, 1973–1990: An Overview* (Ft. Monroe, Va.: TRADOC, 1994) and *The Origins and Development of the National Training Center, 1976–1984* (Ft. Monroe, Va.: TRADOC, 1997).

9. James R. McDonough, *The Defense of Hill 781: An Allegory of Modern Mechanized Combat* (Novato, Calif.: Presidio, 1988), p. 18.

10. Chapman, *National Training Center*, pp. 85–87.

11. Ibid., p. 88.

12. For air assault, see Christopher J. Petty, "Operation Genesis: The Birth of OPFOR Air Assault at the National Training Center," *U.S. Army Aviation Digest*, September–October 1990, pp. 20–23; for the Apaches, see Mark Swanson, "Apaches in the Desert," *U.S. Army Aviation Digest*, September–October 1990, pp. 24–29.

13. Chapman, *National Training Center*, p. 88.

14. Ibid., p. 90. See also Quinn G. Johnson, "They All Hate the Bad Guys of NTC's Mojave," *Army* 37, no. 6, June 1987, pp. 42–49; Dennis Steele, "The OPFOR: Friend and Foe," *Army* 38, no. 12, December 1988, pp. 28–32; and William H. McMichael, "NTC's OPFOR: More Than Home Field Advantage," *Soldiers* 45, no. 3, March 1990, pp. 6–11.

15. McDonough, *Defense of Hill 781*, p. 12.

16. Ibid., pp. 22–23.

17. Ibid., pp. 12–13.

18. See Mark P. Hertling and James Boisselle, "Coming of Age in the Desert: The NTC at 120," *Military Review* 81, no. 5, September–October 2001, pp. 64–71. Colonel Hertling is the commander of the Operations Group, NTC, Ft. Irwin; Lieutenant Colonel Boisselle, his chief of plans. The extract is taken from pp. 66–67.

19. For the BCTP, see Chapman, *The Army's Training Revolution*, p. 26. Tom Clancy with General Fred Franks, Jr., *Into the Storm: A Study in Command* (New York: Putnam, 1997). Pp. 99–104 contain a first-person account of a BCTP-Warfighter exercise from General Franks's days as commander of the 1st Armored Division.

20. Chapman, *The Army's Training Revolution*, pp. 27–30, 44–45.

21. Operation Desert Storm has passed through a number of stages in terms of historiography. There were the "instant works" generated in the immediate wake of the conflict, virtually all of which had a highly positive, even adulatory tone, toward the U.S. effort in the Gulf. See, for example, James Blackwell, *Thunder in the Desert: The Strategy and Tactics of the Persian Gulf War* (New York: Bantam, 1991); Norman Friedman, *Desert Victory, the War for Kuwait* (Annapolis, Md.: Naval Institute Press, 1991); James F. Dunnigan and Austin Bay, *From Shield to Storm: High-Tech Weapons, Military Strategy, and Coalition Warfare in the Persian Gulf* (New York: William Morrow, 1992); and Harry Summers, *On Strategy II: A Critical Analysis of the Gulf War* (New York: Dell Paperback, 1992). None have worn particularly well, and Summers's entry least of all, castigated by one respected analyst as reflecting "no research

base whatever" and having "as much to say about the author's well-known views on the Vietnam War as it did the war in the Persian Gulf." See Richard M. Swain, *"Lucky War": Third Army in Desert Storm* (Ft. Leavenworth, Kans.: U.S. Army Command and General Staff College Press, 1997), p. 365. Blackwell's entry combines solid narration, a good bit of shameless cheerleading, and numerous paeans of praise to the Iraqi army, the last as a means of making the Coalition victory look as grand as possible. One early book that merits some praise, despite the inevitable errors, is *U.S. News and World Report, Triumph Without Victory: The Unreported History of the Gulf War* (New York: Random House-Times Books, 1992). As is clear from the title, it signaled the start of the "morning after" effect, with Saddam in power and the Coalition victory no longer looking so complete; it errs, unfortunately, in placing its emphasis on the U.S. 24th Division, which, after all, functioned mainly as a flank guard on VII Corps's left. Other early works included Lawrence Freedman and Efraim Karsh, *The Gulf Conflict 1990–1991: Diplomacy and War in the New World Order* (Princeton, N.J.: Princeton University Press, 1993), a scholarly analysis of the war's politics and strategy, and Jeffrey Record, *Hollow Victory: A Contrary View of the Gulf War* (McLean, Va.: Brassey's, 1993). Record's work continued the revision of opinion regarding the achievements of the war, pointing out how little it had taught about two key issues: the patience of the U.S. public for protracted conflict with higher casualties, and the "military stamina" of the all-volunteer force (p. 136). Mohamed Heikal, *Illusions of Triumph: An Arab View of the Gulf War* (New York: HarperCollins, 1992) offers a very different pattern of analysis than what most Americans read in their media and for that reason is highly recommended. "The defeat of a Third World army by vastly better-equipped forces could not be compared with the Allied victory over Germany," he argues (p. 316). The work by Rick Atkinson, *Crusade: The Untold Story of the Persian Gulf War* (Boston: Houghton Mifflin, 1993) is the best of the journalistic accounts, although it starts with the shooting, missing the long months of buildup that went before. Finally, the culmination point of the early works is the autobiography of H. Norman Schwarzkopf, written with Peter Petre, *It Doesn't Take a Hero: The Autobiography* (New York: Bantam, 1992). Like its subject, it is oversized, filled with energy, and overflowing with ego; in that sense, it is the perfect autobiography. Most interesting to readers was the animus that Schwarzkopf held toward General Frederick Franks, his VII Corps commander. After the initial spate of works, there was an "operational pause" in the literature, and by 1994, there were already comments that "the Gulf War of 1990–91 has disappeared from public view rather quickly given the extraordinary enthusiasm for anything in desert tan in the spring of 1991." See Richard Swain's review of Freedman/Karsh and Record in *Journal of Military History* 58, no. 1, January 1994, p. 176. By 1998, Alberto Bin, Richard Hill, and Archer Jones published a book called *Desert Storm: A Forgotten War* (Westport, Conn.: Praeger, 1998), thereby resurrecting the hoariest cliché in the military history lexicon. Much of the book consists of huge extracts from first-person testimony, surprising in a work written seven years after the event. Other works of interest cover specific parts of the campaign. James J. Cooke, *100 Miles from Baghdad: With the French in Desert Storm* (Westport, Conn.:

Praeger, 1993) is the account of a U.S. academic and National Guard officer attached to the French Division Daguet; his description of French rations on pp. 48–49 is unforgettable; a marine has his say in Sean T. Coughlin, *Storming the Desert: A Marine Lieutenant's Day-by-Day Chronicle of the Persian Gulf War* (Jefferson, N.C.: McFarland, 1996); the airborne divisions are the subject of Dominic J. Caraccilo, *The Ready Brigade of the 82nd Airborne in Desert Storm: A Combat Memoir by the Headquarters Company Commander* (Jefferson, N.C.: McFarland, 1993) and Edward M. Flanagan, *Lightning: The 101st in the Gulf War* (Washington, D.C.: Brassey's, 1994); for the armor experience, see Alex Vernon, *The Eyes of Orion: Five Tank Lieutenants in the Persian Gulf War* (Kent, Ohio: Kent State University Press, 1999). The official works are indispensable: *The Conduct of the Persian Gulf War: Final Report to Congress Pursuant to Title V of the Persian Gulf Conflict Supplemental Authorization and Personnel Benefits Act of 1991 (Public Law 102-25)*, issued by the Office of the Secretary of Defense in 1992, is massive, comprehensive, and glossy; Schubert and Krauss, *The Whirlwind War* is a shorter, leaner version, but just as handsome; Robert H. Scales, Jr., *Certain Victory: The U.S. Army in the Gulf War* (Washington, D.C.: Brassey's, 1994) is relatively jargon free and intended for the public as well as the military; Perry D. Jamieson's long-awaited air force history, *Lucrative Targets: The U.S. Air Force in the Kuwaiti Theater of Operations* (Washington, D.C.: Air Force History and Museums Program, 2001) is lean and well argued. Finally, special mention is due to two works. Michael R. Gordon and Bernard E. Trainor, *The Generals' War: The Inside Story of the Conflict in the Gulf* (Boston: Little, Brown, 1995) is a fine analysis, buttressed by the authors' numerous contacts in the government and defense establishment. They focus carefully on the abortive Iraqi attack on Khafji as being of crucial importance to the way the U.S. offensive played out: it stimulated the marines into expanding the scope of their "diversionary" effort in the east, forced Schwarzkopf to launch VII Corps prematurely, and thus completely unhinged Desert Storm. Swain, *"Lucky War,"* is an official history written by the command historian of the 3rd Army. It provides the missing link. So much has been written on Schwarzkopf, the theater commander, as well as the various corps commanders; Swain has finally described the role of 3rd Army and its commander, General Yeosock, to whom he credits a great deal of the operation's success. His work is generally a model of how to strike the difficult balance between official history and critical analysis; one negative is his constant carping against military theory in general and the School of Advanced Military Studies in particular, what Swain calls the "red-stripe fraternity," an evil cabal with an "often-scholastic approach to operations" that, he argues, dominated army planning (p. 206). It may be true — if so, he needs to develop these arguments more systematically in another book.

22. Blackwell, *Thunder in the Desert*, p. 69.

23. David H. Hackworth, a well-known military analyst, called Desert Storm "the mother of all military anomalies. It was a war unto itself, not a model for the future." See "Lessons of a Lucky War," *Newsweek*, March 11, 1991, p. 49. See also the fine article by Bo Eldridge, "Desert Storm: Mother of All Battles," *Command* 13, November–December 1991, p. 38.

24. For "Internal Look 90," see Swain, *"Lucky War,"* pp. 9–11.

25. Jamieson, *Lucrative Targets*, pp. 4–6.

26. Blackwell, *Thunder in the Desert*, p. 95.

27. See Schwarzkopf, *It Doesn't Take a Hero*, p. 310; Caraccilo, *Ready Brigade*, p. 29.

28. Blackwell, *Thunder in the Desert*, p. 100.

29. Jamieson, *Lucrative Targets*, p. 7.

30. For this nearly bewildering order of battle, especially of the Arab-Islamic forces, see *Conduct of the Persian Gulf War: Final Report*, pp. 236–237; Schubert and Krauss, *Whirlwind War*, p. 133.

31. For the various claims, see Schwarzkopf, *It Doesn't Take a Hero*, pp. 380–384; Clancy with Franks, *Into the Storm*, pp. 225–235; Swain, *"Lucky War,"* gives a lion's share of the credit to 3rd Army commander Yeosock (pp. 129–131).

32. Schwarzkopf, *It Doesn't Take a Hero*, pp. 381–382.

33. James F. Dunnigan, "How to Fight in the Persian Gulf," *Strategy and Tactics* 139, November 1990, pp. 8–9. The piece is one of the sidebars to Austin Bay, "Arabian Nightmare: The 1990 Crises in the Persian Gulf," *Strategy and Tactics* 139, November 1990, pp. 5–6, 60–61.

34. The "crucial" issue of whether the term "Hail Mary" was an appropriate description of the operation has received much more attention than it deserves. See Clancy with Franks, *Into the Storm*, pp. 452–453, for General Franks's rejection of it. Larry E. Cable, "Playing in the Sandbox: Doctrine, Combat, and Outcome on the Ground," in William Head and Earl H. Tilford, Jr., eds., *The Eagle in the Desert: Looking Back on U.S. Involvement in the Persian Gulf War* (Westport, Conn.: Praeger, 1996), has the definitive discussion of this nonissue (pp. 187–189). Heikal, *Illusions of Triumph*, is the only source to point out that the term "was bad taste from a Muslim point of view" (p. 310).

35. See the article by the command historian of the VII Corps, Peter S. Kindsvatter, "VII Corps in the Gulf War: Deployment and Preparation for Desert Storm," *Military Review* 72, no. 1, January 1992, pp. 2–16. See, in particular, his discussion of the BCTP-led corps map exercises in early January 1991, pp. 12–13.

36. For planning within the XVIII Airborne Corps, see Caraccilo, *Ready Brigade*, and Flanagan, *Lightning: The 101st in the Gulf War*; for questions of corps doctrine, not tied specifically to Desert Storm, see the article by corps commander Gary E. Luck, "The XVIII Airborne Corps: Puttin' Power on the Ground," *Military Review* 72, 4, April 1992, pp. 2–13.

37. See Tom Clancy with General Chuck Horner, *Every Man a Tiger: The Gulf Air War Campaign* (New York: Berkley, 2000). Clancy here employs the same structure that he used in *Into the Storm* with General Franks: lots of Clancy's inimitable technothriller style, combined with a great deal of unadorned first-person testimony from Horner, the latter being of much more use to the historian than the former.

38. Jamieson, *Lucrative Targets*, p. 35.

39. Clancy with Horner, *Every Man a Tiger*, p. 16.

40. Jamieson, *Lucrative Targets*, p. 42.

41. Ibid.

42. The definitive account is James S. Corum, *The Luftwaffe: Creating the Operational Air War, 1918–1940* (Lawrence: University Press of Kansas, 1997).

43. Jamieson, *Lucrative Targets,* pp. 81–83.

44. Coughlin, *Storming the Desert,* pp. 82–83, "Everybody was shocked at how blatantly stupid it seemed to be." Even though he hears all the "maneuver warfare watchwords" being used, about how "quick and violent" the attack is supposed to be, "I just want to know how the Marine Corps commanders are going to practice maneuver warfare if they are just planning to charge straight into the teeth of the Iraqi defenses" (p. 83).

45. For "Division Daguet's" mission in light of traditional French cavalry doctrine, see Raymond E. Bell, Jr., "The French Light Armored Division: The Legacy of the Division Légère Mécanique," *Military Review* 79, no. 6, November–December 1999, pp. 81–84.

46. Cooke, *100 Miles from Baghdad,* p. 100.

47. Office of the Secretary of Defense, *Final Report to Congress,* p. 261; Flanagan, *Lightning: The 101st in the Gulf War,* nuances the language a bit more: "the largest and longest one-day air assault in military history" (p. 167).

48. Office of the Secretary of Defense, *Final Report to Congress,* p. 264.

49. The concept of the "operational pause," its intended duration, even its exact meaning, all continue to elude satisfactory explanation. The best discussion of this "quasi-doctrinal term" is to be found in Swain, *"Lucky War,"* pp. 112–114, 123. As is his wont, he attributes it to the pernicious influence of "the grey hand of the 'SAMS Jedi Knights' and their often scholastic approach to operations" (p. 206).

50. The drive to the Euphrates is covered best in Flanagan, *Lightning: The 101st in the Gulf War,* pp. 179–191.

51. The best accounts of the fight at 73 Easting are found in *U.S. News and World Report, Triumph Without Victory,* pp. 336–342; Blackwell, *Thunder in the Desert,* pp. 201–204; and Eldridge, "Desert Storm: Mother of All Battles," pp. 29, 32.

52. If the gridiron has given its share of metaphors to this campaign, so has the toolbox. Swain, *"Lucky War,"* speaks of "the relentless movement of the drill bit through the coal face" (p. 225); Schwarzkopf, *It Doesn't Take a Hero,* describes the advance of his army as being "like the piston in an enormous cider press" (p. 466).

53. Commander of the 24th Division, General Barry M. McCaffrey, called it "the damnedest thing I ever saw." See Eldridge, "Desert Storm: Mother of All Battles," p. 38.

54. For criticism of such overreaction, see Record, *Hollow Victory,* p. 136.

55. John L. Romjue, *The Army of Excellence: The Development of the 1980's Army* (Ft. Monroe, Va.: TRADOC, 1997), p. 4.

56. Office of the Secretary of Defense, *Final Report to Congress,* pp. 237–238.

57. Swain, *"Lucky War,"* pp. 295–296.

58. Ibid., pp. 117–118, calls it a "highly disciplined, closely controlled maneuver" as opposed to a "devil take the hindmost charge-of-the-light-brigade rash and gallant dash the more romantic critics would seem to have anticipated."

59. For the role that "synchronization" played in leading Franks to a more con-

servative approach, see Stephen E. Hughes, "Desert Storm: Attrition or Maneuver?" (Ft. Leavenworth, Kans.: School of Advanced Military Studies, 1995), a copy of which is on file in the U.S. Army War College Library at Carlisle Barracks in Carlisle, Pennsylvania, especially pp. 31–33.

60. Michael J. Mazarr, Don M. Sinder, and James A. Blackwell, Jr., *Desert Storm: The Gulf War and What We Learned* (Boulder, Colo.: Westview, 1993), p. 154.

61. Ibid., pp. 142–143. See also Dunnigan and Bay, *From Shield to Storm*, pp. 264–265. For the most extreme — and absurd — example of the "non-linearity" argument for Desert Storm, see Shimon Naveh, *In Pursuit of Military Excellence: The Evolution of Operational Theory* (London: Frank Cass, 1997), pp. 323–331. Naveh argues that "The Gulf War brought two schools of military thought into collision. On the one side stood the attrition-oriented, anachronistic school, adhering almost habitually to the nineteenth-century Clausewitzian conception. This school of thought, which crystallized in the prolonged Iran-Iraq War, tended to view warfare through the mechanistic perspective of linear confrontations of masses and resources. It was confronted by a manoeuvre-oriented operational school of thought that had developed during 15 years of vigorous theoretical work" (p. 323). He continues that Operation Desert Storm closed a "broader historical circle." The "operational paradigm which emerged in the United States in the late 1970s was proven, while the traditional dominance of the *Vernichtungsschlacht* paradigm was completely invalidated" (p. 329). It is difficult, given our lack of sources on just what the Iraqi high command thought it was doing, even to entertain the plausibility of an argument that Saddam Hussein's "generalship" has somehow invalidated Clausewitz.

62. Research into the Kosovo War must still rely on government and think-tank documents. There is, as of yet, no body of secondary literature. See Department of Defense, *Report to Congress: Kosovo/Operation Allied Force After-Action Report* (Washington, D.C.: Department of Defense, 2000); Anthony H. Cordesman, "The Lessons and Non-Lessons of the Air and Missile War in Kosovo" (Washington, D.C.: Center for Strategic and International Studies, 1999); and Benjamin S. Lambeth, "NATO's Air War for Kosovo: A Strategic and Operational Assessment" (Washington, D.C.: RAND, 2001). Lambeth has also included a thorough discussion of airpower in Kosovo in *The Transformation of American Air Power* (Ithaca, N.Y.: Cornell University Press, 2000). See also the memoirs of the NATO commander: Wesley K. Clark, *Waging Modern War: Bosnia, Kosovo, and the Future of Combat* (New York: Public Affairs, 2001).

63. Clancy with Franks, *Into the Storm*, p. 513.

64. For Operation Anaconda, see the harrowing journalistic accounts: David Moniz, "Soldiers Describe '18 Hour Miracle,'" *USA Today*, March 7, 2002; Esther Schrader, "Simple Mission Became 18-Hour Fight," *Los Angeles Times*, March 8, 2002; and "Operation Anaconda: What the Pilots Saw," *Newsweek*, April 22, 2002.

65. For a spirited, and often funny, demolition of the entire notion of "information warfare," see R. L. DiNardo and Daniel J. Hughes, "Some Cautionary Thoughts on Information Warfare," *Airpower Journal* 9, no. 4, Winter 1995, pp. 69–79. And for a carefully reasoned, and utterly convincing, argument against discarding Clause-

witz, see Barry D. Watts, "Clausewitzian Friction and Future War," *McNair Paper* 52, revised edition (Washington, D.C.: Institute for National Strategic Studies, 2000). Watts ranges far and wide in this piece, using concepts borrowed from philosophy, physics, the economic theories of Friedrich von Hayek, and the concept of "emergence" in evolutionary biology to argue for the continued existence of friction, no matter what the state of contemporary technology.

66. See, for example, Sean D. Naylor, "Training Command the Hardest Hit in Manning Plan," *Army Times*, September 4, 2000, p. 10; R. W. Rogers and David Lerman, "TRADOC Cash Poor by $360m: Command Hiring Freeze Won't Affect Training, Safety," *Newport News Daily Press*, March 10, 2001; and Mickey McCarter, "GAO Suggests Army Needs Less Money for Training," *Stars and Stripes Omnimedia*, March 27, 2001. No area of army life escaped unscathed in the post-1991 era. See Rowan Scarborough, "Army Running out of Bullets," *Washington Times*, February 7, 2001. This was an era, after all, in which a brigadier general could actually suggest to his officers that they get a subscription to *Army Times* — a commercial publication — to "keep up on new Army policies and concepts." See Donald N. Carr, "Tell Soldiers First — They Are Our Credentials," *Military Review* 79, no. 5 (September–October 1999), p. 77.

67. FM 100-5, "Operations," 1986, p. 6.

68. For a primer on "Transformation," as well as a very gentle treatment of Shinseki that at times ventures into puffery, see Peter J. Boyer, "Is the Army Becoming Irrelevant?" *New Yorker*, July 1, 2002, pp. 54ff. Not to be missed is Dennis Steele, "The Army Magazine Hooah Guide to Army Transformation: A 30-Minute Course on the Army's 30-Year Overhaul" (Association of the United States Army, 2001).

69. For an eloquent argument supporting the "perdurability of ground forces" and the continued existence of a "conventional imperative," see John A. English, *Marching Through Chaos: The Descent of Armies in Theory and Practice* (Westport, Conn.: Praeger, 1996), pp. 153–205.

Conclusion

1. Eliot A. Cohen and John Gooch, *Military Misfortunes: The Anatomy of Failure in War* (New York: Free Press, 1990), p. 236. Quoted in DiNardo and Hughes, "Some Cautionary Thoughts on Information Warfare," p. 76.

2. For a carefully nuanced discussion of the relationship between fire and movement, see John A. English, *The Canadian Army and the Normandy Campaign: A Study of Failure in High Command* (Westport, Conn.: Praeger, 1991), p. 272.

3. For German discussion of this point, see Major Greiner, "Kampf den Reibungen im Kriege durch Erziehung und Ausbildung im Frieden!" *Militär-Wochenblatt* 120, no. 32, February 18, 1936, pp. 1403–1408.

4. See "Introduction," note 7.

Works Cited

The 14-Day War. New Delhi: Publications Division, Government of India, 1972.

Adan, Avraham (Bren). *On the Banks of the Suez: An Israeli General's Personal Account of the Yom Kippur War*. Novato, Calif.: Presidio, 1991.

"Airborne Operations: A German Appraisal." Washington, D.C.: Center of Military History, 1989.

Akbar Khan, Mohammed. "The East Pakistan Crisis — An Analysis." *Defence Journal* 2, no. 12, 1976.

Aker, Frank. *October 1973: The Arab-Israeli War*. Hamden, Conn.: Archon Books, 1985.

Alexander, Bevin. *Korea: The First War We Lost*. New York: Hippocrene, 2000.

Alexander, Joseph H. "Battle of the Barricades: U.S. Marines in the Recapture of Seoul." *Marines in the Korean War Commemorative Series*. Washington, D.C.: U.S. Marine Corps Historical Center, 2000.

———. "Fleet Operations in a Mobile War, September 1950–June 1951." Washington, D.C.: Naval Historical Center, 2001.

Allen, Peter. *The Yom Kippur War*. New York: Charles Scribner's Sons, 1982.

Allon, Yigal. "The Making of Israel's Army: The Development of Military Concepts of Liberation and Defence." In *The Theory and Practice of War*, edited by Michael Howard. Bloomington: Indiana University Press, 1975.

———. *The Making of Israel's Army*. New York: Universe Books, 1970.

Altrock, General Konstantin von. "Sprach- und Schreibdummheiten." *Militär-Wochenblatt* 113, no. 2, July 11, 1928.

Ambrose, Stephen E. *Citizen Soldiers: The U.S. Army from the Normandy Beaches to the Bulge to the Surrender of Germany, May 7, 1944–June 7, 1944*. New York: Touchstone, 1997.

Antal, John F. "Maneuver Versus Attrition: A Historical Perspective." *Military Review* 72, no. 10, October 1992.

Appleman, Roy E. *Disaster in Korea: The Chinese Confront MacArthur*. College Station: Texas A&M University Press, 1989.

———. *East of Chosin: Entrapment and Breakout in Korea, 1950*. College Station: Texas A&M University Press, 1987.

———. *Escaping the Trap: The U.S. Army X Corps in Northeast Korea, 1950*. College Station: Texas A&M University Press, 1990.

———. *South to the Naktong, North to the Yalu: United States Army in the Korean War*. Washington, D.C.: Center of Military History, 1961.

Arrian. *The Campaigns of Alexander*. New York: Penguin, 1982.

Ashmead-Bartlett, Ellis. *With the Turks in Thrace*. New York: George H. Doran, 1913.

Atkinson, Rick. *Crusade: The Untold Story of the Persian Gulf War*. Boston: Houghton Mifflin, 1993.

Attiqur Rahman, Mohammed. *Leadership: Senior Commanders*. Lahore: Ferozsons Book Corp., 1973.

———. *Our Defence Cause: An Analysis of Pakistan's Past and Future Military Role*. London: White Lion, 1976.

"Aus dem Feldzuge in Norwegen." Parts 1 and 2, "Die Kämpfe um die Landverbindung nach Drontheim im April 1940." *Militärwissenschaftliche Rundschau* 6, nos. 2 and 3, 1941.

"Aus dem Feldzuge in Norwegen." Part 3, "Von Drontheim bis Namsos." *Militärwissenschaftliche Rundschau* 6, no. 4, 1941.

Badri, Hassan el, Taha el Magdoub, and Mohammed Dia el Din Zohdy. *The Ramadan War, 1973*. Dunn Loring, Va.: T. N. Dupuy Associates, 1974.

Bakshi, G. D. *The Indian Military Revival: The Saga of the Fateh Shibji*. New Delhi: Lancer International, 1987.

———. "Land Warfare in the Subcontinent: The Indian Quest for Doctrine." *Indian Defence Review Digest* 4, 1992.

———. "The Sino-Vietnam War — 1979: Case Studies in Limited War." *Indian Defence Review* 15, no. 3, July–September 2000.

Baldwin, Hanson. *Battles Lost and Won: Great Campaigns of World War II*. New York: Harper and Row, 1966.

Barber, A. J. *Afrika Korps*. London: Bison, 1977.

Barclay, Cyril N. "A Soldier Looks at the Indo-Pakistani War." *Army* 22, no. 5, May 1972.

Barnett, Correlli. *The Desert Generals*. Bloomington: Indiana University Press, 1982.

Bar-Siman-Tov, Yaacov. *The Israeli-Arab War of Attrition, 1969–70*. New York: Columbia University Press, 1980.

Bateman, Robert L. "What We Haven't Learned." *Military Review* 80, no. 1, January–February 2000.

Bathe, Rolf. *Der Feldzug der 18 Tage: Die Chronik des polnischen Dramas*. Oldenburg: Gerhard Stalling, 1939.

Battles Hitler Lost: First Person Accounts of World War II by Russian Generals on the Eastern Front. New York: Richardson & Steirman, 1986.

Baum, Kim Chull. "The Korean Scholars on the Korean War." In *The Korean War: Handbook of the Literature and Research*, edited by Lester H. Brune. Westport, Conn.: Greenwood Press, 1996.

Bay, Austin. "Arabian Nightmare: The 1990 Crises in the Persian Gulf." *Strategy and Tactics* 139, November 1990.

Beevor, Anthony. *Crete: The Battle and the Resistance*. London: John Murray, 1991.

———. *Stalingrad*. New York: Viking, 1998.

Behrendt, Hans-Otto. *Rommel's Intelligence in the Desert Campaign, 1941–43*. London: William Kimber, 1985.

Bell, Raymond E., Jr. "The French Light Armored Division: The Legacy of the Division Légère Mécanique." *Military Review* 79, no. 6, November–December 1999.

Bennighof, Michael. "Wiedervereinigungskrieg." *Counterattack* 1, October 1987.

Bertkau, Major Friedrich. "Die nachrichtentechnische Führung mechanisierter Verbände." *Militär-Wochenblatt* 120, no. 15, October 18, 1935.

Bin, Alberto, Richard Hill, and Archer Jones. *Desert Storm: A Forgotten War*. Westport, Conn.: Praeger, 1998.

Birtle, Andrew J. "Years of Stalemate, July 1951–July 1953." *The Korean War*. Washington, D.C.: Center of Military History, n.d.

Blackwell, James A. *Thunder in the Desert: The Strategy and Tactics of the Persian Gulf War*. New York: Bantam, 1991.

Blair, Clay. *The Forgotten War: America in Korea, 1950–1953*. New York: Times Books, 1987.

Blumenson, Martin. *Breakout and Pursuit: United States Army in World War II, the European Theater of Operations*. Washington, D.C.: Office of the Chief of Military History, 1961.

———. *The Duel for France, 1944: The Men and Battles That Changed the Fate of Europe*. New York: Da Capo, 2000.

Bohn, Leif. "The Norwegian View." *History of the Second World War*, no. 3, 1978.

Bond, Brian. *Liddell Hart: A Study of His Military Thought*. New Brunswick, N.J.: Rutgers University Press, 1977.

Borgert, Heinz-Ludger. "Grundzüge der Landkriegführung von Schlieffen bis Guderian." *Handbuch zur deutschen Militärgeschichte 1648–1939*. Vol. 9, *Grundzüge der militärischen Kriegführung*. Munich: Bernard & Graefe Verlag, 1979.

Borries, Vance von. "Operation Barbarossa: The Southern Wing." *Schwerpunkt* 1, September 1993.

Boyer, Peter J. "Is the Army Becoming Irrelevant?" *New Yorker*, July 1, 2002.

Bradley, Omar N. *A Soldier's Story*. New York: Henry Holt and Company, 1951.

Brandt, Major Wim. "Bilder aus der Belagerung von Modlin." *Militär-Wochenblatt* 124, no. 30, January 19, 1940.

Braun, Major M. "Gedanken über Kampfwagen- und Fliegerverwendung bei den russischen Herbstmanövern 1936." *Militär-Wochenblatt* 121, no. 28, January 22, 1937.

Brown, Ronald J. "Counteroffensive: U.S. Marines from Pohang to No Name Line." *Marines in the Korean War Commemorative Series*. Washington, D.C.: U.S. Marine Corps Historical Center, 2001.

Brune, Lester H. "The U.S. Navy and Marines in the Korean War." In *The Korean War: Handbook of the Literature and Research*, edited by Lester H. Brune. Westport, Conn.: Greenwood Press, 1996.

———, ed. *The Korean War: Handbook of the Literature and Research*. Westport, Conn.: Greenwood Press, 1996.

Brush, Peter. "The Battle of Khe Sanh, 1968." In *The Tet Offensive*, edited by Marc Jason Gilbert and William Head. Westport, Conn.: Praeger, 1996.

Buckley, Christopher. *Greece and Crete, 1941*. London: H. M. Stationery Office, 1952.

Buell, Thomas B. "Naval Leadership in Korea: The First Six Months." Washington, D.C.: Naval Historical Center, 2002.

Cable, Larry E. "Playing in the Sandbox: Doctrine, Combat, and Outcome on the Ground." In *The Eagle in the Desert: Looking Back on U.S. Involvement in the Persian Gulf War*, edited by William Head and Earl H. Tilford, Jr., Westport, Conn.: Praeger, 1996.

Caraccilo, Dominic J. *The Ready Brigade of the 82nd Airborne in Desert Storm: A Combat Memoir by the Headquarters Company Commander.* Jefferson, N.C.: McFarland, 1993.

Carafano, James Jay. *After D-Day: Operation Cobra and the Normandy Breakout.* Boulder, Colo.: Lynne Rienner, 2000.

Carell, Paul. *Scorched Earth: The Russian-German War, 1943–1944.* Boston: Little, Brown, 1970.

Carr, Donald N. "Tell Soldiers First — They Are Our Credentials." *Military Review* 79, no. 5, September–October 1999.

Carver, Michael. *Dilemmas of the Desert War.* London: Batsford, 1986.

————. *El Alamein.* London: Batsford, 1962.

————. *Tobruk.* London: Batsford, 1964.

————. *War Since 1945.* New York: G. P. Putnam's Sons, 1981.

Cate, Paul. "Large-Unit Operational Doctrine." *Military Review* 58, no. 12, December 1978.

Channow, P. "Conduct of Tanks in Deep Snow." *Krasnaya Zvesda*, December 30, 1939 (translated). Carlisle, Pa.: U.S. Army Military History Institute, 1939.

Chapin, John C. "Fire Brigade: U.S. Marines in the Pusan Perimeter." *Marines in the Korean War Commemorative Series.* Washington, D.C.: U.S. Marine Corps Historical Center, 2000.

Chapman, Anne W. *The Army's Training Revolution, 1973–1990: An Overview.* Ft. Monroe, Va.: TRADOC, 1994.

————. *The Origins and Development of the National Training Center, 1976–1984.* Ft. Monroe, Va.: TRADOC, 1997.

Chew, Allen F. *The White Death: The Epic of the Soviet-Finnish Winter War.* East Lansing: Michigan State University Press, 1971.

Chopra, Maharaj K. "Military Operations in Bangladesh." *Military Review* 52, no. 5, May 1972.

Chopra, Pran. *India's Second Liberation.* Delhi: Vikas, 1973.

Chuikov, V. I. *The Battle for Stalingrad.* New York: Holt, Rinehart and Winston, 1964.

————. *The End of the Third Reich.* Moscow: Progress Publishers, 1978.

Churchill, Randolph S., and Winston S. Churchill. *The Six Day War.* Boston: Houghton Mifflin, 1967.

Citino, Robert M. *Armored Forces: History and Sourcebook.* Westport, Conn.: Greenwood, 1994.

————. "Beyond Fire and Movement: Command, Control, and Information in the German Blitzkrieg." Washington, D.C.: Center for Strategic and Budgetary Assessment, March 2002.

————. " 'Die Gedanken sind frei': The Intellectual Culture of the Interwar German Army." *Army Doctrine and Training Bulletin* 4, no. 3, Fall 2001.

————. *The Path to Blitzkrieg: Doctrine and Training in the German Army, 1920–1939.* Boulder, Colo.: Lynne Rienner, 1999.

————. *Quest for Decisive Victory: From Stalemate to Blitzkrieg in Europe, 1899–1940.* Lawrence: University Press of Kansas, 2002.

————. "Was the Reputation of the Wehrmacht for Military Superiority Deserved?" In *History in Dispute* 4, *World War II, 1939–1945*, edited by Dennis E. Showalter. Detroit: St. James Press, 2000.

————. "The Weimar Roots of German Military Planning." In *Military Planning and the Origins of the Second World War in Europe*, edited by B. J. C. McKercher and Roch Legault. Westport, Conn.: Praeger, 2001.

Claasen, Adam R. A. *Hitler's Northern War: The Luftwaffe's Ill-Fated Campaign, 1940–1945.* Lawrence: University Press of Kansas, 2001.

Clancy, Tom. *Red Storm Rising.* New York: Putnam, 1986.

Clancy, Tom, with General Chuck Horner. *Every Man a Tiger: The Gulf Air War Campaign.* New York: Berkley, 2000.

Clancy, Tom, with General Fred Franks. *Into the Storm: A Study in Command.* New York: Putnam, 1997.

Clark, Alan. *Barbarossa: The Russian-German Conflict, 1941–1945.* New York: Quill, 1985.

————. *The Fall of Crete.* London: A. Blond, 1962.

Clark, Asa. *The Defense Reform Debate.* Baltimore, Md.: Johns Hopkins University Press, 1984.

Clark, Mark W. *Calculated Risk.* New York: Harper, 1950.

Clark, Wesley K. *Waging Modern War: Bosnia, Kosovo, and the Future of Combat.* New York: Public Affairs, 2001.

Clarke, Michael. "AirLand Battle and the Application of New Technology." In *New Conventional Weapons and Western Defence*, edited by Ian Bellamy and Tim Huxley. London: Frank Cass, 1987.

Cloughley, Brian. *A History of the Pakistan Army: Wars and Insurrections; with a New Chapter on the Kargil Issue.* Second Edition. Oxford: Oxford University Press, 2000.

Cohen, Eliot A., and John Gooch. *Military Misfortunes: The Anatomy of Failure in War.* New York: Free Press, 1990.

Coleman, J. D. *Pleiku: The Dawn of Helicopter Warfare in Vietnam.* New York: St. Martin's, 1988.

Collins, J. Lawton. *War in Peacetime: The History and Lessons of Korea.* Boston: Houghton Mifflin, 1969.

Condon, John P. (supplemented by Peter B. Mersky). "Corsairs to Panthers: U.S. Marine Aviation in Korea." *Marines in the Korean War Commemorative Series.* Washington, D.C.: U.S. Marine Corps Historical Center, 2002.

The Conduct of the Persian Gulf War: Final Report to Congress Pursuant to Title V of the Persian Gulf Conflict Supplemental Authorization and Personnel Benefits Act of 1991 (Public Law 102-25). Washington, D.C.: Department of Defense, 1992.

Connell, Jon. *The New Maginot Line.* London: Secker and Warburg, 1986.

Conrath, Paul. "Der Kampf um Sizilien." *German Reports Series,* C-087. Headquarters United States Army, Europe: Foreign Military Studies Branch, 1951.

Cook, Glen Steven. "Korea: No Longer the Forgotten War." *Journal of Military History* 56, no. 3, July 1992.

Cooke, James J. *100 Miles from Baghdad: With the French in Desert Storm.* Westport, Conn.: Praeger, 1993.

Cordesman, Anthony H. *The Iran-Iraq War and Western Security, 1984–1987: Strategic Implications and Policy Options.* London: Janes, 1987.

———. "The Lessons and Non-Lessons of the Air and Missile War in Kosovo." Washington, D.C.: Center for Strategic and International Studies, 1999.

Cordesman, Anthony H., and Abraham R. Wagner. *The Lessons of Modern War.* Vol. 1. *The Arab-Israeli Conflicts, 1973–1989.* Boulder, Colo.: Westview, 1990.

———. *The Lessons of Modern War.* Vol. 2. *The Iran-Iraq War.* Boulder, Colo.: Westview, 1990.

Coroalles, Anthony M. "Implementing a Maneuver Style of War." *Military Review* 62, no. 12, December 1982.

———. "Maneuver to Win: A Realistic Alternative." *Military Review* 61, no. 9, September 1981.

Corum, James S. "Evolution of US Army Doctrine and Current Trends: A Return to Doctrinal Roots." *New Zealand Army Journal,* no. 23, July 2000.

———. "The German Campaign in Norway as a Joint Operation." *Journal of Strategic Studies* 21, no. 4, December 1998.

———. *The Luftwaffe: Creating the Operational Air War, 1918–1940.* Lawrence: University Press of Kansas, 1997.

———. *The Roots of Blitzkrieg: Hans von Seeckt and German Military Reform.* Lawrence: University Press of Kansas, 1992.

Coughlin, Sean T. *Storming the Desert: A Marine Lieutenant's Day-by-Day Chronicle of the Persian Gulf War.* Jefferson, N.C.: McFarland, 1996.

Cox, Geoffrey. *A Tale of Two Battles: A Personal Memoir of Crete and the Western Desert, 1941.* London: William Kimber, 1987.

Coyle, Harold. *Team Yankee: A Novel of World War III.* Novato, Calif.: Presidio, 1987.

Craig, Gordon A. *The Battle of Königgrätz.* Philadelphia: Lippincott, 1964.

Crane, Conrad C. *American Airpower Strategy in Korea, 1950–1953.* Lawrence: University Press of Kansas, 2000.

Creveld, Martin van. "Armed but Not Dangerous: Women in the Israeli Military." *War in History* 7, no. 1, 2000.

———. "Military Lessons of the Yom Kippur War: Historical Perspectives." *Washington Papers* 3, no. 24. Beverly Hills: Sage, 1975.

———. *The Sword and the Olive: A Critical History of the Israeli Defense Force.* New York: Public Affairs, 1998.

Crimp, R. L. *The Diary of a Desert Rat.* London: Leo Cooper, 1971.

Crisp, Robert. *Brazen Chariots.* New York: Ballantine, 1961.

Cross, Robin. *Citadel: The Battle of Kursk.* New York: Barnes & Noble, 1994.

Crutwell, C. R. M. F. *A History of the Great War, 1914–1918.* Chicago: Academy Chicago, 1991.

Cumings, Bruce. *Korea's Place in the Sun: A Modern History.* New York: W. W. Norton, 1997.

———. *The Origins of the Korean War.* Vol. 1. *Liberation and the Emergence of Separate Regimes, 1945–1947.* Princeton, N.J.: Princeton University Press, 1981.

———. *The Origins of the Korean War.* Vol. 2. *The Roaring of the Cataract.* Princeton, N.J.: Princeton University Press, 1990.

Currey, Cecil B. *Victory at Any Cost: The Genius of Viet Nam's General Vo Nguyen Giap.* McLean, Va.: Brassey's, 1997.

———. ("Cincinnatus"). *Self-Destruction: The Disintegration and Decay of the United States Army During the Vietnam Era.* New York: Norton, 1981.

Davies, W. J. K. *German Army Handbook 1939–1945.* New York: Arco, 1973.

Davin, D. M. *Crete: Official History of New Zealand in the Second World War, 1939–45.* Wellington, N.Z.: War History Branch, 1953.

Dayan, Moshe. *Diary of the Sinai Campaign.* New York: Schocken, 1967.

———. *Moshe Dayan: The Story of My Life.* New York: William Morrow, 1975.

Deal, C. Lanier, Jr. "BAI: The Key to the Deep Battle." *Military Review* 62, no. 3, March 1982.

de Czege, Huba Wass. "Army Doctrinal Reform." *The Defense Reform Debate.* Edited by Asa Clark. Baltimore: Johns Hopkins University Press, 1984.

Department of Defense. *Report to Congress: Kosovo/Operation Allied Force After-Action Report.* Washington, D.C.: Department of Defense, 2000. Online.

"Der Abschluss der Vernichtungsschlacht in Flandern und im Artois sowie der Beginn der neuen deutschen Offensive über die Somme und den Oise — Aisne-Kanal in der Woche vom 2. bis 8.6.1940." *Grossdeutschlands Freiheitskrieg 1940,* part 44. *Militär-Wochenblatt* 124, no. 50, June 14, 1940.

"Der Angriffsschlacht von Cambrai vom 30. November bis 6. Dezember 1917." *Militär-Wochenblatt* 112, no. 22, December 11, 1927.

"Der Führer kündigt den Zusammenbruch der Sowjets an." *Grossdeutschlands Freiheitskrieg,* part 113. *Militär-Wochenblatt* 126, no. 15, October 10, 1941.

"Der Stellungskrieg im Osten." *Grossdeutschlands Freiheitskrieg,* part 124. *Militär-Wochenblatt* 126, no. 26, December 26, 1941.

Desch, Michael C., ed. *Soldiers in Cities: Military Operations on Urban Terrain.* Carlisle, Pa.: Strategic Studies Institute, 2001.

D'Este, Carlo W. *Bitter Victory: The Battle for Sicily, 1943.* New York: Dutton, 1988.

———. *Decision in Normandy.* New York: Harper, 1994.

———. *Fatal Decision: Anzio and the Battle for Rome.* New York: HarperCollins, 1986.

"Deutschlands Antwort auf die Kriegserklärung der Weltmächte an die Neutralität: Die Besetzung Dänemarks und Norwegens durch deutsche Truppen." *Grossdeutschlands Freiheitskrieg 1940,* part 36. *Militär-Wochenblatt* 124, no. 42, April 19, 1940.

"Die 7. Woche des Ostkampfes." *Grossdeutschlands Freiheitskrieg,* part 105. *Militär-Wochenblatt* 126, no. 7, August 15, 1941.

"Die Doppelschlacht von Bialystok und Minsk." *Grossdeutschlands Freiheitskrieg*, part 101. *Militär-Wochenblatt* 126, no. 3, July 18, 1941.

"Die Eroberung von Kreta." *Militär-Wochenblatt* 126, no. 6, August 8, 1941.

"Die Vernichtungsschlacht von Bialystok." *Grossdeutschlands Freiheitskrieg*, part 100. *Militär-Wochenblatt* 126, no. 2, July 11, 1941.

DiNardo, R. L., and Daniel J. Hughes. "Some Cautionary Thoughts on Information Warfare." *Airpower Journal* 9, no. 4, Winter 1995.

Dinesh, Deendayal. *Indira Wins the War*. Delhi: Oriental Publishers, 1972.

Dinter, Elmar, and Paddy Griffith. *Not Over by Christmas: NATO's Central Front in World War III*. New York: Hippocrene, 1983.

Doubler, Michael D. *Closing with the Enemy: How GIs Fought the War in Europe, 1944–1945*. Lawrence: University Press of Kansas, 1994.

Doughty, Robert A. *The Breaking Point: Sedan and the Fall of France, 1940*. Hamden, Conn.: Archon, 1990.

———. "The Evolution of U.S. Army Tactical Doctrine, 1946–76." *Leavenworth Paper* no. 1. Ft. Leavenworth, Kans.: Combat Studies Institute, 1979.

Dower, John W. *War Without Mercy: Race and Power in the Pacific War*. New York: Pantheon Books, 1986.

Dunn, Walter S. *Soviet Blitzkrieg: The Battle for White Russia, 1944*. Boulder, Colo.: Lynne Rienner, 2000.

Dunnigan, James F. "How to Fight in the Persian Gulf." *Strategy and Tactics* 139, November 1990.

Dunnigan, James F., and Austin Bay. *From Shield to Storm: High-Tech Weapons, Military Strategy, and Coalition Warfare in the Persian Gulf*. New York: William Morrow, 1992.

Dutt, J. K. "Deep Thrust." *Journal of the United Service Institution of India* 57, no. 450, January–March 1978.

Dworschak, Tom. "Operation Weser Exercise: The German Navy in Norway, 1940." *Command* 39, September 1996.

Echevarria, Antulio J., II. *After Clausewitz: German Military Thinkers Before the Great War*. Lawrence: University Press of Kansas, 2000.

Eden, Steven. "Three Cheers for Attrition Warfare." *Armor* 111, no. 2, March–April 2002.

Edwards, Jill, ed. *Al-Alamein Revisited: The Battle of al-Alamein and Its Historical Implications*. Cairo: American University in Cairo, 2000.

Edwards, Paul M. *To Acknowledge a War: The Korean War in Historical Memory*. Westport, Conn.: Greenwood, 2000.

Edwin, H. Simmons, "Over the Seawall: U.S. Marines at Inchon." *Marines in the Korean War Commemorative Series*. Washington, D.C.: U.S. Marine Corps Historical Center, 2000.

"Einschnürung Leningrads schreitet fort." *Grossdeutschlands Freiheitskrieg*, part 111. *Militär-Wochenblatt* 126, no. 13, September 26, 1941.

Eisenhower, Dwight D. *Crusade in Europe*. Garden City, N.Y.: Doubleday, 1948.

Eisenstadt, Michael, and Kenneth M. Pollack. "Armies of Snow and Armies of Sand:

The Impact of Soviet Military Doctrine on the Arab Militaries." *Middle East Journal* 55, no. 4, Autumn 2002.

Eldridge, Bo. "Desert Storm: Mother of All Battles." *Command* 13, November–December 1991.

Endicott, Judy G., ed. *The USAF in Korea: Campaigns, Units and Stations, 1950–1953.* Maxwell Air Force Base: Air University Library, 2001.

"Englands diplomatische und militärische Niederlage in Norwegen." *Grossdeutschlands Freiheitskrieg 1940*, part 39. *Militär-Wochenblatt* 124, no. 45, May 10, 1940.

Engle, Eloise, and Lauri Paananen. *The Winter War: The Soviet Attack on Finland.* Harrisburg, Pa.: Stackpole Books, 1973.

"Englische motorisierte Versuchsbrigade." *Militär-Wochenblatt* 122, no. 14, October 11, 1927; no. 15, October 18, 1927; no. 16, October 25, 1927.

English, John A. *The Canadian Army and the Normandy Campaign: A Study of Failure in High Command.* Westport, Conn.: Praeger, 1991.

———. *Marching Through Chaos: The Descent of Armies in Theory and Practice.* Westport, Conn.: Praeger, 1996.

Erfurth, Waldemar. "Das Zusammenwirken getrennter Heeresteile." *Militärwissenschaftliche Rundschau* 4, nos. 1–4, 1939.

Erickson, Edward J. *Ordered to Die: A History of the Ottoman Army in the First World War.* Westport, Conn.: Greenwood Press, 2001.

Erickson, John. *The Road to Berlin.* London: Wiedenfeld and Nicolson, 1983.

———. *The Road to Stalingrad.* New York: Harper and Row, 1975.

Eshel, David. *Israel's Armor in Action.* Masada: Eshel Drasmit, 1978.

Fall, Bernard. *Hell in a Very Small Place.* Philadelphia: Lippincott, 1967.

Falls, Cyril. *The Great War.* New York: Capricorn, 1959.

Farwell, Byron. *The Great Anglo-Boer War.* New York: Norton, 1976.

Featherston, Alwyn. *Saving the Breakout: The 30th Division's Heroic Stand at Mortain, August 7–12, 1944.* Novato, Calif.: Presidio, 1993.

Fehrenbach, T. R. *This Kind of War: A Study in Unpreparedness.* New York: Macmillan, 1963.

Field Manual (FM) 100-5. "Operations." Washington, D.C.: Department of the Army, 1976.

Field Manual (FM) 100-5. "Operations." Washington, D.C.: Department of the Army, 1982.

Field Manual (FM) 100-5. "Operations." Washington, D.C.: Department of the Army, 1986.

Field Manual (FM) 100-5. "Operations." Washington, D.C.: Department of the Army, 1993.

Flanagan, Edward M. *Lightning: The 101st in the Gulf War.* Washington, D.C.: Brassey's, 1994.

"Fortschreidender Angriff auf Moskau." *Grossdeutschlands Freiheitskrieg*, part 121. *Militär-Wochenblatt* 126, no. 23, December 5, 1941.

Forty, George. *The Armies of Rommel.* London: Arms and Armour, 1997.

———. *The Battle for Crete.* Hersham, Surrey: Ian Allan, 2001.

―――――. *Desert Rats at War: North Africa*. London: Ian Allan, 1975.

Freedman, Lawrence, and Efraim Karsh. *The Gulf Conflict 1990–1991: Diplomacy and War in the New World Order*. Princeton, N.J.: Princeton University Press, 1993.

"Fremdwort und Heeressprache." *Militär-Wochenblatt* 113, no. 2, July 11, 1928.

Friedman, Norman. *Desert Victory, the War for Kuwait*. Annapolis, Md.: Naval Institute Press, 1991.

Fugate, Bryan. *Operation Barbarossa*. Novato, Calif.: Presidio, 1984.

―――――. *Thunder on the Dnepr: Zhukov-Stalin and the Defeat of Hitler's Blitzkrieg*. Novato, Calif.: Presidio, 1997.

Fuller, J. F. C. *Grant and Lee: A Study in Personality and Generalship*. Bloomington: Indiana University Press, 1957.

Fuppe, Colonel. "Neuzeitliches Nachrichtenverbindungswesen als Führungsmittel im Kriege." *Militärwissenschaftliche Rundschau* 3, no. 6, 1938.

Gabriel, Richard A., and Paul L. Savage. *Crisis in Command: Mismanagement in the Army*. New York: Hill and Wang, 1978.

Gammons, Stephen L. Y. "The UN Offensive, 16 September–2 November 1950." In *The Korean War*. Washington, D.C.: Center of Military History, n.d.

Garland, Albert N., and Howard McGaw Smyth, with Martin Blumenson. *Sicily and the Surrender of Italy: United States Army in World War II, the Mediterranean Theater of Operations*. Washington, D.C.: Center of Military History, 1993.

Gaul, Lieutenant Colonel. "Der Blitzkrieg in Frankreich." *Militär-Wochenblatt* 125, no. 35, February 28, 1941.

Gaylor, John. *Sons of John Company: The Indian and Pakistan Armies 1903–91*. Tunbridge Wells, Kent: Spellmount, 1992.

Geelani, Sultan Ahmad. "The Fourth Arab-Israel War: A Recapitulation." *Defence Journal* 1, nos. 9–10, 1975.

"Generalfeldmarschall Graf von Schlieffen über den großen Feldherrn der preußisch-deutschen Armee." *Militär-Wochenblatt* 125, no. 17, October 25, 1940.

German Experiences in Desert Warfare During World War II. Vol. 1. Fleet Marine Force Reference Publication (FMFRP) 12-96-I. Quantico, Va.: United States Marine Corps, 1990.

German Methods of Warfare in the Libyan Desert. Washington, D.C.: Military Intelligence Service, 1942.

Gibbs, Bill. "Modern Combat Doctrine." *Counterattack* 1, October 1987.

Gibbs, Philip, and Bernard Grant. *The Balkan War: Adventures of War with Cross and Crescent*. Boston: Small, Maynard, and Company, 1913.

Gifford, Jack J. "The U.S. Army in the Korean War." In *The Korean War: Handbook of the Literature and Research*, edited by Lester H. Brune. Westport, Conn.: Greenwood Press, 1996.

Glantz, David M. "Counterpoint to Stalingrad: Operation Mars (November–December 1942): Marshal Zhukov's Greatest Defeat." Ft. Leavenworth, Kans.: Foreign Military Studies Office, 1997. Online. http://rhino.shef.ac.uk:3001/mr-home/rzhev/ rzhev3.html.

————. *From the Don to the Dnepr: Soviet Offensive Operations, December 1942–August 1943*. London: Frank Cass, 1991.

————. *Kharkov 1942: Anatomy of a Military Disaster Through Soviet Eyes*. Shepperton, Surrey: Ian Allan, 1998.

————. "Observing the Soviets: U.S. Army Attachés in Eastern Europe During the 1930s." *Journal of Military History* 55, no. 2, April 1991.

————. *Stumbling Colossus: The Red Army on the Eve of World War II*. Lawrence: University Press of Kansas, 1998.

————. *Zhukov's Greatest Defeat: The Red Army's Epic Disaster in Operation Mars, 1942*. Lawrence: University Press of Kansas, 1999.

Glantz, David M., and Jonathan M. House. *The Battle of Kursk*. Lawrence: University Press of Kansas, 1999.

————. *When Titans Clash: How the Red Army Stopped Hitler*. Lawrence: University Press of Kansas, 1995.

Glantz, David M., and Harold S. Orenstein, eds. *The Battle for Kursk, 1943: The Soviet General Staff Study*. London: Frank Cass, 1999.

Gordon, Michael R., and Bernard E. Trainor. *The Generals' War: The Inside Story of the Conflict in the Gulf*. Boston: Little, Brown, 1995.

Grechko, A. A. *The Armed Forces of the Soviet State: A Soviet View*. Moscow: Voennoe Izdatel'stvo, 1975. Translated and published under the auspices of the United States Air Force. *Soviet Military Thought*, no. 12.

Greiner, Major. "Kampf den Reibungen im Kriege durch Erziehung und Ausbildung im Frieden!" *Militär-Wochenblatt* 120, no. 32, February 18, 1936.

Griffith, Paddy. "British Armoured Warfare in the Western Desert." In *Armoured Warfare*, edited by J. P. Harris and F. H. Toase. London: Batsford, 1990.

————. *Forward into Battle: Fighting Tactics from Waterloo to the Near Future*. Novato, Calif.: Presidio, 1990.

Grove, Eric, Christopher Chant, David Lyon, and Hugh Lyon. *The Military Hardware of World War II: Tanks, Aircraft, and Naval Vessels*. New York: Military Press, 1984.

Guan, Ang Cheng. "Khe Sanh — From the Perspective of the North Vietnamese Communists." *War in History* 8, no. 1, January 2001.

Guderian, Heinz. *Panzer Leader*. New York: Ballantine, 1957.

————. "Die Panzertruppen und ihr Zusammenwirken mit den anderen Waffen." *Militärwissenschaftliche Rundschau* 1, no. 5, 1936.

Gudmundsson, Bruce, ed. *Inside the Afrika Korps*. London: Greenhill Books, 1999.

Gugeler, Russell A. *Combat Actions in Korea*. Washington, D.C.: Office of the Chief of Military History, 1970.

Gunsburg, Jeffrey A. *Divided and Conquered: The French High Command and the Defeat in the West, 1940*. Westport, Conn.: Greenwood, Press, 1979.

Guse, Lieutenant Colonel. "Ein modernes Austerlitz." *Militär-Wochenblatt* 125, no. 20, November 15, 1940.

Hackett, Sir John et al. *The Third World War: August 1985*. New York: Macmillan, 1978.

Hackworth, David H. "Lessons of a Lucky War." *Newsweek*, March 11, 1991.

Halliday, Jon, and Bruce Cumings. *The Unknown War*. New York: Pantheon, 1988.

Hamilton, Sir Ian. *A Staff Officer's Scrap-Book*. London: Edward Arnold, 1912.

Hamilton, Nigel. *Monty*. 3 volumes. London: Hamish Hamilton, 1981–1986.

Hammel, Eric. *Fire in the Streets: The Battle for Hue, Tet 1968*. Chicago: Contemporary Books, 1991.

———. *Six Days in June: How Israel Won the 1967 Arab-Israeli War*. New York: Charles Scribner's Sons, 1992.

Hammond, Grant T. *The Mind of War: John Boyd and American Security*. Washington, D.C.: Smithsonian Institution Press, 2001.

Harkabi, Yehoshaphat. "Basic Factors in the Arab Collapse During the Six-Day War." In *Arab-Israeli Relations: A Collection of Contending Perspectives and Recent Research*. Vol. 3. *From War to War: Israel and the Arabs, 1948–1967*, edited by Ian S. Lustick. New York: Garland, 1994.

Harris, J. P. "British Armour 1918–1949: Doctrine and Development." In *Armoured Warfare*, edited by J. P. Harris and F. H. Toase. London: Batsford, 1990.

Harris, J. P., and F. H. Toase, eds. *Armoured Warfare*. London: Batsford, 1990.

Harrison, Richard W. *The Russian Way of War: Operational Art, 1904–1940*. Lawrence: University Press of Kansas, 2001.

Hart, Russell A. *Clash of Arms: How the Allies Won in Normandy*. Boulder, Colo.: Lynne Rienner, 2001.

"Harte Abwehrkämpfe an der Ostfront." *Grossdeutschlands Freiheitskrieg*, part 125. *Militär-Wochenblatt* 126, no. 27, January 2, 1942.

Hastings, Max. *Overlord: D-Day, June 6, 1944*. New York: Simon and Schuster, 1984.

———. *The Korean War*. New York: Simon and Schuster, 1987.

Hayward, Joel S. A. *Stopped at Stalingrad: The Luftwaffe and Hitler's Defeat in the East, 1942–1943*. Lawrence: University Press of Kansas, 1998.

Head, William, and Earl H. Tilford, Jr., eds. *The Eagle in the Desert: Looking Back on U.S. Involvement in the Persian Gulf War*. Westport, Conn.: Praeger, 1996.

Heckmann, Wolf. *Rommel's War in Africa*. Garden City, N.Y.: Doubleday, 1981.

Heikal, Mohamed. *Illusions of Triumph: An Arab View of the Gulf War*. New York: HarperCollins, 1992.

Henriques, Robert. *A Hundred Hours to Suez*. New York: Viking, 1957.

Herbert, Paul H. "Deciding What Has to Be Done: General William E. DePuy and the 1976 Edition of FM 100-5, Operations." *Leavenworth Paper* no. 16. Ft. Leavenworth, Kans.: Combat Studies Institute, 1988.

Hermes, Walter G. *Truce Tent and Fighting Front: United States Army in the Korean War*. Washington, D.C.: Center of Military History, 1966.

Hertling, Mark P., and James Boisselle. "Coming of Age in the Desert: The NTC at 120." *Military Review* 81, no. 5, September–October 2001.

Herzog, Chaim. "A Military-Strategic Overview." In *The Iran-Iraq War: Impact and Implications*, edited by Efraim Karsh. Tel Aviv: Jaffee Center for Strategic Studies, 1987.

————. *The War of Atonement, October 1973.* Boston: Little, Brown, 1975.

Hetherington, John Aikman. *Airborne Invasion: The Story of the Battle of Crete.* New York: Duell, Sloan and Pearce, 1943.

Hiro, Dilip. *The Longest War: The Iran-Iraq Military Conflict.* New York: Routledge, 1991.

Holder, L. D. "Maneuver in the Deep Battle." *Military Review* 62, no. 5, May 1982.

Hooker, Richard D., Jr., ed. *Maneuver Warfare: An Anthology.* Novato, Calif.: Presidio, 1993.

Hooker, Richard D., Jr., and Christopher Coglianese. "Operation *Weserübung:* A Case Study in the Operational Art." In *Maneuver Warfare: An Anthology,* edited by Richard D. Hooker, Jr. Novato, Calif.: Presidio, 1993.

Horne, Alistair. *To Lose a Battle: France 1940.* Boston: Little, Brown, 1969.

House, Jonathan M. *Combined Arms Warfare in the Twentieth Century.* Lawrence: University Press of Kansas, 2001.

Howard, Michael. "The Battle of al-Alamein." In *Al-Alamein Revisited: The Battle of al-Alamein and Its Historical Implications,* edited by Jill Edwards. Cairo: American University in Cairo, 2000.

Hughes, Daniel J. "Abuses of German Military History." *Military Review* 65, no. 12, December 1986.

————. "Schlichting, Schlieffen, and the Prussian Theory of War in 1914." *Journal of Military History* 59, no. 2, April 1995.

————, ed. *Moltke on the Art of War: Selected Writings.* Novato, Calif.: Presidio, 1993.

Hughes, Stephen E. "Desert Storm: Attrition or Maneuver?" Ft. Leavenworth, Kans.: School of Advanced Military Studies, 1995.

Humayun Amin, Agha. "Tank Ambush at Kushtia." *Defence Journal* 4, no. 4, November 2000.

"Invasion and Battle for Crete." Online. www.feldgrau.com/cretewar.html.

Irving, Frederick F. "The Battle of Hue." *Military Review* 49, no.1, January 1969.

Israel Defense Force. Online. www.idf.il.

Jackson, W. G. F. *The Battle for North Africa, 1940–43.* New York: Mason, Charter, 1975.

Jamieson, Perry D. *Lucrative Targets: The U.S. Air Force in the Kuwaiti Theater of Operations.* Washington, D.C.: Air Force History and Museums Program, 2001.

Jarymowycz, Roman Johann. *Tank Tactics: From Normandy to Lorraine.* Boulder, Colo.: Lynne Rienner, 2001.

Jian, Chen. "Chinese Policy and the Korean War." In *The Korean War: Handbook of the Literature and Research,* edited by Lester H. Brune. Westport, Conn.: Greenwood Press, 1996.

Johnson, David E. *Fast Tanks and Heavy Bombers: Innovation in the U.S. Army, 1917–1945.* Ithaca, N.Y.: Cornell University Press, 1998.

————. "From Frontier Constabulary to Modern Army: The U.S. Army Between the World Wars." In *The Challenge of Change: Military Institutions and New Realities, 1918–1941,* edited by Harold R. Winton and David R. Mets. Lincoln: University of Nebraska Press, 2000.

Johnson, Quinn G. "They All Hate the Bad Guys of NTC's Mojave." *Army* 37, no. 6, June 1987.

Johnston, Paul. "Doctrine Is Not Enough: The Effect of Doctrine on the Behavior of Armies." *Parameters* 30, no. 3, Autumn 2000.

Jomini, Baron Henri Antoine de. *The Art of War.* Westport, Conn.: Greenwood, 1971.

Jones, Archer. "FM 100-5: A View from the Ivory Tower." *Military Review* 64, no. 5, May 1984.

————. "The New FM 100-5: A View from the Ivory Tower." *Military Review* 58, no. 2, February 1978.

Jupa, Richard, and Jim Dingeman. "How Iran Lost/Iraq Won the Gulf War." *Strategy and Tactics* 133, March–April 1990.

Kabisch, General Ernst. "Systemlose Strategie." *Militär-Wochenblatt* 125, no. 26, December 27, 1940.

Kalkat, O. S. "Strike Hard and Deep." *Journal of the United Service Institution of India* 53, no. 432, July–September 1973.

Kamps, Charles T., Jr. "Ardennes of the '90s: The Bavarian Option in the Next War." *Strategy and Tactics* 131, November–December 1989.

————. "The Central Front: The Status of Forces in Europe and the Potential for Conflict." *Strategy and Tactics* 82, September–October 1980.

————. "The Next War: Modern Conflict in Europe." *Strategy and Tactics* 69, July–August 1978.

Karber, Philip A. "The Tactical Revolution in Soviet Military Doctrine." *Military Review* 57, nos. 11–12, November–December 1977.

Karsh, Efraim, ed. *The Iran-Iraq War: Impact and Implications.* Tel Aviv: Jaffee Center for Strategic Studies, 1987.

"Katastrophenanzeichen in der Sowjetunion." *Grossdeutschlands Freiheitskrieg*, part 102. *Militär-Wochenblatt* 126, no. 4, July 25, 1941.

Kathpalia, P. N. *Mission with a Difference: The Exploits of 71 Mountain Brigade.* New Delhi: Lancer International, 1986.

Katz, Samuel M. *Israel's Army.* Novato, Calif.: Presidio, 1990.

Keegan, John, *The First World War.* London: Hutchinson, 1998.

————, ed. *Churchill's Generals.* New York: Grove Weidenfeld, 1991.

Kehrig, Manfred. *Stalingrad: Analyse und Dokumentation einer Schlacht.* Stuttgart: Deutsche-Verlags Anstalt, 1974.

Kennedy, Edwin L., Jr. "Force Protection Implications: TF Smith and the 24th Infantry Division, Korea 1950." *Military Review* 81, no. 3, May–June 2001.

Kessel, Eberhard. "Moltke und die Kriegsgeschichte: Zur Erinnerung an Moltkes Todestag vor 50 Jahren (24 April 1891)." *Militärwissenschaftliche Rundschau* 6, no. 2, 1941.

Khalil Sakakini Cultural Center, "Nakba." Online. www.alnakba.org.

Kiesling, Eugenia C. *Arming Against Hitler: France and the Limits of Military Planning.* Lawrence: University Press of Kansas, 1996.

————. "Debate: Armed but Not Dangerous: Women in the Israeli Military." *War in History* 8, no. 1, January 2001.

Kindsvatter, Peter S. "VII Corps in the Gulf War: Deployment and Preparation for Desert Storm." *Military Review* 72, no. 1, January 1992.

Kinnard, Douglas. *The War Managers.* Hanover, N.H.: University Press of New England, 1977.

Kirkland, Faris. R. "The Attack on Cap Mui Lay, Vietnam, July 1968." *Journal of Military History* 61, no. 4, October 1997.

Köhn, Lieutenant Colonel. "Die Infanterie im 'Blitzkrieg.' " *Militär-Wochenblatt* 125, no. 5, August 2, 1940.

Kolesnikov, I. "Winter Operations," January 12, 1940, *Krasnaya Zvesda* (translated). Carlisle, Pa.: U.S. Army Military History Institute, 1940.

Konev, Ivan. *Year of Victory.* Moscow: Progress Publishers, 1969.

"Kreuzzug gegen den Bolschewismus." *Grossdeutschlands Freiheitskrieg,* part 99. *Militär-Wochenblatt* 126, no. 1, July 4, 1941.

Krishna, Ashok. *India's Armed Forces: Fifty Years of War and Peace.* New Delhi: Lancer Publishers, 1998.

Krohn, Charles A. *The Lost Battalion: Controversy and Casualties in the Battle of Hue.* Westport, Conn.: Praeger, 1993.

Kurowski, Franz. *Der Kampf um Kreta.* Herford, Bonn: Maximilian-Verlag, 1965.

Kutschbach, A. *Die Serben im Balkankrieg 1912–1913 und im Kriege gegen die Bulgaren.* Stuttgart: Frank'sche Verlagshandlung, 1913.

Kutta, Timothy J. "The Capture of Fornebu Airfield." *Command* 39, September 1996.

Lambeth, Benjamin S. "NATO's Air War for Kosovo: A Strategic and Operational Assessment." Washington, D.C.: RAND, 2001.

———. *The Transformation of American Air Power.* Ithaca, N.Y.: Cornell University Press, 2000.

Leary, William M. "Anything, Anywhere, Anytime: Combat Cargo in the Korean War." Maxwell Air Force Base: Air University Library, 2000.

Leonhard, Robert R. *The Art of Maneuver: Maneuver-Warfare Theory and AirLand Battle.* Novato, Calif.: Presidio, 1991.

Lewin, Ronald. *The Life and Death of the Afrika Korps.* London: Batsford, 1977.

———. *Montgomery as Military Commander.* London: Batsford, 1971.

———. *Rommel as Military Commander.* London: Batsford, 1968.

Lewis, Adrian R. *Omaha Beach: A Flawed Victory.* Chapel Hill: University of North Carolina Press, 2001.

Li, Xiaobing, Allan R. Millett, and Bin Yu, eds. *Mao's Generals Remember Korea.* Lawrence: University Press of Kansas, 2001.

Liddell Hart, B. H. *The British Way in Warfare.* London: Faber and Faber, 1932.

———. *The German Generals Talk.* New York: Quill, 1979.

———. *The Real War, 1914–1918.* Boston: Little, Brown, 1930.

———. *Strategy.* New York: Meridian, 1991.

———, ed. *The Rommel Papers.* London: Collins, 1953.

Liddle, Peter H. *The 1916 Battle of the Somme: A Reappraisal.* London: Leo Cooper, 1992.

Lind, William S. *Maneuver Warfare Handbook*. Boulder, Colo.: Westview, 1985.

———. "Some Doctrinal Questions for the United States Army," *Military Review* 57, no. 3, March 1977.

———. "The Theory and Practice of Maneuver Warfare." In *Maneuver Warfare: An Anthology*, edited by Richard D. Hooker, Jr. Novato, Calif.: Presidio, 1993.

Lucas, James. *Battle Group! German Kampfgruppen Action of World War Two*. London: Arms and Armour, 1993.

Luck, Gary E. "The XVIII Airborne Corps: Puttin' Power on the Ground." *Military Review* 72, no. 4, April 1992.

Luck, Hans von. *Panzer Commander*. Westport, Conn.: Praeger, 1989.

Ludewig, Joachim. *Der deutsche Rückzug aus Frankreich 1944*. Freiburg: Rombach, 1995.

Ludwig, General of Artillery. "Der Durchbruch durch die Stalin-Linie." *Militär-Wochenblatt* 126, no. 5, August 1, 1941.

———. "Gedanken über den Angriff im Bewegungskriege." *Militärwissenschaftliche Rundschau* 1, no. 2, 1936.

———. "Moltke als Erzieher." *Militär-Wochenblatt* 125, no. 17, October 25, 1940.

Lukinov, M. I. "Notes on the Polish Campaign (1939) and the War with Finland (1939–1940)." *Journal of Slavic Military Studies* 14, no. 3, September 2001.

Luttwak, Edward, and Dan Horowitz. *The Israeli Army*. New York: Harper and Row, 1975.

MacDonald, Callum A. *Korea: The War Before Vietnam*. New York: Free Press, 1986.

———. *The Lost Battle — Crete, 1941*. New York: Free Press, 1993.

MacDonald, Charles B. *The Mighty Endeavor: The American War in Europe*. New York: Da Capo, 1992.

MacGregor, Knox, and Williamson Murray, eds. *The Dynamics of Military Revolution, 1300–2050*. Cambridge: Cambridge University Press, 2001.

Macher, Major. "Die Besetzung Dänemarks." *Militär-Wochenblatt* 125, no. 45, May 9, 1941.

Macksey, Kenneth. *Armoured Crusader: A Biography of Major-General Sir Percy Hobart*. London: Hutchinson, 1967.

———. *First Clash: Combat Close-up in World War III*. Toronto: Stoddart, 1984.

———. *Rommel: Battles and Campaigns*. London: Arms and Armour, 1979.

———. *Tank Versus Tank: The Illustrated Story of Armored Battlefield Conflict in the Twentieth Century*. New York: Barnes & Noble, 1999.

Mahmud Mukhtar, Pasha. *Meine Führung im Balkankriege 1912*. Berlin: Ernst Siegfried Mittler und Sohn, 1913.

Majdalany, Fred. *The Battle of El Alamein: Fortress in the Sand*. Philadelphia: Lippincott, 1965.

Manstein, Erich von. *Lost Victories*. Novato, Calif.: Presidio, 1982.

Mantey, Colonel. "Praktische Winke für das Anfassen kriegsgeschichtlicher Studien." *Militär-Wochenblatt* 116, no. 24, December 25, 1931.

Mark, Eduard. *Aerial Interdiction in Three Wars*. Washington, D.C.: Center for Air Force History, 1994.

Marshall, S. L. A. *Armies on Wheels*. New York: Morrow, 1941.

————. *Commentary on Infantry Operations and Weapons Usage in Korea, Winter of 1950–51*. Chevy Chase, Md.: Operations Research Office, Johns Hopkins University, 1951.

————. *The River and the Gauntlet: Defeat of the 8th Army by the Chinese Communist Forces November, 1950 in the Battle of the Chongchon River, Korea*. Alexandria, Va.: Time-Life Books, 1982.

Martin, Laurence. *Before the Day After: Can NATO Defend Europe*. Feltham, Middlesex: Newnes Books, 1985.

Mazarr, Michael J., Don M. Sinder, and James A. Blackwell, Jr. *Desert Storm: The Gulf War and What We Learned* (Boulder, Colo.: Westview, 1993).

McCarter, Mickey. "GAO Suggests Army Needs Less Money for Training." *Stars and Stripes Omnimedia*, March 27, 2001.

McDonough, James R. *The Defense of Hill 781: An Allegory of Modern Mechanized Combat*. Novato, Calif.: Presidio, 1988.

————. "The Operational Art: Quo Vadis?" In *Maneuver Warfare: An Anthology*, edited by Richard D. Hooker, Jr., Novato, Calif.: Presidio, 1993.

McGrath, John J. "Restoring the Balance, 25 January–8 July 1951." *The Korean War*. Washington, D.C.: Center of Military History, n.d.

McMichael, William H. "NTC's OPFOR: More Than Home Field Advantage." *Soldiers* 45, no. 3, March 1990.

Megargee, Geoffrey P. *Inside Hitler's High Command*. Lawrence: University Press of Kansas, 2000.

Mellenthin, F. W. von. *Panzer Battles: A Study of the Employment of Armor in the Second World War*. New York: Ballantine, 1956.

Menning, Bruce. *Bayonets Before Bullets: The Imperial Russian Army, 1861–1914*. Bloomington: Indiana University Press, 1992.

————. "The Deep Strike in Russian and Soviet Military History." *Journal of Soviet Military Studies* 1, no. 1, April 1988.

Metcalfe, James S. "Foot Soldiers War." *Infantry Journal* 64, no. 3, March 1949.

Meyer, Henry Cord III, with John Burtt. "The Bundeswehr: Mission, Organization, Doctrine." *Counterattack* 1, October 1987.

Meyer, Hubert. *The History of the 12. SS-Panzerdivision "Hitlerjugend."* Winnipeg: J. J. Fedorowicz, 1994.

Middlebrook, Martin. *The First Day on the Somme: 1 July 1916*. New York: W. W. Norton, 1972.

Mikhailov, P. "Tactical Employment of Ski Troops in Forest Areas." *Krasnaya Zvesda*, January 18, 1940 (translated). Carlisle, Pa.: U.S. Army Military History Institute, 1940.

Miller, Stephen M. *Lord Methuen and the British Army*. London: Frank Cass, 1999.

Miller, Ward A. *The 9th Australian Division Versus the Africa Corps: An Infantry Division Against Tanks — Tobruk, Libya, 1941*. Ft. Leavenworth, Kans.: U.S. Army Command and General Staff College, 1986.

Millett, Allan R. "A Reader's Guide to the Korean War." *Journal of Military History* 61, no. 3, July 1997.

————. "Drive North: U.S. Marines at the Punchbowl." *Marines in the Korean War Commemorative Series.* Washington, D.C.: U.S. Marine Corps Historical Center, 2001.

Milstein, Uri. *History of the War of Independence.* Vols. 1–4. Lanham, Md.: University Press of America, 1996.

Miranda, Joseph. "The First Arab-Israeli War, 1947–49." *Strategy and Tactics* 185, May–June 1997.

Moise, Edwin E. *Historical Dictionary of the Vietnam War.* Lanham, Md.: Scarecrow Press [Rowman & Littlefield], 2001.

————. Vietnam War Bibliography. Online. http://hubcap.clemson.edu/~eemoise/bibliography.html.

Moniz, David. "Soldiers Describe '18 Hour Miracle.'" *USA Today,* March 7, 2002.

Montgomery, Bernard Law. *El Alamein to the River Sangro; Normandy to the Baltic.* London: Barrie and Jenkins, 1973.

————. *Memoirs of Field-Marshal the Viscount Montgomery of Alamein.* Cleveland, Ohio: World, 1968.

Montross, Lynn, and Nicholas A. Canzona. *The Chosin Reservoir Campaign: U.S. Marine Operations in Korea, 1950–1953.* Vol. 3. Washington, D.C.: Historical Branch, HQMC, 1957.

————. *The Inchon-Seoul Operations: U.S. Marine Operations in Korea, 1950–1953.* Vol. 2. Washington, D.C.: Historical Branch, HQMC, 1955.

————. *The Pusan Perimeter: U.S. Marine Operations in Korea, 1950–1953.* Vol. 1. Washington, D.C.: Historical Branch, HQMC, 1954.

Mossman, Billy C. *Ebb and Flow: November 1950–July 1951: United States Army in the Korean War.* Washington, D.C.: Center of Military History, 1990.

Moulton, J. L. "Hitler Strikes North." *History of the Second World War,* no. 3, 1978.

————. "Conquest of Norway," *History of the Second World War,* no. 4, 1978.

Muhleisen, Hans-Otto. *Kreta 1941: Das Unternehemen Merkur, 20. Mai–1. Juni 1941.* Freiburg: Rombach, 1968.

Müller, Rolf-Dieter, and Gerd R. Ueberschär. *Hitler's War in the East, 1941–1945: A Critical Assessment.* Providence, R.I.: Berghahn Books, 1997.

Murray, G. E. Patrick. *Eisenhower Versus Montgomery: The Continuing Debate.* Westport, Conn.: Praeger, 1996.

Murray, Williamson, "May 1940: Contingency and Fragility of the German RMA." In *The Dynamics of Military Revolution, 1300–2050,* edited by MacGregor Knox and Williamson Murray. Cambridge: Cambridge University Press, 2001.

Murray, Williamson, and Allan R. Millett, eds. *Military Innovation in the Interwar Period.* Cambridge: Cambridge University Press, 1996.

Nagaty, Mohammad Ibrahim. "Lessons of Ramadan War." *Defence Journal* 1, nos. 9–10, 1975.

Nalty, Bernard C. *Air Power and the Fight for Khe Sanh.* Washington, D.C.: Office of Air Force History, 1973.

————. "Stalemate: U.S. Marines from Bunker Hill to the Hook." *Marines in the

Korean War Commemorative Series. Washington, D.C.: U.S. Marine Corps Historical Center, 2001.

Nasson, Bill. *The South African War, 1899–1902.* Oxford: Oxford University Press, 2000.

Naveh, Shimon. *In Pursuit of Military Excellence: The Evolution of Operational Theory.* London: Frank Cass, 1997.

Naylor, Sean D. "Training Command the Hardest Hit in Manning Plan." *Army Times,* September 4, 2000.

"Neugestaltung der Kriegführung." *Militär-Wochenblatt* 120, nos. 18–19, November 11, 1935, and November 18, 1935.

Nofi, A. A. "The Desert Fox: Rommel's Campaign for North Africa, April 1941–December 1942." *Strategy and Tactics* 87, July–August 1981.

Nolan, Keith. *Battle for Hue, Tet 1968.* Novato, Calif.: Presidio, 1978.

O'Ballance, Edgar. *The Gulf War.* London: Brassey's, 1988.

———. *No Victor, No Vanquished: The Yom Kippur War.* San Rafael, Calif.: Presidio, 1978.

———. *The Third Arab-Israeli War.* Hamden, Conn.: Archon Books, 1972.

Obkircher, Lieutenant Colonel. "Moltke, der 'unbekannte' General von Königgrätz: Zur Erinnerung an den 75. Gedenktag der Schlacht bei Königgrätz am 3. Juli 1866." *Militär-Wochenblatt* 125, no. 52, June 27, 1941.

Odom, William O. *After the Trenches: The Transformation of U.S. Army Doctrine, 1918–1939.* College Station: Texas A&M University Press, 1999.

Öhquist, General. "Ein finnischer Armeeführer über den Finnisch-Russischen Krieg." *Militär-Wochenblatt* 125, no. 40, April 4, 1941.

"Operation Anaconda: What the Pilots Saw." *Newsweek,* April 22, 2002.

Oren, Michael B. *Six Days of War: June 1967 and the Making of the Modern Middle East.* Oxford: Oxford University Press, 2002.

Paik, Sun Yup. *From Pusan to Panmunjom.* Dulles, Va.: Brassey's, 1992.

Pakenham, Thomas. *The Boer War.* New York: Random House, 1979.

Palit, D. K. *The Lightning Campaign: The Indo-Pakistan War.* Salisbury: Compton, 1972.

Patrick, Stephen B. "Kharkov: The Soviet Spring Offensive," *Strategy and Tactics* 68, June 1978.

Patton, George S. *War as I Knew It.* New York: Bantam Books, 1979.

Pearson, Willard. *The War in the Northern Provinces, 1966–1968.* Washington, D.C.: Department of the Army, 1975.

Pelletiere, Stephen C. *The Iran-Iraq War: Chaos in a Vacuum.* Westport, Conn.: Praeger, 1992.

Pelletiere, Stephen C., and Douglas V. Johnson II. *Lessons Learned: The Iran-Iraq War.* Vol. 1. FMFRP 3-203. Washington, D.C.: U.S. Marine Corps, 1990.

Pemberton, W. Baring. *Battles of the Boer War.* London: Batsford, 1964.

Pendergast, Kerry, and David Ritchie. "Berlin '85: The Enemy at the Gates." *Strategy and Tactics* 79, March–April 1980.

Perrett, Bryan. *Soviet Armor Since 1945.* London: Blandford, 1987.

Petty, Christopher J. "Operation Genesis: The Birth of OPFOR Air Assault at the National Training Center." *U.S. Army Aviation Digest*, September–October 1990.

Philips, William R. *Night of the Silver Stars: The Battle of Lang Vei.* Annapolis, Md.: Naval Institute Press, 1997.

Piekalkiewicz, Janusz. *Moscow 1941.* Novato, Calif.: Presidio, 1981.

Pisor, Robert. *The End of the Line: The Siege of Khe Sanh.* New York: Ballantine, 1982.

Powers, Stephen T. "The Battle of Normandy: The Lingering Controversy." *Journal of Military History* 56, no. 3, July 1992.

Prados, John, and Ray W. Stubbe, *Valley of Decision: The Siege of Khe Sanh.* Boston: Houghton Mifflin, 1991.

Praval, K. C. *Indian Army After Independence.* New Delhi: Lancer International, 1990.

Pyle, Ernie. *Brave Men.* New York: Grosset & Dunlap, 1943.

Raeder, Erich. *Grand Admiral.* New York: Da Capo Press, 2001.

Raza, Maroof. "The 1971 War in Retrospect," *Indian Defence Review* 12, no. 1, January–March 1997.

Reardon, Mark J. *Victory at Mortain: Stopping Hitler's Panzer Counteroffensive.* Lawrence: University Press of Kansas, 2002.

Record, Jeffrey. *Hollow Victory: A Contrary View of the Gulf War.* McLean, Va.: Brassey's, 1993.

Rees, David. *Korea: The Limited War.* New York: St. Martin's, 1964.

Report of the Hamoodur Rehman Commission of Inquiry in the 1971 War: As Declassified by the Government of Pakistan. Lahore: Vanguard, 2000.

Reznichenko, V. G. "Evolution of Tactics in the Great Patriotic War." *Military Thought* 10, no. 5, September–October 2001.

Rezun, Viktor ("Viktor Suvorov"). "Spetsnaz: The Soviet Union's Special Forces," *Military Review* 64, no. 3, March 1984.

———. *Inside the Soviet Army.* New York: Macmillan, 1982.

Richey, Stephen W. "Auftragstaktik, Schwerpunkt, Aufrollen: The Philosophical Basis of the AirLand Battle." *Military Review* 64, no. 5, May 1984.

Ridgway, Matthew B. *The Korean War.* New York: Da Capo, 1967.

Rikhye, Ravi. "U.S. Army Shifts to Armour Warfare." *Journal of the Royal United Service Institution of India*, 105, no. 439.

———. *The War That Never Was.* Delhi: Chanakaya, 1988.

Ritchie, David J. "Korea: The Forgotten War." *Strategy and Tactics* 111, May 1987.

Rogan, Eugene L., and Avi Shlaim, eds. *The War for Palestine: Rewriting the History of 1948.* Cambridge: Cambridge University Press, 2001.

Rogers, R. W., and David Lerman. "TRADOC Cash Poor by $360m: Command Hiring Freeze Won't Affect Training, Safety." *Newport News Daily Press*, March 10, 2001.

Romjue, John L. *American Army Doctrine for the Post-Cold War.* Fort Monroe, Va.: TRADOC, 1997.

———. *The Army of Excellence: The Development of the 1980's Army.* Ft. Monroe, Va.: TRADOC, 1997.

————. *From Active Defense to AirLand Battle: The Development of Army Doctrine, 1973–1982.* Fort Monroe, Va.: TRADOC: 1984.

Ross, Steven S. *From Flintlock to Rifle: Infantry Tactics, 1740–1866.* London: Frank Cass, 1996.

————, ed. *U.S. War Plans, 1938–1945.* Boulder, Colo.: Lynne Rienner, 2002.

Rothbrust, Florian K. *Guderian's XIXth Panzer Corps and the Battle of France: Breakthrough in the Ardennes, May 1940.* Westport, Conn.: Praeger, 1990.

Rothenberg, Gunther E. *The Anatomy of the Israeli Army: The Israel Defence Force, 1948–1978.* New York: Hippocrene, 1979.

Rothwell, Stephen K., with John Desch and Timothy Kutta. "SS Panzer: Bloodbath at Kursk." *Command* 36, March 1996.

Rotundo, Lewis C. *Battle for Stalingrad: The 1943 Soviet General Staff Study.* Washington, D.C.: Pergamon-Brassey's, 1989.

Sagar, Krishna Chandra. *The War of the Twins.* New Delhi: Northern Book Centre, 1997.

Sakurai, Tadayoshi. *Human Bullets: A Soldier's Story of the Russo-Japanese War.* Lincoln: University of Nebraska Press, 1999.

Salik, Siddiq. *Witness to Surrender.* Karachi: Oxford University Press, 1977.

Sandler, Stanley. *The Korean War: No Victors, No Vanquished.* Lexington: University Press of Kentucky, 1999.

Savkin, V. Ye. *The Basic Principles of Operational Art and Tactics: A Soviet View.* Moscow: Voennoe Izdatel'tsvo, 1972. Translated and published under the auspices of the United States Air Force. *Soviet Military Thought*, no. 12.

Scales, Robert H., Jr. *Certain Victory: The U.S. Army in the Gulf War.* Washington, D.C.: Brassey's, 1994.

Scarborough, Rowan. "Army Running out of Bullets." *Washington Times*, February 7, 2001.

Schäfer, Colonel von. "Die Enstehung des Entschlusses zur Offensive auf Lods: Zum Gedenken an General Ludendorff." *Militärwissenschaftliche Rundschau* 3, no. 1, 1938.

Scheben, Thomas. "The German Perspective of War in North Africa, 1940–42: Three-Dimensional, Intercontinental Warfare." In *Al-Alamein Revisited: The Battle of al-Alamein and Its Historical Implications*, edited by Jill Edwards. Cairo: American University in Cairo, 2000.

Schifferle, Peter J. "The Ia Drang Campaign 1965: A Successful Operational Campaign or Mere Tactical Failure?" Ft. Leavenworth, Kans.: School of Advanced Military Studies, 1994.

"Schilderungen aus den Kämpfen der Gebirgsjäger bei der Eroberung von Kreta im Mai 1941." *Militärwissenschaftliche Rundschau* 6, no. 3, 1941.

Schmidt, Heinz Werner. *With Rommel in the Desert.* New York: Bantam, 1977.

Schnabel, James F. *Policy and Direction: The First Year: United States Army in the Korean War.* Washington, D.C.: Center of Military History, 1972.

Schrader, Esther. "Simple Mission Became 18-Hour Fight." *Los Angeles Times*, March 8, 2002.

Schubert, Frank N., and Theresa L. Krauss, eds. *The Whirlwind War: The United States Army in Operations Desert Shield and Desert Storm.* Washington, D.C.: Center of Military History, 1995.

Schuster, Carl O. "Coastal Defense Victory: Blücher at Oslo." *Command* 39, September 1996.

Schwarzkopf, H. Norman, with Peter Petre. *It Doesn't Take a Hero: The Autobiography.* New York: Bantam, 1992.

The Sea Services in the Korean War, 1950–1953 [CD]. Annapolis, Md.: U.S. Naval Institute, 2000.

Seibt, Conrad. "Einsatz Kreta Mai 1941," *German Report Series*, B-641. Headquarters United States Army, Europe: Foreign Military Studies Branch, n.d.

Sharma, B. N. *What They Don't Teach You at Army School: A Critique of Indian Military Thought.* Delhi: Shipra, 1996.

Sharma, Gautam. *Our Armed Forces.* New Delhi: National Book Trust, India, 2000.

Sharma, R. C., ed. *Perspectives on Iraq-Iran Conflict.* New Delhi: Rajesh, 1984.

Sharon, Ariel, with David Chanoff. *Warrior: The Autobiography of Ariel Sharon.* New York: Touchstone, 1989.

Shazly, Saad el. *The Crossing of the Suez.* San Francisco: American Mideast Research, 1980.

Showalter, Dennis E. *Railroads and Rifles: Soldiers, Technology, and the Unification of Germany.* Hamden, Conn.: Archon Books, 1976.

Shulman, Milton. *Defeat in the West.* Waldenbury, East Sussex: Masquerade, 1986.

Simpson, Tony. *Operation Mercury: The Battle for Crete.* London: Hodder and Stoughton, 1981.

Singh, Ajay. "Developing an Information Warfare Strategy." *Indian Defence Review* 13, no. 1, January–March 1998.

Singh, Jagdev. *Dismemberment of Pakistan: 1971 Indo-Pak War.* New Delhi: Lancer International, 1988.

Singh, K. Brahma. "Lest We Forget." *Military Review* 53, no. 1, January 1973.

Singh, K. R. "Iraq-Iran Conflict: Military Dimensions." In *Perspectives on Iran-Iraq Conflict*, edited by R. C. Sharma. New Delhi: Rajesh, 1984.

Singh, Lachman. *Victory in Bangladesh.* Dehra Dun: Natraj Publishers, 1981.

Singh, R. K. "Tank Is Aging — What Next?" *Journal of the United Service Institution of India* 57, no. 450, January–March 1978.

Singh, Sukhwant. *India's Wars Since Independence.* Vol. 1. *The Liberation of Bangladesh.* New Delhi: Vikas, 1980.

———. *India's Wars Since Independence.* Vol. 3. *General Trends.* New Delhi: Vikas, 1982.

Sinha, Anjani Kumar. "Covering the Last 200 Metres and Fighting on the Objective." *Journal of the United Service Institution of India*, 54, no. 437, October–December 1974.

Slater, Robert. *Warrior Statesman: The Life of Moshe Dayan.* New York: St. Martin's Press, 1991.

Smith, Chris. "Strike North: Germany Invades Scandinavia, 1940." *Command* 39, September 1996.

Smith, George W. "The Battle of Hue," *The First and the Finest: U.S. Advisory Team, MACV.* Issues 2–7, 1968.

————. *The Siege at Hue.* Boulder, Colo.: Lynne Rienner, 1999.

Sodhi, H. S. *Operation Windfall: Emergence of Bangladesh.* New Delhi: Allied Publishers, 1980.

————. *Top Brass: A Critical Appraisal of the Indian Military Leadership.* Noida: Trishul, 1993.

Sokolovsky, V. D. "The Battle of Moscow." *Battles Hitler Lost: First Person Accounts of World War II by Russian Generals on the Eastern Front.* New York: Richardson & Steirman, 1986.

Souresrafil, Behrouz. *The Iran-Iraq War.* London: C. C. Press, 1989.

Soutor, Kevin. "To Stem the Red Tide: The German Report Series and Its Effect on American Defense Doctrine, 1948–1954." *Journal of Military History* 57, no. 4, October 1993.

Soviet Military Power. Washington, D.C.: U.S. Department of Defense, 1981.

Soviet Military Power. Washington, D.C.: U.S. Department of Defense, 1983.

Stanley, Owen. "Soviet Conventional Combat Philosophy." *Counterattack* 1, October 1987.

Stanton, Shelby. *America's Tenth Legion: X Corps in Korea, 1950.* Novato, Calif.: Presidio, 1989.

————. *Anatomy of a Division: The 1st Cav in Vietnam.* Novato, Calif.: Presidio, 1987.

Starry, Donn A. "Extending the Battlefield." *Military Review* 61, no. 3, March 1981.

————. *Mounted Combat in Vietnam.* Washington, D.C.: Department of the Army, 1978.

Staudenmaier, William O. "A Strategic Analysis." In *The Iran-Iraq War: New Weapons, Old Conflicts,* edited by Shirin Tahir-Kheli and Shaheen Ayubi. Westport, Conn.: Praeger, 1983.

Steele, Dennis. "The Army Magazine Hooah Guide to Army Transformation: A 30-Minute Course on the Army's 30-Year Overhaul." Association of the United States Army, 2001.

————. "The OPFOR: Friend and Foe." *Army* 38, no. 12, December 1988.

Stewart, Ian McDougall Guthrie. *The Struggle for Crete 20 May–1 June 1941: A Story of Lost Opportunity.* London: Oxford University Press, 1966.

Stewart, Richard W. "The Chinese Intervention, 3 November 1950–24 January 1951." *The Korean War.* Washington, D.C.: Center of Military History, n.d.

————. *Staff Operations: The X Corps in Korea, December 1950.* Ft. Leavenworth, Kans.: Combat Studies Institute, 1991.

Stokesbury, James L. *A Short History of the Korean War.* New York: William Morrow, 1988.

Stuhlmann, F. "Fallschirmjäger." *Militär-Wochenblatt* 125, no. 25, December 20, 1940.

Subrahmanyam, K. "The Lessons of the 1973 Arab-Israeli War." *Institute for Defence Studies and Analyses Journal* 6, no. 3, January 1974.

Summers, Harry. *On Strategy II: A Critical Analysis of the Gulf War*. New York: Dell Paperback, 1992.

Swain, Richard M. *"Lucky War": Third Army in Desert Storm*. Ft. Leavenworth, Kans.: U.S. Army Command and General Staff College Press, 1997.

Swanson, Mark. "Apaches in the Desert." *U.S. Army Aviation Digest*, September–October 1990.

Szabo, Ernest A. "Attrition vs. Maneuver and the Future of War." *Armor* 111, no. 5, September–October 2002.

Tahir-Kheli, Shirin, and Shaheen Ayubi, eds. *The Iran-Iraq War: New Weapons, Old Conflicts*. Westport, Conn.: Praeger, 1983.

Taylor, A. J. P. *The Origins of the Second World War*. London: H. Hamilton, 1961.

Tellier, Jon E. "The Battle for Hue." *Infantry* 85, no. 4, July–August 1995.

Terkel, Studs. *"The Good War": An Oral History of World War Two*. New York: Pantheon Books, 1984.

Theiss, Colonel Rudolf. "Der Panzer in der Weltgeschichte." *Militär-Wochenblatt* 125, no. 15, Ocober 11, 1940.

Thomas, Matthew. "The Airborne Assault Operations in Tangail: Indo-Pak Conflict 1971." *Indian Defence Review Digest* 2, 1992.

Thompson, David G. "Norwegian Military Policy, 1905–1940: A Critical Appraisal and Review of the Literature." *Journal of Military History* 61, no. 3, July 1997.

Thompson, Wayne, and Bernard C. Nalty, "Within Limits: The U.S. Air Force and the Korean War." Maxwell Air Force Base: Air University Library, 1996.

Toase, F. H. "The Israeli Experience of Armoured Warfare." In *Armoured Warfare*, edited by J. P. Harris and F. H. Toase. London: Batsford, 1990.

Tolson, John J. *Airmobility, 1961–1971*. Washington, D.C.: Department of the Army, 1973.

Towles, Robert L. "The Tears of Autumn: Air Assault Operations and Infantry Combat in the Ia Drang Valley, Vietnam, November 1965." Ph.D. diss., Kent State University, 2000.

Travers, Tim. *Gallipoli 1915*. Charleston, S.C.: Tempus, 2001.

———. *The Killing Ground: The British Army, the Western Front, and the Emergence of Modern Warfare, 1900–1918*. London: Allen & Unwin, 1987.

Trest, Warren A. "Air Force Sources: Rethinking the Air War." In *The Korean War: Handbook of the Literature and Research*, edited by Lester H. Brune. Westport, Conn.: Greenwood Press, 1996.

"Troop Training for Winter Operations," *Krasnaya Zvesda*, December 11, 1939 (translated). Carlisle, Pa.: U.S. Army Military History Institute, 1939.

Two Years of War. Tehran: Islamic Revolution's Guards Corps Political Office, 1982.

United States Military Intelligence Reports, Germany, 1919–1941. Frederick, Md.: University Publications of America, 1982.

U.S. News and World Report. Triumph Without Victory: The Unreported History of the Gulf War. New York: Random House-Times Books, 1992.

Utz, Curtis A. "Assault from the Sea: The Amphibious Landing at Inchon." Washington, D.C.: Naval Historical Center, 2000.

van Dyke, Carl. *The Soviet Invasion of Finland, 1939–40.* London: Frank Cass, 1997.

van Hartesveldt, Fred R. *The Boer War: Historiography and Annotated Bibliography.* Westport, Conn.: Greenwood Press, 2000.

"Verlauf und Abschluss der Riesenschlacht von Kiew." *Grossdeutschlands Freiheitskrieg,* part 112. *Militär-Wochenblatt* 126, no. 14, October 3, 1941.

Verma, Ashok Kalyan. *Rivers of Silence: Disaster on River Nam Ka Chu, 1962 and the Dash to Dhaka Across River Meghna During 1971.* New Delhi: Lancer Publishers, 1998.

Vernon, Alex. *The Eyes of Orion: Five Tank Lieutenants in the Persian Gulf War.* Kent, Ohio: Kent State University Press, 1999.

Völkel, Lieutenant Colonel. "Tchingis-Chan als Vorbild und Lehrmeister des modernen Pz.-Kavalleristen." *Militär-Wochenblatt* 126, no. 12, September 19, 1941.

Volkogonov, Dmitri. *Stalin: Triumph and Tragedy.* New York: Grove Weidenfeld, 1991.

von der Heydte, Baron Friedrich August. *Daedalus Returned: Crete 1941.* London: Hutchinson, 1958.

"Vor der Entscheidung im Osten." *Grossdeutschlands Freiheitskrieg,* part 103. *Militär-Wochenblatt* 126, no. 5, August 1, 1941.

Vorobyov, Ivan. "Evolution of Tactics in Wars and Armed Conflicts of the 20th Century." *Military Thought* 11, no. 1, January 2002.

Waddell, Ricky L. "Maneuver Warfare and Low-Intensity Conflict." In *Maneuver Warfare: An Anthology,* edited by Richard D. Hooker, Jr. Novato, Calif.: Presidio, 1993.

Wagner, Hermenegild. *With the Victorious Bulgarians.* Boston: Houghton Mifflin, 1913.

Warlimont, Walter. *Inside Hitler's Headquarters 1939–45.* Novato, Calif.: Presidio, 1964.

Warnock, A. Timothy, ed. *The USAF in Korea: A Chronology 1950–1953.* Maxwell Air Force Base: Air University Library, 2000.

Warr, Nicholas. *Phase Line Green.* Annapolis, Md.: Naval Institute Press, 1998.

Watson, Bruce Allen. *Desert Battle: Comparative Perspectives.* Westport, Conn.: Praeger, 1995.

Watts, Barry D. "Clausewitzian Friction and Future War." *McNair Paper* 52. Revised Edition. Washington, D.C.: Institute for National Strategic Studies, 2000.

Wawro, Geoffrey. *The Austro-Prussian War: Austria's War with Prussia and Italy in 1866.* Cambridge: Cambridge University Press, 1996.

Webb, William J. "The Outbreak, 27 June–15 September 1950." *The Korean War.* Washington, D.C.: Center of Military History, n.d.

Weeks, John. *Men Against Tanks: A History of Antitank Warfare.* New York: Mason/Charter, 1975.

Weigley, Russell F. *The American Way of War: A History of United States Military Strategy and Policy.* Bloomington: Indiana University Press, 1977.

Weinberg, Gerhard. *A World at Arms: A Global History of World War II.* Cambridge: Cambridge University Press, 1994.

Weinert, Richard. "The KATUSA Experience: The Integration of Korean Nationals into the U.S. Army, 1950–1965." *Military Affairs* 38, no. 2, April 1974.

Werth, Alexander. *Russia at War*. New York: Carroll and Graf, 1992.

Westermann, Edward B. *Flak: German Anti-Aircraft Defenses, 1914–1945.* Lawrence: University Press of Kansas, 2001.

Westmoreland, William C. *A Soldier Reports*. Garden City, N.Y.: Doubleday, 1976.

Whence the Threat to Peace? Moscow: Military Publishing House, 1982.

Wieder, Joachim, and Heinrich Graf von Einsiedl (editor). *Stalingrad: Memories and Reassessments*. London: Arms and Armour, 1995.

Wilz, John Edward. "Korea: The Forgotten War." *Journal of Military History* 53, no. 1, January 1989.

Winter, Denis. *Haig's Command: A Reassessment*. London: Viking, 1991.

Winton, Harold R. *To Change an Army: General Sir John Burnett-Stuart and British Armored Doctrine, 1927–1938*. Lawrence: University Press of Kansas, 1988.

Winton, Harold R., and David R. Mets. *The Challenge of Change: Military Institutions and New Realities, 1918–1941*. Lincoln: University of Nebraska Press, 2000.

Wirtz, James, J. "The Battles for Saigon and Hue: Tet 1968." In *Soldiers in Cities: Military Operations on Urban Terrain*, edited by Michael C. Desch. Carlisle, Pa.: Strategic Studies Institute, 2001.

Wortzel, Larry M., ed. *The Chinese Armed Forces in the 21st Century*. Carlisle, Pa.: U.S. Army War College, Strategic Studies Institute, 1999.

Y'Blood, William T. "MiG Alley: The Fight for Air Superiority." Maxwell Air Force Base: Air University Library, 2000.

Yeremenko, Andrei. "Battle of Stalingrad." In *Battles Hitler Lost: First Person Accounts of World War II by Russian Generals on the Eastern Front*. New York: Richardson & Steirman, 1986.

Young, Peter. *The Israeli Campaign 1967*. London: William Kimber, 1967.

Zaloga, Steven J., and Victor Madej. *The Polish Campaign*. New York: Hippocrene, 1991.

"Zentralisation und Dezentralisation." *Militär-Wochenblatt* 115, no. 27, January 18, 1931.

Zettering, Niklas, and Anders Frankson. *Kursk 1943: A Statistical Analysis*. London: Frank Cass, 2000.

Zhang, Shu Guang. *Mao's Military Romanticism: China and the Korean War, 1950–1953*. Lawrence: University Press of Kansas, 1995.

Zhukov, G. K. "The Battle of Moscow." In *Moscow 1941 Stalingrad 1942: Recollections, Stories, Reports*, edited by Vladimir Sevruk. Moscow: Progress Publishers, 1974.

———. *Marshal Zhukov's Greatest Battles*. New York: Harper and Row, 1969.

———. *The Memoirs of Marshal Zhukov*. New York: Delacorte, 1971.

———. "The War Begins." *Battles Hitler Lost: First Person Accounts of World War II by Russian Generals on the Eastern Front*. New York: Richardson & Steirman, 1986.

Index